MODERN INDIAN FAMILY LAW

MODERN INDIAN FAMILY LAW

Werner F. Menski

CURZON

First Published in 2001
by Curzon Press
Richmond, Surrey
http://www.curzonpress.co.uk

Typeset in Sabon by LaserScript Ltd, Mitcham, Surrey
Printed and bound in Great Britain by
TJ International, Padstow, Cornwall

British Library Cataloguing in Publication Data
A catalogue record of this book is available from the British Library

Library of Congress Cataloguing in Publication Data
A catalogue record for this book has been requested

ISBN 0-7007-1316-6

In memory of

Shri M. C. Mathew

Founder-Editor of the Kerala Law Times
(4th June 1920–10th February 1988)

Contents

Acknowledgements

The present volume, built around a framework of essays published earlier, mainly in the *Kerala Law Times* and a number of other South Asian law journals, could not have been produced so speedily without the ready agreement of all copyright holders to have the previously published material reprinted in its present form. I am most grateful to everyone concerned in this regard, especially Advocates Siby Mathew and M. Mathew at the *Kerala Law Times*.

A whole generation of students, sitting through those long Tuesday afternoons of seminars on Law and Society in South Asia, have played much more of a role in preparing this volume than they realise. Contrary to popular assumptions, teachers may learn much from their students, and working with so many bright, occasionally immensely well-informed students from all over the world, and especially from South Asian jurisdictions, has been a privilege and a huge bonus. Without critical inquiry from fresh minds, year after year, the analysis and understanding of South Asian legal developments would have been so much less fun, and probably much less rigid. While I take this occasion to thank all my students in that course over the years, Michael Anderson and Martin Lau, who both became valued colleagues, deserve special mention, as well as Dr. Sangeeta Ahuja, whose recent pioneering work on public interest litigation (Ahuja 1997) relieved me of the pressing task of writing a book on the subject.

In the preparatory work for this volume I was diligently assisted by a number of people. I would like to thank especially Rajesh Bhavsar and Hans Menski for their input at various stages in the preparation of the book. Clare Fazal went through the entire manuscript and made many valuable suggestions.

Martin Daly at SOAS established the initial contact with the publishers and has been a great source of support over many years. I wish him well in his retirement. Jonathan Price, Chief Editor of Curzon Press, provided much encouragement and support.

Finally, it is a pleasant duty to acknowledge the financial support of the

British Academy for the preparation of some of the articles reprinted in this book, as well as the generous assistance of the Nuffield Foundation in London through a Social Science Research Fellowship, which helped to free some time for research on this book.

The law of India is stated as at 1st January 1999. Any mistakes are of course mine, and I would be grateful for corrections and reference to omissions.

Abbreviations

AIR	All India Reporter
All	Allahabad
AllLJ	*Allahabad Law Journal*
AMU	Aligarh Muslim University
AnWR	*Andhra Weekly Reporter*
AP	Andhra Pradesh
ASIL	*Annual Survey of Indian Law*
BLD	*Bangladesh Legal Decisions*
Bom	Bombay
BomLR	*Bombay Law Reporter*
Cal	Calcutta
ch.	chapter
CJ	Chief Justice
CriLJ	*Criminal Law Journal*
CriLR	*Criminal Law Reporter*
CrPC	*Criminal Procedure Code*, 1973
DB	Division Bench
Del	Delhi
DMMA	*Dissolution of Muslim Marriages Act*, 1939
FB	Full Bench
Gau	Gauhati (High Court of Assam)
Guj	Gujarat
HAMA	*Hindu Adoptions and Maintenance Act*, 1956
HMA	*Hindu Marriage Act*, 1955
HP	Himachal Pradesh
HSA	*Hindu Succession Act*, 1956
Hyd	Hyderabad
ILI	Indian Law Institute
ILR	*Indian Law Reports*
IPC	*Indian Penal Code*, 1860
J	Judge, or: Journal
J&K	Jammu and Kashmir

Kant	Karnataka
Ker	Kerala
KLT	Kerala Law Times
Lah	Lahore
Mad	Madras
MLJ	Madras Law Journal
MP	Madhya Pradesh
MWPRDA	Muslim Women (Protection of Rights on Divorce) Act, 1986
Mys	Mysore
NGO	Non-governmental organisation
NOC	Notes of Cases
Ori	Orissa
Pat	Patna (High Court of Bihar)
P&H	Punjab and Haryana
Raj	Rajasthan
Rs.	Rupees
s.	section
SB	Special Bench
SC	Supreme Court
SCC	Supreme Court Cases
SCJ	Supreme Court Journal
SCWR	Supreme Court Weekly Reports
SMA	Special Marriage Act, 1954
SN	Short Note
SOAS	School of Oriental and African Studies
UP	Uttar Pradesh

Introduction

Indian law in the 1980s and 1990s

In the past few decades, especially after the mid-1970s, Indian law has developed at an amazing speed and in very interesting ways which have remained largely unexplored in academic writing. To some extent, such developments have even remained unnoticed, as the image of an unwieldy, non-functioning Indian colossus remains entrenched in the public mind, while some scholars seem to shy away from tackling the complexities of modern India. Somehow, the assumption that nothing works in Indian law has meant that academics in various disciplines have found it easy to disregard the remarkable legal developments that have taken place in India during the 1980s and 1990s. Legal academics, on the other hand, are rare creatures, since almost every Indian law graduate cannot wait to enter the profession and thereafter pays scant attention to the academic development of our field of study. Professional interests and concerns seem not to match those of academic analysis. Thus, for various reasons, writing an analytical book on Indian law these days is a daunting task, hindered further by the new constraints placed on full-time academics by their resource-hungry institutions.

A fresh assessment of recent Indian legal developments has been long overdue. The present volume offers new material to facilitate such assessment and analysis and is primarily aimed at students of South Asian law, researchers and lawyers, but also interested members of the public. Many of the essays in this book were originally written for the benefit of law students and, in at least one case (chapter 3.3) with their active involvement. As time has moved on, and new cohorts of students of South Asian laws at SOAS have brought in fresh concerns and ideas in reaction to more recent developments, a whole body of new material has developed which needs to be shared with a wider public. The present volume aims to stimulate necessary discussions about the main issues in modern Indian law, not only in relation to India or South Asia, but also with reference to the emerging South Asian laws in countries like Britain, Canada, Australia and the USA today.

It is evident in retrospect that the mid-1970s were an important watershed in Indian legal history. Following the Emergency of 1975–1977, imposed by a symbolic, angry Mother India, the legal system of India was restructured in various ways. This was not immediately obvious to scholars and to lawyers. First of all, the realities of the Emergency generated much angry and politically focused reaction, which distracted from deeper reflection. At any rate, scholars often take their time to comment on what they observe while lawyers, as elsewhere, tend to become politicians rather than legal analysts once they have made a decision not to practise law.

More than twenty years later, the implications of those changes display evidence of long-term consequences, which fit well into an overarching historical and conceptual analysis of Indian legal systems. In short, it is evident now that the post-Emergency reforms to Indian laws finally nudged the legal system away from following largely colonial, Western paradigms of legal authority and law-making, shifting legal developments (at first almost imperceptibly) towards a re-consideration of ancient norms inherent in Indian law which do not match with the dominant assumptions of Western legal theories.[1]

When Mrs. Gandhi imposed the Emergency, put scores of people in jail and basically showed everyone how fragile – and how easily rendered defunct – the post-colonial Indian legal and political system had become, she was of course acting like an Austinian model ruler, displaying her power and autocratic indulgence. Surely, she was showing everyone who was boss, but that was manifestly not the complete agenda as far as Indian law making is concerned. While nearly everyone voiced criticism, dissent and disgust about the evident violations of basic human rights and of constitutional propriety, very important hidden developments took place under the mantle of absolutist political power. It was not immediately evident that Mrs. Gandhi also acted like an ancient Indian ruler who perceives an urgent need to control 'the big fish' and to secure a future for the 'little fish'. At first one only saw – and heard of – the interference with 'normal' political arrangements and rules by a crazed, power-hungry individual.

Decades later, the Emergency still sticks in India's collective memory as a bad experience, something that maybe the Pakistanis next door would indulge in for long periods, but not the much more stable Indian democracy. However, Mrs. Gandhi's Emergency was not just a political tool for the ruler, it was also deeply concerned with those sections of the ruled whose rights were manifestly not well enough protected by the way in which Indian law had been developing until the early 1970s.

Around the time of the Emergency, the Indian Constitution was significantly re-structured and partly re-formulated, with enormous consequences for rich and poor alike. For example the fundamental right to property was taken away, and some important new provisions, related to social and economic justice and environmental protection issues, were introduced. Another notable new element of the Indian Constitution was Article 51A, a catalogue of Fundamental Duties to be followed by every citizen. To the outsider, at any rate, conflicting signals were thus given. While the Indian Constitution declared itself to be explicitly secular,[2] at the same time Article 51A reads like a catalogue of Hindu *dharma*, emphasising the obligations and duties of all citizens, as opposed to their individual rights.

Few observers seem to have noticed this subtle re-orientation of Indian laws, reinforced later through post-Emergency top-down reform processes, which re-invigorated bottom-up processes of law-making. The reforms in their totality represent a movement towards a body politic in which every individual citizen is perceived to be visibly and invisibly linked to the microcosmic ordering system of the modern state, a very obviously Hindu-inspired concept. This new emphasis on the citizen's duties asked individuals to be more aware of their roles, holding everyone accountable to what was soon to become defined more clearly as 'public interest'. These reforming pressures look distinctly familiar to those who know about ancient Indian concepts of law, with its emphasis on duties rather than rights, and environmental awareness rather than capitalist and selfish profiteering.[3] In other words, Mrs. Gandhi appears to have actively chosen to behave as the typical Hindu ruler, wielding the ancient stick of *danda*, the punishing rod, to remind all parts of her empire of their mutual interlinkedness, of their respective duties to the whole, rather than just to themselves. Such invisible conceptual connections can of course only strike those observers who are versed in the concepts of ancient Indian society and law – and the number of those has regrettably been shrinking to levels that has given rise to some concern.[4]

These are not simply modern *Hindutva* agenda, then, as much politicised gossip these days would have it, but evidence of a re-alignment of modern Indian law-making processes with ancient socio-cultural (and therefore legal) concepts of organising human life. These have been re-invented for the modern legal restructuring of an unwieldy socialist, secular, democratic system that was, with increasing visibility, violating its own most basic norms of (relative) justice and of concern of all parts for the welfare of the whole. Mrs. Gandhi evidently realised that justice for the common 'little' Indian could never be achieved if modern India continued to follow the supposedly superior Western path of development. A dramatic re-working of Indian law was required to induce the growth of indigenous ways of handling conflicting interests, rather than giving pre-eminence to the adversarial processes of the colonial model and its focus on individual property with its concomitant private interest orientation.

While the Emergency itself looked like a massive violation of fundamental rights, it appears today, contradictory as it may seem, that the fundamental changes it introduced were focused on a concern with justice, a basic justice for all those Indians who would never have the means to engage a lawyer and to claim the wonderful constitutional rights that exist for them on paper. The Emergency was an anti-establishment, pro-poor device to restructure the entire Indian legal system. For the underprivileged sections of Indians, law had manifestly remained a mechanism designed for their harassment and suppression, not as a means of succour. Politicians and lawyers had far too long ignored the real life conditions of common India and of the most deprived sections of the citizenry. Mrs. Gandhi somehow remained attuned to such basic needs and clearly did not only use the prominent slogan 'Defeat poverty' (*garibi hatao*) for electioneering purposes. Through the Emergency, she reminded everyone in India, in the most powerful way possible, of the concerns of those for whom law and all its paraphernalia had come to mean nothing but a distant symbol of exploitation and a means of corrupt governance. Suddenly, with the Constitution and basic fundamental rights suspended, the most powerful politicians, judges and all other 'big' people in the Republic of India were thrown back, so to say, to the level of the almost rightless pavement dweller. This had a cathartic shock value, on which leading analysts like Upendra Baxi were to comment later (see e.g. Baxi 1985).

Related to this catharsis, during the early 1980s, the emergence of public interest litigation in India became a most intriguing new development, which we at SOAS have studied and monitored with growing fascination and enthusiasm almost from its inception. One can now claim that India today leads the world in this area of the law. This has not come about by co-incidence, or as a result of one or two maverick judges who wanted a place in the international limelight. Public interest litigation is, as the name itself says, a public interest-focused method of operating a legal system. It is typically South Asian in its conceptual underpinnings, since this concept emphasises the inevitable interlinkedness between all players in a somewhat open-ended yet global system. I would not say that this is purely a South Asian conceptualisation, however, since traditional African cultures, for example, operate on similar principles. Rather than asking whether public interest litigation is really only an Indian, or even Hindu, construct, we should therefore examine to what extent public interest litigation principles and practices could be translated to other legal systems and to what extent they are conducive to justice.

It is self-evident that public interest concepts could well be perceived as universal. It is no coincidence that they form an intrinsic element of the currently fashionable debates about a global ethics system that a rather diverse cluster of recent scholarship has aimed to construct.[5] Concern for justice and for finding the right balance between rights and duties is certainly not a prerogative of the South Asian socio-cultural complex.

One may observe that Western debates have been much more focused on religion than on social issues. While much of Western scholarship continues to argue over whether 'development' can be something 'secular', South Asians and people from many other countries seek progress within a religio-ethical framework and do not spend mental energy on segregating religious elements. Religion is simply accepted as a part of human existence- one can argue over details, but in principle it is an integral element of public and private life alike. It appears that taking this position frees mental energies to think in more depth about tangible social issues, rather than getting distracted by never-ending religious politics.

South Asia shares with other populous, so-called underdeveloped countries of the South like China, Indonesia or Brazil (to name only the largest) the predicament that wonderful legal concepts and rules will remain hollow paper promises unless the official law is restructured and re-oriented to take more account of social realities. If, from an Indian perspective, law is about the balancing of competing claims, and the achievement of justice for all – remarkably in terms of equity rather than equality, however – then something was needed in post-colonial modern legal systems, such as India's, to keep law and society in some kind of harmony. As it was becoming increasingly evident that the old system was leading to ever-growing disparity between legal claims and social reality, something had to happen – and it did happen. First in India, then in Pakistan, and now elsewhere, too, including Bangladesh, new developments in public interest litigation can be observed. A detailed analysis of this phenomenon must be reserved for a companion volume to the present book.[6]

The two main areas of the law in which the impact of the Emergency-related changes to the Indian legal system could be measured are the vast sphere of constitutional law and the multitude of Indian family laws, which have remained organised on a 'personal law' basis.[7] Western scholarly reactions to this 'personal law' scenario have taken a particular direction, declaring this evident lack of legal uniformity as an indicator of underdevelopment. Thus, a really rather superficial (but nonetheless powerful) impression was created that neither Indian constitutional law nor Indian family laws were developing. In effect, this encourages the view that Indian law would be best ignored and left to disintegrate, thus speeding up the process of catching up with the West.

The main European commentator on classical as well as post-colonial Indian laws, Professor J. Duncan M. Derrett, retired from the School of Oriental and African Studies in the University of London in summer 1981, leaving me to tackle the enormous task of teaching and researching the laws of South Asia *and* of dispelling some negative myths about Indian legal developments. At that time, Derrett's major textbooks were still widely available, but they were written during the 1960s and 1970s and therefore predated the events of the Emergency. Derrett had concentrated his efforts on historical discussions of Hindu law and on modern developments in the Hindu personal laws, so masterly concluded in his 1978 'Epitaph on the rishis' and catchingly entitled *Death of a marriage law*.[8] He had left the study of South Asian Muslim law to others, notably Professor (later Sir) Norman Anderson, as well as Dr. Doreen Hinchcliffe and Dr. David Pearl (as he then was). Professor Derrett had also relied on constitutional law being covered by others, prominently Professor Alan Gledhill, and a number of Indian commentators, many of whom, like Rajeev Dhavan, had been Derrett's students.

Given my academic background as a classical indologist rather than a Western lawyer, my own energies were first of all directed towards linking indology and law through researching key aspects of classical Hindu marriage law (Menski 1984). This material was to be fed directly into our course on Law and Society in South Asia, as well as the exciting, unique course on Legal Systems of Asia and Africa, taught at SOAS as a first year, globalistic introduction to comparative jurisprudence, with its own literature and a gradually emerging critically distanced perspective on what Masaji Chiba (see above, n. 1) came to call 'Western model jurisprudence'. This amounted to a powerful critique of the old, dominant Austinian school of thought, according to which rulers make laws for their people and punish them for violations of those laws, rather similar to the Westminster model. Lawyers growing up in an entirely Western framework of reference might never come to realise that this purportedly universalistic theoretical approach to law may not match with the realities of ancient legal systems like those of the Hindus, the Chinese, and other peoples of the South and their current realities.[9]

During the 1980s and 1990s, the conceptual analysis of ancient and modern Indian laws slowly progressed, if at a snail's pace, due to the many constraints of modern academic life. Yet despite attempts to declare it irrelevant for today's modern world, the study of ancient Hindu jurisprudence is alive and well in London these days. Sadly, however, there are moves to cut down courses which do not attract large numbers of students and, regrettably, politically motivated attempts to restrict thinking about the relevance of ancient Indian concepts for legal developments in modern South Asia. In an institution such as SOAS, this scant concern for the relevance of classical South Asian studies in today's world is indicative of post-modernism's tenuous hold.

Apart from the much-contested arena of constitutional law, the major area of South Asian legal studies at SOAS has been family law, concentrated in the long-established course on Law and Society in South Asia, which was originally developed by Professor Derrett. This detailed study of family laws and constitutional laws was designed for academic as well as practical purposes, and it became an important course for the professional career development of many students. The growing interest of legal practitioners in this subject, both in the subcontinent and in Britain, and the gradually changing composition of our classes, which now attract many second and third generation South Asian students from Britain (and other countries) proved to be important factors in propelling new research. While we watched and monitored, new areas of the law – such as maintenance entitlements for divorced wives, not only for Muslim wives – emerged in front of our eyes during the 1980s, while others became activated, a prominent example being the anti-dowry laws and their recent focus on criminal procedure (see now Menski 1998b).

For anyone wishing to comment on these developments in writing, it becomes clear very soon that academic interest in those subjects has been located mainly in India itself. For a European researcher on Indian law, whose natural readership sits in South Asia, it would therefore be preferable to write for Indian law journals, which are accessible to such a readership.

When I met Shri M. C. Mathew at the Kerala Law Times offices in Ernakulam, Cochin in late 1983, a decision was made that I should publish regularly for the *Kerala Law Times* and thus maintain an old-established link between London-based scholarship and Indian legal developments.[10] Over time, however, the effect of that strategy has been to make my writing on modern South Asian laws almost totally inaccessible in Europe and to a wider public in the West. Few people outside India read the *Kerala Law Times*, although it has long been one of the leading Indian law journals, under the able leadership of the fine gentleman to whose memory this book is dedicated. Few people in Europe have access to other admittedly important publications from India, such as the *Madras Law Journal*, the *Bombay Law Reporter*, or the *Journal of the Indian Law Institute*.

Hence the present volume of essays, comprised almost exclusively of my own articles, which were published originally in several Indian law journals between 1981 and 1996, fulfils an important function in making such analytical discussions about Indian legal developments during the 1980s and 1990s available to a wider readership. These essays are printed in their original form (minus the regrettably frequent typographical errors in their original versions), but they have been supplemented with commentary, updates and, in some cases, with other writing on which a particular article of mine commented, or which it gave rise to. This will allow the reader, and especially future students of South Asian law, who face increasingly cash-starved libraries and torn-out pages from law reports and key textbooks, to retrace details of some of the lively debates conducted around key issues in modern Indian family laws and constitutional law during the 1980s and 1990s.

My coverage of Indian legal issues in those articles published in India was largely unsystematic, often responding to a call for commentary. This often came directly from Shri M. C. Mathew and later his son, Advocate Siby Mathew, who has maintained the *KLT*'s tradition of producing a lively journal section. Some of my essays took up issues that interested us in London and were perceived to be directly relevant to one of the topics we studied and researched. A fuller, more systematic and detailed analysis of Indian family law is in the making, but has turned out to be a daunting task, which requires many years of work. The present volume is much more than a stop-gap measure, however, it lays out the original material published during the last 16 years and guides the reader towards further analysis of the major issues that have developed in modern Indian family laws.

The material in this volume is arranged in six main chapters. Following this introduction, major issues and topics in Indian family law are covered: marriage, divorce, polygamy, maintenance, joint family and succession law, and the tortuous debates over an Indian Uniform Civil Code. The concluding analysis aims to provide an assessment of the current state of Indian family laws and looks towards the future scope for significant legal developments that distinguish the jurisdictions of modern South Asia from others in the world.

Notes

1 The Japanese jurist Masaji Chiba has spoken in this context of 'Western model jurisprudence', in other words, the Austinian model of the sovereign's word as law, or the so-called analytical school of jurisprudence. For details see Chiba (1986) and further below.

2 In the 42nd Amendment of 1976, the Preamble of the Indian Constitution was re-worded to include the word 'secular'. Henceforth the Preamble referred to India as a 'Sovereign Socialist Secular Democratic Republic'. Secularism in India, readers need to be reminded, means in essence 'equidistance from all religions', not total segregation of law and religion. The latter is a concept that Hindus and Muslims can theoretically comprehend, but which to them is unworkable in daily life and therefore of little use as the basis for law-making. On religion in India see authoritatively Madan (1991) and his seminal essay of 1987.

3 For details on the concepts of traditional Hindu law see O'Flaherty and Derrett (1978), Derrett (1968a) and Menski (1997a).

4 Some attempts were made in the 1980s to reinvigorate thinking about the relevance of shastric norms in today's India. A typical, prominent example is Narang (1988). On Indian public law see excellently Jois (1990), but compare Jois (1997), which is much more idealising and paints a too simplistic picture of a glorious past. Important essays in this field were written by Chhatrapati Singh (1990) and Rajeev Dhavan (1992), demonstrating the limits of knowledge for modern scholars of ancient Indian legal traditions.

5 In response to the formulation of a 'Global Ethic' by the Parliament of World Religions in Chicago in 1993 (see Küng and Kuschel 1993), which has been widely perceived as Christian-led and Western-dominated, there has been some interesting writing for all kinds of purposes. While Jois (1997) explores the claims of *dharma* as *the* global ethic and thus explains universalising Hindu concepts, Morgan and Braybrooke (1998) give space to voices from many different religious and cultural perspectives in Britain.

6 For a very detailed overview of Indian public interest litigation see now Ahuja (1997).

7 A system of personal law comprises, in practice, more or less separate legal regulations for members of different religious communities. In Indian law, this involves the Hindus as the majority, and then a number of minority laws for the Muslims, Christians, Parsis, Jews, and an undefined 'other' category of persons who might wish to use the optional secular provisions of the law.

8 His two major assessments of modern Hindu law (Derrett 1963; 1970) have lasting value as analytical tools, although a lot of the legal material itself is now superseded by more recent case law and statutory enactments.

9 This experience is not unique to lawyers. One of my recent students has written about his experience as a young Hindu studying in Canada, finding that he was brainwashed into Western models of thinking that did not match with his life pattern. Hiren Mistry wrote in 'Entrapment and the secular discourse of racism: Some Hindu reflections', published in Trent University's Magazine, *From the Margins* (1997): "The theory I read does not address my Hinduism. The strategies that are devised do not realize that survival for me (and for many) means: tradition, language, prayer, temples, rituals and izzat."

10 Professor Derrett, starting in 1952, appears to have written at least 55 articles for the *Kerala Law Times*, and many more for the *Bombay Law Reporter*. For details of Derrett's enormous bibliography see Sontheimer and Aithal (1982: 413–458).

Chapter One

Marriage

Inability to handle tradition, or skill in abusing it?

1.1 The problem and its socio-legal context

In social reality, and therefore in legal practice, cases often come up in Indian law where one party claims that a particular Hindu marriage does not exist or, more precisely, that there is or was no legally binding marriage between two particular spouses. Such cases may come up many years after the death of a particular spouse, often when a succession is contested. Litigation of this kind is not concerned with exploring the concept of marriage in an academic sense, and is are not designed to clarify the law. Quite on the contrary: litigants (and their professional advisers) often seek to obfuscate and to confuse. Cases of this type tend to arise because one party to a marriage, usually the husband or the husband's relatives, seek to divest a woman (or those claiming entitlements through her) of financial or property entitlements, be it maintenance or inheritance.[1] As we shall see, the resulting problems for claimants may be multiplied if the woman concerned was a wife who had been previously married. Problems over our understanding of customary Hindu marriage rituals and their legal recognition become evident in such complex scenarios, which naturally lend themselves to abuse by ruthless litigants and their unscrupulous professional advisers.

When I started teaching Indian law in London in the early 1980s, writing at the same time my PhD on Hindu marriage concepts and the solemnisation of Hindu marriages (Menski 1984), disputes on marriages were among the first cases that attracted my attention, prompting me to write about the legal problems that emerged in them (see sections 1.2 and 1.3 below). The analysis of those matters remained quite incomplete at that time and I have repeatedly taken up this issue in different contexts. Problems of the legal recognition of customary marriage arrangements also relate to bigamy cases (see chapter 3 below), maintenance law (chapter 4) and joint family property matters (chapter 5).

In some areas of the law, the best example being maintenance law for divorced wives (see chapter 4 below), the last two decades have seen a clear progression from an initial state of confusion and rather unsatisfactory regulation, to an agreeably settled position in the official law. However, this is not the case regarding the law on recognition of customary marriage solemnisation among Hindus in India. Remarkably, the legal problems in this field remain and have re-surfaced with astonishing tenacity even in the most recent Indian law reports. Of course, as a scholar of Indian law writing from London, one should not expect to have a direct impact on Indian legal developments. However, there is a manifest unwillingness – or should one say inability – to handle traditional Hindu concepts of marriage solemnisation in a fair and just way. The temptation remains, for some litigants, to abuse such traditions, and thereby to damage the interests of women, especially widows and remarried women, for obvious pecuniary benefit.

It was evidence of such continuing abuse of tradition which prompted me to write about the topic in the first place. Rather than inability to handle tradition, this appears like a case of devious, litigious exploitation of the vulnerability and weaknesses of hapless women when it comes to defending an action in court. Thus, the case of a remarried widow in the early 1980s, reported in *Bibbe v. Ram Kali*, AIR 1982 All 248, and discussed in section 1.2, is really no different from *Surjit Kaur v. Garja Singh*, AIR 1994 SC 135. In the latter case, the woman was also told that she was not the wife of the deceased and thus had no entitlement to his property, despite the fact that the marriage had even been registered under the relevant law!

The solution to this perennial problem is not, as modernist reformers would immediately be tempted to argue, to get rid of Hindu tradition. That would throw out the baby with the proverbial bathwater. While I was tempted to argue for several reforms during the 1980s, including the suggestion that registration of marriage would be beneficial for women, I am much less optimistic about the impact of such reforms today. Legal changes of this kind are an inappropriate solution because the Indian legal system is clearly not in a position, for financial as well as organisational reasons, to introduce a compulsory marriage registration system as a basis for determining their legal validity. This is of course what has been done in English law and many other Western jurisdictions. However, by the early 1990s, it was becoming increasingly clear that Indian law no longer even tries to follow Western models. The state simply does not have the resources to implement a real welfare state. Then, what would be the point of an elaborate system of marriage registration if the information produced was of no real use to the state at large?

Unlike Western countries, it seems now that India will never be in a position to attach welfare right entitlements to married status. Regarding compulsory official registration of all marriages, therefore, India has neither the resources, nor the will to implement such an important legal change. The legal system therefore continues to rely on old-established customary patterns of marriage solemnisation and the public recognition of status through such social processes.

The British example shows, at any rate, that compulsory registration of all marriages is far from fool-proof. In English marriage law, the main criterion for legal validity of a marriage, whether it was registered by or on behalf of an agent of the state, has been rendered partly defunct by the development of a widespread pattern of unmarried cohabitation, which most Indians would find deeply offensive.[2] Hence, in modern English law, 'cohabitation' is now increasingly equated with formal marriage, at least as far as the consequences in terms of property and succession law, and the implications for any children of the couple, are concerned. Thus, also a modern, bureaucratised, formal system has its limits of effectiveness, its continuing legal insecurities and much potential for abuse. It is therefore widely recognised today that the formal introduction of compulsory registration of all marriages in India would only create many new socio-legal problems. Most crucially, it would not be an effective remedy for women who are in danger of being denied marital status.

When I wrote my first article on the subject in 1983 (see section 1.2), I was not yet sufficiently aware of the difficulties of implementing a registration system for all marriages and overestimated the importance of registration of one's marriage. My recommendation, to the effect that a Hindu woman (or her natal relatives) should insist on official registration of her marriage to safeguard her legal position vis-à-vis the husband and his family, was therefore misguided. Worse, it has meanwhile collapsed altogether. In a number of other cases, but prominently in *Surjit Kaur v. Garja* Singh, AIR 1994 SC 135 – a horrible case to which I shall return quite often – the fact that a Sikh couple's marriage had been legally registered did not appear to mean anything at all to the judges of the court, and not just any court, but the Supreme Court of India! So, what legal security does one achieve by registering a marriage with the organs of the state?

It is thus evident that India has consciously chosen not to follow the route of Western legal systems, which have been making ever-growing use of official administrative processes to determine an individual's status. Today, under the provisions of s. 8 of the *Hindu Marriage Act* of 1955, registration of a Hindu marriage solemnised in India remains merely recommended, but by no means a legal requirement.

This official legal position, which also ensues in Pakistani and Bangladeshi law, (where we deal mainly with Muslim couples under the provisions of the *Muslim Family Laws Ordinance*, 1961) has not stopped British law enforcement agencies, especially the Home Office and its personnel, from insisting that absence of registration of an otherwise valid marriage casts some doubt on the validity of the marriage in question. Such petty cases of tripping up potential immigrants, now that the notorious 'primary purpose rule' has officially been abolished,[3] indicate that there are many ways in which the Hindu law of marriage solemnisation can be abused, not only in Indian law! The British example, as a state-sponsored form of abuse, would appear to teach people to register their marriages, but that, in itself, is clearly not a sufficiently strong safeguard, as the Indian case law itself shows. The stark example of *Surjit Kaur*, in my submission a blatantly wrong decision by two judges of the Indian Supreme Court, confirms my view that Indian law is rightly (for a number of reasons) continuing to rely on customary forms of marriage solemnisation to ascertain the validity of a marriage, but that judges need to be better educated about the potential for legal abuses of such flexible rules.

The relevant legal provisions are found in section 7 of the *Hindu Marriage Act*, 1955, which is quite brief and clear. It reads as follows:

> S. 7 – *Ceremonies for a Hindu marriage.*
> (1) A Hindu marriage may be solemnized in accordance with the customary rites and ceremonies of either party thereto.
> (2) Where such rites and ceremonies include the *saptapadi* (that is, the taking of seven steps by the bridegroom and the bride jointly before the sacred fire), the marriage becomes complete and binding when the seventh step is taken.

Subsection (1) therefore has preserved the old customary position under Hindu law, whereby solemnisation of a marriage is a matter for the families concerned and is to be governed by family, community and caste custom. These vary from locality to locality, from caste to caste, and also from case to case. In other words, the concept of custom is to be interpreted quite flexibly, and undue rigidity is to be avoided. After all, marriage for Hindus is a *samskara*, a sacrament rather than purely a contract. Most importantly, it is not a contract vis-à-vis the state, but falls more or less entirely outside the ambit of the state's law and is a matter for society. For Muslims, where we have a similar situation, the *nikah* being a solemn contract of the two spouses before Allah, somehow lawyers and the state law have been more willing to accept that this is a so-called 'extra-legal' action.

In traditional South Asian laws, in other words, the state has no direct input into the solemnisation of marriages when people marry under traditional Hindu law or Muslim law. However, when the validity of a Hindu marriage is at issue before a court, questions need to be raised about what is customary in a particular kind of marriage. Given the flexible framework of the law, as found in s. 7(1) of the HMA, cited above, several important questions may arise, and legal criteria have to be developed for when an action is to be legally recognised as falling within the ambit of 'custom'. As for the legal validity of customs, section 3 of the *Hindu Marriage Act*, 1955 is the guiding provision. It appears that it is trying to be helpful:

> S. 3 – *Definitions.*
> In this Act, unless the context otherwise requires –
> (a) the expressions "custom" and "usage" signify any rule which, having been continuously and uniformly observed for a long time, has obtained the force of law among Hindus in any local area, tribe, community, group or family;

> Provided that the rule is certain and not unreasonable or opposed to public policy; and
> Provided further that in the case of a rule applicable only to a family it has not been discontinued by the family;

However, what is our understanding of customs and of the nature of a Hindu marriage ceremony? Is it a sequence of ritual steps that rigidly follow some old, traditional pattern? Or is every Hindu marriage rather a specially constructed sequence of ritual steps that have elements of customary tradition in them, but are in essence *ad hoc, ad hominem* constructions? Taking the latter view, as I have always done, of course creates potential clashes with more restrictive understandings of the legal concept of 'custom'. The law seems to assume that Hindu marriages follow set customary patterns, and that families will know what is customary. Such a superficial view of the matter seems to discount the possibility of more or less gradual and subtle changes to customs, assuming that minor modifications are either legally irrelevant or not permitted.

In practice, however, customs are not rigid elements of tradition that never change, but flexible 'bricks' that are re-arranged in accordance with the need of the situation. No two marriage ceremonies are, in principle and probably also in fact, exactly alike. As a result, nobody is likely to question the validity of a marriage between two people from the same caste community or even of different castes, when ritual elements that are clearly recognisable as customary were performed in front of a large public. Problems have arisen, however, when communities have more or less radically changed their customs and have introduced new elements which seem to clash with the provisions of s. 3 HMA. Such changes then open up avenues for devious individuals to claim that the marriage solemnisation did not take place in accordance with ancient custom, and thus resulted in a legally invalid union.

I have slipped in a reference to 'ancient' custom here on purpose. Section 3 of the HMA, as cited above, clearly speaks of customs having been observed 'for a long time'. But how long is 'a long time'? The legal requirement is manifestly not that such customs have to be ancient, but Indian courts have in many instances used precisely that word, and have thus displayed remarkable imprecision in statutory interpretation, which should not have gone unnoticed. However, the so-called leading cases on the subject in Indian law, starting from the well-known case of *Bhaurao Shankar*, AIR 1965 SC 1564, also tend to use the concept of 'ancient' custom. This looks like a relic of British legal education, while in Hindu law there is definitely no such requirement of custom having to be traced 'from time immemorial' in order to be recognised as legally valid and binding.

Because devious, greedy lawyers and litigants seek to misguide the courts, and judges are sometimes less alert than they should be, mistakes have crept in, and this area of the law is still in a state of insecurity and confusion. The oldest case on the matter in independent India is the important Tamil Nadu case of the 'self-respecters', who refused to involve Brahmins and complex Brahmanical rituals in their marriage ceremonies and devised instead new, simpler and cheaper customary forms of marriage solemnisation which were followed by a large number of people. In *Deivaini Achi,* AIR 1954 Mad 657, it was held, in obvious conflict with local social norms, expecting a full-fledged *shastric* marriage ceremony, that such a simple marriage solemnisation did not lead to a legally valid marriage. This decision, against the development of new customs and in favour of high-caste *shastric* norms, created a grave social problem. It invalidated many thousands of otherwise functioning Hindu marriages, and it confused people about their property rights. It took the legislature some time to resolve this conflict. The eventual result was an amendment to s. 7 HMA which applies only in the state of Tamil Nadu. The legislature, thus, gave in to people's law, admitted that *Deivaini Achi* had been wrongly decided, and reversed the legal position, albeit with a delay of 13 years.

The text of the *Hindu Marriage (Madras Amendment) Act*, 1967 is not easy to find and is therefore reprinted here in full to facilitate analysis. This new law inserted a section 7-A after s. 7 HMA in the main Act, for the state of Tamil Nadu (then Madras) only. The new law provided as follows:

> 7-A. *Special provision regarding suyamariyathai and seerthiruththa marriages.*
> (1) This section shall apply to any marriage between any two Hindus, whether called *suyamariyathai* marriage or *seerthiruththa* marriage or by any other name, solemnized in the presence of relatives, friends or other persons –
> (a) by each party to the marriage declaring in any language understood by the parties that each takes the other to be his wife or, as the case may be, her husband; or
> (b) by each party to the marriage garlanding the other or putting a ring upon any finger of the other; or
> (c) by the tying of the thali.
> (2) (a) Notwithstanding anything contained in section 7, but subject to the other provisions of this Act, all marriages to which this section applies solemnized after the commencement of the Hindu Marriage (Madras Amendment) Act, 1967, shall be good and valid in law.
> (b) Notwithstanding anything contained in section 7 or in any text, rule or interpretation of Hindu law or any custom or usage as part of that law in force immediately before the commencement of the Hindu Marriage (Madras Amendment) Act, 1967, or in any other law in force immediately before such commencement or in any judgment, decree or order of any Court, but subject to sub-section (3), all marriages to which this section applies solemnized at any time before such commencement shall be deemed to have been, with effect on and from the date of the solemnization of each such marriage, respectively, good and valid in law.

(3) Nothing contained in this section shall be deemed to –

(a) render valid any marriage referred to in clause (b) of sub-section (2), if before the commencement of the Hindu Marriage (Madras Amendment) Act, 1967, –

(i) such marriage has been dissolved under any custom or law; or

(ii) the woman who was a party to such marriage has, whether during or after the life of the other party thereto, lawfully married another; or

(b) render invalid a marriage between any two Hindus solemnized at any time before such commencement, if such marriage was valid at that time; or

(c) render valid a marriage between any two Hindus solemnized at any time before such commencement, if such marriage was invalid at that time on any ground other than that it was not solemnized in accordance with the customary rites and ceremonies of either party thereto:

Provided that nothing contained in this sub-section shall render any person liable to any punishment whatsoever by reason of anything done or omitted to be done before such commencement.

(4) Any child of the parties to a marriage referred to in clause (b) of sub-section (2) born of such marriage shall be deemed to be their legitimate child:

Provided that in a case falling under sub-clause (i) or sub-clause (ii) of clause (a) of sub-section (3), such child was begotten before the date of the dissolution of the marriage or, as the case may be, before the date of the second of the marriages referred to in the said sub-clause (ii).

Cutting through this jargon, it is evident that this Act represents a resounding victory for custom, and for the legal recognition of the new self-respecters' customs. Not only does the 1967 Act state that henceforth such new customs are virtually equal to the 'customary rites and ceremonies of either party', as provided in s. 7(1) HMA, but s. 2 of the 1967 Act also grants retrospective legal validity to all Hindu marriages in the state of Tamil Nadu (or Madras, as it then was) which fell under the ambit of this Act and were still legally subsisting. The victory of custom could not have been more expansive than this.

However, North Indian courts in particular (among which one must certainly count the Indian Supreme Court), have with great conviction taken the opposite perspective and have in many cases insisted that customs of Hindu marriage solemnisation must be strictly followed, must be 'ancient', and that any deviations from such strict norms would render a marriage legally invalid. Significantly, the leading cases on this point have mainly been bigamy prosecutions, in which the accused husband escapes punishment by claiming that he never married the second wife validly, or indeed he never married any of the women validly! These cases are therefore discussed in the present section rather than in chapter 3 on polygamy, which mainly concerns other issues.

The leading case of *Bhaurao Shankar Lokhande v. State of Maharashtra*, AIR 1965 SC 1564 asserted in essence that, in order to be a legally valid marriage, a Hindu marriage had to be celebrated or performed with proper ceremonies and in due form. What is 'proper' and what amounts to 'due form' was not prescribed in detail, but the indications are clear: In essence, fully ritualised, elaborate ceremonies that involve Hindu priests and Sanskritic rituals would qualify under these criteria, and new simpler ceremonies would not be legally recognised. It was held in the above case, at pp. 1565–1566:

> Merely going through certain ceremonies with the intention that the parties be taken to be married, will not make the ceremonies prescribed by law or approved by any established custom.

It is not evident from the case report that the parties involved were in fact neo-Buddhists in Maharashtra, and that their conversion to Buddhism some time earlier had given rise to several important changes in their marriage rituals. There was no holy fire present during the marriage rituals, and there was also no performance of *saptapadi*, the ritual of seven steps which is explicitly mentioned in s. 7(2) of the HMA as a signifier of legal validity. By assuming that Hindu marriage rituals must include ritual elements around the holy fire and a rite of *saptapadi*, the Supreme Court virtually held that these two rites are essential to a legally valid Hindu marriage, and thus totally overstepped the limits of appropriate statutory interpretation. I have maintained throughout, and continue to argue, that this precedent is a bad case of misguided judicial interpretation and, worse, an obvious example of judicial blindness to social realities.

Bhaurao Shankar was of course decided before the passing of the *Hindu Marriage (Madras Amendment) Act* of 1967. It was soon followed as a precedent in the Supreme Court case of *Kanwal Ram v. The Himachal Pradesh Administration*, AIR 1966 SC 614. This was also a prosecution for bigamy, and this man was also acquitted, again on the ground that the allegedly polygamous marriage he had entered into was not legally valid. Here, almost unbelievably, even the husband's admission that he had taken the second woman as his wife was not accepted as evidence. The Court took a very strict and technical approach on matters of proof and held, at p. 615, that

> ... it is clear that in law such admission is not evidence of the fact of the second marriage having taken place. In a bigamy case, the second marriage as a fact, that is to say, the ceremonies constituting it, must be proved.

Reading the case report, which seems to be more interested in quaint old Scottish marriage folklore than an appreciation of contemporary Indian customs, one can only be puzzled. The appeal against conviction for bigamy succeeded, the Court relying on *Bhaurao Shankar* and the assumption that the essential ceremonies had not been performed. In my submission, not enough thought was given to the particular facts and circumstances of this couple and the question whether perhaps a fully ritualised Hindu marriage ceremony would have been an infringement of customary understandings of propriety in this particular instance.

The resulting official legal position has been that these two Supreme Court cases were taken to determine the issue, and the probability is that a very large number of cases have followed them as precedent. However, by 1981 already, this rather unsatisfactory position was clearly shaken by a case from the Bombay High Court, to which Professor Derrett drew my attention just as he retired.

Baby v. Jayant Mahadeo Jagtap, AIR 1981 Bom 283, being only a High Court case, could of course not overrule the Supreme Court precedents. But the case dented the conviction with which the highest court had asserted its position on proper ceremonies. In *Baby*, also a case on polygamy, the husband and the second wife had been acquitted on the basis of the established case law, as discussed above. The first wife, however, appealed against the acquittal and thus managed to criminalise the husband and his new wife. In this case, it is made evident from the start that the community we are dealing with here is the same as in *Bhaurao Shankar*, namely the neo-Buddhists of Maharashtra. It is shown that millions of people now follow the new modified customary marriage ceremonies of this community, so that it could be argued that the test under s. 3 HMA, to the effect that a custom has to be followed 'for a long time', could be satisfied. This very important case therefore challenges the position that only old-established and fully ritualised customs of Hindu marriage solemnisation could qualify for official legal recognition. However, as a High Court case, it could do nothing to get rid of the unsatisfactory precedent of *Bhaurao Shankar*, to which, for good reasons, no direct reference is made.

Detailed research would show that in many cases, reported and unreported, the strict legal position on 'proper ceremonies' was exploited by ruthless husbands during the 1970s and 1980s to the detriment of women. By the mid-1980s, the abuse became so bad, it would seem, that some Supreme Court judges began to recognise that there could potentially be real social problems if women were divested of their rightful claims simply on the basis of formal invalidity of their marriage. This realisation, it seems to me, went hand in hand with growing judicial activism and awareness about the maintenance rights of divorced wives.[4] However, rather than making a big issue of this and changing the unsatisfactory law on marriage solemnisation by tackling the pernicious precedent of *Bhaurao Shankar*, the Supreme Court chose a soft strategy, making some subtle comments, which most legal analysts did not even notice, and most practising lawyers (who tend to be kept in bread by men) happily overlooked, to the further detriment of women.

One particular case on maintenance rights of women shows that the Supreme Court was not asleep as far as validity of marriages was concerned. In *Sumitra Devi v. Bhikhan Choudhary*, AIR 1985 SC 765, a cunning husband opposed his wife's claim for maintenance by asserting that she was not properly married to him. This very brief case report contains a most important statement from the Supreme Court which nobody seems to have picked up at the time.[5] Thinking that he would get away from this obligation by claiming that he never married his wife in the first place, the husband tried to play down the fact that he was already married to another woman and should thus have been liable for prosecution as a bigamist. The High Court of Patna had refused the wife's claim and had sided with the man. Ranganath Misra J in the Supreme Court criticised the technical approach taken by the lower court and by the High Court, holding at p. 766:

> There is no doubt that in order that there may be a valid marriage according to Hindu law, certain religious rites have to be performed. Invoking the fire and performing Saptapadi around the sacred fire have been considered by this Court to be two of the basic requirements for a traditional marriage. It is equally true that there can be a marriage acceptable in law according to customs which do not insist on performance of such rites as referred to above and marriages of this type give rise to legal relationships which law accepts.

The Court could have taken this as an occasion to overrule the unsatisfactory position of *Bhaurao Shankar* and *Kanwal Ram*, but chose – for whatever reason – not to do so and instead remitted the case to the lower court for disposal. The above words are very clear signals to the effect that the facts and circumstances of individual cases have to be carefully examined before accepting a claim that a particular marriage should not be legally valid. In *Sumitra Devi*, the tangible issue is the entitlement of the wife and her daughter to maintenance from the errant husband, and the learned judge, entirely in line with the new-found judicial activism regarding maintenance law during the mid-1980s (see chapter 4), stresses the entitlement of the child, in particular, to maintenance from the man, irrespective of the precise legal position of the marriage. As a Supreme Court authority, however, *Sumitra Devi* is a weak defence of customary plurality and lacks punch. In addition, the fact that this was primarily a maintenance case may have had the consequence that nobody realised the linkages with the law of marriage solemnisation.

The predicaments of Indian women in relation to marriage solemnisation have been complicated especially in cases where the marriage rituals in question were truncated. This was already the case in *Deivaini Achi*, AIR 1954 Mad 657, and in *Bhaurao Shankar*, AIR 1965 SC 1564 on account of social changes in that particular community. Further problems arise because it is customary among Hindus, if one allows female remarriage at all, to perform marriage rituals for a subsequent marriage that differ from those for a first marriage, in which the woman is (or is at least supposed to be) a virgin. Remarried women, and especially widows marrying a widower, would customarily follow very little ceremonial ritual, and it appears to me that there is, in many cases, even a custom of 'zero-ritual'. In other words, it is customary to perform no rituals at all, just to cohabit and live together as man and wife, in the cases of many remarried women. It then becomes difficult, evidently, to ascertain evidence of the performance of customary marriage rituals.

Detailed research, which remains to be done, would show many customary forms of such truncated or even totally absent marriage rituals and the consequent application of a presumption of marriage.[6] Among recently reported cases, apart from Sikh marriage customs which have always allowed for remarried women, there are cases from Maharashtra,[7] from Kerala,[8] and from other parts of India which accept the legal validity of unusual marriage ceremonies, some of them involving widows.

Some cases during the 1990s, however, indicate that the law in this area still remains far from clear and that women remain at risk from being divested of their entitlements in terms of maintenance and succession rights. It is remarkable that, even today, such problems continue to persist, with conflicting views about this subject matter. Taking a rather cynical approach to the wonderful assumption that a major purpose of legal development is to help clarify the law, it could be argued that some lawyers today evidently seek to exploit the continuing confusion over the precise modalities for getting married under Indian Hindu law, for the benefit of their overwhelmingly male clients as much as their own pockets.

The decision in *Surjit Kaur*, which I was tempted to criticise in much stronger terms (see section 1.4) is evidently based on character assassination of the basest kind. Alleging that the woman claimant to property was not a decent woman, that "Surjit Kaur was in the habit of changing husbands frequently" (p. 136), the deceased husband's agnatic relatives and their immoral lawyer achieve their wicked aim to bend the judges' ears – successfully as it turns out – against listening to the woman's side of the story. Out goes the evidence that this marriage was properly registered and that it fell into the pattern of a Sikh *karewa* marriage, old-established as a custom of remarriage in the Panjab.

Here is strong evidence of lack of judicial sensitivity to gender-related issues and lack of concern for the predicaments caused to women who have to appear in court to defend their rightful claims according to the law of the land. While everyone concerned may be well aware of the inherent rights of the woman, in this type of litigation one side does not wish to accept reality, by hook or crook. It is not unique to Indian law that there are disagreements over what the law should be; there are many examples of Indian litigants who, like Don Quixote, fight windmills to make their futile point.[9]

Remarkably, in the numerous cases decided by the higher courts about the property rights of widows under s. 14 of the *Hindu Succession Act* of

1956, Indian judges have been tough on male claimants. In other cases, to put it bluntly, some judges have either been asleep or otherwise distracted (as manifestly in *Surjit Kaur*), so that their judgements look distinctly misguided and outright wrong.

Unfortunately, in the area of marriage solemnisation, even today, there remains much reason to be highly critical of Indian judges who confuse adherence to tradition with siding with the male litigant's perspectives. There will, of course, always be cases when a woman will be tempted to take advantage of the legal insecurities and will seek to gain from this through going to court. However, the very nature of most of the litigation relating to section 7 HMA shows us *bona fide* petitions by women who desperately seek to defend themselves against the male side's claims that they should not be entitled to anything at all from the man's family. I shall leave it to the reader to decide whether this is evidence of inability to understand tradition, because it is so diverse and complex, or simply male chauvinism.

The three articles reprinted below in this chapter all focus on the courts' inability to handle the ancient traditions of Hindu marriage solemnisation in a fully competent manner. Judges are shown to be less than alert when they come to decisions that are blatantly against the letter of the statute (as in *Bibbe v. Ram Kali* in section 1.2). In other cases, judgements appear to be based on biased, anti-women views or even, as in *Surjit Kaur*, on brutal character assassination of a remarried woman, rather than faithful application of the letter of legal rules that everyone concerned should know and apply. There is much evidence of inability to apply traditional concepts in all their complexity, but an equal measure of deliberate and skilful abuse of legal insecurities can be detected.

1.2 Is there a customary form of widow-remarriage for Hindus?

[From: 1983 *KLT*, Journal section, pp. 69–72]

While this is not the place for a detailed study of the ritual requirements for the remarriage of a Hindu widow, a critical look at a recent case on widow-remarriage may be of immediate interest to the legal profession. Older works focused strongly on the prohibition of such marriage, and its effects,[10] but it seems that widow-remarriage has always, in some form or another, existed in Hindu society.[11] No investigations into the question what rituals would be considered essential to validate such marriages have, so far, come to my knowledge.[12] It is certainly too simple to argue that already S. 6 of the *Hindu Widows' Remarriage Act* of 1856 put widow-remarriages on the same footing as a normal Hindu marriage. The fact that the *Hindu Marriage Act* (HMA) of 1955 does not contain any special provisions for widow-remarriage at all does not entitle us to conclude that the marriage of a Hindu widow is in no way different from that of her unwidowed sister. Striking differences are apparent, and the Hindu public is well aware of them. Can the judiciary ignore this without running the risk of doing injustice in the name of the law? I would very much welcome a student of law with an interest in social reality and a background knowledge of Hindu traditions who was ready to tackle such questions.[13] The work would be much more than a study in legal history or in ritual science, as is becoming obvious in a number of recent cases.[14] A correct answer to the above question may be of crucial importance to a growing number of Hindu litigants.

The case I propose to discuss here is *[Smt.] Bibbe v. [Smt.] Ram Kali and others*, and it is reported at AIR 1982 All 248. It shows how easily injustice can be done by a narrow interpretation of statutes, despite the warnings at Brihaspatismriti 2.12 as repeated by Justice M. Madhavan Nair at *P. V. Kunhikannan v. State of Kerala* (1968 KLT 19, at p. 23).

At first sight one would tend to pass *Bibbe v. Ram Kali* over as yet another dramatic version of that popular Indian game of trying to deprive an unwanted relative of a legitimate share in the family property. Yet there is more to this case. It points to a new version in the abuse of s. 7 HMA, which may become increasingly popular unless the judiciary act with circumspection. I may have misread the report, but it appears that the decision in *Bibbe*'s case is inadequate as it is based on a rigid, technical interpretation of a statutory provision (in this case s. 7 of the HMA). With great respect to the learned Judge (Shri T. S. Misra of the Allahabad High Court) it must be emphasised that a legalistic approach to the problem before the Court left no room for considerations of Hindu cultural tradition and thus reality and could therefore not do justice to the special circumstances of the case. No matter how modern and secular India may now have become, one cannot merely deny the persistence of ancient traditions in our days and refuse to see their implications on questions of law.

In *Bibbe v. Ram Kali* the problem was whether a Hindu widow, who had already been a widow when she married the deceased, could be taken to be one of his legal heirs. The question was not so much whether she rightfully claimed the status of a widow: the real cause of the litigation was a dispute over property rights. Evidently the widow herself had filed a suit for partition of a house left by the deceased and had claimed a 2/3 share for herself and one daughter, leaving a 1/3 share for another daughter, the first defendant in the case for partition. A third daughter, however, the second defendant, asserted her right in the house. All three daughters appear to be born of the first wife of the deceased male. The widow, so we may assume, used some tension between her step-daughters to try and deprive one of them, the second defendant, of her share but was, alas, ousted herself because the second defendant's clever legal adviser managed to persuade the High Court that the step-mother was not a legally wedded wife, merely a kept concubine, and as such not entitled to any share in the deceased male's property.

It appears to me that the learned single Judge who decided this case has deprived a rewidowed woman of her legitimate share in her deceased second husband's property by applying, in an inappropriate manner, the legal test with regard to the validity of a Hindu marriage according to s. 7 HMA. Sub-section (1) of that section reads:

> "A Hindu marriage may be solemnized in accordance with the customary rites and ceremonies of either party thereto."

The learned Judge interpreted, and so far I can follow, that a valid marriage ceremony among any two Hindus must be in accordance with the custom or usage applicable to either party. But then he went on to state that, "The ceremony must be such which is allowed by the *custom of the caste* to which the parties belong".[15] Here, I respectfully submit, is the point where the learned Judge fell in error. A valid custom need not necessarily be that of a particular caste, it may be that of a family, as section 3(a) of the HMA states clearly enough. One may, and must under present circumstances, go even further: the question arises whether the wording "customary rites and ceremonies of either party thereto" in s. 7(1) HMA should not more properly be taken to refer to the individuals who get married. If India wants to be modern and her legislation is drafted accordingly, courts should perhaps not hesitate to follow this move towards individualism. But let this question, which I propose to discuss elsewhere, not distract us here: in general, if the bride or groom is an ordinary member of the respective family, clan, tribe, caste etc., there may be no reason why an individual spouse's "customary rites and ceremonies" of marriage should be any different from that of other individuals belonging to the same social group. But if this is not so, there may be valid reasons for departure from the general ritual standard applicable to that group. Mulla's *Principles of Hindu law*, 14th ed., repr. Bombay 1978, p. 693 is quite clear on this point. There it is argued, with a view to the spouses, that "The question of the requisite ceremonies must be adjusted in accordance with the custom and usage followed by them or either of them". In our present context, the question arises what rituals of marriage will be considered necessary and customary if the bride is a widow.

It is an undisputed fact in *Bibbe v. Ram Kali* that both spouses had been married before. Presumably, both were widowed when they got married some time in 1958.[16] *Bibbe*'s case, instead of emphasising this material fact and its consequences, overlooks or, more seriously, suppresses it. Before Justice Misra, technicalities are pleaded on behalf of the appellant who seeks to oust the widow, Smt. Ram Kali:

> "The submission was that Smt. Ram Kali had not alleged in her plaint that her marriage had been performed in accordance with the customary rites prevailing in her community in the year 1958 and as the same fact had not been pleaded the appellate Court below fell in error in considering the evidence adduced in that behalf and in setting aside the finding reached by the trial court." [17]

So there is evidence of the solemnisation of this marriage, but the appellant tries to prevent that the Judge considers it! It is, of course, not in the appellant's interest to emphasise that we have a marriage before us in which at least one of the spouses was widowed at the time of solemnisation. The widow's lawyer appears to have had little interest in this case. Thus the learned Judge, without delay, follows the appellant's crude and misleading reasoning. Here is a case where speedy justice may not be justice at all.

Merely three cases were cited before the Court, none of them on the point of law that should have been at issue here. Moreover, a recent decision of the Bombay High Court[18] has exposed the pretentiousness of the leading case of *Bhaurao v. State of Maharashtra* (AIR 1965 SC 1564) as a precedent for all cases on s. 7 HMA. The other two cases, *Kanwal Ram v. The Himachal Pradesh Administration* (AIR 1966 SC 614) and *Priya Bala Ghosh v. Suresh Chandra Ghosh* (AIR 1971 SC 1153) appear to have been cited merely to underline the authority of *Bhaurao*'s case. Both are documentary evidence of the legal exploitation of insecurities in the adequate application of s. 7 HMA, which has often enough been used as a bigamist's charter of freedom. I cannot hide my deep dissatisfaction at the superficial level in which the point of law has been discussed in *Bibbe*'s case.

The learned Judge has, as I mentioned, not considered it necessary to distinguish the marriage of Smt. Ram Kali from an ordinary Hindu marriage in which the female spouse is a virgin and was not previously married. In the result, the widow in *Bibbe*'s case is deprived of her status and property because her legal advisers omitted to plead that her marriage was performed in accordance with the alleged custom known as "*kaz*" in the caste to which she belonged. The learned Judge saw no need to inquire into details of this "*kaz*" ceremony. The report does not even make it clear whether it is taken to apply as a custom only to widow-remarriages,[19] or whether it is presumed to be a generally valid customary form of marriage solemnisation in the respondent's community. The learned Justice was satisfied to find that the widow had not established that she followed an ancient, certain and reasonable custom not opposed to public policy. Ironically, he declared that "It is the usage that makes the law and not the reason of the thing,"[20] but did not hesitate to reason away whatever little evidence the widow had been able to bring that some small ceremony of marriage had been performed. Could she reasonably have been expected to adduce more? Did she not act according to customary requirements for a widow-remarriage in that she merely came into her husband's house, after some minimum of ritual, without the *tamasha* that may accompany a Hindu marriage otherwise? Not to do so would have been a violation of ancient customs of widow-remarriage! I remain deeply dissatisfied that nobody in *Bibbe*'s case came to the rescue of this unfortunate widow.

Actually, the disabilities attaching to the remarriage of a Hindu widow may apply to a remarrying widower, too. He may not find it appropriate to undergo another full *samskara*: it appears customary that spouses have a discretion in such matters. One Indian couple I know have recently got married with a minimum of ritual, because the groom was the widowed spouse. They then registered their marriage. The lady, who had never been married before, initially expected to undergo a full marriage ceremony, but has accepted her husband's wish. She is, in the eyes of the law, a wife for all intents and purposes. She would not suffer Ram Kali's fate.

Thus, in view of cases like the one discussed here,[21] one must strongly recommend that a Hindu woman, or her natal family, insist on registration of the marriage. This alone insures the female spouse against later greedy claims of the husband's relatives who resent the presence of the somewhat superfluous female, and may, à la *Bibbe*, succeed in ousting the widow by applying S. 7 HMA with the help of clever legal advisers. *Bibbe v. Ram Kali* must not be allowed to become a precedent; I hope the case has gone to the Supreme Court for review.

1.3 Solemnisation of Hindu marriages: The law and reality

[From: 1985 *KLT*, Journal section, pp. 1–10]

It is no secret that with regard to ancient Indian societies and their manifestations many wrong notions and inadequate theories persist; the incomplete state of our present knowledge about ancient Indian marriage rituals need not be emphasised here in so many words. The dangers for an approach which focuses exclusively on contemporary phenomena cannot be discussed here in any depth, but they must be pointed out with some force: the premises we are applying in our studies of contemporary South Asian societies may well be wrong unless we have made efforts to co-relate present day societal phenomena with medieval and more ancient evidence that may be available, but may not be easily accessible to the researcher for a number of reasons. To pretend that what we do not know does not exist, and has never existed, may lead us further into the jungle of misconceptions about South Asian societies.

In our present context, a categorical statement that there has never been a period of Hindu cultural history in which patterns of marriage solemnisation could be characterised as uniform is not at all unjustified.[22] If the string of ancient scriptural sources that we are so lucky to possess has tended to create an impression of uniformity, this is clearly wrong.[23] Moreover, these sources must be taken as selective rather than comprehensive evidence, and their use as a mirror of ancient and medieval Hindu social reality is most obviously very limited.

Statements frequently found to the effect that contemporary Hindu marriage rituals have basically remained the same for thousands of years[24] seem to rely on historical evidence that has been created by taking the, at times rather inadequate, writings of earlier authors as documents of historical value.[25] That there has been continuous change within Hindu traditions of marriage solemnisation has become overwhelmingly apparent from my own recent studies of the subject.[26]

Now in contemporary India we find a strange situation and a new constellation with regard to marriage solemnisation. We observe not merely the familiar pattern of diversity of Hindu traditions, but apparent misconceptions of these traditions and their genesis, and obvious contradictions between what people do and what the modern laws of India have to say on this particular topic of marriage solemnisation. This, ultimately, is an unsatisfactory state of affairs, and the difficulties should be explained and adequate solutions found.

Expressed in a simple way, the basic underlying contradiction in the present context is this: traditionally, Hindu marriage has been considered a sacrament (*samskara*), which leads to a life-long union of the spouses. The modern Hindu law, however, has emphasised the contractual aspects of marriage and has legislated away the expectation that a Hindu marriage should be a supernaturally sanctioned, indissoluble union. We could go a step further and say that, nowadays, a Hindu marriage, *when solemnised*, may be conceived of as a *samskara*, but at any point thereafter, when it pleases either spouse, or another interested party, one may use the provisions of the modern Hindu law to break the marital tie. The result, as is gradually becoming more evident, is growing insecurity, especially among female Hindu spouses, about their position in law, and in life, but we are not directly concerned with such questions here.[27] The solemnisation of marriage, which is our central concern here, should normally involve a dramatic expression of expectations connected with the respective marriage, or with marriage in general terms.

Here the contradictions between the modern Hindu law and social reality in contemporary India become most obvious. Many years ago it has been stated, rather cautiously, that "[t]he law seems to have taken little account of the facts here."[28] We must not only ask here why this is so, but should become alerted to the consequences of the modern legal approach to Hindu marriage, consequences for the law itself as well as for the spouses, and last, but not least, for Hindu marriage as an institution.

The claim that the spirit of Hindu marriage was finally buried in 1976 when further amendments to the *Hindu Marriage Act* (HMA) of 1955 made it even less difficult for a Hindu spouse (normally the male partner) to get out of a marriage, appears justified.[29] Yet while the Western expert deplored these changes and emphasised the dangers of a legislative 'overkill', one of the leading Indian scholars of Hindu law felt one had not gone far enough, and the changes had long been overdue anyway.[30] It seems that the consequences of these modern enactments and their repercussions on the patterns of marriage solemnisation among Hindus have so far not been discussed adequately, and that confusion reigns in this particular area of Hindu law.

To begin with, section 7 of the HMA of 1955, dealing with the solemnisation of Hindu marriages, has never been amended, for the whole of India,[31] so as to fall in line with recent developments in other fields of law. An additional provision explicitly allowing a secular mode of marriage solemnisation has been suggested,[32] but the legislative bodies seem unwilling to act. It may well be that one is afraid of the consequences.

The courts, having to bear the brunt of the present unsatisfactory situation and having to ascertain in each case whether the marriage rituals have been performed in a manner creating legal validity,[33] have, at times, anticipated legislative innovations.[34]

We must clearly see, however, that the fathers of the HMA have exclusively concerned themselves with the end of marriage,[35] and have never applied their mind (as we shall see) to its beginning. We would find a blatant imbalance here within the HMA, had s. 7 not remained very general and almost insignificant in view of India's social reality. The wording of this curious section deserves our attention now.

> *S. 7 Ceremonies for a Hindu marriage*
> (1) A Hindu marriage may be solemnized in accordance with the customary rites and ceremonies of either party thereto.
> (2) Where such rites and ceremonies include the *saptapadi* (that is the taking of seven steps by the bridegroom and the bride jointly before the sacred fire), the marriage becomes complete and binding when the seventh step is taken.

Unfortunately, a number of textbooks on Hindu law are rather confused when it comes to interpreting this section.[36] The task has not been made easier by the decisions of Indian courts.[37]

The first major confusion arises with regard to the role of the Sanskritic model of marriage solemnisation. It is clearly wrong to state from the outset that "[p]erformance of certain *shastric* ceremonies is still necessary for a valid Hindu marriage".[38] The, as we must presume, age-old co-existence of non-Sanskritic and Sanskritic customary forms of marriage solemnisation has been preserved in s. 7 HMA, and there are good reasons for that.[39]

One gets the impression that, subconsciously or even purposely, the Sanskritic models of marriage solemnisation, which tend to involve considerable ritual detail and necessitate the employment of a Hindu priest, have been protected by the HMA. Strictly speaking, there was no necessity for s. 7(2) of the HMA, because the determination of validity of the marriage on the seventh step of the *saptapadi* does not cover all cases where a Sanskritic ritual is employed. One wonders, thus, why the ritual element of *saptapadi* has found special mention in the HMA at all.

The professional involvement of priests in Hindu marriage rituals has been remarkably absent in most discussions of the present topic. A recent work, though in a different context, has alluded to the potentially detrimental effects of priestly interest in, and control over, Hindu marriage solemnisation.[40] It cannot be overlooked that solemnisation of marriage is a lucrative branch of priestly business in India and, with few exceptions, wherever else Hindus have settled. This, by itself, is not a negative phenomenon. But much concern of the priestly officiants over the size of their remuneration, rather than the socio-religious and educative public role they have been playing appears to have contributed significantly to the deterioration of Hindu marriage into an expensive show, a *tamasha* of *shadi* rather than a solemn *vivaha*. Serious research works on Hindu rituals have not avoided some criticism of the priestly role in the context of marriage solemnisation. The problems extend, however, much beyond the realm of socio-economic questions.[41]

Here we come to the second major confusion, the meaning of certain Hindu marriage rituals that are supposed to be performed. In the present context we can only concentrate on the *saptapadi*.

This ritual, in its long history, seems to have been undergoing considerable changes; it may not be irrelevant, in our present context, to outline them.[42] Apparently the taking of seven steps was originally a friendship ritual, performed by two allies who made a pact, in the presence of the holy fire. So far, I have not found any evidence that verses should be spoken while these seven steps are taken. On the other hand, in the marriage hymn of the Atharvaveda (14.2.53–58) we find a ritual of endowment of the bride with the auspicious qualities of the cow. Here we have only *mantras* and no evidence of ritual actions. It appears that these two rituals have been merged at a later stage and have been employed specifically in the context of marriage. One of the oldest *Grihyasutras*, that of Baudhayana, has, it appears, preserved the intermediate position: the bride's father walks seven steps with his daughter, in front of the groom, before the latter receives the bride.[43] All other old *Grihyasutras* depict the bride taking the seven steps by herself. Since this is an apparent deviation from the ancient model, at a later stage of re-interpretation again two persons take the seven steps together, now the bride and the groom. Significantly, in all those cases the *saptapadi* is the last major marriage ritual.

The decisive ritual element validating the performance of the marriage rituals in the *Grihyasutras* is, however, not the *saptapadi*, but the ritual of *panigrahana*, the seizing of the bride's hand, most obviously a *rite of incorporation*. This may also bring with it, in the majority of cases, the first direct physical contact between the spouses. This ritual lost its dominant position, so it seems, because in the *dharma* texts rules regarding intercaste marriage destroyed its uniform ritual pattern;[44] this opened the way for the *saptapadi*, already the final ritual of marriage (as far as the major ceremony is concerned), to become the *decisive* marriage ritual. Precisely this position is depicted in *Manusmriti* 8.227, which says that the *mantras* pertaining to the seizing of the hand are a certain proof only that a marriage has been solemnised, while legal validity arises only when the seventh step has been taken. The underlying idea seems to be that the completion of the totality of the marriage rituals signifies legal validity, not so much any particular ritual element. Such conclusions are supported by observations that one may make at Hindu weddings nowadays: a large number of people may be physically present during the solemnisation of the marriage, but the guests may rather have a good time chatting with each other than paying attention to the actual solemnisation of the marriage, not to speak of any ritual detail.

The *saptapadi*, it appears, has been performed in various ways, accompanied by a number of ritual *mantras*. Evidence about the latter, which is forthcoming from the various *grihya* texts, gives a coherent conceptual development, but the details of ritual practice may vary considerably.[45] Already *Manusmriti* 8.227 is not concerned with this diversity; it merely wants to emphasise the instance of completion of the marriage ceremonies.

The concept of *saptapadi* in s. 7 HMA appears to have been taken directly from *Manusmriti* 8.227 in an effort to preserve cultural continuity.[46] This may be due to the prominent position given to 'Manu's law-book' which had been taken to represent authoritatively 'the ancient Hindu law'. In fact, that very verse of the *Manusmriti* seems to have been added to the text subsequently by a commentator.[47] The explanation of *saptapadi* provided in brackets in the text of the HMA itself, viz. "(that is the taking of seven steps by the bridegroom and the bride jointly before the sacred fire)" merely allows a glimpse of the extent of the underlying conceptual 'unity in diversity': the fact that we find an explanation here is significant by itself. Whether this represents an effort at unification is difficult to say. Contemporary India does indeed know several concepts of *saptapadi*.

The tremendous ritual changes since the time of the *Manusmriti* cannot be outlined here in detail, but it may have become clear that here is one case where a comprehensive study of contemporary Hindu phenomena cannot proceed very far without better knowledge of earlier stages of development.

With reference to the performance of the *saptapadi* in our days, further ritual changes have become apparent. In some parts of India (I know, so far, only about Gujarat) the *saptapadi* and the *agniparinayana*, the walking of the spouses around the sacred fire, three or four (less often five, but sometimes seven) times have been merged into one ritual. I was told very often that going around the fire is *saptapadi*. This innovation has also been noticed by some Indian scholars of law. Prof. Diwan finds it necessary (and he is quite right, if I may say so) to emphasise that *saptapadi* means seven steps and not seven rounds.[48] Naturally enough, under the above circumstances the question arises how one could determine the seventh step. For this very reason, some communities seem to circumambulate the fire seven times.

The extent of this ritual diversity is creating some confusion, as is apparent from a little passage in a recent textbook of Hindu law.[49] The author's comment that the legal requirement is the taking of seven steps *round* the sacred fire is clearly wrong (see s. 7 HMA).

My own fieldwork shows that even in one and the same locality the various communities perform marriage rituals in quite different ways, and that the *saptapadi* in one case may well involve the taking of seven steps by the couple, while their immediate neighbours from a different community may merely circumambulate the fire four times. I was told by a learned Hindu priest that the Sanskrit verses spoken during the latter ritual could well be those pertaining to the *saptapadi*, with the result that after the fourth round the priest may speak – presumably in an astonishing speed – the remaining three *mantras* that would belong here.

In view of the fact that there is little agreement in the ancient texts as to what *mantras* should be used, and that the priest generally does not bother to instruct the spouses, we can thus hardly expect that the couple have got the slightest idea of what has been expressed on their behalf.

Medieval[50] practices that seem to have connected the ritual of *saptapadi* with the stepping (of the bride alone!) on seven lines, or into seven circles, appear to have been abandoned in our days, but seem to live on in the popular notion that *saptapadi* has got something to do with the vows (*vrata*) of the spouses. Apparently these vows may be ritually dramatised in a number of ways. So far my rather random search has yielded some further examples of ritual sevenness: the couple may worship seven betel nuts (*supari*) that have been placed in a row in front of them and have been decorated with various ritual ingredients. In South India, not surprisingly, totally different combinations of ritual elements can be found; I may merely point to an example of blending the *saptapadi* with the ancient ritual of stepping on a stone.[51]

The crucial role of the Hindu priesthood in determining *what* rituals are to be performed and *how* they should be performed, cannot be overemphasised. While ritual details may well be predetermined by customary practice in the respective communities of the spouses, with old ladies, in particular, watching over their 'correctness', the priest appears to have wide discretion with regard to the *mantras* chosen. I was given examples how one and the same priest performs quite different marriage rituals for spouses from neighbouring, yet different communities. The priest normally knows the customary requirements of the respective social groups[52] and solemnises the union accordingly. There are, however, elements of innovation. As far as the priests' choice of solemn verses is concerned, few Hindus will be able to question or even scrutinise the criteria of selection. There is evidence that priests do not merely stick to one particular ritual text, but may, for a number of reasons, compose their own version of marriage *mantras* from various sources. Thus, if the *saptapadi mantras* are at times spoken while the ritual of circumambulation of the sacred fire is performed, our conception of 'popular customs' remains imperfect unless we take notice of the potential importance of priestly interference.

Apart from ignorance of the average Hindu about the role of priests in marriage solemnisation, and a general, growing dissatisfaction with, and disregard for, the requirement to conform with ancient patterns whose usefulness, due to lack of cultural insight, one does no longer understand, a number of other factors have been contributing to the rise of varying patterns of Hindu marriage solemnisation and, in the extreme, to the *ad hoc* performance of certain rituals that are taken to constitute a full marriage ceremony. Such developments have been unduly disregarded and have not been taken seriously enough.[53] Evidently legal science, with its tendency to emphasise order, in the broadest sense, will seek to delimit the scope for such 'chaotic cases'. Certain doubts have been cast, however, from time to time and Prof. Derrett has pointed out that:

> It seems hard that new customs can never be formed in such a significant connection as marriage.[54]

That particular communities may adjust to new environmental circumstances, whatever, for the moment, these may be, should not surprise us at all. The immense adaptive potential of South Asians, and Hindus in particular, becomes apparent here again.[55] Thus among communities of Hindus living in foreign countries, new customs of marriage solemnisation have been developing, at times under the explicit influence of legal requirements of the new *lex loci*.[56] Minor elements of change are easily perceived: in England some Hindu brides now wear a white wedding *sari*, and the ceremonial cutting of the English wedding cake has become ubiquitous.

It would be interesting to see, however, as far as Indian evidence is concerned, whether migrant communities have, in a new socio-ecological environment, also changed their customary forms of marriage solemnisation; whether for example, the working-class Tamil communities of Bombay or Delhi have been developing their own customs, which may differ considerably from the original models. Again, the warning that what we do not know may well exist, must be emphasised. An Indian High Court has recently had to face precisely this situation, and the modern Hindu law has had to concede defeat in view of the strength of customary practices. The decision in *Baby v. Jayant Mahadeo Jagtap and another* (reported at AIR 1981 Bombay 283) is of eminent interest in our present context.

In this instance, *prima facie* a bigamy case, the husband had married twice, both times in a Buddhist ceremony (the community concerned is that of the Mahars of Maharashtra, who converted to Buddhism some time around 1956). Undoubtedly with a view to the lenient attitude of many Indian courts towards bigamists (they often got away with it because it was held that one of their marriages was not appropriately solemnised and thus not valid in law),[57] it was pleaded on behalf of the husband that the first marriage had been validly dissolved by a customary divorce. The learned Judge explicitly distinguished the present case from an earlier decision of the same Court (reported at *Shakuntala v. Nilkanth* (1973) *Maharashtra Law Journal* 310) and held that the complainant, the first wife, had successfully proved the customary form of marriage undergone by herself and the second 'wife' of the husband. In the result, the husband was convicted of bigamy and the second wife punished for having abetted the accused.

The importance of this judgment lies in its explicit recognition of neo-Buddhist marriage ceremonies. Those had been continuously performed for the last 25 years and could no longer be denied (as in *Shakuntala*'s case) legal recognition without adverse legal consequences for the millions of people affected by this decision. *Baby*'s case shows that modern Indian judges may do well to adopt an approach of realism, which also includes consideration of the implications of their decisions for the litigants and their communities.

Baby's case also contains an appeal to the Government of Maharashtra to persuade the Government of India to introduce changes to s. 7 HMA 1955 that have been recommended by the Ninth Report of the Maharashtra State Law Commission, which suggests amendments to the above section in order to simplify the ceremonies of marriage amongst Hindus. I would not be surprised to hear that nothing has happened since. It must be seen very clearly that the major problem is not one of simplification of marriage rituals, because simple rituals of marriage have always co-existed with the more elaborate models in all parts of India. The real problem is that simple marriage rituals may be denied legal recognition by some Indian courts at any time, and that this has already happened rather often. In view of the well-documented strictness of Indian courts when it comes to the definition of 'customary', and especially in view of the fact that courts have at times found it necessary to rule that *saptapadi* and *homa* (sacrifices into the sacred fire, at any rate, the presence of fire) are essential ceremonies for *all* Hindu marriages, the suggestions made *appear* appropriate. But, should one not ask who should adjust to whom? It appears as though here we have an example of the limits of law.[58] If s. 7 HMA did not disturb the ancient patterns of marriage solemnisation among Hindus and has adopted a course of non-interference, apart from its Sanskritic bias, it can hardly be the task of a more modern version of this section to prescribe marriage rituals to all Hindus. One could have removed the Sanskritic bias, but then the Supreme Court of India could have achieved this a long time ago.

Actually, the Indian Constitution, by directing in Article 44 that the State shall endeavour to secure for all citizens a Uniform Civil Code has already predetermined the issue to the effect that modern Indian laws should not be concerned with religious matters, or issues that vitally affect one of the religious communities of India. Then, the desirable procedure can certainly not be to amend and re-amend s. 7 HMA; it is undesirable that thousands of pieces of legislation should be created to ensure legal validity for all customary forms of Hindu, Sikh, Jaina and Buddhist marriage solemnisation found on Indian soil. The aim must be to create uniform legal provisions that will, moreover, relieve Indian courts from their present, arduous task of ascertaining the validity of individual marriages. It must be clearly said that *Baby*'s case was easy to decide because of the large number of people directly affected by that particular decision. The learned Judge in this case has, appropriately, demonstrated a sense of social responsibility. The problem is much greater, and the position of the female spouse concerned much more vulnerable, if marriage rituals have been performed that may now be fashionable in India, but could not claim to be customary, or if, due to ignorance of traditions, negligence, or whatever other reason *ad hoc* ceremonies have been performed with the genuine intention of the spouses to become husband and wife. Even if one made 'intention to marry' a legal criterion, judges will find it difficult to determine this intention unless there is some concrete evidence of manifestations of this intention.[59] Thus, despite growing evidence of individualism in contemporary India, the modern Hindu law would not necessarily uphold a marriage solemnised in disregard of custom and tradition; in fact the strict letter of the law as it stands at present would demand that such marriages be declared invalid.

In discussions of the secular nature of modern Indian matrimonial laws it has recently been suggested that the law should abolish the institution of Hindu marriage altogether:

> It should be either amended suitably so as to break the religious shield of the marriage or be removed completely from the statute book.[60]

With respect, such utopian suggestions of an apparently over-enthusiastic legal scholar who seems to be anxious to abolish all fetters of the past regardless of the consequences, need not be discussed here at length. How the modern 'secular' laws of India should achieve abolition of religion and its manifestations is, to my knowledge, not clear to anyone. The modern law can, however, *paying a certain price*, abandon its concern over 'religious' issues and may restrict its demands to minimal formal requirements.

In the present context the obvious secular solution to the problem of determination of legal validity of a Hindu marriage, in fact of all marriages in India, would be a uniform legal provision for the compulsory registration of all marriages. S. 7 HMA could then be declared redundant, and s. 8 HMA, which contains the rudiments of legal provisions regarding registration, could be enlarged, or could make way for a completely new legal provision that may be drafted according to the model of the *Special Marriage Act*, 1954. One would, moreover, achieve a number of positive side-effects, e.g. better legal control over the problem of child marriages.[61]

Here we must actually leave our present topic. The customary forms of marriage solemnisation among the Hindus and others governed by Hindu law would cease to be of much interest to the student of law. The example of the 'Asians' in Britain shows a somewhat happy co-existence of the formal legal requirement of registration and the traditional Hindu wedding. It is up to the spouses and their families to decide which mode of marriage solemnisation they recognise as the most important one, and whether they wish to continue their Hindu traditions.

The situation in India would be very much the same, though it may take longer than in Britain to drive home the message that registration of all marriages is a definite legal requirement. How this could be achieved at all in India is not our concern here, but it seems that the Hindu priests may play a crucial role in this context as they, currently, are the dominant agents of Hindu marriage solemnisation.

We must note, finally, that the introduction of uniform legal provisions in India with regard to marriage solemnisation would be a great step towards the somewhat utopian Uniform Civil Code, but that it would by no means abolish the traditional heterogeneity of normative traditions with regard to marriage solemnisation among Hindus. One may ask whether this is a useful result of legal uniformity. In view of the current, growing confusion over the legal value of the innumerable customary forms of Hindu marriage solemnisations, registration, if effectively implemented and strictly controlled, could indeed relieve the Indian judiciary of an arduous problem.

1.4 Widow's right to property. Prejudices against remarried women

[From: No. 89 [July–August 1995] *Manushi*, pp. 15–16]

A bad case of male bias and judicial inconsistency has appeared in *Surjit Kaur v. Garja Singh and others,* reported at AIR 1994 SC 135. Decided by a bench of two judges on October 27, 1993, this case creates a potentially dangerous situation of legal uncertainty for many Hindu, Sikh, Jain and Buddhist women in India. The implications of such a decision for Indian women need to be addressed.

The details of the case can be quickly summarised. It is a simple, almost everyday case, a property dispute, quite familiar in modern India. A certain Gulaba Singh had died in 1969, leaving behind no offspring. A woman by the name of Surjit Kaur claimed to be his rightful wife. As his widow, she prepared to take over his property. However, she was prevented from doing so by Singh's male relatives who claimed to be the rightful heirs, producing dubious evidence of a will in their favour. In addition, most relevant for us here, they insisted that Surjit Kaur had no rightful claim to the property since she had not been validly married to the deceased.

This case illustrates the problems that arise due to section 7 of the *Hindu Marriage Act* of 1955. This Act has time and again proved to be an ideal tool for unscrupulous litigants. Usually these are men who seek to avoid a prosecution for bigamy, who want to evade payment of maintenance, or, as in this case, seek to defeat a widow's claim to inheritance. It particularly affects women who remarry after a divorce, or after the death of their first husband.

For some strange reason, many lawyers do not want to accept what most Indians know very well: in such situations it is customary not to have the full marriage rituals performed as done for a first marriage. In fact, in some situations it will be customary to have virtually no marriage rituals at all. There are many cases in which a man and a woman simply contract to marry, and whether this is done in writing or not is immaterial. In the case of Surjit Kaur and Singh, some *gur* (jaggery) was distributed to friends of the newly married couple. There was thus public recognition of the marriage and, in addition, the marriage was registered.

A legal presumption of marriage in such situations is a well-known concept in the personal laws of India. In this case, however, the higher courts refused to accept such evidence of simple marriage solemnisation. Why then, did the lower courts recognise the same marriage as valid? The Supreme Court declared an absence of proof that the ceremonies required by custom had been followed to the last detail. Surely, this demanded an unnecessarily strict burden of proof?

Sub-section 1 of s. 7 simply lays down that Hindus can create a valid marriage by performing the customary rites and ceremonies of either party to the marriage. Of course, what is customary depends on a variety of social facts, different from case to case. Sub-section 2 provides that: "Where such rites and ceremonies include the *saptapadi* (the taking of seven steps by the bridegroom and the bride jointly before the sacred fire), the marriage becomes complete and binding when the seventh step is taken." Clearly, the wording of these sections confirms that it is perfectly possible to enter a legally valid Hindu marriage without going through elaborate Sanskritic rituals. However, this is where complex problems of proof arise and where widows and divorcees have to be extremely careful. In Surjit Kaur's case, her opponents succeeded in exploiting the legal insecurities about recognition of informal marriages in which Sanskritic rituals such as *homa* and *saptapadi* have not been performed.

Even before the *Hindu Marriage Act* came into force in 1955, the law showed signs of confusion. The *Deivaini Achi* case (AIR 1954 Madras 657) resulted in a large number of Tamil couples being told that they were not legally married since they had only followed simple marriage rituals. However, these marriages were subsequently approved by the law when the *Hindu Marriage (Madras Amendment) Act* of 1967 came into force. This example confirms that, in South India, there is much more awareness about the scope for customary variations.

The *Surjit Kaur* case looks even more out of line if we consider that, exactly two weeks earlier, and reported immediately before it in the same issue of AIR, there is a case from Madras which relaxes the burden of proof and holds the exact opposite: never mind the absence of evidence of full rituals, we apply a presumption of marriage because not to do so would be unjust. (See *S. P. S. Balasubramanyam* AIR 1994 SC 133). This again confirms the North-South divide in India's legal approaches to women.

The High Court dismissed Surjit Kaur's claim of being married on the basis of lack of evidence and accepted the allegation that she was a loose woman cleverly fishing for property rights. One sentence on page 136 of the case report suggests the Court's perspective: "Surjit Kaur was in the habit of changing husbands frequently." One suspects that this was part of the strategy to get rid of this problematic woman once and for all by killing her socially and legally. In a desperate plea for justice, Surjit Kaur went in appeal to the Supreme Court, but all she got was another judicial slap in the face. Apparently, Justice Mohan in the Supreme Court did not look through the scheming pleas of the male relatives and simply proceeded to address the legal technicalities of Hindu marriage law. One suspects that the learned judge was so impressed with the statement of the High Court about the doubtful character of the woman, that he saw no need to question its basis.

It is almost beyond belief that in a case like this, where there is public recognition, evidence of marriage solemnisation, and even registration of the marriage, a presumption of marriage is simply ruled out. Obviously, moral judgment was passed here on a woman who had remarried. What about a legal presumption of marriage in such situations, a well-known concept in the personal laws of India? If there is a *de facto* marriage in an adversarial court setting, judicial attention should also investigate the motives of litigants for questioning such a marriage. Merely accepting wild allegations about a woman's morals cannot be a proper response in a case about property rights.

Depriving women like Kaur of any right in their deceased husband's property means that these women are forced back into the old pattern of looking for another man to support them. If this is what modern Indian law does to its resourceful women, one can imagine the lurking dangers for those whose cases do not even reach the courts. Bad decisions of this kind no doubt contribute to keeping women in subordination.

1.5 Marriage solemnisation and protection of women's rights

Re-reading the case material presented in the three reprinted articles above, published between 1983 and 1995, has fortified my view that such litigation is not really designed to clarify the law. It is mere adversarial bargaining in front of judges, instead of fighting this out in living rooms or arguing under shady spaces below pipal trees. In other words, it looks as though recourse to the modern state law, and even to the highest court of the land, does not necessarily help women to assert their rightful claims to entitlements from the husband's family, as they arise out of marriage arrangements. It all depends, to a large extent, on the politics of the case, and it seems to matter where the case comes from: There is much evidence that North Indian courts, particularly the High Courts of Punjab & Haryana, of Delhi and of Uttar Pradesh, are prone to male chauvinist infections which create blurred vision for the rule of law.[62] Sometimes therefore, far too often for some observers, the official legal mechanisms fail to protect women's rightful claims from greedy predators. As such, what happens in Indian courts probably reflects what goes on in society, too.

As legal observers of the Indian system (and for that matter, of any other legal system), we should of course not behave as though all important disputes go to courts. As the *Manushi* article of 1995 (see 1.4 above) indicates in the conclusion, however, if modern Indian law treats even resourceful women like Surjit Kaur so badly and evidently unfairly, what does life have in store for all those Indian women who never make it to a courtroom to plead their case? We have no proper answer to such questions. However, the assumption that recourse to courts will necessarily bring relief tends to lead to disappointment for one side in an adversarial court setting, where only one party is likely to come out as the winner, while the other will be labelled as the loser. The politics of the courtroom are not easily subjected to academic analysis, nor do they necessarily result in situational justice. Saying this, one admits that mistakes do happen, and oversights occur, but when it comes to the law of marriage solemnisation, there seems to be too much evidence of abuse to allow us to be content.

On the other hand, it would not be fair to assume that all women whose cases do not reach the courts, or who do go to court, fare badly in Indian law and society. In South India, at any rate, many women own property in their own right, and the same is true for North Indians, albeit to a lesser extent. Many women have been able to assert their rightful claims, but we do not know how often this is the case. I am not aware of studies that provide us precise factual details, although they may well exist for some parts of the country. At last, the subject of women's property rights is beginning to be tackled in more depth now by some enterprising and forceful enquiries.[63]

The unsatisfactory state of the law on marriage solemnisation at present affects not only the subject of women's property. Marriage solemnisation is also a connecting factor for women's maintenance rights and for their legal position in cases of polygamy (see chapter 3 below). The modalities of getting married therefore impact on a woman's legal position in several most elementary ways. As we saw, even when contested cases go to the highest court in the land, this often brings bad news for women, especially remarried women. Monitoring of legal developments in this field will need to remain alert and more research in this particular area of the law is urgently needed. Meanwhile, a new PhD project, embarked upon recently by Ms. Livia Sorrentino at SOAS, on the legal roles of North Indian women in negotiating their own remarriages, may throw further light on the question of women's agency in the context of arranging marriages, but also with regard to property entitlements.

Three questions need to be pursued here to conclude this chapter on marriage solemnisation and its implications. First, what has happened in this field of law since the outrageously negative decision of *Surjit Kaur* in 1994? Second, is there any way of protecting Indian women, and remarried women in particular, against persistent male assaults on their legal rights through arguments over marriage solemnisation and what progress have the courts made in this respect? Finally, given that the prevailing picture appears to be one of continuing abuse of tradition and exploitation of some women's weak position, what reform measures can we suggest for Indian law in this regard?

Regarding developments after *Surjit Kaur*, my earlier writing and my article in *Manushi* (see section 1.4 above) seem to have had no impact whatsoever. While this may be frustrating, this is not unexpected. On the other hand, nobody has so far suggested that my interpretation of the *Surjit Kaur* case is wrong, either.[64] Do we find a picture of embarrassed silence, or is this subject simply not considered important enough to warrant attention? There are a number of recent cases on the subject, but no academic debate of any substance is tackling the continuing abuse of tradition and the purposeful twisting of remarried women's cases to suit the whims of male chauvinism. Instead, older and more recent academic comments recite the purportedly well-established *mantras* of the essential nature of elaborate Sanskritic ritual elements such as *homa* and *saptapadi*.

The relevant case law contains conflicting material and yields as a first impression the unsatisfactory conclusion that the courts still seem to be confused, or at any rate inconsistent, in their treatment of evidence regarding marriage solemnisation. In one case, there is insistence on strict proof of customary rituals, even of performance of specific rituals like the *saptapadi*, while in other cases, such evidence is not even required and wide-ranging presumptions are applied.

Thus, printed immediately before *Surjit Kaur v. Garja Singh*, AIR 1994 SC 135, we find *S. P. S. Balasubramanyam v. Sutturayan*, AIR 1994 SC 133, a case concerning property rights, which also turns on the question of legal validity of a marriage, entered into a long time ago, in fact in 1920. The headnote of the case indicates that this litigation concerns evidence law, the subject being to what extent a presumption of marriage may be applied. This is a case that came up from Madras, and it firmly upholds the strong presumption of validity of marriage between two people who have been known to be husband and wife for many years, irrespective of precise proof of the marriage rituals that were performed. It was held, at p. 134:

> What has been settled by this Court is that if a man and woman live together for long years as husband and wife then a presumption of marriage arises in law of legality of marriage existing between the two. But the presumption is rebuttable.

The confident tone of this statement is, however, slightly tinged if one reads the immediately following judgement in *Surjit Kaur v. Garja Singh*, AIR 1994 SC 135, which refuses to accept such a presumption on a number of grounds. My 1995 article, reprinted in section 1.4 above, vigorously criticised that decision, and I am still of the view that it is blatantly wrong. It is also quite strange that in both cases, the second judge on the bench, Mr. Justice S. R. Pandian, does not comment at all, so we do not know about his views.

While there is evidence of several other cases during the mid-1990s which held that strict proof of customary rituals is essential, it must be noted that all these cases were bigamy prosecutions, where the courts appear to retain their male-biased interpretation of s. 7 HMA as the bigamist's charter of freedom. That does seem to make a difference.

In *Nirmala v. Rukminibai*, AIR 1994 Kant 247, which is also a bigamy case, the main legal dispute was over entitlements to substantial property. Here a man, who died in 1978, had taken a second wife in 1948. Only some time after his death did the first wife and those siding with her start alleging that the second wife had always been merely a concubine. Two learned judges in the High Court of Karnataka patiently heard out the parties (even though the second wife had died in the meantime) and firmly upheld the presumption of marriage in cases of long cohabitation. The case report not only contains a detailed discussion of the case law on presumptions of marriage, but also tackles the question of performance of customary ceremonies.

It had been alleged by the first wife's side that there was no evidence that the alleged second marriage had been performed in accordance with customary rituals. The learned judge, reminding everyone that the marriage in question took place in 1948, found it unfair to demand such evidence and proceeded to apply a further presumption, holding at p. 255:

> When there is a presumption that there is a legal and valid marriage, there is also equally a presumption that all the formalities and customs have been duly performed at the time of the said marriage. Therefore, in view of that presumption also the trial court was not justified in holding that the marriage ... was not performed in accordance with the customs and rituals of the community ...

Significantly, the lawyer for the first wife sought to rely on *Surjit Kaur v. Garja Singh*, AIR 1994 SC 135, and extracts from that case are even quoted *verbatim* and at length in this report (pp. 255–256). However, and this is quite remarkable, the High Court of Karnataka asserted that the facts of the case before it were different from those of *Surjit Kaur* and hence proceeded to decree that the second wife had a valid claim to the full status of wife, while her six children were legitimate offspring and were entitled to succeed to the property of their deceased father. This instructive case, therefore, although only a High Court case, correctly uses the flexible provisions of Hindu law and of modern Indian procedural law to uphold the presumption of a valid marriage on the basis of long cohabitation. Together with the Supreme Court case of *S. P. S. Balasubramanyam v. Sutturayan*, AIR 1994 SC 133, which clearly decides a similar matter to the same effect, this presents a formidable challenge to the biased position taken in *Surjit Kaur v. Garja Singh*, AIR 1994 SC 135.

Another recent case from the Supreme Court confirms that the welfare of women and children must rank above male chauvinist predilections and, in this very interesting brief case, high-caste Hindu prejudices as well. In *M. Govindaraju v. K. Munisami Gounder*, AIR 1997 SC 10, the validity of a marriage and entitlement to property were at issue in a case concerning, above all, the legitimacy of a Shudra child. The matter was heard by M. M. Punchhi J and Mrs. Justice Sujata Manohar. Their excellent, well-focused judgement pinpoints the key issues admirably well. The mother of this child had been married before to another man, and had then started to live with the father of the child in question some time during the 1940s. The High Court had taken a technical approach and had declared the child illegitimate, because there was insufficient proof of the performance of marriage rituals. The Supreme Court held that the High Court had overlooked the caste factor in this case, "which would have a great bearing in order to establish the relationship between the parties" (p. 11). Thus, as stated at p. 11:

> Hindu law is clear on the subject that if a Shudra woman is turned out of the house by her husband, or she wilfully abandons him and is not pursued to be brought back as wife a divorce in fact takes place, sometimes regulated by custom, and then each spouse is entitled to re-arrange his/her life in marriage with other marrying partners.

In view of explicit recognition of the man's membership of the clan in question (which occurred through giving him a first cousin in marriage, as the learned judges perceptively noted as well), there could be no doubt that this child, now a grown-up man, was all along recognised as legitimate offspring. The Supreme Court of India has here again shown, in 1997, that we need not be confused about marital statuses, even of Shudras, who have their own customary, very informal and flexible rules about how to handle marital relationships.

Cases after the questionable 1994 decision by the Supreme Court in *Surjit Kaur* therefore continue to yield an overall picture of confusion, but only as long as we mix cases on prosecution of male polygamists and cases about women's and children's entitlements to property and maintenance together. The inadequate analysis in present legal writing, and in some courtrooms, may be improved by drawing clear distinctions between such categories of cases. The present discussion shows that Indian courts have continued to allow Hindu bigamists to plead performance of incomplete or otherwise truncated rituals of marriage to escape prosecution. This shows us that Indian law is still not ready to fully penalise polygamous males (see chapter 4 below).

However, whenever the property entitlements of women or children are at stake, such preferential treatment for male claims has now very clearly been abandoned – with the exception of one case, the Supreme Court's decision in *Surjit Kaur*, which therefore sticks out all the more as a sorely misguided verdict on a badly treated and very unfortunate Sikh widow. Her case should really be taken up again, since it reeks of blatant injustice.

Notably, not all recent cases under this rubric concern the rights of remarried women. Two interesting case reports from the Chennai High Court in Madras involve young women who claim to have been duped into a marriage they did not want. These cases are relevant here because they also tell us about how courts in India today treat evidence of registration of marriages. In *Shaji v. Gopinath*, AIR 1995 Mad 161, a young BSc student claimed that a promising young man had fraudulently registered a marriage with her:

> The defendant gave a flowery picture of the education and the status in life and represented to her that he was going to U.S.A. soon and he

could get a visa for her too. He promised to get her a good employment in U.S.A. immediately on her completion of education. He took her signatures in the forms of application for passport ... fraudulently representing to her that a marriage certificate should be obtained for the purpose of getting a Visa in her name and she should be described as wife. The plaintiff signed the necessary forms before the Registrar and false declarations were given by the defendant in the office of the Registrar. Thereafter they went to their respective houses and they never lived together as husband and wife. (p. 161).

It is quite evident that this young woman foolishly colluded with the charming young man, but later came to regret that step. The 'couple' – being modern young people – did not even attempt to solemnise a Hindu marriage and simply relied on registration procedures. Significantly, the Family Court of Madras rejected the woman's petition for nullity. It appears that this judge was totally disgusted with the facts and, by refusing relief, simply exercised a moral judgment. On appeal before the Madras High Court, the young lady again sought nullity of her 'marriage', on the ground that mere registration of the marriage does not amount to a legally valid marriage. The 'husband' had not even bothered to appear in court and remained *ex parte* throughout. This judgement rehearses how Hindu marriages may be solemnised in Tamil Nadu,[65] and is quite instructive about the basic rules on registration of a Hindu marriage under s. 8 HMA. Before there can be such a registration, the relevant Hindu rites and ceremonies have to be performed. It is evident that in the state of Tamil Nadu, a wide variety of rituals is explicitly permitted. In the present case, however, no proper evidence of the performance of any Hindu marriage rituals was provided at all, and the young woman easily freed herself from the yoke of this unwanted marital arrangement which was certainly not a Hindu marriage.

The odd but interesting case of *S. C. Shanthi v. P. Venkatesh*, AIR 1996 Mad 150 also concerns two young people whose marriage remained dysfunctional. Again it is a woman's appeal against the lower court's refusal to grant her nullity of marriage. She claims that at the time of her marriage she was only 18 years old, did not consent to the marriage and that she was induced to perform certain rituals through misrepresentation. The marriage was not consummated. The husband, whose motives never become clear, pleaded that this was a love marriage and that the woman had fully agreed to the marriage. Further, he sought to rely on the fact that the marriage had been registered.

From the marriage certificate, it appeared that the marriage had allegedly been conducted in accordance with s. 7-A of the HMA, as applied in Tamil Nadu. However, it was held, at p. 151:

For a Hindu Form of marriage, three essential features are necessary, viz (i) Homam; (ii) Tying of 'thali', and (iii) 'Saptapadi' [sic]. Neither.

> ... speaks about these essential features. ... In the absence of any evidence to show that the marriage took place in accordance with the Hindu Customary Rites, it cannot be stated that it is a valid marriage.

Relying on *Shaji v. Gopinath* (see above), decided in the same High Court a year earlier, Jagadeesan J in the Madras High Court then proceeded to hold, at p. 151, that "even for registration of the marriage, the marriage ought to have been solemnised in accordance with the provisions of the Hindu Marriage Act". Accordingly, nullity was granted to the woman, since the husband was manifestly unable to prove details of the performance of the Hindu marriage rituals.

Cases of this nature are bound to occur from time to time as young Indian people increasingly make their own arrangements without the involvement of elders and then may find, some time later, that this was not in their own interest and/or is not considered acceptable. In these cases we find confirmation that merely registering a Hindu marriage is not treated in modern Indian law as proof of a valid Hindu marriage. What continues to matter in Hindu law is the performance of the requisite rites and ceremonies, so all the time we are thrown back to this confusing key issue.

Of course, Parliament could have stepped in and laid down that registration of marriages should become the sole criterion of legal validity, following Western legal systems. Indeed, this has been suggested as a remedy by several commentators, prominently Paras Diwan (see further below). However, this step was not taken. In this context, we should perhaps remember that statutory reforms to the Hindu personal law have not been introduced since 1976, although several attempts in this respect have been made. Indian law makers have clearly become more circumspect and no longer rush in with good-looking copies of Western legal models.[66] This situation confirms my assessment that Indian law remains unwilling to follow the Western route of making registration of marriage the sole or even the main criterion of legal validity.[67]

In some cases, courts still behave as though *homa* and *saptapadi* are the absolutely essential ritual elements of every Hindu marriage and require evidence of the performance of 'proper' rituals. This stance makes absolute sense, and the court may sometimes be right to apply such a strict test – depending on the nature of the problem to be solved.

We saw earlier that the issue of solemnisation of Hindu marriages is intimately linked to control (or rather, the absence of effective control) of polygamy among Hindus. When it comes to protecting Hindu men from criminalisation for polygamy, commentators still insist, as before, that the essentials of a Hindu marriage must be proved to sustain a prosecution for bigamy under s. 494 of the *Indian Penal Code*. For example, citing *Laxmi Sahuani v. Maheswar Sahu*, AIR 1985 Ori 11 as the then most recent case on the subject, one of the leading Indian commentators on Hindu law, Professor Paras Diwan, wrote in 1985:

> It is an established proposition of Hindu Law that the offence of bigamy is committed only if it is conclusively established that the required ceremonies of marriage were performed; the second marriage cannot be taken to be proved by the mere admission of parties and it is incumbent on the petitioner to prove that the essential ceremonies and rites were performed.[68]

This evidently biased, male-centred position was maintained by the learned author throughout,[69] but it is increasingly questionable today whether that is the correct position to take in all cases concerning marriage solemnisation. While some recent case law still favours men and manifestly protects those men who indulge in polygamy (see also chapter 3 below), there is now growing evidence of more judicial concern about the position of women and children, and hence more recourse to presumptions of marriage to achieve the desired result of social protection (on this see in detail chapter 4 below).

As it were, the flip side of leniency towards polygamous men now shows more concern for the predicaments of women who are an unwilling party to such marriages. This could be interpreted, above all, as a move towards outrightly activist protection of the maintenance rights of women who are party to such legally invalid marriages (see section 4.3 below). A novel element in this respect has been the recent award of Rs. 30,000 to a polygamously married wife (who also had a child from that marriage) as damages for the husband's misdeeds, as reported in *Ranjit Kumar Bhattacharyya v. Sabita Bhattacharyya*, AIR 1996 Cal 301.

Given that the Indian courts seem, after all, perfectly able to handle traditions of marriage solemnisation – if they apply their minds – and can control the skillful abuse of the legal flexibilities surrounding marriage solemnisation, what remedies do we need to suggest for the improvement of the law? Professor Diwan (1995: 105) has for a long time claimed that "[t]he solution lies in prescribing one ceremony for all Hindu marriages, and by providing for registration of marriages".

The same argument is taken up and elaborated by Singh (1991: 44–47), who also submits that s. 7 HMA should be amended and that the emphasis should be on intention of the spouses rather than the performance of certain rituals. However, this merely reproduces arguments which were advanced during the 1970s by Paras Diwan and others, but have not been found convincing. How does one measure intention to marry? Is it merely through express consent to the marriage? Without corresponding registration of all marriages, this is not a workable method. I have already argued that a system of compulsory registration of all Indian marriages is neither feasible financially nor workable in practice.

Vyas (1993: 194–196) suggests that how a marriage is to be performed and solemnised may be left to religious rites and practices of the various communities and turns his attention to polygamy, rather than the issue of solemnisation of marriages. Apart from an earlier discussion about legal reforms in this area of the law,[70] the debate about the issue of marriage solemnisation and the real problems that it throws up in the case law has remained seriously underdeveloped. The present summary is merely a first step to an urgently needed deeper analysis. As it stands, the current Indian law on Hindu marriage solemnisation has made definite advances in protecting the legitimate interests of women and children, but as my article of 1995 (see section 1.4) showed, dangerous cases like *Surjit Kaur* still offer women and children only shaky security, not a fully guaranteed legal position of entitlement. Saying that, I would not claim that any foolproof system could ever be developed. What is required, therefore, is continuing judicial vigilance and sensitivity to the needs of situational justice.

Notes

1 In the British legal context, such cases arise today to divest South Asian women of rights of entry to the UK as the spouse of a man they lawfully married under Indian law.

2 Indeed, Asians in Britain do not, with few exceptions, partake in this pattern of cohabitation and for Muslims, at any rate, this would amount to illicit sex (*zina*).

3 On the primary purpose rule and its implications for South Asians in Britain see Sachdeva (1993).

4 An excellent and influential case on this matter is *Soundarammal v. Sundara Mahalinga Nadar*, AIR 1980 Mad 294.

5 For example, the normally meticulous and quite comprehensive *Annual Survey of Indian Law* for 1986 does not mention this case at all, and it was also overlooked (or purposely ignored?) by other commentators.

6 On presumption of marriage see very clearly Desai (1990: 639), a leading practitioners' handbook from India.

7 *Ningu Vithu Bamane v. Sadashiv Ningu Bamane*, AIR 1987 Bom 27 recognises a *pat* marriage as an approved and customary form of marriage among Hindus in Maharashtra and followed an earlier case to that effect.

8 *Narayanan Namboodiri v. Bhargavi Amma*, 1989(1) KLT 547, explicitly relies on *Sumitra Devi*, AIR 1985 SC 765 when holding that the customary local form of marriage known in Kerala as *sambandam* was fully recognised by the law.

9 I have referred in this context repeatedly to the funny case of *Partap Singh v. Union of India*, AIR 1985 SC 1695, where the bone of contention is the extent of absolute property rights of Sikh widows under the provisions of s. 14 of the *Hindu Succession Act*, 1956.

10 See Mitra, Trailokyanath: *The law relating to the Hindu widow.* Calcutta 1881 (Tagore Law Lectures 1879).

11 For some evidence see Derrett, J. Duncan M.: *Religion, law and the state in India.* London 1968, p. 110, 235 n, 301 and 320, with some references to the *Hindu Widows' Remarriage Act* of 1856. I am grateful to Dr. L. C. Stout of Cambridge for permission to use an interesting, so far unpublished contribution on the early judicial action to this Act: 'Law, custom and statutory social reform: The Hindu Widows' Remarriage Act of 1856'. Much material is found in Kapadia, K. M.: *Marriage and family in India.* Calcutta 3rd ed. 1966, repr. 1972.

12 Many cases, of course, contain some remarks on such questions; these deserve to be put together in a systematic study. I would be most grateful if any reader could inform me of such studies where they exist.

13 Many readers may not be aware that I am continuing the work begun here in London by Professor J. D. M. Derrett who, as far as Hindu law is concerned, has entered the stage of *vanaprastha*. For a broad outline of his ideas on socio-legal studies see "Sociology and family law in India: The problem of the Hindu marriage". In: Gupta, Giri Raj (ed.): *Family and social change in modern India*. New Delhi 1976, pp. 47–61.

14 On marriage ceremonies in general: *Ram Awadh v. Krishna Nand Lal* AIR 1981 All 432, but see p. 436 on widow remarriage. On the latter: *Parameshwari Bai v. Muthojirao Scindia* AIR 1981 Kant 40; *Rasamani Das v. Patrabala Devi* AIR 1981 Gau 42. See below, n. 12.

15 At p. 249 of the AIR report, emphasis supplied.

16 There is a possibility that the husband remarried because his first wife bore only daughters; the report does not supply details on this point.

17 At p. 249 para 2 of the AIR report.

18 *Baby v. Jayant Mahadeo Jagtap*, reported at AIR 1981 Bom 283 was decided on 29–1–1981 and should have been known in Allahabad by 6–1–1982, the date on which *Bibbe*'s case was decided. Of course legalists will say that it is not a Supreme Court case.

19 This would be suggested, for example, by Crooke, W.: *The tribes and castes of the North Western India*. Repr. Delhi 1974, Vol. II, p. 14.

20 This appears quoted *verbatim* from *Mulla's Principles of Hindu law* (see above), p. 83 and 693.

21 Mention must also be made of *Muthyya v. Kamu*, AIR 1981 NOC 172 (Mad), a case fully reported at 1981 1 MLJ 107. There the "widow" was somewhat luckier, because the very man who divested her of whatever rights she may have had offered to pay Rs. 50,000 for her maintenance and that of her two daughters. This may not be out of pure benevolence.

22 Already the (rather old) standard work on ancient Hindu marriage rituals makes this clear, not only by the choice of sub-title. I refer to Winternitz, Moritz: *Das altindische Hochzeitsrituell. Nach dem Apastambiya-Grihyasutra und einigen anderen verwandten Werken*. Wien 1892 (Denkschriften der Kaiserlichen Akademie der Wissenschaften. Philosophisch-Historische Classe. Vierzigster Band).

23 *Ibid.*, esp. p. 4. The intensive search for Indo-Aryan common elements seems to have supported such notions of uniformity.

24 See e.g. Edwardes, Michael: *Everyday life in early India*. London 1969, p. 36.

25 In a different context, it strikes me that a modern Indian sociologist can describe the traditional husband-wife relationship in terms of statements by the famous Abbé Dubois. See Narain, Dhirendra: 'Interpersonal relationships in the Hindu family'. In: Hill, Reuben and René König (eds.): *Families in East and West*. Paris and The Hague 1970, pp. 454–480, at pp. 456–457.

26 Menski, W. F.: *Role and ritual in the Hindu marriage*. London 1984 (Unpublished PhD thesis).

27 I refer to Mehta, Rama: *Divorced Hindu woman*. New Delhi 1975 for a number of excellent case studies. On the difficult position of 'modern' women in India see also *Shanti Nigam v. Ramesh Chandra Nigam* at 1971 Allahabad Law Journal 67.

28 Derrett, J. Duncan M.: *A critique of modern Hindu law*. Bombay 1970, p. 296.

29 Derrett, J. Duncan M.: *The death of a marriage law*. New Delhi 1978. The relevant legal provision is the *Marriage Laws (Amendment) Act*, 1976 (Act 68 of 1976), which introduced divorce by mutual consent and provided additional grounds for divorce, not yet, however, 'irretrievable breakdown of marriage'.

30 Diwan, Paras: "Marriage and divorce law reforms". In: (1977) *Supreme Court Cases*, Journal section, pp. 1–11, esp. p. 11.

31 On the *Hindu Marriage (Madras Amendment) Act*, 1967 (Madras Act 21 of 1967) see Derrett, *Critique*, pp. 299–300 and Venkata Subbarao, G. C.: *Family law in India*. Madras 1979, pp. 47–48.
32 Sampath, B. N.: 'Hindus and civil marriage: An unresolved dilemma". In: Bagga, V. (ed.): *Studies in the Hindu Marriage and the Special Marriage Acts*. Bombay 1978, pp. 270–278, at p. 277; Diwan, *Marriage* . . ., p. 4.
33 Gupte, S. V.: *Hindu law of marriage*. 2nd ed. Bombay 1976, p. 154.
34 *Ibid*., p. 155 gives the example of the Madras High Court which has held (in *Raghuvir Kumar v. Shanmugvadiar* at AIR 1971 Madras 330) that mere execution of a document by the spouses will amount to a declaration of intention to be husband and wife under s.7 HMA as amended for Tamil Nadu.
35 Diwan, *Marriage*, p. 4 emphasises the importance of the reforms in divorce law.
36 I find Kulshrestha, A. K.: *Marriage and divorce*. Chandigarh 1979, pp. 31–33 very confusing. Diwan, Paras: *Modern Hindu law*. 4th ed. Allahabad 1979, pp. 78–83 presents a disorderly mess of statements; the problems are too numerous to be discussed here in detail.
37 Gupte, *Hindu law*, pp. 153–154 is not an improvement on the first edition (of 1961), because the author has relied on inadequate judicial decisions.
38 Diwan, *Modern Hindu law*, p. 78.
39 On this point see in particular Gour, Hari Singh: *Hindu law of marriage and divorce*. Rev. ed. Allahabad 1977 (with addenda), p. 91.
40 Sagade, Jaya: 'Law and social reform in rural India. With special reference to child marriages'. In: 1981 *Supreme Court Journal*, Journal section, pp. 27–35, at p. 34.
41 For details I must here refer to Pandey, Raj Bali: *Hindu samskaras*. 2nd rev. ed Delhi 1969.
42 For further details I refer to Menski, *Role and ritual*, esp. pp. 580ff.
43 *Ibid*., p. 581 and esp. pp. 584ff.; Winternitz, *Das altindische Hochzeitsrituell*, pp. 18–19.
44 Menski, *Role and ritual*, esp. pp. 707ff.
45 *Ibid*., pp. 582–583 give a synopsis of the elements of the *saptapadi* in the various texts.
46 *Ibid*., p. 727.
47 *Ibid*., p. 796.
48 Diwan, *Marriage*, p. 4.
49 Chadha, Prem Nath: *Hindu law*. 4th ed. with supplement, Lucknow 1978, p. 93 points to an incompetently decided case in which the couple had only taken five rounds and the marriage was held bad in law.
50 This already includes the *Kauśikasutra* (cf. Winternitz, *Das altindische Hochzeitsrituell*, p. 52), where more recent models are briefly described. Further details are found at Menski, *Role and ritual*, pp. 617ff. and pp. 849–879, where a *vivahapaddhati* and a *vivahakaumudi* have been analysed.
51 Thurston, Edgar: *Ethnographic notes in Southern India*. Madras 1906, p. 1.
52 If this is not the case, the role of old women as guardians of tradition is, at times, significantly enhanced. For an example see Menski, *Role and ritual*, pp. 875ff.
53 Derrett, *Critique*, pp. 297–298 refers to the famous case of a lady who 'married' her 'husband' three times and still did not convince the Court that she was validly married.
54 *Ibid*., p. 299.
55 Derrett, J. Duncan M.: *Religion, law and the state in India*. London 1968, pp. 56–74 gives background material; cf. also: Ross, Aileen D.: *The Hindu family in its urban setting*. Repr. Delhi 1973.
56 An essay by myself and Ismail Mehta on 'Patterns of marriage solemnisation among 'Asians' in the UK' is currently being prepared.

57 This has changed more recently. See the strong words of India's highest judicial authority at *Gopal Lal v. State of Rajasthan,* AIR 1979 SC 713.
58 Allott, Anthony N.: *The limits of law.* London 1980.
59 This topic has been widely discussed. I may refer to Derrett, *Critique*, pp. 300–301 and Diwan, *Modern Hindu law*, pp. 82–83 for details that do not interest us here.
60 Rao, R. Jaganmohan: "The law of marriage and social change". In: Bagga, V. (ed.): *Studies*, p. 68.
61 Sagade, 'Law and social reform.', p. 34.
62 This is not merely my personal view, but an established fact, documented in numerous Supreme Court decisions which have been critical of judgments passed by those High Courts. For stark examples see *Pratibha Rani v. Sushil Kumar*, AIR 1985 SC 628, criticising the decision in *Vinod Kumar v. State of Haryana*, AIR 1982 P&H 372FB, which virtually held that women are owned by men. The Allahabad High Court was subjected to serious criticism recently in a case of dowry murder, see *State of UP v. Ramesh Prasad Misra*, AIR 1996 SC 2766.
63 I would point here in particular to the excellent work of Bina Agarwal (1994). The subject is further discussed in chapter 5 below.
64 Malhotra and Malhotra (1998) mention the *Surjit Kaur* case and appear to agree with its position, but their discussion omits any reference to the fact that this lady was a remarried woman. Unfortunately, the article as a whole does not define what precisely is meant by 'cohabitation' and therefore misleads a Western-oriented readership into assuming that it has the same meaning as, for example, in English law.
65 See section 1.1 above on the provisions of the *Hindu Marriage (Madras Amendment) Act*, 1967 and its implications.
66 The fate of the *Marriage Laws (Amendment) Bill*, 1981 was an early case in point. During the 1990s, there was further evidence of the Centre's reluctance to reform family laws when the *Marriage Bill*, 1994 also failed.
67 This was held most recently in *Ranjit Kumar Bhattacharyya v. Sabita Bhattacharyya*, AIR 1996 Cal 301, where the husband's first marriage had been conducted under Christian law, but the second marriage was under Hindu law. Under the Christian law of India, the registration document of a marriage is treated as conclusive proof of the existence of a valid Christian marriage.
68 Diwan (1985: 100), which is a part of the authoritative *Annual Survey of Indian Law.* Regrettably, Professor Diwan was killed in an armed robbery in 1997.
69 See *ibid.*: 104–105, as well as Malhotra and Malhotra (1998).
70 On this see Jain (1961) and Mathur (1962). A fairly recent book on traditional Hindu marriages, Mishra (1994), is useful for the study of the customary elements.

Chapter Two

Divorce

Following the West?

2.1 Indian divorce law: An overview

Chapter 1 showed that modern Indian law continues to treat Hindu marriage ideologically and in practical terms as a sacramental union (*samskara*) at its inception, remaining at the same time aware of its inherent contractual elements with their manifold socio-legal consequences. Hand in hand with this, the modern law, as manifested in legislation and even the most recent decisions of the superior courts, has insisted that reliance on traditional patterns of marriage solemnisation, in all their confusing variety, remains the most efficient method of ascertaining the validity of any particular Hindu marriage. We saw, in other words, that the modern Indian state has declined jurisdiction and primary responsibility in this matter and has placed the onus of maintaining social cohesion and legal statuses in this regard on the people themselves. The courts, as chapter 1 showed, would only come into the picture if there were persisting doubts about the validity of a particular marriage, or if someone tried to abuse the confusing patterns of traditional diversity in this field for their own selfish means.

The present chapter briefly discusses key issues in the development of modern Indian divorce law. A detailed analysis of this subject could easily fill a whole book.[1] Regarding the issue of exit from marriage, the developments in modern Hindu divorce law during the past few decades signify a definite shift towards, but not the total embracing of, contractual rather than sacramental elements of marriage. The modern law, thus, seems to operate in favour of divorce and facilitates it on certain fault grounds. Occasionally, judges have gone as far as dissolving marriages on the ground of irretrievable breakdown, but recent cases firmly assert that this has to remain an exception in the modern law of India.[2] Hindu divorce law as a whole has thereby moved progressively further away from the old *samskara* ideal, according to which divorce among Hindus would not be permitted at all, but India is not copying the West.

Let us clarify straight away, however, that this denial of traditional Hindu divorce has always been an ideological assertion rather than social reality – Hindu law has, right from its inception, certainly known various forms of dissolution of marriage. While treating this as a definite deviation from the ideal, Hindu ideology and Hindu law have always justified breakdown of marriage and the consequent separation of spouses in various ways.[3] As we shall see, the crucial issue here is in what situations, and on what conditions, a modern legal system in the Southern hemisphere should today operate in favour of easy divorce.

English law has insisted since the early 1970s that marriages are only legally valid if registered with the involvement of the state, and all divorces in English law now have to be processed by the state legal system. In other words, the state has completely seized jurisdiction in this matter and has given itself the exclusive right to determine the legal validity of all marriages and divorces.[4]

Modern Indian divorce law has most definitely not followed that model. First of all, within the personal law system, Muslims in India have continued to be governed by the principles of *shariat* law. Almost the entire Indian Muslim law on marriage solemnisation and on divorce (with the exception of divorce initiated by women under the *Dissolution of Muslim Marriages Act*, 1939) has remained outside the ambit of the state's direct authority. We shall see further below that this has given rise to interesting discussions.

For a long time, and certainly during Professor Derrett's time at the helm of South Asian legal studies at SOAS, it looked like modern Indian legal developments and reforms in divorce law would follow Western legal developments.[5] A number of statutory grounds for divorce were introduced into modern Hindu law by s. 13 of the HMA in 1955.[6] These grounds were further enlarged by the *Hindu Marriage (Amendment) Act*, 1964 and then the important *Marriage Laws (Amendment) Act* of 1976, which created several new divorce grounds and potentially opened the floodgates for easier divorce. These modernising and secularising reforms were introduced to put modern Hindu law still more in line with the provisions of the *Special Marriage Act* of 1954, India's optional Uniform Civil Code, about which more will be said in chapter 6 below. In fact, Professor Derrett anticipated to some extent that Hindu law might be abolished altogether, given that its spirit had been buried by the reforming efforts of 1976.

The progression of the statutory law towards more and more grounds for divorce (and also easier nullity under s. 12(1)(c) of the HMA) began to create the powerful impression, during the late 1970s and early 1980s, that modern Hindu divorce law had now fully developed and was actually closely following the 'breakdown theory' of modern English divorce law.

However, that has simply not happened. Today, we can see clearly that the tide turned already by the early 1980s, when the *Marriage Laws (Amendment) Bill*, 1981 failed in Parliament because women's groups protested that full introduction of the breakdown principle would make it still easier for husbands to simply abandon their wives. Although this supposedly important Bill had failed to become law, it still seemed for some time as though Indian law would warmly embrace the breakdown principle, and a large number of cases were reported which clearly used that concept. For example, in *Bimla Devi v. Singh Raj*, AIR 1977 P&H 167 (FB), a wife was demanding divorce before a Full Bench of three judges of the High Court. The marriage had apparently only lasted a day; something must have gone wrong in the first night. The wife strenuously alleged that fraud had been practised on her and evidently did not want anything to do with her husband. It was held, at p. 177:

> The concept of wrong disability which was hitherto the sole basis of relief under the Act has now, in part, given way to the concept of a broken-down marriage, irrespective of wrong or disability.

It was therefore almost a forgone conclusion that this non-functioning marital union should be legally dissolved, although judges might still take the view that the couple should try once again.[7] However, not all cases were as evidently suitable for the application of the breakdown principle as this one and the development of a case-law in which divorcing men were taking advantage of their own wrong has been characterised as creating blatant injustice (Derrett 1975; 1981). Professor Derrett, who had warned in his *Death of a marriage law* in 1978 that India's Hindu law was in danger of being killed off, remained vigilant in criticising a number of court decisions which definitely damaged the best interests of women. Other research on divorce in the 1970s (Mehta 1975) as well as during the 1980s (Dhagamwar 1987) continued to show that rushing into divorce would be particularly costly, and detrimental in many ways, for most of India's women.

Few writers addressed the resulting problems for children at that time. Indian child law has really only begun to develop during the early 1990s. I shall show in more detail in section 2.5 below how during the 1980s the Indian High Courts and the Supreme Court developed a jurisprudence of liberty, focused on freeing unhappy spouses from the shackles of a broken marriage. However, as divorce and nullity decrees were handed out more and more freely by the judges, it began to dawn on lawyers, policy makers and the public alike that the new dispensation favoured the stronger party – normally the man – over the weaker litigant, and that the modernising trends in Hindu divorce law were creating their own social problems for women and children. Professor Derrett, after all, had been right to warn about abuses of a too liberal divorce system and about the poisoned gift of 'divorce for all', which he had wisely depicted as a Trojan horse (Derrett 1978: 97).

In this context, we also need to discuss briefly the development of a not so new phenomenon, namely divorce by mutual consent, which was made available under s. 13(B) of the HMA by the 1976 amendments. Such forms of divorce were already an element of the old customary patterns of divorce, so it could be argued that this was really nothing new. However, if more than 98% of all divorces in England today fall under the category of divorce by mutual consent, is this a pattern that India will eventually follow? I am not aware of any statistics that would tell us how frequently such petitions are made and what share of the market, as it were, they have reached in India. It is certain that such divorces are on the increase, and if we count those together with the many millions of customary divorces in India, then it may be possible to say that in India, too, divorce by mutual consent is actually the dominant element of the divorce law. However, asserting that position, we must be aware that most of such divorces have never gone through any state-sponsored forum. In other words, the Indian state actually has quite limited jurisdiction over the field of divorce and it would appear that this, as in the field of marriage, has become officially accepted as the most efficient strategy.[8] Again we see that the sheer cost of administering a fool-proof divorce system for all Indians would be prohibitive. In the field of divorce law, too, therefore, the Indian state has continued to rely on society and on social processes, rather than on formal legal control mechanisms.

In the official, state-sponsored divorce law, one particular recent trend deserves to be explicitly mentioned and highlighted here. I shall further elaborate on this new development in chapter 2.5 below to provide a fuller update. Despite the prominence of the breakdown principle as a rhetorical tool, it seems that since about 1988 the Indian High Courts and now also the Supreme Court have been signalling to Hindu litigants that divorce will no longer be granted on the flimsiest of grounds. In other words, Indian judicial thinking has to some extent been moving away from the breakdown theory and from the simple, but ultimately socially destructive strategy of granting divorce to anyone who cares to ask for it. During the early 1990s, judges have been writing a growing number of judgments that read like moral admonishments to warring couples, to the effect that some small disagreements will inevitably arise in any marriage, and that couples should not rush to court in such circumstances to file for divorce. A good example of this kind of judicial intervention is found in *Rajendra Agrawal v. Sharda Devi*, AIR 1993 MP 142, where we read at p. 144:

> Before passing a decree for divorce, the court must bear in mind that for a Hindu marriage, if there is any chance of reconciliation between the husband and the wife, the Court should be slow in granting a decree of divorce. Under the Hindu Law, the marriage is a sacrament and not a contract, and therefore, there should always be an effort to save the marriage tie than to break it, but once the Court is satisfied that there is no chance of the marriage tie being continued, then it would be desirable to dissolve it rather than to continue.

Indeed, in view of the prolonged breakdown of the marital relations in this case, the judge proceeded to grant a divorce, but this judicial statement captures the balancing act which Indian judges during the 1990s have been trying to perform. Torn between individualistic notions and the desire to free spouses from an unwanted marriage, on the one hand, and social concerns and the desire to preserve marriages, wherever possible, judges have produced a mass of reported decisions which nobody today could survey in their entirety – there are just too many reported cases in too many different law reports. India's enormous size defeats even the most energetic researcher.

Still, the direction of recent developments in modern Hindu divorce law is evident. Judges are increasingly ambivalent when faced with arguments that a marriage has broken down irretrievably and are manifestly searching for ways of keeping couples together. On the other hand, when the facts of irretrievable breakdown speak for themselves, Indian courts can be very quick to pronounce divorce decrees.[9] Judges are under multiple pressures from backlogs of cases and many other, conflicting obligations. They are increasingly aware, so they tell us, that Indian society can never be like American society, that there is no state welfare net to take care of discarded wives and abandoned children. Consequently, the social costs of allowing breakdown freely would be unmanageable and ultimately disastrous for Indian society in the 21st century. We shall seek to analyse in section 2.5 below whether this partial return to traditional concepts of Hindu marriage and divorce implies the re-invention and operation of neo-Hindu concepts, or rather a reaction to the manifest social problems created by high divorce rates in the West.

The public impression of very widespread increase in divorces in Indian society today may have its roots in another phenomenon, which is often overlooked in legal analyses. While judges, practising lawyers and legal scholarship have seen their attention directed towards the new state-sponsored methods of seeking divorce through the courts, the innocuous yet powerful and wide-ranging saving provision in s. 29(2) of the HMA of 1955 has actually preserved the pre-existing law of customary divorces among Hindus. Largely unnoticed, this has allowed literally hundreds of millions of Hindus in India to seek divorce without the involvement of any court whatsoever![10] The acceptability of this position, at the highest judicial level, was impressively reiterated in an important 1997 Supreme Court case which we have already referred to, *M. Govindaraju v. K. Munisami Gounder*, AIR 1997 SC 10.

Understandably, India's lawyers have not really been interested in that provision, since it is bad for their business. S. 29(2) of the HMA provides as follows:

> Nothing contained in this Act shall be deemed to affect any right recognised by custom or conferred by any special enactment to obtain the dissolution of a Hindu marriage, whether solemnized before or after the commencement of this Act.

This clearly implies that there is no need for lawyers to get involved in customary Hindu divorces, and the field of customary divorces has indeed remained, as Professor Derrett (1963a: 169) called it, a "world of its own". While that is still true today, a remarkably interesting case law has developed under s. 29(2) HMA. To date this has only been analysed by one of my postgraduate students, whose work has regrettably not been published (Weber 1997). The reported cases (which are of course only an immensely tiny minority of all actual cases) show that there is often much judicial reluctance to allow customary Hindu divorces, especially when the couple belong to a 'higher' caste,[11] but there are other cases in which the court virtually told couples not to waste precious judicial time and sent them away to sort out their difficulties at home in accordance with customary traditions.[12]

In the Christian personal law of India, too, there have been some important developments, which we cannot discuss here in detail. During the 1980s, there were constant and increasingly loud calls for reforms to the seriously outdated Indian Christian law, but these voices remained unheard for a long time. Significant progress was then made during the early 1990s, when the judges, notably not the legislature, relaxed the traditional strictness of Indian Christian law where divorce had been virtually unobtainable. While Parliament has been either unable or unwilling to legislate on this matter, the judges of the Kerala High Court, always alert to questions of women's rights and social justice in their multi-religious state, have rewritten certain provisions of the Indian Christian law on divorce.[13] Today, it is therefore possible for Christian men and women in India to seek divorce on the fairly unencumbered, wide ground of cruelty. Recent cases confirm that this approach is also being adopted by other High Courts in India.[14] This strategy of law reform is most interesting. since it leads towards uniformisation of legal provisions across personal laws, a matter for discussion in ch. 6 below.

Such new developments add, of course, to the growing perception in India that divorces have become more frequent. Further, if the law now has the effect that women of any community can seek divorce more easily, men can no longer rely on sacramental ties to bind their wives to home and hearth, while they enjoy wider freedoms. The resulting re-balancing of gender relations has not even begun to be researched in depth.

Parallel recent developments in South Asian Muslim divorce law have led to what can only be called an 'equality of misery'. In South Asian Muslim law today, most evidently in Pakistan, a Muslim husband's traditional prerogative to terminate the marriage unilaterally by *talaq*, irrespective of whether the wife agrees or not, is now matched by the wife's right to do the same through *khul*.[15] While the procedure is slightly different, in that a Muslim wife normally has to go through a court, this has now become simple and easy, if still daunting for women, as Pakistani judges well recognise and actually take into account. Today, any married Muslim woman who dares to stand up in a Pakistani court to say that she cannot live any longer with her husband 'within the limits of Allah' thereby claims – and by some accounts obtains without further questions – an instant divorce through the court. Muslim husbands anywhere in South Asia, but most evidently in Pakistan today, are now equally powerless as their women to oppose a unilateral divorce. Because of the Islamic nature of the Muslim wife's argument for freedom from the marital tie, this new development has literally put 'the fear of God' into many Muslim husbands in South Asia. It will be interesting to examine what kinds of socio-legal developments the rapidly rising figures for Muslim divorces of this kind will lead to in the future.

In Indian Muslim divorce law, where of course s. 8 of the *Muslim Family Laws Ordinance* of 1961 does not apply, unhappy wives can still seek dissolution of their marriage under the *Dissolution of Marriages Act*, 1939. While there are hardly any cases reported under that statute now, we should not assume that Indian Muslim wives do not seek divorce in this way.[16] Further, for Indian Muslims, too, manifold forms of customary divorces do exist, if informally, and the activities (as in Britain, by the way) of various Shariat Councils and other advisory bodies that exercise quasi-judicial functions in this field should be researched by socio-legal scholars. These are extremely sensitive matters, though, and they will be easily politicised.

Much less noticed, but with persistent determination, the tiny Parsi community of India has managed to persuade Parliament during the 1980s to legislate for a modern Parsi law of divorce.[17] The *Parsi Marriage and Divorce (Amendment) Act*, 1988 follows, almost *verbatim*, the relevant provisions of modern Hindu law and of the *Special Marriage Act*, 1954, as amended together by the *Marriage Laws (Amendment) Act*, 1976. The politics of this scenario are highly relevant for the debates on India's Uniform Civil Code (see chapter 6 below) and the legal amendments were mainly designed, it appears, to assert the position of Parsi law as a separate personal law system within modern Indian law. Little is known about cases on Parsi divorce law, but the divorce rate among this community has traditionally been high. It may be assumed, therefore, that definite social policy aims were also behind the moves to reform the Parsi divorce law, rather than just the assertion of separate personal law status.

Taken overall, the perception that more Indians divorce these days is not just a superficial impression, it is a hard fact, discussed at great length in innumerable newspaper columns, several issues of *India Today*, and by a public that is aware of the many negative consequences of mass breakdown of marriages. This is where the tempting images of the West become tainted: the Western path of easy breakdown of marriages and of 'serial monogamy' (one of the favourite slogans of Professor Tahir Mahmood, see chapter 3 below), is not really perceived as morally and socially ideal for South Asian societies by a public that would like to be seen as 'modern' but continues to value 'tradition' in many ways.

Thus, the issue of divorce in modern India is now increasingly treated as a matter of great concern in terms of social policy, highlighting no longer so strongly, as before, the need to free shackled individuals, especially women, from unwanted ties. Rather, current debates and concerns emphasise the social problems that arise as a result of growing evidence of breakdown of family life and in particular of the destitution that may befall members of broken families.

While marriage is still seen by a good number of feminist writers as the classic suppression mechanism developed by mankind, and matrimony is portrayed as a burdensome social obligation, together with childbirth, housework and all other marital duties, most Indian women appear to seek some sort of financial security and support, if nothing else, within the marital framework. Single women, whether unmarried spinsters, divorcees, widows or abandoned wives, continue to find it hard to survive on their own unless they have the courage and the financial resources to arrange a comfortable life for themselves, which will be an exception rather than the rule. The stigma of divorce continues to make itself felt, although Khan (1999: 52) correctly emphasises that "[i]n recent years, the profound societal taboo against divorce has relaxed a little". This is clearly an issue also in recent reported cases.[18] However, according to some literature, many poor women find it more agreeable to fight for themselves and their children than to carry the added burden of an unreliable husband.[19]

Too few people think and write about the fact that all of this may not really be very different for Indian men, who experience their own difficulties with getting married and staying in matrimony, once the knot has been tied. Reading cases does not give us a full picture of Indian socio-legal realities with regard to marital relations – or indeed anything else. Unquestionably, it is especially hard to be a poor person in India, whether male or female, married or unmarried, and of whatever age, caste, religion or social background. How this impacts on marital relations and their nature does not appear to have been researched in depth. I know from fieldwork experience that it is hard work to live among really poor people and to try to understand their ways of life, which differ so much from normative textbook descriptions.

Why do I bring such issues into a discussion of divorce in modern Indian law? Does this not distract from the topic? My argument, in brief, is that the significant changes which we currently witness in Indian divorce laws for Hindus are so intimately linked with socio-economic policy matters that one cannot afford to look at the law of divorce in isolation. To put it in a nutshell, the current restrictive approaches towards divorce, as evidenced by a whole series of cases from the High Courts and the Supreme Court during the late 1980s and through the 1990s, are in my interpretation a key indicator not only of the fact that the tide is turning in some way against easy divorce and towards reminding couples again of their duty to try and work together, but also of changing public policy concerns when it comes to the consequences of breakdown of marriage in Indian society.

More precisely, the key to understanding India's recently reformulated restrictive approach to easy divorces may therefore lie in understanding the financial implications of massive marriage breakdown for women and children. This has many potential knock-on effects for the resources of a welfare state which can definitely not afford to implement its wonderful constitutional guarantees to all citizens. By reminding couples that it is their obligation to try their best to make a success of married life by co-operating and staying together, rather than following egoistic, individualistic strategies for leading one's life, judges are implicitly activating the provisions on fundamental duties under Article 51-A in the Indian Constitution,[20] applying thereby, in effect, wider public interest arguments to private relations between citizens. If we learn to look at the problems of divorce in this way, we need to see as well that the policy of the Indian state to leave the issues of marriage and divorce largely to the citizens ties in admirably with this particular policy approach. It is simply not in the public interest that warring couples should be allowed to clog up the modern adjudication system of India at the higher levels with their litigious outpourings. The courts are too hard-pressed with more important matters, and some case reports (see section 2.5 below) now provide evidence of impatience with such couples who indulge in manipulative litigation at everyone else's cost. Behind the various reforms of modern Indian divorce law, therefore, lurk definite social and fiscal agenda, which we will further explore in sections 2.5 and 4.3 below.

The three reprinted essays in this chapter capture the spirit of the discussions about divorce in India during the 1980s and do not discuss, evidently, what happened in this field during the 1990s. Hence I have decided to produce a more detailed update about the Indian case law during the 1990s in section 2.5 below, to trace the emergence of the recently more restrictive approach to divorces for Hindus and to analyse its consequences.

The argument proposed by Mr. Haq's article in section 2.2 below, to the effect that divorce should be made easier for Hindus, written as it was in 1988, probably did not take into account that by then the 'liberating' reforms of 1976 had made themselves felt more widely. While conceptual elements of *samskara* were still strong in the public's perception, the case law during the late 1970s and in the 1980s had actually begun to seriously challenge the sacramental undertones of Hindu marriage and had emphasised the ease with which marital unions could now be broken. The stance taken by Mr. Haq appears to confirm that it takes some time until such case reports and their contents have filtered down into public consciousness. Mr. Sivaraman (section 2.3) would appear to suggest that Mr. Haq was not even sufficiently aware of the statutory changes to modern Hindu law which had actually made divorce easier. That may well be too harsh.

Mr. Haq was pursuing some other agenda as well, though, and these have become quite relevant to our discussion. By suggesting that the Muslim divorce law, as an extra-judicial regulatory system, could be a useful model for Hindus, the learned writer was doing more than playing communal politics. He recommended, in effect, that a system allowing extra-judicial divorces, rather than full jurisdiction of the state over all divorces, would be useful. To that extent at least, Mr. Haq's essay made a most valuable contribution to the present discussion, although it could be charged that he was only playing Muslim communal politics.

As I shall show in section 2.5 below, the rubber-like and ultimately too wide extension of divorce grounds like 'cruelty' by the judges during the

1980s confirms that Mr. Haq's argument about Hindus having problems with access to divorce needs to be taken with a pinch of salt. Ideologically, of course, Hindu reservations about divorce as such remain largely in place, but in effect the law had already made divorce so easy for Hindu men, in particular, that commentators would soon ask for restrictions on this freedom of men to unilaterally divorce their wives. This viewpoint is shared by Mr. Sivaraman in section 2.3 below. It appears, and this is a point which our essays in the late 1980s did not bring out well enough, that any modern system of divorce regulation which allows easy divorce will end up permitting one spouse to divorce the other more or less unilaterally. In this respect, the traditional Muslim law of *talaq*, its modern counterpart of liberalised *khul*, and the most modern Western manifestations of the breakdown principle all have the same social effect: by allowing spouses to abandon their partners – and often enough their responsibilities to these partners and any children of the marriage. A so-called modern system of divorce regulation, thus, inevitably sets up costly consequences, which a country like India cannot possibly bear from public funds.[21]

The response by Mr. Sivaraman, and my own essay of 1989, show that in the debate about divorce reforms the issue of uniform legal regulation took centre stage for much of the time and somewhat distracted us all from the much more important issue of financial consequences of easier divorces. When I responded to Mr. Haq in 1989, I was not yet sufficiently aware of the financial implications of India's new divorce regime to formulate a response along those lines, but the beginnings of this argument were then gradually developing. Mr. Justice Sathiadev in the important case of *Soundarammal v. Sundara Mahalinga Nadar*, AIR 1980 Mad 294, had already issued his serious warning that Indian society was heading for disaster of epic proportions if divorces were made too easily available and corresponding maintenance provisions were not made. The important *Shah Bano* case of 1985, *Mohd. Ahmed Khan v. Shah Bano Begum*, AIR 1985 SC 945, had led to the promulgation of the *Muslim Women (Protection of Rights on Divorce) Act* in 1986. Still, at that time, I too was blinded by Muslim and anti-Congress propaganda and did not properly understand that this 1986 Act had not actually taken away the maintenance entitlements of divorced Muslim wives.

Today, we know better, and we can appreciate that significant progress has been made in matching easier divorce for Hindus with stricter requirements for divorcing men to provide for divorced wives (and, of course, children) through periodic maintenance payments, lump sum arrangements or in other ways.[22] At the same time, manifestly less progress has been achieved on the issue of a Uniform Civil Code (see the discussion in chapter 6 below).

It seems evident, therefore, that research about the development of Indian divorce law during the 1990s needs to be fully aware of the close links between legal policy on divorces and on post-divorce maintenance regulations, as well as the intricate links of the sphere of family law with considerations of public interest in general and public finance in particular. India is not only culturally different from the West, and a developing country seeking to modernise in its own way, it is also facing severe financial challenges. All these factors, as is beginning to emerge more clearly from our current analysis of recent developments in family law, are contributing to the emergence of a unique system of family law regulation, premised on state supervision, but conscious of a large extent of self-controlled order in the realm of society. This remains a typically South Asian form of legal regulation, with very selective borrowings from the West, and no chance at all of wholesale copying of any Western system of regulation. While registration of marriages has remained voluntary for most Indians, most of the exit routes from marriage are also not policed and guarded by the modern Indian state, but are left to the discretion of the couple within their social context. To speak in this context of an officially sanctioned tendency towards DIY divorce within the Indian legal system, rather than watertight state control, would be no exaggeration.

2.2 Amend the law and make divorce easy for Hindus

M. Fazlul Haq

[From: 1988(1) *KLT*, Journal section, pp. 45–47]

Divorce is discouraged by all religions.

Manu, who is described as the father of mankind; the founder of social and moral order; a ruler of men; a 'Rishi' to whom sacred texts were revealed and the author of legal maxims, has said: "He only is a perfect of men who consists (of three persons united) his wife, himself, and his offsprings; thus (says the Veda) and (learned) Brahmanas propound this (maxim) likewise, "The husband is declared to be one with the wife. Neither by sale nor by repudiation is a wife released from her husband; such we know the law to be, which the Lord of Creatures ... made of old" (see G. Buehler: *Laws of Manu*, IX, 44 to 46).

Jesus has said: "It was also said, 'whoever divorces his wife, let him give her a certificate of divorce.' But, I say to you that every one who divorces his wife, except on the ground of unchastity, makes her an adulteress; and whoever marries a divorced woman commits adultery" (Mathew: 31).

Prophet Muhammad has said: "The most detestable of lawful things near God is divorce" (Abu Daud) and "whichever woman asks her husband for divorce without his fault, the fragrance of Paradise is forbidden to her" (Ahmad).

But nobody can plead for continuance of marriage in cases where the parties are bound together by a marital tie which is better untied (see, for instance, *Ms. Jorden Diengdeh v. S. S. Chopra* (1985) 3 SCC 62). In this case the Supreme Court has observed:

> ... there is no point or purpose to be served by the continuance of a marriage which has so completely and signally broken down. We suggest that the time has come for the intervention of the Legislature in these matters to provide for a uniform code of marriage and divorce and ... to provide by law for a way out of the unhappy situations in which couples like the present have found themselves in. We direct that a copy of this order may be forwarded to the Ministry of Law and Justice for such action as they may deem fit to take (paras 4 and 7).

We must not overlook the fact, in this connection, that a marriage may break down for reasons which cannot be proved in a court of law and, even if proved, will not come within the scope of any of the grounds defined in the statute.

In (1985) 3 SCC 62 (*supra*), the wife prayed for a declaration of nullity of marriage on the ground of impotence of the husband in that though the husband is capable of achieving erection and penetration, he ejaculates prematurely before the wife has an orgasm, leaving the wife totally unsatisfied and frustrated. It is absolutely impossible to prove allegations of this kind in a Court of law, if refuted by the opposite party. The prayer for declaration of nullity of marriage was disallowed by the High Court. The wife filed a petition for special leave to appeal before the Supreme Court against the judgement of the High Court and the Supreme Court pointed out:

> At this stage, we are not concerned with the question how far the wife has been able to establish her case. The real problem now is that the marriage appears to have broken down irretrievably. Yet, if the findings of the High Court stand, there is no way out for the couple, they will continue to be tied to each other since neither mutual consent nor irretrievable breakdown of marriage is a ground for divorce. ... We may also notice that irretrievable breakdown of marriage is yet no ground for dissolution of marriage under the Hindu Marriage Act also.

Cruelty and adultery are the main grounds mentioned in s. 13(1) of the *Hindu Marriage Act*, for divorce.

But, the Act does not define 'cruelty' and it is not a word that can be precisely defined, too.

> The question whether the misconduct complained of constitutes cruelty and the like for divorce purposes is determined primarily by its effect upon the particular person complaining of the acts. The question is not whether the conduct would be cruel to a reasonable person or a person of average or normal sensibilities, but whether it would have that effect upon the aggrieved spouse. That which may be cruel to one person may be laughed off by another, and what may not be cruel to an individual under one set of circumstances may be

> cruelty under another set of circumstances. (*American Jurisprudence* 2nd edn, Vol. 24, p. 206).
>
> The court has to deal not with an ideal husband and an ideal wife (assuming any such exist) but with the particular man and woman before it. The ideal couple or a near-ideal one will probably have no occasion to go to a matrimonial court for, even if they may not be able to drown their differences, their ideal attitudes may help them overlook or gloss over mutual faults and failures. (*Dastane v. Dastane*, AIR 1975 SC 1534).

Coming to 'adultery', the definition in s. 13(1)(i) of the said Act is not at all conducive to Indian culture; and under this section, a marriage may be dissolved by a decree of divorce if the other party has, after the solemnization of the marriage, had voluntary sexual intercourse with any person other than his or her spouse.

There is many a Hindu who still believes that the law given by Manu is the divine law, according to whom (even) offering presents (to a woman), romping (with her), touching her ornaments and dress, sitting with her on a bed and touching a woman in a place (which ought) not (to be touched) or allows (oneself to be touched in such a spot) are all considered to be adulterous acts: (*Manusmriti* VIII, 357–358). However, a learned Indian Judge has declared:

> All that the petitioner has deposed is that her husband and the girl of 11 to 12 years of age were indulging in indecent acts and were naked in a room. Even while describing the incident on the second occasion she deposed that the respondent was lying on the girl with his hand on the private part of the girl. ... There is not even an allegation in the petition or a suggestion in the evidence that there was any penetration by the man of the girl. At best these could be said to be indecent acts of sexual gratification and as long as they are unaccompanied by some penetration they cannot amount to adultery. (*C. Howell v. R. S. Howell*, AIR 1982 Delhi 328, at p. 331).

It cannot be hoped that after a prolonged legal battle for divorce, which invariably involves washing one's dirty-linen in [a] public place, the parties will forget and forgive the charge of adultery and resume the matrimonial life, merely because the aggrieved spouse fails to prove the charge of adultery and the plea for divorce is disallowed by a court of law. Even if divorce is allowed, the inordinate delay in getting the final verdict under the Act will defeat the very purpose of the petition for divorce.

This state of affairs has been causing irreparable hardship to the Hindu spouses; and it is wonderful why the Parliament is not focusing its attention on this vital problem adversely affecting the life of a major section of the Indian people.

It is submitted that the whole procedure can be simplified by amending the Act to include a provision for efforts for effecting reconciliation between the spouses concerned in all contested cases for divorce and allowing divorce if those efforts fail, without going into the grounds for it.

In the early days of Islam, following the procedure laid down in Chap 4 Verse 35, 128 and 130 of the Qur'an, the judge was required to appoint two arbiters: one belonging to the wife's family and the other to the husband's. These two arbiters will find out the facts, but their objectives must be to effect a re-conciliation between the parties. If all hopes of re-conciliation fail, a divorce is allowed: (See Moulana Muhammad Ali: *The Holy Quran*, p. 200). This procedure has been incorporated in the *Marriage Law of the Peoples' Republic of China* and in the *Legislation on Marriage and Family in [the] U.S.S.R.*

Under Article 17 of the Marriage Law of China, in the event of either husband or wife alone insisting upon divorce, it may be granted, only when mediation by the District People's Government and the Judicial Organ fail to bring about a reconciliation. Article 14 of the Legislation on Marriage and Family in the U.S.S.R. provides that a marriage shall be dissolved by the court when, on taking steps to reconcile the spouses by the court, it is established that further co-habitation of the spouses and the preservation of their family have become impossible.

A reflection on the provision of the *Ezhava Act* (III of 1100) regarding divorce, also, will be highly useful for finding out a solution to this problem. Under that Act, on payment of compensation provided therein and without going into the grounds of the proposed dissolution, the marriage shall be dissolved if the petition is not withdrawn within six months after the service of the copy of the petition on the respondent. The only complaint that may, probably, be made against the said Act is that the compensation provided therein is inadequate.

It is suggested that the *Hindu Marriage Act* may be amended so as to enable the spouses desiring divorce to get it without proving any ground therefor. We must not lose sight of the fact that the question to continue or not to continue the marriage tie is one which can, properly, be decided by the aggrieved spouse alone. Let them live in a becoming manner or separate in a becoming manner. Divorce proceedings which cause the parties to throw mud at each other can, in no way, be described as progressive ones.

2.3 On marriage laws

S. Sivaraman

[From: 1988(2) *KLT*, Journal section, pp. 3–4]

Sri M. Fazlul Haq has tried to render some service to Hindus by highlighting the inadequacies and deficiencies in the statute governing them regarding divorce – vide 1988(1) KLT Journal 45. He has also suggested that the *Hindu Marriage Act* may be amended so as to enable the spouses desiring divorce to get it without proving any ground therefore.

It appears Sri Haq has overlooked s. 13-B of the said Act which provides for divorce by mutual consent. It applies to marriages solemnised before or after the commencement of the *Marriage Laws (Amendment) Act*, 1976. All that is necessary to aver is that the parties have been living separately for a period of one year or more, that they have not been able to live together and that they have mutually agreed that the marriage should be dissolved. Subsection 2 of s. 13-B describes the further formalities to be observed in the matter and if the averments in the petition are true, the court shall pass a decree of divorce.

S. 14 of the Act has curtailed the period of waiting for presentation of a petition for divorce from 3 years to one year, since the date of marriage. Though this amendment was effected in 1976, the marginal note to that section has not been amended and the marginal note says that no petition for divorce is to be presented within 3 years of marriage.

At the same time, let us take a quick survey at the laws now in force governing divorce among Christians and Muslims. The law governing Christians viz. the *Indian Divorce Act* has long completed a century of its existence, it having been enacted on 26-2-1869. It is rather surprising that such a measure has stood without reflecting the changes and trends in modern society. Despite this aspect being brought to the notice of the authorities by courts on various occasions, the antiquarian, antediluvian and anachronistic Act still continues in the statute book. Even the sweeping and revolutionary changes made in the law of succession among Christians have [sic] left the *Indian Divorce Act* untouched and unscathed.

S. 7 of this Act says that the court has to act on principles of English Divorce Courts. The law in England has been liberalised but still there is judicial conflict in India as to whether the changes brought about in the Divorce Law in England subsequent to 1869 can be applied in India. That is because one view is that the section covers only principles and rules followed by English courts and they will not cover statutory provisions or statutory rules.

Different grounds are provided for petitions for divorce filed by a husband and by a wife. This itself is discriminatory.

So far as Muslims are concerned, there is the *Dissolution of Muslim Marriages Act* 1939. That however governs only applications for divorce to be filed by a woman. Muslim men still retain power for instant divorce by the magic word of '*Talaq*'.

Regarding conversion of one of the spouses to the marriage to another religion, it is interesting to note that the law is different for Hindus, Christians and Muslims. S. 13 of the *Hindu Marriage Act* which narrates the grounds for divorce is applicable equally to petitions whether filed by the husband or the wife. One ground is that the respondent has ceased to be a Hindu by conversion to another religion. In the *Indian Divorce Act*, the only ground available to the husband is that his wife has, since the solemnisation of the marriage, been guilty of adultery. But in a wife's petition, a ground is available to her that since the solemnisation of the marriage, her husband has exchanged his profession of Christianity for the profession of some other religion and gone through a form of marriage with another woman. This gives a limited ground to the wife to invoke the ground of change of religion. It appears, if the wife has renounced Christianity, that will afford no ground to the husband to seek a divorce. On the other hand, if the husband has exchanged the profession of Christianity, that could be the basis for divorce provided, along with the change of religion, the husband has gone through a form of marriage with another woman. Coming to the *Dissolution of Muslim Marriages Act*, s. 4 thereof enjoins that the renunciation of Islam by a married Muslim woman or her conversion to a faith other than Islam shall not by itself operate to dissolve her marriage.

There are wide disparities in other respects also. Maintenance pendente lite and expenses of proceedings are dealt with in s. 24 of the *Hindu Marriage Act*. Such relief can be given either to the wife or to the husband. So also the provision for permanent alimony and maintenance is dealt with under s. 25. The *Indian Divorce Act*, however, safeguards only the right of the wife to alimony whether pendente lite or permanent. There is no provision regarding expenses of proceedings. Under the *Indian Divorce Act*, it is also stipulated that alimony pending the suit shall in no case exceed 1/5th of the husband's average net income for the preceding 3 years. No such protection is provided to a Muslim wife.

Under the *Indian Divorce Act*, a District Court can only pass a decree for dissolution which shall be a decree nisi and such decree has to be confirmed by the High Court to become absolute. The reference to the High Court has to be heard by 3 Judges vide sections 16 and 17 of the Act. No such restrictions are provided in the *Hindu Marriage Act*.

The above anomalous position only points to the imperative, compelling and urgent need to bring about a uniform marriage law for all Indians. This has been envisaged in the Constitution in Article 44 which provides that the State shall endeavour to secure for the citizens a uniform civil code throughout the territory of India. The fact that this question has not so far received unbiased attention from the authorities is evident. The enactment of the *Muslim Women (Protection of Rights on Divorce) Act*, 1986 only shows that 'politics' are at the root and that no Government tries to study the question in an impartial manner, eschewed of all other extraneous and narrow political considerations. In fact, in the ruling of the Supreme Court referred to by Sri Haq, 1985 (3) SCC 62 the Supreme Court has pointed out that the time has come for the intervention of the Legislature to provide for a uniform code of marriage and divorce.

It is a fallacious and erroneous concept to think that enactment of a uniform law will cause interference in personal laws. In expressing this view point, the difference between personal laws and personal belief is conveniently forgotten. In any case, the mandate of the Legislature must certainly prevail even if it abrogates what is thought to be the law till then. This aspect is emphasised by courts now and then as for example in 1987(1) KLT 409.

To conclude, the need of the hour is the enactment of a uniform law of marriage and divorce to govern all citizens in India irrespective of religious faith. And this can brook no further delay.

2.4 Hindu talaq: On a progressive divorce law for India

[From: 1989(1) *KLT*, Journal section, pp. 23–30]

A very interesting contribution to the debate about a uniform divorce law for all Indians and about the place of the principle of 'irretrievable breakdown' is now found at 1988(1) KLT, J 45–47. The article by Shri M. Fazlul Haq appears prima facie to be concerned with reforms to the Hindu divorce law, the argument being that divorce should be made easier for the Hindus, that a modern, secular and progressive divorce law should enable spouses to "live in a becoming manner or separate in a becoming manner" (p. 47). This becoming manner, it is put forward, should not involve judicial proceedings which may "cause the parties to throw mud at each other" (*id.*). So it is suggested that the *Hindu Marriage Act* should be amended to enable spouses desiring divorce to obtain it without proving any ground for it, in other words, divorce should be freely available on demand.

It is left open whether such amended divorce law should involve any judicial proceedings at all; very probably the answer would be in the negative. One could think of a form of divorce by mutual consent, subsequently ratified in a quasi-judicial but in reality administrative act, such as practised in the Special Procedure of the English 'quickie divorce'. But Shri Haq does not view consensual divorces with any favour; his proposal aims to allow a unilateral repudiation of the marital tie, also against the wishes of the other spouse. In fact, the proposal amounts to saying that the Hindu law of India should be reformed in such a way as to incorporate the standard rule of the Muslim law of India in this regard. It is all too obvious that the Muslim *talaq*, divorce as a unilateral repudiation of the marital tie, primarily by the husband, who need not give any ground for his decision, is here sought to be applied to the Hindus. One could say that the learned author seeks to extend the benefits of the Muslim *talaq* to his Hindu compatriots. One needs to ask, though, whether this would bring about a useful improvement of the existing Hindu law of divorce; further, whether the proposal offers a viable solution to the tricky problem of formulating divorce rules for a uniform civil code for all Indians.

I gave Shri Haq's essay to my students in our course on 'Law and Society in South Asia', instructing them to write a discussion of the proposed reform. We had just studied the Indian and Pakistani law of divorce. The responses to the essay ranged from confusion and bewilderment to substantial criticisms. Everybody felt that the Hindu law of divorce was already very liberal, too liberal at times to protect the interests of women well. Few students detected that Shri Haq proposed to introduce the Muslim law rule into Hindu law, though many commented on the desirability or otherwise of a Uniform Civil Code. One clever student found that the proposal was bad news for lawyers, since a substantial slice of business might shrink if one allowed too much extra-judicial divorce.

Many students felt, very rightly, uncomfortable about the way in which the case for the reform of Hindu law had been argued. They detected serious flaws in the argument that the present Hindu law does not allow easy divorce: far from it, they said, divorce has become very easy, apart from delays and costs, since there are many grounds available. Shri Haq has apparently overlooked how much the Indian courts have extended the definition of cruelty: much has happened after *Dastane*'s case in 1975 by way of judicial expansion of the meaning of 'cruelty'. Divorce by mutual consent has been made available since 1976, so has a much more flexible law of nullity for fraud under s. 12(1)(c) of the HMA; s. 29(2) of the HMA continues to secure the right of very many Hindus to bring about a customary divorce. It was also noted that many Indian judges are now applying the principle of 'irretrievable breakdown' although the formal introduction of this ground was explicitly rejected when the *Marriage Laws (Amendment) Bill*, 1981 failed. Our opinion was certainly not that the Hindu divorce law needed an amendment to make divorce yet easier.

We noted, though, that the cases used by Shri Haq to illustrate the problems of Hindu divorce law were in fact cases under the *Indian Divorce Act* of 1869, pertaining to the indeed outdated Christian law of India. We do not know how, after looking at such cases, the conclusion could be drawn that the Hindu law needs further amendment. The learned author, it was felt by some of us, either was not up to date on the current state of the law, or deliberately misguided his readers.

Meanwhile, at 1988(2) KLT, J 3–4 Shri S. Sivaraman has responded to Shri Haq's proposal with great diplomacy. He points out that in his attempt to render some service to Hindus Shri Haq may have overlooked s.13(B) of the HMA and the fact that the waiting period for presenting a divorce petition was reduced to one year in 1976. The point being made about the marginal note is indeed marginal and quite unnecessary: surely the law was so amended.

Shri Sivaraman then proceeds to look at some incongruities in the various personal laws of India. No clear picture emerges, but the author is right to emphasise the need for reform. Whether this has to take the form of a uniform civil code is another matter, and we must note again that the issue has not been raised explicitly by Shri Haq.

I liked the point that "it is a fallacious and erroneous concept to think that enactment of a uniform law will cause interference in personal laws" (p. 4). The argument seems to be, though, that how one divorces may have little to do with one's personal belief. Surely, this line of argument is going to run into difficulties in India and elsewhere; to many people, religion is as much a way of life as a matter of personal belief. This reasoning will be killed off by 'politics', as referred to by Shri Sivaraman himself. This – is it not? – is the reason why India has so far made little progress in developing a uniform divorce law. Shri Haq's proposal would, however, warrant a more serious and deeper analysis.

Without doubt, India has more urgent items on her agenda for law reform than the introduction of a Uniform Civil Code. Nevertheless, let us first contemplate the benefits that Shri Haq's proposal may bring in terms of uniformity before we come to a second major point that his essay raises, namely an appropriate evaluation of the current state of Hindu divorce law.

Under Article 44 of the Constitution, the State is under a strong, yet not justiciable obligation "to endeavour to secure for the citizens a uniform civil code throughout the territory of India". The progress made since 1950 has been visible in one particular area: the personal law of the Hindus, as the law of the overwhelming majority, was codified (although not completely) and secularised in 1955–6, apparently to make it ultimately suitable as a uniform law for all Indians. Further reforms to this law, introduced in 1964 and 1976, continued this process of secularisation, to the extent that claims were heard that Hindu law had been killed off (J. D. M. Derrett: *The death of a marriage law*. New Delhi 1978). The new reforms also brought the modern Hindu law of India more and more in line with the provisions of the *Special Marriage Act* of 1954, that much underrated nucleus of a uniform civil code for the country. The SMA is so secularised (though there have been many allegations that it remains rather Hindu in nature) that it could indeed be the law of any Western country on marriage, divorce and related matters. The trouble with the SMA is, of course, that it remains optional for most Indians and appears to be known only to very few people, who may or may not use its provisions. Generally speaking, a progression can be noticed in the Indian legal system towards applying a secular, formalised legal regime of marriage and divorce to all Indians, and Mr. Haq's proposal can be seen in this context.

But India is still not ready for the uniform regulation of divorce laws. One cannot be sure, anyway, that legal uniformity is a desirable aim for such a huge and diverse country. For example, many Sikhs are not happy about the implications of having Hindu law applied to them; in *Partap Singh* (AIR. 1985 SC 1695) a valiant male fights the windmills of the modern legal system quite in vain. Calls for the reinstatement of the Sikh personal law are not just a political football, they reflect serious discomfort about State interference in intensely personal matters, something that the traditional Indian ruler, of whatever religion, would not have contemplated lightly as an expedient means of exerting his influence.

The Muslims of India have, for well-known reasons, not been subjected to many family law reforms. To this day, the Indian Muslim laws of marriage and divorce remain almost completely outside the purview of the courtroom law. Divorce, apart from the regime of the DMMA, 1939, is an extra-judicial matter leaving much discretion to the spouses. Or should we say, rather, to the stronger and more powerful spouse, in all probability the man? The divorce laws of the small minorities of Christians and Parsis continue to be governed by outdated legislation that has quite rightly prompted the Supreme Court to point out the need for more uniform regulation (See *Ms. Jorden Diengdeh* (1985) 3 SCC 62 and AIR 1985 SC 935). The tiny Parsi minority, propelled by anxious community leaders, has already accepted the need for certain modern reforms. But the situation at present is still one of legalised inequality, of differential treatment of spouses according to their religion, and whether this is, in a modern secular republic, a reasonable system of classification, remains debatable.

In this context, the reform suggested by Shri Haq seems eminently sensible at first sight. Avoid lengthy court battles, he says, avoid judicial proceedings with all their problems altogether, let us make a progressive rule that allows self-regulation of society in this quite crucial area of the law. Give power to the individual.

One should not throw out this proposal merely on the ground that it seeks to re-invigorate a traditional Muslim concept. Such concepts could become traditional, in the first place, only because they proved useful to someone; otherwise society would not have maintained such a tradition over a long time. There is, thus, an inherent merit in this proposal. But can we imagine that a Hindu divorce law that contains the option of an extra-judicial *talaq*-like divorce would be acceptable to the Muslims of India after the totally secularised *Hindu Marriage Act* had been re-named 'Uniform Civil Code'? If that were the case, we should warmly embrace the proposal as a pathbreaking, in fact breath-taking and indeed progressive measure. But are not the political realities such that the Muslims would not accept this? Tahir Mahmood, among others, reminds us of Muslim sensibilities time and again, and the current trend in political expediency goes certainly the other way: Shah Bano and Salman Rushdie's 'satanic' writings are living proof of this.

So what is the purpose of the proposal made by Shri Haq? He has left us to draw our own conclusions. Shri Sivaraman took the matter slightly further by arguing, as indicated, that a uniform law need not cause interference in personal laws. While I do not go along with that, I still think that it would make sense to incorporate Shri Haq's proposal as an amendment to the HMA, provided the Muslims could then be persuaded to use this very same legislative provision to regulate their divorces under the new Uniform Civil Code. In real life, probably nothing would change: the traditional *talaq* would be deemed to take effect under the new Code, and corresponding provisions on maintenance for wives and children could ensure that the *shariat* principles are continued under the ambit of the new uniform law, which would then not be very uniform in reality, but in name only. But if that is what India needs so urgently, as Shri Sivaraman and many others have argued, it can be done very soon and with a few strokes of the pen. I gather Shri Haq did not intend his proposal to be used in the way suggested here, but we should give him much credit for promoting some thinking on the subject.

Let us ask now whether the Hindus of India would be ready to adopt the proposed amendment. The cruel truth is, beyond doubt, that such a new rule might please many Hindu husbands. It might even slightly reduce the number of dowry deaths. Then, would the legislature perhaps be willing to introduce this reform? Leaving all anti-Muslim biases aside (they did not prevent the 'option of puberty' being introduced into the Hindu divorce law in 1976), my view is that the legislature will not be ready to contemplate this.

The explanation lies in the fate of the *Marriage Laws (Amendment) Bill*, 1981, which has apparently been shelved indefinitely. It went too far for India in seeking to introduce 'irretrievable breakdown' as a ground for divorce. To allow unilateral divorce without giving a ground would go even further than the failed Bill. It would also leave Hindu women unprotected against male whims, or the politics of the husband's family, as the case may be. Women's groups would do well to raise a massive protest against such an amendment, and we can be sure that they would be alert to the new dangers.

The issue here is not one of communalism, then, but at stake is the equitable distribution of rights and duties between males and females in modern India. As indicated, following Shri Haq's proposal would tip the balance further in favour of male chauvinist discretion to dispose of females when and how one likes. Precisely this modern India cannot allow to happen. A country that sports one of the most progressive Constitutions in the world cannot allow half its population to be treated as society's major commodity item, to be acquired and disposed of by those that can afford to do so. If we take the Constitution seriously and give its Articles proper meaning, greater rights of the individual need to be matched with greater duties towards those that are affected by one's actions.

Thus, as the Prime Minister is ultimately, in principle, accountable to every citizen, every citizen is accountable to society, to the public interest; it could not be in the public interest that women may be bought and sold, or merely picked up and abandoned by those individuals who can afford to have it their way. India's present constitutional guarantees to the individual imply that there can be no absolute individualism in modern India. The constitutional amendments in 1976 and 1978 have made this message explicitly clear, not only in Article 51-A in the context of Fundamental Duties. The development of public interest litigation in the present decade and the application of its principles in all areas of Indian law exclude the possibility of acceptance of Shri Haq's proposals for Hindus without adequate and effective safeguards for divorced women and for children. The proposal may sound progressive and useful in our modern age, but total individual discretion as implied in unilateral termination of a marital tie without any need to give grounds violates a number of constitutional principles.

The proposal would look different if corresponding maintenance provisions had been suggested. We know that up to date satisfactory maintenance arrangements for divorced spouses and their children are at best existing on paper. The forceful lecture to the nation by Mr. Justice Sathiadev in *Soundarammal* (AIR 1980 Mad 294) has certainly not been forgotten, but there is no reason to be satisfied with the present legal position, which perpetuates injustices in many cases, though we may detect some movement in the right direction in the many reported cases under s. 24 HMA now. Difficulties over maintenance exist as much for the Hindus as for Muslim divorcees, who by the *Muslim Women (Protection of Rights on Divorce) Act*, 1986 have been explicitly deprived of appropriate legal protection, a position not taken in the very interesting case of *Ali v. Sufaira*, 1988(2) KLT 94. The *Shah Bano* issue also showed that the modern Indian welfare state is not in a position to rescue the victims of an excessively liberal divorce law of any community. As in modern China, the onus to maintain indigent individual falls to the family, not the state (see also *Vijaya*, AIR 1987 SC 1100). In such circumstances, the state has a strong obligation to protect individuals from the negative side-effects of divorce, and of unilateral divorce in particular.

Further, one fails to see how the legal safeguard of reconciliation procedures, as suggested by Shri Haq, can help the victim of a unilateral divorce. Surely, pleading for the absolute freedom of a spouse to sever the marital tie and suggesting reconciliation procedures do not go together well. Not only China and Russia have such procedures, as Shri Haq points out, also Pakistan and Bangladesh include them under the provisions of the *Muslim Family Laws Ordinance*, 1961. In either case, I am reliably informed, such procedures are not an effective safeguard once the husband has made up his mind to utter the *talaq* or has already pronounced it.

On the other hand, there is much evidence to show that strengthening maintenance provisions may be a powerful deterrent to divorce. We know that the deferred Muslim *mehr* is now increasingly being used as a deterrent against unilateral divorce. A man faced with the binding obligation to pay a huge lump sum will think twice before divorcing his wife in a moment of anger. The evidence of vastly increased stipulated sums of deferred *mehr* in India, Pakistan, Bangladesh, and also in Britain, shows well how a traditional customary legal system can adapt to changing circumstances, seeking to maintain a reasonable balance of rights and duties between the spouses. Not surprisingly, the invidious arguments that women in India now marry with an eye to maintenance provisions has begun to appear (Tahir Mahmood: *Personal laws in crisis*. New Delhi 1986, pp. 127–130).

However, the reality for most Indian women is still, as a recent study shows very convincingly, that wives are in danger of falling between two stools if they accept a divorce (Vasudha Dhagamwar: *Women and divorce*. Poona 1986). They would lose the roof over their head and may have nowhere to go if their natal family does not help them. As a result, Dhagamwar found among women of all communities that wives may put up with matrimonial violence too cruel to describe just in order to remain married. This goes not only for poor, illiterate women, who may in fact be very strong when it comes to fending for themselves (see Leela Gulati: *Profiles in female poverty*. Delhi 1981, a study of women in Kerala), but for their educated professional middle-class sisters, too, who may bitterly regret having agreed to a divorce once it is too late (see Rama Mehta: *Divorced Hindu woman*. Delhi 1975).

To allow Hindu husbands unilateral repudiation of the marital tie without giving any grounds would lead to much more suffering among Hindu women. For all the reasons outlined above, Shri Haq's proposal for the amendment of [the] HMA is entirely unacceptable.

Let us now finally turn to one important issue indicated above, namely the question whether the present Hindu law of divorce is really as restrictive as Shri Haq claims. It appears, indeed, that he has based his case for the reform of Hindu divorce law on a strangely misguided evaluation of the present legal position.

To begin with, clever Hindu spouses can now invoke with great ease the law of nullity for fraud immediately after a disappointing first night. HMA s. 12(1)(c) was much liberalised in 1976 and now allows instant repudiation of the marital tie if one can show that "any material fact or circumstance concerning the respondent" was not disclosed prior to the marriage. Especially in Northern India, courts have been ready to annul marriages on the flimsiest of grounds (see e.g. *Bikkar*, AIR 1981 P&H 391, *Balbir*, AIR 1984 P&H 417, *Som Dutt*, AIR 1986 P&H 191). Nobody seems to have asked the respondents whether they have any interest in the marriage. The victim may well be the husband, too, as in *Rajinder*, AIR 1987 Del 285, where he had not disclosed his previous marriage, and the lady walked off in disgust. The statutory amendment and its judicial operationalisation have strengthened individualism so much that the slightest non-fulfilment of expectations or the tiniest defect in a spouse can now be used as a ground for nullity. The traditional ideal of a sacramental union has all but disappeared here.

In the alternative, one waits a year and lets the usual wear and tear of married life take its toll. Accusing one's spouse of cruelty has now become such a rubber-like judicially expanded ground for terminating a marriage under Hindu law that it is bound to become increasingly popular with unscrupulous husbands and scheming relatives. Recent law reports, again mainly from North India, make depressing reading: take the subject index of AIR 1987 Delhi under HMA s. 13, where no less than seven cases on cruelty are listed. Here, too, the victim is by no means always the wife. Reports of the recent formation of the "All India Front Against Wives' Atrocities" in New Delhi strengthen the impression of a brutalisation process in contemporary Indian society which is made worse by judicial connivance and a lack of understanding about the consequences of modern law reforms. How can India at the same time decry the Western decadence of high divorce rates and lack of care for each other, and then proceed to follow in the same direction?

A subtler way of getting rid of one's unwanted spouse before a court of law is, of course, to arrange a divorce by mutual consent under s. 13(B) of the HMA, as introduced in 1976. The language of this section is clear and unambiguous, little needs to be proved before the court proceeds to grant a decree, and there are few reported cases. A recent controversy has been over whether a spouse, having consented to such a divorce petition, may then withdraw such a consent. The courts are consistently answering this in the affirmative now (see *Harcharan*, AIR 1988 P&H 27 and *K. I. Mohanan*, AIR 1988 Ker 28), and one may note also the preference for informality expressed in *Krishna*, AIR 1987 P&H 191.

It would be very useful to know how many such petitions are made every year and whether they are successful. If one plays one's cards well, so that the judge does not notice the element of duress where it exists, this is an unexpectedly easy exit from matrimony. It is not surprising that 97% of all divorces in English law are thus 'settled' now. This always happens in court since English law does no longer allow extra-judicial divorces since 1973. But much hidden duress is involved; the courts here are not under an obligation to be satisfied, as under Hindu law in India, that consent of either party was not obtained by force, fraud or undue influence. Looking at England, one may anticipate that divorces by mutual consent will become, in due course, the most popular means to terminate a marriage in India.

The myth that traditional Hindu law did not allow divorce is still restated quite often; the point is also made in an odd interpretation of some verses of the *Manusmriti* by Shri Haq (p. 45). But the facts are very different from the *dharmic* ideal, and s. 29(2) of the HMA explicitly safeguarded the position of Hindu customary divorces. It had been known for a long time that such divorces remain very popular (see J. D. M. Derrett: 'Divorce by caste custom' at (1963) 65 BomLR, J 161–169), but just how frequent are such divorces after the many modern law reforms? Recent research by one of my postgraduates, to be included in a forthcoming book on family law in India, found that customary divorces among Hindus have consistently been underrated: not only low-caste Hindus have customary forms of divorce, there are also many cases among the higher castes, even Brahmins (Simon Beckwith: *The Hindu customary law of divorce*. London 1988). Such arrangements may not be accepted by the courts (see the adverse comments in *Nitaben* (1984) 1 Guj LR 276) and may therefore lead to people learning to use the official law of divorce by mutual consent, which means, perhaps, little else than going to court to have the family arrangement rubber stamped. Notwithstanding the official legal position, informal customary divorce arrangements continue to exist in many communities right through the caste spectrum (see also P. K. Virdi: *The grounds for divorce in Hindu and English law*. Delhi 1972, pp. 25–36). Such divorce arrangements are often much less informal than the textbooks and court decisions would seem to suggest. Since few people question such customary and normally extra-judicial family arrangements, courts are not in a strong position to lay down the law on s. 29(2) HMA, and we find much evidence of unilateral repudiation of the marital tie here among Hindus, again without any need to give grounds.

Such findings do not automatically make Shri Haq's proposal look any better, but I would suggest that in substance there is indeed much less difference than is commonly admitted between the Muslims and the Hindus in their treatment of divorce. Male chauvinism exists everywhere. The communal differences, it appears, have been exaggerated by constant pigeon-holing of the Muslim *talaq* as a mischievous unilateral tool of suppression of women and the Hindu ideal of *samskara*. In reality, though, Muslims are not divorcing as indiscriminately as is occasionally alleged, and many Hindus divorce their wives, despite assertions by Hindu chauvinists that their women are like goddesses, and divorce is taboo.

It is indeed right, as Shri Haq stated in his very first sentence, that divorce is discouraged by all religions. And it seems useful to retain those customary and religious reservations. Where they do not exist, however, women may indeed get a rough deal; modern secularising law reforms, by themselves, cannot guarantee women a better place in society.

Muslims will argue, quite rightly, that the Islamic form of unilateral repudiation of the marital tie has not led to a high divorce rate overall. In the absence of reliable statistics on this, we may perhaps conclude that Western dimensions of breakdown of marriage have not been reached; the same is apparently true for Hindus in India. It would seem that traditional South Asian reservations against easy divorce have prevented the extra-judicial *talaq* as well as extra-judicial Hindu customary divorces from taking on epidemic proportions. But there is much evidence that divorce is becoming more common now in India, and Shri Haq's proposal is not to be welcomed in this context, too, since it strengthens the position of the ruthless individual at the cost of those less able to defend themselves.

Evidence of the clever fabrication of grounds for divorce (one may refer here to the tricky 'own wrong' problem that seems now solved by judicial alertness) and prolonged court battles, plus the fact that 'progressive' judges have not always been alert enough to avoid injustice in the name of the law, do not at all lead to the logical conclusion that it is better not to have to prove any grounds for divorce.

So Shri Haq's proposal fails on all counts. It proceeds from the quite mistaken assumption that the Hindu divorce law today is not liberal enough and that the model of the Muslim *talaq* would be useful for a modern uniform regulation of Indian divorce law. My view is clearly that a progressive divorce law for India must be one which restricts individual discretion to divorce and promotes a sense of responsibility and concern for one's spouse and his or her future. To encourage, in young people, the egoistic exploitation of the other's weaknesses and lack of tolerance of even minor divergence from the ideal will mean a progression into disaster. India does not need a billion of selfish, pampered egoists, but must require her people's concern for co-humans in every possible way, otherwise a ruthless 'survival of the fittest' will become inevitable. Quite clearly one can apply Article 51-A of the Constitution here in principle. In a society where arranged marriages continue to be the norm, and will so continue, and where self-arranged unions may (as elsewhere) not stand the test of time, giving absolute discretion to an 'aggrieved spouse' over the fate of a marriage is a step in the wrong direction, whether it be for Muslims or Hindus, or anyone else. Marriage involves at least two people, and anyone entering into marriage cannot, in my submission, reasonably expect to remain an independent individual. Therefore, any uniform regulation of Indian divorce law that does not protect the weaker spouse adequately against the 'big fish' would violate all underlying legal postulates of modern India's Constitution, of *dharma*, *shariat* and morality in general, and would be a slap in the face for most women of India. To offer the Hindus of India the equivalent of the Muslim *talaq* is neither a reasonable improvement of the Hindu law nor a viable solution for the distant mirage of the uniform civil code.

2.5 Divorce law in modern India: Balancing breakdown, social cohesion and financial viability

As we saw in chapter 2.1, during the 1970s and early 1980s, Indian divorce law was still expected to become more 'liberal', in the sense of freeing spouses from an unwanted marriage. The breakdown principle, which Lord Denning in Britain so persuasively held up as the most humane way to end messy marital relationships with the minimum of fuss and without washing 'dirty linen' in public, had impressed Indian policy makers, lawyers, legal commentators, and some judges. The Indian Law Commission, in its 59th Report, had recommended widening the statutory grounds for divorce and the *Marriage Laws (Amendment) Act*, 1976 had introduced several new grounds for divorce, including cruelty and divorce by mutual consent, the latter under a new s. 13B of the HMA. Indian judges, too, were taken in by the assumption that it was better to avoid lengthy court battles if either spouse felt that the marriage was dead. 'Irretrievable breakdown' was not included as a ground for divorce under modern Hindu law, but the concept somehow floated around and looked attractive to many judges.

Thus it came that in modern Indian divorce law the breakdown principle has remained a prominent and powerful concept, although it never took statutory form. As we saw, by 1981, when the *Marriage Laws (Amendment) Bill* failed in Parliament because women's groups opposed it so vigorously, a process of slow re-orientation began. Meanwhile, however, during the early 1980s, the ideology of breakdown still exercised considerable influence over Indian judges, litigants as well as lawyers. It is perhaps only commonsensical that a man who wants to get rid of his wife will argue for the operation of the breakdown principle, and so will a wife who wants to end her marriage. However, this leads to massive unilateral repudiation of marriages, and in most cases we are going to see husbands, rather than wives, as the petitioner for such divorces.

Faced with persuasive pleadings about the facts of marital breakdown in innumerable cases, many judges initially used their discretion to enlarge the grounds for divorce and for nullity, as provided by statutory reforms through the *Marriage Laws (Amendment) Act*, 1976. In the process, they created a case law that was decidedly individualistic, using the slightest dissatisfaction, or alleged fault in a spouse, as a ground for divorce or nullity. But what legal protection would this give to the respondent? It seems that too little thought was initially given to this aspect of divorce and nullity litigation. However, during the late 1980s, if not before, Indian courts became more alert about gender imbalances in the law and, as chapter 2.1 emphasised, about social and financial considerations in relation to divorce litigation.

In this chapter, I shall first discuss in some detail, taking examples from various areas of the law, how this process of liberalisation and of judicial enlargement of divorce grounds during the 1980s worked. Our case analysis will seek to indicate what conceptual and social problems these developments gave rise to. We shall concentrate on cruelty as a ground for divorce and the reformed law on nullity for fraud under s. 12(1)(c) of the HMA, with brief comments on the 'own wrong' problem, which created so many manifestly bad decisions (see Derrett 1981) and on the new law on divorce by mutual consent. All these areas moved initially towards facilitating divorce, based on the assumption that once a marital relationship had broken down, it should be terminated as quickly as possible. Given that this was such a dominant policy objective, the immediate and long-term consequences of a growing rate of marital breakdown in the country were not recognised as an important factor.

During the late 1980s, however, Indian judges seem to have become more alert to the moral, social and financial consequences of widespread marital breakdown. It also appears that judges began to examine their supposedly liberal approach more carefully. Was it really that liberal to ignore the respondent's concerns? Was it actually desirable, on all counts, to allow Hindu men to divorce their wife as and when they pleased? Should it be acceptable in modern Indian law and society that either spouse could unilaterally terminate the marital union, as in the much-criticised Muslim law? My analysis of the Indian case law on Hindu divorces from the 1980s and 1990s demonstrates a definite change of judicial approaches to facilitating divorces during this period. Quite what the nature of that change is, we shall have to see. We will also need to examine, as indicated, whether the new-found conservatism is a consequence of ideological influences from Indian religious traditions, or whether the judges are actually aware (and, telling us about) the negative impact of too liberal divorce policies on women or on socio-economic developments in modern India. While it appears that even fiscal concerns have played a large role in this context, to what extent have the judges been saying, in this particular context, that blindly following the West is not a useful strategy for modern India? We need to reserve judgment on all these questions until we have analysed the most recent cohorts of cases from the various Indian High Courts and the Supreme Court.

Divorce based on cruelty during the 1980s: enlarging the scope for divorce

While cruelty had been a ground for judicial separation under s. 10 of the HMA 1955, but not a ground for divorce, this was changed in 1976. S. 10(1)(b) of the unreformed HMA 1955 provided:

> 10. *Judicial separation.* –
> (1) Either party to a marriage, whether solemnized before or after the commencement of this Act, may present a petition to the District Court praying for a decree for judicial separation on the ground that the other party –
> (a) ......
> (b) has treated the petitioner with such cruelty as to cause a reasonable apprehension in the mind of the petitioner that it will be harmful or injurious for the petitioner to live with the other party; or ...

The interpretation of this section has been fairly strict. Given that this ground was introduced into the HMA to support a case for judicial separation, not for divorce, there are also many reported cases in which the courts found evidence of cruelty, as a fact, and granted the petitioner the desired relief. However, this still meant that the Hindu marriage would subsist in law, and so the concept of *samskara* was impaired, but not outrightly challenged.

The word 'cruelty' was not defined in the HMA, nor in any other enactment, hence the judges had much room to exercise their discretion – and they did so. Older writers have a tendency to stress the influence of English legal concepts. Thus, Gupte (1976: 198) emphasised that "... the Courts in England as well as in India have consistently held that the cruelty must be such as to create a reasonable apprehension of harm or injury, physical or mental".

The *Marriage Laws (Amendment) Act*, 1976 left cruelty as a ground for judicial separation under s. 10 of the Act, but now also introduced cruelty as a ground for divorce under s. 13(1)(ia) of the amended HMA. However, the relevant section has a different, shorter wording, which became crucial, since the new law laid down that cruelty *simpliciter* should be the yardstick. While Gupte's definition, as given above, still requires proof that the cruelty concerned must have created harmful consequences, it would now perhaps no longer be necessary to prove actual harm to the petitioner. In accordance with the ideology of 'irretrievable breakdown', simply cruelty by itself could now be considered as sufficient ground for granting divorce. The new provision reads:

> 13. – *Divorce*
> (1) Any marriage solemnized, whether before or after the commencement of this Act, may, on a petition presented by either the husband or

> the wife, be dissolved by a decree of divorce on the ground that the other party....
>
> (i) .....
>
> (ia) has, after the solemnization of the marriage, treated the petitioner with cruelty, or ...

Legal commentary has been to the effect that this statutory change facilitated a liberal construction of divorce regulation (e.g. Sampath 1983: 298). Desai (1990: 658) comments generally that, "[i]t has now become the settled practice of the courts to give liberal interpretation to the provisions of this Act in the method of certain reliefs to be granted under it". More specifically, Desai (1990: 662–663) discussed the implications of the legal change on the law relating to cruelty:

> By the amendment the Legislature must, therefore, be understood to have left to the courts to determine on the facts and circumstances of each case whether the conduct amounts to cruelty. This is just as well since actions of men are so diverse and infinite that it is almost impossible to expect a general definition which could be exhaustive and not fail in some cases. It seems permissible, therefore, to enter a caveat against any judicial attempt in that direction.

Since the 1976 amendment has simplified the concept of cruelty under the HMA, as Desai (1990: 663) notes, there has indeed been a definite movement towards what everybody called 'liberalisation' of divorce on the ground of cruelty. Desai refers in this context to the important old leading case of *Dastane v. Dastane*, AIR 1975 SC 1534, which contributed to the new liberalisation as a pre-reform case on the matter. Desai (1990: 665) also notes that the court's assessment of what amounts to cruelty needs to be comprehensive, taking a picture of the domestic life of the spouses as a whole. The learned author further, at p. 664, emphasised the need to examine the facts and circumstances of each case in the light of the changing cultural context of Indian society:

> There has been such a marked change in the notions of matrimonial duties and obligations of husband and wife in the present generation in India that it will be incumbent on the court to be extremely careful in the matter of seeking assistance and guidance from decisions arrived at under any previous legislation in India or England even when the rules may be similarly worded and blind adherence to any of those decisions must be depreciated and particularly when they relate to persons whose customs, manners and modes of life may be different.

This statement appears to suggest that in the late 1970s and 1980s, India was perfectly able to develop her own policies of divorce regulation and that the need to rely on foreign models was no longer there (if indeed it had ever been). Divorce petitions on the ground of cruelty soon became statistically the most prominent element of modern Indian divorce law and an immense number of cases have been reported.[23] I shall pick out a number of cases which illustrate how far the Indian courts went, during the early 1980s in particular, in freeing petitioners from the company of a less than ideal spouse who could be said to be guilty of some act of cruelty.[24]

In *Rajinder Singh Joon v. Tara Wati*, AIR 1980 Del 213, a husband appealed against refusal of a decree for divorce on the ground of cruelty. The husband, who was employed in the army, had met with a serious accident in far-away Assam and was hospitalised there for 8 months. The wife did not go to visit him there, nor did she visit her sick husband after his transfer to Delhi. The lower court judge had apparently accepted the wife's excuse that she had no money to go to Assam, but in the High Court, the judge took a dim view of the wife's behaviour and, in essence, passed a moral judgment on her when he held at p. 214:

> In my opinion the conduct was such that it can properly and rationally be stigmatised by the word "cruelty" in its ordinary acceptation. It was not a trivial incident. It was a matter at once "grave and weighty". It was a question of life and death of the husband. The wife's callous indifference and neglect is inexcusable and unforgivable.

Since the wife had, in addition, indicated to the judge that she would not oppose a divorce, and since the financial matters between the parties were sorted out before the court (notably the wife claimed back Rs. 5,000/- of dowry money), the husband's appeal was allowed and divorce was granted.

The disturbing case of *Kiran Kapoor v. Surinder Kumar Kapoor*, AIR 1982 Del 543, involves allegations by the wife that she was put under pressure to bring more dowry. When no such money was forthcoming, she was treated with cruelty by the husband and his parents. However, this was a husband's petition for divorce. His case was that she had been cruel to him by complaining about the dowry demands to official authorities, and she had also been cruel to him on many other occasions, small and large, not allowing him sexual intercourse, refusing to make tea for his friends, and turning up at his factory to discuss the marital difficulties and have him dismissed from his job. The learned judge carefully examined the various allegations and confirmed the decree of divorce on the ground of cruelty. Evidently, he found it impossible to accept the version of the wife and held, at p. 549:

> I am satisfied that the wife by making these allegations had exceeded her right to protest against the alleged highhandedness of the husband and his family. As far as this aspect of the case is concerned it cannot be said that the husband is taking any advantage of his own wrong.

This case, badly pleaded, convoluted and quite labour-intensive for the judge, seems to be decided also on the basis that the marriage between the spouses had anyway broken down, though that is only indicated very subtly

(p. 549). Interestingly, while the judge notes that smaller matters, like not making tea, would not amount to cruelty, complaining about the husband to public bodies was treated as a grave issue and definitely qualified as cruelty. The judge does not appear to have accepted the wife's allegations about dowry-related violence, and one wonders whether this was justified.[25]

A number of cases have focused on the expectation that married women should bear children, so that a Hindu wife's refusal to do so, whether through denial of intercourse, secret sterilisation, or abortion of the foetus, was held to amount to cruelty towards the husband. In *Satya v. Siri Ram*, AIR 1983 P&H 252, the wife had twice terminated her pregnancy and the husband had been granted divorce on the ground of cruelty on that basis. In her weak appeal before the High Court, she foolishly tried to suggest that it was not even established that she had been pregnant. This definitely turned the judge against her. Scathing in his criticism of the wife's actions, he said at p. 253:

> Now if the wife deliberately and consistently refuses to satisfy [the] husband's natural and legitimate craving to have a child, the deprivation reduces him to despair and it naturally affects his mental health. This is more so in the case in hand where the parties to the litigation are Hindus. In this sort of case the Court has to attach due weight to the general principle underlying the Hindu law of marriage and sonship and the importance attached by Hindus to the principle of spiritual benefit of having a son who can offer a funeral cake and libation of water to the manes of his ancestors. It would be no answer to say that it is now open to the respondent to adopt a son.

The judge also noted explicitly (at p. 253) that the 1976 Amendment Act had introduced divorce on the ground of cruelty and had omitted the requirement that any cruelty must be such as to cause a reasonable apprehension in the mind of the petitioner that it would be injurious to live with the respondent. Hence, there was no doubt in the judge's mind that this was a fit case for a decree of divorce in favour of the husband. This case was discussed by Sampath (1983: 299), who strongly agrees with the decision itself, but raises interesting comments on the scope for difference of opinion about the need for sons and the underlying ideological burden on women.

A similar case is *Sushil Kumar Verma v. Usha*, AIR 1987 Del 86, a husband's successful appeal against the lower court's refusal to grant him a divorce. Here, the wife had left the husband about 4 months after the marriage and had had an abortion. The judge clearly found that unacceptable, while he also noted the change in the law on cruelty, saying at p. 89:

> In this country everyone wants to have at least one child, if not more, and in fact one of the primary ends of the marriage ... is to have progeny ...

> I am of the view that aborting the foetus in the very first pregnancy by a deliberate act, without the consent of the husband, would amount to cruelty. It is important to bear in mind that it is no more the requirement of law that cruelty must be of such kind that it should be a cause of danger to life and limb.

While the law would appear to place married Hindu women under certain obligations in terms of cohabitation and even child-bearing, it is too often ignored that Hindu men are under matrimonial obligations, too. Thus, as Diwan (1987: 294) emphasises, either party's refusal to have sexual intercourse amounts to cruelty and hence becomes a ground for divorce. In *Anil Bhardwaj v. Nirmlesh Bhardwaj*, AIR 1987 Del 111, it appears that it was the wife who had refused sexual intercourse, as indeed in most reported cases. There were so many disagreements between the couple that it must have been difficult for the judge to make sense of the totally contradictory pleadings. Apart from dowry demands and probably resulting violence, the wife insisted that she wanted to stay separately from her in-laws, complained about the burden of housework and, by all accounts, had refused to consummate the marriage. The couple had only stayed together for less than 6 weeks. The judge referred to earlier cases on the point,[26] and swiftly granted the husband a divorce.

Keshaorao Krishnaji Londhe v. Nisha Londhe, AIR 1984 Bom 413 has been considered an important case on cruelty (Diwan 1984: 265). The judge reviewed a large number of cases on cruelty and the case illustrates well how some judges in the 1980s may have been confused about the objectives of the legislative changes of 1976 and their relationship to the early leading case of *Dastane v. Dastane*, AIR 1975 SC 1534. Although it had been clearly stated by the 59th Report of the Indian Law Commission that cruelty *simpliciter* should be made a ground for divorce to liberalise the legal provisions, and this had been implemented in 1976, some judges were refusing to take notice of such evidence. It was held in this case, at pp. 416–417:

> New trend of thinking has developed in society. The thinking was that there is no use maintaining the marriage as a facade in the absence of emotional and other bonds which are the very essence of the marriage. It was considered better in the interest of healthy society to dissolve the marriage than meaninglessly to try it to limp along. The fault theory was thus considered as outdated and the "irretrievable breakdown theory" became favourite.

Diwan (1985: 106) emphasises in this respect that the change in the law in 1976 had made a real difference:

> After the 1976 amendment redefining cruelty it is no longer necessary for the petitioner to establish that respondent's cruelty has caused reasonable apprehension in his or her mind that it would be harmful or injurious to live with the respondent.

However, at the same time, when there were difficulties in the marital relationship, but it was not impossible for the spouses to continue to live together, divorce decrees were refused in quite a few reported cases. In *Rita v. Brij Kishore Gandhi*, AIR 1984 Del 291, the husband was a habitual drunkard, which caused the wife great distress. While the court branded excessive drinking as a vice, the wife's appeal failed and she was not granted a decree of divorce, probably because she had not pleaded that it was unsafe for her, and injurious for her health, to stay with the husband (Diwan 1984: 265).

Such cases may make us wonder if it mattered in practice, perhaps, whether the spouse seeking divorce on the basis of cruelty was the husband or the wife. It appears that in the majority of cases, when a husband sought divorce on the basis of the wife's alleged cruelty, it was more easily granted than if the wife had been the petitioner. Such cases are, for example, found in the *Annual Survey of Indian Law 1985* (Diwan 1985: 104–106), although in *Asha Handa v. Baldev Raj Handa*, AIR 1984 Del 76 the wife's case was accepted.

It became a well-established proposition in law during the early 1980s that false charges of unchastity, adultery, or illicit relationship amounted to cruelty.[27] In those cases, either side could be granted divorce. Another line of cases, stretching back at least to the 1960s, concerns disagreements between spouses if the wife has a job and wants to – or needs to – stay at a different place from the husband. Technically falling under restitution of conjugal rights (covered by s. 9 HMA) and desertion (covered by s. 13(1)(ib) of the HMA, as amended in 1976), such cases have often involved allegations of cruelty, have mostly – but notably not exclusively – blamed the wife and have led to many divorce decrees in favour of men.[28]

By the late 1980s, demanding dowry became a ground for divorce on the basis of cruelty. In distinct contrast to *Kiran Kapoor*, AIR 1982 Del 543, the Supreme Court of India took a totally negative stance against husbands who demand dowry from their wife and held, in *Shobha Rani v. Madhukar Reddi*, AIR 1988 SC 121, that this amounted to cruelty and was a ground for divorce for the wife.[29] This decision reflects, very interestingly, the significant development of Indian anti-dowry legislation in the mid-1980s and signals a tougher stance of the highest court against abuses of the dowry system. Jagannatha Shetty J noted that "cruelty simpliciter is now a ground for divorce" (p. 123) and proceeded (*id.*):

> The word "cruelty" has not been defined. Indeed it could not have been defined. It has been used in relation to human conduct or human behaviour. It is the conduct in relation to or in respect of matrimonial duties and obligations. It is a course of conduct of one which is adversely affecting the other. The cruelty may be mental or physical, intentional or unintentional. If it is physical the court will have no problem to determine it. It is a question of fact and degree. If it is mental the problem presents difficulty. First, the enquiry must begin as

> to the nature of the cruel treatment. Second, the impact of such treatment in the mind of the spouse. Whether it caused reasonable apprehension that it would be harmful or injurious to live with the other. Ultimately, it is a matter of inference to be drawn by taking into account the nature of the conduct and its effect on the complaining spouse. There may, however, be cases where the conduct complained of itself is bad enough and per se unlawful or illegal. Then the impact or the injurious effect on the other spouse need not be enquired into. In such cases, the cruelty will be established if the conduct itself is proved or admitted.

Next, the judge commented on changing social conditions and gave some important pointers for how cruelty was being assessed, saying at p. 123:

> It will be necessary to bear in mind that there has been marked change in life around us. In matrimonial duties and responsibilities in particular, we find a sea change. They are of varying degrees from house to house or person to person. Therefore, when a spouse makes complaint about the treatment of cruelty by the partner in life or relations, the court should not search for standard in life. A set of facts stigmatised as cruelty in one case may not be so in another case. The cruelty alleged may largely depend upon the type of life the parties are accustomed to or their economic and social conditions. It may also depend upon their culture and human values to which they attach importance. We, the Judges and lawyers, therefore, should not import our own notions of life. We may not go in parallel with them. There may be a generation gap between us and the parties. It would be better if we keep aside our customs and manners. It would be also better if we less depend upon precedents. . . . Among the human beings there is no limit to the kind of conduct which may constitute cruelty. New type of cruelty may crop up in any case depending upon the human behaviour, capacity or incapability to tolerate the conduct complained of. Such is the wonderful realm of cruelty.

In this case, the judge refers to the newly introduced provisions in s. 498 of the *Indian Penal Code*, 1860 concerning cruelty against married women in the context of the anti-dowry legislation. Thus, he shows his awareness of what he calls, at p. 124, "a new dimension of cruelty", which in dowry cases often drives women to suicide. The High Court of Andhra Pradesh, which had refused the wife a decree of divorce and had, amazingly, found nothing wrong with the husband demanding money from the wife, found itself criticised at p. 126:

> The High Court appears to have misunderstood the case. It has evidently proceeded on a wrong basis. It proceeded on the ground that the husband wanted some money for his personal expenses. If the demand was only of such nature we would have thrown this appeal

> away. The wife must extend all help to husband and so too the husband to wife. They are partners in life. They must equally share happiness and sorrow. They must help each other. One cannot take pleasure at the cost of the other. But the case on hand is not a failure on that front. It has been admitted by the husband himself . . . that his parents demanded dowry.

Hence, the conclusion was reached (p. 127) that the demands for dowry, in itself prohibited under the law, amounted to cruelty against the wife. By freeing this wife from the marital bond while she was under pressure to provide more dowry, the court may well have saved her life. It is evident from the judgment that the judges were aware of the grave risk to the wife's life and limb and were further motivated by this concern. *Shobha Rani*, AIR 1988 SC 121, therefore marks a point of departure in the modern Indian law on cruelty in that the legitimate concerns and expectations of married women are being recognised with more sensitivity. If we look back at the earlier cases on cruelty, most of them were actually about claims by husbands that their wife had been cruel to them, one way or the other. By giving more attention to the woman's perspective, as the Supreme Court shows in *Shobha Rani*, a more appropriate gender balance appears to be achieved in the case law on cruelty.

Towards the end of the 1980s, we find an increasing number of cases in which the judges display some concern about preserving marriages and later, as we shall see, make explicit reference to the need to protect the interests of married women.

In *Shyam Lata v. Suresh Kumar*, AIR 1986 P&H 383, the husband had constantly ill-treated the wife. When she complained to the police, the husband sought divorce, claiming cruelty. Yet this was not granted, evidently because the judge took the view that the wife's action was not of such a magnitude as to come within cruelty. While in quite a few such cases the judges do not tell us in more detail why they refused a divorce decree, already in the 1980s, some Indian judges began to say that ordinary wear and tear in a marriage should not be confused with cruelty and thus signalled that it was perhaps time to reconsider the liberal approach to granting divorces. This might also have the effect that in more cases where the husband had been granted divorce by the lower court, the wife would win on appeal. However, it appears that in the mid-1980s, such cases still mostly ended in a divorce. A useful case on this subject is *Neelam v. Vinod Kumar*, AIR 1986 P&H 253. There were some disputes over dowry, and the couple had only lived together for about a month. S. S. Sodhi J broached the subject of the court's role in maintaining marriages and held, at p. 256:

> In dealing with matrimonial matters, it must be recognized that even to this day, more often than not, marriages are still arranged by parents, with the boy and girl having little or no opportunity of meeting each other before their marriage. Marriage is a very close and

> intimate relationship between a man and a woman and when two persons almost strangers to each other are suddenly thrown together into such a relationship, it is inherent in the situation that they must go through a period of adjustment, which may be rough or smooth, depending upon the parties concerned. What happens during this period has, therefore, to be seen in this context. In other words, if courts are to help preserve marriages too much should not be made of petty instances of things said or done, until parties have had little time to know each other and settle down. There can of course be no hard and fast rule for this as each case has to be considered in its own set of circumstances. In the present case, when the husband says that he and his wife lived together for only a month the instances of cruelty pleaded by him as also those deposed to by him, do not warrant the finding of cruelty of such nature as could measure up to the standard required for it to constitute a ground for divorce.

However, because it was evident that this marriage had completely broken down and the parties were also litigating over other matters, divorce was granted to the husband on the basis of the wife's desertion. Such cases seem to show that the principle of 'irretrievable breakdown' became prominent in the minds of judges and served as a powerful trigger for divorce decrees, thus counterbalancing any socially motivated desire for preserving marriages. It seems that cases, at this time, could go either way. Quite similar on facts is *Snehlata Seth v. Kewal Krishan Seth*, AIR 1986 Del 162, where the lower court had simplistically concluded that the marriage had broken down irretrievably and had granted divorce to the husband on the basis of the wife's desertion, even though it was evident that she had had to leave the matrimonial home, probably because of dowry-related ill-feeling. On appeal before the Delhi High Court, D. R. Khanna J noted that the husband was in fact taking advantage of his own wrong, and promptly allowed the wife's appeal.

A wife's demands that the husband should live separately from his parents – an argument often heard – does not necessarily amount to cruelty according to some interesting cases. In *Om Parkash v. Rajni*, AIR 1988 Del 107, S. S. Chadha J held at p. 109, dismissing the husband's appeal:

> It is not that every time a wife says that the husband should live separately from his mother and the husband refuses to do so, it would be an unreasonable behaviour on the part of the wife and that it would amount to cruelty. A decision which affects both the parties and their children has to be taken together by the parties. It is the obligation of the parties to decide these questions by agreement, by give and take and not by the imposition of the will of the one over the other.

Where older couples seek divorce, the courts have often taken into account the position and concerns of the children and have refused a decree of divorce. The Supreme Court, in *J. L. Nanda v. Veena Nanda*, AIR 1988 SC 407, heard such a case, in which the couple experienced difficulties early on in their marital relationship but then settled down after the birth of a son. The couple, married in 1961, had lived separately since 1971. The wife had earlier successfully appealed to the Delhi High Court against a decree of divorce granted by the lower court, the husband had lost a further appeal before a Division Bench and now appealed to the Supreme Court. The learned judges called the couple in person and sought to bring about a reconciliation, but this was not possible. Nevertheless, the husband's appeal was dismissed and divorce was not granted. It was held, at p. 408:

> It is no doubt an unfortunate state of affairs but it could not be held that the respondent was behaving with the appellant in a manner which could be termed as cruelty which would [have] entitled the appellant to a decree for divorce. Sometimes the temperament of the parties may not be so conducive to each other which may result in petty quarrels and troubles although it was contended by the appellant that he had to suffer various ailments on account of this kind of behaviour meted out to him by the wife; but it could not be held on the basis of any material that ailment of the appellant was the direct result of her (respondent's) conduct.

This case report does not give us definite hints about the rationale for upholding the legal status of a marriage that had evidently broken down many years ago. The wife, having opposed the earlier divorce decree, had given clear signals that she wanted to remain married. Maybe this is what turned the judges away from applying, as they could well have done, the concept of 'irretrievable breakdown'. Or is it that, by 1988, Indian judges were becoming more alert to the negative consequences of dissolving every marriage that was questioned before them? Did the Supreme Court give some kind of subtle indication in this case that preserving marriages would be socially (and perhaps financially) desirable?

Also in 1988, the High Court of Kerala refused a husband a decree for divorce on the ground of cruelty, despite the allegation that the wife had falsely accused the husband of adultery, in fact of incest.[30] In *Somasekharan v. Thankamma*, AIR 1988 Ker 244, K. G. Balakrishnan J held, at pp. 310–311, noting that the word 'cruelty' had not been defined in the HMA:

> There cannot be any hard and fast rule in interpreting this word. It must be judged on the facts of each case having regard to surrounding circumstances. Whether one spouse is guilty of cruelty is essentially a question of fact and the court must consider the social status, environment and physical conditions and customs and manners of the parties. In a case of matrimonial proceedings the whole matrimonial relationship has to be taken into account. It is true that making false allegations about the character of the husband and his family

> members so as to injure the reputation of the husband amounts to cruelty.

However, even though the allegations about the husband's misdemeanours appeared to have some basis, the learned judge refused to grant a decree of divorce to the husband and dismissed the appeal. It appears that, even though unsuccessful attempts were made to patch up the differences between the parties, the marriage was not entirely unworkable. More importantly, there were two children; the wife had been given custody of them, while the husband was employed in the Indian Military Service. The learned judge concluded, at p. 311:

> We do not think that even now the relationship between the appellant and the respondent is so embittered that the marital tie is snapped [sic] forever. Better counsel may prevail on both of them and an amicable settlement may be made.

Here, then, is another case in which the breakdown principle could easily have been applied, but this was manifestly not done. Also in 1988 and in the same High Court, *Gangadharan v. T. K. Thankam*, AIR 1988 Ker 244 contains a detailed examination of the law on cruelty by Shamsuddin J which ends in a refusal of divorce to the appellant husband. The husband had also tried to bring about a customary divorce (p. 245), but the wife seems to have resisted this, despite her alleged actions of publicly disowning the marital relationship. The husband strenuously argued that the wife had treated him with cruelty of all kinds and had deserted him. The judge reviewed the case law on cruelty and implicitly linked the definition of 'cruelty' and the principle of marital breakdown, concluding at p. 249:

> In our view the cruelty should be of such a nature as to satisfy the conscience of the court that the relationship between the parties had deteriorated to such an extent that it would be impossible for them to live together without mental agony, torture or distress to entitle the party to secure divorce. Physical violence is not absolutely essential [sic] to constitute cruelty and a consistent course of conduct inflicting immeasurable mental agony and torture may well constitute cruelty within the meaning of the Act. Mental cruelty may consist of verbal abuses and insults by using filthy and abusive language leading to constant disturbance of mental peace of the other party.

However, the learned judge found no acceptable evidence in this case to show that the wife had treated the husband with cruelty. Noting evidence of the wife's affection towards the husband, the court found, rather, that the husband had been cruel to the wife. The husband's appeal was, therefore, dismissed. Where, however, a frail-looking young man had been married to a robust and heavily built wife, and she had started thrashing the entire family, including the husband, S. S. Sodhi J in *Rani Devi v. Hussan Lal*, AIR 1988 P&H 65, swiftly confirmed a decree for judicial separation in favour of the husband. The wife had tried to claim that she was under pressure to bring more dowry, but this was found to be an entirely false allegation. The judge concluded, at p. 66:

> 'Cruelty' on the part of the wife stands writ large by the evidence brought forth by the husband and there are no mitigating circumstances in favour of the wife to absolve her from the blame accruing to her on this account. Such being the situation, there is clearly no occasion provided here for interfering with the decree of judicial separation as granted to the husband.

Notably, this was not a divorce decree, so the marriage is preserved in this case. In the case law on desertion, too, there is growing evidence at this time of courts refusing divorce decrees to spouses, mainly husbands, who ride roughshod over the emotions of their partner. In *Kamal Kumar Basu v. Kalyani Basu*, AIR 1988 Cal 111, the husband had insisted that he and his wife should stay together with his widowed elder sister, who was like a mother to him, while his wife had refused to do so and had left the husband. Was the action of the wife reasonable? The elder sister had insisted that she would not stay with her brother if he lived together with his wife, so the husband evidently faced a real dilemma. Having chosen to side with his sister, a typical case of feeble manhood perhaps, on which Professor Derrett would have commented with relish, the troubled man had virtually forced his wife to desert him. A. M. Bhattacharjee J brought in the heavy guns of constitutional law and produced a most interesting discussion on the changing position of women in India which is relevant to the present debate. It was said, at p. 114:

> Manu, our ancient law-giver,[31] was not confronted with Art. 14 and Art. 15 of the Constitution mandating equality before the law and countermanding all discrimination on the ground of sex and thus could issue a peremptory fiat condemning women to perpetual tutelage . . . and commanding a wife not go against her husband [sic] in mind, body, words or deeds . . . we must not be taken to have advocated the husband's shedding off his aged parents or other aged relatives to infirmaries and to build a home only for his wife and minor children. But in the context of the set up of our modern society, we cannot, with Art. 14 and Art. 15 staring at our face, take that view of the law which would expose [a] wife to unreasonable unpleasantness from the relations of her husband in her matrimonial home. The wife is entitled to the society, comfort and consortium of the husband and those rights would come within her rights to "personal liberty" under Art. 21 of the Constitution, now that the said Article has been expanded with the widest possible amplitude by the Supreme Court . . .
>
> And if those rights stand the risk of being subverted because of the presence of and provocation from other relations, the law should allow the wife to insist for a separate home away from those relations.

> In the modern setup of our present-day society, the husband cannot have either a casting vote or a veto in the matter of choosing the matrimonial home or the members thereof and reference in this connection may be made to a decision of the Madras High Court in *M. Ponnambalam v. Saraswathi*, AIR 1957 Mad 693 where Ramaswami, J (as His Lordship then was) observed (at p. 694) that "at times the husband may have to choose between parents, mother and wife" and "that it is now the settled law in England, America and India that a wife is entitled to insist that she should not be exposed to the unpleasantness of the relatives of her husband and that suitable provisions should be made for her to live with the husband in privacy". And if on the failure of the husband to provide such a home, the wife leaves the home while indicating all the time her readiness and willingness to join the husband as and when such a home is provided, she cannot be branded as a deserting spouse ...

Following such an elaborate and wide-ranging discourse, it was evident that the husband could not hope to achieve a decree of divorce and his appeal was dismissed. This case, therefore, elaborately protects the position and the manifest interests of Indian wives in a marital relationship and even introduces weighty constitutional provisions in this respect.

By 1989, accusations of adultery, so often used by litigious or simply desperate Indian spouses to bring about a quick divorce, were subjected by the courts to much stricter requirements of proof.[32] Courts also toughened up on husbands' allegations of the wife's desertion and cruelty when it was found, as in *Tapankumar Chatterjee v. Kamala Chatterjee*, AIR 1989 Cal 74, that there had actually been much dowry-related violence against the wife, forcing her to leave the matrimonial home. As stated at p. 79,

> ... if cruelty had ever been perpetrated upon anybody it was on her by the petitioner and members of his family. It so appears from evidence on record that she tolerated and swallowed all these ignominies without making any fuss, with a view to purchase family peace.

Growing judicial awareness about the abuse of divorce proceedings under Hindu law by men is brought out well in the dowry-related case of *Ashok Kumar Bhatnagar v. Shabnam Bhatnagar*, AIR 1989 Del 121. The husband had sought divorce on the ground of the wife's cruelty and desertion and was also alleging that the marriage had broken down irretrievably. In reality, this was a case of dowry-related violence perpetrated against the wife. The marital relations lasted only for about 7 months in 1976. There was a child of this marriage, born in 1977, but the husband had persistently refused to acknowledge his son and had certainly not provided any maintenance for him. The wife, in defence, had emphasised that the husband was taking advantage of his own wrong and should not be allowed to do so. She made it quite clear that her mother-in-law's greed for more dowry and gifts had been the root cause of all troubles. The court held, in light of the facts, that "although ostensibly the respondent was away from the matrimonial home but it was the appellant who is blatantly guilty of expulsive conduct" (p. 135).

Following strong words on the harassment of young brides for dowry (p. 136–137), Santosh Duggal J observed, at p. 139, that "the respondent had done everything in her power to adjust to the family atmosphere" and, at p. 142, that "[a]ll this establishes without a shadow of doubt that the appellant has failed to establish his allegations of desertion on part of the respondent".

The husband's argument was that the marriage had broken down irretrievably and "that it was futile for the parties to keep up a pretence of this relationship, and that the same be better dissolved by a decree of the Court" (p. 142). The learned judge was not persuaded at all, saying at p. 142:

> We ... fail to find any support for the proposition ... that in case a marriage is found to have been broken down to an extent, that it was beyond all rapprochement or reconciliation, then whether any ground as laid down by law exists or not, the Court ought to, or can take this circumstance alone, as a ground for dissolving the marriage.

The decision was then concluded at p. 143:

> Irretrievable break down of the marriage is not contemplated to be one of the grounds for dissolution of the marriage, in the Scheme of the Hindu Marriage Act, and as such cannot be by itself taken as a ground for a decree of dissolution of marriage. It is pertinent to note that [in] the law as it stands, the causes of action for a decree of dissolution of marriage are either fault oriented or defect based. In spite of recommendations of the Law Commission in its 71st Report, the legislature did not consider it advisable to introduce irretrievable break down of marriage, as one of the grounds for a decree of divorce. We, therefore, cannot take into consideration, any such situation, as not recognised by law, to pass a decree of dissolution of marriage between the parties.

One may perhaps ask whether such a decision is socially desirable, since the husband so evidently did not want to contemplate the return of his wife to the matrimonial home. Since this is also a dowry-related case, again I am concerned that a wife who, in such circumstances, attempts to return to the matrimonial home, may simply be killed. There are too many recent cases of this kind to dismiss this argument as scaremongering.[33] What will husbands (and their mothers!) do, once they are told by the courts, time and again, that they cannot just throw out a wife or daughter-in-law as they please? Are the courts here engaged in some, perhaps not so subtle, exercise of social engineering? Only deeper analysis can answer that question and we do not have the space at present to go into such questions.

Divorce cases on cruelty in the 1990s

Divorce cases based on cruelty during the 1990s continue the line of argument that granting easy divorces for all kinds of small faults or misbehaviour is not a desirable policy. In *K. Narayanan v. K. Sreedevi*, AIR 1990 Ker 151, the husband alleged desertion and cruelty on the part of the wife. It is noted, at p. 154, that "there is no evidence to show that the wife wanted to stop cohabitation permanently with the husband". He worked in the Army and had stayed away from home since 1978, leaving his old mother in the care of his wife. After his mother's death, this man petitioned for divorce; plainly, he no longer needed the services of his mother's nurse and the wife subtly suggested that he had taken no real interest in matrimonial relations. In the Kerala High Court, Varghese Kalliath J was unwilling to grant a divorce to the husband on the grounds of cruelty or desertion, but explicitly noted the judicial trend towards liberalisation of divorce, saying at p. 155:

> Of course the courts are taking a liberal view in the matter of grounds based on cruelty in the matter of allowing divorce. But whatever liberal approach that is to be adopted, the court can find cruelty [sic] only on some legal evidence. Here the evidence is insufficient ...

While refusing the husband a decree of divorce, judicial guidance was given on filing a joint petition for divorce under s. 13B of the HMA, "since it is seen that the husband and wife are not living together for a considerable number of years" (pp. 155–6).

In the same High Court, Fathima Beevi J did not hesitate to hold that harassing a wife with a view to extorting more dowry amounted to cruelty, and thus became a ground for divorce. In *Rajani v. Subramonian*, AIR 1990 Ker 1, the couple had been married for ten years and had three young children when the wife, a young practising lawyer, asked for divorce on the ground of cruelty. The judges found that the marriage could not be rescued and it was said, at p. 2:

> From the attitude of the parties it is abundantly clear that there is no chance for any reunion and that the marriage is irretrievably broken. It is only in the interests of the children who are in the age group of 6 to 12 years that a chance appears to have been given by the learned Subordinate Judge for the parents to reunite.
>
> ... We are satisfied that the appellant has no intention to join the husband and the offer made by the respondent to provide an ideal matrimonial home, congenial to the welfare of the children and the happiness of the wife, lacks bona fides. It is only [a] ruse to avoid legal consequences. In such circumstances, we have to examine the evidence on record dispassionately ...

Here we find a brief discourse by Fathima Beevi J, who went on to become India's first female Muslim Supreme Court judge, on matrimonial conduct and the role of cruelty as a ground for divorce. We read, at pp. 2–3:

> Matrimonial conduct constituting cruelty is treatment in respect of matrimonial duties and obligations. Mutual love and affection and the concern of one for the opposite spouse form the foundation of a happy family life. The court is not certainly concerned with ideals in family life. The Court has only to understand the spouses concerned and consider their particular grievance. The cruelty alleged may largely depend upon the type of life the parties are accustomed to or their economic and social conditions, their culture and human values to which they attach importance. Judged by standards of modern civilization in the background of the cultural heritage and traditions of our society, a young educated woman is not expected to endure the harassment in domestic life whether mental or physical, intentional orunintentional. Her sentiments have to be respected, her ambitions and aspirations taken into account, in making adjustments and her basic needs provided, though grievances arising from temperamental disharmony is irrelevant. If she resents unfair or unreasonable demand for dowry and decides to keep away from the husband on account of the persistent and dubious approach to compel her parents to yield, the wife cannot be found fault with. This is what has been brought to light in this case.

Referring to the Supreme Court case of *Shobha Rani v. Madhukar Reddi*, AIR 1988 SC 121, the learned judge criticised the lack of alertness on the part of the lower court to the manifest evidence of dowry demands in the present case. Granting the wife divorce, it was held, at p. 3:

> She has unfolded the course of conduct of the husband over the years, the nature of the physical torture and the mental agony she has suffered. The version is consistent and convincing. Without compelling reasons an educated young woman, the mother of three children would not leave the husband and shoulder the burden of earning and educating the children and suffering the humiliation of continuing as dependant in the family of birth.

In *Nitu v. Krishan Lal*, AIR 1990 Del 1, the husband had sought divorce based on the wife's desertion, but it was manifest that he was taking advantage of his own wrong by treating her in a most contemptible manner. The High Court of Delhi had earlier granted the husband a divorce based on the wife's desertion,[34] but on appeal by the wife the husband was refused a divorce decree. Here again, it appears that North Indian courts, too, are becoming more alert to the need to protect the position of married women. The judge held, at p. 12, that "sensitivity is not the exclusive preserve of a husband. The wife is also entitled to expect such a treatment from her husband as is consistent with her self-respect and dignity".

In this case, counsel for the husband also tried to press the argument that the marriage had irretrievably broken down, but with reference to *Ashok Kumar Bhatnagar v. Shabnam Bhatnagar*, AIR 1989 Del 121, it was firmly held, at p. 12, that "irretrievable break down of marriage is not contemplated to be one of the grounds for dissolution of marriage, in the scheme of the Hindu Marriage Act, and thus by itself it cannot be taken to be a ground for decree of dissolution of marriage".

Nirmala Manohar Jagesha v. Mahohar Shivram Jagesha, AIR 1991 Bom 259 contains an interesting, detailed discussion by Savant J on the definition and scope of cruelty. In this case the couple were unwilling to be reconciled and had already lived separately for more than ten years. It was held at pp. 266–267:

> . . . it is now well-settled that the conduct complained of should be so grave and weighty as to come to the conclusion that the husband cannot reasonably be expected to live with the wife. It must be more serious than the ordinary wear and tear of married life. The cumulative conduct, taking into consideration the circumstances and background of the parties has to be examined to reach the conclusion whether the conduct complained of amounts to cruelty in the matrimonial law.

Commenting on this case, Diwan (1991: 87–88) emphasises that, therefore, cruelty cannot be a basis for divorce unless something has gone drastically wrong. He wrote at p. 88:

> But merely by showing that the parties are unhappy because of the unruly temper of a spouse or matrimonial wranglings falls considerably short of the conduct which can amount to cruel treatment. It would not be sufficient to show that the other spouse is moody, whimsical, exacting, inconsiderate and irascible. Defects of temperament must ordinarily be accepted for better or for worse. Therefore, there may be unhappiness in a marriage and the court cannot for that cause alone find cruelty.

In the present case, relations between the parties were evidently not cordial, and mutual accusations of impotence, frigidity and other defects had been made.[35] Savant J examined in detail a large number of reported cases on the legal effects of such allegations, focusing on the wife's "irresponsible, wild and baseless allegations of impotency and lack of manliness in the husband" (p. 268). It was finally held, at p. 272, that this entitled the husband to a decree of divorce on this ground alone, since, in the words of the learned judge, "[t]he making of wild, reckless and baseless allegations of impotency and lack of manliness – itself amount to cruelty in the matrimonial law". It was also held to be immaterial whether the wife actually intended to be cruel or not. Not much was said in this case about the fact that the husband had made similar allegations. However, in other cases it has been held that a suspicious husband casting wild aspersions on the character of the wife is guilty of cruelty – and thus not entitled to a decree of divorce against the wife.[36]

Diwan (1992: 158) rightly welcomed the fact that attempts to formalise cruelty as a ground for divorce had not been successful. This means that the decision in each case depended on the particular facts and circumstances. In *Sukumar Mukherjee v. Tripti Mukherjee*, AIR 1992 Pat 32, the husband had made all kinds of allegations against the wife, but it transpired that he was unhappy with her because her family had refused to accede to dowry demands. Relying, quite appropriately, on the earlier dowry demand case in the Supreme Court, *Shobha Rani v. Madhukar Reddi*, AIR 1988 SC 121, it was held that the husband had proved neither desertion nor cruelty. Significantly, the husband was ordered to pay the wife's legal costs, perhaps a sign that the courts are beginning to get more alert about *mala fide* cases.

Interestingly, Diwan (1992: 158) referred to a number of reported cases in 1992 in which different forms of unjustified allegations were held to be a ground for divorce. In *Ashok Kumar v. Vijay Laxmi*, AIR 1992 Del 182, the wife had falsely claimed that the husband had doused her in kerosene oil to burn her. The husband's appeal against a refusal to grant him divorce on this basis was allowed. In *Pushpa Datt Mishra v. Archana Mishra*, AIR 1992 MP 260, the wife had made reckless allegations that the husband had been adulterous and a divorce decree in his favour was confirmed.[37]

In other cases, minor quarrels were held not to be sufficient grounds for divorce. In *Yashoda Bai v. Krishnamoorthy Bhimappa Katavkar*, AIR 1992 Kant 368, the husband had asked for divorce but the lower court had granted him judicial separation on the ground of cruelty. The wife appealed and thereby signalled her interest in the full continuation of this marriage. The judge in this case showed himself aware of the importance of settling family disputes without delay, "... having regard to the importance of the subject matter ... as well as the need for protecting the interests of the parties in matrimonial cases, which in their very nature, do not brook any delay" (p. 370). The judge was not ready to terminate this marriage and it was held, at p. 370:

> Marriage [sic] is considered a sacrament under the customary Hindu Law and, therefore, is not amenable to dissolution easily. The Act has provided grounds to male spouse in Hindu Society and also to give relief to women who are considered to belong to the weaker section of the society. Notwithstanding the religious tenets, whatever may be the compelling reason, all that may be stated is that, so far as the Hindu Marriage and divorce is concerned, the law is yet developing, particularly with reference to cruelty.

In the present case, the husband's allegation was to the effect that the wife had been cruel to her mother-in-law by insisting that she wanted to live separately from the joint family. The judge clearly saw the social tensions and said, at p. 371:

> We see from the evidence ... that, there was constant quarrel between him and his wife...on account of his refusing to set up a separate family for himself and his wife and their children which caused him terrible mental agony as he loved his mother and would not think of

> having a separate establishment, wherein, he could not personally take care of his mother. This is the problem of most of the Hindu Undivided Families.

Mindful of the frequency with which such disputes arise in Indian society, it was therefore held, at p. 371, while setting aside the decree for judicial separation, even after such a long time:

> Mere domestic quarrels on account of the presence of the mother-in-law in the family would not constitute mental cruelty. If so, then the Courts could hardly refuse dissolution of marriage to any husband who approaches with such a story and prays for dissolution of his marriage.

Powerful expressions of the need for judicial alertness in divorce litigation are found in the important case of *Vimlesh v. Prakash Chand Sharma*, AIR 1992 All 260. Here, the wife had persistently appealed against the granting of a divorce to the husband, while he had already married after the decision of the lower court and had, thus, created irrefutable facts, as he thought.

He husband had alleged cruelty, evidenced by a number of facts which were disputed in court. The judge carefully examined letters written by the wife and came to the conclusion that the wife had never stated her desire to leave the husband and appeared to be a totally devoted Hindu wife (p. 266). Some fine points were made at p. 266:

> It may be noticed that this is law of nature to keep husband and wife together and to maintain their union ...
>
> ... There is steep decline of the norms in the society. Amongst Hindus marriage was a sacrament [sic] and not a contract. With the ever growing trend of family disputes, a Court deciding disputes between wife and husband, is called upon to discharge a very delicate duty where the grievances of either party are brought before the Court.

Next, B. L. Yadav J emphasised the social context of matrimonial litigation and said, at p. 267:

> While considering [the] concept of cruelty it may be noticed that [the] Hindu Marriage Act is a social benevolent legislation and the approach of [the] Court interpreting social legislations should be the approach to a statute of predominant [sic] social nature in that light. The judges must take a broad view of the background and policy of the statute in question ...
>
> ... Beneficial and social statutes should not be construed too rigidly as it was for the protection of certain class of persons that the statute was enacted. The intention of the legislature and the policy underlying it has also to be kept in mind. As far as possible the language of the statute, unless it goes against the intention of the specific provisions must be construed consistent with the changing social attitudes.

> ... It would not be inapt to state that in such matters where the Court has been assigned duty by the Legislature to bring about the reconciliation between the parties, I am of the view that the Court is expected to make sincere efforts to preserve the marriage tie and the same appears to be the policy behind such legislation unless the same becomes impossible. The jurisdiction in matrimonial matters is remedial and cannot be assumed to be punitive. The Court is expected to remedy a matrimonial wrong ... the duty of the Court ought to be to make efforts for settlement. To put it differently in matrimonial matters the Court becomes a Court of conscience and the satisfaction of the Court ought to be the good conscience of the Court.

In light of the above, it was held, at p. 267:

> ... the solitary instance of cruelty would not constitute cruelty so as to grant a decree for divorce rather the behaviour of the other party ... has to be persistently and repeatedly treating the respondent with such cruelty so as to cause a reasonable apprehension in the mind of the respondent that it will be harmful and injurious for the respondent to live with the appellant.

This same point was also reiterated at p. 269 of the judgment, and the wife's appeal was allowed, which meant that the couple were still married. But what about the fact that the husband had already married another woman after the lower court had granted him a decree of divorce? His lawyer was, of course, instructed to plead that the first marriage could not possibly be resuscitated at this late stage? Do we find here a case of court-induced polygamy?

The judge referred everyone to *Lata Kamat v. Vilas*, AIR 1989 SC 1477. In that case, the husband had married another woman before his first wife could file an appeal against the grant of nullity to her husband on the basis of the wife's pregnancy before the marriage. The lower court had held that the husband's second marriage was legally valid and thus the first wife no longer had a right to appeal against the nullity decree. The first wife continued to appeal, however. The Bombay High Court,[38] asked to consider the position under s. 15 HMA,[39] found it "crystal clear" (p. 234) that this section only applies to cases of dissolution of the marriage by divorce and thus dismissed the first wife's appeal. It was held at p. 235:

> The respondent remarried after having obtained the decree of nullity annulling his marriage with the appellant. He was perfectly within his right to do so ... the respondent was no more the husband of the appellant and there was no provision of law which created any impediment in the marriage.

The first wife's appeal was therefore held to be infructuous, but she appealed further to the Supreme Court, as seen in *Lata Kamat v. Vilas*, AIR 1989 SC 1477. Mr. Justice Oza gave a carefully reasoned judgment which basically allowed the wife's appeal and required the lower court to decide the matter afresh.

In *Vimlesh v. Prakash Chand Sharma*, AIR 1992 All 260, at p. 269, therefore, it was held that the wife's appeal against the divorce decree succeeded, so this couple was still legally married despite the existence of the husband's second marriage.[40]

It appears that most of the reported cases from 1993 tended to operate in favour of preserving marriages, provided the marriage could be saved in some form. However, the courts are not forthcoming with many explanations as to why they make such decisions, so we have to interpolate the results. In *Rajinder Bhardwaj v. Anita Sharma*, AIR 1993 Del 135, the marriage had only lasted about five months and had irretrievably broken down, as noted at p. 146. P. N. Nag J was clear about the fact that it was not open to him to grant a decree of divorce on the ground of breakdown. However, since the wife had evidently acted with persistent cruelty towards the husband, and was also not genuinely interested in the continuation of the marriage, divorce was granted.

A v. H., AIR 1993 Bom 70 involved a highly educated mature couple with grown-up daughters, whose lives had gradually drifted apart. This case appears to establish the proposition that the cruel acts of the respondent must relate to the period prior to filing the petition for divorce (p. 75), even though the appeal proceedings themselves took place a long time after the breakdown of marital relations. The wife had appealed against the divorce decree given to the husband on the ground of cruelty and irretrievable breakdown, and she succeeded on both counts. It was held, at p. 76, with reference to the breakdown principle, that judges are not free to create a new ground for divorce.

Indira Gangele v. Shailendra Kumar Gangele, AIR 1993 MP 59, is another case in which the husband had been granted divorce by the lower court on the basis of cruelty and desertion. The wife appealed to the High Court challenging the legality of the decree – and duly won her appeal. The judge in this case referred back to a Supreme Court case of almost two decades ago, *Swarajya Lakshmi v. G. G. Padma Rao*, AIR 1974 SC 165, a divorce case on the basis of the wife's leprosy, to justify the refusal of a divorce for the husband.

In *Swarajya*, a medical doctor had been married to a young woman who, as soon transpired, was suffering from virulent leprosy. After some time, having failed to cure his wife, the husband petitioned for divorce, which was granted on the basis of the wife's virulent illness. It was held, at p. 166, interpreting the provisions of s. 13 HMA:

> In construing these provisions one has to remember that divorce is not generally favoured or encouraged by courts and is permitted only for very serious and grave reasons.
>
> ... Clearly enough, the conditions under which divorce is to be allowed are far more stringent than the conditions under which judicial separation may be granted.

Given the medical condition of the wife, however, divorce was granted to the husband, with the following concluding comment at p. 170:

> We have no doubt in our minds that the law-makers do not treat the subject of divorce lightly and must have taken into consideration the consequences of one spouse being compelled to live intimately with another spouse who suffers from leprosy when they provided for a way out for the former.

Thus, a quote clipped from an old case was used in *Indira Gangele* in 1993 to justify taking a stricter view on divorces than was done a few years before. The judge refers to this liberalised view at p. 63 of the judgement but refuses to come to a finding of serious cruelty, holding instead, with reference to a number of decided cases and the facts before the court, at p. 63:

> What has been established is only some misunderstanding between the parties in the beginning of their matrimonial journey. Merely saying that parties are unhappy is not enough not even the unruly temper of a spouse or whimsical nature of a spouse is enough. The cruelty must not only consist of intentional act of the appellant, but also result in a reasonable apprehension in the mind of the appellant that it is not possible to continue the married life.

This wording is different from earlier formulations to the effect that any cruelty must create an apprehension of harm, physical or mental, and now emphasises the appellant's assessment of the chances of continued married life. A decidedly modern note, another glimpse of a more evidently gendered perspective, may be detected at p. 63:

> It must be realised that [the] age of Saint-Tulsi-Das, who propounded that women deserve tobe chastised is long past and we are living in a country where equity is constitutionally guaranteed. Under the circumstances, it will not be possible to accept the appellant in any way inferior, as in the past and, therefore, she will not be expected to bear taunts or indifference, as in the past. Therefore, if the appellant made a complaint to the respondent, she cannot be said to have done anything, which would amount to cruelty. Her not returning home because of her studies can also not amount to cruelty, because she is entitled to prosecute her studies to develop her own personality and to find her own place in the society. . . .

Concerning the ground of desertion, which the husband had also advanced, the learned judge was equally scathing about the husband's lack of understanding. It may well be that the young wife in this case, a successful law graduate, benefited from a legal sympathy factor. The judge even ventured to tutor the husband in law and said, at p. 64:

> Adopting an attitude that reconciliation was out of place, the respondent seems to have false notions about his right as a husband.

> He also does not seem to be properly educated in divorce jurisprudence and is perhaps not aware of the fact that divorce in this country is not granted merely because it is asked for. These facts, in the opinion of this Court, do not justify a conclusion of desertion. The learned District Judge has unfortunately not considered this matter in the proper perspective and has reached the conclusion, which is not only illegal, but wholly unjustified.

Other cases came to similar conclusions. In *Tapan Chakraborty v. Anjali Chakraborty*, AIR 1993 Cal 10, the husband was held not entitled to divorce on the ground of cruelty, since the instances alleged were all in the nature of ordinary quarrels between husband and wife. It was held, at p. 13, that "[m]arriage cannot be so frail and fragile that it should be wrecked because of some quarrels of the couple or on account of some frailty on the part of this or that spouse". Noting that the couple had continued to live under the same roof, with both spouses looking after the children, it was evident that "it cannot be said that the marriage has irretrievably broken down" (p. 14) and, at any rate, as was explicitly noted (*id.*), irretrievable breakdown itself is not a ground for divorce. Similarly, in *Devidas v. Gyanwati*, AIR 1993 MP 14, it was held that where a couple lived together for several months after the husband had made allegations of cruelty, this amounted to condonation, and the husband's divorce petition could not succeed.

In *Madan Mohan Manna v. Chitra Manna*, AIR 1993 Cal 33, it appears that the husband was already staying with another woman when he brought his wife home. After about seven days, the new bride was taken away by her father and never returned. The husband petitioned for divorce on the basis on desertion and cruelty, but this had been refused. On appeal before the Calcutta High Court, it was noted (at p. 34) that the husband had refused to pay his wife maintenance of Rs. 100/- per month, had vaguely tried to question her moral character (pp. 34–35), and that his whole story was a distorted version of the true facts (p. 37). The judge found that a newly married woman could not be expected to live with her husband in such circumstances and held, at p. 37:

> She could not be compelled to live in the same house under the same roof with another woman not related to the husband. If she was so compelled, that itself would have amounted to cruelty.

The husband's lawyer also tried to raise the ground of irretrievable breakdown of the marriage. The parties had been married in 1980, but the judge's response in 1993 was firm, as shown at p. 37:

> We find that very often this argument is advanced. We think that the arguments advanced that the marriage is to be annulled simply because a party has asked for [it], on the ground that the marriage has become irretrievable, are based on some misconceptions. Decisions

> are cited, but we feel that they are not always appreciated in their proper sense.

Contrasting two earlier decisions with the facts of the present case, the judge firmly refused to grant a divorce to the husband. It was held at p. 38, dismissing the husband's appeal:

> The wife is still willing to join the matrimonial home, if Malina be not there. We cannot say at once that the marriage has broken down. Moreover, the petitioner cannot take advantage of his own wrong. Here if the petitioner is granted a decree simply for his asking, it would be allowing to take advantage of his own wrong, in view of the objective situation referred to by us. If a person is allowed to file a suit solely according to his whims and caprice and get a decree only on the ground that the marriage has broken down because of his attitude, then the whole of the Hindu Marriage Act would become otiose [sic]. The institution of marriage itself would be imperilled ... the whole institution of marriage itself would be seriously shaken if such liberty is given to a person.

Such judicial statements are supported by a prominent general comment on the grounds of divorce, found in Vol. 27 of the most recent set of the AIR Manual (Manohar and Chitaley 1989: 26):

> Although the grounds for divorce have been liberalised, they nevertheless continue to form an exception to the general principle favouring the continuation of the marital tie. The language of the section cannot be extended by adding new grounds not enumerated in the section.

Similarly, at p. 27 of the same source, we find:

> While exercising matrimonial jurisdiction a court is not merely concerned with the rights of the private parties but it has to keep in view the matters of public policy as well. In spite of the fact that divorce proceedings have now been made by the legislature much less stringent, it is in public interest that marriage should not be annulled on lighter grounds.

Where, however, a married couple have argued themselves into an intractable mess, even though breakdown as such is not a ground for divorce under Hindu law, this could be granted in the interest of maintaining dignity and, it must be said, of saving precious judicial time. In *V. Bhagat v. D. Bhagat*, AIR 1994 SC 710,[41] the Supreme Court of India was faced with an embarrassing dilemma. Here was a couple of mature age and seniority (the husband was a practising lawyer in the Supreme Court), with grown-up children, who had turned their marriage into a living hell (p. 715) and had already spent years arguing their case before various courts. Terminating the pending appeal proceedings in the Delhi High

Court, the Supreme Court displayed boldness as well as a remarkable awareness of *izzat*, the all-important element of status, social standing and reputation in society.

Emphasising, right at the start (p. 712), that "[t]his is an unusual case which calls for an unusual solution", the two judges (Kuldip Singh J and B. P. Jeevan Reddy J, who spoke for the court), solved the dilemma by finally granting the husband a divorce on the ground of the wife's cruelty, while recognising publicly that this marriage had broken down irretrievably due to their bitter drawn-out battle over many years. Great care was taken to emphasise that this case was not to be read by anyone as a precedent for introducing the breakdown principle into modern Hindu divorce law. It was held, at pp. 720–1:

> Having regard to the peculiar features of this case, we are of the opinion that the marriage between the parties should be dissolved under Section 13(1)(ia) of [the] Hindu Marriage Act and we do so accordingly. Having regard to the peculiar facts and circumstances of this case, and its progress over the last eight years ... we are of the opinion that it is a fit case for cutting across the procedural objections to give a quietus to the matter.
>
> Before parting with this case, we think it necessary to append a clarification. Merely because there are allegations and counter-allegations, a decree of divorce cannot follow. Nor is mere delay in disposal of the divorce proceedings by itself a ground. There must be really some extraordinary features [sic] to warrant grant of divorce on the basis of pleadings (and other admitted material) without a full trial. Irretrievable break-down of the marriage is not a ground by itself. But while scrutinising the evidence on record to determine whether the ground(s) alleged is made out and in determining the relief to be granted, the said circumstances can certainly be borne in mind. The unusual step as the one taken by us herein can be resorted to only to clear up an insoluble mess, when the court finds it in the interest of both the parties.

The approach taken by the court here is certainly motivated by social realism, but probably also by a concern to save precious court time. Thus, while dissolving this particular marriage, important reservations were made to prevent this case from turning into a precedent justifying the breakdown principle. Significantly, the learned judges also sought to vindicate the honour and character of the wife by stating, finally, at p. 721, that "[i]n the circumstances, the allegations levelled by the petitioner against the wife are held 'not proved'". This is a very significant example of *izzat*-awareness on the part of Indian Supreme Court judges.

Other cases reported in 1994 have tended to uphold marriages, wherever possible. In *Katari Subba Rao v. Katari Seetha Mahalakshmi*, AIR 1994 AP 364, the husband tried once more to get rid of his wife by appealing against a refusal of divorce on the grounds of cruelty, desertion, and invalidity of the marriage. He was not successful in proving any of his allegations. In *Meera v. Vijay Shankar Talchidia*, AIR 1994 Raj 33, the wife appealed against a divorce decree granted to the husband and succeeded. The court reiterated, at p. 35, the basic parameters of cruelty as applied after the 1976 amendments to the HMA:

> Cruelty in such cases has to be of the type which should satisfy the conscience of the Court to believe that the relations between the parties had deteriorated to such an extent due to the conduct of one of the spouses that it has become impossible for them to live together without mental agony, torture or distress.

It was noted, therefore, that "[i]t is not that every insignificant or trifling conduct could constitute cruelty of one on the other" (p. 35), and the husband's case collapsed due to lack of proper evidence. In *Sunil Kumar v. Usha*, AIR 1994 MP 1, the husband had alleged cruelty because the wife had refused to engage in sexual intercourse and had deserted him. The lower court had not accepted this and the husband appealed. The parties, married in 1986, had only lived together for about two weeks. The wife had declared her willingness to return to the husband, but he objected to that. A. R. Tiwari J found strong words to criticise husbands who keep their wives out of the matrimonial home and then claim desertion and cruelty, saying at p. 4:

> In modern society, the wife is certainly entitled to comfort and company of the husband and has a right to live with dignity. The husband cannot have vote or veto. The wife has to be treated properly. If the wife is forced to leave [the] matrimonial home on failure of the husband to provide her [a] home of congenial atmosphere and to provide her with protective umbrella of safety, then such an act, decreed by fate, cannot be given insignia of desertion ...

The judge even brought in the Fundamental Duties in Article 51-A of the Constitution of India and held, at p. 4, that one of the duties is to "renounce practice derogatory to the dignity of women". Finally, the judge commented on the need to uphold marriages, saying that "it is apt to remember that the institution of marriage is not in the need of being damaged or destroyed" (*id.*). The husband's recalcitrant attitude was a clear violation of his marital obligations, and the divorce decree should not be granted. Whether such court-induced reminders of matrimonial obligations, executed in stilted language, will have any effect in society is of course a matter of conjecture.

Leela Devi v. Suresh Kumar, AIR 1994 Raj 128, on the other hand, is a case in which the court is impressed with the husband's evidence that the wife treated him with cruelty, deserted him and is unwilling to return. Divorce was, accordingly, granted to the husband. In *Parimi Mehar Seshu v. Parimi Nageswara Sastry*, AIR 1994 AP 92, too, the court found that the wife had treated the husband with cruelty and had been responsible for the breakdown of the marriage. The wife's appeal against the divorce decree was therefore dismissed.

In *Uma Wanti v. Arjan Dev*, AIR 1995 P&H 312, the wife opposed a decree for divorce granted to the husband on the ground of her mental unsoundness and resulting cruelty to the husband. The court granted the husband divorce, but only after ordering him to pay the wife a substantial sum as permanent alimony. Explicit protection of the position of the wife is also evident in *Teerth Ram v. Parvati Devi*, AIR 1995 Raj 86, where the wife had abandoned the husband in 1978 after arguments over establishing a separate residence, away from the husband's parents. The husband had filed a petition for divorce 11 years later and his petition had been dismissed by the lower court on the ground of delay. His appeal before the High Court was not successful and it was held, at p. 87:

> We are not satisfied that the husband has established a ground to have a decree for divorce. It cannot be held that [the] wife has permanently deserted the husband with no intention to come back. The wife has no intention to break the matrimonial home for good. On the contrary, she wants the husband to establish an independent matrimonial home where she would live with him as the other brother of the husband has done. In this case, it cannot be held that [the] wife will be considered to have deserted the husband without sufficient reasons.

Devinder Pal Singh v. Sanjogta Rani, AIR 1995 P&H 274 was a husband's appeal against refusal to grant him divorce on the basis of the wife's cruelty and desertion. The appeal was dismissed as "meritless" (p. 278) since the facts showed that the husband had forsaken the wife, rather than *vice versa*. In *Devakumar v. Thilagavathy*, AIR 1995 Mad 116, the wife had attempted to commit suicide soon after the marriage. The husband used this, and other evidence, to support his allegation of her cruelty towards him. The husband's appeal was, predictably, dismissed. In the early 1980s, such a case would have gone the other way and divorce would in all probability have been decreed on the ground of the wife's cruelty.

In *Rajan Vasant Revankar v. Shobha Rajan Revankar*, AIR 1995 Bom 246, the husband had petitioned for divorce on the ground of cruelty but had not been successful. On appeal to the Bombay High Court, the matter was heard at great length. It is noteworthy that the judges relate this case (at p. 263) to *V. Bhagat v. D. Bhagat*, AIR 1994 SC 710, where divorce had been granted because the marriage had irretrievably broken down and the parties kept on arguing, thereby wasting precious judicial time. Here, the dramatic pleadings and counter-allegations were also spun out in great detail. It was held that the wife had treated the husband with cruelty, but the additional factor of the manifest breakdown of the marriage also weighed with the judges (p. 263) in granting the husband divorce.

Romesh Chander v. Savitri, AIR 1995 SC 851 also follows *V. Bhagat* and thus signals that this important case could be used by courts to justify the dissolution of marriages on the breakdown principle, although the Supreme

Court had been so careful to say that this case should not become a precedent in that direction. In *Romesh Chander*, the question before the court was immediately stated by R. M. Sahai J at p. 851:

> Should a marriage which is otherwise dead emotionally and practically be continued for name-sake is the issue for consideration in this appeal.
>
> Twenty-five years have elapsed since the appellant ... and the respondent ... have enjoyed the company of each other as husband and wife. Within these 25 years this is the second round of litigation which ... has reached this court.[42]

This case report also refers to another case decided by the Supreme Court, *Chanderkala Trivedi v. S. P. Trivedi*, (1993) 4 SCC 232, in which it had been held that if a marriage was dead and there was no chance of saving it, it would be better to bring it to an end.[43] It had been held by R. M. Sahai J, at p. 233:

> We do share [the] feelings of [the] wife expressed by the learned counsel that a conservative Hindu lady would not prefer to be known as a divorcee in the society. At the same time, we cannot be oblivious to the impossible situation in which the parties have landed themselves which indeed is unfortunate.

It appears that, based on these two earlier cases of total breakdown of marital relations, R. M. Sahai J then held at p. 852 in *Romesh Chander*:

> In this case the marriage is dead both emotionally and practically. Continuance of marital alliance for name-sake is prolonging the agony and affliction. It cannot be disputed that the husband has not been dutiful and conscious of his responsibilities either towards his wife or his son. He did not contribute any thing towards upbringing of the child. Yet the marriage being dead, the continuance of it would be cruelty, specially when the child born out of the wedlock ... as far back as 1968 having now grown and being in service.

This extremely brief case does not go into any further detail on the judicial reasoning. However, a important element of this case lies in the financial arrangements, over which the court casts a critical eye. It was held, at p. 852:

> The appellant has expressed remorse for his conduct and is willing to compensate for his past mistakes by transferring the only house in his name in favour of his wife.
>
> Considering the facts and circumstances of this case we, in exercise of power under Article 142 of the Constitution of India, direct that the marriage between [the] appellant and the respondent shall stand dissolved subject to the appellant transferring the house in the name of his wife. The house shall be transferred within four months from

today. The dissolution shall come into effect from the date the house is transferred and possession is handed over to the respondent.

It is relevant to look here briefly at the constitutional framework within which this case was decided.[44] Article 142(1) of the Constitution of India is the relevant instrument, emphasising the need for 'complete justice' as follows:

> 142. *Enforcement of decrees and orders of Supreme Court and orders as to discovery etc.* –
> (1) The Supreme Court in the exercise of its jurisdiction may pass such decree or make such order as is necessary for doing complete justice in any cause or matter pending before it, and any decree so passed or order so made shall be enforceable throughout the territory of India in such manner as may be prescribed by or under any law made by Parliament and, until provision in that behalf is so made, in such manner as the President may by order prescribe.

Another case under Article 142 of the Constitution is *Kanchan Devi v. Promod Kumar Mittal*, AIR 1996 SC 3192. Here, A. S. Anand J (as he then was) and Faizan Uddin J found that a couple had been living apart for more than a decade and the wife had unsuccessfully applied for maintenance. The facts were that the wife had given birth to four daughters and had then been thrown out of the matrimonial home. After lengthy court battles, a compromise was reached and the wife returned home, but only to be turned away again.

The learned judges formed the impression that "there was no possibility of any reconciliation between the parties and that the marriage between them had irretrievably broken down" (p. 3193). In 1995, the wife had asked for a lump sum of Rs. 60,000/- in settlement of her claims, to which the husband had agreed. An out-of-court agreement was endorsed by the Supreme Court when it was held, at p. 3193:

> In view of the peculiar facts and circumstances of the case and being satisfied that the marriage between the appellant and the respondent has irretrievably broken down and that there is no possibility of reconciliation, we in exercise of our powers under Art. 142 of the Constitution of India hereby direct that the marriage between the appellant and the respondent shall stand dissolved by a decree of divorce. All pending cases ... between the parties shall stand disposed of.

Narayan Shankar Gokhale v. Sudha Narayan Gokhale, AIR 1996 Bom 380 concerns the definition of 'cohabitation' for the purposes of ascertaining whether a couple living under a decree of judicial separation had resumed cohabitation or not. It was found, as a matter of fact, that the couple had occasionally visited a juice bar, a temple and some friends together, but that did not, in the opinion of the court, amount to cohabitation. Hence, the marriage was dissolved on the basis of non-resumption of cohabitation after a decree for judicial separation, in other words, on the basis that the marital relations had irretrievably broken down.

In *Alka v. R. K. Gautam*, AIR 1996 Del 276, divorce was granted to the husband despite the wife's appeal to the High Court against an earlier decree of divorce. The couple, both doctors, did not develop harmonious matrimonial relations and various accusations of cruelty were made against the wife by an evidently frustrated husband. This case discusses a lot of old English cases, which seem of little relevance, but then turns to a number of Indian decisions, among them *V. Bhagat v. D. Bhagat*, AIR 1994 SC 710. In the spirit of that decision and its approach to the breakdown principle, it was finally held in the present case, at p. 284, dismissing the wife's appeal against divorce:

> This is one of those unfortunate cases where every effort to save the marriage or in other words all efforts for reconciliations have miserably failed. When all the facts, circumstances and evidence on record are comprehensively taken into consideration, then it is not possible to arrive at any other conclusion ...

In *Vimla Ladkani v. Chandra Prakash Ladkani*, AIR 1996 MP 86, the wife had allegedly had an affair with another man, who was even present in court. Her conduct in responding to these allegations with slanderous counter-allegations was held to amount to cruelty and it was said, at p. 90, that "[m]aking false allegations in open Court about the character of the husband and the family members so as to injure the reputation of the husband amounts to cruelty". Divorce was accordingly granted. It should be noted, however, that the court did not rush into giving a divorce decree, expressing much caution on p. 89 by saying that, "[n]ormally, the Court should be reluctant to grant a decree for divorce and every effort should be made to bring the parties to terms so that they may lead a happy married life".

In *Rajee v. Baburao*, AIR 1996 Mad 262, the lower court had granted the husband a divorce on the basis of his allegations of the wife's adultery. The couple had three grown-up children and the husband claimed to have delayed his divorce petition until after the marriage of the younger daughter. S. S. Subramani J in the Madras High Court carefully went through the evidence and disagreed with the findings of the lower court. It was finally held, at p. 270:

> In this case, the appellant has been insulted. Her character [sic] has been assassinated without any reason. The appellant had to stay away while her husband behaved in the way spoken to by her. On going through the evidence in this case, this Court feels that the doubt expressed by the appellant is genuine. When a dependant and obedient servant has been falsely implicated and witnesses have been brought to Court to ruin the entire family, the conduct of the

> respondent can never be justified to vindicate her conduct. I award the appellant exemplary costs, and I allow her to recover the same from her husband or from his assets. I quantify the same as Rs. 10,000/-.

This tough line, obviously a clear warning signal to *mala fide* litigants, ties in well with other attempts to protect women against being thrown out of marriages for no rhyme or reason. In a similar vein, it was held in *P. K. Vijayappan Nair v. J. Ammini Amma*, AIR 1997 Ker 170, that where a wife maliciously files one case after the other against the husband, this satisfies the test of cruelty and amounts to a valid ground for divorce. It was stated, at p. 172, highlighting the fact that cruelty *simpliciter* would suffice:

> After the Hindu Marriage (Amendment) Act, 1976, the petitioner need only establish that the respondent had treated him with cruelty. He need not show that cruelty must be such as to cause reasonable apprehension that it would be harmful or injurious to the appellant. Cruelty should be of the type which will satisfy the conscience of the Court that the relationship between the parties has deteriorated to such an extent that it has become impossible for them to live together without mental agony.

Satish Kumari v. Ranjit Singh, AIR 1997 H&P 16, is a wife's appeal against refusal of a decree for divorce on the basis of cruelty and desertion. However, the High Court, too, could not find any evidence that the wife had been treated with cruelty and thus dismissed the wife's appeal. The couple had three daughters of marriageable age. It may well be that the judges took that into account, since there is explicit reference to their ages and the fact that they are "quite grown up" (p. 16). *Archana Mahajan v. Vinod Mahajan*, AIR 1998 MP 220, is a wife's appeal against a divorce decree passed in favour of the husband on the basis of the wife's cruelty. She had alleged that her husband had a relationship with another woman, and the lower court judge had disbelieved her story. On appeal before the MP High Court, Chitre J was invited by counsel for the husband to follow the reasoning in *V. Bhagat v. D. Bhagat*, AIR 1994 SC 710 and to confirm the divorce decree on the basis of cruelty because of the wife's baseless allegations. The learned judge discussed *V. Bhagat* but then turned to s. 13 HMA, finding at pp. 223–224:

> Mental cruelty in Section 13(1)(ia) can broadly be defined as that conduct which inflicts upon the other party such mental pain and suffering as would make it not possible for that party to live with the other. In other words, mental cruelty must be of such a nature that the parties cannot reasonably be expected to live together. The situation must be such that the wronged party can not reasonably be asked to put up with such conduct and continue to live with the other party.

In view of the evidence and also because of the presence of two young children, Chitre J took the view that this marriage was redeemable and that the couple's quarrels were in the nature of ordinary wear and tear of married life. The wife's appeal was therefore allowed and the divorce decree was set aside. In *Karthikeyan v. Sarojini*, AIR 1998 Ker 136, Mohammed J produced a judgment which ended in a decree for judicial separation instead of divorce, as wanted by the husband, who claimed that the marriage had irretrievably broken down due to the wife's adultery and cruelty. The learned judges in this case were not willing to be swayed by mere allegations and it was held by Mohammed J, at p. 137, that "adultery and cruelty are not grounds which can easily be inferred from certain averments. For establishing them there shall be cogent materials constituting legal proof".

On the other hand, the spouses agreed that the marriage had irretrievably broken down. The learned judges were aware of two recent Supreme Court cases in which divorce had been granted on the basis of breakdown of the marital relationship. Mohammed J referred to *Chanderkala Trivedi v. S. P. Trivedi* (1993) 4 SCC 232 and *Romesh Chander*, AIR 1995 SC 851, but was not willing to apply the breakdown principle.[45] Considering instead the possibility of granting a decree for judicial separation, although this had not been asked for, it was held, at p. 138:

> In this case ... both sides appear to be uniform in their submission that the marriage between the spouses is irretrievably broken and it is emotionally and practically dead though the grounds of adultery and cruelty have not been convincingly established ...
>
> Thus for the last about fourteen years the spouses spent their precious life in the legal battle. This Court can definitely perceive the perpetual mental agony and despair in their family life and thus the marriage between them is [sic] emotionally and practically dead. Therefore, we are of the view that this Court can definitely exercise the power for passing a decree for judicial separation ...
>
> We are, therefore, strongly convinced that the circumstances of this case justify a decree for judicial separation.

It is noteworthy that this decree was coupled with two measures to protect the financial circumstances of the wife. Firstly, it was decreed that the maintenance arrangements in favour of the wife should remain undisturbed. Secondly, her legal costs were to be borne by the husband who was directed to pay Rs. 2,000/- in this respect.

The most recent divorce cases under Hindu law, mainly on the grounds of cruelty and desertion, therefore confirm that the superior courts of India are not rushing to divorce couples. While the Supreme Court has given itself room for discretion to intervene in cases of irretrievable breakdown, most evidently in *V. Bhagat v. D. Bhagat*, AIR 1994 SC 710, all courts remain alert to the need to preserve marriages, and divorce is not available for the asking. As noted earlier, Vol. 27 of the new AIR Manual also emphasises the exceptional character of divorce (see Manohar and Chitaley 1989: 26).

Thus courts and commentators alike remain aware of the need to protect marital relations against quarrelsome pleadings that amount to unilateral repudiation without concern for the spouse's welfare. In addition, during the 1990s, we definitely see more judicial awareness of the need to make adequate financial arrangements to protect the position of women and children.

Nullity for fraud: the slightest fault becomes a ground

A parallel picture emerges if we consider briefly the legal developments under s. 12 HMA, which concerns nullity petitions on a variety of grounds. Under the original HMA of 1955, it was almost impossible to obtain nullity for fraud, evidently an appropriate policy to adopt in view of the arranged nature of most Indian marriages and the potential for interference in marital relations by members of either spouse's family. However, the old legal position meant that once a couple had been married, the spouses would be forced to remain married even though one spouse felt cheated and more or less dissatisfied. This could of course be abused by devious families who, as it were, might be tempted to 'palm off' deficient spouses to unsuspecting partners.

Through the *Marriage Laws (Amendment) Act* of 1976, a new rule regarding nullity for fraud was introduced by s. 12(1)(c) of the HMA, which now reads as follows:

> 12. *Voidable marriages.* –
> (1) Any marriage solemnized, whether before or after the commencement of this Act, shall be voidable and may be annulled by a decree of nullity on any of the following grounds, namely: .....
> (c) that the consent of the petitioner, or where the consent of the guardian in marriage of the petitioner was required under section 5 as it stood immediately before the commencement of the Child Marriage Restraint (Amendment) Act, 1978, the consent of such guardian was obtained by force or fraud as to the nature of the ceremony or to any material fact or circumstance concerning the respondent; or ...

While earlier, it had been most difficult to obtain nullity on the ground of fraud,[46] a flood of cases from the late 1970s and especially in the early 1980s showed that the interpretation of what constituted a "material fact or circumstance concerning the respondent" under s. 12(1)(c) could be taken to dangerous extremes. In *Asha Srivastava v. R. K. Srivastava*, AIR 1981 Del 253, it was alleged that the wife was suffering from incurable schizophrenia which had not been disclosed to the husband. The lower court had granted nullity. The wife appealed to the High Court, opposing this decree but also asking for divorce against the husband on the ground of his adultery and cruelty. It was held at p. 259, in view of the new law on nullity for fraud, that the wife's appeal would have to fail:

> A marriage cannot be annulled on the basis of any and every misrepresentation or concealment. However, if there is a misrepresentation or concealment regarding a material fact concerning the respondent then the provisions contained in Section 12(1)(c) would definitely be attracted. Concealment about the ailment of schizophrenia, which is a mental illness and is incurable according to ... would, in my opinion, amount to obtaining the consent of the respondent by fraud as to any material fact concerning the appellant.

In *Bikkar Singh v. Mohinder Kaur*, AIR 1981 P&H 391, it was alleged that fraud had been played on the husband. Before the marriage, he had been shown a beautiful girl from a distance, but had been married to another woman, who was allegedly about 40 years old, had grey hair, some artificial teeth, and was suffering from venereal disease and other ailments. While all this seems hardly believable, the husband had actually consummated the marriage on the first night. Therefore, the wife was now claiming that this barred a nullity petition because he had condoned the fraud and impersonation. Would a single act of intercourse amount to condonation of the fraud practised on the appellant husband? It was held that "a solitary act of sexual intercourse without more" (p. 394) would not bar a nullity decree. A similar case, also involving concealment of the wife's real age and doubts about her mental state, is *Som Dutt v. Raj Kumari*, AIR 1986 P&H 191, where nullity was also granted to the husband on appeal.

In *Balbir Kaur v. Maghar Singh*, AIR 1984 P&H 417, the facts were that the wife's left hand had been partially disabled because of polio in her childhood. This had not been disclosed to the husband and the question before the court was whether this was a material fact and circumstance. It was held, at p. 418, dismissing the wife's appeal against nullity:

> The deformity found by the doctor cannot be ignored and to my mind it is [a] deformity of material nature and it was the duty of the parents of the girl to clearly disclose the deformity so that it could be open to the husband to marry or not. Once this was withheld it clearly amounted to fraud and the husband has rightly been granted a decree of nullity of marriage by the Court.
>
> Marriage is partnership for the life and is not a child's play. Parliament was conscious of it and that is why a new provision was inserted by the 1976 Amendment. A spouse may not like to marry a person who may be suffering from physical deformity/disability due to polio ... No hard and fast rule can be laid. However, the facts of each case will have to be seen.

In *Rajinder Singh v. Pomilla*, AIR 1987 Del 285, the husband had not disclosed the fact that he had been married before, and the wife had successfully petitioned for nullity. On appeal to the Delhi High Court, this decision was confirmed.

There have been few cases under this section during the early to mid-1980s in which a marriage has been upheld. Later cases introduced interesting arguments over who would need to be told of a potential spouse's deficiencies. Was it the family or the individual who was supposed to marry? In *Ruby Roy v. Sudarshan Roy*, AIR 1988 Cal 210, the marriage had been annulled by the lower court and the wife appealed. The husband claimed that his consent had been obtained by the non-disclosure of material facts concerning the wife, who was devoid of female organs and incapable of cohabitation (p. 211). It transpired that this had been an arranged marriage and the father of the husband had known of the wife's condition – but had not told his son. The wife, therefore, argued that her physical defects had been duly disclosed and no nullity should be given. A. M. Bhattacharjee J held, at p. 212:

> If an obedient son, who is on good terms with his father, authorises his father to negotiate for and settle his marriage including the selection of the bride, and the father selects a bride after full knowledge about her physical defects and the son marries that bride, the son cannot thereafter be allowed to turn round and to have the marriage annulled on the ground that he would not have consented if the defects were made known to him. A marriage may not be a contract only; but is nevertheless a contract also; it may be that all the principles of law of contract may not apply with all their rigour to a contract of marriage; but there can be no reason why the fundamental principle, so well-known in the Law of Agency ... he who acts through another acts himself, shall not apply where, as here, the petitioner has held out his father as the authority to finalise the negotiation and to select the bride and has not disputed that the father was given such authority.

Diwan (1988: 302) vigorously criticised the application of the principle of agency in this case as "grotesque". It is doubtful whether such a decision is socially acceptable and that the marriage will have lasted long. This case was referred to, with some element of approval, in *Alka Sharma v. Abhinash Chandra Sharma*, AIR 1991 MP 205, a wife's appeal against nullity granted to the husband on a number of grounds, including fraud. Dharmadhikari J first held, at p. 209:

> I have to keep in mind that Marriage Laws (Amendment) Act 66 of 1976 has introduced farreaching changes in the original Act of 1955 and the provisions regulating the relationship of marriage between the Hindus have [sic] been, to a very large extent, liberalised, keeping in view the recent modern trends on the subject all over the world. The orthodox concept of unbreakable marriage tie between two Hindus based on 'Sanskara' has to a very large extent modulated because it resulted, sometimes, in extreme hardship and tragedy to the party [who] suffered or [was] aggrieved due to the serious handicap or position of the opposite party.

It was further held that mental disorder and related inability to procreate may not be a sufficient ground for nullity in all cases. The judge continued at p. 211:

> We can envisage a spouse marrying at a late age or a mental disorder of such a type where he or she is unable to complete a sexual act or a man or woman having no sexual organ for procreation of children but he or she may be otherwise completely fit as a marriage partner irrespective of a mental disorder disabling her/him from procreating children. In such a case permitting dissolution or nullification of marriage would break the marriage tie on an unsubstantial ground. In a given situation, where the parties are young and the mental disorder is of such a type that sexual act and procreation of children is not possible it may furnish a good ground for nullifying the marriage because to beget children from a wedlock is one of the principal aims of Hindu marriage where Sanskar of marriage is advised for progeny and offsprings.

On the question of fraud, it transpired that the mother and grandmother of the husband, who had negotiated the marriage, had not been told of the wife's medical condition. Hence, fraud had been practised and the wife's appeal against nullity was dismissed, despite her fervent pleas that this would be a social disaster for her.

Where the husband, at the time of the marriage, was aware of the fact that the wife was pregnant, and marital intercourse did take place, he could not then seek nullity. This was held in *C. S. Rangabhattar v. C. Choodamani*, AIR 1992 AP 103. This was actually the husband's second marriage. He had already three children from his first wife, who had died, and badly needed someone to look after his children. In a very perceptive judgment, it was held at p. 107:

> . . . the probabilities of the case clearly point to the fact that since the husband himself was undergoing a second marriage and was having three children from out of the wedlock of the first marriage apart from having undergone vasectomy operation, he could not have been looking for a marriage with an ideal girl for a second marriage in the context of things as they were existing at that time. Therefore, there is every reason to believe that he was prepared to compromise with the situation and to settle down for a marital life which may not be equal to the expectations that one may have in looking for a partner in life.

This decision shows social awareness and realism on the part of the judge. Dismissing the husband's appeal and refusing him a decree of nullity, it was finally held, at p. 109:

> Since the marital intercourse with the consent of the petitioner has taken place after discovery by the petitioner of the pregnancy of the wife, we are not inclined to believe the story of the petitioner that he

> was unaware of the pregnancy till the child was actually born to the respondent . . .

On the other hand, in *Gitika Bagchi v. Subhabrota Bagchi*, AIR 1996 Cal 246, a case under s. 25(iii) of the *Special Marriage Act*, 1954 regarding consent obtained by fraud, the wife's appeal against a decree for nullity was dismissed. This is a sad, confused case, involving two people who had a long-standing cohabitation arrangement and then fell out once they formally married. It is probably appropriate that this 'modern' marriage was terminated.

Fraud cases in the late 1990s: Opposing misrepresentations

Cases on nullity for fraud seem to have become rarer during the 1990s, at least they are now hardly found in the case reports. Either the law is now so clear and well-established that there is no need for case reports, or it may be that nullity petitions under s. 12(1)(c) on the ground of fraud are no longer as easily granted as during the 1980s, and thus less attractive to petitioners. Confirmation of this may be found in *Sujatha v. C. D. Hariharan*, 1995 (II) MLJ 327, where a husband was unsuccessful in pleading that he had been the victim of misrepresentation. He had complained about the fact that his wife was wearing contact lenses. This was held not to be a material fact concerning the respondent, and his application failed.

Briefly examining the most recent cases on nullity of marriage, we find confirmation that in this area of the law, too, Indian judges are now less inclined to dissolve marriages at the behest of any claimant than they were in the 1970s and 1980s. However, there are exceptions, since so much depends on the facts and circumstances of individual cases. Further, the courts are becoming increasingly aware of the scope for misrepresentations made in marriage advertisements. In other words, modern practices of arranging marriages with media help, and with less direct family involvement, offer greater scope for hiding material facts and consequently present a higher risk of misrepresentation and outright fraud. Since such considerations weigh on the judges' minds, as we shall see, nullity is being granted in some cases under s. 12(1)(c) HMA.

In *Rama Kanta v. Mohinder Laxmidas Bhandula*, AIR 1996 P&H 98, the husband had perhaps been more interested in his financial benefits from the marriage than in checking the credentials of the wife, who came from a prosperous family but had, unknown to him, already been married twice before and had given birth to a son. The learned judge, Dr. (Mrs.) Saksena J, considered the evidence before her in detail and came to the conclusion that the husband was entitled to a decree of nullity based on fraud as well as a decree of divorce on the ground of cruelty. He had been cheated, and had also been treated badly by the wife, whose conduct had made it impossible for him to enjoy a peaceful married life. Whether this actually amounts to a breakdown argument is not evident from the case report itself.

In *A. Premchand v. V. Padmapriya*, AIR 1997 Mad 135, the husband claimed that his wife's age had been misrepresented to him. Hence the horoscope given on that basis could not be accepted and the marriage should be annulled for fraud, or divorce should be granted. However, the court found, as a matter of fact, that the husband knew the wife's true age at the time of the solemnisation of the marriage. Since this was manifestly not a case of fraud, the husband's appeal failed.[47] The court made no explicit comments about preserving marriages and seems entirely focused on the facts and a detailed perusal of relevant cases.

More instructive is *Anurag Anand v. Sunita Anand*, AIR 1997 Del 94, a typical modern case, in which the husband had allegedly concealed material facts regarding his income and property. This was a husband's appeal against a decree of nullity awarded to the wife. It appears that, soon after the marriage, the wife had lodged a complaint to the Dowry Cell of the Delhi Police, the couple had fallen out, and had ceased to cohabit. The wife claimed that the husband had misrepresented his age (by one year), had inflated his income and exaggerated his property status. The judge was unwilling to accept that a difference of one year in age would constitute a material circumstance (p. 99), but found that "the bio data of the appellant regarding his salary and property status was inflated and false" (p. 101). Would this qualify as 'material facts and circumstances'? A. K. Srivastava J produced an elaborate definition, which is relevant for our present discussion, at p. 102:

> The material facts and circumstances [sic] are those vital and important facts and circumstances which would induce or influence the mind of a party to give or withhold the consent to marry. This would appear to be the intention of the Legislature while enacting Section 12 of the Hindu Marriage Act. Having this interpretation in view it has to be seen as to what would be the material facts and circumstances . . . The marriage is a union between a man and a woman and while accepting any person as a husband or wife there are certain vital considerations which are definitely looked into before the parties or their parents give their consent for the marriage proposal. These considerations may be age, educational qualifications, income, caste, marital status, family status coupled with financial status, religion or nationality of the other party. They may be termed as material facts and circumstances. This list may not be exhaustive, as between certain parties some other factors may as well be material facts and circumstances depending upon the facts and circumstances of their case.

The relevance of financial considerations in modern Indian society is elaborately discussed in this judgment. We read, immediately following the above quote at pp. 102–103:

> For a girl to give her consent to a marriage proposal unless it is a love marriage, financial status of the other party is quite an important

> factor. Why? It [sic] is because everyone wants to have a comfortable living. For that a level of monthly income and a level of property status of the other party are required. In addition to monthly income of the other party his property status is assuming considerable importance. One needs financial security in time of need to fall back. This level of monthly income and property status would differ from case to case depending upon the status of the girl. Further, if the girl is herself working then it also becomes her aspiration to marry a boy who is earning more than her. A girl would definitely prefer a boy in marriage whose parents have already sufficient landed property and thus she has not to curtail her monthly expenditure for acquiring landed property to fall back in emergent needs. She needs a minimum level of expenditure capacity in the house of her husband. She may not accept a marriage proposal if she does not find the aforesaid.

Thus, it was held, at p. 103, that "the monthly income and the property status of the appellant can easily be called material facts and circumstance concerning him as envisaged in Section 12 of the Hindu Marriage Act". But would it amount to fraud if one did not declare the full particulars to an intending spouse? Again, the learned judge provided a detailed social commentary, saying at p. 103:

> Earlier common friends and relatives used to be involved in getting the marriages settled and whatever information they used to give to both the parties were depended upon and the marriages were solemnised. If after the marriage any fraud was detected the parties could do nothing as there was nothing in writing. Now marriages are to a large extent being settled through advertisements and exchange of bio data. Joint family living is dissipating and individual units have emerged. The result is that it is rather difficult to ascertain correct facts and the parties are largely [sic] dependent upon the bio datas exchanged. Therefore, it becomes very necessary for the parties to issue correct bio datas and to see that the bio datas do not contain any inflated or false information.

The potential abuse of such modern arrangements was explicitly highlighted by the judge further below at p. 103:

> The tendency to give false and inflated information regarding material facts in the bio datas exchanged in marriage negotiations should be curbed. They are generally given for eliciting better proposals and if the other party is hooked the purpose is served. Therefore, this tendency is not to be allowed to prosper. Benefit of said section must be given to the party which has suffered the fraud.

Noting that in the present case, because of the rush in making the marriage arrangements, there had been no proper chance to verify the assertions in the bio datas, it was held, at p. 103:

> Even if there could have been time for such ascertainment, I am not prepared to excuse a party which had issued a false bio data. The other party could act on the basis of the bio data issued for giving his/her consent for marriage with the other party. If the material facts and circumstances declared in the bio data are found to be false and the falsity is striking the very foundation of the marriage [it] becomes shaky. Mutual confidence is gone. Then what is the purpose of a married life unless the love still remains and the erring party is excused or forgiven.

It was then held, at p. 103, that "[i]n the present case the falsity on the part of the appellant is significant and can be called deception or misrepresentation. The respondent has not excused the appellant". In response to the assertions of appellant's counsel that these misrepresentations were not really of a serious nature, the judge reiterated the educative message of this particular decision, saying at p. 104:

> Though the general tendency of the Courts is that the marriage should be sustained as far as possible and this tendency is no doubt good for a laudable object but at the same time the Courts have also to take into consideration that by their reluctance to set aside a marriage brought out by fraud [sic] the Courts may be encouraging such false representations in the bio datas issued for attracting better proposals.

Finally, in *V. Shankar Ram v. Sukanya*, AIR 1997 Mad 394, the husband, a successful businessman, claimed to have been given assurances that his bride-to-be would be a suitable wife for him and daughter-in-law to the family. However, she turned out to be, so he claimed, a self-centred, childish and uncooperative partner, so that he could not even consummate the marriage and found his marital life very stressful. The husband alleged fraud and misrepresentation regarding material facts and circumstances concerning the respondent. He filed a petition for nullity, which had been refused by the Family Court, hence his appeal. It was also submitted on behalf of the husband that the marriage had broken down irretrievably. We read at p. 398:

> ... both parties are living apart ... for about 8 years and three months. They have lived together only for about 8 months, but they have no children. The appellant is aged 44 now and the respondent is 34 and according to the appellant the marriage which is otherwise dead emotionally and practically be continued for name sake and therefore, considering the facts and circumstances of the case, this Court should exercise its power and direct the dissolution of the same subject to any condition of payment of money or otherwise.

It was held at pp. 399–400 by A. R. Lakshmanan J:

> A decree of nullity can be granted under this section only on the grounds mentioned in the section and not merely because the parties to the marriage cannot live happily together for any domestic reason.

The learned judge was not convinced of the husband's evidence regarding fraud (p. 402), non-consummation of the marriage or impotence (p. 403). With reference to three Supreme Court cases in which a broken marriage had been dissolved under Article 142 of the Constitution, it was then pleaded on behalf of the husband that his marriage should be dissolved because it had broken down, and he even offered to "pay her any amount which this Court may fix for her livelihood" (p. 405). Referring to *Chanderkala Trivedi v. Dr. S. P. Trivedi*, 1993 (4) SCC 232, it was noted that the husband in that case had agreed to purchase the wife a flat in Bombay as well as provide her a lump sum of Rs. 200,000/-. Also *V. Bhagat v. D. Bhagat*, AIR 1994 SC 710 was cited, as well as *Romesh Chander v. Savitri*, AIR 1995 SC 851. As we saw, in the latter case, the husband had agreed to transfer the only house in his name to the wife as part of the divorce deal brokered by the Supreme Court.

Lakshmanan J remained unimpressed and declared that the facts of the present case were different. Having interviewed the wife, he had found that she still wanted to live with the husband and dismissed the husband's appeal, saying at p. 406:

> The assertion of the wife during our interview in Chamber that she wants to live with her husband even now appears to us to be true. Mr. C. Hariskrishnan is not fully correct when he says that dislike for each other was burning hot. The wife in her evidence says that she likes her husband and still wants to live with him. We do share the feelings of the wife expressed before us that a conservative Hindu Brahmin family girl would not prefer to be known as divorcee . . . in the society.
>
> Before parting with this case we think it necessary to say the following. Marriages are made in heaven. Both parties, in our opinion, have not crossed the point of no return. A workable solution is certainly possible if the parties reconcile themselves and live together forgetting their past as a bad dream.

Significantly, the learned judge totally ignored the husband's offer to buy his freedom and therefore clearly puts the sacramental notion of Hindu marriage higher than adequate financial arrangements for the wife. The latest case law on nullity for fraud shows, then, that the High Courts are beginning to be well aware of the recent Supreme Court cases which granted couples divorce on the ground of irretrievable breakdown, but there is clearly no floodgate effect. Where, however, fraud has manifestly been practised, the courts will not hesitate to grant nullity. In *R. Sankaranarayanan v. Anandhavalli*, AIR 1998 Mad 198, the husband's nullity petition on the ground of the wife's undisclosed schizophrenia had been refused and he appealed. It was found that this condition had not been disclosed to the husband and that it was a vital fact, thus this appeal was allowed and nullity granted.

The 'own wrong' problem

Regarding this area of divorce litigation among Hindus, too, my observations in this chapter continue to hold: Up to the early 1980s, courts were sometimes willing to grant divorces irrespective of the negative effects on the respondent, normally the wife. However, during the late 1980s, the courts became much more alert to the potential for injustice by overlooking the petitioner's – mainly the husband's – 'own wrong'. The courts have therefore taken a more explicitly gendered position and have become more sensitive to achieving justice, rather than merely applying the fashionable breakdown principle when urged to do so by forceful litigants.

The own wrong problem was explained in some detail by Professor Derrett (1981). It arose when the *Hindu Marriage (Amendment) Act*, 1964 introduced two new grounds for divorce under s. 13 (1A) HMA, which provided as follows:

> (1A) Either party to a marriage, whether solemnised before or after the commencement of this Act, may also present a petition for dissolution of the marriage by a decree for divorce on the ground –
>
> (i) that there has been no resumption of cohabitation as between the parties to the marriage for a period of two years or upwards after the passing of a decree for judicial separation in a proceeding to which they were parties; or
>
> (ii) that there has been no restitution of conjugal rights as between the parties to the marriage for a period of two years or upwards after the passing of a decree for restitution of conjugal rights in a proceeding to which they were parties.[48]

Reported cases soon showed that it was possible for petitioners to abuse these provisions by engineering a breakdown of the marriage and then seeking to take advantage of their own wrong by claiming a divorce. The relevant law is well explained in *Laxmibai v. Laxmichand*, AIR 1968 Bom 332, a 'good' case in many ways. There had been an earlier decree of restitution of conjugal rights in favour of the wife, the husband had wilfully refused to comply with that decree and had then petitioned for divorce on the ground of non-resumption of cohabitation, a classic case of taking advantage of one's own wrong. Divorce had been granted by the lower court, forcing the wife to appeal to the High Court. It was held that s. 23(1)(a) HMA, which requires a court to ascertain that "the petitioner is not in any way taking advantage of his or her own wrong or disability for the purpose of such relief" applied to such cases. Thus the wife's appeal was allowed and the marriage continued to exist.

However, the important case of *Bimla Devi v. Singh Raj*, AIR 1977 P&H 167, a Full Bench decision of the Punjab&Haryana High Court, vigorously dissented from *Laxmibai*. Here, there had been a decree of restitution of conjugal rights in favour of the husband and the wife had not complied with the decree for more than two years. The question before the court was whether the wife would nevertheless be able to secure a divorce. The marriage had lasted one day, the wife alleged fraud and refused to return to the husband. B. S. Dhillon J found at p. 172:

> From the various amendments made in the provisions of S. 13 by the Parliament, one thing is obvious that the Parliament sought it fit to liberalise the dissolution of marriage between the parties where there is no possibility of the spouses continuing matrimonial relations.

In view of these notions, reiterated at p. 175, this judge argued that the wife's refusal to return to the husband could not be treated as an 'own wrong' under s. 23 HMA and therefore she was not barred from obtaining a decree for divorce. It was held, at p. 175:

> It would further be seen that a spouse who has suffered a decree of restitution of conjugal rights, has already been adjudged to have left the company of the other spouse without reasonable excuse. The said wrong was committed much before the passing of the decree for restitution of conjugal rights ... Moreover, living separately from the spouse cannot be regarded as a wrong as the term 'wrong' ... contemplates causing some injury to the other side.

O. Chinnappa Reddy J agreed with Dhillon J, tracing the history of the legislative reforms in Hindu divorce law from an initial focus on fault-disability towards the breakdown principle. It was held at p. 177, allowing the wife's appeal and dissolving the marriage:

> The concept of wrong disability which was hitherto the sole basis of relief under the Act has now, in part, given way to the concept of a broken-down marriage irrespective of wrong or disability. To my mind it is not permissible to apply the provisions of S. 23(1)(a) based as they are on the concept of wrong-disability ...
>
> ... To probe into the question as to who was responsible for the non-resumption of cohabitation or non-restitution of conjugal rights and to deny relief on the ground that the petitioner was the guilty party would be to nullify the very object of the 1964 amendment.

This view was followed in a large number of cases and it became a more or less fully established position that non-resumption of cohabitation within two years (one year after the 1976 Amendment Act) meant that the marriage was irredeemable and a divorce decree should be given. For example, in *Jaswinder Kaur v. Kulwant Singh*, AIR 1980 P&H 220, the husband was allowed to take advantage of his own wrong and the wife's appeal against divorce was dismissed. This is what prompted Professor Derrett, in a series of articles during the 1970s, to warn against injustice perpetrated against women in the name of the law.[49] Professor Derrett

(1978: 97) candidly admitted that nobody, including himself, had realised at the time that "the gift of divorce in a cosmopolitan form to the large number of respectable castes was a Trojan horse, a poisoned gift".

When did the tide turn? The leading case of *Dharmendra Kumar v. Usha Kumar*, AIR 1977 SC 2218, attempted to redefine 'wrong' within the context of s. 23(1)(a) of the HMA but this case was strange because it was, remarkably and unusually, a husband's appeal against a decree of divorce granted to the wife. He alleged that she had taken advantage of her 'own wrong' by making it impossible for the couple to come together again. It was held that s. 13 HMA continues to be subject to the provisions of s. 23(1)(a) HMA. However, the 1964 Amendment had introduced two new grounds of divorce which stood intact. Thus, it was finally held, at p. 2220:

> Therefore, it would not be very reasonable to think that the relief which is available to the spouse against whom a decree for restitution of conjugal rights has been passed, should be denied to the one who does not insist on compliance with the decree passed in his or her favour. In order to be a 'wrong' within the meaning of Section 23(1)(a), the conduct alleged has to be something more than a mere disinclination to agree to an offer of reunion, it must be misconduct serious enough to justify denial of the relief to which the husband or the wife is otherwise entitled.

In the present case, this meant that the wife's action of refusing to respond to the husband's conciliatory letters did not qualify as a serious wrong. In the words of the judge, at p. 2220, it "does not amount to misconduct grave enough to disentitle the petitioner to the relief she has asked for". The husband's appeal was thus dismissed and his wife had finally managed to gain freedom from the matrimonial ties.

Diwan (1984: 261) reported that the Supreme Court's precedent in *Dharmendra* had remained ineffective to some extent and that "[t]his decision has not dampened the enthusiasm to advance the argument based on taking advantage of one's own wrong clause". Among the cases reported in the mid-1980s, there are many in which divorce was refused. *O. P. Mehta v. Saroj Mehta*, AIR 1984 Del 159, is a husband's appeal against the refusal to grant him divorce on the basis of non-resumption of cohabitation. The wife's defence was that the husband had maliciously accused her of adultery, and he was thus taking advantage of his own wrong through the divorce petition. This was accepted and the husband's appeal was refused.[50] In *Veena Handa v. Avinash Handa*, AIR 1984 Del 445, the wife had obtained a decree for restitution of conjugal rights and the husband had subsequently managed to be granted a divorce on the more or less automatic basis of non-resumption of cohabitation for a year. The husband had in fact remarried while the wife was in appeal against that decree.[51] M. L. Jain J was strongly critical of the behaviour of the husband, who had duped his wife in various ways and was refusing to maintain her and a child appropriately. Thus, he refused to uphold the divorce decree. It is quite evident from this case that the earlier liberality in 'own wrong' cases had been re-thought.

From a perusal of such cases it appears to me that the powerful comments of Sathiadev J in *Soundarammal v. Sundara Mahalinga Nadar*, AIR 1980 Mad 294, have had much effect on subsequent judicial decisions. It was held in that case, at pp. 301–2, with pointed reference to interpreting the interaction of sections 13 and 23 HMA:

> If for sustaining amendments a harmonious construction is to be resorted, and it is to result in a wrongdoer to be helped, of all things in the world by legal provisions, then it will lead to disastrous situations and would be the easiest handle for the wrongdoer to wriggle himself out of his marital obligations on his whims and fancies by committing deliberate acts to disrupt marital life. No law can be conceived of to give relief to a wrongdoer, the foundation of which is based on his own wrongs. In attempting to make a harmonious construction of the sections in the amended Act, merely because the subsequent amendments are claimed to usher in liberalisation on the aspect of divorce, the court cannot bring about an interpretation which would give a helping hand to the wrongdoer to get relief based on his wrongs, commissions and omissions which are against law. Illegality and immorality cannot be countenanced as aids for a person to secure relief in matrimonial matters ... Therefore even though the defaulting spouse is now enabled to file a petition for divorce, if the wrong is of a continuing nature, it cannot be held that ... it cannot be taken note of for finding out whether such a conduct of the defaulting person is reprehensible enough to constitute a 'wrong' on the date of the presentation of the petition by him.

During the late 1980s, a growing number of 'own wrong' cases ended in dismissal of the divorce petition. Such cases are, for example, *O. P. Mehta v. Saroj Mehta*, AIR 1986 Del 327 and *Ashok Kumar Bhatnagar v. Shabnam Bhatnagar*, AIR 1989 Del 121, discussed further above, where the husband did not succeed because he had manifestly been cruel to the wife in demanding dowry. In *Sumitra Manna v. Gobinda Chandra Manna*, AIR 1988 Cal 192, however, divorce was granted to the husband despite his 'own wrong'. There had been an earlier decree for judicial separation at the instance of the wife. It was held that the husband's refusal to resume cohabitation and to pay the wife maintenance did not amount to taking advantage of his own wrong.

While judges like Sathiadev J in the Madras High Court opposed the breakdown principle, it is interesting to observe that Professor Paras Diwan and other scholars supported it. Diwan (1985: 112) argued with reference to *Santosh Kumari v. Krishan Sabharwal*, AIR 1985 Del 393, that the judge should have treated the marriage as irretrievably broken down:

> The socially just solution would have been to dissolve the marriage and grant her fair maintenance and make it a charge on the husband's property. The judge himself has observed that where a marriage has completely broken down, it would be a practical and realistic approach to dissolve it. Yet he did not grant relief in this case.

In the same vein, Boparai (1984: 286) argued in favour of the breakdown principle and concluded his study on bars to divorce by saying:

> It is submitted that the application of the presently prescribed bars, especially to the "marriage breakdown" grounds for divorce, is wholly inappropriate. Separation as evidence of irretrievable breakdown is based on a no-fault concept. There would be nothing to connive at or condone. Similarly the petitioner's adultery or desertion would seem to have no serious bearing on the fact of the separation. Traditionally it has been argued that the application of these bars aims at maintaining an equilibrium between the sanctity of marriage and the liberalisation of divorce. However, times have changed and the application of these bars today tends to defeat the very purpose of modern divorce legislation. To apply these bars to keep alive a marriage which is nothing but an empty shell results in a lot of harm to the spouses, to the children of the marriage and to the society in general.

Thus, while scholars have continued to argue for the breakdown principle, and have largely been willing to overlook the 'own wrong' problem, the Indian courts have become more alert to the damaging socio-economic consequences of granting divorce to anyone who asks for it.[52] Strangely, in the 1990s, the case law under this rubric seems to have dried up and attention has shifted to the law on divorce by mutual consent. It is not clear at present why this should be so.

Divorce by mutual consent: Teething troubles

The legal provisions for divorce by mutual consent were also introduced into the HMA by the *Marriage Laws (Amendment) Act*, 1976. It has taken this section a while to be noticed, and to be interpreted by the judges. The wording of s. 13B is as follows:

> 13B. *Divorce by mutual consent.* –
> (1) Subject to the provisions of this Act a petition for dissolution of marriage by a decree of divorce may be presented to the district court by both the parties to a marriage together, whether such marriage was solemnized before or after the commencement of the Marriage Laws (Amendment) Act, 1976, on the ground that they have been living separately for a period of one year or more, that they have not been able to live together and that they have mutually agreed that the marriage should be dissolved.

(2) On the motion of both the parties made not earlier than six months after the date of the presentation of the petition referred to in sub-section (1) and not later than eighteen months after the said date, if the petition is not withdrawn in the meantime, the court shall, on being satisfied, after hearing the parties and after making such inquiry as it thinks fit, that a marriage has been solemnized and that the averments in the petition are true, pass a decree of divorce declaring the marriage to be dissolved with effect from the date of the decree.

The main technical question arising under this section was whether any one of the parties to a petition could withdraw consent at any time. Again, the resulting discussions concern the balance between the breakdown principle as an ideological tool and recognition of the socio-economic implications of increased marital instability.

The legal struggles over the right to withdraw a petition under this section were, thus, not only a technical or procedural matter. Refusing to acknowledge that one of the spouses might wish to pull out of an agreement to divorce would amount to putting a check on the breakdown principle. For, how could a spouse decide in one moment that the marriage had irretrievably broken down, and change his/her mind the next? Again, as in the 'own wrong' debates, the interaction of this part of s. 13 HMA and of s. 23 HMA became an important element in this context. For, Indian Hindu law explicitly recognises that a spouse (normally of course the wife) may have been forced to agree to a divorce petition by mutual consent, when in effect such consent has been obtained by duress of some kind.

It is not unrealistic to imagine a scenario where a Hindu wife finds herself asked to choose whether she wants to die or agree to a divorce. Indian law makers have been acutely aware of that possibility,[53] and the law has eventually been clarified to the effect that either spouse may withdraw consent at any time of the proceedings.

The earlier cases, however, were quite restrictive and thus reflect a preponderance of sentiments in favour of the breakdown principle. *Jayashree Ramesh Londhe v. Ramesh Bhikaji Londhe*, AIR 1984 Bom 302, is a somewhat untypical case in that it is the wife who appeals against the dismissal of a divorce decree on the basis of mutual consent. The marriage had lasted only for three months. The wife had initiated divorce proceedings, which were later changed to a joint petition for divorce under s. 13B HMA. The husband then reconsidered and, as the judge noted at p. 303, "has started feeling that he and his wife would live together happily and that, therefore the marriage should not be dissolved". In view of this, the lower court had refused to grant a divorce.

The Bombay High Court applied certain provisions of the *Code of Civil Procedure*, 1908 which deal with abandonment of a suit. Doing so, the social dimensions of a divorce petition were suppressed and the case was decided as a matter of legal technicality. It was held at p. 304 that "in any case one of the co-plaintiffs would not be able to abandon the suit more particularly when the other co-plaintiff has not consented to such abandonment". It was also held, at p. 305, that "there should be a consent for mutual divorce at the time when the petition is filed". Thus, as held at p. 305:

> It will not be possible for any party to voluntarily agree to have a divorce by mutual consent or to revoke or withdraw that consent at a later stage. Such permission would nullify the very purpose of a joint application.

Thus, in effect, it would not be possible for a spouse to reconsider, once a petition for divorce by mutual consent had been filed. It was finally held, at p. 306, that "[t]he fact that at a later stage either party does not want a divorce would be irrelevant". There is clearly no concern here for the preservation of marriages and rather an assumption that evidence of marital breakdown should automatically lead to a divorce decree. This view was questioned by Kusum (1987), one of India's leading writers on matrimonial law, who appeared to be in favour of the breakdown principle, but argued for caution, concluding her discussion at p. 114 by saying that "mutuality and consent should continue until the divorce decree is passed; then and then alone can a divorce be called a divorce by mutual consent". This view was later to be endorsed by the courts.

The breakdown principle was, as ever, vigorously supported by Diwan (1986: 136–137) with reference to further cases.[54] In *K. Omprakash v. K. Nalini*, AIR 1986 AP 167, there were mutual allegations of unfaithfulness and the marriage had clearly broken down. The judge applied the concept of breakdown and said, at p. 168:

> ... we entertain no doubt that it would be in the best interests of the parties to order the dissolution of the marriage. We are of the clear opinion that the marriage between the parties had broken down irretrievably and that there is no reasonable chance for reunion of the parties ... Any prolongation of the legal status of marriage is not likely to bring about reconciliation. It can only help to accentuate their unhappiness by further fomenting their mutual jealousies. This long separation strengthened by the serious charges of unfaithfulness made against each other must have drained off the matrimony its last drops of sweetness. The parties are fighting relentlessly in Courts against each other on the basis of those allegations ...
>
> We have no doubt that the differences between the parties are long-standing and deep rooted and that this Court would only be acting just to decree dissolution of the marriage here and now on the basis of their mutual consent.

Thus, it was finally held, at p. 170:

> S. 13B(2), no doubt cautions the Courts of its duty to fight the last ditch battle to save the marriage; but when the Court is fully satisfied, on the basis of the proved facts, that in the interests of justice of the

> society and the individuals marriage tie should be put asunder immediately, S. 13-B(2) does not impose any fetter on the powers of the Court to grant instant decree of divorce ... The great Telugu poet Vemana said that the broken iron can be joined together, but not broken hearts. Parties have been living apart for long and their wedlock has now virtually become a deadlock. Chances of reunion had completely faded away. In these circumstances, we think it just and proper to grant a decree of divorce straightway.

Remarkably, the judge emphasised in his very last sentence, at p. 170, that this decision had been made on the basis of mutual consent, not application of the breakdown principle. This confirms judicial awareness of the law: of course, breakdown as such is not a ground for divorce under Hindu law. Diwan (1986: 137) of course warmly welcomed this decision.

Courts will overlook procedural niceties if they realise that to refuse a divorce decree will create new social problems. In this regard, *Santosh Kumari v. Virendra Kumar*, AIR 1986 Raj 128, is instructive.[55] Here, the wife had appealed against a decree for divorce, but both parties had actually remarried. The judge granted divorce to this couple on the basis of breakdown facts and said, at p. 130:

> It was, therefore, abundantly clear that the parties did not want to live together and were desirous of getting a decree of divorce. In these circumstances, the insistence on the form of the application would be improper and unnecessary because if the decree is refused on such a ground, the agony between the parties will continue and will hamper in their way of settling by their fresh marriages.

It was, however, also held at pp. 130–131 that either party had the right to withdraw from a joint petition, a position which Diwan (1986: 137) vigorously disagreed with, while Kusum (1987) clearly took the opposite view. Here again, we see that male scholars have argued ideologically in favour of breakdown concepts, while judges and female scholars seem much more focused on matching the law with social realities.

By 1988, however, this area of the law also experienced a re-orientation, duly noted by Diwan (1988: 307). Remarkably, Diwan himself (1988: 307–308) continued to argue vigorously for refusal of the right to withdraw consent at any time and in favour of the breakdown principle. At this point, he did so with reference to *Dhiran Harilal Garasia v. N. Mansu*, AIR 1988 Guj 159, a case which went as far as holding that a decree for divorce by mutual consent could be passed before the expiry of six months from the date of filing the petition.[56] The court had ascertained that both parties desired divorce and made elaborate arrangements for maintenance for the children. It was held at p. 161:

> The Legislature has by enacting S. 13-B of the Act liberalised the tendency of providing relief to parties on the basis of their mutual

> consent from their broken marriages. This relief is granted by bringing out a profound alteration in the concept of a Hindu marriage from that of a sacrament to a contract. By that alteration, law has definitely set its face against forcible perpetuation of the status of matrimony between unwilling parties.

Significantly, this decision was not made without some cautious words (at p. 162), thus not completely underwriting the breakdown principle. This kind of decision, by emphasising the paramountcy of facts and circumstances of every case, can also be read to confirm that where either party withdraws consent to the divorce, a decree may not be granted.

The case law, from 1988 onwards, moved swiftly towards growing recognition that either spouse's consent may be withdrawn at any time. Thus, in *Harcharan Kaur v. Nachhattar Singh*, AIR 1988 P&H 27, the Punjab and Haryana High Court overruled *Nachhattar Singh v. Harcharan Kaur*, AIR 1986 P&H 201 and dissented from *Jayashree Ramesh Londhe*, AIR 1984 Bom 302. It was held that either party is at liberty to revoke consent at any time before the petition is finally disposed of. The court emphasised that a refusal to grant divorce under s. 13B did not amount to eternal matrimonial misery. It was held, at p. 30:

> The object of S. 13-B is to provide an additional speedy remedy to the husband and wife to have the marriage dissolved if even after sufficient efflux of time both of them find, that it is not possible for them to continue as husband and wife any further. Obviously, if both the parties agree, the decree of divorce can be granted by mutual consent under S. 13-B and if one of them fails to agree and does not want to oblige the other party by extending the requisite consent to the divorce, decree of divorce cannot be passed under S. 13-B of the Act. For that, other provisions of the Act would have to be resorted to.

K. I. Mohanan v. Jeejabai, AIR 1988 Ker 28 also dissented from the Bombay High Court decision in *Jayashree Ramesh Londhe*, AIR 1984 Bom 302. It was held that the provisions of Order 23 Rule 1 of the *Code of Civil Procedure*, 1908 are not appropriate for divorce cases. The final concluding comment of the learned judge, at p. 30, is significant:

> We would also add that it will militate against the letter and spirit of S. 13B of the Hindu Marriage Act, which contemplates an opportunity for reconciliation within a period of six months, or an extended period of eighteen months to say that once an application is signed, a reconciliation or a withdrawal must be completely ruled out.

N. G. Rama Prasad v. B. C. Vanamala, AIR 1988 Kant 162 also dissented from *Nachhattar Singh*, AIR 1986 P&H 201 and held that a court cannot proceed to consider a case under s. 13B HMA if one of the parties had withdrawn consent.[57] The controversy continued in 1989, with Professor

Paras Diwan sticking to his guns, now finding support only from the Delhi High Court in *Chander Kanta v. Hans Kumar*, AIR 1989 Del 73, holding that unilateral withdrawal of consent without evidence of force, fraud or duress was not permissible. At the same time, the Punjab & Haryana High Court in *Parkash Kaur v. Bikramjit Singh*, AIR 1989 P&H 46, followed *Harcharan Kaur*, AIR 1988 P&H 27, to the effect that consent can be withdrawn unilaterally at any time. It is evident that the Indian High Courts were becoming increasingly polarised on this matter and there was a need for the Supreme Court to clarify and unify the position.

In *Leela Mahadeo Joshi v. Mahadeo Sitaram Joshi*, AIR 1991 Bom 105, it was even held that once all the conditions of s. 13B HMA are fulfilled, it is mandatory on the part of the Court to grant a divorce decree. Saldanha J provided an elaborate reasoning on why this should be so at pp. 107–8:

> Prior to 1976, dissolution of marriage by mutual consent was not permissible under the provisions of the Hindu Marriage Act, but it was found advisable by the Legislature to introduce this provision so that in those of the cases where the other grounds for dissolution of marriage do not exist, i.e. cases where the parties find it impossible and inadvisable to continue living together, must also qualify for the relief. In doing so, the Legislature brought the Hindu Marriage Act in line with matrimonial statutes in other parts of the world where temperamental incompatibility is regarded as a valid ground for dissolution of a marriage. After incorporation of this provision, a duty is cast on the Court, where the ingredients of the section are satisfied, to pass a decree without going into an investigation of other extraneous issues.

However, this did not amount to a full endorsement of the breakdown principle without further consideration. It was further held by the learned judge, at p. 108:

> S. 13B presupposes only those cases where cohabitation, which is the essential ingredient of a valid and subsisting marriage, has come to an end because of a total break-down of the matrimonial relationship. Again, the Legislature has provided a further safeguard, namely that the period of such separation should be at least one year prior to the date when the petition is presented. Obviously, the reason for prescribing this period is that in cases of estrangement or separation on flimsy or frivolous grounds, the Court would be justified in not passing a decree unless the facts disclose that the breach has not only been serious but such as to have lasted for at least for one year.

Where, however, all the conditions under s. 13B HMA had been fulfilled, it was mandatory on the court to grant a divorce (p. 108). This case could therefore also be used to support the breakdown principle.

The long-awaited Supreme Court decision on this matter is found in *Sureshta Devi v. Om Prakash*, AIR 1992 SC 1904, which firmly held that consent to a joint petition can be unilaterally withdrawn at any time and that such consent must continue until the divorce decree is passed. In this case, the wife had claimed that her initial consent to the divorce petition had been given under duress. The High Court of Himachal Pradesh had granted divorce, taking the position that consent, once given, could not be revoked, hence the wife appealed to the Supreme Court. It is explicitly mentioned at p. 1907 that "[t]he need for a detailed study on the question has arisen because of the fact that the High Courts do not speak with one voice on this aspect". The judge, at p. 1907, first clarified the meaning of certain key phrases in s. 13B HMA:[58]

> The 'living separately' for a period of one year should be immediately preceding the presentation of the petition. . . . The expression 'living separately', connotes to our mind not living like husband and wife. It has no reference to the place of living. The parties may live under the same roof by force of circumstances, and yet they may not be living as husband and wife. The parties may be living in different houses and yet they could live as husband and wife. What seems to be necessary is that they have no desire to perform marital obligations and with that mental attitude they have been living separately . . .
>
> . . . The second requirement that they 'have not been able to live together' seems to indicate the concept of broken down marriage and it would not be possible to reconcile themselves. The third requirement is that they have mutually agreed that the marriage should be dissolved.

The main issue was whether one of the parties could withdraw consent to the joint petition. Analysing s.13B, it was held, at pp. 1907–8, allowing the wife's appeal:

> . . . it will be apparent that the filing of the petition with mutual consent does not authorise the court to make a decree for divorce. There is a period of waiting from 6 to 18 months. This interregnum was obviously intended to give time and opportunity to the parties to reflect on their move and seek advice from relations and friends. In this transitional period one of the parties may have a second thought and change the mind not to proceed with the petition . . . There is nothing in the Section which prevents such course. The Section does not provide that if there is a change of mind it should not be by one party alone, but by both . . .
>
> . . . At the time of the petition by mutual consent, the parties are not unaware that their petition does not by itself snap marital ties. They know that they have to take a further step to snap marital ties. Sub-section (2) of Section 13-B is clear on this point. . . . What is significant in this provision is that there should also be mutual consent when they move the Court with a request to pass a decree of divorce. . . . If there is no mutual consent at the time of the enquiry, the Court gets no jurisdiction to make a decree for divorce.

> ... If the Court is held to have the power to make a decree solely based on the initial petition, it negates the whole idea of mutuality and consent for divorce. Mutual consent to the divorce is a sine qua non for passing a decree for divorce under Section 13-B. Mutual consent should continue till the divorce decree is passed.

This case certainly settled the law, and the early 1990s saw very few reported cases on divorce by mutual consent. In *Preeti Singh v. Sandeep Singh*, AIR 1995 SC 1851, we catch a glimpse of the vigilance with which the Supreme Court now monitors the financial arrangements between the parties to a divorce by mutual consent. Applying the Supreme Court decision of *Sureshta Devi*, AIR 1992 SC 1904, Dhinakar J in the Kerala High Court held in *Girija Kumari v. Vijayanandan*, AIR 1995 Ker 159, that where a spouse's agreement to a divorce decree by mutual consent is not given, such a decree becomes invalid and the court has no authority to grant a divorce. Such decisions on appeal seem to show that knowledge of the law laid down by the Supreme Court in *Sureshta Devi* took time to filter down to the Family Courts, in particular.

This is certainly the impression one gets from reading *Satyabhama Nayak v. Narendra Kumar Nayak*, AIR 1997 Ori 47, a wife's appeal against a decree of divorce by mutual consent – in a sense a contradiction in terms. It appears that the Family Court had rushed into granting the couple divorce on the basis of mutual consent, but had also taken care to provide the woman and the couple's son a safety net of maintenance provisions. Both aspects of the case were struck down by the High Court and the case was sent back to the lower court for making a decision in accordance with the law. Since the wife now objected to a decree for divorce, this would probably mean that the marriage would legally subsist, while the husband would still have to pay maintenance for the wife and the son.

This case is very relevant for the present discussion because Pasayat J seems to be well-read and eager to comment on the social dimensions of modern divorce law. At p. 49, it was said, *inter alia*:

> The institution of marriage is of vital importance to society... . Sick marital relations pose a problem not merely for the related spouses, they have much wider implication. They have their repercussions and impact upon society and the same give rise to social problems. Harmony in society is inconceivable where there are dissatisfied parties that make a home which is one of the most crucial units in the hierarchy of social institutions. Emotional stability of society is linked with the institution of marriage. Concepts underlying matrimonial relations affect not only happiness of the individuals, they are also concerned with social norms and ethical mores. The institution of marriage has facets which are both public as well as private in nature. They impinge, as inevitably they would, upon our actions of public and private morality. Broken homes and strained marital relationships

> are not only a source of extreme anguish for the individuals concerned, they are also symptomatic of a social malaise and call for rational and sympathetic approach.

On divorce, and importantly also on customary divorce, the learned judge commented at p. 49:

> Divorce is sometimes described as a social innovation and an escape valve for the inevitable tension of marriage ...
>
> Wedded as it was to the doctrine of indissolubility of marriage (marriage being a sacramental union was an inviolable and immutable union thus even death did not dissolve the marriage), the Dharmashastra did not recognise divorce, and any attempt to deduce from stray Smriti [sic] texts the proposition that divorce was recognised by some Smritikars [sic] is nothing but one's inability to comprehend the basic concepts that the Dharmashastra propounded. However, the Dharmashastra's adherence to the doctrine of indissolubility of marriage did not hamper the recognition of the people's need for divorce, and a large section of Hindus (i.e. the lower classes) did enjoy the right of divorce. This was under the custom which prevailed over the sacred law. Customary modes of divorce were easy. In some cases a marriage could be dissolved by mutual consent. Sometimes divorce could also be purchased, very little formalities for dissolving a marriage were needed. Many a time it was purely a private act of parties. In some communities a forum was necessary it was either a Panchayat or a family council. Customary divorce was the privilege of the lower castes and higher castes seldom had a custom which permitted divorce.

It was noted that divorce in the Christian world was not made available and the judge continued, at p. 50:

> It was this rigid adherence to the doctrine of indissolubility of marriage which is partially responsible for the recognition of divorce later on. Largely, divorce came to be recognised in England and other Protestant countries on account of new ideas of liberty and equality generated by the Industrial Revolution. When marriage was accepted as essentially a contract, it was [the] next logical step to recognise divorce. However, marriage was not equated with a commercial contract. It was accepted that marriage being a social institution, there was a social interest in its preservation and protection. Thus it came to be accepted that marriage could be dissolved only in those cases where a party to the marriage by his act fundamentally undermined the marriage.

The theme that divorce should not be lightly given was further explored by the learned judge at p. 51:

> Divorce by mutual consent is one of the modes of easy divorce. Divorce was not known to the ancient Hindu law. The reason is that a marriage from the Hindu point of view creates an indissoluble tie between the husband and the wife. Neither party, therefore, can divorce the other unless divorce is allowed by custom.

However, given that s. 13 HMA had been introduced in 1955, and s. 13B had been added in 1976, divorce by mutual consent was now available for Hindus. It was held, at pp. 51–52:

> Section 13B deals with divorce in the case of broken down marriage by mutual agreement in order that they must apply for divorce as early as possible to obviate further emotional turmoil. As provided under sub-section (2), party to the prayer for divorce by a mutual consent may withdraw the consent. . . .
>
> . . . From a bare reading of the provision, it will be apparent that the filing of the petition with mutual consent does not authorise the Court to make a decree for divorce . . .
>
> . . . Mutual consent to the divorce is a sine qua non for passing a decree for divorce under Section 13-B.

Thus, *Sureshta Devi* is here being paraphrased, and it was held, at p. 52, that instant acceptance of a joint petition was not permissible. Thus, both the divorce decree itself, as well as the financial arrangements worked out by the Family Court, were struck down. One could argue that the High Court was here holding on to the power to refuse a divorce, although it is doubtful whether that is an effective strategy for upholding marriages in the long run. It should be noted, however, that the wife in the present case had appealed against the divorce, so how could this be a case of divorce by mutual consent? The case report does not enlighten us on whether the wife had earlier been under some duress to agree to the divorce, or whether she simply wanted the husband to state in court that he was willing to offer certain sums as maintenance for herself and the son. Both interpretations seem possible.

In *Ashok Hurra v. Rupa Bipin Zaveri*, AIR 1997 SC 1266, the strands of the case law under s. 13B and on irretrievable breakdown seem to converge in a very interesting way. The couple had been married in 1970, had no children and seem to have lived together until 1983.[59] There had been protracted litigation since 1984, including a divorce petition by mutual consent, an application by the wife in 1986 to withdraw her consent, and many failed attempts at reconciliation. The husband was trying to obtain a divorce despite the wife's refusal to consent, hoping that the earlier case law (as discussed above) would assist him. In 1996, the Gujarat High Court refused to grant him a divorce because the wife had withdrawn her consent, and the husband appealed to the Supreme Court after *Sureshta Devi* had been decided. There is much evidence of mutual allegations of inappropriate behaviour. This was clearly an intractable case, with the wife continuing her refusal to consent to divorce and relying on *Sureshta Devi*, AIR 1992 SC 1904. The husband argued that this decision required reconsideration and that 'complete justice' needed to be done.

We have come across the phrase 'complete justice' before in cases where couples were battling over their divorce for years and the Supreme Court finally intervened to terminate the marital relationship to avoid further waste of energies and resources. Not surprisingly, in the present case, too, the husband's legal representatives had argued for applying the principle of breakdown of the marriage as used in *V. Bhagat v. D. Bhagat*, AIR 1994 SC 710 and had thus brought in Article 142 of the Constitution, from which this phrase is taken. The High Court, as is noted at p. 1272, could not have applied Article 142.

The Supreme Court refused to depart from *Sureshta Devi*, however, and merely said, at p. 1271, that this case "may require reconsideration in an appropriate case. We leave it there". However, in view of the evident breakdown of the marriage and the long-standing battle between the spouses, this was considered a fit case to apply the Court's discretion under Article 142 of the Constitution (p. 1273). Again, the Supreme Court was much concerned about adequate financial arrangements for the wife,[60] and further justified its approach of granting a divorce on p. 1273:

> There is no useful purpose served in prolonging the agony any further and the curtain should be rung at some stage. In coming to the above conclusion, we have not lost sight of the fact that the conduct of the husband is blameworthy in that he married a second time and got a child during the pendency of the proceedings. But that factor cannot be blown out of proportion or viewed in isolation, nor can [it] deter this Court to take a total and broad view of the ground realities of the situation when we deal with adjustment of human relationship.

The Court also referred to the 71st Report of the Law Commission of India on the HMA (dated 7th April 1978), focusing on irretrievable breakdown of marriage, and quoted several key passages to underline its reasoning that in cases of prolonged litigation between warring spouses, where the marriage is indeed irretrievable, divorce should be granted under s. 13B of the HMA. This was done on condition that the husband made the substantial payments which the Court had ordered for the benefit of the wife.

Thus, under the legal rubric of 'divorce by mutual consent' we now have a remarkably similar picture as under the law relating to cruelty. In either case, the Supreme Court has clearly asserted its authority to terminate protracted proceedings and to dissolve a dead marriage. However, this does not amount to allowing the principle of 'irretrievable breakdown' a free run throughout the modern Hindu law on divorce. I therefore disagree to some extent with Sharma and Nagpal (1992: 92) who have written:

> Since its incorporation S. 13(B) has come for interpretation before the courts. The way it has been interpreted by the courts not only makes it

> a valid and a sound ground for consent theory but also increasingly it is becoming a fertile ground for the growth of breakdown principle in India.

As many other reported cases in the past few years show, the High Courts, in particular, need to remain extremely alert to ensure that spouses are not taking advantage of their own wrong and that respondents – in particular women, and obviously women who have to look after children – are not pushed out of a marriage without adequate safeguards of a financial nature. This often means that the courts will refuse pleadings that the marriage is irretrievably broken down and will uphold marriages. This goes for cases under s. 13B as well as other divorce cases.[61] The extent of accompanying financial safeguards, clearly an issue of growing prominence, will be further explored in chapter 4.3 below. It can be stated firmly here, however, that the most recent developments of Hindu divorce law and of maintenance law go neatly hand in hand in that they appear to protect women and children much better than a few years ago.

Conclusion

Despite further movement towards application of the principle of 'irretrievable breakdown' therefore, the modern Indian divorce law for Hindus does not simply follow the individualistic tendencies and parameters of Western laws. Sharma (1994: 150), like so many other Indian scholars, seems to assume that the English legal principles have been gradually adopted but argues against the blind copying of Western concepts, saying at p. 150:

> Actually the mentality and the socio-economic conditions of Hindu society cannot be equated with Western society. Therefore, we should not blindly borrow any Western [sic] concept and incorporate it in any Indian legislation without looking into its pros and cons.

The author refers in this context particularly to the financial arrangements for women and children (see chapter 4.3 below), emphasising in the conclusion, at pp. 363–364, that "if divorce becomes easier, it will harm women, as it will provide a unilateral right of divorce to men". A balance has to be found, therefore, between acceptance of the supposedly modern breakdown principle and protection of the individual rights of citizens.

It seems to me that most Indian judges are acutely aware of the need to protect spouses – and women in particular – against ruthless partners who unilaterally abandon marital relationships that might as yet flourish.[62] It appears that many judges have been at pains to develop a system of handling cases of marital breakdown which takes account of Indian socio-economic realities and thus gives more importance to the wider social dimension than individualistic reasoning. As we saw, citing the example of *V. Shankar Ram v. Sukanya*, AIR 1997 Mad 394, there is also evidence that some judges are concerned about the negative status implications of divorce for Hindu wives and may take this into account. However, in comparison to the social and financial considerations, this aspect of the matter seems to be distinctly less prominent in the judicial minds. Further, as in *Chanderkala Trivedi*, (1993) 4 SCC 232, when the marriage has really broken down, ideological *mantras* about the stigma of divorce for Hindu wives are of little help to a wife who has not exactly behaved like a dutiful Hindu wife herself.

Thus, if a Hindu wife were to signal to the court that she is not willing to undergo a divorce, and she is not herself responsible for the breakdown of the marital relationship and actively engaged in fomenting the dispute, the likelihood is now that a divorce may not be granted to the husband, unless he makes tempting financial offers which might help to cushion the wife against the negative consequences of divorce. Conversely, where a Hindu husband insists on divorce, he can no longer take easy advantage, in the divorce law as it currently stands under the HMA, either of simple pleadings of cruelty, fraud, non-recognition of his own wrong, or the unthinking application of the breakdown principle, which could earlier so often be interpreted as male-focused collusion.

A few recent cases illustrate these points well and allow us further insight into current judicial thinking about Hindu marriage and divorce. *Love Kumar v. Sunita Puri*, AIR 1997 P&H 189, is a husband's appeal against divorce, granted in favour of the wife on the grounds of cruelty and desertion. The wife had alleged dowry abuse and had claimed that it was not safe for her to live with the husband and his family. Her story – all too familiar today – was not believed, however, and it was found that the husband should have been given proper opportunity to put his version to the court. Dr. (Mrs.) Saksena J said, at p. 192, that "[i]n our Indian society, we treat the marriage as sacrosanct and in [the] past divorce was not favoured/approved by the society" and then held, with regard to the court's obligations, at p. 193:

> Under S. 23(2) of the Act it is incumbent on the matrimonial Court, to endeavour to bring about reconciliation between the parties, a great responsibility is cast on the Court. A Hindu marriage is not contractual but sacrosanct, it is not easy to create such ties but more difficult to break them; once annulled, it cannot be restored. A Judge should actively stimulate [the] rapproachment process. It is fundamental that reconciliation of a ruptured marriage is the first duty of the Judge. The sanctity of marriage is the corner stone of civilisation. The object and purpose of this provision is obvious. The State is interested in the security and preservation of the institution of marriage and for this the Court is required to make attempt to bring about a reconciliation between the parties.

Thus, the learned lady judge took the view that this divorce petition had been decided "in unwarranted hot haste" (p. 194) in favour of the wife and remanded the case to the trial court. However, in *Satya Narain v. Mamta*, AIR 1997 Raj 118, the husband's alleged dowry-related cruelty was held to be a proper ground for granting the wife a divorce decree. Here again, much depends on the evidence before the court.

In *Balwinder Kaur v. Hardeep Singh*, AIR 1998 SC 764, the wife had been duped into signing a divorce petition by mutual consent, but the High Court of Punjab&Haryana had overlooked this and had granted divorce to the husband. The wife appealed to the Supreme Court, where D. P. Wadhwa J held, at pp. 766–7, that the courts have particular duties in matrimonial litigation:

> A petition for divorce is not like any other commercial suit. A divorce not only affects the parties, their children, if any, and their families but the society also feels its reverberations. Stress should always be on preserving the institution of marriage That is the requirement of law. One may refer to the Objects and Reasons which led to setting up of Family Courts under the Family Courts Act, 1984. For the purpose of settlement of family disputes emphasis is "laid on conciliation and achieving socially desirable results" and eliminating adherence to rigid rules of procedure and evidence ...
>
> ... Even where the Family Courts are not functioning, the objects and principles underlying the constitution of these Courts can be kept in view by the civil Courts trying matrimonial cases.

Since the High Court had not acted in accordance with the law, the wife's appeal was allowed and divorce was refused. In *Guru Bachan Kaur v. Preetam Singh*, AIR 1998 All 140, a Sikh wife appealed against a decree of divorce on the ground of irretrievable breakdown – and succeeded. This case also revisits the predicaments of professional couples living in different places. There had been an allegation of mutual desertion, which does not exist as a legal ground. The Family Court was severely criticised for giving a patently wrong and illegal decision and for taking many years to do so. While it was accepted that this marriage had broken down irretrievably, and *V. Bhagat*, AIR 1994 SC 710 and other cases were referred to as authorities for applying the breakdown principle, we know that the High Courts cannot dissolve a marriage under Article 142 of the Constitution. In the present case, too, therefore, the dam which the Indian Supreme Court has erected against the continuous flood of breakdown arguments held up well. The wife's appeal was allowed and the couple were sent on their way with a final judicial blessing, worth quoting here because it seems to encapsulate much of today's judicial thinking. We read at p. 145:

> We hope and trust that still good sense will prevail on the husband to adopt attitude of forgiveness and forgetness. We hope that GOD will bless them. It is never to be too late to start a married life.

This is much more than a few pious word, before the judges move on to the next case on their list. While many scholars and researchers have argued vigorously in favour of the breakdown principle, Indian judges have continued to take a more complex view. It has been too simple to assume that the scholars are modern and the judges are somehow tradition-focused. For, the judiciary's main concern would appear to be justice, which one attempts to find on the basis of the facts and circumstances of the individual case. In real cases, this may sometimes mean instant dissolution of a hopeless marriage, but in other cases the judges send a couple home with their blessings for matrimonial bliss, as we saw above.

This is not evidence of judicial confusion, but a reflection of the basic principle in Indian law that justice can only be done by considering the facts and circumstances of the case, not by following some uniform statute or a universally binding principle. We have seen that the Indian judiciary has soundly rebuked the assumption that just because a couple have ended up in court, their marriage must be ended. Compared to scholars, Indian judges seem to be much better placed to feel the pulse of modern Indian society and, as members of that society (however elitist and removed) they have their 'ear to the ground', much more than scholars who may have read a lot of foreign material and come out thoroughly confused.

I find it significant in this context that Paras Diwan, by many counts the leading scholarly commentator on modern Indian family law, consistently overlooked the potential for the abuse of individualistic, modern divorce strategies by litigious individuals. The Supreme Court, on the other hand, has led the Indian judiciary in developing a unique approach to Hindu divorce law, which is at the same time conservative and modern, individualistic and socially-focused, open to arguments of total breakdown, yet seeking to preserve social cohesion. Added to this complex scenario, as is now absolutely evident, are several important financial considerations surrounding marriage breakdown in modern Indian society. The Indian judiciary, thus, is found to be engaged in a most exciting and challenging continuous balancing act between breakdown and social cohesion.[63] This occurs within a secular framework and yet in typical Hindu fashion, where no law ever applies to everyone, where nothing is ever crystal-clear, and where finding the correct balance for India's contemporary social order is a never-ending task.

Notes

1 On Muslim laws of divorce in South Asia see now in much detail Pearl and Menski (1998, ch. 9).
2 See authoritatively *V. Bhagat v. D. Bhagat*, AIR 1994 SC 710.
3 For an interesting article on the subject of ancient Hindu divorce see Larivière (1991).
4 Pearl and Menski (1998) show in detail which difficulties this has been causing to South Asians resident in Britain, who now find, with few exceptions, that they have to marry and divorce twice to follow the requirements of the two legal systems to which they are subject, notwithstanding the official stance of English law, which sees itself alone as the relevant 'law'.

5 Derrett (1957: 111) asserted that "[i]t is evident that in making provision for divorce the Indian Parliament has not been uninfluenced by English experience".
6 On details of the law see, with approval, Derrett (1963b) and Derrett (1970).
7 Indeed, more recent cases have done this. For details see chapter 2.5 below.
8 Parashar (1992: 119) confirms that "[n]o systematic study of even a part of those customs followed by eighty per cent of Hindus had been made to determine their contents. These customs did not form part of the public debate on Hindu law reform at any stage". Derrett (1978: 97) suggested that there was "general agreement that castes that had customary divorce should not be deprived of it".
9 The most powerful case remains *V. Bhagat v. D. Bhagat*, AIR 1994 SC 710.
10 See n. 8 above for Parashar's probably valid assertion that 80% of Hindus can avail themselves of such customs.
11 See e.g. *Nitaben v. Dhirendra Chandrakant Shukla* (1984) 1 GujLR 276.
12 A good example of this type of case is the confusing but funny appeal by a military man's wife, who was simply too fat for his liking. The case is also instructive on the law of cruelty. See *Parihar v. Parihar*, AIR 1978 Raj 140.
13 The key cases on this subject are *Mary Soniz Zachariah v. Union of India*, 1990(1) KLT 130, which still asks the government for legislative action, while in *Mary Sonia Zachariah v. Union of India*, 1995(1) KLT 644 (FB), the judges rewrite the statute themselves and then apply this law in *A. v. B.*, 1996(1) KLT 275.
14 *Urmila M. Ram v. Patras Masih* AIR 1993 P&H 121(SB) is a case on reference to a Special Bench of the High Court and confirms a divorce decree in view of the husband's persistent cruelty.
15 In Pakistan, this used to occur under s. 2(ix) of the *Dissolution of Muslim Marriages Act*, 1939 but the new case law is now mainly found under s. 8 of the *Muslim Family Laws Ordinance* of 1961, which applies to forms of divorce open to Muslim wives, such as *khul*, and treats them as corresponding to the *talaq*. For details on Muslim divorce laws in South Asia see now Pearl and Menski (1998, chapter 9).
16 But see *K. P. Y. Siddhique v. Amina*, AIR 1996 Ker 140, a petition based on the husband's cruelty.
17 Deshta (1995: 62) confirms that important spokespersons of the small Parsi community (who often studied law at SOAS) expressed themselves strongly against a uniform civil code because it obviously meant the formal end of legal recognition for such minority personal laws.
18 See the statement of Lakshmanan J in *V. Shankar Ram v. Sukanya*, AIR 1997 Mad 394, at p. 406: "We do share the feelings of the wife expressed before us that a conservative Hindu Brahmin family girl would not prefer to be known as divorcee . . . in the society".
19 See e.g. Gulati (1981).
20 For an example see *Sunil Kumar v. Usha*, AIR 1994 MP 1, at p. 4.
21 The problems are not germane to so-called developing countries. Current attempts in the UK to make absent fathers more strictly responsible for the maintenance of their abandoned offspring reflect the same concerns in a post-modern Western system of family law regulation.
22 Under section 25 of the HMA 1955, women are potentially liable for the maintenance of a husband who is indigent. There is some recent case law which ridicules men who seek to rely on their ex-wife for maintenance. See *Kanchan v. Kamalendra*, AIR 1992 Bom 493, where the husband was told in no uncertain terms that an able-bodied person has a duty to work and that a grant of maintenance to a man in such circumstances would promote idleness.

23 Diwan (1988: 303) confirms that "most of the divorce petitions in the courts are on the basis of fault ground of cruelty". Diwan (1994: 296) states that "[c]ruelty continues to be the favoured ground of divorce. Thereafter comes desertion". Dhagamwar (1987: 20) reports on a survey in which cruelty leads the table with 28% of all cases, while mutual consent accounts for 1%.

24 Where courts refused to grant divorce, as in the amusing case of *P. v. P.*, AIR 1983 Bom 8, where the wife's persistent adultery neither qualified in its own right nor as evidence of cruelty, academic comment was quick to criticise the judge: see Sampath (1983: 296–297).

25 If one looks at the case law on dowry at the same time, one notices a parallel, in that judges at that time are not aware of the scale of dowry-related violence against women in Indian society and favour the man's arguments. For details see Menski (1998b).

26 *Rita Nijhawan v. Balkishan Nijhawan*, AIR 1973 Del 200 is a nullity case on impotence. *Shakuntala Kumari v. Om Prakash Ghai*, AIR 1981 Del 53 is a wife's unsuccessful appeal against divorce. A number of other cases are cited in *Anil Bhardwaj* at p. 115.

27 Diwan (1986: 132). See *A. v. B.*, AIR 1985 Guj 121; *Kamini Gupta v. Mukesh Kumar Gupta*, AIR 1985 Del 221.

28 For instructive earlier cases see *Gaya Prasad v. Bhagwati*, AIR 1966 MP 212, discussing wifely duties in traditional terms, while *Sadhu Singh v. Jagdish Kaur*, AIR 1969 P&H 139, contains a wide-ranging discussion on the predicaments of spouses in such situations and comes down in favour of the wife. To my knowledge, more recent cases have not been analysed comprehensively. It may be anticipated that such analysis could provide important pointers for understanding changes to marital relationships in modern India, given that an increasing number of wives find that they have to work to make ends meet.

29 This is of course a wife's petition, which again makes all the difference. A year earlier, in *Adarsh Parkash Srivastava v. Sarita Srivastava*, AIR 1987 Del 203, a greedy husband was refused a divorce decree when it transpired that he had demanded dowry and had then turned round to accuse his wife of cruelty to get rid of her and to take dowry from elsewhere. Nobody commented on the fact that this decision might put the wife in mortal danger and it is not mentioned in the case report whether the wife would have been agreeable to a divorce.

30 It is interesting to note that Diwan (1988: 304) vigorously opposed this decision, arguing that "[t]here cannot be a greater mental cruelty than such allegations".

31 I cannot resist entering a protest here about the way in which the mythical author of the *Manusmriti* is uncritically treated as a legislator, when this is so manifestly not a historical fact. This confirms the point I made in the introduction to this book, to the effect that Indian legal scholars themselves have today difficulties in understanding details of their legal past.

32 In *Parvati v. Shiv Ram*, AIR 1989 HP 29, the husband's unspecific pleadings of adultery were not accepted and the wife won her appeal against divorce.

33 On such murder cases, see in detail ch. 6 in Menski (1998b).

34 See *Krishan Lal v. Nitu*, AIR 1986 Del 460, now obviously overruled by the present case.

35 This was also a case regarding the effects of the wife's mental instability, an allegation by the husband which was not accepted by the learned judge.

36 See e.g. *Alka Bhaskar Bakre v. Bhaskar Satchidanand Bakre*, AIR 1991 Bom 164.

37 In *V. Bhagat v. D. Bhagat*, AIR 1992 Del 267, the wife had alleged that the husband (who was a practising lawyer in the Supreme Court) was insane and was a lunatic. Still, on technical grounds, the husband's case was thrown out. This case went on to the Supreme Court and is discussed further below.

38 That case is reported as *Lata v. Vilas*, AIR 1987 Bom 231.
39 S. 15 of the HMA provides as follows:

> 15. Divorced persons when may marry again. –
> When a marriage has been dissolved by a decree of divorce and either there is no legal right of appeal against the decree or, if there is such a right of appeal, the time for appealing has expired without an appeal having been presented, or an appeal has been presented but has been dismissed, it shall be lawful for either party to the marriage to marry again.
>
> Provided that it shall not be lawful for the respective parties to marry again unless at the date of such marriage at least one year has elapsed from the date of the decree in the court of the first instance.

40 On this matter, see further section 3.6 below.
41 See n. 37 above for the High Court stage of this case.
42 The earlier case does not appear to have been reported. It must have been one of those innumerable cases in which divorce was refused by the court, leaving the spouses to their own devices.
43 This case was also cited with approval at p. 719 of *V. Bhagat v. D. Bhagat*, AIR 1994 SC 710.
44 Article 142 of the Constitution was not referred to in *V. Bhagat v. D. Bhagat*, AIR 1994 SC 710.
45 It must be noted, however, that action under Article 142 is only available to Supreme Court judges and not the High Courts.
46 For example in *Padmaja v. Sivaraman*, 1975 KLT 213, it was held that consent to marry, obtained on the basis of a false horoscope, was not a ground for annulment of the marriage.
47 It appears that this is a somewhat typical dowry case, in that the husband was seeking to extract more money from the wife's family, and probably used his knowledge of her real age to extract yet more. The outcome of the case means that the husband failed on both fronts.
48 In both cases, the waiting period of two years was reduced to one year by the *Marriage Laws (Amendment) Act* of 1976.
49 Derrett (1973: 105) emphasised in strong words that the scheme of the 1964 Act can be "shockingly abused". Derrett 1975 correctly advised that women should petition for restitution of conjugal rights rather than judicial separation if they valued the continuation of their marriage. Derrett 1981 found it "ridiculous" to treat matrimonial litigation in accordance with the breakdown principle.
50 See similarly *Pavuluri Murahari Rao v. Povuluri Vasantha Manohari*, AIR 1984 AP 54, where the husband's appeal against refusal to grant divorce was thrown out. It was evident that he was trying to get money from the wife's parents and there was "absolutely no trace of genuineness" (p. 59) in this matter.
51 A very similar case is *Santosh Kumari v. Krishan Sabharwal*, AIR 1985 Del 393. Here the appellant wife was defending herself against a decree of divorce. The husband had taken her back into the matrimonial home for a short while but then had turned her out again. The husband's actions were severely criticised by the judge.
52 Where, however, a wife blatantly abused legal processes to retain married status without fulfilling any duties, the husband was granted a divorce on the ground of non-resumption of cohabitation and the wife lost her appeal. See *Kumud Wadhwa v. Mahender Kumar Wadhwa*, AIR 1998 P&H 65.
53 It is similarly clear that modern English law, with its absolute emphasis on 'quickie divorce' and divorce by mutual consent, has not built such safeguards

into its regulatory framework to be able to assist wives who are pushed out of marriages. In practice, one does come across cases where the wife was forced to renounce not only the marriage but also a variety of ancillary reliefs that should have been available to her.

54 See *Nachhattar Singh v. Harcharan Kaur*, AIR 1986 P&H 201. There is no statutory requirement to allow the parties to rethink, as shown by *In the matter of Sharan Kumar*, AIR 1986 P&H 213.

55 See also *Krishna v. Satish Lal*, AIR 1987 P&H 191, where the judge turns a fault-based petition into one for divorce by mutual consent, recognising the breakdown of the marital relations.

56 This was also held in *Dhanjit Vadra v. Beena Vadra*, AIR 1990 Del 146, which also recognised the breakdown of the marital relationship and thus elicited favourable comment from Professor Diwan (1990a: 128). See, however, *Kanchan Mohanty v. Kulamani Mohanty*, AIR 1992 Ori 165, which holds the opposite and is critically referred to by Diwan (1992: 162). See further *Roopa Reddy v. Prabhakar Reddy*, AIR 1994 Kant 12, which also recognised the liberalising intentions of the legislature and granted a divorce by mutual consent without further delay.

57 Interestingly, the judge referred to an earlier decision of the same High Court which supports this view, *K. Krishnamurthy Rao v. Kamalakshi*, AIR 1983 Kant 235. In that case, it had been held that there was a positive duty on the Court to ascertain that the consent of the wife was freely given, more so where the parties were not very educated.

58 On the meaning of 'not living together as husband and wife' see further *Kiritbhai Girdharbhai Patel v. Prafulaben Kiritbhai Patel*, AIR 1993 Guj 111, where it was held that going abroad jointly and living under one roof did not amount to living together as husband and wife.

59 The case report confusingly prints 1993, which appears to be wrong in view of the history of the litigation.

60 The relevant judicial statements, quoted from p. 1273, are found below in chapter 4.3.

61 See e.g. *Anil Kumar Banerjee v. Sefali Banerjee*, AIR 1997 Cal 6, a case on cruelty and desertion, holding that even though the couple had lived separately for nearly twenty years, the wife did not consider the marriage as finished and thus divorce should not be granted to the husband. In *Tapan Kumar Chakraborty v. Jyotsna Chakraborty*, AIR 1997 Cal 134, the court refused a divorce on the basis of cruelty as well as breakdown and ordered judicial separation instead. In *Pratap Lal v. Kundana*, AIR 1997 Raj 158, the husband had petitioned for divorce on the ground of the wife's mental disorder and leprosy, but the court found no such evidence and refused the decree. *Om Prakash v. Madhu*, AIR 1997 Raj 214, is an own wrong case in which the husband was alleging child marriage, non-consummation, and was seeking to argue irretrievable breakdown of the marriage, even with reference to *V. Bhagat*, AIR 1994 SC 710. The husband's case was soundly dismissed by an alert judge. In *Sukhdev v. Santosh*, AIR 1998 Raj 12, a husband's appeal against refusal of a divorce decree on the basis of desertion was dismissed when it was found that the wife had been forced to live apart and had no desire to break the marital tie. *K. (Chandana) Dhanum Kumari v. K. Venkata Vara Prasad*, AIR 1998 AP 225, is another case where the wife, to pursue her career, insisted on living in a separate place and ended up being accused of desertion. The court found that in the circumstances the wife could not be held guilty of desertion and set aside the divorce decree. In *Rajashri Rajendra Shasane v. Rajendra Babulal Shasane*, AIR 1997 Bom 65, the Family Court had granted a couple divorce by mutual consent, even though this had not been petitioned for. The High Court sent the case back for reconsideration.

62 Where, however, a wife abuses her knowledge of the law and causes misery to the husband, the courts will not take the woman's side, showing that women's 'own wrong' cases receive more scrutiny now as well. *Adhyaatmam Bhaamini v. Jagdish Ambalal Shah*, AIR 1997 SC 1180, confirms that the Supreme Court will not protect a procrastinating wife against a decree for divorce, especially if she can be awarded financial support from the husband. This is an unsuccessful appeal by a wife against divorce. It was found that she was not unfamiliar with court proceedings and was deliberately protracting the case, so that it was her own fault that the proceedings against her went *ex parte*. Thus, the divorce was confirmed, but the wife was also awarded Rs. 5,000/- maintenance per month.

63 I do not accept the argument put forward by Sharma and Nagpal (1992: 85) that the courts have been confused and their decisions unsystematic. As the example of divorce by mutual consent shows, there have been phases of insecurity, but since 1988 or so, judicial thinking on divorce has developed with greater consistency than scholars seem to realise so far.

Chapter Three

Polygamy

Favourable treatment for Muslims?

3.1 Playing to different arenas: Indian polygamy between international stage and local forum

While the enormously complex recent developments in Hindu divorce law have passed almost unnoticed, there has been continuing debate over the issue of triple *talaqs* among Muslims (see in detail Ahmad 1994). However, that undoubtedly contentious topic pales in comparison with the public and international opposition to polygamy, especially the assumed right of the Muslim husband to have up to four wives at the same time. At first sight, the topic of polygamy raises totally different issues. However, as we shall see further below, these are also linked to the other main agenda of modern Indian law.

The present section provides an overview of Indian law and policy on the suppression (or rather toleration, as we shall see) of polygamous marriages. It is evident that polygamy is widely seen as inherently bad and is frequently linked to Islam, thus adding to Islamophobic trends and current processes of 'othering' anything that concerns Muslims in many parts of the world. Unsurprisingly, much of the academic writing on polygamy is instantly linkable to this great internationally contested issue, often envisaged as a struggle between tradition and modernity, an important battle between uncivilised non-Europeans and civilised Europeans, often more narrowly just between Muslims and the rest of the world.

Such ideological standpoints are often challenged – and yet reproduced – by Muslim writers in an outrightly defensive fashion. Frequently this is done in a way which actually makes the pseudo-conflict worse and entrenches conflicting positions. For example, the author of section 3.2 below, an Indian Muslim academic from a leading research institution, highlights immediately in the first sentence his perception of Western criticism of Islamic family law. Writing of this kind puts polygamy right at the top of a mountain of contested issues between Muslims and non-Muslims.

At the international, national, local and personal level, polygamy remains a difficult subject which excites common people, scholars and international conferences alike, regularly eliciting often much emotional comment. In the national theatre of the South Asian jurisdictions, this international debate has created its own dramatic reverberations. Thus, any continuing evidence of polygamy, and more so of state-sanctioned allowances for plural marriages, will come in for serious criticism, with potential implications, today, for international aid mechanisms. For countries like India, with an entrenched personal law system, this means that the Muslim personal law, which alone continues to permit polygamy for men at an official level, will come under particularly strong ideological attack and will be subject to much socio-political criticism. This has come from many quarters and has been expressed in many different ways. It is not surprising that Muslim scholars and other spokespersons have long been on the defensive against those who are perceived to be criticising not only polygamy but the social laws of the Qur'an and the socio-legal arrangements among Muslims in India.

Probably the most prominent protagonist of the defensive approach has been Professor Tahir Mahmood (see especially 1986: 68–71), who has written much on the subject. Mahmood (1986: 70) emphasised that until 1947, both Hindu law and Islamic law in India permitted polygamy. While the West ridiculed and rebuked both, the Hindus alone were overawed by such criticism and legislated for a type of Western-based absolute prohibition on polygamy.[1] Mahmood asserts that the Hindus were, in their reformist zeal, unaware that the West could only achieve an absolute legal prohibition of polygamy "at the cost of first ignoring mass-scale adultery and finally legalising it and also various forms of sexual perversion" (Mahmood 1986: 70). While this may sound as though such practices do not occur in Muslim societies or when polygamy is legally allowed, Mahmood is of course making the well-known point, without saying it clearly, that in traditional Muslim law the prohibition on any form of extra-marital sex (*zina*) is a dominant value and overriding public policy concern. The tempting assumption is that by allowing plural marriages for men, the supreme aim of reducing *zina* can be achieved. But does this really lead to a morally superior society, as many Muslim authors appear to claim?

It is too simple for Muslim writers to assert that the 'serial monogamy' of the West is a device to hide polygamous inclinations. It is similarly dishonest if Muslims pretend that polygamy solves all social ills.[2] Nobody responded to my suggestion (see ch. 3.5 below) that shedding crocodile tears for prostitutes was not good enough – should Muslim polygamists today not 'rescue' prostitutes and their children if they were really so concerned about social welfare?

An important issue that has been overlooked in such polemics is the fact that the Muslim defence of polygamy in India denies – or at least obstructs – the state's authority to make rules for all its people. One senses that at least some of the objections to permitting polygamy amongst Indian Muslims can be traced to apprehensions about permitting a 'state within a state', or an extent of communal self-control which legal centralists find hard, if not impossible, to accept. But we are operating here within the context of a personal law system, not a unified, stratified 'rule of law' model. The links with the debates about a uniform civil code for India, which would have to tackle the issue of polygamy head-on, are obvious (see further chapter 6.1 below).

I have previously written in qualified defence of polygamy (chapter 3.3 below), but this was in response to an article by a Muslim scholar who, it seemed to us in London, had gone too far in justifying polygamy as a moral safety valve for greedy males. The argument that men are by nature polygamous, while women would by nature be monogamous (see section 3.2 below), seemed less than honest and twisted the issue by justifying male chauvinism and almost unfettered male discretion over sexual relations. Clearly, the Qur'anic prohibition on more than four wives does not mean that a man, in the course of his life, could not have a very large number of wives.[3] Such perspectives, where they operate, still relegate women to the position of sexual objects. Not surprisingly, my lively South Asian law class of 1989/90 had much to say on that topic (see ch. 3.3 below).

It is of course a fact that the Qur'anic permission of polygamy for Muslim men with up to four wives was, in its time and historical context, a significant social reform in favour of women. They were no longer to be treated merely as objects of transfer and sale and were to be given legal rights of their own. It is evident that the Qur'anic reservations about polygamy, in terms of equal treatment of co-wives, were later interpreted by the majority of Muslim jurists as a general permission for polygamy with certain rather mild restrictions. The minority view, however, that no man could possibly treat two women equally and that therefore polygamy should not be permitted, was never totally absent. It has resurfaced in the context of Islamic family law reforms in Muslim countries like Tunisia,[4] Syria,[5] and now in Bangladesh, where a recent judgment interestingly questions the Islamic standing of s. 6 of the *Muslim Family Laws Ordinance*, 1961.[6]

Within the Indian personal law system, given that the post-colonial Indian state did not find it feasible to interfere in the Muslim personal law on marriage and divorce, the traditional juristic majority view was therefore retained as the official, state-sanctioned norm. As all textbooks confirm, polygamy remains permitted among Indian Muslims, while it has been outlawed under all other Indian personal laws. If we restrict our purview to statute law for the moment, then this conclusion is correct. It raises at once important questions of equal treatment under one legal system and Constitution, and has led to the widespread and popular assertion that undue favours have been given to the Muslims of India.

Apart from the polemic about whether allowing any man the right to be polygamously married really constitutes a great favour, several serious policy questions arise. First, a key issue for the modern Indian legal system with regard to polygamy has clearly been whether the state can justify virtual non-interference in Muslim polygamy if all other personal laws in Indian law now prohibit plural marriages. This looks at first sight like a straightforward problem with a tempting, simple solution. Cannot the modern state just pass another Act in order to supersede, or at least reform, the Muslim personal law on polygamy by imposing a legal prohibition on Muslim polygamy? If Turkey could do it, and later Tunisia, then why not India?

Anyone with the slightest knowledge of Indian political realities will realise that, as a Hindu-dominated state, India cannot simply legislate on Muslim law without facing massive popular objections. At least that is the view widely taken. The familiar cry of 'religion in danger' would be immediately raised. England with its now close to two million Muslims hides, so far successfully, behind the axioms of assimilation for migrants and the sovereignty of Parliament as a maker of uniform laws for all, while overlooking the social realities around Muslim polygamy in Britain today.[7] In the Indian legal system with its personal law set-up, legislation on Muslim law has always been a stressful – and therefore, it seems, very rare – experience. Except for the *Muslim Women (Protection of Rights on Divorce) Act* of 1986 (see chapter 4), post-Independence India has not even attempted to legislate on Muslim law. It would probably create grave unrest if India were to criminalise and outlaw Muslim polygamy.

This stalemate scenario raises big issues in itself over the value of having a national legal system with a Constitution and equal protection guarantees for all citizens. Criticism notwithstanding, we must realise that India's legal system is a major model of active and successful legal pluralism in the world today, functioning in ways which modern Western lawyers do not easily understand. South Asians and other 'Southerners', on the other hand, have lived and worked in such a system all their lives and often do not appreciate the need to explain to the uninitiated Westerner how radically different South Asian laws have been developing. Here, as elsewhere, the colonial myths are still very strong and the expectation that the South should just follow the North seems all too persuasive.

In terms of policy towards Muslim polygamy, so much is certain: Because Indian Muslims are as much part of the secular Indian state as other citizens, and since it appears to be the community's wish – whatever 'community' in this context precisely means – not to be subjected to legislative interference on this matter, modern India has rightly and wisely refrained from legally prescribing monogamy to its Muslim citizens.

The second issue is, then, having decided that Muslim polygamy could not be legally abolished, as for everybody else in India, whether the Indian state should interfere in the sphere of Muslim personal law at all if a woman were to complain about being subject to polygamy. In other words, should the modern state wash its hands entirely of any responsibility for those Indian Muslim wives who might object to being party to a polygamous marriage? While the answer to that question should be in the negative, popular opinion is to the effect that Muslim wives in such predicaments have no legal support mechanisms because the modern law continues to favour men. However, that is not factually correct, since Indian Muslim law as it stands today offers aggrieved women quite powerful remedies.

We must not overlook the fact that already the classical Muslim divorce law allowed a woman several escape routes from an unsatisfactory or unwanted polygamous marriage.[8] Being based on the traditional *shariat*, the modern South Asian Muslim law on polygamy does the same. Apart from negotiations between the spouses or within the families concerned, s. 2 (viii)(f) of the *Dissolution of Muslim Marriages Act*, 1939 reflects this by allowing a Muslim wife to petition for a decree of divorce on the basis of the husband's cruelty, that is to say:

> (f) if he has more wives than one, does not treat her equitably in accordance with the injunctions of the Quran.

This is one little section of an important British-made statute that clearly aimed to empower Muslim women to free themselves from a polygamous marriage they could not tolerate any longer. There is considerable evidence to the effect that this statute was not imposed on Muslims against their wishes, but had been asked for in a complex trade-off, one major aim being to stop desperate Muslim wives from abandoning Islam in order to terminate a hopeless marriage.[9] Modern South Asian law, being built to some extent on Anglo-Indian structures, has adopted this legislation and thereby incorporated the traditional reservations of the Qur'an towards polygamous arrangements.[10] Whether these will actually be activated in social reality has probably been less a matter of state law than a function of social conditions in a woman's particular circumstances. As we saw in the chapter on divorce laws, legally empowering women to demand a divorce by constructing 'cosmopolitan grounds' in certain situations does not automatically mean that women will then be economically and socially in a position to take up such offers. But the absence of prominent law reports on the subject does not, as such, prove that there is no such law, or that it cannot be effective. A South Asian woman who has to choose between being divorced or putting up with polygamy may indeed opt for the latter, for a variety of reasons.[11] While one could argue here about the quality of such freedom of choice, it is a fact that many South Asian women object to polygamy, but in social reality some women argue and act in favour of it. Clear signals that the official law would assist a woman who complained about polygamy would seem desirable in this regard. It is well possible that by exerting pressure on their women not to approach the state fora for dispute settlement, Indian Muslim leaders seek to maintain the current status quo.[12]

The third issue is whether Indian Muslim and Hindu law really treat polygamy so very differently. Looking solely at the letter of the statutory law, it seems impossible to argue that Hindus and Muslims are treated alike. However, if we add to our analytical equation how the Hindu case law on polygamy has developed, the argument takes quite a different turn. As we shall see in more detail in chapter 3.6 below, an analysis of the modern case law shows that the official legal prohibition of polygamy in Hindu law has not in fact been strictly implemented and has been systematically undermined in various ways. Thus, the contrast between Muslim and Hindu personal laws is much less pronounced than appears at first sight. In reality, Indian Muslim personal law permits polygamy with considerable social reservations which are expressed by the judges. As we saw above, a legal escape route for polygamously married Muslim wives who are dissatisfied does exist. The Hindu personal law, on the other hand, tolerates a modicum of polygamy despite the official legal proscription. This is not surprising, given the traditionally fairly positive approach to polygamy among Hindus as a safety valve for imperfect marriages.[13]

The somewhat clandestine legal tolerance of Hindu polygamy in India today is a complex issue in itself. To some extent, it feeds on traditional patriarchal predilections towards allowing men discretion over how to arrange matters in their home sphere. It reflects on the growing re-assertion of the private sphere vis-à-vis the public realm, while at the same time recognising the supremacy of overriding public interest concepts. This is still the rule of law, but it is manifestly of a different type than in Western legal systems. At the same time, the modern Indian state's evident lack of enthusiasm for imposing its normative framework of reference on the legal postulates of every Indian home is also becoming more evident in this area of family law. In addition, the widespread non-prosecution of polygamous Hindu males appears to be socially and economically motivated to protect the interests of women. Apart from that, of course, many polygamous marriages among Hindus never come to the attention of the legal authorities, and nobody complains.

When cases do go to court under the relevant provisions, s. 494 of the *Indian Penal Code* and s. 17 HMA, prosecutions are deflected through intricate legal arguments about validity of marriages under s. 7 HMA, as we began to see in chapter 1.5 above. The strand of case law under s. 7 HMA concerning the legal position of polygamous marriages has led to that section being characterised as a kind of bigamist's charter of freedom. Professor Derrett (1970: 307) was highly critical:

> The criminal courts are sympathetic to bigamists, holding that in order to commit the crime the ceremony must have been such a ceremony that, according to the custom of the parties, a valid marriage would have been contracted but for the first marriage. This is unfair ...
>
> ... The whole law on bigamy by Hindus is unsatisfactory, since Parliament's intention has been turned into oppression.

Even in the rare cases where convictions for polygamy have been the result, the punishments given, as far as we can ascertain from the case reports, remain lenient, notwithstanding the tough rhetoric of the Supreme Court in *Gopal Lal v. State of Rajasthan*, AIR 1979 SC 713. Here, explicit reference is made to the maximum penalty of seven years' rigorous imprisonment, but the polygamous husband is let off lightly. It was held by Fazal Ali J, at pp. 715–716, dismissing the husband's appeal and yet treating him with leniency:

> Bigamy is a serious offence and the maximum punishment under Section 494 is seven years. Therefore, where the offence of bigamy is proved the court cannot take a very lenient view. In the instant case the appellant was sentenced to two years and a fine of Rs. 2,000/-. It appears that the appellant has already paid a fine of Rs. 2,000/. In these circumstances therefore, we feel that the ends of justice will be met by reducing the sentence of imprisonment from two years to one year but maintaining the sentence of fine. With this modification the appeal is dismissed. The appellant will now surrender and serve out the remaining portion of the sentence.

Such ambivalous treatment of a Hindu polygamist does not amount to a total toleration of polygamy, but it comes close to it. The modern Indian state, thus, does not really favour Muslim polygamists in any meaningful sense, it simply refuses to implement an outright, strict legal prohibition of polygamy for all Indians because, so it seems, that is now seen as culturally and socially inappropriate for South Asia. The realisation that this is so was already reflected, several decades ago, in a comment made by Derrett (1970: 310) to the effect that "the rash abolition of polygamy in a euphoric moment is not working out satisfactorily". In addition, there is an economic dimension to this issue, which we need to discuss further below in section 3.6 and chapter 4.

One can easily interpret this scenario as a devious form of double-speak on the tricky subject of polygamy, but it appears to me rather as an integral element of the purposeful, and to some extent planned and conscious, South Asian re-assertion of indigenous legal postulates for the reconstruction of post-modern South Asian family laws. Mindful of international opinion, no doubt, the modern Indian state has taken the internationally sanctioned and politically correct path of officially prohibiting polygamy for the majority of Indians and has, as in other fields, bowed to Muslim pressure to preserve the *shariat* as the personal law for Indian Muslims. At the same time, the modern state has pursued its ancient, time-tested policy of flexibly adjusting to various new circumstances in order to survive as a politically acceptable unit, a 'soft state', not becoming the maker of universally binding legal rules in the fashion of Western legal centralist assumptions.

A brief look across the borders to Pakistan and Bangladesh confirms this analysis with an almost exact mirror image. India has reformed the majority Hindu personal law and prohibited polygamy for the Hindus while ignoring Muslim law. Pakistan has ignored Hindu law and reformed only the Muslim majority personal law. The modern Pakistani state, similarly mindful of international opinion and political correctness as the Indian state, appears to have prohibited Muslim polygamy in s. 6 of the *Muslim Family Laws Ordinance*, 1961 but has left the Hindu personal law untouched, albeit for different political reasons. Thus, Hindus in Pakistan and Bangladesh continue to enjoy the discretion of unlimited polygamy,[14] while Pakistani and Bangladeshi Muslim husbands, despite the control mechanisms of s. 6 of the 1961 Ordinance, remain at best punishable only if they do not follow the letter of the law. The stipulated power of refusal of the existing wife's or wives' consent under s. 6 is not in fact fatal to a subsequent polygamous marriage in Pakistan or Bangladesh, nor does the state law even attempt to invalidate such marriages.[15]

For the analysis of India's law on polygamy, this means that the modern state relied, first of all, on the edifice of the colonial period with some relevant provisions of the *Indian Penal Code*, 1860 in particular, which outlawed and criminalised polygamy. Modern India could have chosen to ignore the pressure towards explicit legal control of polygamy for Hindus, but in the reformist spirit of the 1950s, that was not on the cards, hence the HMA appears to outlaw polygamy in clear terms. Once the modern state had legislated for the abolition of polygamy among Hindus, however, the legal job was deemed to be done. The relevant legal facts had been created; international opinion should thereby be satisfied about the Indians as good pupils of the Western civilising model and master. Significantly, the modern Indian state has not interfered further in this area of the law since 1955. There is no evidence of legislative activity beyond the legal prohibition of polygamy in sections 5(i), 11 and 17 of the HMA, 1955. There are no subsequent amendments to those provisions, no increase of penalties for violations of the law, as we clearly see in other areas of the law, notably with regard to dowry (see now Menski 1998). There is no evidence of judicial or other activism, which does not mean to say that there is no judicial concern for the legal position of wives who are confronted with polygamy. Consequently, there is little reported case law, and the few reported cases often raise other matters. Polygamy is frequently linked to certain aspects of women's rights, mainly concerning property and maintenance.

It is significant that in certain situations, therefore, modern Indian Hindu law will treat a polygamous Hindu marriage not as a total nullity for all intents and purposes. Several groups of cases show that socially recognising the factum of a legally void polygamous marriage, and taking legal notice of it in interesting ways that make sense to Indians, allows the courts to grant such women substantial financial relief.[16] This is not a new issue at all, but it is remarkable that cases like *C. Obula Konda Reddy*, AIR 1976 AP 43, do not just represent a stray phenomenon but indicate deeper concerns which we can now bring out more clearly. These centre on judicial protection of the economic interests of women in situations of family conflict, a concern which has been allowed to override the moral and ideological objections to polygamy as such.

The most prominent conclusion from this particular legal development matches the conclusions from our chapter on divorce above remarkably well. While it appeared for a long time suspiciously as though male-dominated Indian courts were merely helping men in bailing them out of criminal prosecutions for bigamy, the implications of India's new gender awareness in law go beyond male-dominated agenda and are again linked to fiscal concerns. When it comes to polygamy, modern Indian law has also been refocused on protecting the material interests of individual women caught up in polygamy. Thus, rather than underwriting the ideological axioms of anti-polygamy rhetoric and thereby in effect punishing women for becoming involved in polygamy, the modern Indian state places concern for the social welfare of disadvantaged female claimants higher than ideological compliance with the expectations of Western modernity. Legal modernity in South Asian laws, therefore, as we see here again, involves developing an economically focused, welfare-based safety net for claimants in society, in this case polygamously married women. The state's approach relegates the ideological demands of anti-bigamist rhetoric to the back and emphasises social welfare measures that could be of real benefit to the women concerned. I must admit that I find little fault with this approach, even though it is achieved at the cost of taking official legal account of polygamy.[17]

A prominent diversion from such issues and thus a confusing element in the debates on polygamy in India has been the long-standing assertion that many Hindu men would convert to Islam merely to be able to enjoy the freedom of polygamy. This argument reinforces, of course, and is in turn based on, the assumption that there is a huge difference between Hindu and Muslim law on the subject. This is an old issue, much commented on by Professor Derrett several decades ago.[18] More recently, too, this has given rise to some interesting litigation, including the famous case of *Sarla Mudgal v. Union of India*, AIR 1995 SC 1531, briefly discussed in section 3.6 below.

Given that modern Hindu law does not actually seem to implement its anti-polygamy statutory rules, there should be little need for such conversions by Hindu men, and it does not seem to be a big issue in practice. It is well possible that this whole matter has been blown out of proportion for political and 'communal' reasons. This issue is constantly debated and is currently in the headlines not only in relation to Muslims but now rather with reference to Christians. It seems, then, that the polygamy debates are being used as a surrogate for inter-communal rivalries and as a political football.

The four essays reprinted in this chapter constitute an attempt, roughly ten years ago, to generate a discussion about some policy issues surrounding Muslim polygamy in India. These essays, though rich in content and detail, are full of rhetoric and polemical comments; they tell us little about the actual Indian law on the subject. In section 3.6 below, I shall therefore turn to the relevant statute law and reported cases to analyse the legal development of Hindu polygamy in India, particularly during the past few decades.

3.2 Islamic polygamy – A blessing in disguise

*M. Mustafa Ali Khan**

[From: 1989(1) *KLT*, Journal section, pp. 47–58]

The most criticised aspect of Islamic family law is that which permits polygamy. Partial and jealous writers in the West have generally misrepresented Islam. Particular care was taken by Western & non-Muslim writers to keep the real Islam out of the reach of their folk and to present such caricature of Islam that would be repulsive even to look at. The West accordingly levelled the charge of originating and advocating polygamy against Islam and its Prophet (SAW). The same has now started in free India by enemies of Islam. To know the truth behind this malicious allegation it is necessary to make a brief survey of the world history relating to polygamy.

History reveals that in all periods of human civilisation polygamy has remained, and even today is, an important social institution.[19] M. Letournean in his renowned [sic] work *Evolution of marriages* says "the most civilised nations have begun with polygamy. It is a law which has few exceptions".[20]

Isaac Taylor[21] writes that polygamy is a most difficult question. Nearly all the Prophets mentioned in the Talmud, the Old Testament and the Qur'an were polygamous. It was practised by religious leaders and reformers in different stages of history. Non-Muslim writers who condemn Islam on the score that it allowed polygamy forget that their own religions have not expressly prohibited polygamy.[22] For Jews and Christians polygamy was an accepted way of life. Moses did not prohibit it. The practice was expressly recognised in Mosaic law. It was prevalent among Israelis and continued even after Moses.[23] [The] Bible set no limit to the number of wives and/or concubines a man might take. It was not directly forbidden even in the New Testament. Even Jesus Christ did not expressly forbid polygamy.[24] John Milton in his *Treatise on Christian doctrine* quotes many passages from the Bible in defence of polygamy.[25] Polygamy was practised by Christian kings without the disapproval of [the] Church.[26] Writers like Westermarck,[27] Linton[28] and Roberts[29] observe that polygamy was not unknown during the reign of Charlemagne even among priests.

No Church Council in earlier centuries opposed polygamy. Nor was any obstacle placed in the way of its practice. Day notes: "In the judges' time, plural marriages were undoubtedly common".[30]

Among the Romans the freedom of women, the looseness of the tie which bound them to man, the frequency with which the wives were changed or transferred, be taken, in fact, the prevalence of polygamy under different names.[31] Westermarck observed that "Greco-Roman marriage

*Reader, Faculty of Law, AMU, Aligarh, UP. The notes to this article have been reproduced with limited editorial changes to achieve some consistency.

was opposed to the monogamous form of marriage and liaisons between married men and mistresses [sic] were not uncommon".[32]

To the Athenians, the most civilised and cultured of all nations of the antiquity, the wife was a mere chattel [sic], marketable and transferable to others and a subject of testamentary disposition. An Athenian was free to have any number of wives.[33] So among the Christians, polygamy flourished in a more or less pronounced form until forbidden by the laws of Justinian. It, however, still continued in practice until condemned by the modern society. St. Augustin himself seems to have observed in it no intrinsic immorality or sinfulness, and declared that polygamy was not a crime where it was the legal institution of a country.[34]

About the middle of the 16th century, Burnardo Ochinus, General of the Order of Capuchins, wrote in favour of polygamy. In 1531 the Anabaptists [sic] openly preached that a true Christian must have several wives.[35] The doctrine of the Mormons is well known.[36] Even today some African bishops support polygamy on moral grounds and in preference to other alternatives.

Henry Hallam,[37] in his *Constitutional history of England*, points out that German reformers even as [sic] late as the 16th century admitted the validity of a second or a third marriage contemporaneously with the first, in default of issue or other similar circumstances. Higher classes of Germans, as also many English aristocrats [sic] and royals [sic], indulged in polygamous marriages even up to the 19th century. The Emperor Valentine II, by an edict, allowed all his subjects if they pleased to have several wives. The succeeding Emperors practised polygamy and people generally followed their examples.

Among all the Eastern nations polygamy was a recognised institution. Among the Medes, Babylonians, Assyrians, Chinese and Japanese there was no restriction as to the number of wives a man could have.[38]

Seldon proves in his *Uxor Hebraica* that polygamy was allowed not only among Jews but likewise among all other nations.[39] Among the Syro-Phoenician races, whom the Israelis replaced, polygamy was degraded into bestiality.[40] In Sparta, because of female infanticide, the institution of polygamy and wife lending was recognised and practised. The corruptness of morals in Persia, about the time of the prophet of Islam (SAW) was deplorable.[41] Men were notoriously voluptuous and to them women were [sic] nothing more than an object of the gratification of their passions. The Persians went for a multitude [of] regular matrimonial connections besides having a number of concubines [sic]. Hindu laws and customs were, till recently, extremely unfavourable to women. Before the enactment of the *Hindu Marriage Act*, 1955 by Indian Parliament, there was unrestricted polygamy in the Hindu society.[42] [The] Vedas mention polygamy as an established institution. Manu is mentioned to have [had] 10 wives at a time.[43] Even at the present day polygamy is as common as it is permissible. Among Brahmins and other high caste Hindus in Bombay and Madras it is permitted and practised.[44]

According to [the] Smritis, sterility of the first wife or existing wives was the usual cause of polygamy.[45] Kapadia[46] observes that the institution of polygamy was socially approved from the Vedic period. According to him it persisted right from the Vedic time to the present day. Manu and Kautilya recognised and sanctioned it.[47] Besides polygamy Hindus also practised Tibetan, Nair and fraternal polyandry which is still in vogue both in the hilly North and Southern India.[48] Kapadia cites many well-known examples, including that of Draupadi and Mamata, from ancient Indian history in support of his assertion that polyandry as an institution existed from Vedic time.[49]

Schopenhauer frankly admits, "we all live, at any rate, for a time and most of us always, in polygamy". The great philosopher further exclaims, "there is no use arguing about polygamy, it must be taken as defacto existing everywhere and the only question is how to regulate it".[50]

Probably a majority of primitive tribes permitted polygamy; biological and social conditions of the societies restricted its prevalence.[51] In the great majority of preliterate cultures polygamy is the preferred type of family organisation.[52]

Thus we see that when Prophet Mohammad (SAW) came with the laws of Islam, more than 600 years after Christ, polygamy was an established institution in all countries and in all religions. It had been rather an established institution from time immemorial. No religion or social system seriously condemned it. At the dawn of Islam polygamy was prevalent in Arabia as in other parts of the world, the Arabs, had, however, corrupted it.[53]

Islam purged it of those corruptions; and as a result of that, it was fully reformed. Islam did what it considered necessary, keeping in view the social, moral, and the natural requirements of the society and humanity. Islam, by limiting the number of wives to four and laying down strict conditions for having more than one wife at a time, has introduced a radical change and reform in the social conditions of human society. Polygamy is, therefore, both checked and regulated in Islam. The brief historical facts about polygamy, mentioned above, prove, more than adequately, that Islam neither originated nor advocated nor even encouraged it.

Nature and extent of polygamy recognised in Islam

Sura Nisa verse 3 is the only verse of [the] Qur'an from which the permission to marry more than one wife is derived. The verse may be translated as "Take in marriage such women as please you, two, or three or four, and not more. But if you fear, that you cannot act equitably towards so many, marry only one or what your right hand possesses; this is more proper than you deviate not from the right path".[54]

The important point to be carefully noted here is that this verse does not enjoin polygamy. It only permits polygamy and that permission, too, is given on a very strict condition i.e. if one can be just and equitable between the wives. If he cannot be equitable, he is bidden in plain language to marry only one. The Qur'an is unequivocal in stating that if there is fear of injustice a man should marry only one wife.[55] This qualification constitutes one of the religious-moral limitations which Islam has placed on polygamy. The verse was revealed not to legalise polygamy but to control and restrict the already prevalent polygamy, by subjecting it to the conditions of equality and justice among wives. In no way the verse can be constituted to indicate any new permission. The new and most important thing in the verse is restriction on number and equal treatment. Justice and equality here mean equal treatment of wives as regards conjugal relations, maintenance and upkeep.[56] Equality in love and inclination is, however, beyond human competence and that is why Shariah has not made it necessary. What the Qur'an requires is what is humanly attainable,[57] i.e. justice in terms of companionship, provisions, considerateness and such controllable aspects of family life.[58] At the same time it does not condone discrimination. Maulana Mohammad Ali, in his translation of the Holy Qur'an observes that the said verse permits polygamy under certain circumstances, it does not enjoin it nor even permit it unconditionally. The verse when analysed and examined proves to be a barrier against the practice of polygamy, instead of being a certificate for indulgence in polygamy.[59]

The condition of equality between wives, in theory, is a near impossibility in practice. The Qur'an itself indicates the implication of this proviso of equality. Verse 129 of the same Sura states: "Ye will not be able to deal equally between (your) wives however much ye wish (to do so). But turn not altogether away (from one), leaving her as in suspense. If ye come to a friendly understanding and practise self-restraint. Allah is ever forgiving, merciful".[60]

The ignorant and biased critics have also tried to create misunderstanding by distorting the meaning of verse 129 of Sura Nisa. They try to take advantage of the opening part of the verse, i.e. it is not within your power to be perfectly equitable with all your wives. They assert that this verse takes away the permission of polygamy given in verse 3 of the same Sura. They take the plea that the permission is conditional and when God Himself declares that equality (the condition) is not possible then the permission is withdrawn defacto. Keeping in view the life of the Holy Prophet (SAW) and that of his companions (most of them had more than one wife at a time) and the later part of the verse (129) itself only an ignorant and prejudicial person can reach the above mentioned conclusion.[61] There cannot be any greater absurdity than the misleading interpretation put forward by such critics. To demonstrate the absurdity and futility of their opinion, I put forward the following arguments:

The verse (129) in its later part "... therefore (in order to satisfy the dictates of Divine Law) do not lean wholly towards one wife so as to leave the other in a state of suspense ..." makes the intention of Allah quite clear and plain, that what Allah demands is not the equal inclination of heart, love and affection, but the outward and material treatment. Maulana Abul

Ala Maudoodi,[62] Maulana A. Majid Daryabadi,[63] Maulana Mohamad Ali[64] and all other renowned commentators of the holy Qur'an are in perfect agreement to this interpretation. As a matter of fact Allah defined the meaning and concept of equality and justice in this later part of the verse.

Hazrat Aisha (RA) reports that the Prophet of Allah declared that he treats all his wives equally but has no control over his love and inclination and for that he seeks the forgiveness of Allah, the Most Merciful.[65]

Being the best interpreter of the Book of Allah, the Holy Prophet (SAW) demonstrated this very meaning of the verse (iv: 102).[66] Most of his companions, including the rightly guided Caliphs had more than one wife at a time and acted justly and equally among them all. History does not record any case where a complaint of this nature was made to the Holy Prophet (SAW). They cannot be said to be acting against the will of Allah.

If the interpretation of the ignorant and biased critics is accepted verse 3 (iv: 3) stands abrogated by verse 129 (iv: 129) which is never claimed by anyone and the Holy Qur'an nowhere contradicts itself.

Those introducing their own interpretation are among wrong doers sternly warned by the Prophet (SAW) of Allah:

> "If anyone interprets the Book of Allah in the light of his opinion even if he is right he has erred".[67]

Sura Al-Ahzab mentions "God has not given man two hears within him".[68] These verses (iv: 129 and xxxiii: 4) read with Sura Nisa verse three have no room for any doubt and speculation that Islam has checked and discouraged polygamy and has adopted in doing so, its usual course of appealing to human nature. In fact, these verses favour the natural course of monogamy as a general rule and permission of polygamy as exceptional provision.

The real perspective of verse three of Sura Nisa can be well gauged by comparing it with a similar verse in the Qur'an dealing with permission of divorce, i.e. Sura Baqara verse 229. This verse may be translated: "Divorce is to be pronounced twice and then the wife must be either retained in honour or released in kindness". Is this verse a proof of permissibility of divorce? Like polygamy, unrestricted divorce was prevalent in pre-Islamic Arabia and other parts of the world. Men kept divorcing their wives and taking them back in their wedlock and there was no limit to it, that left the poor woman in distress. She was neither treated as a wife nor set free to marry someone else. The said verse (ii: 229) put an end to this inhumane [sic] practice and atrocities by fixing the number of the reversible divorces (*talaq-e-rajaee*) to two; and the succeeding verse (ii: 230) declared that a third pronouncement effects a final irrevocable '*talaq*'. It is no more a matter of dispute but a well-settled principle of Shariah that the intention of verse 229 of Sura Baqara is not to introduce, permit, or legalise divorce but to rectify, check and reform the already prevalent practice of unlimited number of divorces.

The same is the case with polygamy referred to in Sura Nisa, verse 3. It was in fact revealed to put a stop to the existing practice of unrestricted polygamy, and to unequal treatment of wives. Islam, according to Martin,[69] puts a check on the unlimited polygamy, limiting the number of wives to four, a man could simultaneously marry under unavoidable circumstances, provided he could do and show equal justice and material favour to them all, while prescribing monogamy for all who could not act equitably and justly towards and make provision for more than one wife and thus closing practically the doors of polygamy for the vast majority of Muslims. Dr. W. Leitner rightly remarked, "now, as practically, none can be, as a rule, equally fair to two or more wives, the spirit of Islam is clearly in favour of monogamy".[70] In Islam monogamy is [the] rule and polygamy an exception.

Ignorant writers have not only attributed polygamy to Islam, as if it was [a] purely Islamic institution, but have tried to show that Islam makes it obligatory for every Muslim to have more than one wife. The explanation of Sura Nisa verse 3 as discussed above and the fact that there is no other verse in the Qur'an permitting polygamy, makes the point crystal clear that polygamy is, by no means, obligatory upon Muslims, on the contrary, those Muslims who indulge in polygamy and do not observe equality between the wives or do not fulfil the financial obligations, they commit a sin, because, they go against the plain injunction of the Qur'an to be monogamous if they cannot be equitable and discharge the financial obligation. IS THERE ANY RELIGION WHICH MAKES POLYGAMY A SIN EVEN IN PARTICULAR CIRCUMSTANCES?

So the attitude of Islam towards polygamy may be summed up as under. The uncontrolled polygamy is, as much, opposed to the teachings of Islam as it is to the general progress of civilised society and true culture.

Islam is as much monogamous as other religions, the difference being that the former makes provision to solve exceptional and urgent social, moral and natural problems, with due regard to the conjugal rights of wives, but the latter [sic] leaves them unsolved.[71] Islam permits plurality of wives as a voluntary behavioural measure which the individual may or may not abrogate. Polygamy, in Islam, is in the nature of remedial or auxiliary provision to be resorted to in cases of emergency created by natural design. Islam recognises it as an institution of exceptional cases. Polygamy in Islam, is, in a word, a remedy. It is [the] exception rather than the rule. It has its uses and abuses.[72] Islam guards against the latter and allows the former under restrictions and within stringent limits. It is neither an offence nor an injunction and nor an article of faith. The status of polygamy in Islam is no more and no less than of a permissible act. And polygamy, like any other legal and permissible act becomes undesirable and, therefore, forbidden if [it] leads to unlawful consequences, such as injustice and discrimination. Islam neither instituted it nor ignored its reality and occurrence, it only adopted a middle course between categorical prohibition and unqualified liberalisation. Galwash rightly observed: "Besides the substantial laws, the code of Islam, as every wise legislation must do, provides certain ordinances which may be looked upon as auxiliary or remedial laws, with an elasticity to meet the contingencies of place and time. It deprecates their abuses, and lays down proper restrictions as to their use".[73]

For non-Muslims who do not believe in Qur'an and Sunna and for those Muslims, who by words and actions prove [that they] do not respect Qur'an and Sunna and want to judge everything from [a] material point of view and from their own imperfect standard I want to discuss the problem from that angle too.

Social, moral and natural justification of polygamy

A question may arise, why did Islam even permit polygamy under any circumstances? Or why Islam did not abolish it completely? The answer is that Islam permitted, restricted polygamy with a view to meet social, moral, economic and natural eventualities. An outright prohibition would probably remain an 'ideal' but hardly a pattern of actual behaviour. What Islam considered 1400 years ago as right is now being accepted as natural and inevitable by modern researchers, philosophers, scientists and reformers all over the world. The aforesaid verse of the Qur'an[74] which conditionally permits polygamy was revealed after a murderous battle, the battle of Uhud. Several Muslims were killed reducing the male population. Many young girls who had become orphans and the widows of the martyrs required support, shelter and protection. There was then a situation which made polygamy a necessity. The constitution of human society is such that on particular occasions men are more wasted. Hazards of life are greater for males than for the females.[75] In Europe the I and II World Wars created a similar situation. Because of freedom movements similar situations arose in Algeria and Vietnam. In [the] Middle East, South Africa, Afghanistan, Ethiopia, the Philippines, Sri Lanka and many other countries facing freedom movements a similar situation is being created. A similar situation may arise any time and anywhere in the world. [The] Prophet of Islam (SAW) was a religious teacher. He was a moralist. He, therefore, could not recognise unmarried mothers, and war babies nor could he ignore human nature. Single life for a woman is not natural. A woman in health and with natural vigour, if condemned to single life, will suffer the consequences of ignoring the demands of nature. Modern society may condone or connive at adultery, Mohammad (peace be on him) the Prophet of Islam could not. He had only two alternatives, either to permit polygamy under restrictions or to encourage immorality, corruption, adultery and illicit sexual connection. He selected the former, the natural course.

Stern[76] properly understood the position when he remarked that the introduction of the regularised and controlled polygamy by Islam was to solve emergent social and moral problems. Westermarck quotes a number of writers who advocate the legislation of polygamy on different grounds.[77] French sexologist Dr. Le Bon[78] has predicted that European legislation in future will recognise polygamy. He further observes that a return to polygamy, the natural relationship between the sexes, would be a remedy for evils like prostitution, venereal diseases, abortion, the misery of millions of unmarried women and mothers, adultery and even jealousy.

According to Havelock Ellis in *Psychology of sex*, James Hinton observes: "A forced monogamy is responsible for many of the evils of prostitution and leads to hatred, quarrels, intense jealousy and to an insistence on the mere physical relationship which turns purity into corruption. The women's natural jealousy is not so much at a man's loving another, but at his forsaking her".[79]

Dr. Norman Haire[80] maintains that legally controlled polygamy would offer many advantages to the majority of people. He further argues that if the children are supported by the State there need be no limit to the number of legal mates. This implies that if there is no economic constraint, a man may have as many wives as he can afford to.

Westermarck further observes that due to disproportion between the number of men and women of marriageable age about four per cent women are compelled to lead a single life in a monogamous system like ours. Polygamy, therefore, in such situation, becomes a social necessity provided it is on a restricted scale as permitted in Islam.

Mr. Mazharaddin Siddiqui in *Women in Islam* observes that in England, proposals were made in the 17th and 18th centuries, to legalise polygamy as a means of restraining infanticide, adultery, prostitution and the consequential evils of extra-marital sex relation.[81]

Bernard Shaw, the well-known thinker and writer advised his brethren in the West to adopt polygamy in order to save Europe from the inundation of adultery and prostitution.

Finally a return to polygamy has been proposed in several European countries following the two world wars, which threw the sex ratio far off balance and doomed millions of women to spinsterhood.[82]

According to McFarlane, polygamy is not contrary to the highest standard of civilisation. The suggestion offers a practical remedy for the Western problem of the destitute, unwanted females, the continued prostitution, concubinage and distressing spinsterhood.[83]

Nature also seems to favour polygamy. "Man" says Dr. Robinson, "is [a] strongly polygamous or varietist animal".[84] One of the grounds on which polygamy may be justified, according to Westermarck, is the strong and innate polygamous instinct of men as contrasted with women who are generally monogamous by nature. "The man's taste for variety in sex experience," says Westermarck, "is more intense than the woman's and this has led to the often repeated statement that he is instinctively polygamous".[85]

George Raleigh Scott declared that by nature man is essentially and intrinsically polygamous. Michels observes: "We regard it as beyond doubt that there is no man of whatever degree of virtue, who has not at least in imagination or in dream life, possessed more women than one".[86]

Miesel-Hess remarks that "in the man satiety ensues as soon as he has gained the goal of his desire. He wishes to pass on in search of fresh sexual experience, whereas the woman who has given herself up to a man clings to this person all the more firmly to him".[87]

According to Forel, woman is generally much more particular than man, in giving her love: While the normal man is, as a rule, attracted to coitus by nearly every more or less young and healthy woman, this by no means is the case in the normal woman. It is really impossible for her to experience sexual desire for several men at one and the same time.[88]

It is obvious that if a man is by nature, more strongly polygamous, the marriage law should not lose sight of this important fact and some provisions should be made for men in whom sexual instinct is more than normal, otherwise illegitimate sexual relations are likely to become more frequent.[89] If the society is to be saved from the evils of adultery, concubinage, prostitution and immorality, the laws and custom of the country must take full notice of man's nature and his biological needs.

Dr. Rom Landon observes: "In an imperfect world, such as we live in, polygamy must be considered both natural and legitimate. To eliminate polygamy we should first have to change entire character of our society and civilisation, the nature of man and finally the nature herself".[90] On the evidence of history and science it is imperative that polygamy should be recognised more honestly.[91] Prof. N. W. Ingells in an essay 'Biology of sex' says: "Man as an animal is anything but monogamous, and one would have great difficulty in explaining, biologically, such a sudden change of heart, the transition to a single [sic] wife.[92] So the recognition of polygamy in Islam is to check nature, to regulate nature, to improve nature but not to defy nature.

On socio-economic grounds a second marriage becomes inevitable under certain special circumstances e.g., wife's barrenness, perpetual illness leading to prolonged sexual abstinence and frigidity, unsuitability of cohabitation and the like. A complete prohibition of polygamy under any one of these circumstances commonly drives men to adultery and extra marital sex indulgence. A dissolution of the first marriage on the other hand is bound to be a curse rather than a blessing to the divorced wife in any of the above circumstances. History provides glaring examples of such miserable situation.[93] Modern research has shown that polygamy is not always a privilege of the man and a curse for the woman. Nor it is altogether anti-social.

Even Prof. J. N. Anderson,[94] a protagonist and staunch critic of Islamic law, had to concede that it would certainly be more beneficial to women to permit polygamy under specific conditions. He further observed that complete prohibition of polygamy in combination with ever increasing facilities of divorce would be a retrograde rather than progressive step, for it would mean that a man compelled or determined to marry a second wife would feel compelled to get the marriage dissolved taking help of extra-judicial or judicial procedure even by concocting false and indecent allegations against [the] first wife. The result will not be a different one, i.e. a second marriage as desired by the husband, but at the cost of total destruction of the first wife's personality and position in the society. This is in fact what a strictly monogamous system has to present to society.

Strict monogamy is bound to weaken the tie of marriage and encourage its dissolution. It is also bound to encourage infidelity, promiscuity, adultery, debauchery and extra-marital sex indulgence, as is now becoming common in the so called civilised West. They may even encourage the killing of wives as is the case among Hindus in India.

Dr. Rom Landon remarks that though [the] West prohibits polygamy [it] is forced to condone it, in times, by granting and liberalising divorce.[95]

Permission in Islam to have more than one wife at a time is an instant necessity. It sometimes becomes absolutely necessary for the preservation of social values and for safeguarding society against evils like debauchery, immorality and promiscuity. Islam permitted polygamy as a solution to social ills and has rightly allowed a certain degree of latitude to human nature.

The permission given by the Qur'an for controlled polygamy arose out of natural need and particular circumstances since nature is eternal and these circumstances are likely to recur now and then in the life of the Muslim community and since there will always be individual cases where polygamy may become necessary to avoid more serious moral and social evils. As a complex phenomenon, polygamy may help to solve some personal and social problems.

The above-mentioned reasons are more than enough to appreciate why Islam did not deem it expedient to abolish the institution of polygamy altogether. Islam restricted it by making conditional that full justice should be done to all wives. It was further discouraged by express provision that if one was afraid that he could not do justice he should limit himself to only one wife.[96]

Mr. Gustave Le Bon[97] says that so-called monogamy in most of the European countries is a sort of compromise between celibacy and polygamy. He further remarks that monogamy exists in modern Christian lands in books only. It is not practised and so although there is no legal validity for polygamy, the condition of society is worse than it would have been under a polygamous system. According to him, the statistics show that in France adultery increased 10 times after 1826, the year in which polygamy was legally prohibited. In America and Scandinavian countries, the concept of virginity is becoming [a] concept of history. In so-called monogamous countries of the West, cases of explicit and disguised polygamy are multiplying and are becoming quite common. The evidence shows that the West is de facto polygamous.[98] The new *Encyclopaedia Britannica* asserts that as an institution polygamy exists in all parts of the world.[99]

In *The conventional lies of our civilisation*, p. 301, Max Norden writes that man lives in a state of polygamy in so-called civilised countries in spite of the monogamy enforced by law. While M. Leplay goes a step further and says that polygamy is a social necessity under certain conditions of the society. Mrs. Annie Besant[100] says: "The true and righteous sex relation between one man and one woman is preached as an ideal in most of the western countries but is generally practised in none".

Islam permits conditional polygamy. Christiandom forbids but winks at it provided that no legal tie exists with more than one woman. There is pretended monogamy in the West, but in fact there is polygamy without responsibility. The mistress is cast off when the man becomes weary of her and she sinks generally to be the woman of the street, for the lover has no responsibility for her future and she is [a] hundred times worse than the sheltered wife and mother in a polygamous Muslim family. When we see thousands of miserable women who crowd the streets of towns in the West during night, we surely feel that it does not lie in the Western mouth to reproach Islam for its polygamy.

Prof. Gibs at the end of his book, *Modern trends in Islam*, rightly remarks: "Until the Western world puts its own house in order, it is no use asking the Islamic world to do the same".

Dr. Billy Graham honestly remarks:

> "Christianity cannot compromise on the question of polygamy. If present day Christianity cannot do so, it is to its own detriment. Islam has permitted polygamy as a solution to social ills and has allowed a certain degree of latitude to human nature but only within the strictly defined framework of the law. Christian countries make a great show of monogamy but actually they practice polygamy. No one is unaware of the part mistresses [sic] play in Western society. In this respect Islam is [a] fundamentally honest religion and permits a Muslim to marry a second wife if he must strictly forbidding [sic] all clandestine amatory associations in order to safeguard the moral polity of the community".[101]

So polygamy with all its evils has counter-balancing advantages. The strictly regulated polygamy in Islam is infinitely less degrading than the promiscuous polyandry which is the course of most of the 'so-called' civilised nations of the West.

It is better and happier and more respectful for a woman to live in an Islamic polygamy, united to one man only with the legitimate child in her arms, surrounded with respect and clothed with many matrimonial rights and privileges than to be seduced, cast out into [the] street perhaps with an illegitimate child outside the pale of law, unsheltered and uncared for, to become the victim of any passer-by, rendered incapable of motherhood, despised by all.

There is one more point which should not be lost sight of in this connection. It is this that woman herself is responsible, to a great extent, for the existence of the institution of polygamy. If all women were to refuse to marry a polygamous man there would have been no polygamy left. The

New *Encyclopaedia Britannica* mentions that women themselves prefer it for shared labour. Inspite of permitting polygamy Islam gives complete freedom and option to women in marriage. To secure, preserve and enjoy her peace of mind and happiness if a woman does not like to marry someone already having a wife, Islam does not compel her to marry such a suitor. In Nigeria, African and Middle Eastern countries girls, well-educated coming from well-to-do and respectable families, willingly opt for [a] polygamous home. The existence of polygamy proves that women tolerate it. And if this tolerance is, as it always was, to avoid a greater evil, then polygamy, as restricted in Islam, is not a curse but a blessing.

Western critics generally base their criticism on [the] presumption that polygamy breeds hatred, jealousy and non co-operation among co-wives which in turn [sic] wrecks the matrimonial life. But the fact that a Muslim woman, educated and financially well-off, having an option to reject a polygamous suitor and opt for a monogamous marriage (under [the] statutory system) does not generally resort to this option but happily settles down with a husband along with his existing wife/wives and children is enough proof that the criticism is not based on fact but on prejudice and imagination.

Polygamy, with all its incidents and consequences, in the context of African and Middle Eastern social life, is more than enough proof that a controlled polygamy, as permitted by Islam, is more a blessing than a curse. The cordiality, cooperation and understanding between co-wives in an African or Middle Eastern Muslim family is enough to shut the mouth of critics and enemies of Islam on the basis of its qualified permission of polygamy. Considering the above mentioned social, moral, economic, natural and special factors in support of polygamy, it was quite prudent and logical for Islam to recognise and tolerate, in a limited form, this important social institution. The beauty of Islam is that while it has stopped immorality and purified the society, it has by no means encouraged polygamy.

More knowledge of human needs and exigencies would enlighten the world and enable it to see the necessity of allowing and recognising an institution like polygamy with its rare and limited use as in Islam.

Relating to the question of validity or otherwise of modern legislations in the name of reforms, enacted by various Muslim countries in Asia and Africa, I have only to say that religiously and legally speaking, the State has no power and justification to abrogate, change or even modify the substantive provision of law expressly ordained in the Qur'an, clearly explained and illustrated by the Prophet (SAW) of Islam and unanimously practised by the companions of the Prophet (SAW) especially the rightly guided Caliphs (Khulfa El-Rashideen). Such an attempt is a clear case of *bidah*, i.e. innovation, which is strictly forbidden by Prophet Mohammed (SAW). He is reported to have said that all religious innovations stray you from the right path and all that strays you from the right path leads to hell.[102]

It is, therefore, religiously not permissible to abolish polygamy altogether. And what is not allowed religiously should not be legally done. But there is no harm, even very desirable and commendable, if [the] state in consultation with and approval of Ulemas and jurists of renowned [sic] legal and religious fame, evolve a procedure which tends to regulate and restrict polygamy as enjoined by the Qur'an and the Prophet of Islam. Even this needs expert investigation, analysis, assessment and a proper legislation. This is both desirable and necessary to curb the misuse of the permission accorded in the Holy Qur'an.[103]

Before I conclude it will be in the fitness of things to emphasise the most important aspect of the problem that Islamic law is a believers' law and, therefore, rests on faith and conviction. Islamic law, being purely religious in nature, is clearly outside the realm of academicians and secular authorities. Its responsibility lies only on the generality of the Muslims. They are the subjects of the law, they represent the law and the law represents them, they are loyal to the law, for the law articulates their beliefs, ideals and aspirations and sets forth their rights and duties. The academicians live outside this realm for they live in [a] dream world, unrelated to the people. The secular authorities also live outside this realm for they are bent on furthering so called secularism at the cost of religious beliefs. Islamic law, as it rests on faith and convictions can operate only when the believers consciously decide to implement it. Legal sanctions, no matter how effective, can be of no benefit.

3.3 Comparative legal training in action: A reluctant defence of polygamy

[From: 1990(2) *KLT*, Journal section, pp. 50–69]

This article responds partly to an essay at 1989(1) KLT J 47–58 (Khan 1989). As the title indicates ('Islamic polygamy – a blessing in disguise'), Mr. Khan wrote in defence of polygamy as an institution. However, while some points raised by the learned author are quite acceptable, his chain of argumentation shows serious flaws and logical fallacies which need comment in the wider context of the communal politics of modern Indian law and the debate on the Uniform Civil Code.

The essay appeared at a convenient time for me to use it as a tool to train students in the skills of dismantling a legal argument and of constructing an adequate response, with the aim of encouraging constructive criticism, an art that needs to be practised. Our resulting comments are here prefaced with some remarks on teaching young lawyers appropriate skills.

The need for more appropriate legal training

Legal practice, we are often told, is centrally concerned with justice and the public interest. In real life, though, lawyers are frequently tempted to put narrower or private interest first. Does legal training encourage deviousness?

There are remarkably many lawyer-politicians in the world, certainly not for want of legal business. The consequences for legal development, and for development processes generally, may become significant, especially if certain class interests gain priority (for India see Bardhan, 1984).[104] In such contexts, there are many incentives to play tricks on justice; in fact, the image of a blindfolded Justitia may have helped to encourage such attitudes.

Notably, the ancient Chinese, in line with many other traditional cultures, maintained a sceptical view of the role of lawyers, who were described as something like 'litigation tricksters' and whose activities were officially discouraged (van der Sprenkel, 1977: 69). Aspiring government officials were expected to study the Confucian classics rather than law, for which, like in ancient India, there was no exact equivalent in the language. Contemporary China, too, has not developed a consistent attitude of faith in lawyers and legal studies and remains distrustful of a specialist science that often holds itself out as divorced not only from religion and morality, but also separate from philosophy, sociology and related academic disciplines.

In any legal system, in my submission, the training of young lawyers is much more than a matter of academic or practical routine. One is at the same time in the business of forming personalities and character-building, increasing knowledge and developing skills. A holistic view of legal training is, however, not often taken, and is certainly not taken seriously enough, in Britain as well as in India, with the inevitable result that much lawyering remains not only bad craftsmanship but often morally dubitable.

Solid legal training must insist that students pay attention to the grand concepts of law as much as to little technical details. In my experience, young lawyers who do not bother to spell correctly will also not follow precision in their argument. The same individuals may also show scant regard for the moral dimensions of legal work. If such individuals 'make it' to the profession, all too often, in the end, the burden falls on an already overworked judiciary to tutor and correct such lawyers and to keep them in check. For it is ultimately the judiciary that has to ensure that the often feeble voice of justice is heard in the jungle of conflicting and sometimes self-contradictory submissions with its cacophony of disharmonious and twisted noises from a variety of sources. Indian law has a number of fine examples of judicial perceptiveness in this regard, even in such grand cases as *Kesavananda Bharati* [(1973) 4 SCC 225].

Concern with developing appropriate forms of legal training leads one to the idea that, apart from teaching 'the law', we must focus student attention on legal methods and skills. But it is not sufficient to nurture the art of developing one's own argument in a coherent fashion; equal importance must be given to the cultivation of another, closely related skill, taking a critical view of one's own or, better at first, someone else's product or argument.

Thus, I now regularly expect students to produce a critical analysis of a piece of academic legal writing, be it a learned article, a chapter from a book or a case report. This may be hard initially, as one has to overcome certain barriers, but the capacity for critical and rational analysis of arguments put forward by another person is a crucially important skill, not only for lawyers. This technique is also practised in moot competitions, though in a more instant and therefore often haphazard fashion; it is much needed in later life, in court as well as in office situations.

There are obvious differences between responding to an argument in a courtroom situation and answering a point made in writing. Some of us are good in one, but not the other. Ideally, both types of skill should be taught, and they can be taught! It seems to me, however, that the academic stage of legal training, in Britain as well as in India, does not pay sufficient attention to this aspect. Some recognition of this deficiency is now evident in Britain: the professional stage of legal training at the Bar has been restructured to place greater emphasis on practical skills rather than the unreflected acquisition of masses of information. India, too, would benefit from some reform in this area, though an appropriate training 'on the job' does often take care of this matter.

With these issues in mind, I invited my students of 'Law and Society in South Asia' to sharpen their skills of analysis and adequate response. Mr. Khan's essay, on a tricky issue of family law, proved ideal for this. Last year's group had done a similar exercise on an article on divorce (see Haq 1988 and Menski 1989),[105] now the issue was polygamy, or was it Islamic polygamy? Or what was it really?

An Indian lawyer's defence of polygamy

The article we comment on here was written by a Reader in Law at Aligarh Muslim University, no doubt a respectable place of learning in India. It appears to be a serious piece of scholarship, but it combines a number of skillfully constructed arguments with a few academically questionable elements. The resulting self-contradictions are not difficult to locate, but to fully disentangle the complex network of logically sound and unsound arguments and to separate fact and ideology in this article was a hard nut to crack. Most of my 20 students, who come from all over the world, have no axe to grind with the author, and include many Muslims, found themselves shocked into action by this essay. The present response is to a considerable extent based on our collective efforts.

It is fairly apparent that the article falls basically into three parts. The first, after a short introduction (the first para), argues that polygamy was, and continues to be, a universal phenomenon (pp. 47–49) and, less convincingly, that it remains 'an important social institution' (p. 47). The second part (pp. 50–53) focuses on the nature and extent of polygamy in Islam, while the third (pp. 53–58) presents a range of social, moral and even natural justifications for polygamy. The article concludes, in the last three paras, with some important comments on the place of polygamy in modern Indian law. We shall have to return to those comments later, for only at this late point, as it were, is the *parda* of rhetoric, in which the arguments are clothed, slightly lifted to reveal a glimpse of the true message of this article: Hands off Islam and Islamic law! Hands off Muslim polygamy! No state interference in Islamic law in India!

The underlying central argument of the essay is remarkably similar to that advanced a few years ago by the leading Muslim law scholar in modern India (Mahmood 1986) and is in line with the reasoning of other Muslim scholars (e.g. Haq 1988) that Islamic law provides a useful model for the development of modern Indian family laws. In principle, the essay adds nothing new to the discussion, but it introduces an unfortunate tone and goes too far in its advocacy of polygamy.

It is probably common knowledge that the introductory and concluding parts of a piece of writing often provide much insight into the author's arguments. We have just looked at the conclusion, let us now turn to the introduction, which contains several crucial clues about how the writer perceives the issue under debate and how he intends to argue. Since he starts, in my submission, on the wrong foot, we need a disproportionate amount of comment on this short paragraph.

The argument begins in a very defensive mould, stating at once that polygamy is the most criticised aspect of Islamic family law and that Islam has been misrepresented by Western and non-Muslim writers so as to make it look repulsive. This is, of course, to an extent, true not only for polygamy, but for many aspects of Islamic law, notably criminal laws. By adopting a defensive posture, characteristic of minorities who see themselves as oppressed or threatened, Mr. Khan introduces at once an unfortunate antagonistic undertone which had evidently distracted from the real issue. Instead, a rather demagogic strand of argument continues. Thus I doubt whether it is factually correct to state generally that Islam has been charged by the West or now, more recently, "in free India by enemies of Islam" with "originating and advocating polygamy" (p. 47).

It would be wise to rely on historical facts here rather than bloated arguments: Nobody could reasonably maintain that Islam invented polygamy. As a late-comer to the club of world religions, it could not really be charged with 'originating' very much, least of all polygamy! Mr. Khan himself clarifies this later by emphasising, correctly, that early Islam modified and in fact improved the existing rules on polygamy in pre-Islamic Arabic societies (p. 49). Here, then, is a purposely exaggerated claim, perhaps put up to rally Muslim support, but easily demolished.

That leaves the charge of advocating polygamy. It is no malicious allegation to say that Islam does this: it is the truth, though only to a certain extent, as it were, since we must point out at once that all Muslims do not speak with one voice on this issue. The reason is well-known: the interpretation of the small amount of Qur'anic material on polygamy is, for good reasons, heavily disputed. Many Muslims in the world accept the so-called liberal Tunisian approach, which has led to an official ban on polygamous marriages imposed in a Muslim country. Syria, another

Muslim country, has developed the idea that polygamy must be strictly controlled.

It would, thus, be wrong for anyone to allege in sweeping terms that Islam advocates polygamy. The truth is, rather, that many spokesmen of Islam do this, including Mr. Khan, who has thus debarred himself from employing the above liberal arguments to protect Islam against unjustified charges. The reason must be that he sees the Tunisian reforms as wrong, which is probably why he does not even mention them. But for how long can one make unpalatable facts non-existent by keeping quiet about them and ignoring them in scholarly articles? The essay is, unfortunately, also a blatant attempt to repress diversity of opinions in Islam by the way it attacks any innovations as "strictly forbidden" (p. 58).

Sensibly enough, yet only much later, and too late to be convincing, it is stated that Islam does not really advocate polygamy, but merely allows it and seeks to regulate it (p. 49). These are again defensive comments which are very much contradicted by the subsequent crass argument that polygamy is a natural necessity for men.

We are not re-writing Mr. Khan's essay here, but is would have been much more honest to state, at the outset, some basic legal facts: in the context of modern Indian law, Islamic law is the only legal system that continues to allow polygamous marriages today. The issue would then at once have been whether a Uniform Civil Code for India, envisaged as an ultimate goal by Article 44 of the Constitution of India, should respect this element of Indian Muslim law and how it should regulate polygamy. It is significant that the learned author meticulously avoids any reference to the Uniform Civil Code throughout the essay. This technique to ignore crucial realities and real issues that one does not like, or that do not fit one's argument or theory, as already observed, does not augur well for a scholarly enquiry. As a result, several of us were tempted to dismiss the whole piece as cheap demagogic, but this would do injustice to the learned author and would not be a constructive criticism.

The first substantive part of the essay (pp. 47–49) focuses on the universality of polygamy. The major argument is that in all periods of human civilisation, and even today, polygamy has had an established place as an important social institution (p. 47). A very mixed bag of evidence is provided, jumping a bit too rapidly from one country and period to another, so that the polyandry of Draupadi, for example, is instantly followed by the German philosopher Schopenhauer's views on polygamy. More could, no doubt, have been said about the important discussion of polygamy in Africa, where the Christian churches continue to face much opposition to their teaching on the need for monogamy.

While there is much truth in the general argument that polygamy was, in the past, a more or less universal phenomenon, some assertions found here do go too far and invite odd interpretations. Thus, the portrayal of polygamy as a "law which has few exceptions" (p. 47) must be read in context, and to argue that polygamy was "an established institution from time immemorial" (p. 49) should not be misinterpreted: it is doubtful whether polygamy was ever a binding norm in any society. To say that it was "an accepted way of life" (p. 47) or even "the preferred type" of family organisation in certain societies (p. 49) probably goes too far. The repeated statement that certain religious traditions did not explicitly prohibit polygamy is certainly a valid point, but the inference drawn can hardly be that such traditions, therefore, freely allowed polygamy.

The chain of arguments becomes seriously flawed when we turn to present-day conditions. Apart from a general indication that polygamy has become condemned by modern society (p. 48), there is no evidence that this difficult aspect of the question has been addressed at all. Instead, the issue is obfuscated by an odd attack on Hindu culture as, till recently, "extremely unfavourable to women" (p.49). It is not clear how this fits in with the advocacy of polygamy as a universal phenomenon. Further, the author advances proof that Hindus in various parts of the country still practice polygamy under Hindu law, overlooking the perhaps rather crucial fact that the recent edition of a famous book on Hindu law (Jolly 1975) is a reprint of a work which was originally published in German in 1896 and first appeared in English in 1928! At that time, of course, Hindus could legally indulge in polygamy. One hopes that any Indian law student in his/her first year would instantly spot this confusion, which, moreover, deprives the author of a potentially valuable argument: he overlooks that modern Hindu law has outlawed polygamy by sections 5(i) and 11 of the *Hindu Marriage Act* of 1955, but that, in fact, many Hindus continue to make polygamous arrangements despite this drastic change in the law, which criminalises bigamists in section 17 of the same Act. He could also have used such evidence to strengthen the fruitful line of argument that many legal systems appears to have allowed polygamy in certain situations and on specific conditions. Of course, such reasoning is not really viable if one actually wants to argue, as the author later proceeds to do, that men should be free to make any polygamous arrangements they like.

This part ends (in the last two paras of p. 49) with the familiar reasoning that Islamic law is more advanced in regulating bigamy than other legal systems. The claim is that it reformed and improved the existing law, limiting the number of wives to four, and "laying down strict conditions for having more than one wife at a time" (p. 49). As a result, the author argues that polygamy "is therefore, both checked and regulated in Islam" which, then, "neither originated nor advocated nor even encouraged it" (p. 49). This conclusion sounds convincing and correct at this point of the essay.

In the next major part (pp. 50–53) which focuses on the nature and extent of polygamy recognised in Islam, the author elaborates on the nature of the Qur'anic injunctions regarding polygamy and their interpretation. Sensibly, the discussion starts with reference to the only Qur'anic verse on polygamy, verse 3 in Sura Nisa. It is rightly pointed out that this does not enjoin polygamy, but permits it under strict conditions, which, it is argued with considerable force, must be understood to mean equal treatment of wives in terms of material provisions and favours only, not in terms of emotions and affections. This is so because equality of treatment in that area is not humanly possible and therefore it could not have been intended by Allah to make such a tight condition. The ease with which certain motives are here presumed in the actions of the Islamic God is truly amazing. Considerable effort is then made to argue that all renowned commentators on the Holy Qur'an "are in perfect agreement to this interpretation" (p. 51).

This, of course, is less than honest. The author gives this away by making repeated reference to "ignorant and biased critics", who apparently include not only Western non-believers, but many 'misguided' Muslims with their "imperfect standard" (p. 53). Sadly, by setting his own interpretation up as the only correct one, it would appear that our learned author does exactly what the Prophet said one should not do (see p. 51 and note 49)!

Despite the above-mentioned reservations, the conclusions reached in this part, too, remain convincing and proper: Uncontrolled polygamy is opposed to the teachings of Islam, keeping it, as the author is keen to emphasise, in line with the ideas of civilised society and "true culture" (p. 52). Thus, not only is Islamic polygamy an exception rather than the rule, Islam also provides safeguards against its abuses and has evolved stringent limits for that purpose. In sum, Islam adopted what appears to be a reasonable "middle course between categorical prohibition and unqualified liberalisation" (p. 53).

So far, so good, it seemed to us. But at the same time the learned author has already made some disturbing asides that shatter the aura of reasonableness created around Islamic polygamy. The full impact of that message is only brought home on the last few pages of the article. Yet the issue is anticipated here: Polygamy is held up as a remedy to solve exceptional and urgent social, moral and natural problems (p. 52). It is described as being "in the nature of a remedial or auxiliary provision to be resorted to in cases of emergency created by natural design" (p. 53). What this may mean or imply is not explained at this point. We are merely assured that due regard is given to the conjugal rights of wives (p. 52) and the voluntary nature of this remedy is pointed out in general terms (p. 53).

Only in the third part of the essay does the author reveal his actual position. Under the heading "social, moral and natural justification of polygamy" (pp. 53–58), we find a remarkable volte-face, a chain of argumentation that virtually destroys all the valuable work in the first two parts.

The author first argues that an outright prohibition of polygamy would hardly lead to a pattern of actual behaviour. Having studied bigamy in modern Hindu law and the Supreme Court's collusion in its perpetuation, and being familiar with Eugen Ehrlich's theory of the universal phenomenon of 'living law', my students readily accepted that comment. Detailed socio-legal enquiry on this point could have provided useful arguments for the author.

But he was single-mindedly concerned to pursue the issue of the need for polygamy, which is taken up once again. Now the answer is slightly more vague than a moment ago: Islam permitted and restricted polygamy "with a view to meet social, moral, economic and natural *eventualities* (our emphasis) (p. 53). Then the argument is advanced that Islam was the first to see the positive side of polygamy and that, 1400 years later, this "is now being accepted as natural and inevitable by modern researchers, philosophers, scientists and reformers all over the world" (p. 53). This goes, of course, much further than saying that polygamy is a remedy in exceptional cases. Here the author begins to argue for polygamy as a necessary institution, on several grounds. The first one is well-known in Islamic studies and relates to the situation after a famous battle, which left many women and children without male protection. The same situation, the author argues, occured in many European countries as a result of the two world wars, and has arisen in many other parts of the world. In Mr. Khan's submission, Islam showed the right path by allowing polygamy with some restrictions, and the world would do well to follow this model. His argument may be respected, but the actual facts are different: in several European countries, especially Germany, millions of women did not become polygamous, but remained unmarried because of unavailability of men in their age groups; this has become socially acceptable and has caused no noticeable adverse moral effects. The facts are that many women in those countries, and elsewhere, have become self-supporting. Polygamy is, therefore, only one possible way to alleviate particular social problems.

Interestingly enough, in Britain today, an odd artificial shortage of marriageable Asian males has been created by the impact of the immigration laws, in particular the notorious "primary purpose" rule, whose declared aim is to destroy transnational arranged marriage patterns among Asians. As a result, many young (and now not so young!) Asian women in Britain today, whether Hindu, Muslim or Sikh, face an agonising choice between remaining unmarried or marrying 'out of caste', which often means marrying a European. Two other commonly employed strategies carry considerable risks: to keep looking for the right spouse may lead to ultimate spinsterhood, while the decision to move out of the UK for the purpose of marriage means added disruptions for such women and may not be an attractive option at all. I have not yet heard of calls for the re-introduction of polygamy in this context, but this may be expected.

Our learned author next progresses to a powerful religious and moral reason to justify not only Islamic polygamy, but polygamy generally: The Prophet of Islam, as a religious teacher and moralist, "could not recognise unmarried mothers and war babies nor could he ignore human nature" (p. 53). The switching of words here is significant: war widows and orphans have suddenly turned into "unmarried mothers" and "war babies", i.e. illicit sexual relations are ominously hinted at. Worse, the author suddenly argues that "single life for a woman is not natural" (p. 53), that such a woman will suffer and that this would lead to adultery. Therefore, the author concludes with characteristic omniscience, the Prophet of Islam did the right thing by allowing polygamy to males.

We are not told why it is that women cannot bear living a single life. The hidden argument here is, of course, a very familiar one for Hindus and Sikhs, too: women are not trustworthy and must be kept under male control all their lives. Otherwise unchastity will result. This obsessive fear of violation of the chastity principle, linked with *izzat* (honour) in many parts of South Asia, and powerfully expressed in the Islamic concept of *zina* remains, of course, a major axis of sexual morality in all South Asian societies, even abroad. But we cannot overlook the oddly justified sexual discrimination in this approach: nowhere, at this point, is there a reference to male sexuality and the danger of seduction by men who, as is powerfully argued further below, have by nature an insatiable appetite for sex.

The present one-sided and twisted argumentation, therefore, does not disclose openly that it is abhorrence of *zina* which is here used to justify a basic rule that every woman must be married to one man, while any one man may be allowed several wives. Females in general, and unmarried females in particular, are thus in the familiar way portrayed as a moral danger to society. As a result, to permit polygamy was "the natural course" (p. 53) and a little later polygamy is even advanced as "the natural relationship between the sexes" (p. 54), apparently because it facilitates legalised sexual relations. The argument then turns again to Western scholars who made comments in favour of polygamy, against forced monogamy and for the re-introduction of polygamy into European countries to alleviate the miseries of millions of "doomed" women, plus all kinds of social evils. Not content with such sweeping array of arguments in favour of polygamy, the author then proceeds to his final invincible argument: "Nature also seems to favour polygamy" (p. 54). Some of my students could hardly believe what they read: it is argued here that males need polygamy, that they are by nature polygamous!

What about women, then? Somebody noted that the argument was, a page earlier, that women will suffer if sex was denied to them. If men are by nature polygamous, are women by nature polyandrous? One female student declared herself ready to accept polygamy, provided polyandry was also legally recognised.

It is fascinating to follow up how our learned author has arrived at his odd conclusion. He has taken a general reference to "man" (p. 54) as referring to "men" only! It does not help the learned scholar to rely on Westermarck, no doubt a great authority, but seriously outdated in many respects today. The conclusion drawn is, thus, simply bogus and unscientific.

Now, if men are according to Westermarck and Khan, "instinctively polygamous" (p. 55), while women find it "impossible ... to experience sexual desire for several men at one and the same time" (*id.*), should not a reasonable law protect men from their own desires, and women from male lasciviousness, rather than the other way round? How, we may ask, can women be blamed for sexual immorality in the world if Mother Nature has given insatiable sexual appetite to "the normal man" (p. 55), while the "normal woman" (*id.*) clings to the one man she knows? A serious attempt to devise a law of polygamy that protects women, if that is indeed the aim (which, of course, it is not in Mr. Khan's argumentation!) must obviously advocate the restriction of male sexuality. This may well be what the Qur'an intended, but the present twisted demagogic, dressed up as an academic discussion, leads only to further distortions.

For, the argument proceeds to inject the important comment that a good marriage law should not lose sight of natural realities. Fully agreed, in principle. But our suggestions vary dramatically: We have just argued for controlled bigamy to discourage male sexual greed. Mr. Khan pleads ominously that "some provisions should be made for men in whom sexual instinct is more than normal, otherwise illegitimate sexual relations are likely to become more frequent" (p. 55).

What does this suggestion amount to? The author's argument is now no longer that polygamy is a social necessity to take care of certain women and children, now it is held up as a natural necessity. To restrict polygamy would be to defy nature. At this point, more than anywhere else, Mr. Khan is clearly most concerned with avoidance of *zina*, which is later referred to as "a greater evil" than polygamy (p. 57).

Allowing polygamy, in this context, is thus nothing but a clever device to legitimise sexual relations that may otherwise be illicit. This could almost mean a return to pre-Islamic conditions, since, as one of us discovered, a man who had exhausted his quota of four sex partners would presumably not automatically lose his appetite for more. Divorce law is mentioned, but our learned author is careful not to indicate the possibility of getting rid of wives who may no longer be sexually attractive. We may need to be reminded here of the facts in the *Shah Bano* case; the mere possibility of abuse is reason enough to build in some restrictions. The author is equally careful not to make any reference to *mut'a* marriages, only allowed to Shia Muslims, of course, which serve precisely the same purpose, i.e. to avoid a charge of *zina*.

In the end, the attempted portrayal of Islamic polygamy as a blessing in disguise has badly backfired. Worst of all, it has done much damage to the rightful argument by the Muslims of India that their personal law should be respected in an acceptable form and democratically impeccable way. That polygamy can be a useful legal remedy in certain difficult social situations may not be deniable. A blanket allowance for polygamy – for this is what the argument amounts to in the end – may indeed help to solve some problems, in particular it may reduce *zina*, but it would certainly create new problems and is clearly unacceptable as it stands here.

Summary of our objections

We found Mr. Khan's hesitating argument that women would benefit from polygamous arrangements only partly acceptable and were not at all convinced that Muslim women had as much choice in the matter as one would make us believe. It seemed typical male arrogance to even suggest that women themselves were responsible for polygamy. The author's twisted logic has clearly enough shown the overriding concern that male sexual caprice should not be discouraged to avoid the "greater evil" of *zina*. Some of us found it ludicrous to say that women prefer polygamy, and several commented to the effect that women may have no option but to accept a man's polygamous arrangements, particularly in a society which sees polygamy as more than a remedy for certain socio-economic difficulties. There would, then, be little hope for individual women to keep out of such arrangements; many may have no option but to accept. Therefore the apparent toleration of polygamy by women in a society does not prove anything at all.

This does not mean that one has to argue immediately for a total and absolute ban on bigamy. Several of us remain convinced that carefully regulated bigamy, in the sense referred to by Derrett (1970: 309), can be justified on social, economic and moral grounds. While we also have doubts whether the copying of Western legal models, such as compulsory monogamy, makes sense in Indian conditions, we have been objecting here to the way in which an Indian Muslim law teacher argues for virtually unlimited polygamy. We were amazed, if not shocked, about the irrationality of some arguments, especially the grossly exaggerated distinctions between male and female nature. We found this an unfortunate piece of legal writing, irresponsibly demagogic, damaging to community relations by the way it snipes at Hindus and at the West, seeking, ultimately, to portray the Islamic perspective as superior, though it is apparent that there is no consensus about polygamy among all Muslims and that Muslim polygamy, as it exists in India, is a far cry from the original ideal.

We accept that the regulation of Islamic polygamy 1400 years ago may have been a wise and bold innovation inspired by the ideals of Islam. But Mr. Khan shows that, unfortunately, such high ideals have been adulterated over time. The author's attempt to declare as outlawed all innovation in Islam seems, thus, particularly obnoxious and is symptomatic of a siege mentality. At he end, the author himself is so confused that in an attempt to declare academics as useless day-dreamers he pulls the rug from under his own feet. The only real message, finally, is that the state in modern India has no right to regulate any aspect of Islamic law. If that was all the learned author really wanted to say, he could have done so in a less cumbersome way, making a constructive contribution to the present Indian debate on how to regulate polygamy. In fact, the author has done a great disservice to the Muslim position on this question, inviting harsh criticism not only of himself, but of that Muslim position which he so vigorously portrays as the 'true' one.

While we respect the stance of the Muslim believers, we are here responding to a piece of legal writing in a learned legal journal. One may, therefore, expect certain minimum standards of academic and legal reasoning; these seem to have been debased here. While superficially controlled polygamy is subtly offered to the world as an ideal model, in a second strand of arguments closer to reality, it serves obviously to legitimise the passions of some rich, sex-hungry men. This exercise in bigotry offers a slightly too cheap accommodating measure for the lack of self-control of man as understood by Mr. Khan.

It is a dubious argument that most civilised societies *began* with polygamy, since there is an obvious difference between not directly forbidding something and expressly allowing it. The fact that polygamy existed earlier does not mean much today, and the essay certainly failed to address the question why polygamy has fallen into such disrepute, even among Muslims. His distinctions between past and present are shaky, to say the least, he makes sweeping statements and holds obscure views on the natural differentials of the sexes, and uses simplistic generalised assumptions about the West. We were not concerned to defend the Western system as such: it is a valid assertion that the relaxation of divorce laws has encouraged serial polygamy and a less responsible attitude towards marriage. Unfortunately the same is now largely true of countries like India that have found it wise to follow the Western model. Thus, such points do not allow a conclusion that "the West is de facto polygamous" (p. 56), and it certainly goes over the top to depict thousands of miserable women crowding the streets of Western cities at night or to assert that every man in the West has a mistress. What Mr. Khan really objects to is hidden away in a verbose aside, arguing that Muslim polygamy is "infinitely less degrading than the promiscuous polyandry . . . of the West" (p. 57). So here we are again: it is fine for men to philander, but women must stick to one man! Apparently our learned author did not realise that his system of respecting the natural urges of men must inevitably lead to serial polyandry.

For, is there any evidence, one must ask, that the law of nature changes for an Islamic husband after the fourth marriage? To give a free rein to 'natural' male urges makes nonsense of the whole Islamic system of controlled polygamy with its requirement of equal treatment and shows how ingenious the *mut'a* concept really is, as was, by the way, the Chinese system of allowing a man one 'wife', but a number of 'concubines', if he could cope with that. What Mr. Khan has not told us, of course, is that a Muslim divorce can be brought about faster than a marriage, that a Muslim wife has really no 'locus standi' in such 'proceedings', which are still giving so much discomfort also to judges in Britain. Most Muslim wives remain defenseless against male caprice of any kind. While the author attacks Western men for discarding women when they are weary of them, he fails to admit that Muslim husbands may be no better. To give an idealised picture of Islamic law and the real picture of Western practices is clearly not a fair method of comparative study, and one is constrained to make the point again that this essay is a model exercise in academic deviousness.

It is, thus, quite apparent that any system of Islamic polygamy does not magically cure all social evils in Islamic societies. Worse, the way Islamic polygamy is advertised here gives quite unlimited discretion to male indulgence. It will encourage men to think that they have a God-given natural right to several women, while women are told to remain fixed to one man. Such crass biological determinism left more than half of my class angry and disgusted, which clearly shows that Mr. Khan runs a danger of creating enemies of Islam, giving people a good reason to 'bash the Muslims'. His arrogantly biased and hence internally contradictory piece of legal writing, which hides, in the end, behind religious authority to justify its aggressive, male chauvinist stance, which does not appear to us as purely Islamic, makes such an attempt at legal scholarship liable not only to misunderstanding, but also to misuse. We have tried here to develop constructive criticisms, but this has been very difficult throughout, especially in view of the antagonistic tone and the author's chameleon-like practice to change colours as he goes along, turning an initially acceptable and reasonable argument into quite reprehensible pseudo-scholarship that hides behind Islamic authority as a smokescreen.

In reluctant defence of polygamy

Despite our objections to the mischievous argumentation above and a variety of reservations against polygamy *per se*, there are several valid grounds to suggest that, in certain situations and on certain conditions, polygamous marital arrangements may be a desirable remedy for some problematic social and economic situations. This, in my submission, and from a comparative legal viewpoint that questions the axiom of the inherent superiority of everything Western, should be recognised by an appropriate legal system.

Thus, one can hardly fault the rationale of early Islam that not only allowed, but virtually expected men to take care of war widows and orphans. Whether support must necessarily be given by actually marrying the women is, however, questionable. Could genuine assistance not just as well be achieved by a form of charity, such as *zakat*, so that polygamy would here still be an excuse for male possessiveness? I disagree: merely to provide for the material needs of a person deprives him, or her, as the case may be, of equally important emotional and other social comforts. The same objection is, in principle, valid against modern forms of state welfare, which may provide some material benefits, but leave recipients in social isolation, if not permanently degraded because of the status differentiation that has been created and is perpetuated in this way. We must understand, I think, that such impersonal forms of welfare benefit leave people in an emotional vacuum and can never be a full replacement of supportive personal relationships that integrate or re-incorporate the individuals concerned into their particular social spheres. Oriental legal systems have no difficulties seeing the matter in this way. Of course, a purely individualistic rationale will be opposed to this kind of argumentation, but total individualism, while not absent as a concept in Oriental laws, does not make much sense there as a basic principle of organising human existence.

As we saw, the Islamic argument for allowing polygamous arrangements seems to be conducted on two level: (i) let us take care of individuals in society that are in need of support and (ii) let us avoid *zina*.

In a society where women do not object to such 'protection', the law would indeed do well to recognise such polygamous arrangements and I would agree that Islamic law developed, in this regard, a reasonable approach to a complex problem. It would be helpful, though, to have some material and evidence from the experts on some crucial questions: To what extent have Muslim women in various parts of the world a real choice between taking up an offer of male protection, support from charitable funds, or other sources of sustenance? Does tradition provide authoritative guidance on this point, and what evidence can be found in various Muslim societies? If it could be shown that Muslim women have indeed a choice here, not just in theory, but in practice, then I would find such a system more acceptable.

Traditional Hindu law appears to have devised another system of looking after potentially destitute women without the need for polygamous unions. Vasudha Dhagamwar has recently made reference to Panjab cases where young widowed women (Sikhs, apparently) needed a customary divorce from their father-in-law if they wanted to re-marry within their community (Dhagamwar, 1989: 65). To see this as evidence of actual polygamy or of de-facto marriage between these two partners may be going a bit too far. It is known that some traditional forms of Hindu law saw marriage, in principle, as transfer of the procreative potential of the bride to a family rather than to an individual man. Should the husband die, the wife would be provided for in the family, often, but not necessarily, as far as I am aware, by marrying a family member. From this tradition follows the fact that "levirate marriages are not unknown to North India" (Dhagamwar, 1989: 65; see also Diwan, 1980). But levirate marriages are not actually polygamous unions, and the fact that, as Dhagamwar reports, such women are apparently allowed to marry a man from outside the family shows that an element of female choice is not excluded. Similar to Islamic law, though, this phenomenon of Hindu law is designed to take care, in every respect, of a woman who has lost her husband. Again, if a woman agrees to such arrangements, what is wrong with them? One gets a feeling that much modern legal scholarship in India objects to tradition *per se* without bothering to consider the potential positive sides of non-state legal systems. A somewhat precarious balance will need to be struck in many cases.

Both the Islamic approach to polygamy and the Hindu system of levirate developed many centuries ago. Both reacted, presumably and sensibly, to social realities at that time. However, socio-economic conditions have since changed: war widows and orphans are more commonly taken care of, in economic terms, by state benefits of various kinds, at least in most developed countries and, with some hitches, as *Ram Pyari*, AIR 1988 Raj 124 shows, also in some developing countries, yet by no means everywhere. It would appear, though, that more and more women have become (or have had to become) economically independent to a larger extent, and thus able to stand on their own feet. In such situations it is seen again that economic factors have an important bearing, but with differential social consequences: while a rich man may be able to afford several sets of wives and offspring, a reasonably well-to-do woman, especially in the lower classes, where women have traditionally been less dependent on status considerations that demand their dependence on males, can buy herself at least some independence (see Gulati, 1981), often by divorcing herself from a male parasite.

For different kinds of middle class women, Rama Mehta (1975) has shown us clear distinctions in their extent and perception of freedom, while a more recent socio-legal study (Dhagamwar, 1987) has provided evidence that many women are prevented by economic factors from actively seeking divorce to free themselves from unacceptable domestic situations. We are, thus, though at tremendous cost, reaching a situation in India that divorce is becoming more and more common and, as a result, more women prefer to stay on their own, either as spinsters, refusing marriage altogether, or not remarrying after a divorce or the death of the spouse. Very many women would find the thought of being part of a polygamous arrangement quite repulsive.

Of course, Mr. Khan never considered the issue from the female perspective. But he would, no doubt, concur with a recent study that deplores the ease with which women can gain divorce and can thus treat divorce as "a sort of an insurance deal offering far more lucrative benefits than available in marriage" (Mahmood, 1986: 127). This line of argument indicates, apart from unease, to put it mildly, about the development of modern India's laws on maintenance for divorced women, that the really objectionable development is, in the eyes of many South Asian men, that more and more women manage to survive decently without male protection. The viability, and almost possibility of this happening, is constantly denied by dubious implication, especially when charges of prostitution are raised against any unattached woman. Female independence seems clearly anathema to the rationale of Mr. Khan and like-minded men and they would prefer to see them securely locked away in polygamous unions rather then 'roaming the streets at night'.

I am not arguing that it is ideal for anyone to stay on their own, since the price one may have to pay in emotional terms may be very huge. Yet it is a fact of life that modern societies tend to emphasise individualism and allow many of us to stay on our own if we can afford to do so in economic and emotional terms. A major difficulty is, perhaps, that most of us really cannot bear the solitude of individual freedom for long. The remedy is not, in the views of many people today, to enter a marriage, and certainly not to enter polygamous marriages. Critics of the Western system have a point, though, when they refer generally to dishonesty in this regard

(Mahmood, 1986: 115) or point to "pretended monogamy" with further consequences for sexual morality (Khan, 1989: 57). While marriage today seems indeed a bit less of the universal phenomenon that it probably used to be, and the pressure to enter polygamous unions will have become even less as a result, Western Casanovas may prefer to remain unmarried altogether, while their Oriental counterparts receive welcome assistance by constructions of new justifications for polygamy.

The above-mentioned factors all serve to reduce the need for polygamous arrangements of the traditional type as envisaged by Islam. In what situations, then, may polygamy still be a reasonable remedy in modern Indian law today?

One situation that comes to mind first is childlessness of a couple (see also Derrett, 1970: 307). The instant answer to that, today, is often that one should not be too concerned, as there are already many people in the world, but that is a cruel response to a couple desperately wishing to have children. The other remedy often instantly offered is adoption, but the Indian laws on adoption do not exactly inspire confidence. Many people, at any rate, are not swayed by the legal fiction of adoption, even if it were easily accomplished. So neither way may recommend itself to all couples. The intense interest with which advances on the medical front in remedying infertility are followed, not just in the West, speaks volumes for the desire of people to have their own child, and many gods would be 'out of business' if childlessness were not an important concern.

Childnessness, of course, may be due to a defect in the husband rather than the wife, though South Asians generally tend to blame the wife for this, as well as, even more irrationally, for producing children of the 'wrong' sex. I have so far found little evidence through fieldwork in India that men whose wives bore only daughters would want to look for a second wife, or another wife. There are, however, as only reading law reports, often between the lines, can teach, a lot of cases where a marriage has remained issueless for one reason or another, and the couple end up in court. If the reason is obviously the wife's infertility, as in *Vinod Chandra Dube*, AIR 1977 Del 24, a conscientious husband may be at great pains to make new arrangements; the modern Hindu law would not allow any polygamous arrangement, of course. But it is common knowledge that a sizeable number of Hindu men take more than one wife (Derrett, 1970: 297; Mahmood, 1986: 116; now Dhagamwar, 1989: 31). The judges, too, have treated the issue with remarkable nonchalance and leniency, for decades lending a helping hand to their fellow-men by discharging the clever bigamist (Derrett, 1970: 308). Only more recent cases (*Baby*, AIR 1981 Bom 283, see Menski 1985)[106] have begun to change this, and we now find cautious beginnings of judicial activism in this area (*Sumitra Devi*, AIR 1985 SC 713), which may mean that the Supreme Court will finally implement its rhetoric threat, issued in *Gopal Lal*, AIR 1979 SC 713, that bigamists should be treated harshly by the law. An analysis of this area of the law as it stands at present clearly confirms Derrett's view of two decades ago that "the rash abolition of polygamy in a euphoric moment is not working out satisfactorily" (Derrett, 1970: 310).

If that is the case, and we hear consistent calls for polygamy to be allowed in certain controlled situations, why bury one's head in the sand and plead that our notion of progress will be violated if modern India were to re-introduce, as it would look, the legal recognition of polygamy? I find myself in agreement with Derrett (1970: 309–310) that one should not pay the lightest attention to such difficulties and should instead be concerned, for example, that a couple who love each other, but are unable to have children together should not be forced by the modern state law to arrange a divorce so that the husband (or, more often, his family), can be allowed to make arrangements for procreation with another wife. For any state law to legislate against people's wish to have children, or even male children, as modern China's example shows, seems more than slightly overambitious.

A law that prohibits polygamy even in those limited few cases where there are genuine reasons for it, and where all parties concerned agree to it, is in my view not a good law, since it causes hardship rather than helping people order their lives sensibly. That there must be some situations in which women willingly consent to polygamous arrangements in India is evidenced by a reference made by Vasudha Dhagamwar (1989: 31) to the "curious institution of committing bigamy with the wife's consent".

I remain as concerned as Dhagamwar and others working towards harmonisation of modern Indian laws that we must try to achieve the best possible legal reforms that ensure better treatment for women and children. But we are dealing with a huge and diverse country, not a place where individualism is the most highly-prized commodity. Nor will this, in my view, ever be the case, for obvious cultural reasons, which no amount of legal and secularising reforms will ever undo. It is, thus, not necessarily correct to argue that women from all social classes and parts of India must be and are opposed to polygamous arrangements. One of my students rightly remarked that it would be just as unacceptable for Mr. Khan's model to be imposed on a society as it would be for polygamy to be completely outlawed in India.

The question of polygamy needs to be debated from all angles and with great depth, since despite modern uniformising trends, present India continues to exhibit a bewildering variety of diverse legal systems, whether state law or non-state law, which often vie for the allegiance of one and the same individual, offering a possibility for devious people to choose the law that seems best suited to their interests. In this particular context one allegation is often heard, that of Indian men becoming Muslims merely for the purpose of allowing themselves more than one wife. If that was indeed such a problem as popular conversation on the issue would suggest, the Indian state, despite its secular image, would probably have reacted some time ago by re-allowing Hindus their cherished polygamy to avoid further defections from the rank of the majority that now feels so threatened. Perhaps this issue even provides an added explanation for the remarkable leniency of the Indian state towards Hindu bigamists until today. Seen from this perspective, allowing qualified bigamy for Hindus could get rid of one sore point, at least, in community relations, though I doubt whether we would want to see the comparatively lenient approach of Indian Muslim law applied to the Hindus.

Having pointed out the potential value of tradition, whether tribal or highly Sanskritic, I want to refer here to the *shastric* idea that it would be an issueless woman's *dharma* to allow the husband, even to encourage him, to take another wife. This, in the past, was probably quite sensible, especially since the same *dharma* complex required the husband to maintain such a wife who had, as it were, stepped back as an individual for the benefit of a greater whole. Especially where relations between the women involved are good, and remain good, what is wrong with such arrangements? There are many societies the world over in which women see advantages in sharing a man, who may often be a rather precious figurehead and less of an economic asset, if not a definite liability. I continue to feel that Western feminists and other enlightened protagonists of gender equality have no right to condemn such societies and their time-tested opinions as backward or barbarous. They are alternative views of ordering society, and ultimately of law, and they deserve respect in their own right.

In my submission, the legal debate on polygamy must prominently address the needs of individual Indian women. Polygamy may, with much justification, be commonly perceived as injurious to women, but if the women concerned agree out of their own free will to a polygamous arrangement, then it is likely that this is a reasonable remedy, which must be respected by a reasonable law. I continue to hold that there are no universal standards, social or legal, on such matters; India must find her own workable compromise between uniform legal regulation and the diversity of her people's socio-economic needs in the widest sense.

It is surely agreed without question that monogamy must remain the norm (Mahmood, 1986: 116). Thus, a controlled acceptance of polygamy does not amount to a blank cheque for bigamists. Rather, the need for it would only arise in certain social situations, which a law that is concerned to keep in line with society would do well to respect. Suggesting this does not mean total renunciation of the 'social engineering through law' approach. I would certainly argue, though, that modern legal systems in many Asian and African countries have become too ambitious, fired on, as they often are, by the enthusiasm of an elite that makes law reforms for itself rather than for the benefit of all citizens. The most recent suggestion that I have come across, symptomatic of this approach, is found in a rather ambivalent advocacy for the compulsory introduction of a Uniform Civil Code in India irrespective of the fact that "there is a possibility of a deep period of social unrest taking place" (Dhagamwar, 1989: 76), which, it is indicated, must be ridden out by a government that is serious about the matter. I could never see that happen, and it is possible that Dhagamwar's guarded words indicate just as much.

Total harmonisation of all differences in India is, quite clearly, a nonsensical aim. Development strategies follow here, without admitting this, the by now obsolete Western ideas of integration and assimilation that have largely proved unworkable in the multi-ethnic realities that we see today all over the world. There are hopeful signs that modern India, still in the process of shedding her colonial heritage through important cases like *M. C. Mehta* (AIR 1987 SC 1086, at 1099), is beginning to see the customary ethnic diversities and differences as an asset rather than a liability. It is part of Indian culture that it is a multi-ethnic experience, and any attempt to implement a truly uniform legal regime, whether in the context of a Uniform Civil Code or a uniform law on polygamy, will not only be doomed to failure, but is a patently retrograde step. In fact, it promotes communalism by allowing communal identities to be played off against each other. This would not happen under a system that respects and accepts all parts of the whole as integral elements.

Having said this, however, does not mean that one needs to be happy with the present legal position. Modern Indian law has got itself into communal troubles by inconsistency in its implementation of gradual harmonisation of family laws. By continuing to allow Indian Muslims polygamy within the rather vague limits of *shariat* (we have seen that this could mean no limit!) but denying, officially at least, the same right to all other communities, it has even not achieved a satisfactory half-way house to proper legal reform. It is a bit like the Salman Rushdie affair in Britain, where it was said that the state should either protect all or none, but should not differentiate on the ground of religion alone, as is clearly the case in both legal systems, though for different historical reasons. The present Indian legal regulation of polygamy not only encourages deviousness, right up to the Supreme Court, as we saw, it also contributes probably to the growing number of desertions of women, and worst of all, it offers no reasonable remedy, in some communities, in those *bona fide* cases where polygamous arrangements, as explained, may be seen by all concerned as the best solution.

I am, therefore, though with some reluctance, suggesting that modern Indian law, which should not give up the idea of working towards greater legal uniformity in principle, cannot go for an outright ban on all forms of polygamous marriages. The only reasonable path is to make allowances for certain polygamous arrangements, as and when they become necessary in particular conditions. These could be specified to prevent that the natural urges of the male sub-species, as perceived by Mr. Khan, do still get an upper hand. And, of course, modern India, wanting the best of both worlds, would perhaps not get away with allowing polygyny only!

To safeguard the position of all participants in polygamous arrangements, certain minimum standards might be contemplated. The law should probably insist that all parties must be asked, without compulsion from any party, whether they are happy with the proposed arrangements. Adequate financial provisions and safeguards for future contingencies should reasonably be made, since there is perhaps a particular risk that such arrangements may be modified over time and may, indeed, come to an end, by dissolution or death.

As it were, Islamic law with its idea of contractual elements in marriage and the concept of deferred *mahr*, in particular, offers useful models in this regard that could be used, in principle, to safeguard especially the position of the spouses that share the partner. Since absolutely equal treatment seems impossible to achieve, one should not be concerned about this point as long as all spouses are indeed happy. How to ascertain this, admittedly, will always remain a problem. But as all marriages, polygamous unions will be open to dissolution, a point that seems to have been overlooked in the heat of the debate.

If the law were to allow polygamy in this limited way, without placing too many hurdles before people, there should in theory be no need for clandestine arrangements that are so common today, where wife 1 may not even know of the existence of wife 2, as in a recent English case that ended in the man's death at the hands of a third party. Moreover, if such arrangements were properly registered and documented, the state's task in keeping a check on marital statuses would be made even easier than in a society like Britain, where often not even first marriages are brought to the attention of the authorities, i.e. where people simply cohabit as husband and wife without official legal sanction. In India, as the study of the emergent Asian laws in Britain shows (Menski, 1988), this will be an effective, though not absolutely watertight remedy, as women and those concerned about their status will quickly learn that state registration of such unusual marriages safeguards the legal position of the women involved far more effectively than any community law could possibly do.

While I am, thus, certainly not advocating the open introduction of polygamy, because this would be abused and exploited by men, a qualified permission for polygamous arrangements of any combination seems a reasonable way forward for modern Indian law.

In the light of Ehrlich's concept of 'living law', though, I see no solution to a major perennial problem of law reform by the state. Despite the new law, Indians of any community will probably continue to make such family arrangements as they consider most appropriate. This may happen with one eye to the official law, so as not to fall foul of its letter, as the example of Asians in Britain shows in so many ways. But it will probably remain a fact of life that in the presence of state laws there can never be total harmony between law and society.

Even ardent reformers admit that India has many tribal societies whose values are worth preserving (Dhagamwar, 1989: 63). Since so-called modern legal development tends to see progress only in a denial of the value of differential statuses and of integration of religion and law, we are in an another deep conceptual impasse.

Finally, I would strongly urge two points: Firstly, that a re-assessment of the various Indian forms of traditional non-state legal systems and more official laws (the borders are obviously more fluid than Professor Baxi sees them) would be a useful exercise. This could be the topic of one, if not several fine PhD theses in law, vitally needed studies in today's communally charged legal universe. Secondly, a re-assessment of the 'living law' theory of the German scholar Eugen Ehrlich should be undertaken, since that evidently sensible theory, not just in my view (see Baxi, 1982: ix), could help train law-makers to learn to be less self-confident about their powers to change societies by the stroke of a pen. Law reform here seems rather like a chemical process: what goes into the glass reacts with what is there already to produce something new, depending on a number of factors. In chemistry, one may have means to calculate and predict the intended results. Social engineering through law depends much more on trial and error, it appears. This is another reason why the present defence of polygamy is a reluctant one.

3.4 Polygamy in Islam: Misrepresented and ill-judged

M. Fazlul Haq

[From: 1990(2) *KLT*, Journal section, pp. 14–18]

Dr. W. F. Menski has written an elaborate reply ('Comparative legal training in action: a reluctant defence of polygamy', 1990(1) KLT, J pp. 50–69) to Mr. Mustafa Ali Khan on his essay, 'Islamic polygamy – a blessing in disguise' (1989(1) KLT J pp. 47–58).

In a discussion on the subject: 'Polygamy in Islam', two points crop up for consideration:

(1) What are the injunctions of Islam?
(2) What is the relevancy of those injunctions in the modern world?

On the first point, as observed by the Allahabad High Court (DB) in a recent decision, the Qur'anic injunctions are clear, but misrepresented and ill-judged by laymen outside the religion of Islam.

The Court held: "... It is a dangerous game to tear tenets [sic] from another person's religion out of their context for one's personal advantage. Polygamy under Islam was always an exception, and never a generality. Then polygamy went and goes with the obligation of equality, equity, justice to be discharged or dispensed amongst more than one wife. The Koran speaks of conscience as an obligation on the husband before taking two, or three or four wives. It speaks of equality of love amongst wives, and equality which is within the sole perception of the woman not the male. It is a hard discipline of the Islamic religion which requires perfection as any wife in a polygamous marriage can as of right speak out in a case of unequal treatment, and make matters difficult for a husband. Thus, a polygamous marriage, under Islam, is exception with a mathematical justice of equality amongst the wives – the woman is the keeper of conscience. The husband only discharges it with an effort which borders on justice. The scales are with all the wives. If one complains of in-equality no one can question her. Such is the discipline of the Koran. ... The concept of marriage and polygamy under Islam and as is referred to in the Koran is clear, but misrepresented and ill-judged by laymen outside this religion ...". (See *Chandrapal and others v. Keshav Deo and others*, 1990(1) Civil Law, J 790).

In the above case, a Hindu husband who was prosecuted for bigamy challenged the prosecution by a petition under Articles 226 and 227 of the Constitution of India, contending that s. 17 of the *Hindu Marriage Act*, 1955, is ultra vires of the equality clause under the Constitution because if he were a Muslim he would get away with it and can not be prosecuted under s. 494, IPC and consequently the petitioner contended that even s. 494, IPC is ultra vires. Dismissing the petition the Court further held: "... The petitioner's contention that s. 17 of the Hindu Marriage Act, 1955 or s. 494 of the Indian Penal Code, 1860, are ultra vires as they offend his liberty as he understands it, under Article 21 of the Constitution of India is a myth of his own making and an immorality engineered by him and it effects neither religion to which he belongs nor any concept of marriage under Islam ...".

Only a layman can say that a Muslim has a right to have four wives; it may also be noted that no marriage, polygamous or otherwise be solemnised without the free consent of the woman. So, even if a man proposes to contract a polygamous marriage, if no woman is willing, his wish will remain as a mere dream. So, it is respectfully submitted that there is no reason why Dr. Menski and the like-minded scholars should shed crocodile-tears for the women in the name of polygamy.

Let us now, come to the Qur'anic injunctions on the point:–

"In the name of the merciful and compassionate God;

(1) O Ye folk! Fear your Lord, who created you from one soul, and created there from its mate, and diffused from them twain many men and women. And fear God, in whose name Ye beg of one another, and the wombs; verily God over you doth watch;

(2) And give unto the orphans their property, and give them not the vile in exchange for the good, and devour not their property to your own property; verily that were a great sin. But if you fear that Ye can not do justice *between orphans*, then marry what seems good to you of women, by twos, or threes, or fours;

(3) If you fear that Ye can not be equitable then only one ... That keeps you nearer to not being partial;

(4) And give women their dowries freely;

(5) Ye are not able, it may be, to act equitably to your wives, even though Ye covet it; do not however be quite partial, and leave one as it were in suspense ...". (E. H. Palmer: *The Qur'an*, the Chapter of Women (IV) 1–4, 125–130).

The Qur'an, thus, permits polygamy as a part of religious duty to do justice between orphans; not as a sexual variety entertainment. Dr. Menski's comment on the subject is only superficial and biased; and the learned author has not attempted to study the Qur'anic law on the point; at any rate, his article is silent on that aspect, presumably with ulterior motives.

Let me quote Moulana Muhammad Ali regarding the scope of the above verses; "... The care of the orphan was one of the earliest injunctions that Islam gave, and the Prophet had always shown a deep anxiety for the welfare of the poor and the orphans. ... This Chapter was revealed to guide the Muslims under the conditions which followed the battle of Uhud. ... Now, in the battle 70 men out of 700 Muslims had been slain, and this decimation had largely decreased. ... Thus, many orphans would be left in the charge of widows, who would find it difficult to procure the necessary means of support. ... We are told that if they could not do justice to the orphans, they might marry the widows whose children would thus become their own children; and as the number of women was now much greater than the number of men, they were permitted to marry even two or three or four women. It would thus be clear that the permission to have more wives than one was given under the peculiar circumstances of the Muslim society; and the Prophet's action in marrying widows, as well as the example of many of his companions corroborates this statement. Marriage with orphan girls is also sanctioned in this passage for there were the same difficulties in the case of orphan girls as in the case of widows ...". (*The Holy Qur'an*, p. 187).

It has been rightly held that polygamy is encouraged or permitted by Islam as an exception and not as a rule. Islam has its own conception of marriage; and does not permit extra-marital relations, which have become the very foundation of what is called the Western culture; aptly described as bourgeois, way of life by communists. For example,

"Manifesto of the Communist Party" says:–

"Our bourgeois, not content with having the wives and daughters of their proletarians at their disposal, not to speak of common prostitutes, take the greatest pleasure in seducing each other's wives. Bourgeois marriage is in reality a system of wives in common ..." (K. Marx and F. Engels, p. 88, 1955 ed.).

Dr. Menski's comment contains contradictory [sic] and mutually destructive arguments. While pointing out that polygamy is only one possible way to alleviate particular social problems and is a useful legal remedy in certain difficult social situations, and that a qualified permission for polygamous arrangements of any combination seems a reasonable way forward for modern India, the learned author contradicts himself by saying that allowing polygamy is nothing but a clever device to legitimise sexual relations that may otherwise be illicit. He also states that a female student declared herself ready to accept polygamy provided polyandry was legally recognised. We find in this a plea in disguise for legalisation of extra-marital sexual relations which have demoralised the Western social life. If the Western-minded people, who are described as bourgeois, by Marx and Engels, want such a legislation to legalise their present immoral life, which is immersed in the "Pleasure in seducing each other's wives", let them have it. It appears that the "qualified permission" which Dr. Menski has in his mind may be the above condition of his female student. On the matters of this kind the Qur'an urges the Muslims to say, "Ye have your religion, and I have my religion" (Chapter 109).

The question is whether Dr. Menski admits that Mr. Khan has correctly cited in his essay the Islamic law on the subject. If so, his criticism will be a fruitless exercise so far as the Muslims are concerned who will ignore it as anti-Islamic.

Here, it may be remembered that prostitution, the greatest evil of civilisation which is a real canker, with its concomitant increase of bastardity is practically unknown to countries where polygamy is allowed as a remedial measure (Moulana Muhammad Ali, *ibid.*, p. 188).

As a matter of fact, in India, the Muslim community is not confronted with any serious problem arising out of or connected with polygamous marriages.

As held by the Allahabad High Court (*ibid.*, p. 795): "... As social conditions in the nation and throughout the world continue to change, the reality of life is that even without a code on personal law of Muslims in so far as the marriage is concerned, polygamy is going into oblivion. Education, changing patterns of the family structure, the structure of a family in the context of reality of the world, and economic necessities are on their own precipitating a situation where monogamy is becoming the reality though the religion permits a Muslim with such sanction of conscience to venture into polygamy. But, the code upon which polygamy rests in Islam is strict and difficult to keep. Let no man misunderstand another's religion". (See also *Islamic law in modern India*, by Indian Law Institute, 1972 ed., p. 154).

But, prostitution and extra-marital relations create grave danger to social life in India too because of the influence of the bourgeois way of life or the Western culture. The West is now, punished by God through the fatal disease: AIDS for their promiscuous sexual life. "This (the Qur'an) is a guidance, and those who misbelieve in the signs of their Lord, to them is torment of a grievous plague" (Chapter 45: 12).

The problem of prostitution has now, come up for consideration before the Supreme Court of India, in *G. Jain v. Union of India*, AIR 1990 SC 292. In this case, an application under Art. 32 of the Constitution was filed asking for direction to the Union of India and others for making provision of separate hostels for children of prostitutes. The Court observed: "... Legislation has been brought to control prostitution. Prostitution has, however, been on the increase and what was once restricted to certain areas of human habitation has now spread in several localities. The problem has, therefore, become one of serious nature and requires considerable and effective attention ...".

The court, therefore, constituted a committee to examine the material aspects of the problem and submit a report containing recommendations to the court. How did these women become prostitutes? Who are responsible for the same? Can it be said that polygamy has produced prostitution? What are the remedial measures to be taken for rehabilitation of prostitutes and their children? All these aspects require investigation and serious thoughts.

Though Marx and Engels have visualised that abolition of the present system of production must bring with it the abolition of the community of women springing from that system, i.e. of prostitution both public and private (*ibid.*, p. 89), it is not clear whether in countries under the rule of communism this has been achieved.

Dr. Menski says that in several European countries, esp. Germany, millions of women did not become polygamous but remained unmarried because of unavailability of men in their age groups. This has become socially acceptable and has caused no noticeable adverse moral effects, and the facts are that many women in those countries, and elsewhere, have become self-supporting.

But, if these women, who have become self-supporting and at the same time remain un-married, are leading a chaste life also, that is well and good. How many of them lead a chaste life is a matter which is to be enquired into.

However, when the orphans or widows including the prostitutes and their children cannot otherwise be protected or rehabilitated, polygamous marriages should be encouraged as a remedial measure. Thus, the Islamic law on polygamy holds considerable importance in the modern times, too.

3.5 Crocodile tears and Muslim polygamy in India

[From: 1991(2) *KLT*, Journal section, pp. 20–24]

At 1990(2) KLT, J 14–18, I stand accused by my learned friend M. Fazlul Haq of misrepresenting and ill-judging polygamy in Islam and of shedding crocodile tears over Muslim women in India. It is regrettable that my exercise in comparative legal study, found at 1990(1) KLT, J 50–69, appears to have offended some Muslim sensibilities and is portrayed as anti-Islamic (p. 17). I rather expected feminist attacks or human rights objections to our qualified defence of polygamy in India. Here now is my response, not so much a defence of the earlier reluctant defence of polygamy, which was mainly designed as a critique of what I called ‘a model exercise in academic deviousness’ (p. 61), but a clarification of some of the points that Mr. Haq has raised to take the discussion further. Since the KLT has a long tradition of encouraging scholarly debate on legal issues, surely a major reason why its much-revered and well-remembered founder editor was able to turn it into one of the leading law journals in India, it is hoped that a spirit of constructive criticism can be maintained here.

To clarify two small issues first, raised by Mr. Haq at various points: Firstly, it is quite improper to suggest any ulterior motives on my part in writing about Muslim polygamy coupled with the term 'layman', which Mr. Haq uses quite liberally, why this paranoia when a non-Muslim writes about Islamic law? Various people may resent the fact that someone who appeared to be appointed to teach Hindu law in London more than a decade ago has found it just as interesting to write on Muslim law in the subcontinent. May be I soon found out that one cannot really teach and write about Indian law today without knowing about Islamic law? I am sure this has been true for a long time. Thus I follow here in the footsteps of Professor J. N. D. Anderson rather than the famous Professor J. D. M. Derrett. At any rate, my brief to cover Hindu and modern South Asian Law certainly includes several jurisdictions dominated by Islamic law.

Further, to answer the last point of Mr. Haq's essay (at p. 18), there is no question for me that the Islamic law on polygamy holds considerable importance also today, not only in India, but worldwide. At 1988(1) KLT, J 56–66 I argued that Indian laws are also important in Britain today; I have since gone much further in writing about the re-creation of Asian laws in Britain and have made particular reference to British Muslim law. My students' ongoing enthusiasm in contributing to this discussion readily confirms the relevance of the topic of bigamy/polygamy, too.

Mr. Haq rightly identifies (at p. 15) two major points for a discussion of polygamy in Islam, i.e., what are the injunctions of Islam and what is the relevance of those injunctions in the modern world? This is, of course, a rather Islam-centric perspective, emphasising the importance of Islamic rules rather than, in the second question, those of modern state law. But the above remains a valid approach: If Muslims believe that the Qur'an regulates polygamy, then what is the claim to authority of the modern state law in this field? Below, I shall elaborate on this point with particular reference to modern India.

Readers will have noted that Mr. Haq avoids reference to the latter point as much as possible and merely insinuates that I am incompetent to discuss his first question and not interested in the second. In my view, the underlying suggestion that a non-Muslim is forever unable to make sense of Islamic law is plain nonsense, though such charges are still regularly made. Perhaps the learned author would like to consider that some people may not be Muslim precisely because they know much about Islam. The result need not be an unsympathetic attitude, but a tolerant 'live and let live' approach. I was happy to see this twice referred to in Mr. Haq's article and hope I am right in reading it in that spirit.

It is quite wrong (but see p. 16) that my lengthy response to the earlier article of Mr. Khan at 1989(1) KLT, J 47–58 is silent on the Qur'anic law, which Mr. Haq has now laid out in some detail. I trusted that the learned readers of KLT would make sense of my comments on Mr. Khan's discussion of these provisions (see for example pp. 53–54 and the first para of p. 56) and see no justification for laying them out in detail myself, just to show that I have studied them. There are many textbooks on Islamic law which contain these provisions and discuss them. I certainly did not wish to increase the length of my earlier article by a mechanical display of basic sources. If that is called superficial, so be it.

Readers will remember that I constructed my response to Mr. Khan's essay as an exercise in comparative legal training, not an in-depth treatment of one particular legal system. A comparative lawyer must be able to view the world through another culture's eyes and to understand and appreciate different legal traditions, but this does not mean uncritical acceptance of the stated axioms of any one particular tradition. If some legal writers in India today have problems with that approach, it is in my view symptomatic of the urgent need to strengthen comparative legal training in Indian law schools to enable lawyers to understand the difficult issues that a modern plural legal system has to grapple with. A narrow communalist approach is not good enough to make sense of any aspect of modern Indian law!

Since it is plain that there is no disagreement between Mr. Haq and myself on the fact that the Qur'anic provisions permit polygamy in certain situations and under certain conditions, why all this fuss and twisted argument? My learned friend seems to disagree with Mr. Khan's rather than my argument. Certainly, I have never said that it is a rule in Islamic law that a husband should have up to four wives. If fact, my major criticism of Mr. Khan's argument was precisely that he attempted to show, in the later part of his article, how 'normal' polygamy was.

Layman or not, it remains correct to say that Islamic law allows a man four wives in certain circumstances, i.e. that many Muslim men have, in principle, a right to have up to four wives. Indian state law has, as far as I am aware, never circumscribed this right, while Pakistani law has done so (however ineffectively) in s. 6 of the *Muslim Family Laws Ordinance*, 1961. Since we all know that in *shariat* law as it stands in India limited polygamy is a qualified right, why this quibbling over a few words taken out of context? The real issue in this debate, and that is what I objected to in Mr. Khan's chain of arguments, is that some Muslims use the Qur'anic provisions to justify what Mr. Haq aptly calls 'sexual variety entertainment' (p. 16). I did note that my learned friend does not like this idea, but he also does not simply argue that Muslims live by the letter of the Qur'an; instead he quotes a number of scholarly opinions, Marxist clippings and a few case notes.

Whatever words or quotes one uses here, the fact remains that polygamy continues to exist on a small scale in India today, clearly both among Muslims and in other communities. I have tried to argue, and I am sorry if this was not clear enough, that polygamy itself is not really a grave problem, but that Indian law should take account of this social fact without discriminating between members of different religious groups. Saying this implied some criticism of modern India's handling of the law of bigamy, not of Islamic law. The recent case of an angry Hindu bigamist, prosecuted for an action that his Muslim neighbour would be allowed to take is cited by Mr. Haq. It is rather helpful to my argument and highlights the point that I was trying to make: Hindus in India have become increasingly resentful of what they see as the 'preferential treatment' of Muslims by the state legal system. The present differential treatment of Muslim men by modern Indian law, allowing them alone more than one spouse, while denying the same right to all other citizens, is fundamentally wrong on many counts. In other words, I defended the position that bigamy, under carefully controlled conditions, may have a useful role to play in modern India's legal system, but I neither argued for a re-instatement of virtually unfettered male discretion in this area, nor have I said that Muslims should be forced to accept the total criminalisation of polygamy.

But I have also not explicitly defended Muslim polygamy, firstly because Indian Muslims are subject to Indian law and secondly because of doubts over the effectiveness of Islamic law safeguards against abuse of the polygamy provisions. I am, of course, aware of the argument by some Muslim scholars that the rules of Islamic law offer themselves as an ideal blueprint for the whole of Indian law today. Clearly, this avenue for legal reform seems just as unacceptable as the imposition of a uniform civil code on all communities. It would, in principle, lead to the same 'period of deep social unrest' of which Vasudha Dhagamwar has recently warned us in her excellent study *Towards the Uniform Civil Code* (Bombay: Tripathi 1989: p. 76).

What, then, would be the potential justifications for polygamy today? Mr. Haq agrees with me on the factum of restrictions and conditions, but in what circumstances should one allow bigamous arrangements? Classical Islamic law saw the rescue of widows and orphans from battlefields as a valid ground. This, today, is not such a big issue, though the age of *jihad* is evidently not over. I would accept, however, that the battlefield of life itself leaves many casualties that need to be taken care of. Whether one thinks of Bhopal, communal riots or other disasters, large or small, there are certainly many situations in which helpless women and children need assistance, and might wish male protection. But I am not sure that this alone will explain or justify the incidence of polygamy in any community. What we clearly need is detailed fieldwork to ascertain in what situational contexts men and women in South Asia today make polygamous arrangements. I am not aware of any such work and do not wish to speculate here without substance. But from talking to people about this and from the literature that I know, I anticipate that two other grounds are likely to appear as prominent: infertility of a marriage and sexual or status desire of the man.

In my earlier article (at p. 61), I have already argued that male protection can be given to hapless women and their offspring through charity rather than polygamy, i.e. a form of help that does not involve sexual relations. Islam, in the institutions of *zakat* and *waqf*, has excellent models for such charitable support as may be required from time to time, or even over a longer time. One may note that Mr. Haq agrees with me that 'polygamy is only one possible way to alleviate particular social problems and is a useful legal remedy in certain difficult situations' (p. 17). Readers will have noted that Mr. Haq extends this now to rescuing prostitutes and their offspring, an issue which will be debated below.

The real problem, in my view, is the uncomfortable truth of promiscuity in human society. It should not happen, in the view of many, but it does. Here Mr. Haq prefers blinkered self-righteousness to good reason. He throws in a few comments about the devious and corrupted bourgeois West, about Marxist manifestos and AIDS as divine punishment for the West. On the latter, unfortunately, he has not got his facts right, and his comments are just as unacceptable as those of Western writers who have tried to blame the Africans, suggesting that it served them right. Unfortunately, AIDS is now a problem anywhere in the world and respects neither the borders of Muslim countries nor the sensitivities of Indian society. But dragging such topics into our discussion does not lead us anywhere.

I fully understand, though, that my learned friend found it difficult to believe that millions of unmarried German women could maintain chastity. How can one 'prove' this to alleviate the doubts of Mr. Haq? There is specialist literature about this, but I have mainly relied on my personal knowledge, derived from growing up in Germany and meeting such women daily as teachers, relatives and fellow citizens. I did make the more important point, however (at p. 57), that a similar development is beginning to take place among South Asian women in Britain. Some research on this is now under way and our preliminary findings are that single Asian women in Britain can well be trusted to maintain chastity. The absolute necessity of male protection is just a convenient and powerful myth, perpetuated not only in India, but also in Britain; it means little in reality for such women. To enter polygamous unions, interestingly, does not figure among the ambitions of our respondents, many of whom see men as exploiters rather than protectors.

Finally, two points remains to be resolved. Mr. Haq demanded to know (p. 17) if in my view Mr. Khan had correctly cited the Islamic law on the subject. I think I answered that on p. 56 of my article and need not add any further comment.

As far as the position of Islamic law in modern Indian law is concerned, I argued above for a less Islam-centric approach than Mr. Haq appeared to take, for the simple and obvious reason that the relevance of the injunctions of Islam in modern India has to be worked out by reference to India's legal system, in which Muslim law is, for better or worse, just one component. Our discussion, then, cannot focus on Islamic law alone but must be put into appropriate context.

With reference to polygamy, we have agreed on the position of the classical law as allowing a Muslim husband up to four wives subject to certain conditions. A major concern of the present exercise was to work out a viable legal rule on polygamy for the whole of India, taking account of the needs of various communities. As we all know, Indian state law has not interfered in the Muslim law on polygamy, for a number of reasons, but has reformed other personal laws on this very issue. At the risk of repeating myself, I can only say that the development of a uniform legal rule on polygamy for all communities in India will need to take account of the fact that in certain social situations, including the fact that the parties are Muslims, polygamy may continue to be seen as desirable, whether on grounds of religion, mere sexual greed or anything else.

Mr. Haq seems to suggest that there are certain situations in which polygamous unions make good sense both socially and legally. With reference to *Gaurav Jain* at AIR 1990 SC 292, he has invited us to consider an extension of the beneficial rules of Islamic law on polygamy to prostitutes and their children, whose lives, according to this reasoning, could be significantly improved in this way. I dare say this will not get rid of prostitution and its related problems, but modern Indian law, as it stands at present, would not have any objections to such a solution from within Islamic law, since it appears to have almost completely refrained from regulating Muslim family law. But does this suggestion make sense or does Mr. Haq shed crocodile tears over the prostitutes? I am sure other readers of KLT may have something to say on this.

3.6 No continuing favours for men? The post-modern reconstruction of Indian laws on polygamy

As we saw in chapter 3.1 above, to some extent it has been a politically and legally convenient myth that Muslims in India have been given preferential treatment regarding polygamy. Official legal recognition that polygamous marriages among Muslims may be arranged without any risk of legal penalties, so many commentators argue, gives the wrong messages to precisely those Muslim men who are most ready to abuse such liberal-looking provisions and wish to exploit them for their own selfish reasons. On the other hand, this then allows the ever-present 'enemies of Islam' to criticise Muslims for exploiting polygamy. In addition, we find a situation today where some Indian Muslims will assert their traditional rights under *shariat* just for the sake of demonstrating to the state that they consider *shariat* the supreme law and that they can claim the freedom to enter polygamous unions. One can see some of the politicised foundations here for debates about Muslim loyalty in India and threats to the concepts of 'state' and 'rule of law'.

While such real issues cannot be brushed aside as irrelevant, a comprehensive analysis of modern India's laws on polygamy should not stop at this level of enquiry. I have asserted in section 3.1 above that Muslim polygamy in India, despite the absence of legislative prohibition, is not such a huge issue that it is necessary to demand the abolition of Muslim polygamy under Indian law forthwith. Doing so will undoubtedly please international opinion, but it might immediately create some public order problems in India itself.[107] Still, that may not be the major argument for non-action on this issue through the legislative pen. In the long run, abolishing polygamy by law would only drive it underground, as has clearly happened with Hindu polygamy in India and Muslim polygamy in many other countries.[108] My argument is, therefore, that the legal abolition of Muslim polygamy would not tackle the real problems for women which we seek to address. Further, some scholars need to be reminded that no law can just abolish what people see – rightly or wrongly – as an aspect of their religion.

However, such arguments do not amount to total or even partial condonation of Muslim polygamy, or uncritical acceptance of the Muslim juristic pronouncements on the acceptability of polygamy for Muslims. I have all along tried to argue for socio-legal solutions to problems in Indian law and society that reflect legal realism, not for building legal dream castles in the air. I remain unimpressed, therefore, by the criticisms regarding polygamy coming from the detailed Report of the Committee on the Status of Women in India (1974: 104–111). The comments in this Report were made from the premise of demanding and expecting full equality of sexes (see the very first sentence at p. 104), so it is evident that the Committee would oppose any legal system or regulatory framework which permits polygamy and any social system which tolerates it. In other words, again, refusing to follow Western models would be *per se* treated as unacceptable. One wonders whether that approach, implying an outright rejection of South Asian socio-legal postulates, can be an appropriate starting point for a debate about this issue in Indian law.

At p. 108 of the same Report, Professor Derrett (1970:309) and his suggestions concerning the potential usefulness of regulated bigamy are criticised as giving "a misleading impression of being in the interests of women and as it is likely to be advanced in the context of Muslim law also, it needs to be rebutted in full". I share the apprehensions of the Committee, but it was not factually correct to deny any evidence of sympathy for bigamous unions or an opinion in favour of them, since the Committee itself provided just such evidence at p. 104. I find this Report useful in that it appears to oppose the assertion that there would be public unrest if Muslim polygamy were to be legally abolished (p. 105), but I am not convinced that it would be 'safe' for the state to attempt any outright legislation. There may be more effective methods of reaching the same goal. Indeed, further below we will examine how far modern Indian law has gone in opposing and putting actual checks on Muslim polygamy by other means than outright legislation.

I also argued in section 3.1 that the legislative prohibitions on Hindu polygamy in the HMA have not been effectively implemented and thus the situation is almost equally bad 'on the ground' for Hindu women and for Muslim women. Turning to the socio-legal realities of Hindu polygamy in India today, we have already found that the official legal prohibition of polygamy has not been effective and did not have the desired social effects. I have already cited Derrett (1970: 307–308) and his strongly worded criticism of the unsatisfactory operation of this law.

Such criticism has continued to be voiced also in more recent academic writing. Sharma (1994: 85–128) has written a whole chapter on legal provisions for monogamy and their ineffectiveness and finally recommends, in essence, stricter legal enforcement of the prohibition.[109] This even includes illegitimising the children of polygamous unions (Sharma 1994: 361), which clearly goes too far, forgetting again the basic rule that the innocent victims of polygamy should not be punished. Vyas (1993: 194–196) briefly discusses polygamy in the context of obstacles to national integration and argues that continuance of polygamy should not be regarded as a requirement of any religion. Again, we find the all too familiar picture of enthusiastic socio-legal scholars who publish books full of wonderful ideas and prescriptions for social reforms, without thinking in sufficient depth about the actual consequences of their suggestions. The main issue in India's polygamy law is clearly not whether or not to abolish it by legislation. This appears to be the main issue only in terms of playing to an international arena. Surely, India's reputation in the world would be tainted if one were to remove the legislative prohibitions on polygamy and were to allow it for all citizens, even on strict conditions. However, an outright legal prohibition of polygamy is no magic cure to its potential manifestations as a social evil.

We know only too well that polygamy has probably never really been a binding norm of any society, rather it has been an exception to the general rule of monogamy.[110] Mankind has not moved, in the classic linear progression model of modernisation theories, from a stage of primitive polygamy to a modern stage of monogamy. Monogamy and polygamy have always co-existed and – dare one suggest it in these times of political correctness – will always co-exist in human societies, irrespective of state laws. We are talking about questions of extent here, not universal prohibition or acceptance.

It is probably uncontested by now that all traditional societies seem to have made allowances for polygamy in certain situations, whether these were reflective of family emergencies such as infertility, the economic or social standing of particular men, or chauvinistic exploitation of male claims to superior status.[111] Many writers have discussed polygamy in the context of Islam.[112] Altekar (1978: 115–116) pinpoints the key issue well in terms of classical Hindu concepts when he writes:

> The main reason, however, for the occasional occurrence of polygamy even among ordinary classes was the great anxiety that was felt for the preservation and continuance of the family. For offering the prescribed oblations to ancestors so as to secure their continuance in heaven, a son was absolutely necessary, and so society permitted the husband to take a second wife, if the first one was barren. Nay, we find some writers laying down that it was the duty of the wife to urge her husband to contract a second marriage if she had failed to present a son to him.

Such arguments cannot just be brushed aside by modern, secular reformers who do not care an *iota* about other people's religious beliefs and social organisation. Hindus themselves have not so much claimed religious necessity as blamed the Muslims. I find it a significant argument in this context that the widely perceived decline of women's status in the subcontinent during medieval times is prominently linked to Muslim influence. While this view is often put forward by Hindu or Sikh writers (see e.g. Singh 1992: 48), not only Muslim writers claim that Hindus are more polygamous than Muslims.[113] Since one prominent aspect of the perceived deterioration of female status relates to the increased practice of polygamy, it was only a little step beyond such perceptions to call for legislative controls in post-Independence India.

The above discussion, as well as the outline provided in ch. 3.1 above, suggest three major tasks for the present chapter. First, it will be useful to provide an overview of the development of statutory prohibitions of polygamy in Indian law. Then, it is my aim to substantiate the argument that Muslim polygamy in independent India has not remained without legal controls. Finally, we should investigate in more detail why and how the legal prohibitions on Hindu polygamy have not been effective in social reality. The final section will discuss possible ways forward to achieve better control women over the decision-making processes regarding polygamous arrangements, where these are found to be useful or preferable.

The progress of statutory prohibitions regarding polygamy

During the British period, the first major enactment regarding polygamy was made in sections 494 and 495 of the *Indian Penal Code* of 1860, which provide as follows:

> 494. *Marrying again during lifetime of husband or wife.* –
> Whoever, having a husband or wife living, marries in any case in which such marriage is void by reason of its taking place during the life of such husband or wife, shall be punished with imprisonment of either description for a term which may extend to seven years, and shall also be liable to fine.
>
> *Exception.*–
> This section does not extend to any person whose marriage with such husband or wife has been declared void by a Court of competent jurisdiction,
>
> nor to any person who contracts a marriage during the life of a former husband or wife, if such husband or wife, at the time of the subsequent marriage, shall have beencontinually absent from such person for the space of seven years, and shall not have been heard of by such person as being alive within that time, provided the person contracting such subsequent marriage shall, before such marriage takes place, inform the person with whom such marriage is contracted of the real state of facts so far as the same are within his or her knowledge.

> 495. *Same offence with concealment of former marriage from person with whom subsequent marriage is contracted.* –
> Whoever commits the offence defined in the last preceding section having concealed from the person with whom the subsequent marriage is contracted, the fact of the former marriage, shall be punished with imprisonment of either description for a term which may extend to ten years, and shall also be liable to fine.

This enactment clearly does not apply to persons whose polygamous marriage is legally valid under any of India's personal laws. Thus, at the time of its original enactment, the provisions of section 494 and 495 would mainly have applied to Christians in India, but not to Hindus and Muslims, and today they still do not apply to Muslims in India.[114]

The exceptions to s. 494 shows that the law was as much concerned to protect abandoned spouses who were contemplating remarriage against subsequent prosecutions as it was to outlaw polygamy as such. The offence in s. 495 is treated as an aggravated form of the offence under s. 494, reflected in the potentially higher jail sentence.

In post-colonial India, when the provisions of the HMA, 1955 were drafted, Hindus were brought under the provisions of s. 494 and 495 of the *Indian Penal Code*. The three relevant sections of the HMA are closely linked. The first is found in s. 5(i):

> 5. *Conditions for a Hindu marriage.*–
> A marriage may be solemnized between any two Hindus, if the following conditions are fulfilled, namely: –
> (i) neither party has a spouse living at the time of the marriage;

This clear rule of monogamy is then reinforced by s. 11 HMA, which reads:

> 11. *Void marriage.*–
> Any marriage solemnized after the commencement of this Act shall be null and void and may, on a petition presented by either party thereto, be so declared by a decree of nullity if it contravenes any one of the conditions specified in clauses (i), (iv) and (v) of section 5.

Such a marriage is null and void *ab initio* and need not be so declared by a court,[115] but where spouses find it desirable to have an official court document, then such a decree may be given. The HMA contains one further provision on polygamy in s. 17, relating to punishment:

> 17. *Punishment of bigamy.* –
> Any marriage between two Hindus solemnized after the commencement of this Act is void if at the time of such marriage either party had a husband or wife living; and the provisions of sections 494 and 495 of the Indian Penal Code (XLV of 1860) shall apply accordingly.

Merely looking at the letter of the statute law, therefore, one cannot be blamed for coming to the conclusion that Hindu polygamy has been outlawed by the modern Indian legal system. As we saw already, there are no such legislative provisions for Muslims in India. Does this mean, then, that Muslim polygamy in India is unfettered?

Restraints on Muslim polygamy in India

In this section, I elaborate the argument that there have been several restraints on Muslim polygamy in the subcontinent under British rule as well as in post-Independence India, despite the absence of official legal prohibition. This is not to say that such restraints would be absolutely effective in society, but they set signals for Muslim women who wish to oppose polygamous arrangements made by men without their agreement. The point to make here is that the presence of such opposition cannot be denied just because it is not legally visible in statute books. Why do we have to stick to the axiom that legislation alone will be an effective means of social reform? Maybe it is precisely because signposts and directives provided by the courts work more directly in the social sphere, in which we should certainly include the law courts, that they may in fact be more effective than legal dictates in statutes alone. We shall have more to say about this issue at the end of the chapter.

The legislative non-action with regard to Muslim polygamy in India has of course been criticised on constitutional grounds. Many authors have produced vigorous arguments on this point.[116] Bhatnagar (1992: 99) not only opposes the basic interpretation that Muslim law permitted polygamy but extends his opposition to Muslim polygamy into the common argument that recognition of Muslim polygamy clashes with the Indian Constitution. We then read at pp. 99–100:

> It is surprising that dubious religious interpretations with values valid in a bygone age are being enforced in the current times by civil courts in our professedly secular State when those values have become mere legal superstitions, if not anathema for the community at large, out of a false sense of solicitude to a fancied section of society. The Indian Constitution directs that the State should endeavour to have a uniform civil code applicable to the entire Indian community . . .[117]

Bhatty (1991: 148) argues that "[i]n a secular country, where monogamy is the rule for all citizens [sic], there is no justification for a Muslim man enjoying a singularly unique privilege which even Islamic countries are abandoning". She continues at p. 149:

> While [the] Indian constitution guarantees equality irrespective of gender for its citizens, Indian Muslim women are denied this fundamental right in the name of religion and the state has been safeguarding the superior right of Muslim males over Muslim women in violation of the Constitution. It is precisely this issue which makes the status of Indian Muslim women a concern for all Indian citizens . . .

However, does evident legislative acquiescence necessarily become condonation and acceptance? Outwardly, it appears that way, and the ongoing debates about Indian polygamy have simply assumed this. Thus, Deshpande (1993) opposes the discrimination against Muslim women on the grounds of religion and suggests that the current position is unconstitutional on a number of grounds. In the context of arguments for the uniform civil code (see chapter 6), Shiv Sahai Singh (1993: 10–11) argues that the modern state has the right to override religious norms and asserts that "[t]he state, therefore, can validly enact measures of social welfare and reform with respect to the matters governed by the Muslim law".

It is evident from such arguments that the nature of the co-existence between a unified constitutional framework and a personal law system in modern Indian law has not been sufficiently well understood by some authors who blindly argue for following Western models. Equality in diversity, or equity in otherwise plural situations, continues to puzzle many scholars, who find it easier to follow Western model concepts of uniformity and of the state's legislative power.

While India has not, for better or worse, used the legislative route to control and outlaw Muslim polygamy, Muslim wives who wish to complain against polygamous arrangements are not without remedies. First of all, within the conceptual context of *shariat* as the yardstick for the Muslim personal law, the primary control mechanisms for Muslim men with polygamous inclinations or intentions arise out of the Qur'an itself. These restraints impact on the conscience of the individual believer and may, therefore, not be effective in checking an individual's selfish behaviour. Religious law, after all, faces the same issues of potential social obstinacy as the modern state law.

The general classical rules on Muslim polygamy are well-known and do not need to be repeated here.[118] Tahir Mahmood (1976: 77) suggested – and he is not alone in this – that "certain aspects of the Muslim personal law presently prevailing in India have outlived their utility and do need a reconsideration", listing at p. 78 explicitly:

> Man's uncontrolled freedom to contract a bigamous marriage, without even informing his first wife about it, irrespective of whether he really needs another wife and can equitably maintain the co-wives satisfying, in any degree, the demands of the *Qur'an* from a polygamous husband ...

Already in British India, the traditional minority view of Muslim jurists, that polygamy is not really allowed by the Qur'an, as treating two wives equally is humanly impossible, received much attention. This is reflected, for example, in a surprisingly 'activist' statement by Verma (1988: 56), which is as much based on the spirit of judicial decisions as on strict interpretation of the Qur'an:

> It is unlawful for a male Muslim to have more wives than one and for a Muslim woman to have more husbands than one at one and the same time.

This is not a single pronouncement by a maverick scholar but reflects the considered views of many Anglo-Indian judges and their successors. Pre-Independence judicial decisions were to the effect that controlled polygamy was permitted to Muslim men, but only if equal treatment could be ensured.[119] In independent India, the early leading case of *Itwari v. Asghari*, AIR 1960 All 684, established famously that a Muslim wife faced with unwanted polygamous arrangements could claim cruelty as a ground for divorce and ancillary relief against her husband.[120] This was not such a unique case as has been made out – there are many others.[121] Bhatnagar (1992: 13) asserts that, depending on the circumstances, a first wife has the right to separate from a polygamous Muslim husband and that "[i]n any event, there is no compulsion for a wife to share her husband with another co-wife". This author, too, takes a dim view of the polygamous husband's capacity to treat his wives equally, saying at p. 40:

> The failure to treat all wives equally in providing services and supplies in life material and mental is a foregone [sic] conclusion and foreign to human conduct cutting right across the Divine will in exercise of mutual rights or performance of duties *inter se*.

Already during British rule, therefore, while the right of the Muslim husband to marry polygamously was officially respected, the judges did not encourage polygamy and assisted women who complained about their polygamous husband. As Bhatnagar (1992: 67) put it, "[t]hus the Indian Courts tolerate polygamy amongst Mohammedans but do not encourage it".[122]

One could produce here a long analysis of the relevant Indian case law to reinforce this point. Since we have to be brief, only two major cases have been selected to illustrate the main point to be made here, namely that judicial opposition to Muslim polygamy in India has remained strong, vocal and effective. Further, it has acquired new vigour due to the judicial activism in granting divorced Muslim wives maintenance rights beyond the *iddat* period (see chapter 4).

This may well have had the effect that Muslim men will seek to restrain their women from bringing cases to the official courts in the first place. One technique to achieve this, and to develop more socially appropriate methods of dispute processing, may be to strengthen the profile of informal Muslim bodies of dispute settlement, similar to the Shariat Councils now operating unofficially in Britain (Pearl and Menski 1998: 77–80). As in the UK, these fora may not operate to the full advantage of women, but it is too simple to dismiss them rashly as agents of male chauvinism. If such bodies were not listening to distressed Muslim women's pleas, they would not be approached by such women and they would lose credibility in the wider community. As in Britain, there is an urgent need for further research on the activities, and the socio-legal impact, of such informal Muslim bodies.[123]

Regarding the Indian case law on the subject, we turn first to *Shahulameedu v. Subaida Beevi*, 1970 KLT 4, decided by India's equivalent of Lord Denning, V. R. Krishna Iyer J (as he then was) in the Kerala High Court. This was a Muslim husband's appeal against an award of maintenance under s. 488(3) of the *Criminal Procedure Code* of 1898 for the princely sum of Rs. 120/- per month in favour of his first wife and their four children. The lady had refused to live with her husband after he took a second wife and the husband had refused to pay her maintenance unless she lived with him again. He had thereafter pronounced *talaq*. Iyer J speedily disposed of the husband's objections to the size of the maintenance award (p. 5) and then turned to s. 488(3) of the *Code of Criminal Procedure*. Here the question was, as stated at p. 6, whether "the refusal of the wife to live with the husband who has married another is just in the case of Muslims whose personal law permits a male to marry up to four women at a time".

The learned judge combined express concern for the material welfare of women and children (this portion of the quote is found in chapter 4.3 below) with social opposition to polygamy and held with regard to the latter, at p. 6:

> But the amendment incorporated by Act 9 of 1949 expresses the moral consensus of the community that a woman should not be driven to live with her husband who has transferred his affections to another woman either by marrying her or by keeping her as his mistress. The argument is that while this wholesome rule may apply to the rest of Indian humanity, Muslims should be excused out of this civilized law, because the fundamental assumption in the provision is that it is obnoxious to marry a second wife while the first is alive and this assumption does not hold good in the case of the Muslims of India who under their personal law enjoy the privilege of four wives simultaneously.

Referring to a number of decided cases in which Muslim men had unsuccessfully entered special pleadings about their right to be polygamous,[124] the learned judge found himself fortified in taking a strong view against Muslim polygamy. It was said at p. 9:

> The starting point of all this argument that the Muslim Law actively permits multi-marriages is itself open to serious doubt, as I will presently show. Moreover, it is distressing for a Court to discriminate against Muslim women who have for ages been subjected to several social disabilities clamped down on them in the name of personal laws. It is surprising that dubious religious interpretations with values valid in a bygone age are being enforced in the current times by civil courts in our professedly secular State when those values have become

> mere legal superstitions, if not anathema for the community at large, out of a false sense of solicitude for a fancied section of society.

With reference to the policy aim of a uniform civil code and the social welfare objectives of s. 488(3) of the *Criminal Procedure Code*, it was therefore held, in strong words (pp. 9–10, cited in chapter 4.3 below) that Muslim women could not be treated differently from the rest of Indians. Considering the Qur'anic provisions on polygamy, which were cited in court, the learned judge further held, at p. 10:

> It follows from these passages that the Koranic injunction has to be understood in the perspective of prevalent unrestricted polygamy and in the context of the battle in which most males perished, leaving many females or orphans and that the holy prophet himself recognised the difficulty of treating two or more wives with equal justice and, in such a situation, directed that an individual should have only one wife. In short, the Koran enjoined monogamy and departure therefrom as an exception. That is why, in the true spirit of the Koran, a number of Muslim countries have codified the personal law wherein the practice of polygamy has been either totally prohibited or severely restricted ...

This interpretation was supported by reference to a number of Muslim scholars, and the husband's objections were therefore rejected. This case, therefore, gave a strong signal to Muslims in modern India, to the effect that a wife objecting to the husband's polygamy would be entitled to separate maintenance.

It is well-known that the easiest remedy for a Muslim husband in that situation would be to simply divorce his wife by *talaq* and wash his hands of any further liability for her (and often the children, too).[125] This is precisely what the appellant husband in the above case had done, thereby following a devious and socially disruptive route which the law needed to block with some urgency. The story of that legal amendment, the introduction of the re-worked *Criminal Procedure Code* of 1973, relates to the issue of maintenance and is therefore found in chapter 4 below.

Following the high-profile *Shah Bano* case,[126] an interesting question arose in *Subanu v. A. M. Abdul Gafoor*, AIR 1987 SC 1103, a case on appeal from Kerala. The editorial note at pp. 1103–1104 explains:

> In this case the question that came up for consideration before the Supreme Court was whether a Muslim wife whose husband has married again is worse off under law than a Muslim wife whose husband has taken a mistress to claim maintenance from her husband. The main defence raised was that since the husband is permitted by Muslim law to take more than one wife his second marriage cannot afford a legal ground to the wife to live separately and claim maintenance. The Supreme Court held that irrespective of the

> husband's right under his personal law to take more than one wife, his first wife would be entitled to claim maintenance and separate residence if he takes a second wife.

This case, therefore, is not really on a new point of law regarding polygamy as such and merely reiterates and confirms what was held in *Shahulameedu v. Subaida Beevi*, 1970 KLT 4, as discussed above. However, this decision updates the position of Indian law towards Muslim claims to separate treatment after the promulgation of the *Criminal Procedure Code*, 1973 and reiterates the position taken in the *Shah Bano* case, namely that the provisions of the general law override the personal law. In addition, it adamantly refuses to make a distinction between Muslim men who formally marry a second wife and those who merely take a mistress. It was held, at pp. 1107–1108:

> We would like to point out that the Explanation contemplates two kinds of matrimonial injury to a wife, viz. by the husband either marrying again or taking a mistress. The Explanation places a second wife and mistress on the same footing and does not make any differentiation between them on the basis of their status under matrimonial law. If we ponder over the matter we can clearly visualise the reason for a second wife or a mistress being treated alike. The purpose of the Explanation is not to affect the rights of a Muslim husband to take more than one wife or to denigrate in any manner the legal and social status of a second wife to which she is entitled to as a legally married wife, as compared to a mistress, but to place on an equal footing the matrimonial injury suffered by the first wife on account of the husband marrying again or taking a mistress during the subsistence of the marriage with her. From the point of view of the neglected wife, for whose benefit the Explanation has been provided, it will make no difference whether the woman intruding into her matrimonial life and taking her place in the matrimonial bed is another wife permitted under law to be married and not a mistress. The legal status of the woman to whom a husband has transferred his affections cannot lessen her distress or her feelings of neglect. In fact from one point of view the taking of another wife portends a more permanent destruction of her matrimonial life than the taking of a mistress by the husband. Be that as it may, can it be said that a second wife would be more tolerant and sympathetic than a mistress so as to persuade the wife to rejoin her husband and lead life with him and his second wife in one and the same house. It will undoubtedly lead to a strange situation if it were to be held that a wife will be entitled to refuse to live with her husband if he has taken a mistress but she cannot refuse likewise if he has married a second wife. The Explanation has to be construed from the point of view of the injury to the matrimonial rights of the wife and not with reference to the

> husband's right to marry again. The Explanation has, therefore, to be seen in its full perspective and not disjunctively. Otherwise it will lead to discriminatory treatment between wives whose husbands have lawfully married again and wives whose husbands have taken mistresses.

If we look at this scenario in a wider perspective, what the Supreme Court is also saying here is that Muslim men can keep their right to be polygamous, if they wish to claim it. However, they will have to pay for this by having to make appropriate financial arrangements for those women whom they have chosen to discard or to drive out of the marriage. It is evident that the enormous developments in Indian post-divorce maintenance law after 1985, which we chart in section 4.3 below, have had much impact on how the Supreme Court viewed the issue of Muslim polygamy. This is well-illustrated by how Natarajan J in the present case firmly dismissed the husband's make-believe offer to take his wife back and swiftly proceeded to determine an appropriate quantum of maintenance for her. The husband had claimed to have only an income of Rs. 1,000/- per month, while the wife alleged that he earned altogether closer to Rs. 2,000/- per month. The wife was awarded only Rs. 300/- per month, but backdated to the time when the husband had married the second wife. He was ordered to pay the (by this time quite substantial) arrears in five equal instalments and was also told to pay an additional Rs. 200/- per month for the maintenance of his daughter, increased from Rs. 100/- monthly. We see here further evidence of the activism of the Supreme Court in leading the drive towards ensuring adequate maintenance provisions for women and children who find themselves destitute and pushed out of marriages. As indicated in ch. 3.1 above, at the end of the day, this is what counts more in Indian law today than ideological debates about the right to polygamy.

Academic comment on the issue of Muslim polygamy has been quite diffuse. Asif (1991: 6–7) refers to the traditional grounds for Muslim husbands taking more than one wife and confirms the entitlement of an aggrieved wife or wives to reside separately from such a husband and to get maintenance from him for such separate residence. At p. 39, this author therefore welcomes the decision of the Supreme Court in *Subanu*, obliging a Muslim husband who took a second wife to maintain the first wife separately. It is also indicated that this decision has since been followed by the High Courts.

Economic agenda and financial – even fiscal – considerations have therefore also influenced the current Indian legal approach to Muslim polygamy. In the 1970s, this was not yet clear. Qureshi (1978: 52) distinguishes different types of polygamy among Muslims in India and observes, at pp. 52–53:

> According to most observers, the largest number of bigamous marriages found among Indian Muslims are not cases where the

> husband lives with and supports two wives, which few can afford to do. In most cases of bigamy, the husband abandons his first wife (and frequently children as well) and goes off to marry another woman.
>
> Most of these people do not divorce their wives who are legally bound to them. Frequently, the second wife knows nothing about the earlier marriage, nor of the children, even though these may at a later date, vitally affect her own rights of inheritance as well as the rights of her children. Can this behaviour, by any stretch of imagination, be justified by the two verses of Quran quoted above? This is nothing but simple desertion, followed by bigamy. And yet, the present law of polygamy upholds it.

With respect, this does not appear to me as a scenario of bigamy as much as a consequence of the less than strict approach of Muslim divorce law to the obligations of the divorcing husband. As indicated, all over South Asia today, this is a grave social problem, with which even the Pakistani government has now begun to grapple, notably through islamisation techniques. While it is perfectly legitimate for the government of an avowedly Islamic state to remind its Muslim male population of the Qur'anic obligations in terms of proper divorce rules (and maintenance provisions, it should be added), this option is not really open to the secular Indian government.

While Qureshi rightly highlights the pernicious combination of male desertion and subsequent second marriage, official legal prohibitions on polygamy would, in my submission, make little difference. What counts, at the end of the day, is the tightness of financial obligations through which deserting husbands and fathers can be bound to their duties. Qureshi (1978: 53–55) focuses further on the economic dependence of women in situations of polygamy and concludes at p. 55:

> Polygamy depends on the socio-economic conditions of people. The socio-economic conditions of Indians and specially Muslims are not sound. Comparatively, Muslims are more backward than their brothers of other communities. In the circumstances the institution of polygamy should be completely controlled by the state. The abolition of polygamy will definitely increase the status of the common Muslims.

This well-meaning advice is again based on the simplistic belief in the power of statutory law. It is evidently built on the author's facile assumption (see p. 54) that if many Muslim countries can abolish polygamy through law, then Indian law can and should do the same. This argument is problematic in many ways, though. The legal abolition of polygamy in Turkey, for example, has not totally eradicated the practice, and I do not believe that other Muslim countries, such as Tunisia, have actually succeeded in controlling polygamy. Rather, the various forms of legislative intervention appear to look very impressive, but they have only driven polygamy underground, as several studies from Turkey, for example, have confirmed.[127]

In the 1990s, too, blue-eyed legal optimism is frequently found in the academic writing on Indian family laws. Midha (1990) is a typical modern Indian writer who uncritically eulogises the powers of law and finds blockages for modern development merely in the lack of female education about the legal system. While I do not disagree for a moment with the need for women's legal education, I find this approach too simple, and ultimately wrong. Midha (1990: 78) writes:

> Law, as an instrument of social change, is a potent force, especially in [a] heterogeneous society like ours, not only regulating social relations but also relations between State and society. To make it really effective, women should also be educated on every aspect of legislations concerning them to give them the maximum benefit of such legislations. A realistic and progressive change in law in the light of [the] constitutional mandate for equality and its effective implementation, making the rule of law the way of life, is the *modus operandi* by which social justice for women can be achieved.[128]

Midha (1990: 73) further criticises that polygamy, though illegal for other communities, "is still accepted under Muslim law", as though the religious law could just be modified by legislation. She then writes very interestingly about the lack of legal remedies for Muslim wives in India and their financial predicaments (*id.*):

> Muslim law regards marriage as a contract and some jurists have advocated the adoption of a standard contract providing, inter alia, that the wife shall have the power to divorce her husband if he takes on a second wife. This remedy, however, will not provide any substantial relief to the first wife and children, as the Muslim law absolves the husband of the duty to maintain the divorced wife. the responsibility of maintaining a divorced woman beyond the *iddat* rests on the reluctant relatives. Women, from among the poor are especially vulnerable to practices like polygamy and *talaq*. Often they are mentally and physically tortured by a husband especially if the *mehar* is of reasonable amount. ...

This author, like so many others, was evidently not aware of the substantial legal change introduced by the *Muslim Women (Protection of Rights on Divorce) Act* of 1986, which was passed in reaction to the famous *Shah Bano* case and was widely misunderstood to have taken away the rights of divorced Muslim wives to post-divorce maintenance from the former husband (see in detail chapter 4.3 below). She therefore was not yet able to see that the newly invigorated judicial activism of the Indian courts on female maintenance entitlements would counteract the undoubtedly grave bullying indulged in by Muslim husbands, who force their wives to put up with polygamous marriages or drive them to exercise *khul* rights, thereby forfeiting important entitlements to financial benefits. As we now know, the agenda for the legal abolition of Muslim polygamy have been taken over by financial pressure on polygamous husbands by the superior courts in India.

Singh (1990: 62–63) refers to another form of Muslim polygamy which has underlying economic motives and looks rather like a form of bonded labour coupled with polygamy.[129] She refers to reports from Karnataka about Muslim men engaged in lacquer work. Those men find the religious allowance to marry up to four wives useful, and make these women work for them, "for what they gain by having extra hands to work is much more than what they have to spend on their keep" (p. 63). I have no doubt that Singh is right to emphasise that "there is no doubt that the prevalence of legal sanction for polygyny caused widespread resentment among women of this community" (*id.*), but the legal abolition of polygamy would not rescue such poor women from their economic predicaments, in fact it might make a lot of young women jobless.[130] In other words, this example demonstrates the interrelationship of polygamy with other social phenomena.

Similarly, the popular feminist scholarly argument that "[o]ne of the most terrifying threats that a mother-in-law can hold over a quaking daughter-in-law is that of finding another wife for her son" (*id.*) can of course be related to polygamy, but it is indicative of the impaired bargaining power of many women in Indian socio-legal reality, rather than an indictment of the legal system as such, or a direct consequence of the legal allowances made for polygamy. To reiterate, law by itself cannot create better socio-economic conditions for women, though I accept that the symbolic significance of outlawing polygamy should not be entirely discarded.

Few writers have attempted to produce constructive suggestions for legal reforms. Iyer (1987: 68) severely criticised Professor Derrett for making suggestions about qualified polygamy and writes polemically:

> His error is in reading the Prophet as conferring a polygamous franchise, coupled with mawkish solicitude for Indian Muslim 'religiosity'. Many Indian Muslims need to be saved from their friends. In fairness to Islam and with an eye on reforms, we must repudiate the anti-contextual perversion of western scholarship that prohibition of extravagant polygamy implies permission of limited polygamy. Any dynamic Indian judge, jurist or legislator could have reasonably spelt out monogamy from the original text read in modern Indian circumstances. Living law has to be interpreted in a living way. The words of the Holy *Qur'an* say that if a man cannot treat his two wives with perfect equality, he is enjoined to marry only one wife. It is obvious that in modern Indian conditions, however financially, psychically, sexually potent a husband may be, it is beyond him to show equal justice in every respect to a plurality of wives. The Qur'anic *sine qua non* being impossible now, a court, a legislator and truly religious Muslim would be right in insisting on monogamy.

With great respect to the learned author, he uses the wonderful concept of 'living law' but seems to overlook that not all Muslim men are concerned to be 'truly religious' and some would thus, whether the law allows it or not, make polygamous arrangements. I do not find this kind of discussion fruitful.

Lateef (1990: 11) rightly points out that Muslim resistance to legal changes, such as a ban on polygamy, is not to a change in customs as such, but to formalising such a change through the modern state's legislation. Indu Prakash Singh (1992: 58–59) also confirms that many Muslim women resent polygamy and argues fervently in favour of legislative changes. She recognises that changes in the law would not necessarily eradicate the practice itself, but holds that continuing liberality towards Muslim polygamy by the statute law perpetuates it and gives the wrong social signals. Her assumption that legislated law can directly act as a social norm setter seems too optimistic in view of the development of Indian legal history. This impression is also confirmed by our analysis below of the development of socio-legal realities around the Hindu anti-polygamy law in India.

The Hindu case law on polygamous marriages

We have already seen above how the interplay of three sections in the HMA has comprehensively outlawed polygamy. Before 1955, it had been argued vigorously that polygamy was an integral part of Hindu religion. This was also the reasoning of a Hindu male who did not have a son with his first wife, and claimed that as a Hindu he would be entitled to contract a second marriage in order to obtain a son for religious purposes. This reliance on Hindu freedom of religion, under India's then new and largely untested Constitution, was soundly rejected by Chagla J in *State of Bombay v. Narasu Appa Mali*, AIR 1952 Bom 34.[131] The judge drew a distinction between religious faith and belief, on the one hand, and religious practices on the other, holding that if a religious practice runs counter to public order, morality or health, then it cannot be upheld. In the same case, Gajendragadkar J held that the provisions of personal laws permitting polygamy cannot be said to offend against Article 15(1) of the Constitution of India, i.e. were not discriminatory on the basis of religion, race, caste, sex or place of birth.

This case has given rise to a lively discussion about the extent of discrimination based on gender and religion in Indian law.[132] Cases like *Ram Prasad v. State of U. P.*, AIR 1957 All 411, unsuccessfully challenged those provisions of the HMA which restrict polygamy as unconstitutional and as an infringement of the fundamental right of Hindus to freedom of religion.[133]

Despite the legislative prohibition of Hindu polygamy, however, all writers concur that the legislative abolition of Hindu polygamy has not been effective.[134] Qureshi (1978: 51) pointedly hits the target when he specifically comments on s. 5(i) HMA:

> However, the above provision exists only in theory. Although the number of bigamous marriages has been declining considerably during the last 20 years, the practice has not been eliminated. One of the reasons is the reluctance of the aggrieved wife to go to the court. She is between the devil and the deep sea: if she takes recourse to the law, her husband may be sent to jail (which she does not want) and if she does not, she has to share her husband with another woman.

Mahmood (1986: 115–117), in a section on 'Monogamy at the cost of dishonesty' has this to say at pp. 115–116:

> The West regards monogamy as an absolute ideal in itself and would never pardon the East for any of its laws that may permit the slightest deviation from this western ideal even in the most abnormal circumstances of an individual couple.

He then asks, at p. 116, in view of the abolition of Hindu polygamy in Indian law:

> The question, however, is what relief does the Indian law give to a Hindu, Buddhist, Jain or Sikh wife whose husband unscrupulously plans to marry again for no rhyme or reason? . . . Can prosecution of a bigamist in a criminal court help his first wife? . . .

Finding that no proper relief is available to wronged women, Mahmood (1986: 116–117) goes further:

> Then, has the law as now in force really succeeded in its aim of eradicating bigamy? Bigamous marriages continue to take place as freely as they did before 1955. A Hindu, Buddhist, Jain or Sikh husband who has contracted such a marriage would, if prosecuted, prove to the satisfaction of even the highest court of justice that his second marriage did not at all amount to a "marriage" within the meaning of that term under the Hindu Marriage Act as it lacked in some minute detail of the customary ceremony that was allegedly adhered to.

This entirely appropriate criticism is made with specific reference to the leading case on the matter, *Bhaurao Shankar Lokhande v. State of Maharashtra*, AIR 1965 SC 1564, which we already discussed in chapter 1 above. This was a case involving people from a former low-caste Hindu and now neo-Buddhist community in Maharashtra, recently converted to Buddhism. As a result, they had modified their marriage customs. However, this is not clearly evident from the case report itself and only transpires from later cases in which *Bhaurao Shankar* is referred to.

The husband in this case had married his first wife in 1956 and the second in 1962. He had been convicted by all three lower courts for the offence of polygamy under s. 494 of the *Indian Penal Code*, 1860. On appeal to the Supreme Court, the husband claimed that the essential ceremonies for a valid marriage were not performed when he underwent the second marriage ceremony in 1962. Considering the wording of s. 17 HMA, the Supreme Court concentrated on the word 'solemnised' and held, at pp. 1565–1566, that it is "essential for the purpose of s. 17 of the Act, that the marriage ... should have been celebrated with proper ceremonies and in due form. Merely going through certain ceremonies with the intention that the parties be taken to be married, will not make the ceremonies prescribed by law or approved by any established custom". Seeking to determine what the essential ceremonies for a valid marriage between the parties would be, the court consulted the 12th edition of Mulla's *Hindu law*, in which it was stated, at p. 615:

> (1) There are two ceremonies essential to the validity of a marriage, whether the marriage be in the Brahma form or the Asura form, namely –
> (1) invocation before the sacred fire, and
> (2) saptapadi, that is, the taking of seven steps by the bridegroom and the bride jointly before the sacred fire.
> (2) A marriage may be completed by the performance of ceremonies other than those referred to in sub-section (1), where it is allowed by the custom of the caste to which the parties belong.

The Supreme Court found that in the present case the two essential ceremonies listed above were not performed and that there was no dispute about this. The Court then took an extremely technical approach and held, at p. 1566:

> There is no evidence on record to establish that the performance of these two essential ceremonies has been abrogated by the custom prevalent in their community ... There ought to have been definite evidence to establish that the custom prevalent in the community had abrogated these ceremonies for such form of marriage.

The evidence before the court related to a simple marriage ceremony involving mutual garlanding and minimal ritual, in particular the touching of the foreheads of bride and groom, which seemed to constitute the final rite.[135] This was not found to be sufficient proof of 'proper rituals' and of customary ceremonies. The Court was evidently hesitant to accept evidence of changed customs during the past five or seven years, saying at p. 1567 that "the departure from the essentials cannot be said to have become a custom, as contemplated by the Hindu Marriage Act".

In the context of our present discussion, the important consequence was that the husband's appeal against conviction for bigamy was therefore allowed. This case soon became the leading precedent, extremely convenient and much-used by Hindu polygamists ever since to escape conviction.[136] Following the judicial reasoning of this case, husbands faced with a prosecution for bigamy would simply try to argue that the form of marriage they had undergone did not lead to a legally valid Hindu marriage.

In *Kanwal Ram v. The Himachal Pradesh Administration*, AIR 1966 SC 614, it was held by the Supreme Court, following *Bhaurao Shankar*, that a conviction for bigamy was not justified if it could not be shown that the essential ceremonies for a valid Hindu marriage had been performed. Remarkably, it was held at p. 615 that this was so even where the husband had admitted that he had married the second wife because "it is clear that in law such admission is not evidence of the fact of the second marriage having taken place" (*id.*).

In *Priya Bala Ghosh v. Suresh Chandra Ghosh*, AIR 1971 SC 1153, this basic position was reiterated. This was a first wife's appeal against acquittal of her husband, indicating that she was keen to have him punished for polygamy. She got married to him in 1948, was then allegedly driven out of the house and by 1962 the husband had married a second wife. The husband, in defence, attempted a final blow to his obstinate first wife by claiming that he had never validly married her, but he admitted the fact of the second marriage. The Magistrate's Court had found the husband guilty of bigamy and had sentenced him to rigorous imprisonment for one year and a fine of Rs. 500/-, with half the fine to be paid to the complainant wife. On appeal before the Sessions Judge, the husband had been acquitted because it had been held that both his marriages were legally invalid. The High Court upheld the validity of the first marriage but confirmed the husband's acquittal, hence the wife's appeal to the Supreme Court.

Vaidialingam J in the Supreme Court carefully examined the rival contentions and came to the conclusion that the first marriage was not validly solemnised and therefore dismissed the wife's appeal. This is another technical, totally unsatisfactory decision, which merely relies on the two earlier cases and refuses to consider in any detail the social circumstances of this particular couple. This particular wife must have been devastated, and the decision does not inspire faith in the law at all.[137]

The resulting acquittals of men who had allegedly or actually married polygamously were interpreted by some commentators as a result of judicial caution about evidence. The Committee on the Status of Women in India (1974: 108) wrote:

> While judicial decisions have rendered the enforcement of the penal provision against bigamy in section 17 of the Hindu Marriage Act, 1955 difficult, it would only be fair to say that this stemmed not from a sentiment in favour of bigamy, but from a deep seated judicial attitude that penal provisions should be construed strictly.

Sharma (1994: 85–128) contains an elaborate, useful discussion of India's law on polygamy and criticises the technical constructions placed by the courts on s. 17 HMA, which have had the effect that "[f]or decades, the Judges have treated the issue with remarkable nonchalance and leniency, thus, lending a helping hand to their fellow men by discharging the clever bigamist" (Sharma 1994: 95).

Other scholars, however, have been taking the male perspective and have thereby contributed to a continuation of the unsatisfactory situation in this area of the law. Diwan (1985: 100) uncritically reiterated the standard position, with reference to *Laxmi Sahuani v. Maheswar Sahu*, AIR 1985 Ori 11, and wrote:

> It is an established proposition of Hindu law that the offence of bigamy is committed only if it is conclusively established that the required ceremonies of marriage were performed; the second marriage cannot be taken to be proved by a mere admission of parties and it is incumbent on the petitioner to prove that the essential ceremonies and rites were performed.

This learned author, one of the leading authorities on modern Hindu law, still justified the actions of men in the same fashion ten years later (Diwan and Diwan 1995: 104–105):

> A prosecution for bigamy will fail if what is established is that some sort of ceremonies (not the essential ceremonies as prescribed by law or custom) were performed with the avowed purpose that the parties were to be taken as married, and it is immaterial even if it is established that the parties intended seriously to marry and thought that the ceremonies performed by them would confer marital status on them. It is now established that if the second marriage of the accused is declared void before the prosecution is commenced, no prosecution for bigamy can be made. The mere intention of parties, however serious, will not make them husband and wife and the accused will escape prosecution even if he deliberately performed defective ceremonies.

With respect, this was not the correct position at all if we look at the case law as a whole and not just the cases that suited Professor Diwan's argument in this particular context.[138] It is notable that the above reasoning entirely omits reference to the operative concept of presumption of a valid Hindu marriage and in fact refutes the idea that such a concept may come into play. Turning to the 16th edition of the old practitioners' text of Mulla's *Hindu law*, here cited as Desai (1990: 639), we find at once a very different perspective:

> There is an extremely strong presumption in favour of the validity of a marriage and the legitimacy of its offspring if from the time of the alleged marriage the parties are recognised by all persons concerned as man and wife and are so described in important documents and on important occasions. The like presumption applies to the question whether the formal requisites of a valid marriage ceremony were satisfied. Similarly the fact that a woman was living under the protection of a man who generally lived with her and acknowledged her children raises a strong presumption that she is the wife of that

> man. But this presumption may be rebutted by proof of facts showing that no marriage could have taken place.[139]

Therefore, it is clearly not the whole truth that the Supreme Court of India inevitably had to acquit Hindu polygamists because of the nature of Hindu law, as Diwan and Diwan (1995: 105) try to suggest, when they conclude with reference to the issues of uniformisation and bureaucratisation of modern Indian laws. These authors clearly had different agenda altogether:

> The solution lies in prescribing one ceremony for all Hindu marriages, and by providing for registration of marriages. So long as we recognize all sorts of ceremonies, such things are bound to happen; dupes may take advantage and innocent persons may become their victims.

Vijay Sharma (1994: 108) argues similarly about the need to have "independent and infallible proof of a marriage" and thus falls into the same trap of demanding legal certainty and uniformity, when it should be clear that Indian culture – and certainly the Hindu law of marriage solemnisation – consistently operate against such rigid uniformity. However, she takes an overall much more appropriate socio-legal perspective and notes, for example, that "most second marriages are celebrated without pomp and publicity" (Sharma 1994: 102). Remarkably, as we saw in chapter 1.5 already, the Indian Supreme Court in *M. Govindaraju v. K. Munisami Gounder*, AIR 1997 SC 10, has now explicitly recognised that the Hindu law of marriage and divorce depends to a large extent on caste customs and that courts, also today, have to take appropriate account of them in order to achieve justice.

Sharma (1994) also refers to a number of more recent cases and thus begins to see that the Indian courts have very well been able to use the presumption of marriage in a constructive fashion. Almost everyone, however, seems to have overlooked the small but important Supreme Court case of *Sumitra Devi v. Bhikan Choudhary*, AIR 1985 SC 765, which held that various customary forms of marriage are just as acceptable as the high-caste, ritualised Sanskritic forms of Hindu marriage. This case impliedly challenged *Bhaurao Shankar* and the case law following that precedent, but it was reported as though it was a case under maintenance law. Hence, it appears, nobody made the necessary connections between the presumption of marriage applied in this case and the refusal to recognise presumptions in the line of cases following *Bhaurao Shankar*. It was held in *Sumitra Devi*, at p. 766:

> There is no doubt that in order that there may be a valid marriage according to Hindu law, certain religious rites have to be performed. Invoking the fire and performing Saptapadi around the sacred fire have been considered by this Court to be two of the basic requirements for a traditional marriage. It is equally true that there

> can be a marriage acceptable in law according to customs which do not insist on performance of such rites as referred to above and marriages of this type give rise to [a] legal relationship which law accepts.

As indicated, this case appears to have been overlooked by Professor Diwan and others who regularly commented on Hindu law in India. Apart from this case, it is of course not entirely new that the Indian courts were gradually modifying their approach to the recognition of customary marriages in divergence from the assumed precedent of *Bhaurao Shankar*. For example, in *Baby v. Jayant Mahadeo Jagtap*, AIR 1981 Bom 283, the Bombay High Court had held, in no uncertain terms, that customary forms of marriage among persons governed by the HMA could be modified over time and that the new marriage customs among the neo-Buddhists of Maharashtra would be entitled to full legal recognition. It was held in *Baby*, at p. 294:

> ... this court can take a judicial notice that during the last 25 years a different form of marriage has been devised and adopted by these Buddhists or those who were converted from the scheduled caste to Buddhist faith at least in this part of the country. This different form is not only adopted but has been recognised as of a valid marriage amongst these people. Thousands of marriages are solemnised in this new form and according to these customary rites and ceremonies of marriage. It is not the case of either of the parties that any other rites or ceremonies of marriage are performed amongst people belonging to this community. No argument is advanced before this court that 'Saptapadi' and 'Lajja Homa' were ever part of their marriage rites and ceremonies in the community to which the parties belong. As 'Saptapadi' and 'Lajja Homa' were not parts of the rites and ceremonies of the marriage, the only question is whether the ceremonies which have been proved by evidence on record in this case are the rites and ceremonies according to custom of either or both of the parties. As observed earlier, there is no dispute that these rites and ceremonies are the only ones adopted and followed uniformly amongst the members of this community for more than last 25 years. The refusal to recognise the solemnization of such ceremonies of marriage as a valid and legal marriage will visit these people with untold miseries of grave social consequences.

The court also held, at pp. 294–295:

> ... over the last 25 years several forms of marriage aimed at simplicity and economy have been adopted by different sects of Hindus ...
>
> ... If a different and new form or variation in the ceremonies and rites of marriage are adopted by a particular community, the law has to take cognizance of the same at some point of time and accord them

> recognition in the eye of law. If the courts refuse to recognize such forms of marriages, it will bring, as stated earlier, untold miseries to the members of this community.

The result of this perceptive and socially alert judicial approach was that the bigamous husband in this case would be found guilty of the crime. On the offence of bigamy, the Court had this to say at p. 299:

> Once the offence of bigamy is proved, the court cannot take a lenient view regarding the sentence. In this country specially in this part of the country, it is not infrequent that the husband marries [a] second time and leaves the first wife to her fate to lead a life of untold miseries for the rest of her life. No sympathy can be shown to such persons . . .
>
> . . . The attitude of such persons who marry the second time is not only a cavalier one but a wanton one. Such types of persons allow themselves to be under the impression that the long arm of the law cannot touch them inasmuch as there can be no proof of the solemnization of the second marriage,

The husband was, therefore, sentenced to two years of rigorous imprisonment and a fine of Rs. 1,000/-. The court also took steps to disseminate this judgment to law officials in the state of Maharashtra. However, this was not a Supreme Court case, so it could only shake the authority of *Bhaurao Shankar* but could not topple it as a precedent.[140]

In *Santi Deb Berma v. Kanchan Prava Devi*, AIR 1991 SC 816, we still find an unsatisfactory Supreme Court case which frees a bigamous husband. This is a bigamous husband's appeal against conviction by the High Court of Gauhati, which had applied a presumption of performance of all the required ceremonies, in view of the evidence that the husband and his second wife had lived like a married couple. However, it was held by the Supreme Court, at p. 817, that "the High Court is not at all justified in drawing such an inference in the absence of any reliable and acceptable evidence, in regard to the performance of Saptapadi". The second marriage was therefore declared invalid, and the husband was swiftly acquitted. The insistence on performance of *saptapadi* by the Supreme Court in this case, inspired by the earlier leading cases and perhaps Sanskritic judicial bias, seems entirely misguided.

More recent case law has shown two trends, already discussed in chapter 1.5 above. In cases where polygamists are on trial, the courts will still often collude with the male and will acquit the bigamist, hiding behind the law as stated in *Bhaurao Shankar*. In most other cases,[141] however, the factual situation is different, in that the husband attempts to deny the factum of the marriage because he wants to evade his financial or social responsibilities. In such cases, of which there are now many, as we also saw in chapter 1.5 above, the Indian courts have, since the mid-1980s, taken a rather different approach to the question of validity of Hindu marriages. They have liberally applied presumptions of marriage, trying to protect women and to allow them a basis for claims of maintenance or other relief.[142] The same goes for the position of children and protection of their legal status, despite the fact that the marriage of their parents may be void.[143]

We have already seen that the deeply unsatisfactory case of *Surjit Kaur v. Garja Singh*, AIR 1994 SC 135, was seriously out of line in that it was treated by the judges like a (female) polygamy case, so that legal validity of the marriage undergone by the couple was refused and the widow was sent away in disgrace.[144] Happily, *Surjit Kaur* is really an exception. The Indian courts are demonstrating that they can handle the complex law of marriage solemnisation with compassion and an eye to the needs of women and children, but they still have a soft spot for the Hindu polygamist faced with a jail sentence. *Bhaurao Shankar* is still widely presumed to be the leading case on the subject and legal advice to any potential complainant would probably be given on that basis.[145]

Our analysis confirms, therefore, that despite the legislative prohibition of Hindu polygamy, the courts have been far too lenient towards polygamous men and appear to have inclined towards protecting them. Thapalyal (1986: 11) has rightly commented that "[t]he interpretation of this law by contemporary Indian courts ... has created tremendous confusion and made evasion of the law all too easy", noting that "prosecution does not often lead to conviction" (*id.*). If the courts were to become more aware of the manifest abuse of the law on marriage solemnisation in relation to cases of polygamy, then indeed Hindu wives would be better protected against the polygynous inclinations of Hindu men. The statute law by itself has not created a situation where Hindu polygamy has been wiped off the legal map altogether.

Conversion as a distracting issue

Mahmood (1986: 117) has highlighted this problem in the context of inefficient legal control of Hindu polygamy:

> A husband who is more cautious, and does not want to incur even the risk of prosecution, would announce a sham conversion to Islam and then marry again under an absolutely fallacious belief that Islamic law comes to his shelter.

Apart from Mahmood,[146] several authors have been fascinated by this topic, on which many years earlier Professor Derrett wrote many articles.[147] Diwan (1993b: 240) raised in particular the question how, under private international law, such marriages should be treated.

The well-publicised recent case of *Sarla Mudgal v. Union of India*, AIR 1995 SC 1531, was a case concerning the allegedly widespread practice of Hindu husbands who chose conversion to Islam to escape conviction for polygamy and evasion of their socio-economic responsibilities. This case was brought to the Supreme Court by a social actions group concerned about women's rights and several women who were directly affected by the husband's polygamy and conversion.

Kuldip Singh J, in his judgment, took as a powerful starting point (p. 1532) the argument that modern Indian law should by now really have implemented a uniform civil code (see ch. 6 below). The main question in the case related to the extent of criminal penalties for a Hindu husband who converts to Islam and married another wife. Would such a man be guilty of polygamy under s. 494 of the *Indian Penal Code*? Kuldip Singh, J commented on marriage in the following terms at p. 1533:

> Marriage is the very foundation of the civilised society. The relation once formed, the law steps in and binds the parties to various obligations and liabilities thereunder. Marriage is an institution in the maintenance of which the public at large is deeply interested. It is the foundation of the family and in turn of the society without which no civilisation can exist.

However, as the learned judge portrayed it, the security of marriage was under threat from the plurality of legal systems in Indian law. It was stated, at p. 1533:

> Till the time we achieve the goal – uniform civil code for all the citizens of India – there is an open inducement to a Hindu husband, who wants to enter into a second marriage while the first marriage is subsisting, to become a Muslim. Since monogamy is the law for Hindus and the Muslim law permits as many as four wives in India, [an] errand Hindu husband embraces Islam to circumvent the provisions of the Hindu law and to escape from penal consequences.

It was noted (at p. 1533) that under the traditional Hindu law, conversion to another religion would not have had the effect of dissolving a Hindu marriage. The case law in this regard, discussed by the learned judge, shows the influence of the Hindu concept of marriage as a sacrament (*samskara*).[148] The position was summed up at p. 1536:

> It is, thus, obvious from the catena of case-law that a marriage celebrated under a particular personal law cannot be dissolved by the application of another personal law to which one of the spouses converts and the other refuses to do so. Where a marriage takes place under Hindu Law the parties acquire a status and certain rights by the marriage itself under the law governing the Hindu Marriage and if one of the parties is allowed to dissolve the marriage by adopting and enforcing a new personal law, it would [be] tantamount to destroying the existing rights of the other spouse who continues to be Hindu. We, therefore, hold that under the Hindu Personal Law as it existed prior to its codification in 1955, a Hindu marriage continued to subsist even after one of the spouses converted to Islam. There was no automatic dissolution of the marriage.

> The position has not changed after coming into force of the Hindu Marriage Act, 1955 (the Act) rather it has become worse for the apostate....

Considering various provisions of the HMA, it was then held, at p. 1536:

> It is obvious from the various provisions of the Act that the modern Hindu Law strictly enforces monogamy. A marriage performed under the Act cannot be dissolved except on the grounds available under Section 13 of the Act.[149] In that situation parties who have solemnised the marriage under the Act remain married even when the husband embraces Islam in pursuit of [an] other wife. A second marriage by an apostate under the shelter of conversion to Islam would nevertheless be a marriage in violation of the provisions of the Act by which he would be continuing to be governed so far as his first marriage under the Act is concerned despite his conversion to Islam. The second marriage of an apostate would, therefore, be an illegal marriage *qua* his wife who married him under the Act and continues to be Hindu. Between the apostate and his Hindu wife the second marriage is in violation of the provisions of the Act and as such would be non est.

Having briefly looked at the provisions of s. 494 of the *Indian Penal Code*, the learned judge continued, at pp. 1536–1537:

> It is no doubt correct that the marriage solemnised by a Hindu husband after embracing Islam may not be strictly a void marriage under the Act because he is no longer a Hindu, but the fact remains that the said marriage would be in violation of the Act which strictly professes monogamy.

On the question of void marriages, it was held at p. 1537:

> A Hindu marriage solemnised under the Act can only be dissolved on any of the grounds specified under the Act.[150] Till the time a Hindu marriage is dissolved under the Act none of the spouses can contract [a] second marriage. Conversion to Islam and marrying again would not, by itself, dissolve the Hindu marriage under the Act. The second marriage by a convert would therefore be in violation of the Act and as such void in terms of Section 494, I. P. C. Any act which is in violation of mandatory provisions of law is per se void.
>
> The real reason for the voidness of the second marriage is the subsisting of the first marriage which is not dissolved even by the conversion of the husband. It would be giving a go-bye to the substance of the matter and acting against the spirit of the Statute if the second marriage of the convert is held to be legal.

Kuldip Singh J asserted, at p. 1537, that this approach to the matter was also in line with 'justice, equity and good conscience' and with the principles of natural justice. Thus, it was held, at p. 1537:

> The interpretation we have given to Section 494, I.P.C. would advance the interest of justice. It is necessary that there should be harmony between the two systems of law just as there should be harmony between the two communities. Result of the interpretation we have given ... would be that the Hindu Law on the one hand and the Muslim Law on the other hand would operate within their respective ambits without trespassing on the personal laws of each other. Since it is not the object of Islam nor is the intention of the enlightened [sic] Muslim community that the Hindu husband should be encouraged to become Muslims merely for the purpose of evading their own personal laws by marrying again, the Courts can be persuaded to adopt a construction of the laws resulting in denying the Hindu husband converted to Islam the right to marry again without having his existing marriage dissolved in accordance with law.
>
> ... We, therefore, hold that the second marriage of a Hindu husband after his conversion to Islam is a void marriage in terms of Section 494, I.P.C.

Noting that "[m]uch misapprehension prevails about bigamy in Islam" (p. 1540), R. M. Sahai J concurred with the judgment by Kuldip Singh J and added, at p. 1540, some comments of his own regarding the further legislative control of cross-religious polygamy:

> The Government may also consider [the] feasibility of appointing a Committee to enact Conversion of Religion Act, immediately, to check the abuse of religion by any person. The law may provide that every citizen who changes his religion cannot marry another wife unless he divorces his first wife. The provision should be made applicable to every person whether he is a Hindu or a Muslim or a Christian or a Sikh or a Parsi or a Budh. Provision may be made for maintenance and succession etc. also to avoid clash of interest after death.
>
> This would go a long way to solve the problem and pave the way for a unified civil code.

Significantly, these comments only concern men and do not appear to take into account that women may wish to change their religion, too. This important judgment takes explicit notice of a problem which has exist in South Asian societies for a long time, as the judgment fully acknowledges. It may be doubted whether the legislative prescription of automatic divorce on conversion would find much favour. After all, the *Dissolution of Muslim Marriages* Act, 1939 was partly put on the statute book to avoid this very scenario when Muslim women converted to another religion.

The decision in *Sarla Mudgal*, nullifying and criminalising a convert's polygamous marriage represents a significant inroad into the legislative non-intervention in Muslim polygamy. This case, therefore, should be read as further evidence that Muslim polygamy in modern India is not as uncontrolled as has been commonly assumed. Significantly, the two learned judges in *Sarla Mudgal* also raised the concomitant issue of financial provisions for the dependants of men who seek to marry polygamously. In the concluding section, we take up this theme again, and thus link the recent legal developments on the Indian law of polygamy with those regarding marriage and divorce.

Conclusion: No favours for polygamists: Pay up or marry one wife only

In the various communities of India, polygamy appears in all kinds of forms. The reported cases most certainly only scratch the surface of a deep bowl of hidden practices. For example, in a number of recent cases we find evidence of husbands remarrying while an appeal relating to their divorce is still pending.[151] I am sure that this is not a new phenomenon, but it has achieved some notoriety. Diwan (1992: 206) found strong words to criticise this practice, but most courts seem to be too busy to take explicit notice of such obvious contempt of court.[152] This may lead to strange results, such as court-induced polygamy, when the divorce decree is refused, but the husband has already married another wife in the meantime.

The case of a Hindu woman from Himachal Pradesh who went to court asking for her husband to be granted the right to marry polygamously is probably more than an amazing exception. *Santosh Kumari v. Surjit Singh*, AIR 1990 HP 77, was decided by the learned Chief Justice himself, N. M. Kasliwal. A District Magistrate had permitted a man to contract a second marriage because his existing wife was weak and ailing. The judge had ruled that the existing wife should remain the legally wedded wife and she and her daughter should be entitled to appropriate maintenance for life and, in the case of the daughter, until her marriage. It was held, at p. 78, that "[t]he above order is absolutely wrong and illegal and against the clear provisions of the Hindu Marriage Act, 1955". The lower court judge was severely reprimanded for his lack of knowledge of the relevant law and the order was set aside, at pp. 78–79:

> The Sub Judge has clearly ignored the provisions of the Hindu Marriage Act as well as the Indian Penal Code in this regard. The Sub Judge is expected to know such elementary principle of law and it is a gross mistake on his part to have ignored such principle of law and to have given a decree contrary to the provisions of [the] Hindu Marriage Act and perpetuate a criminal offence of bigamy punishable under the Indian Penal Code.

It was of course an entirely proper course of action on the part of the High Court to make this decision, and to publish it in those terms.[153] However, this does not solve the social dilemmas of any couple in India who seem to have agreed that a polygamous arrangement may suit them best. To be sent away from the official courts in such a situation creates an obvious communication block between law and society and does not allow for an open debate about the best possible solution to a particular family's difficulties. Here we see that the absolute legal prohibition of polygamy prevents the courts from playing a role in consensual arrangements – while they do of course have a crucial role when any arrangements are contested. Many socio-legal researchers are aware of the fact that only certain disputes, or certain segments of disputes are brought to the official courts.[154] The key lesson from *Santosh Kumari* is therefore that a couple who agree to arrange polygamy within the family should not approach an official court to have this family arrangement formally sanctified. It clearly violates basic principles of current Indian public policy. If, however, the modern Indian system of family law regulation relies, as it clearly does, more and more on self-help and extra-judicial arrangements, then this does not preclude bigamous family arrangements unless anyone complains.

Such distractions and concerns notwithstanding, there can be no doubt, on the other hand, that most Indian women do not like polygamy and would presumably oppose such family arrangements. Alka Singh (1992: 82–85) provides a report on fieldwork among Muslim women in Lucknow and Delhi and shows that only a tiny minority of women found polygamy acceptable:

> The data show that in Lucknow 95.33 per cent women spoke against it. However, 4.66 per cent thought it to be acceptable under certain specific conditions such as barrenness of the first wife or in the case where the first wife is not keeping in good health.
>
> Similarly, in Delhi, 3.33 per cent spoke in favour of polygamy whereas 96.6 per cent firmly believed that the present-day circumstances including social and economic factors do not leave any scope for men to marry more than one time.

Singh also found that in most cases, the first wife did not know of the existence of the second marriage, and often vice versa. Her research contains a clear call for "some legislation putting a ban on this practice" (Singh 1992: 84). She also cites, at p. 85, a Muslim author from the 1970s to the effect that "[t]he state can validly enact measures of social welfare and reforms in respect of the matter governed by the Muslim Law".[155] Such comments display considerable confusion – certainly a notable lack of clarity – about the potential role of the law makers. Do the various authors ask for legislation, or do they recognise that judges can also make law? Judges certainly can and do make law in the Indian legal system, despite pious lipservice to some colonial concepts of judicial restraint. Such lack of clarity is also evident in the comments by Agrawala and Ramanamma on bigamy (1994: 257):

> The law of bigamy, and the judicial interpretation under the Hindu Marriage Act, 1955, are no deterrent to the Hindu husband. This attitude of law evidently discourages the Indian woman from expecting relief under the formal amended law. Underlying this is

> probably a compromise of the Indian legislator and the judge to help the woman while yet not being too hard on the man. This ambivalence of the legislator and the judge is, however, at the cost of the woman's interests. Be that as it may, it amply establishes lack of conviction of the lawgivers in the offence of bigamy.

Is it really justifiable to group legislators and judges together in this way? Other commentators have brought law enforcement agencies into the picture. Thus, Sharma (1994: 111–112) criticises that the legal provisions against Hindu polygamy suffer from being non-cognizable, to the effect that courts can only act if an aggrieved person makes a complaint. She writes at p. 112:

> Therefore, the police and the law enforcing authority should be empowered to act on their own since the status of marriage is one in which the whole of society has an interest and not just parties to the marriage. Thus, the evil practice of bigamy can be effectively put down if the offence is made cognizable.

With respect, this does not appear to be a satisfactory solution because of the way in which law enforcement agencies like the police work in India. Instead of arresting a bigamous husband, officers would probably try to extract money from him. The track record of such authorities in promoting justice is not at all impressive and gives rise to many concerns about a police state.[156]

In her recommendations, Vijay Singh (1994: 357–361) identifies the lack of official documentation of marriages as a problem. She writes, at p. 358:

> There exists, therefore, a need for an independent and infallible proof of marriage. Compulsory registration of marriage provides a proof of marriage and it would help those women whose husbands disown them for lack of proof of marriage.

However, is it realistic to expect the Indian state to introduce a complex bureaucracy of compulsory marriage solemnisation, which anyway would not be foolproof and would be undermined in many different ways?[157] In the context of a detailed, very engaged article arguing in favour of compulsory registration of all Hindu marriages, Ranbir Singh (1991: 44–47) also argues that the solution lies in prescribing one ceremony for all Hindu marriages and by providing for registration of such marriages. It should be noted that his arguments are almost verbatim copied from Professor Paras Diwan, whose views on the subject we have already discussed.

It is of course correct, as Singh (1994: 359) reiterates, that many Indian judges have helped polygamists by insisting on impossible standards of proof of 'solemnisation'. However, to discard the element of marriage solemnisation and to argue for compulsory registration would be a classic example of throwing out the baby with the bath water. I can only reiterate my observation that the Indian state has many more important things to do than trying to establish a fool-proof marriage registration system in order to control polygamy. In view of the case law relating to Hindu marriage solemnisation and its link with polygamy, it is more than evident that the most cost-effective method to protect Indian wives against allegations that their marriage was not valid is the liberal use of presumptions of marriage, already a well-known and well-used concept.

Overall, as in the reform debates on Indian marriage and divorce, I find that most of the wonderful scholarly and activist suggestions about how to protect women from modern Indian society's ills are not realistic remedies. We have much evidence that the modern state is barring itself from playing an active role in the arrangements that people wish to make on their own terms. This is exactly parallel to the scenario of a divorcing couple who agree that their marriage is at an end. They, too, using customary norms, may remain outside the official fora to make their own consensual agreements. I have argued in chapters 1 and 2 above that the modern Indian state appears to be happy to delegate jurisdiction over many matters to society and to act – rather in the manner of the ancient Indian ruler – as a safety valve or watchdog over justice. It is therefore important to facilitate access to courts for those individuals who wish to make a *bona fide* complaint. However, if members of society are willing to tolerate local arrangements made for them, then the law should not pretend that it has an obligation to interfere because we are more concerned to follow international political correctness than to achieve locally sustainable arrangements for people in their daily lives. The ever-ready assumption that formally uneducated rustics 'suffer' from their customary legal arrangements is highly questionable – such people would not have such rules if they were really so bad.

On the other hand, UN Charters and legislative enactments do not feed people in their villages. Saying this, I am of course aware that the voices of women and children may not be adequately heard in the local bargaining over rule systems. But again, an adequate solution lies less in top-down legal models that interfere in people's daily lives on ideological or legal centralist grounds. What is needed, rather, are support mechanisms that allow such unheard voices to be heard. This is not primarily a law job.

My argument regarding the legal regulation of polygamy in India is, therefore, that the state cannot, in this field of law, suddenly take a different stance from that taken in marriage and divorce law and insist on being involved in all arrangements within society. The modern law cannot construct a system of rules which amounts to virtual permission for DIY marriages and divorces and then expect to control polygamous arrangements. Legislation or no legislation, the courts should be there to assist women and children if polygamous arrangements are made that clearly cause them distress and disadvantage, but it is not the state law's task to lay down binding statutory norms for everyone's private life.

The fact that using the official mechanisms of the state law may be counterproductive becomes evident also if we look briefly at another recent case, which is not exceptional in its facts and conclusion. *Sanjay Mishra v. Eveline Jobe*, AIR 1993 MP 54, concerns a Hindu man and an Indian Christian woman who allegedly married, but the 'husband' refused to acknowledge that a lawful marriage had taken place. The woman had distributed copies of a marriage registration document under the *Special Marriage Act*, 1954 among her friends, while the man admitted to having signed certain marriage registration documents in a Registrar's office, but this had happened under duress. The woman alleged that the couple had got married in a famous Hindu temple in Calcutta some time in 1985 in accordance with Hindu customs and rites and had thereafter lived as husband and wife.

The judge found, correctly, that under the provisions of the HMA, a Hindu man and a Christian woman could not validly marry, thus the 'wife's' claim to have followed Hindu customary rituals of marriage collapsed. Significantly, the lower court was criticised for overlooking such crucial facts regarding the personal law of the parties and it was said, at p. 58:

> The trial court has merely gone by the registration certificate; but such registration is valid only when it is found that there is a valid marriage. Where the factum itself is disputed, essential ceremony constituting the marriage in the instant case in accordance with Hindu rites must be pleaded and proved and the performance of such rites must be brought on records.

It was quite inappropriate for the court in the present case to have presumed (see para 23 at p. 58) that rituals like the *saptapadi* are an essential element of a valid Hindu marriage. However, the decision reached is perfectly correct. The registration document pertaining to this 'marriage' cannot be effective in law since there was no evidence of a properly solemnised marriage between the parties, merely the registration document itself. The young man's appeal was therefore allowed.

This kind of case, which of course does not concern polygamy, rather a lovers' liaison that did not work out, reinforces the picture that I have painted of the modern Indian state's deliberate and purposeful refusal to claim full jurisdiction over all marriage-related matters. With specific reference to the control of polygamy, Mahmood (1986: 117) made some comments which are relevant to the present debate:[158]

> Much more effective than legislative abolition of bigamy would, in fact, be its judicial control. A legal provision to the effect that whoever is once married under the Hindu Marriage Act – *whether he remains a Hindu or not* – cannot under any circumstances marry again without prior permission of the court, coupled with powers conferred on the courts to effectively prevent a proposed bigamous marriage likely to be contracted without its prior consent, would yield much better results. Under such a law, in a case of exceptional hardship the court can even give permission for a second marriage,

> instantly dissolving the first marriage at the same time, should the other spouse insist on it. Similar provisions may be introduced, *mutatis mutandis*, into the Special Marriage Act, 1954

In view of the decision in *Sarla Mudgal*, AIR 1995 SC 1531, we see that the first point in Mahmood's argument has actually been followed by the case law. However, the Indian courts, as we saw above in *Santosh Kumari v. Surjit Singh*, AIR 1990 HP 77, would not be prepared to underwrite polygamous arrangements made by the spouses, even if the existing wife expressly agreed to this. Professor Mahmood (1986: 117) rightly sensed that this would not be agreeable to the Indian courts:

> For appreciating and accepting these suggestions we shall, of course, have to give up our blind imitation of the West in regarding monogamy as an ideal in itself and not as one of the means to attain the real ideal – *viz.*, mutual welfare of the couple.

In conversations with Indians, I have been amazed about the strength of popular assumptions, in India and among Indians abroad, that the Muslims of Pakistan, through s. 6 of the *Muslim Family Laws Ordinance*, 1961 have effectively been prohibited from practising polygamy. This assumption is then used for the further argument that it is therefore entirely unreasonable for the Indian Muslims to oppose state-sponsored legal controls on Muslim polygamy. This is also reflected in the scholarly literature. For example, Verma (1988: 57) asserts that "[i]n Pakistan it is not possible to practise polygamy without permission from the Arbitration Council". This is a convenient myth, however, since even the slightest perusal of the relevant case law in Pakistan confirms that any polygamous marriage in contravention of s. 6 of the Ordinance remains legally valid.[159] So much for the power of statutory law!

Purporting to outlaw Muslim polygamy through the *Muslim Family Laws Ordinance* of 1961, while actually tolerating it in practice, then, Pakistan merely pretends to have followed the Western anti-polygamy model. The socio-legal reality in India and in Pakistan, despite legislative control of Muslim polygamy in one country and no legislative control in the other, has remained quite the same, however. In either country, if a woman were to complain to a court about the husband's polygamy, the judges would in all probability help her to obtain financial relief and other provisions. While it seems fully recognised everywhere that courts cannot repair broken marital relationships, they have a definite role in re-balancing gender relations.

Already Qureshi (1978: 54) noted that in India, where Muslim polygamy has not been prohibited by law, the judiciary has at least tried to play a beneficial role:

> Though no reforms have been made in India either to restrict or abolish polygamy among Muslims, the courts have always tried to control this practice.

Similarly, Ganai (1990: 423–424) commented in detail on the positive evidence of helpful judicial intervention on behalf of wronged Muslim wives in India. At p. 424, he concluded:

> The judiciary can still play an important role in liberalising and modernising the rules of Muslim law relating to marriage and divorce. The need for doing so is greater today then ever before, in view of the changing socio-economic conditions. Innovative exercises on the part of the judges in re-defining and re-interpreting uncodified Muslim matrimonial law by making use of the diversity of opinions among the Muslim jurists themselves is the need of the time. There is larger scope for uninhibited judicial adventure in that part of the Muslim matrimonial law which is codified, since in that case the courts are called upon to interpret statute law which has already replaced traditional law. Reforms by judicial law-making may, in familial matters, achieve objectives probable if not impossible of realisation by political processes and without the public outcry that political debate engenders.

Comparing this to the comments by Qureshi (1978: 51) on Hindu polygamy and his argument that despite the legislative prohibition of polygamy among Hindus the practice continues and does not appear to be controlled by the judiciary, we see that the ironic circle is almost complete. Qureshi blames only the predicaments of Hindu wives for the lack of implementation of the anti-polygamy law, when in fact he should have said quite a bit about the clever abuse of s. 7 HMA by male polygamists pleading mercy before a male-dominated judiciary. It might then have become clearer that the statutory abolition of Hindu polygamy in India seems to have led to defensive judicial moves in favour of husbands under threat of criminalisation, while the Muslim husband's legalised discretion to contract polygamous marriages has triggered off judicial paternalism towards wronged wives and children.

It must therefore be argued that the much-criticised rash legislative intervention in India's cauldron of polygamy appears to have been counterproductive. One could take this argument one step further and call, with some trepidation and a modicum of mischief, for the reintroduction of some form of 'controlled' polygamy into modern Indian law. However, as the discussion in this chapter has shown, the most important guarantor of ultimate justice in Indian matrimonial law is not some type of uniform legislation, but the judicial supervision of justice on a case-by-case basis.

Perhaps the time has come for countries of the South to assert themselves against the dominant legal models of the North and to openly go their own way, rather than pretending all the time to follow the West. At the end of the day, as one could discuss at great length, there may be little real difference between following international standards of human rights norms and indigenous values of equitable justice. One senses, though, that it is a matter of pride for Western observers as well as many members of the

Indian élite (among whom, no doubt, we have to count the judges) to be following Western 'rule of law' models based on equality and uniformity rather than indigenous traditions of relative justice and equity between diverse, unequal (and thereby ultimately again equal) partners. It behoves the secular legal model of India, purportedly based on equidistance from all religions, to stop worrying about Hindu domination (or the corresponding Muslim apprehensions of minority suppression) and to get down to the real issues of substantive justice. Looking back at the legal position concerning polygamy in modern Indian law, it has come as a bit of a surprise to find that most judges are so well-focused on the job in hand that women and children who suffer from the consequences of polygamy can actually expect a sympathetic hearing.

Notes

1 As I show further below, this assertion is not correct for South Asia as a whole. If we draw Pakistan into the same picture, we see the impact of Western expectations on the family law reforms of the 1960s in that country, too.

2 Iqbal (1989: 165–175) provides an elaborate defence of polygamy under Islam and emphasises at p. 171 that the practice of polygamy in any society ensures a sharp drop in crimes such as adultery, prostitution and problems of spinsterhood, which is why Muslim women do not have the problem of sharing their husbands with 'keeps' and mistresses. The idealising assertions of this female Pakistani writer are seriously contradicted by evidence from case reports from both India and Pakistan.

3 In this context, it is still considered newsworthy, from time to time, that aged Muslim men marry yet again, this time a very young woman who could be their great-granddaughter. A recent example from Egypt was reported in the *Asian Times* of 2nd March 1999, concerning a man allegedly 114 years old who was about to marry a girl of 17 years. Not surprisingly, there was opposition to this proposed marriage from his own family.

4 Tunisia abolished polygamy through legislative reforms in 1956. For details see Pearl and Menski (1998: 241–242).

5 Syria enacted a law in 1953 to the effect that financial ability of the husband should be the major criterion for ascertaining whether a Muslim husband should be allowed to take a further wife. For details see *id.*

6 For details see *Jesmin Sultana v. Mohammad Elias* (1997) 17 BLD 4; Pearl and Menski (1998: 271).

7 See now *ibid.*: 273–278.

8 It is, of course, another misguided stereotype about Muslim law that it only allows the husband to repudiate the marital contract.

9 For details see Pearl and Menski (1998: 301–302).

10 The 1939 Act applies also in Pakistan and Bangladesh and has given rise to a remarkable case law, details of which are found in relevant sections of Pearl and Menski (1998).

11 In that regard, the excellent fieldwork-based study of Khanam (1960) deserves special notice, since it brings out so very well the dilemmas of women who have to make decisions by weighing the pros and cons of divorce with tolerating polygamy.

12 As we shall see in chapter 4.1 below, the important *Shah Bano* case and its aftermath taught Indian Muslims that getting involved with the Supreme Court would subject Muslim practices to constitutional and public interest tests.

13 Several authors have provided brief comments about the Vedic, classical and medieval periods of Hindu law in relation to polygamy. Choudhary (1988: 2) reiterates that polygamy was rare in ancient times. Sharma (1994: 16–17) comments that polygamy was never recommended openly, though it was generally tolerated in the Vedic period and he writes, at pp. 24–25, that polygamy in the post-Vedic period was not held in contempt. Shastri (1990: 29–30 and 53–54) discusses polygamy in the Vedic and post-Vedic period and concludes, at p. 54, that "generally monogamy was followed by the vast majority of the people. It was only in special circumstances that a second marriage was resorted to". See also Vyas (1993: 194–196) and in much detail Mishra (1994: 158–166).

14 Significantly, nobody claims, to my knowledge, that they have been given any undue favours.

15 For details see Pearl and Menski (1998: 247–273). In Pakistan, the case of *Faheemuddin v. Sabeeha Begum*, PLD 1991 SC 1074, contains a recent example of judicial social criticism, directed at a man who failed to tell his second wife that he was already married.

16 A case in point is *C. Obula Konda Reddy v. C. Pedda Venkata Lakshamma*, AIR 1976 AP 43, where a woman who was party to a polygamous and therefore legally void marriage was nevertheless granted maintenance from the 'husband'.

17 Precisely the same argument applies to the modern Indian state's policy towards the legal validity of child marriages. Here, too, despite ideological objections, the protection of the tangible interests of women and children is considered more important than obedience to dominant, metropolitan gender ideology. My arguments are supported by the only case on the subject found in the *All India Reporter* during the 1990s, *Gajara Naran Bhura* AIR 1997 Guj 185.

18 See for example Derrett (1967), his most important article on bigamous marriages. More recently, Parashar (1994) has focused on legal conflicts which arise in situations of conversion to another religion.

19 The new *Encyclopaedia Britannica*, Vol. VIII, 15th ed. p. 97; *Encyclopaedia Biblica*, Vol. 3, pp. 2946–2947; W. Goodsell, *A history of marriage and the family*, Rev. ed. New York, pp. 59–60.

20 1st ed., p. 134.

21 Quotes Hammudah Abdul Ali, *The family structure in Islam*, p. 111.

22 Goodsell, supra; Abdul Ali, supra, pp. 111–112; M. Masharuddin Siddiqui, *Women in Islam*, 1980, pp. 110–111; *Encyclopaedia Biblica*, Vol. 3, p. 2946.

23 Goodsell, supra; Deuteronomy, XXI–15; *The Standard Jewish Encyclopaedia*, p. 1526.

24 *Encyclopaedia Britannica*, Vol. V; Abdul Ali, supra, p. 113.

25 1st ed., pp. 39–40.

26 Siddiqui, supra, p. 113.

27 Edward Alexander Westermarck, *The history of human marriage*, New York, 1922, Vol. 1, pp. 43–44.

28 Ralph Linton, *The study of man*, New York, 1936, p. 27.

29 Robert Roberts, *The social laws of the Qur'an*, 1977, pp. 8–9.

30 Edward Day, *The social life of the Hebrew*, New York, 1901, pp. 38 and 41.

31 Goodsell, supra, p. 63; Weh Lecky, *History of European morals*, Vol. 2, p. 349.

32 Westermarck, supra, Vol. 1, p. 495; Vol. 2, p. 392; Vol. 3, pp. 233–235. Also see G. R. Leslie, *The family in social context*, 1967, p. 169.

33 Goodsell, supra, pp. 21 and 60; R. H. Lowie, *Primitive society*, 1960, p. 42.

34 Abdul Ali, supra, pp. 112–116.

35 *Ibid.*, pp. 113–114. Lecky, supra, p. 343.

36 A. Schopenhauer, *Selected essays*, 1900, pp. 338–339.

37 Vol. 1, p. 68.

38 Roberts, supra, pp. 7–9; Fida Hussain, *Wives of the Prophet (SAW)*, 1st ed. p. 64; Westermarck, supra, Vol. 1, pp. 44–48; Al-Haj M. Ullah Jung, *The Muslim law of marriage*, 1986, p. XXXI.
39 2nd ed., pp. 29–30.
40 Lecky, supra, p. 343; Abdul Ali, supra, p. 114.
41 A. Michels, *Sparta*, 1952, p. 34; S. G. Wilson, *Persian life and customs*, 1st ed., pp. 2292ff.
42 K. M. Kapadia, *Marriage and family in India*, pp. 54–58; Paras Diwan, *Modern Hindu law*, 4th ed., p. 96.
43 Julius Jolly, *Hindu law and custom*, 1975, p. 140.
44 *Ibid.*, p. 146.
45 Id.
46 Kapadia, supra, pp. 92–98.
47 *Ibid.*, pp. 98–100.
48 R. Smith, *Kinship and marriage in Arabia*, 1903, pp. 145–146 and 157; Kapadia, supra, pp. 52–85.
49 *Id.*
50 E. Belfort Bax, *Selected essays of Arthur Schopenhauer*, 1900, pp. 350–351.
51 Lowie, supra, p. 42.
52 M. F. Nimkoff, *Marriage and the family*, Boston, p. 42.
53 Roberts, supra, p. 9; Smith, supra, p. 157.
54 Qur'an, iv: 3.
55 *Id.*
56 Maulana Abdul Majid Daryabadi, *Tafsirul Qur'an*, Vol. I., pp. 372–373.
57 Maulana Mohammad Ali, *Translation of Qur'an*, 1928, p. 99, n. 3, Maulana A. Yusuf Ali, *The Holy Qur'an. Text, translation and commentary*, n. 639: "Allah tasketh not a soul beyond its scope (capacity)": Qur'an, ii: 286.
58 Daryabadi, supra.
59 *Ibid.*, p. 95.
60 Qur'an, iv: 1291.
61 Even a staunch critic like J. N. D. Anderson remarks, "It is only fair to add, however ... that the Qur'an must not lightly be regarded as contradicting itself, and that the equal justice demanded by the verse of polygamy must therefore be interpreted in terms of those favours which a husband has controls not the instinctive inclination". (*Islamic law in the modern world*, 1959, p. 49).
62 *The meaning of the Qur'an*, Vol. I. The English translation of 'Tafheemul Qur'an' 1982, pp. 375–378, n. 161. The Maulana comments that what is required here is not the equal love and affection, but the outward treatment and that the husband should not, so to say, keep the other in a state of suspense as if she was not a wife.
63 *Tafsirul Qur'an*, Vol. I, pp. 372–373. In interpreting the verse, [the] Maulana comments that the verse demands the husband to hold the balance (not equality) even in love and affection, which feelings are of involuntary nature and beyond human control. The verse demands that the husband should not incline to one wife in his dealing, in his voluntary conduct, even when absolute justice and perfect equality are impossible.
64 *Translation of Qur'an*, 1928, p. 99, n. 3. The Maulana comments: "When conditions for resort to polygamy are met with, equal love cannot be insisted upon but there must be equality in outward treatment".
65 Bukhari, Vol. 7, *Kitab al nikah*, Chapters nos. 4, 100, 101, 102, 105 and 106; Muslim, Vol. 2, Chapters DLXX, DLXXI, DLXXII; Sunan Darmi, Chapter 727, Tradition no. 2181 and Chapter 728, Tradition no. 2182.
66 Qur'an XXXIII: 21: "Verily in the Messenger of Allah ye have a good example for him who looketh unto Allah and the Last Day and rememberth Allah much". Also see Qur'an VII: 54 and 157; XVI: 16 and XLV: 18.

67 Sunan Abu Dawud, Vol. III, Tradition no. 3644.
68 Qur'an, xxxiii: 4.
69 *Great religious teachers of the East*, pp. 263–264.
70 *Muhammadanism*, 1st ed., p. 297.
71 Ahmad A. Galwash, *The religion of Islam*, New York, p. 92.
72 *Ibid.*, p. 96.
73 *Ibid.*, p. 93.
74 iv: 3.
75 [no text given].
76 G. H. Stern, *Marriage in early Islam*, London, 1939, p. 81.
77 Edward Alexander Westermarck, *The future of marriage in Western civilisation*, 1st ed., pp. 182–188; Westermarck, supra, Vol. I, pp. 42–44 and 72–88, Vol. 2, pp. 392–396, Vol. 3, pp. 157–160.
78 Quoted *id.*
79 New York 1954, p. 280.
80 Quoted by Westermarck, *The future of marriage*, supra, pp. 182–183.
81 Siddiqui, supra, p. 112.
82 Barber, *Marriage and family*, 2nd ed., p. 577.
83 J. E. McFarlane, *The case for polygamy*, 1st ed., p. 126.
84 Quotes Siddiqui, supra, p. 114.
85 *Id.*; Westermarck, supra, Vol. 1, pp. 230–239.
86 Hymen of the future of marriage, London, 1927, pp. 161–162.
87 Quoted by Siddiqui, supra, p. 115.
88 *Id.*
89 *Ibid.*, pp. 127 and 217.
90 *Sex, life and faith*, 1946, p. 136.
91 *Ibid.*, p. 137.
92 Ira G. Wile (ed.), *Sex life of the unmarried adults*, 1946, p. 88.
93 Napoleon had to divorce his beloved wife, Josephine, and King Reza Shah Pahlevi of Iran was compelled to divorce Queen Suraiya. These well-known tragedies would not have occurred had the Islamic type of polygamy been allowed. For such social and individual problems, Islamic polygamy becomes [a] blessing.
94 *Patriarchal family*, London, 1967, pp. 228–229.
95 Supra, p. 138.
96 Qur'an, iv: 3.
97 Quoted by Westermarck, supra, pp. 182–183.
98 Zaibunnisa Hamidullah, *Sixty days in America*, p. 134.
99 Vol. VIII, 15th ed., p. 97.
100 For detail and reference see my article, 'Polygamy in Islam' in *Muslim personal law*, edited by F. R. Faridi and M. N. Siddiqui, Islamic Research Circle, 1973, pp. 50–51.
101 *Peace with God*, New York, 1953, pp. 93–94.
102 Bukhari and Muslim, referred to by Mishkatul Masabih, Vol. I. Traditions nos. 140–146.
103 Qur'an, v: 3.
104 The bibliographical details of this article have been included in the main bibliography of the book.
105 See now chapters 2.2 and 2.4 above.
106 See now chapter 1.3 in the present book.
107 It is an interesting question just how much impact international opinion may have on developments in India's legal system. Public acknowledgement of such influence may also be interpreted as admission that India is open to outside pressures, hence the issue is immensely complex and involves post-colonial sensitivities about national sovereignty as well as considerations of domestic legal policy.

108 This is clearly the evidence from Britain today, where the state's total prohibition on polygamy does not prevent British Muslims from arranging a variety of polygamous unions under *angrezi shariat*. For details see esp. Pearl and Menski (1998: 273–278).

109 See in detail Sharma (1994: 359–361). Gupta (1979: 155–176) provides an overview of statute and case law. Baxi (1986: 62–63) remarks that knowledge of the law against bigamy or polygamy is very meagre. Sharma (1994: 85–128) comments in detail on the legal provisions regarding polygamy and emphasises their ineffectiveness. She also notes discrepancies between cases where the judges appear to decriminalise polygamy and cases of maintenance, where different criteria are evidently applied.

110 Interestingly, Muslim understandings of the pre-Islamic period support the notion that controlled polygamy is an indicator of civilisation, while the modern argument clearly is that such limited form of control is not good enough. It is debatable, though, whether pre-Islamic Middle Eastern societies ever practised polygamy as a binding norm. All we seem to know is that there were few fetters on male discretion.

111 See Singh (1993: 20–23) on general concepts of Hindu marriage. Sharma (1993: 103–119) discusses monogamy, polygamy and polyandry with reference to classical texts. Sinha (1992: 81) suggests that in ancient India polyandry and polygamy were almost the prevailing custom, but the succeeding ages preferred monogamy. Mishra (1994: 151–168) produces a useful brief chapter on polyandry and polygamy. Diwan (1995: 65) emphasises the element of male chauvinism with some fascination. Harman (1989: 13) writes that "tradition allows for the possibility that any form of sexual intercourse between a man and a woman *ipso facto* creates a marriage" and indicates the potential links with divine models for Hindus, saying that "[f]or deities, polygamy and reappearances ... are always possible: this enables them to have many wives, in many places, under many circumstances, and under several guises".

112 See e.g. Arora (1986: 368–375); Engineer (1992: 21–22 and 100–104); Ali (1993: 24). An interesting recent contribution by Subhash Chandra Singh (1996) deserves attention.

113 The Report of the Committee on the Status of Women in India (1974: 108) puts the figure for Muslim polygamy slightly lower than that for Hindus, see in detail *ibid.*: 66–67 with statistics. Shiv Sahai Singh (1993: 29–30) points out that certain statistics show more evidence of Hindu polygamy than Muslim polygamy and therefore concludes, at p. 30, that "it will hardly hurt the Muslims if monogamy legislatively be made the rule for them". Like many other Muslim authors, Mahmood (1986: 71) alleges that Muslims are less polygamous than others without providing detailed evidence.

114 Section 4 of the *Parsi Marriage and Divorce Act*, 1865 prohibited polygamy for Parsis, see also s. 5 of the *Parsi Marriage and Divorce Act*, 1936. For Christians, s. 60 of the *Indian Christian Marriage Act*, 1872 is the relevant enactment, superseding Church law on the matter.

115 See to this effect also Desai (1990: 635): "... the bigamous marriage is non-existent and simply because there is no recourse to the court it cannot be said that it exists unless and until a decree is passed declaring it to be null and void".

116 See generally Bhattacharjee (1985 [1994a], 1994b and 1996) Bhattacharjee (1985: 128–141) focuses particularly on bigamy. Midha (1990: 72) complains that the constitutional mandates for equality and justice have been considerably diluted by a parallel regime of personal laws which continue to discriminate against women. Even most recent studies do not accept personal laws as an integral element of the Indian legal system. Deshta (1995: 2) treats

personal laws as "a medieval concept" and argues for their replacement by a uniform civil code.

117 This is actually an almost verbatim quote taken from the decision of V. R. Krishna Iyer J in *Shahulameedu v. Subaida Beevi*, 1970 KLT 4, discussed further below.

118 For details see Pearl and Menski (1998: 237–247) with further references.

119 See e.g. *Zubaida Begum v. Sardar Shah*, AIR 1943 Lah 310.

120 For details see also Pearl and Menski (1998: 249–250). Mahmood (1976: 15) suggested that this decision "was, in effect, a judicial effort to prepare the Muslims psychologically to accept the ideal of monogamy".

121 Older cases on Muslim women's right to divorce in case of polygamy are discussed by Bhatnagar (1992: 13–14 and 40–41). Shabbir (1988: 31–65) contains a useful, detailed discussion of such cases.

122 Ganai (1990: 423) emphasises that the courts have interpreted Muslim law in a progressive spirit, thereby controlling the practice of polygamy. This was done by recognising the right of delegated divorce in favour of the wife in the event of the husband taking another wife, by refusing restitution of conjugal rights to a bigamous husband, or by holding that a husband's second marriage may constitute cruelty.

123 For a discussion on the activities of Shariat Councils in Britain see Pearl and Menski (1998: 273–278 and especially 77–80).

124 Two decisions that supported the male perspective were cited before the learned judge, as noted at pp. 8–9, but they were not found acceptable.

125 Worse than this, as many authors confirm, plain desertion of the wife and children is a major social problem in all South Asian countries.

126 *Mohd. Ahmed Khan v. Shah Bano Begum*, AIR 1985 SC 945. This case concerned the rights to post-divorce maintenance of a divorced Muslim wife and held that Muslim husbands were liable to maintain their divorced wives beyond the *iddat* period. The decision led to riots and new legislation (see ch. 4 below).

127 For details see e.g. Abadan-Unat (1986: 173) and Cosar (1978). A detailed comparative study of Muslim polygamy in Britain, Turkey and Pakistan is now found in Yilmaz 1999. It confirms the social reality of Muslim polygamy in all three jurisdictions.

128 Midha (1990: 73) further asserts simplistically that "[c]ompulsory registration of all marriages can prove an effective check upon bigamous marriages as well as on child marriages".

129 On women being bought and sold, and the links with polygamy, see Dhagamwar (1992).

130 This, then, is related to the predicament of bonded labourers in South Asia who may well be freed by the Court's reiteration of their constitutional rights, but who will feed them and their children?

131 See also *Shrinivasa Aiyer v. Saraswati Ammal*, AIR 1952 Mad 193 to the same effect.

132 For good material and discussions on the subject see Indu Prakash Singh (1989: 60–63); also Mukhopadhyay (1985: 14); Sorabjee (1991: 262–263).

133 See also *Haisnam Baruniton Singh v. T. N. H. O. B. Devi*, AIR 1959 Manipur 20. Such legal actions could no longer occur if Indian law were to prohibit Muslim polygamy, since there is now no community left that receives 'favourable treatment'.

134 A very useful chapter on polygamy is found in Nijjar (1994: 20–64).

135 This appears to be a modified, simple form of the *saptapadi* ritual, which is widely considered to be the crucial marriage ritual for high caste Hindu marriages. In the present case, involving neo-Buddhists, this was evidently a fairly new custom, which the Court was quite unwilling to recognise.

136 This is also reflected in the more recent editions of Mulla's *Hindu law*, see now Desai (1990: 638–639), which is still misleading and has given rise to wrong decisions (see esp. chapter 1. 4 above).
137 Another Supreme Court case which frees the polygamist is *Lingari Obulamma v. L. Venkata Reddy*, AIR 1979 SC 848.
138 Professor Diwan was of course well aware of the concept of presumption and actually expresses himself in favour of a decision recognising an unusual marriage (Diwan 1986: 128). Elsewhere, too, the learned author emphasises the role of presumptions. See Diwan (1987: 292) with reference to *Ningu Vithu Bamane*, AIR 1987 Bom 27. See, however, the contradictory statement at Diwan (1989: 213) that "it is essential that such ceremonies and rites must be proved to be ancient, continuous and definite and that these should have been recognised either in the community of the bride or bridegroom". The reference to the requirement of 'ancient' custom is not appropriate in view of s. 3(a) HMA.
139 This presumption was applied in many recent cases, e.g. *S. P. S. Balasubrahmanyam v. Suruttayan*, AIR 1994 SC 133.
140 *Sumitra Devi* was subsequently applied in *Narayanan Namboodiri v. Bhargavi Amma*, 1989(1) KLT 547, which concerned the form of marriage called *sambandam* in local Kerala custom.
141 The interesting case of *Ningu Vithu Bamane v. Sadashiv Ningu Bamane*, AIR 1987 Bom 27 concerned widow remarriage and also applies a presumption of validity to protect the property entitlements of the claimants.
142 See *Sumitra* Devi, AIR 1985 SC 765, discussed above. An instructive and more recent example is found in *Vimala v. Veeraswamy*, (1991)2 SCC 375, where a husband was seeking to defeat his second wife's claim for maintenance on the ground that her marriage was void, but did not succeed. *Nirmala v. Rukminibai*, AIR 1994 Kant 247, achieves a truly equitable result by applying a presumption of validity of marriage and of the required rituals, thus distributing the contested property to all claimants rather than one winning party.
143 See e.g. *Laxmibai Nagappa Maliwadar v. Limbabai Nagappa Maliwadar*, AIR 1983 Bom 222, where it is held under s. 16 HMA that the children born of a void marriage are not disentitled to inherit from their parents. *Perumal Gounder v. Pachayappan*, AIR 1990 Mad 110, clarifies the legal position of illegitimate children in terms of their status as coparceners in the joint family. While this right is denied to them, they are entitled to inheritance on the death of the parents.
144 The comments on this case by Diwan (1991: 83–84) were made when the case had been decided by the High Court in Chandigarh. Evidently, in view of what I say here, I disagree with the learned author's interpretation and reasoning, as well as with his comments on the same case in 1994 (Diwan 1994: 295–296).
145 However, *Sumitra Devi*, AIR 1985 SC 765, has also been followed by some courts. See *Narayanan Namboodiri v. Bhargavi Amma*, 1989(1) KLT 547.
146 See also Mahmood (1991: 77–79). Deshpande (1993: 22–33) emphasises the negative implications for women. Shabbir (1991: 13, 15 and 46–47) discusses the issue with reference to Parsi law.
147 A search of Derrett's *Essays in Classical and Modern Hindu Law* leads to many and wide-ranging discussions about this wider topic during the 1960s and 1970s. See also Derrett (1967) with particular reference to bigamy.
148 Case law involved also the corresponding Christian approach to marriage as a sacrament, as in *Emperor v. Ruri*, AIR 1919 Lah 389, and Jewish law as well as Zoroastrian law (see for details p. 1534 of *Sarla Mudgal*).
149 With respect, this statement overlooks the provisions of s. 29(2) HMA, discussed in detail in ch. 2.5 above.

150 This form of words sounds more correct.
151 I have referred to some of these cases in chapter 2.5 above.
152 See for example *Katari Subba Rao v. Katari Seetha Mahalakshmi*, AIR 1994 AP 364.
153 See also the comments of Diwan (1990a: 125) on this case.
154 See Dhagamwar (1992); Agrawala and Ramanamma (1994) discuss this issue in detail.
155 See Ghouse (1973). The research by Khanam (1960) in Pakistan is also relevant in the present context, coming to similar findings about the difficulties caused to Muslim wives by traditional allowances for polygamy.
156 On cases about police powers see in detail Ahuja (1997: Vol. I, pp. 90–146). On the ineffectiveness of the police in relation to dowry-related violence see Chowdhary (1998).
157 See Allott (1980: 259–286) with a powerful critique of English law in this respect, emphasising the limits of law.
158 Similarly Ganai (1990: 423) observes that over time, the development of Indian Muslim law has been shaped not only by *sharia*, but in particular by judicial power.
159 The same goes for Bangladesh. For details of relevant cases see Pearl and Menski (1998: 256–273).

Chapter Four

Maintenance

Saving the welfare state money

4.1 Rethinking the welfare state

We have already seen above, with reference to marriage, divorce and polygamy in modern Indian law, that protecting the financial interests and claims of women and children has become an increasingly central concern of Indian judges. It appears that this is now considered more important than paying lipservice to modernising reforms *per se*.[1] As we saw, the post-modern reconstruction of India's laws on polygamy does no longer allow the simple, plain conclusion that polygamous Indian men, of any religion, are given favours by the statute law and the judges. The picture today is more and more that if a man has the means to maintain several women, nobody may complain and the state will never come to know – and does not really want to know. On the other hand, if a polygamist neglects his marital or parental obligations, the courts are there to receive complaints, and they have become remarkably activist and outspoken in protecting women and children.

Such findings show that, during the past few decades, Indian judges have become increasingly aware of the socio-economic dimensions of matrimonial law. They realise now, more clearly than before, that their decisions do have social and economic impacts. More judges also seem to be aware now that they are producing gendered dicta, which may have considerable financial implications. Judges also recognise more readily now that their decisions may throw already desperate individuals into further hopelessness and thus contribute to growing loss of faith in the legal system.

As concern about basic issues of justice has risen on the judicial agenda, which were earlier dominated by technical and procedural preoccupations, the Indian judiciary has become more inward-looking and thus of necessity more Indian, a subject on which Professor Derrett had much to say during the 1970s.[2] This indigenisation was achieved not so much by returning to the revered (but largely forgotten or incompletely remembered) élitist models of an ancient past as by becoming more aware of the social realities of people who appear before the courts, and by focusing more attention on their often rather unsophisticated concerns. Litigation, it seems, is no longer seen and treated merely as an abstract, technical mechanism to settle disputes. It is increasingly being understood, and used by the Indian judiciary, as a socially involved process, as much a means of settling disputes in accordance with the law as a tool of social engineering.

I am arguing here, with specific reference to the development of Indian maintenance law for divorced wives, and its implications for children, that the Indian judiciary has in this field of law achieved a real revolution during the past two decades. The most direct effect of this has been a transformation of the entire field of matrimonial litigation, which seems to be anchored in hotly contested questions regarding maintenance law. After all, most people litigate for money and property, not to clarify a principle that has remained unclear. While the potential abuse of tradition in the field of marriage solemnisation (see ch. 1) is also relevant here, the close links between divorce law and maintenance law have become particularly evident in our analysis of modern Indian divorce laws in chapters 2.1 and 2.5 above. In addition, we found that polygamy and financial arrangements are closely linked issues in real life, too.

In modern India, the judiciary has now largely moved away from its earlier focus on protecting men and family property to an explicit concern for safeguarding the survival of women and children as individuals in a society that has no all-encompassing social welfare net paid for by the state. This, in itself, is a most significant shift. Realising that modern India will never be in a position to introduce a state-sponsored welfare system along Western lines, the judiciary appears to have become more and more bold in exploring the limits of a welfare system which does not need to rely on the resources of an impoverished state.[3] In the absence of a state that could take on the role of provider of basic needs for all those who are destitute – an impossible scenario for any huge country in the South – some alternative remedy had to be found. It appears that in this way modern Indian law has rediscovered the usefulness of the family (see further ch. 5. 1 below).

Realising that many of the huge constitutional and legislative promises of the modern Indian state are programmatic rather than reflective of social reality, the judges, more than anyone else,[4] have recognised that the ancient models of family support remain essential in modern India. While scholars continued to argue for modernity models, the judges, in order to protect divorced wives and their children, went back to traditional family concepts. By developing new techniques to hold men liable for the financial protection of women and children, the modern statute law as well as judicial activism in this field created a scenario in which women and children are often manifestly dependent on the male-dominated resources of joint families. This must have been ideologically unpalatable to many writers, but this has not been openly acknowledged.

Matters came to a head in the famous, highly politicised *Shah Bano* controversy, which we will need to discuss in some detail in ch. 4.3 below. There was almost universal agreement among modernists that the decision in this case, assisting an old Muslim divorcée in obtaining post-*iddat* maintenance from her former husband, who was a rich lawyer, was a landmark in Indian law. Actually, this was not so, since the relevant law had already been laid down a few years earlier in the important case of *Bai Tahira v. Ali Hussain Fissalli Chothia*, AIR 1979 SC 362.

The politicised nature of the *Shah Bano* controversy was highlighted by Muslim riots in protest of the judgment and vitriolic attacks against the implications of this judgment for Muslim ex-husbands. The heat was further raised by forthright statements of the five Hindu Supreme Court judges in this case about interpretation of the Qur'an and, in particular, the need for a uniform civil code for modern India, which further antagonised many Muslims.

The aftermath of this case culminated in the rapid promulgation of an important Act of Parliament, the *Muslim Women (Protection of Rights of Divorce) Act*, 1986. This Act has been misread, by almost everyone,[5] to the effect that it nullified the position of the *Shah Bano* case and deprived divorced Muslim wives of their entitlements to post-*iddat* maintenance from the former husband. The modernising ideologies of virtually every commentator created blinkers that even respectable publications like *India Today* have not dropped. Journalists and scholars alike continue to peddle the myth today that the 1986 Act nullified the modern achievements of the *Shah Bano* case and signify the ineptness of the modern Indian state in solving social problems and helping destitute women.

I found it almost amusing to watch, during the past decade, how scholars and commentators desperately clung to this myth, while the case law under the 1986 Act proclaimed exactly the opposite. Politicised scholars did not care to read law reports from the various High Courts in India. Even leading scholars of Indian law were caught out politicking instead of reporting on the cases that had been decided by the courts.

By 1994, I was sufficiently frustrated about this to publish an article in the *Kerala Law Times* (here reprinted in ch. 4.2 below), which pointed out that the High Court of Kerala, in particular, had actually produced an authoritative interpretation of the relevant sections in the 1986 Act which meant that *Shah Bano* had not been nullified and that life had now become even tougher for Muslim men who divorce their wives and seek to abandon them without proper maintenance. Provided the man has money (for otherwise, both spouses have to suffer poverty in silence) a divorced Muslim wife is today better off than her co-citizens of different religions, who could at best obtain a decree for Rs. 500/- per month. There are no financial limits under the provisions of the 1986 Act, so that a millionaire wife who gets divorced and wants more money from the former husband stands a good chance of success.

The Indian judges, as we shall see with very few exceptions, have therefore driven a coach and horses through the masses of blindly politicking commentators who accused the Indian government of giving in to the Muslims and abandoning the concerns of divorced Muslim wives.

Many people have reason to eat their words, but if even *India Today* persistently continues to peddle politicised nonsense about the 1986 Act, the educational standards of the supposedly educated élite will remain deficient.

I have to assert here, therefore, that many of the legal and ideological confusions that have marked, and in effect marred, our understanding of Indian maintenance law during the late 1980s and early 1990s have been caused by vigorous, almost fanatical objections which have turned out to be high-society fiction.[6] One can explain such misguided constructions and blinkered perceptions by the domination of middle and upper class concerns in drawing room debates and in modernist scholarly analyses, which have developed their own distortions and politicised biases. Women, so the argument of modernity, should be empowered by the law to be free and independent individuals. While reliance on family handouts was seen as ideologically unacceptable, when it came to divorced wives, middle class self-interest somehow prevailed over ideology. It is notable that the vigorous arguments in favour of post-divorce maintenance are often fuelled by the claims of middle-class women to an adequate life-style after divorce, not by concern about the survival of desperately poor women on a day-to-day basis. Professor Tahir Mahmood (1986: 127), ever-vigilant in spotting abuses of Muslim law, picked this up and was scathing in his comments:

> Under our modern personal law enactments there is not as much stress on the mutual obligations of the married couples as on the rights of divorcees. Particularly, women who have been divorced [or have obtained divorce at their own initiative] are provided with all sorts of legal reliefs under the civil and criminal laws of the country. To use Justice V. R. Krishna Iyer's terminology, by a process of "sociological decoding" and a "telelogical interpretation" of the modern laws of alimony and maintenance our "functionally sensitised" judiciary is gradually turning divorce into a sort of an insurance deal offering far more lucrative benefits than available in marriage. In return for the social and economic security offered to women through marriage, our traditional laws imposed on them domestic responsibilities and an obligation to respect all reasonable wishes of the husband. The modern Indian laws of divorce, as judicially interpreted, absolve divorced wives of all these obligations without depriving them of the benefits that were available to them in married life. The only constraint that these laws impose on divorced women is a forced celibacy; "unchastity" being fatal to the privilege of being maintained by the former husband.

In other words, apart from communal politics, the social agenda of the rich and of privileged women dominated the discussion, as in the above quote, and determined in which direction further blinkers would be applied. It is crystal clear today that the judges, but not academic and other writers, despite all their professed social concerns, were the ones that really came to the rescue of destitute Indian divorcées. The interpretation of s. 3 in the MWPRDA 1986, which we will examine in detail in ch. 4.3 below, is hard-hitting and – as far as I can see – much more effective than most women had dared to hope. Especially for those divorced women who cannot stand on their own feet economically, this offers a fast remedy, provided of course that the husband actually has money to share, and the woman has the courage and the means to approach a court.

In a sense, then, the new developments in Indian post-maintenance law – which are by no means restricted to divorced Muslim women – have ushered in a new socio-economic realism. The new law takes more explicit account of life's realities than of socially removed deliberations and abstract principles of gender relations. By holding married men responsible for the life-long maintenance of a former wife – unless she were to remarry or become 'unchaste' – the modern law relies on distinctly non-modern principles, to the effect that women are dependent on men. Modern commentators, it would seem, developed filters that shut out this non-modern justification for male responsibility, while maintaining the female claim to post-divorce financial support. We can see here that the two approaches are not in fact totally disjointed, even though this may not be evident at first sight.

I have not been satisfied with the interpretation that the modern post-divorce maintenance law of India protects women against destitution. The agenda of the state in cleverly redrafting the statute law, first the all-important *Criminal Procedure Code* of 1973, which redefined 'wife as including a divorced wife, signalled the impecunious welfare state's intention to shift the burden onto husbands. The absolutely ingenious wording of s. 3 of the *Muslim Women (Protection of Rights on Divorce) Act*, 1986 is in my interpretation a rock solid consolidation of a policy that has its roots in 1973, thus even before the Emergency. The 1986 Act is not an accident of history, then, or a hyped-up aftermath of the *Shah Bano* issue. It is to be seen in the wider context of a process of development towards holding Indian men liable for their broken marriages. It constitutes at the same time a systematic step in the somewhat hidden agenda of protecting the Indian state from social welfare claims by indigent women and children. In other words, it is evidence of a fiscal strategy that is, seen from this angle, primarily designed to protect the state, rather than women and children.

I doubt whether there have ever been any directives to the Indian judges, as there are apparently to judges in England, that they must first and foremost consider the impact of their decisions on public funds. This is so especially in matrimonial litigation when questions of ancillary relief arise. Gone are the days, in England, when the husband could expect to shift the burden of housing and maintaining the former wife onto the welfare agencies of the state. While Western state welfare systems were beginning to experience scenarios of collapse and cash crisis, and English judges were told to work out viable compromises that would leave the state's emptying coffers untouched, Indian judges looking westwards found something to emulate. They saw the welfare state's crisis and realised that India would never be able to afford such a system in the first place. They decided for themselves, without telling us in so many words, that modern India would be better off with a sustainable strategy of development that exonerates the state and utilises the considerable resources hidden within the wide mantle of society.

Turning again to English law for a moment, we must note that English judges today are under exactly the same obligation towards the state when it comes to divorce petitions and the often arduous and painful processes of sorting out matters of ancillary relief. The first duty of judges here is, as they often remind everyone in the courtroom, to ensure that there is no resulting liability on public funds from their judgment. If equitable distribution of marital assets is such a hugely important matter in English law today, then, as in modern Indian law, the purpose of this exercise is not only to help wives and children, and to avoid that they fall destitute. Here, too, the major purpose is to save the state from claims by its stranded citizens on scarce and (at least in the Indian case) non-existent social welfare funds.

In this far-sighted process of reformulating and reshifting a prominent social burden, the Indian courts have used moralising reminders about the duties of humans and the responsibilities of spouses to each other. We can see more clearly now why the most recent Indian case law operates in favour of refusing couples easy divorces and reminds them of their obligations to each other. Marriage involves commitments for life, significantly and more so, as we now learn, for the man than the woman. This is another lesson that blinkered women-centred thinking about 'traditional' marriage arrangements had systematically shut out.

The topic of maintenance has come alive in Indian law really only after the old s. 488 of the *Criminal Procedure Code*, 1898 was redrafted in 1973 and the new sections 125–127 of the *Criminal Procedure Code*, 1973 were promulgated. While it took a few years for cases to come up under this new Act, once the courts got into action, they rapidly changed the face of modern Indian law. The case law involved prominently Hindus as well as Muslims, but of late Christian wives have joined the battle. From the late 1970s onwards, as Muslim husbands continued to fight against what they saw as new liabilities for post-divorce maintenance, some judges produced amazing judgments, such as *Bai Tahira*, AIR 1979 SC 362, which reflected the enormous changes which were developing within the complex field of Indian family laws. With the hugely politicised *Shah Bano* case of 1985, a second phase of important changes began, signalling that the modern Indian state would not shy away from using socio-religious traditions creatively and to its own advantage, putting ideology behind practicality and sustainability in the agenda of the modern state.

The outcome, apart from multiple confusions which continued even during the late 1990s, has been a new regime of Indian post-divorce maintenance law. The MWPRDA 1986 appears to violate all norms of modern legality because it is India's first enactment on Muslim personal law for many decades. Going by the loud protests, the 1986 Act should have been held unconstitutional on many counts, but the Indian Supreme Court has sat on those petitions and has refused to comment, until recently. At the same time, the MWPRDA, as its name indicates, is tough on men and has the twin objects, as we saw, of protecting women and children and the state itself. The new law expects men or their families to take care of women whom they once married but then chose to discard. This law hurts the man's pocket. It is a form of individualised taxation, a form of social tax on divorce, so to say. From this perspective, as we saw, even the new legal approach to polygamy makes sense, similarly imposing an extra tax on the polygamous husband for the privilege of multiple marriage. This could indeed represent a disincentive for some polygynously inclined men. However, as we argued already, by itself this will not control polygamy.

The modern Indian law, thus, has creatively used concepts of traditional gender relations for the purpose of protecting women and children in today's society with its many consumerist and individualising temptations. Far from the favourite feminist *mantra* that Indian traditions keep women dependent on men at all stages of their life, the socio-legal reality has been that men are at all times responsible for the welfare of women in their family, even if they divorced their wife. This is remarkably similar to traditional Indian scenarios about the responsibilities of the joint family towards the individual and the duties of the husband towards a wife, irrespective of whether she is still his wife or an ex-wife. The progressive encroachment of the statute law in this area has created protective mechanisms for women who face destitution and is thus part of the modern state's strategy of avoiding multiple social stress.

I shall argue further in chapter 5.1 below that this scenario may well be treated as ideologically suspect by those who believe in axioms of equality and individualism. However, if India's new policies on securing maintenance for women and children do the job of ensuring the dignified survival of otherwise indigent and stranded individuals, perhaps the modern ideologies and axioms require some re-assessment in the light of socio-economic realities in modern India. It would appear that an analysis of India's modern law on post-divorce maintenance involves a detailed re-assessment of the role of the welfare state. From an Indian perspective, distinct from Western models which promise so much but cannot deliver everything a person needs to survive as a full human being, directing indigent persons back to the family is not merely the only financially realistic option, it is also a strategy which teaches people, every day of their life, that they are inevitably interlinked with others and cannot behave as autonomous individuals. To that extent, the modern Indian laws on post-divorce maintenance also reinforce deeply cultural messages that are not unique to South Asia but are distinct from individualising, supposedly modern perspectives on life.

4.2 Maintenance for divorced Muslim wives

[From: 1994(1) *KLT*, Journal section, pp. 45–52]

Two recent decisions of the Kerala High Court, reported as *Mytheen v. Saphiya* at 1993(2) KLT 322 and *Hassainar v. Raziya* at 1993(2) KLT 805, are of considerable interest for the development of the law and prompt me to make some more general comments about maintenance for divorced wives in India. The subject is of immerse importance and is in urgent need of detailed analysis. At the University of London, we are presently preparing two major studies on this topic; they will hopefully be available in print during 1995. Our research shows that maintenance, because it concerns money, is one of the central areas of South Asian family law in which tempers run high and confusion reigns supreme.

Maintenance for divorced wives is not only an Indian or a Muslim problem, it is a universal predicament. Once a marriage breaks up, does either spouse have any continuing obligation towards the other? If so, for how long? Should the end of a marriage not signify the end of financial liabilities, at least for the ex-spouse, if not for any children from this marriage? Various legal systems have handled this problem in quite different ways.

As for children, the argument that their parents must have a moral and legal duty to maintain them till they can look after themselves may sound correct. But when is that? The law may stipulate certain norms, but these are not matched with actions in so many cases. Here, we are not concerned with maintenance for children from marriages that break up and focus on divorced spouses.

In India, modern Hindu law lays down that a divorced woman may have to provide maintenance for the husband under Sections 24 and 25 of the *Hindu Marriage Act*, 1955. Few other legal systems in the world go along that extreme path of gender equality. Most laws rely on patriarchal notions and place an obligation on the divorcing man to provide for the woman and to maintain any children from the marriage, too. Obviously, if a wife's continuing liability from a broken marriage is to look after the children, that should be reflected in her own maintenance arrangements. Our research in London shows that, to some extent, Indian law has been ready to recognise this basic principle. But what about maintaining the divorced woman herself?

The duty to maintain an ex-wife is, in a sense, the flip side of patriarchal chauvinism. A wife may have spent many years producing, bringing up and looking after children and after the husband himself, who acquired not only a wife, but multiple benefits arising from unpaid women's work, which is so little recognised in this male-focused world. Does all this give any divorced wife an inherent claim to financial support beyond the duration of the marriage? What about the rights of the man, who may find it attractive to remarry and who may need his resources for that purpose? Should he be allowed to lavish attention on the new arrangement only and simply forget about the past?

Few societies will find it agreeable that a spouse should be able to simply throw the other spouse out of the home at his or her whim and fancy. At the same time, it remains reality that marital breakdown happens more often than official statistics record, in all societies, not only among Muslims, and not always because the man has behaved in such a way as to make continued marital relations possible. Rightly or wrongly, attention has focused on male action to terminate marriages; in the extreme, we come across every shade of human depravity. Atrocity takes different forms, but mainly targets women: in Britain, as elsewhere, wives find themselves locked out of the home and thrown onto the street, or they have to escape from unbearable domestic violence. A growing number of such women are assisted by a network of women's refuges. In North India and the Pakistani Punjab, so-called dowry murders are sometimes used to get rid of unwanted wives. In a recent field study in Lahore, we found that men in certain neighbourhoods used 'accidental' fires fuelled by kerosine as the cheapest possible method of an instant divorce. The rationale is convincing: A dead wife can make no claims to maintenance.

In a high-level conference in Bangladesh in autumn 1992, it was significant that women's groups argued against a right to maintenance for divorced wives, of any community, 'till death or remarriage'. The preferred wording was a telling comment on human perversion: such a right should extend to her 'as long as she lives and remains unmarried'. Such subtleties of drafting disclose very perceptive nuances of the problem from a victim perspective and should be taken seriously. Getting rid of the woman by murder even saves on any form of *mahr* money or *iddat* payment and can now perhaps be seen as another form of the dreaded *talaq-al-bida*. But let us make no communalistic mistake: whether Hindu, Muslim, Sikh, Jain, or Christian – there is evidence of a despicable uniformity of cruelty and meanness accompanying marital breakdown. At the same time, it remains a remarkable but not unsurprising feature of Indian law that the leading cases assisting wives in securing maintenance have come from South India rather than the more chauvinistic North. Anybody with doubts should re-read *Soundarammal* (AIR 1980 Mad 294) and a whole row of cases in the KLT under the *Muslim Women (Protection of Rights on Divorce) Act*, 1986 (see below). It is probably also no accident of history that the infamous *Shah Bano* case (*Mohammed Ahmed Khan*, AIR 1985 SC 945) does not come from Southern India.

Modern Western legal systems have shifted the burden of maintaining divorced women to the welfare state. The notion that Muslim Waqf Boards should take care of such women has been floated in India and has led to anguished litigation (see e.g. *Syed Fazal Pookoya Thangal* at 1993(1) KLT 860). The verdict in that case is clear, but the case itself shows that public policy in India is confused about whether payment of maintenance for ex-spouses should be a matter for the state, some other agency, or rather for the families concerned. I have begun to argue against a welfare state approach (see now 1993(2) KLT J 57–58). Much more remains to be said about that issue, but not in the present article.

First of all, we must draw attention to a remarkable legal development in Indian maintenance law which has been covered up and misunderstood far too long. Virtually unnoticed in India, and certainly abroad, where an outmoded image of Indian family law as medieval is being cultivated even by some professed 'experts', a quiet revolution has followed India's hasty promulgation of the *Muslim Women (Protection of Rights on Divorce) Act,* 1986. A remarkable line of progressive cases has come mainly from Kerala: *Ali* 1988(2) KLT 94; *Aliyar* 1988(2) KLT 446; *Shamsudeen* 1988(2) KLT 392; *Ahammed* 1990(1) KLT 172; *Abdul Sathar* 1991(1) KLT SN No. 22; *Alavi* 1992(1) KLT 649; *Hyderkhan* 1992(2) KLT 330; *Syed Fazal Pookoya Thangal* 1993(1) KLT 860 and now also *Hassainar* 1993(2) KLT 805. Other High Courts, too, have given divorced Muslim wives surprisingly generous treatment, based on an entirely correct and solid interpretation of the letter and spirit of the 1986 Act (see e.g. *Arab* AIR 1988 Guj 141).

There have been a few indignant murmurs of dissent, as in *Usman Khan* AIR 1990 AP 225 FB and *Raja Mohammed* 1992(2) KLT SN 1. The latter is a Madras case, explicitly opposing the Kerala High Court's interpretations. More recently, *Mytheen* 1993(2) KLT 322 tests the strength of Kerala's concern for divorced women's maintenance and seems to favour the man's position. It must be emphasised that there is no authoritative all-India decision on the point, but the Kerala High Court's detailed interpretations of the 1986 Act make sense in legal as well as social terms. Thus, Muslim men, like all other Indian men, have been held accountable to pay maintenance for ex-wives and children. I am certainly not saying that the law is perfect in its application, but the state's strategy to have the costs of broken marriages paid by the spouses themselves has worked out for the benefit of many women. That women continue to bear the brunt of the costs of marital breakdown, in financial as well as emotional terms, is so obviously clear that it need not be emphasised in many words.

It is, of course, entirely right that the courts have concluded from the 1986 Act that a divorcing husband has, in law and in principle, some responsibility towards the woman he divorces. What is disputed, in fact, is no longer the factum of this responsibility, but the extent of provision to be made by the man. The high-profile dispute in modern Indian law has been mainly about the obligation of Muslim husbands to pay maintenance to divorced wives which extends beyond the traditionally stipulated limit of the *iddat* period. Our current research in London, based first of all on Arabic sources, has shown that Quranic law put a definite moral obligation on the husband to maintain an ex-wife decently; yet the Quran does not say for how long this should be done. The dilemma for Muslim jurisprudence, as we can now see so clearly, is that this general rule in the Quran raises all the basic issues of interpretation in Muslim law and distracts from any policy discussion about the maintenance for divorced wives by reference to inter-communal and intra-communal politics. At the end of the day, the Shah Bano decision, confirming the general principle that a divorcing husband should be considerate and remains in some way responsible for the welfare of his former wife, gave a correct interpretation of the basic ground rule of Islamic law on this point, despite the fact that it was reached by five Hindu judges.

It will be general knowledge that Muslim jurisprudence has gradually defined away and whittled down the original Quranic obligation of the divorcing husband to be kind to the woman he sends away. This is what led, as every lawyer in India must be presumed to know, to the famous *Shah Bano* situation, faced by *lakhs* of women in India from any community. After the *Muslim Women (Protection of Rights on Divorce) Act* of 1986, the Kerala High Court has courageously taken the lead in showing that the 1986 Act was not a retrograde step taken by an intimidated government but a firmly pro-women statute which does not violate the basic Quranic principles but contradicts subsequent juristic interpretations. Inevitably, this has again raised the perennial question about the primary sources of Islamic law. If the clear answer ought to be that it is Allah's law of the Quran, rather than man-made interpretations of it, the 1986 Act cannot be faulted. Conversely, juristic definitions of what constitutes adequate maintenance for divorced Muslim wives cannot be entitled to judicial recognition in any modern state if they violate the basic Quranic requirement of being considerate. Again, thus what one argues about is the extent of this considerate [sic] behaviour. This, I would suggest, can only be determined by reference to the facts and circumstances of each individual case. At least with regard to maintenance, Islamic law never purported to establish a rule of law model in which everybody was to be treated equally. Reported cases in modern Indian law also tell us that if both spouses are poor, they have to starve together, whether Hindu or Muslim, or anybody else. Not untypically, the cases that go to court involve spouses who have money but cannot agree on how to allocate it.

The public discussion of this legal problem in India has remained overshadowed and confused by communal politics. In return, Western audiences and readers have been misled, mainly by the media, into believing that Muslim women's struggles for maintenance rights are a matter of communal politics, when in fact they are a question, first and foremost, of financial liability and the rights of women. Far too many writers, whether in law journals, newspapers like the Indian Express or India Today, have continued to repeat politicised nonsense about the 1986 Act, showing their ignorance of the legal facts which it undoubtedly created. This has only served to increase confusion. In view of this, the Kerala High Court's clear-sighted position on the letter and spirit of the 1986 Act is a remarkable example of judicial independence and of skilful application of a controversial statute. This is not judicial lawmaking, it is, I humbly submit, evidence of the best of judicial craftsmanship.

For years, we were told that highly charged and politically motivated petitions, challenging the constitutional *vires* of the 1986 Act, have been pending before the Supreme Court of India. The apex court may be too busy, or have its own reasons for seeking to delay a decision. But what about *Syed Fazal Pookaya Thangal* at 1993(1) KLT 860? Here a learned single Judge, Mr. Justice Viswanatha Iyer, held that the 1986 Act was not violative of Articles 25 and 26 of the Constitution. That case did not answer some to the questions carried to the Supreme Court, but it strengthens the entirely reasonable and logical stance taken by the Kerala High Court so far, standing up to male chauvinism and seeking to protect disadvantaged women as far as possible.

Indian law had imposed, in sections 125–127 of the *Criminal Procedure Code* of 1973, a uniform rule system that studiously avoids placing a burden on the state in terms of maintaining divorced persons and their offspring. Following the high drama of the *Shah Bano* case, that uniform regime was only formally broken up by the 1986 Act, which continues in effect the same ground rules as the 1973 Code. If anything, Muslim ex-husbands in India today are worse off: even though the wife may be rich herself, she can still ask for more (see *Ahammed* 1990(1) KLT 172).

Given that a Muslim husband in India, after divorce in any form, now has few excuses left not to pay some form of permanent maintenance to his divorced wife, it was inevitable that a test case on the legal strength of mutual agreements about non-payment of maintenance would be brought. To what extent would the modern, professedly secular law uphold private agreements made under the personal law? This is precisely what *Mytheen v. Saphiya* at 1993(2) KLT 322 is about. I see it as a test case in this regard, perhaps a victory for common sense and flexibility at this stage, but an ambivalent precedent which can easily be overturned. In *Mytheen*, the man appears to win, but his gain is not a victory for Muslim chauvinism; it puts the onus on Indian Muslim to come up with an acceptable solution to an age-old problem. If this is what Tahir Mahmood and other spokesmen of Muslim interests have been asking for, here is their opportunity to become creative: The case offers a good change for South Asian Muslims to develop an extra-legal Islamic rule system regarding maintenance of divorced wives which satisfies both the Quranic requirement of being considerate and the modern state's expectation that the breakdown of a marriage should not impose any costs on the public purse and still allow the divorced woman to survive in dignity.

Mytheen establishes, for Kerala at any rate, that if a Muslim woman has signed away her entitlement to maintenance, she cannot later go to court and seek to use the 1986 Act to fill her pockets or make her life easier. Some Muslim strategists will have been jubilant: all a husband has to do now is count on his wife's ignorance about the law and get an agreement out of her that she renounces any expectation of permanent maintenance after divorce. If the 1986 Act cannot be challenged in a court of law, can it be circumvented by social engineering in the community itself?

My view is that simple social facts will foil such facile ploys: I venture to predict that Muslim families will learn very fast that what helps a husband to save maintenance cannot help the wife, who is, after all, somebody else's daughter, sister and niece. Thus, in the negotiations prior to a marriage, there will be some social pressure to ensure that women get a fair deal. As stipulated by Shahdeen Malik in 'Saga of divorced women: Once again Shah Bano, maintenance, and the scope for marriage contracts', published at 42 *Dhaka Law Reports* (1990), Journal section 34–40, Muslim families in South Asia can make good use of the old-established institution of pre-nuptial contracts to safeguard the position of their female members at the point of entry into a marriage. This may sound like planning the break-up of a marriage before it has even started, but good marital planning these days may mean precisely what the Islamic law has always advised: Putting contentious matter down in writing eases problems of evidence and can be used by a petitioner to have one's right upheld in a court of law, if necessary. It is an insurance policy; emotional barriers may work against making such arrangements, but the interests of the women concerned should be paramount.

Mytheen helps the husband to assert his position that he is not liable to pay more maintenance to his wife than was originally agreed. But, given inflation and other changes in circumstances, we will inevitably come across situations of the *Bai Tahira* type (AIR 1979 SC 362), in which the learned V. R. Krishna Iyer very appropriately ruled that a meaningful maintenance settlement that expects to be upheld by modern state law has to be such that it enables the wife to keep body and soul together. In *Mytheen*, it does not appear that the wife desperately needed the extra money. Rather, she embarked on a fishing trip and perhaps wanted to achieve what Tahir Mahmood has castigated as abuse of divorced Muslim men's rights; in such situations, the woman (as Saphiya here did) remains unburdened by a further marriage but expects her former husband to pay for that privilege.

The critical question in *Mytheen* was whether a court should re-open an existing maintenance agreement and how this could be harmonised with public policy. The facts in the reported case are not detailed enough to allow much comment on this particular issue, but the principle itself is important: a court will not re-open an existing settlement if the wife simply wants more money. The decision might have been different if the wife, in *Bai Tahira* style, had justified her claim by reference to inflation or changed circumstances. Of this, there is no evidence in the reported case, where we merely find an indication of the wife's expedient move to ask for more because the law changed in her favour. It should at least be noted that in *Shamsudeen*, reported at 1988(2) KLT 392, a Muslim husband's misguided attempt to play a similar trick misfired: he trusted political gossip and thought the law had changed in his favour!

We can be quite sure that Indian Courts have not spoken the last word about this kind of situation. *Mytheen* gives a clear message to Muslim women and their male protectors that it is wise to anticipate marital trouble and to ensure that a premarital contractual agreement or any other agreement made during the marriage (especially if its purpose is to terminate that marriage, as in this case) allows for adequate post-divorce maintenance for the woman. The kind of financial vetting that South Asian marriage often involves should help to give substance to such agreements.

Let it be emphasised again, lest there is any doubt: Maintenance law in India does not guarantee food for all people to an imaginary level of 'breadline', as the English law purported to do till this eyewash strategy of the benevolent welfare state ran into trouble because it became too costly. In English law, the state's direct financial involvement in maintenance arrangements has recently prompted a large-scale reopening of existing agreements between divorced couples. This has led to much enhanced demands on ex-husbands to pay more maintenance for their children from a former marriage. Purportedly, the recent reforms in English law were introduced for the benefit of the children, in an allegedly child-centred family law system. However, the fact that most such men had remarried and had new families to look after was quite brutally discounted, leading to several suicides and large-scale demonstrations against the new rules. Most obviously, at the end of the day, the divorced women concerned are no better off financially: the new rules simply effected a shifting of the financial burden for child maintenance from the state, desperate to save money, to the ex-husbands, who of course remain the fathers of the children they produced. The current shambles in Britain over the Child Support Agency and its disastrous trail of misery must be the subject of a separate article.

In my view, the current events in Britain show that Indian family law is wise to keep state interference in post-divorce maintenance arrangements to a minimum. Let the spouses work it out, in accordance with their means and expectations, let the increasingly operational family courts play a useful role in strengthening such settlements. If the people of India have to pay for post-divorce maintenance rather than the welfare state, then the state should keep its finger out of the maintenance pie. If we read *Mytheen* as a decision that seeks to strengthen the powers of individuals to make their own reasonable arrangements, I have little to quarrel with that decision. If we choose to read it as a victory for male irresponsibility, it will not carry much weight. At the same time, it gives a warning to Indian women that they cannot hope to abuse procedural loopholes to plead for more maintenance unless they can show real need. After *Mytheen*, one must wonder how courts will deal with the legitimate expectation, expressed in *Bai Tahira* at AIR 1979 SC 362 by Kerala's learned philosopher-judge Krishna Iyer, that maintenance payments must enable divorced women to live in dignity.

Male litigants will seek to ignore such principles with the same ease with which the Quranic stipulation about being considerate has been marginalised. *Hassainar v. Raziya* at 1993(2) KLT 805 provides further evidence that some divorcing men will seek to fight against reasonableness in order to save money. In this case, the 'ingenious contention' (p. 806) that the wife's claim was barred by limitation had been produced. Mr. Justice K. T. Thomas gave short thrift to this argument, upholding – at least this is a possible interpretation – the right of a divorced woman to demand reasonable maintenance any time after the divorce. The case reported is appropriately technical, given the nature of the suit. I shall venture here to add some comments of a socio-legal nature about the important questions raised by this case, because it is bound to be misused in future cases.

It seems as though the process of learning about the 1986 Act and her rights under it took the divorced lady in *Hassainar* more than six years. Again, it is not an issue in the case whether she actually needed extra money; we also do not know whether she had to look after the two children from the marriage. The husband's reaction to her petition is significant: he searches for a procedural loophole rather than addressing the substance of the ex-wife's claim. We could expect him to do that, well and good, but is this what lawyers do, and are paid to do? In the process, the court was not given a full picture of the complex issues that this case raises.

Apart from technicalities about limitation, what about the nature of the ex-wife's claim? One issue in the case is at what point the ex-wife's claim actually arose. It seems that the ex-husband's ingenious contention is matched by a more ingenious answer from the court, basically telling the husband that, because he just slipped away from his responsibilities, he cannot now claim that his action gave rise to a cause at some point in the past which should now be covered by limitation. Thus, it seems, the husband got beaten at his own devious game.

But that does not answer the real question which lies at the root of this case. If a woman is unaware of a law beneficial to her for so many years, does she lose the protection of that law because of limitation? In other words, could ignorance of the law be a valid defence here? There will be many Raziyas who are simply abandoned without sufficient arrangements for their maintenance, with nobody telling them about Kerala High Court cases which could mean a significant financial improvement for them. *Hassainar* should not be read to mean that such women lose their claim for ever.

When, however, does such a woman's claim arise? I would have thought that the right to claim under the 1986 Act arises when the husband has refused to make reasonable arrangements, as is his duty according to this Act. If the couple never discuss maintenance arrangements, for whatever reason, a woman may not know whether the man will make any reasonable provision till the *iddat* period has expired. Under the 1986 Act, according to the Kerala High Court cases of 1988 cited above, he is under an obligation to make proper arrangements for the time after the *iddat* period during this period. Unless he explicitly refuses to provide for the woman prior to the expiry of the *iddat* period, she could not really file a petition till after the end of her *iddat*. Contrary to the statement in *Hassainar*, thus, the divorced woman's right to apply for maintenance may arise precisely at the end of the *iddat* period.

But can she still claim this right many years after it actually arose? While *Hassainar* is, no doubt, an appropriate response to the skimpy husband in this case, it does not settle the law as fully as one would hope for. Given the nature of the subject, we can look forward to further test cases. In principle, though, it is now quite certain that divorced Muslim wives in India are entitled to reasonable maintenance beyond the *iddat* period. This not only gives food for thought to policy planners in other jurisdictions, but strengthens the claim of modern Indian law to be able to work out secular solutions that do not infringe on basic religious principles. Dissent there will be, anywhere, especially when money, power and male egos are involved. But it is long overdue that India as a whole and people abroad recognise the importance of the legal groundwork on maintenance for divorced Muslim wives under the 1986 Act, so painstakingly laid by the Kerala High Court. It is extremely unlikely that this pioneering position will be undermined by verdicts from other High Courts. Commonsense does not depend on any one religion, nor on state boundaries. In our present context, reasonableness and commonsense would seem to indicate that in a huge country without the resources to pay for the casualties of broken marriages, most divorcing men will need to face up to continuing responsibilities beyond the duration of the marriage, while women, at the same time, must be prevented from exploiting a law that is appropriately weighted in their favour. As always in family law, a gendered imbalance has to be harmonised with the need for achieving relative justice. There is no easy prescription for this, but judicial vigilance, such as evidenced in Kerala, is an essential precondition.

4.3 Maintenance law for divorced wives in Indian law today: Taxing men for the privilege of divorce

The issue of maintenance law did not become prominent in Indian law until the mid-1970s. Significant developments have taken place in this field during the last ten years or so, both in Hindu and Muslim law. The starting point for modern Indian maintenance laws lies in traditional assumptions about the issue. These were clearly focused on the welfare of women and children, seeking to protect them from destitution.[7] This has remained a major concern, first during the colonial period with its criminal legal sanctions for men who failed to maintain their wives,[8] and later in independent India. We shall see in detail below how vigorously the modern Indian law on this issue has developed.

In a nutshell, the legal framework for maintenance law has grown from a less than adequate welfare net into the much more effective system of protection which we see today. During the 1960s and 1970s, the relevant law still left many married women and their children destitute, so the relevant law was changed by re-drafting the 1973 *Criminal Procedure Code*. This brought in much tougher rules that now hold men, in principle, liable for life for the maintenance of women they married and children they fathered. This is typical modern Indian, duty-based jurisprudence, defining the rights of individuals through the duties of others, not as an obligation on the modern welfare state.

While we find clear indication that modern Indian family laws have become much more welfare-centred, this is not the whole story. As we saw already with regard to marriage, divorce and polygamy, the modern Indian state's activism in developing a stronger law on post-divorce maintenance for women, in particular, looks like a fiscal self-protection device, rather than primarily a measure to protect the basic human rights of women. The result for Indian men is absolutely evident today: men have to pay for the privilege of marriage, the consequences of divorce, and the implications of polygamy. One can of course ask whether there was really any other option for the Indian state in policy terms, but the effects of this development have not dawned on most current commentators on Indian law, who continue to use welfare ideologies that merely exist in the realm of imagination but most definitely not in Indian social reality. Therefore, it needs to be expressed clearly in the academic literature now that the modern Indian welfare state has skilfully managed to shift such burdens away from itself into the realm of society. Modern Indian law is thus engaged in the complex process of developing a financially sustainable and yet legally and socially effective system of social welfare. While this welfare net is certainly not without loopholes, it is now definitely much more effective than a few years ago.

In the present chapter, we move from a brief consideration of the relevant traditional Hindu and Muslim law to the statutory enactments and their socio-legal implications. The enormous case law that has built up under the various statutes provides excellent examples to illustrate the progress of the law and the confusions that arose on the way to today's tough regime of responsibilities for Indian men.

The traditional law

Both in traditional Hindu and Muslim law, a wife was entitled to maintenance from the husband during the pendency of the marriage. Traditional Hindu law had a number of complicated rules about when a wife would lose her right to maintenance from the husband or his joint family.[9] Such rules are obviously linked with different positions regarding divorce. Given that divorce was treated as a deviation from the ideal of marriage as a binding sacrament (*samskara*), the general position became that a woman, once married through the *shastric* system, would remain entitled to maintenance from the husband or his clan, in one way or another.[10] This basic principle partly explains institutions like *niyoga*, the customary remarriage of a widow with the husband's younger brother or another close relative, while customary traditions in many communities allowed for fairly informal marriages and divorces.[11] In effect, traditional Hindu joint family law had many ways of seeking to ensure that married women would not fall destitute and would be maintained till death or, alternatively, until they married a man who did not belong to the former husband's family. All of this was arranged and achieved without outside interference.

The assumption that women could stand on their own feet in economic terms, while certainly not unknown to the ancient Hindus,[12] did not receive prominence in the classical texts. I have already indicated that the dominant assumption appears to have been that Hindu women, at all stages of their life, had a claim to be maintained by a close male relative, the father in childhood, the husband during marriage, and the son after that.[13] We shall see that modern Hindu law has explicitly built on such concepts to safeguard, for example, the inheritance rights of widows,[14] as well as the post-divorce entitlements of Hindu wives.

In traditional Muslim law, the wife's entitlement to maintenance during the subsistence of the marriage was a cornerstone of matrimonial law.[15] Already in the classical law, Muslim women could have this entitlement written into the marriage contract and could specify an appropriate sum for eventualities. Arrears of maintenance could be charged to the husband's estate under South Asian Muslim law. Muslim husbands who attempted to plead poverty have elicited no sympathy from the courts, as the recent, interesting case of a Gulf returnee in Kerala clearly shows.[16]

Muslim law operates the principle that a wife who is 'disobedient' in some form loses her entitlement to maintenance from the husband. Such situations may arise if the wife returns to her parental home without the husband's agreement, refuses him sexual intercourse, or otherwise does not follow his wishes. Diwan and Diwan (1991: 135) reiterate the general rule that "the husband's obligation to maintain his wife exists only so long as the wife remains faithful to him and obeys all his reasonable orders".

Traditional Muslim law carried many differences of opinion about the quantum of maintenance. Should the husband's means alone be taken into account, or was the socio-economic standing of the wife also a factor? South Asian Muslim law has tended to reflect the Hanafi position, as for example found in the *Hedaya* (Hamilton 1891) and provided that the quantum of maintenance should be determined by taking into account the position of both spouses, while the main criterion under Shafi'i law (which is often applied in South India) would be the husband's means. Shi'a law places emphasis on the needs of the wife and her requirements in accordance with her status. Overall, these criteria have remained flexible and constantly contested in society; much would depend on the facts and circumstances of a particular case.

In traditional Muslim law, after the husband's death, the wife's right to maintenance ceased and, in theory if not in practice, inheritance law should take care of her needs.[17] In cases where the marriage was dissolved by divorce, classical Muslim jurisprudence developed the general rule that the wife would be entitled to maintenance during the *iddat* period.[18] However, if a wife is pregnant at the time of the divorce, the husband's liability for her maintenance continues until the birth of the child. Normally, the three months (or three menstrual cycles) of the *iddat* period start from the date of pronouncement of *talaq*, and the wife's right to maintenance during this period should be secured. However, there may be multiple problems for a wife in securing maintenance for herself and her children. If the husband simply does not pronounce the *talaq* but abandons the wife and fails to maintain her, she still has a claim towards him, but what if his whereabouts are unknown? If the wife does not even have knowledge of the *talaq*, her entitlement starts when she comes to know of the divorce (Verma 1988: 330).

Such examples begin to indicate that women are likely to face many problems in implementing maintenance rights that the traditional systems promised but would have found difficult to implement in social reality. Not every man, clearly, is a good Hindu or Muslim whose conscience and awareness of obligations protect women and children in society. Somehow, when it comes to monetary matters, selfishness often prevails over a sense of social obligation. Not surprisingly, therefore, the issue of post-divorce maintenance has remained a major area of concern in modern South Asian laws and has led to much activity by the official law.

Colonial intervention

It appears that in view of the many problems in South Asian societies surrounding maintenance arrangements, the British colonial administration began to interfere as a matter of social welfare policy. However, not unlike the modern Indian state today, the colonial state refused to bear any direct financial liability. It merely offered to help abandoned wives and children by passing relevant legislation that strengthened their traditional legal and moral claims to maintenance. In addition to the pre-existing personal law rules, therefore, South Asian law began to develop a general law on maintenance, notably with a criminal law emphasis. The first relevant enactment is found in s. 488 of the *Code of Criminal Procedure*, 1898. This section enabled a wife of any religion to apply for maintenance, provided she could prove that her husband had sufficient means and had failed to maintain her.[19] Section 488 is no longer in operation in India because it was replaced by sections 125–127 of the *Criminal Procedure Code*, 1973 (see further below). The original section read as follows:

> 488. *Order for maintenance of wives and children.* –
> (1) If any person having sufficient means neglects or refuses to maintain his wife or his legitimate or illegitimate child unable to maintain itself, a Magistrate of the first class may, upon proof of such neglect or refusal, order such person to make a monthly allowance for the maintenance of his wife or such child, at such monthly rate, not exceeding five hundred rupees in the whole, as such Magistrate thinks fit, and to pay the same to such person as the Magistrate from time to time directs.

> (2) Such allowance shall be payable from the date of the order, or if so ordered from the date of the application for maintenance.

The stated aim of this section, to provide financial support to all Indian wives neglected by their husbands, did not please the latter, of course. The various provisos of this section enabled a wife, including a wife whose husband had taken another wife or wives, to refuse cohabitation, while claiming maintenance under this section. Not surprisingly, this provision was challenged with particular vigour by Muslim husbands on the ground that it conflicted with traditional *shariat* rules. While most of these petitions were turned down,[20] it soon transpired that the fastest remedy for a Muslim husband faced with claims to maintenance from a 'disobedient' wife was simply to divorce her by *talaq*, thus freeing himself from the burden imposed by s. 488.[21] The section thus lost much of its protective energy through the easy device of the husband's instant *talaq*. Not surprisingly, the Anglo-Indian judges were not pleased. Early judicial criticism is recorded in *Ahmad Kasim Molla v. Khatun Bibi*, ILR [1932] 59 Cal 833, at p. 848, where it was held by Costello J:

> I am bound to say that, in my opinion, it does seem harsh that, at any time, a Mahomedan husband can, of his own power, put an end to any proceedings his wife may take under section 488 of the Code of Criminal Procedure, and it may be that some day this matter will have to be seriously considered by the members of the Mahomedan community and the legislature with a view to determining whether such arbitrary power in the hands of the husband is not now an anachronism inconsistent with present day ideas and incompatible with modern conditions.

Various subsequent enactments have sought to strengthen the position of wives in relation to maintenance during the subsistence of the marriage. Section 2(ii) of the DMMA 1939 gives a Muslim woman the right to claim divorce if her husband fails to maintain her for a period of two years. But how will a woman survive in the meantime? The relevant legal provisions were not effective enough to protect destitute women and their children if the husband did not fulfill the traditional obligations under the respective personal law.

Post-Independence developments

After Independence, India soon activated further legal mechanisms to protect the maintenance rights of wives generally, and of Muslim wives in particular. While this was an important social welfare measure, it raised large jurisprudential questions in Indian law about the role and position of the Muslim dower (*mahr*) and its relationship with other financial consequences of a marriage. In particular, the question arose whether the *mahr* is linked to divorce, whether it is therefore a kind of maintenance payment, or whether it constitutes a more general entitlement.

During the early 1970s, too, there was some interesting Indian case law on maintenance rights which identified the nature of the problems created in society. In *Shahulameedu v. Subaida Beevi*, 1970 KLT 4, decided by India's Lord Denning, V. R. Krishna Iyer J, a Muslim wife was asking for maintenance under s. 488 although she was refusing to live with her husband, who had taken another wife. The husband sought to rely on traditional Muslim law principles. Krishna Iyer J put social welfare higher than so-called religious concerns and said at p. 6:

> 70 years ago a law was enacted in India to prevent vagrancy by insisting on those who had a moral obligation to maintain a deserted wife or neglected child to pay, provided they had sufficient means, monthly allowances for the maintenance of the wife or the child. No civilised State can relax its duty in this regard and so this humane law deserves to be enforced sternly in a country and at a time when the paramount law of the land breathes the spirit of social justice.

It was therefore held in this case that such a wife was certainly entitled to a decree for maintenance. In *A. Yousuf Rawther v. Sowramma*, AIR 1971 Ker 261, Krishna Iyer J heard another case concerning the implications of a Muslim wife's right to maintenance. This was a husband's appeal against a decree of divorce in favour of his wife, given on the ground of non-maintenance. It was firmly held that a Muslim wife had a right to claim divorce on the basis of the husband's non-maintenance for two years. The judge emphasised social realism, holding at p. 270:

> For all these reasons, I hold that a Muslim woman, under Section 2(ii) of the Act, can sue for dissolution on the score that she has not as a fact been maintained even if there is good cause for it – the voice of the law, echoing public policy is often that of the realist, not of the moralist.

This decision was criticised by Muslim law specialists for going too far with regard to a Muslim wife's entitlement to maintenance in cases where she had abandoned the husband.[22] Since both spouses had remarried in the meantime, the question of further maintenance payments from the wife's former husband did not arise.

Problems regarding maintenance entitlement for divorced wives arose not only with regard to Muslims, of course. Such problems might be litigated under s. 488, but after the implementation of the HMA and the *Hindu Adoptions and Maintenance* Act, 1956 maintenance cases appeared also under those statutes and gave rise to interesting case law which we cannot possibly cover here in detail.

One example of a case which is certainly no longer good law must suffice here to illustrate the potential problems for Hindu wives during the 1960s and early 1970s. In *Akasam Chinna Babu v. Akasam Parbati*, AIR 1967

Ori 163, a Hindu wife had asked for a maintenance allowance *pendente lite* under s. 24 HMA and for maintenance for herself and her daughter under s. 25 HMA. The husband alleged that the wife had left him and was living in adultery with her maternal uncle. The wife's case was that the husband and his mother had been guilty of cruelty towards her, and that her husband had committed adultery. The husband had also refused to acknowledge paternity of a daughter born to the wife. Before the High Court, the husband appealed against a decree refusing him divorce, but awarding maintenance to the wife, at the rate of Rs. 30/- per month plus Rs. 10/- for the daughter.

It was found, at p. 164, that "[i]n view of the evidence and circumstances of the case, the learned trial court rightly held that a case of adultery had not been established". The judge then considered the relevant provisions of the HMA and held, at p. 164:

> In view of the clear provisions in Section 24, there cannot be any dispute that the wife is entitled to a pendente lite maintenance when she has no independent income sufficient for her support, and also the necessary expenses of the proceedings. There is no evidence in this case that the wife had sufficient income for her support. In that view of the matter the order for pendente lite maintenance ... at the rate of Rs. 30 must be maintained. Section 24, however, does not authorise grant of any pendente lite maintenance to the daughter ... The maintenance of Rs. 10 awarded in favour of the daughter must therefore be set aside.

This evidently technical decision may have been procedurally correct, but socially it was absolutely inadequate.[23] It blatantly refuses to consider the full extent of the needs of the abandoned woman and her daughter, throwing them back to depend on the generosity of the wife's maternal uncle. This case, as well as another unsatisfactory early decision,[24] were dissented from in *Monoj Kr. Jaiswal v. Lila Jaiswal*, AIR 1987 Cal 230, which reflects the remarkable progress made in judicial awareness in the 20 years between *Akasam* and *Monoj*. In the latter case, it was held, at pp. 231–232, that decisions like *Akasam* were inadequate:

> ... these decisions have adopted a rather technical and literal approach and the effect and impact of S. 26 of the Hindu Marriage Act have not at all been considered in these decisions.[25]

Husbands would obviously seek to argue, wherever possible, that their wives had their own income and thus required no maintenance. In *Bhagwan Dutt v. Kamla Devi*, AIR 1975 SC 83, the Supreme Court heard a husband's appeal against an award of maintenance to the wife under s. 488 of the *Criminal Procedure Code*, 1898. Both spouses in this case were fairly poor people. The facts were clear-cut and the husband basically sought to argue that the wife had enough income to maintain herself and the child. The question for the Supreme Court, therefore, was whether the income of the wife can be taken into account in determining the amount of maintenance payable to her under s. 488.

The Supreme Court compared the relevant provisions of s. 488 and of s. 125 of the new *Criminal Procedure Code* of 1973, which had meanwhile been enacted. Examining the provisions of s. 488 and related sections, it was held at p. 85:

> These provisions are intended to fulfil a social purpose. Their object is to compel a man to perform the moral obligation which he owes to society in respect of his wife and children. By providing a simple, speedy but limited relief, they seek to ensure that the neglected wife and children are not left beggared and destituted on the scrap-heap of society and thereby driven to a life of vagrancy, immorality and crime for their subsistence.

It was further held, at p. 86:

> The object of those provisions being to prevent vagrancy and destitution, the Magistrate has to find out as to what is required by the wife to maintain a standard of living which is neither luxurious nor penurious, but is modestly consistent with the status of the family. The needs and requirements of the wife for such moderate living can be fairly determined, only if her separate income, also, is taken into account together with the earnings of the husband and his commitments.
>
> There is nothing in these provisions to show that in determining the maintenance and its rate, the Magistrate has to inquire into the means of the husband, alone, and exclude the means of the wife altogether from consideration. ...
>
> Keeping in view the object, scheme, setting and the language of these associate provisions ..., it seems to us clear that in determining the amount of maintenance under s. 488(1), the Magistrate is competent to take into consideration the separate income and means of the wife.

Before remitting the case to the Magistrate with instructions to re-fix the amount of maintenance for the wife and the child in accordance with the Supreme Court's interpretation of the law, it was therefore held, at p. 87:

> We have said and it needs to be said again, that Section 488 is intended to serve a social purpose. It provides a machinery for summary enforcement of the moral obligations of a man towards his wife and children so that they may not out of sheer destitution become a hazard to the well-being of orderly society.

This is an ambivalent case, therefore, reflecting to some extent the change-over in Indian judicial approaches to maintenance arrangements. This is not yet an outrightly activist stance, as taken later by judges like Krishna Iyer, but it projects adequately the social needs of potentially destitute women and children in Indian society.

The new maintenance law of the 1970s

Given that a Muslim husband could easily defeat a wife's claim for maintenance under s. 488 of the 1898 Code by simply divorcing her,[26] modern Indian law extended the statutory definition of 'wife' for the purposes of maintenance law in 1973 to include 'divorced wife'. To some extent, this has been seen as an anti-Muslim measure, targeting Muslim men, but detailed research would show much evidence to the effect that this was a social welfare measure designed to make all Indian husbands and fathers accountable, not just Muslim men. Case law, too, has emphasised the social rather than the penal nature of the new legal provisions.[27] Of course, this change in the general statute law immediately raised fresh conflicts about the supposedly unfettered right of a Muslim husband to cast off a disobedient wife and about the financial consequences of such a wife's action. Would a Muslim husband in India now have to pay maintenance to his divorced wife until she died or remarried? It seems obvious today, with the benefit of hindsight, that the Indian legislature tried to find a compromise between social welfare concerns and respect for Muslim personal law. Again, we see that while the compromise chosen by modern India favoured the social welfare of women, it was at the same time designed to protect the non-existent coffers of the welfare state. The final outcome of this complex strategy has been, as we shall see further below, to make divorcing husbands of any religious background potentially liable for the permanent maintenance of their former wives. As I have indicated in the analysis of chapter 2, this may very well be read as an indirect encouragement for Indian men to make their marriages work, rather than risk divorce and its accompanying financial penalties.

In view of multiple problems over maintenance entitlements for women in the various communities, s. 488 of the *Code of Criminal Procedure,* 1898 was replaced in India by s. 125 of the new *Code of Criminal Procedure,* 1973. The relevant parts of this section read as follows:

> 125. *Order for maintenance of wives, children and parents.* –
> (1) If any person having sufficient means neglects or refuses to maintain –
> (a) his wife, unable to maintain herself, or
> (b) his legitimate or illegitimate minor child, whether married or not, unable to maintain itself, or
> (c) his legitimate or illegitimate child (not being a married daughter) who has attained majority, where such child is, by reason of any physical or mental abnormality or injury unable to maintain itself, or
> (d) his father or mother, unable to maintain himself or herself,
> a Magistrate of the first class may, upon proof of such neglect or refusal, order such person to make a monthly allowance for the maintenance of his wife or such child, father or mother, at such

monthly rate not exceeding five hundred rupees in the whole, as such Magistrate thinks fit, and to pay the same to such person as the Magistrate may from time to time direct.

Provided that the Magistrate may order the father of a minor female child referred to in clause (b) to make allowance, until she attains her majority, if the Magistrate is satisfied that the husband of such minor female child, if married, is not possessed of sufficient means.

Explanations. – For the purposes of this chapter, –

...

(b) "wife" includes a woman who has been divorced by, or has obtained a divorce from, her husband and has not remarried.

By including a divorced wife in the definition of 'wife', this section opened the way for maintenance payments to be awarded to a divorced woman until her death or remarriage. While this concept was known to Hindu law, it evidently conflicted with classical juristic interpretations and the popular understanding of Muslim law rules, according to which maintenance payments to a divorced wife are assumed to cease at the end of the *iddat* period, while the Muslim husband remains certainly responsible for his wife's maintenance during the *iddat* period. As a result of political pressure from Muslims,[28] an additional provision was therefore inserted into the Code as s. 127(3)(b), taking account of customary Muslim institutions like *mahr* and *iddat*.[29] This section states:

127. *Alteration in allowances.*–

(1) On proof of a change in the circumstances of any person, receiving, under section 125 a monthly allowance, or ordered under the same section to pay a monthly allowance to his wife, child, father or mother, as the case may be, the Magistrate may make such alteration in the allowance as he thinks fit:

Provided that if he increases the allowance, the monthly rate of five hundred rupees in the whole shall not be exceeded.

...

(3) Where any order has been made under section 125 in favour of a woman who has been divorced by, or has obtained a divorce from, her husband, the Magistrate shall, if he is satisfied that

(a) the woman has, after the date of such divorce, remarried, cancel such order as from the date of her remarriage;

(b) the woman has been divorced by her husband and that she has received, whether before or after the date of the said order, the whole of the sum which, under any customary or personal law applicable to the parties, was payable on such divorce, cancel such order. –

...

(c) the woman has obtained a divorce from her husband and that she had voluntarily surrendered her rights to maintenance after her divorce, cancel the order from the date thereof.

The appropriate interpretation of s. 127(3)(b) read with s. 125 became the subject of much litigation from the mid-1970s until 1985. It raised afresh the key question of whether dower was an amount payable by the Muslim husband to the wife on divorce, or whether it played a role in the context of maintenance.[30] Below, we now turn first to the case law involving Muslim couples, up to and including the famous *Shah Bano* case of 1985.

Muslim cases under sections 125–127 of the 1973 Code

As expected, constitutional challenges to the new regime of maintenance law were soon brought to the courts. In *Kunhi Moyin v. Pathumma* 1976 KLT 87, the constitutional validity of s. 125 of the 1973 Code was questioned. Khalid J characterised the new legislation, at p. 91, as "a milestone in the social legislation conferring benefits to a particular group of women who is in need of help ... the object being to prevent vagrancy and to protect such women from poverty and starvation". The main charge was that the new law violated Muslim law and constituted "an invasion of the personal law of Muslims" (*id.*) because it effectively changed, with retrospective effect, the conditions under which Muslim spouses had entered their marriages. This was answered by the learned judge with a long discussion of the social conditions of divorced women in India and the abuse of liberal divorce laws. Finally, it was held, at p. 96, concerning the import of s. 127(3)(b):

> We would like to make it clear that section 127(3)(b) refers not to maintenance during the period of iddat or payment of dower. ... It is therefore not a sum of money which under the personal law is payable on divorce.

The husband's claim that he should not be liable to payment of maintenance was therefore refused. In another important case, *Muhammed v. Sainabi* 1976 KLT 711, Khalid J in the High Court of Kerala reiterated that the dower payment is outside the purview of s. 127(3)(b), reasoning that such dower payments tended to be insufficient to provide for the needs of divorced women, anyway. Khalid J restated the traditional understanding of Muslim law and then, turning to the impact of the 1973 Code, said at p. 712:

> Under the Muslim Personal Law, as applied by Courts in India, a divorced wife is entitled to claim maintenance after divorce only for the period of iddath. Even here, there is difference between Shaffi and Hanafi Law. S. 125 Cr.P.C. imports a legal fiction, which is that a divorced wife continues to be a wife notwithstanding the divorce, in her claim for maintenance until she remarries. The husband, under the new clause, can successfully resist the claim of the wife for maintenance only if he establishes a custom, that certain customary dues, if paid, at the time of the divorce, would disentitle the wife from

> claiming maintenance. What exactly is meant by customary dues I do not propose to examine here.

Concerning the role of *mahr* in this context, the learned judge said, at p. 713:

> Mahar is an amount payable by the husband to the wife either prompt or deferred. Payment of Mahar will not effect a discharge of a claim for maintenance, because the claim for mahar is a valuable right available to the wife and this claim is a charge over the properties of the husband. Therefore, mention of payment of mahar ... will not also operate as payment of customary dues in discharge of the claim for maintenance.

It was, however, held in the Bombay High Court that the payment of *mahr* on divorce would satisfy s. 127(3)(b), so that a court would have no jurisdiction to make an order for further maintenance under s. 125.[31] A number of further High Court cases followed and judicial alertness to this thorny problem grew.[32] In one of those cases, the wife refused to accept the meagre sum offered by the husband and had thus, according to s. 127(3)(b) of the 1973 Code, not 'received' the customary dues.[33] The husband had paid the wife Rs. 27.50/- as prompt *mahr* at the time of the marriage and had offered to pay her a further Rs. 100/- as deferred *mahr*. He had deposited this sum in court and claimed that he had thereby discharged his liability under the 1973 Code. The judge held that, in view of the social welfare objectives of the new law, any liberal interpretation was uncalled for.

Three Supreme Court cases then took up the debate, which was ultimately decided, as expected, in favour of the socially conscious Kerala decisions rather than technical reliance on certain words.[34] In *Bai Tahira*, AIR 1979 SC 362, the wife had received a divorce settlement through a consent decree. This included a flat, which had been transferred into her name, shares of a housing society, a *mahr* of Rs. 5,000/- and Rs. 180/- as *iddat* money. Following the change in the law, and suffering from the effects of inflation, this divorced wife then made an application under s. 125 of the 1973 Code for a further decree of maintenance in favour of herself and her son. Krishna Iyer J said, at pp. 365–366:

> Payment of mehar money, as a customary discharge, is within the cognisance of that provision. But what was the amount of mehar? Rs. 5000/-, interest from which could not keep the woman's body and soul together for a day, ... unless she was ready to sell her body and give up her soul! ... Where the husband, by customary payment at the time of divorce, has adequately provided for the divorcee, a subsequent series of recurrent doles is contra-indicated and the husband liberated. This is the teleological interpretation, the sociological decoding of the text of S. 127. The key-note thought is

> adequacy of payment which will take reasonable care of her maintenance. The payment of illusory amounts by way of customary or personal law requirement will be considered in the reduction of maintenance rate but cannot annihilate that rate unless it is a reasonable substitute. The legal sanctity of the payment is certified by the fulfilment of the social obligation, not by a ritual exercise rooted in custom.... The proposition, therefore, is that no husband can claim under Section 127 (3) absolution from his obligation under S. 125 towards a divorced wife except on proof of payment of a sum stipulated by customary or personal law whose quantum is more or less sufficient to do duty for maintenance allowance.

This "enlightened judicial approach" (Kusum 1980: 412) was widely praised, but it was also rapidly opposed through a Private Member's Bill in Parliament, which sought to restrict the maintenance rights of divorced Muslim wives.[35] Krishna Iyer J, giving judgment in *Fuzlunbi v. K. Khader Vali*, AIR 1980 SC 1730, applied the principles laid down in *Bai Tahira*. Here the husband had paid his wife Rs. 500/- by way of dower and now claimed exemption from the effect of s. 125 of the 1973 Code. The learned judge said at p. 1731:

> No one in his senses can contend that the mahar of Rs. 500/- will yield income sufficient to maintain a woman even if she were to live on city pavements! What is the intendment of S.127(3)(b)? What is the scheme of relief for driftwood and destitute wives and divorcees discarded by heartless husbands? ...
>
> What, in short is the text and texture of the provision, if read in the light of the mischief to be avoided, the justice to be advanced?[36]

V. R. Krishna Iyer J answered these questions, as in *Bai Tahira*, by stating categorically that the payment of illusory amounts by way of customary or personal law requirements would be considered in the reduction of maintenance awarded, but that it could not wipe out the divorcing husband's liability unless what he offered amounted to a reasonable provision for the former wife.

Another case in the Indian Supreme Court, *Zohara Khatoon v. Mhd. Ibrahim*, AIR 1981 SC 1243, permitted a Muslim wife who had earlier obtained a divorce under the *Dissolution of Muslim Marriages Act*, 1939 to secure maintenance under s. 125 of the 1973 Code. The main point of contention in this case concerned the legal position of a wife who had divorced the husband, rather than being divorced by him. Would she still be a 'wife' for the purposes of the 1973 Code and thus remain entitled to maintenance? The court referred to s. 127(3)(c) of the Code, but the dicta of Krishna Iyer J in this case created the impression that there was still some doubt as to the exact meaning and extent of s. 127(3)(b).

This lingering insecurity, as well as the continuing opposition of Indian Muslims to the implications of the new maintenance law, set the scene for the famous *Shah Bano* case of 1985. Reported as *Mohd. Ahmed Khan v. Shah Bano Begum*, AIR 1985 SC 945, this case involved a prosperous husband, a senior advocate by profession, who had married Shah Bano in 1932 and had three sons and two daughters from her. He claimed that this was never a happy marriage and eventually took a second wife. In 1975, he drove Shah Bano, by now an old lady, out of the house. In April 1978, she filed a petition claiming Rs. 500/- monthly maintenance under the 1973 Code. It speaks volumes for the legal approach to women's claims at the time, even in the case of privileged Muslim wives such as Shah Bano, that the magistrate awarded her merely Rs. 25/- per month. Then, in November 1978 the husband divorced her by *talaq* and his defence to Shah Bano's maintenance claim now became that she was no longer his wife, that he had paid her Rs. 3,000/- as *mahr*, and hence was under no further obligations to her. The High Court of Madhya Pradesh awarded Shah Bano Rs. 179.20 per month as maintenance and the husband appealed against that to the Supreme Court.

A bench of two judges took the stance that *Bai Tahira* and *Fuzlunbi* were incorrectly decided and that the law was not clear. Therefore, they referred the matter to a full bench of five judges, headed by Chief Justice Chandrachud. While one of the two judges who referred the case had been a Muslim, the fact that all five judges on this full bench were Hindus became a political issue, as the case involved an analysis of the Qur'anic foundations of Muslim law.

In his judgment, the Chief Justice first reiterated (at p. 949) the well-established position that s. 125 of the *Criminal Procedure Code* was part of the general law and thus overrides the personal law in any case of conflict. There was also no doubt that the extended definition of 'wife' under the 1973 Code was beyond dispute. Chandrachud CJ then went on to examine the question whether there was in fact any conflict between the Muslim personal law and the general law. This is a new element in the case law, which led to intense anguish and some additional politicking, because five Hindu judges were here seen interpreting the principles of Muslim law. The most important reason for Muslim male opposition was, however, that this case would have huge financial implications and would hit the pockets of many Muslim men.

The learned judges went through the statements of several specialist authors and found that "these statements in the text books are inadequate to establish the proposition that the Muslim husband is not under an obligation to provide for the maintenance of his divorced wife, *who is unable to maintain herself*" (underlining in the original text, at p. 950). Chandrachud CJ then stated, at pp. 950–951:

> Since the Muslim Personal Law, which limits the husband's liability to provide for the maintenance of the divorced wife to the period of iddat, does not contemplate or countenance the situation envisaged by section 125, it would be wrong to hold that the Muslim husband,

according to his personal law, is not under an obligation to provide maintenance, beyond the period of iddat, to his divorced wife who is unable to maintain herself ... The true position is that, if the divorced wife is able to maintain herself, the husband's liability to provide maintenance for her ceases with the expiration of the period of iddat. If she is unable to maintain herself, she is entitled to take recourse to section 125 of the Code. The outcome of this discussion is that there is no conflict between the provisions of section 125 and those of the Muslim Personal Law on the question of the Muslim husband's obligation to provide maintenance for a divorced wife who is unable to maintain herself.

This conclusion was supported by reference to Qur'anic verses (Sura 2, verses 241 and 242), according to which reasonable maintenance should be provided to divorced women as a matter of duty for righteous Muslim men.[37] Having gone through various English translations of the Arabic text, the Chief Justice concluded, at p. 952:

> These Aiyats leave no doubt that the Quran imposes an obligation on the Muslim husband to make provision for or to provide maintenance to the divorced wife. The contrary argument does less than justice to the teachings of the Quran.

Next, the learned Chief Justice turned to the question of *mahr.* He refused to accept the interpretation of *mahr* as an amount payable by the husband to the wife on divorce and held, at pp. 952–953:

> If Mahr is an amount which the wife is entitled to receive from the husband in consideration of the marriage, that is the very opposite of the amount being payable in consideration of divorce. Divorce dissolves the marriage. Therefore, no amount which is payable in consideration of the marriage can possibly be described as an amount payable in consideration of divorce. The alternative premise that Mahr is an obligation imposed upon the husband as a mark of respect for the wife is wholly detrimental to the stance that it is an amount payable to the wife on divorce. A man may marry a woman for love, looks, learning or nothing at all. And, he may settle a sum upon her as a mark of respect for her. But he does not divorce her as a mark of respect. Therefore, a sum payable to the wife out of respect cannot be a sum payable 'on divorce'.

Other parts of this judgment are not relevant to the present discussion (see ch. 6. 8 below on the uniform civil code issue). The *Shah Bano* case had firmly reiterated the liability of the divorcing Muslim husband for his former wife's welfare beyond the narrow confines of the *iddat* period.[38]

The pressure exerted by this decision was well-reflected in the violent public reactions of protesters on the streets and scholars with sharp pens and tongues.[39] The *Shah Bano* case became the catalyst for a most interesting re-assessment of the basic principles of Muslim law on post-divorce maintenance in modern South Asia.[40] As we shall see in more detail further below, it has now been well-established in modern Indian law that there is really no conflict between the Qur'anic pronouncements about the husband's obligations towards a divorced wife and the welfare-based statutes of the modern Indian state, since both place an obligation on divorcing husbands to look after the future welfare of their ex-wives, which cannot be a matter for the state in either case, but must remain a matter for society. While this basic message has not been lost in Middle Eastern and North African Muslim law, it competes of course with traditional juristic reasoning to the effect that the liability of Muslim husbands for an ex-wife ceases at the end of the *iddat* period. Who, then, is to take care of such women if they need help? As we shall see in more detail below, modern Indian Muslim law, in particular the *Muslim Women (Protection of Rights on Divorce) Act* of 1986, has made creative use of the benevolent Qur'anic foundations by establishing a multi-tiered, tightly framed and time-bound system for defining and implementing the rights of the divorced Muslim wife in modern Indian law. Before we turn to that important, recent development in Indian maintenance law, we should now consider in some detail the implications of growing judicial activism for the maintenance claims of Hindu women in post-Emergency India.

New activism in Hindu maintenance law

There can be no doubt that India's judicial activism in the field of maintenance law, which so prominently focused on Muslim cases during the 1980s, has also influenced cases involving Hindus and the parallel Hindu law on maintenance, as found in various personal law statutes. However, there are other reasons for this new activism, which will become more obvious during the present discussion. While this field has not been researched in much detail until the late 1980s, new studies are now beginning to appear, reflecting the increased activism of the Indian courts also with regard to Hindu couples.[41]

When we discussed the contentious and difficult issue of marriage solemnisation in ch. 1.5 above, it became clear that judicial approaches to the validity of Hindu marriages brought immediate consequences for maintenance law, for both women and children. This has now fully dawned on the Indian courts. In the context of marriage and divorce laws therefore, claims by husbands that they did not validly marry a particular wife – and hence should not be liable to maintenance claims – have been increasingly answered by strong judicial emphasis on presumptions of marriage.[42] There is a long line of cases concerning presumptions of marriage in this context. It appears that since the 1980s most such cases were decided in favour of the wife, thereby protecting women's financial interests and entitlements.

In *Boli Narajan Pawye v. Shiddheswari Morang*, 1981 CriLJ 674 (Gau), the Gauhati High Court rejected the husband's argument that strict proof of marriage with all attending ceremonies is a *sine qua non* to prove the status of wife under s. 125(1)(a) of the 1973 Code. It was held that a void or voidable marriage does not disentitle a wife to maintenance in the absence of a final declaration from a competent court. Any proposition to the contrary would throw millions of women on the streets, and would amount to granting a licence to men to go through void or voidable marriages.[43]

With regard to polygamous marriages, too, the courts have been concerned to protect wives and to make husbands liable for maintenance payments, even where the marriage of the woman concerned is in all probability void in law. This follows on from the earlier case of *C. Obula Konda Reddy*, AIR 1976 AP 43, in which it had been held that under s. 18 of the *Hindu Adoptions and Maintenance Act*, 1956 the expression 'Hindu wife' means "a Hindu wife whose marriage is solemnized" (p. 44), including a Hindu wife who is party to a polygamous marriage. Similarly, in *Rudramma v. H. R. Pattaveerabhadrappa*, (1987) CriLJ 677 (Ker), it was held by the High Court of Kerala that a court before which a maintenance petition is filed cannot go into the validity of the marriage. This was held even though it was evident from the facts of the case that the claimant wife was the second wife of a polygamously married Hindu man.[44] *Shantaram Tukaram Patil v. Dagubai Tukaram Patil*, AIR 1987 Bom 182, firmly held, at p. 191, that "Section 25, Hindu Marriage Act, confers upon a woman, whose marriage is void or is declared to be void, a right of maintenance against her husband". Vijay Sharma (1994: 271–273) discusses a number of such cases and refers (at p. 271) to a decision by Fathima Beevi J,[45] holding that a husband who married a further wife was liable to pay maintenance to his second 'wife' even if she was able to look after herself and the maintenance amount was beyond his means.

The social responsibility of family members for others in the family who may be indigent has been powerfully reinforced by the Supreme Court in a number of cases. These deserve careful analysis in the context of social welfare strategies.[46] *Vijaya Manohar Arhat v. Kashirao Rajaram Sawai*, AIR 1987 SC 1100 involved a maintenance claim filed by an aged father (who had remarried) against a married daughter who had become a medical practitioner. The court held that the word 'his' in clause (d) of s. 125 of the Criminal Procedure Code includes both male and female children and thus held the daughter liable for the maintenance of her aged father and his second wife. So much for gender equity! It could not be argued that only men are targeted by modern India's comprehensive re-definition – or re-discovery – of social welfare arrangements; this is a task for society as a whole.

As indicated, Indian courts have come down heavily, and with scathing criticism, on men who claim inability to maintain their dependants and are simply unwilling to fulfil their obligations. In *Jai Singh v. Khimi Bhiklu*, AIR 1978 HP 45, the judge made strong comments about the husband's recalcitrance and expressed the view, at pp. 47–48, that asking an impecunious wife to take out execution proceedings and contempt proceedings would only delay the matter beyond tolerable levels. This case refers to a number of other decisions, indicating that this was a common problem experienced by the High Courts at that time.

In *Durga Singh Lodhi v. Prembai*, 1990 CriLJ 2065 (MP), an evidently able-bodied husband was refusing to pay maintenance. The question before the Court was whether he could be imprisoned for default, even though he had no property. It was held, significantly, that the term 'means' included not only real property, but also the capacity to earn. It was held at p. 2067, confirming the order of imprisonment, that a man could not avoid his liability under s. 125 of the 1973 Code,

> merely because he has no tangible real property or income, but is otherwise able-bodied and healthy and has capacity to earn. The presumption should be that such an able-bodied healthy person is possessed of sufficient means and it is for him to show that by accident, disease or the condition of the labour market or otherwise, he is not capable of earning anything.

In a case concerning a poor couple, the wife and child had been awarded Rs. 300/- per month as interim maintenance and the husband appealed. *Sivankutty v. S. Komalakumari*, AIR 1989 Ker 124, is a useful case on the ambit of s. 18 HAMA and confirms the wife's right to maintenance under that section. It was held, at p. 125:

> The right of the wife to claim maintenance is an incident of the status of matrimony. The section emphasises that when once the relationship of husband or wife is established, the wife gets the entitlement to maintenance. Though the claim to maintenance or the obligation of the husband to maintain the wife springs from the consortium of the wife with the husband, under certain circumstances enumerated in the section, where the wife is allowed by the statute to live separately from her husband, the wife will not lose her right to maintenance.

However, judicial realism prevailed over pro-women activism. Although there was a well-recognised general principle to the effect that a married man had to maintain his wife and offspring, a proper balance would have to be achieved. It was held at p. 129:

> I do not think that a man who is incapable of earning any income should be compelled by a court to pay maintenance to the wife on the principle that it is a personal obligation on the part of the husband to maintain his wife. In a case where the husband happens to be an indigent person or becomes an indigent person, it is a misfortune that has to be shared by the wife also.

Evidently, in the present case the learned judge saw a genuine appellant, not a work-shy man who wanted to evade his responsibilities. Since the husband's monthly income was only Rs. 623/-, the amount of maintenance payable was reduced from Rs. 300/- to Rs. 250/-.

Husbands will seek to hide their income from the courts, or will simply prevaricate, but in a number of recent cases this strategy has not been successful and has led to strong judicial comments. In *Vinod Kumar Kejriwal v. Usha Vinod Kejriwal*, AIR 1993 Bom 160, referred to by the judge as "an unfortunate litigation" (p. 161) at the very start of the judgment, the husband opposed an order for maintenance *pendente lite* in favour of the wife. The husband had made repeated "wild and baseless allegations" (p. 171) about the unfaithful and adulterous behaviour of his wife and had clearly hidden his substantial income to avoid payment of considerable arrears to the wife. The learned judge found no reason to accept the husband's story and decreed that unless the husband deposited a substantial sum of money in the Family Court, which would then be passed over to the wife, any further relief would be refused.

In *Anil Kumar v. Laxmi Devi*, AIR 1994 NOC 61 (Raj), it was held that s. 24 of the HMA gives a wide discretion to the court in matters of fixing maintenance payments. It was said by B. R. Arora J, at p. 31:

> It is the duty of the able-bodied person to earn enough to discharge his legal obligations to maintain his wife and to provide for the subsistence so that the wife is not driven to destitution even when the husband is not earning sufficient money. The provisions have been made to protect the neglected wife against starvation and to tide over the immediate difficulties and to protect her interest during the proceedings which have been foisted upon her by the husband. The proceedings under S. 24 of the Hindu Marriage Act are to be decided in a summary manner and the Court is not expected to try the issue at length.

Significantly, the judge here gives short thrift to the husband, and he also puts the financial liability on him for starting judicial proceedings and effectively wasting judicial time. This is well in line with our analysis to the effect that divorce litigation in modern India is not being encouraged by the state. Again, the message to husbands is that they are free to litigate, but they will have to pay for this privilege.

Where, as is possible under the gender-balanced provisions of sections 24 and 25 HMA, a former husband is seeking maintenance from his ex-wife, the judges have not found this acceptable where the man was manifestly unwilling to work or hiding his real income. In *Kanchan v. Kamalendra*, AIR 1992 Bom 493, a wife appealed against a decree of maintenance in favour of the husband. He had been awarded Rs. 100/- per month as maintenance *pendente lite* and Rs. 500/- towards his litigation expenses. The court found that s. 24 HMA gave an equal entitlement to Hindu husbands, who can in certain circumstances claim maintenance *pendente lite* against the wife. However, such a husband would have to satisfy the court that he was unable to maintain himself (p. 493). It was then held, at p. 494, setting aside the maintenance order:

> The non-applicant husband is [a] mentally and physically well-bodied person. He has a skill of a particular business. There is no handicap for him to earn bare minimum to support his livelihood. Merely because his business is closed, it cannot be held that he has no source to earn. Since the wife is in the employment, the husband cannot make himself wholly dependent on her income through a device of S. 24 of the Act. In absence of any handicap or impediment to earn, to grant maintenance to such able bodied person equipped with skill would promote idleness. It is opposed to [the] spirit of S. 24 of the Act.

Constitutional challenges have sometimes been mounted against the law's new strictness on maintenance arrangements. In *P. S. Krishna Murthy v. P. S. Umadevi*, AIR 1987 AP 237, a clever husband was seeking to challenge the constitutional validity of s. 24 HMA on the ground that it was discriminatory and violative of Article 14 of the Constitution. He claimed unlawful discrimination on the basis of religion, since under s. 36 of the *Indian Divorce Act*, 1869 the maximum amount of interim maintenance that could be granted to a wife is only one-fifth of the husband's average net income for the three years preceding the order. Under s. 24 HMA, on the other hand, the husband's liability is unspecified. The court did not agree that there was any invidious discrimination in this provision.

Regarding ceilings for maintenance payments, Diwan (1990b: 6) reports that the Indian Law Commission made a recommendation on s. 125 of the *Criminal Procedure Code*, 1973 to the effect that the statutory ceiling of Rs. 500/- should be removed in view of inflation or should be increased to Rs. 4,500 (Diwan, 1990b: 11). Diwan himself suggested a ceiling of Rs. 1,000/- or Rs. 1,500, noting at p. 11:

> The provision is not meant to provide maintenance to the claimant in accordance with his or her status. The amount of maintenance in accordance with the status or station in life is the criterion under personal law and matrimonial statutes. It should not be so under Section 125, the avowed object of which is the prevention of destitution and vagrancy.

Nothing was done on this front, however, and the emergency nature of the protection scheme under s. 125 has been maintained. If we abandon middle class perceptions of this issue, we might see that Rs. 500/- is still a substantial amount of money for desperately poor women and children in Indian society today.

In the most recent case law, as noted in the context of divorce litigation in ch. 2.5 above, we find much evidence that the Indian courts have become especially concerned about finding appropriate methods to safeguard the financial interests of women and children after a broken marriage. During the 1980s, this matter was still perceived in a much more individualistic fashion. This is well-reflected in a statement by Boparai (1984: 286–287), who argued in favour of the breakdown principle and self-reliance of women, concluding his study on bars to divorce by saying:

> It seems to us, however, that no marriage should be maintained without the full and free consent of the spouses. The maintenance of children or a needy spouse are important questions but can be provided for otherwise. The doctrine of assumed dependence of a wife is quite out of keeping with modern times. Women today, not only in Canada and other developed countries but in developing countries like India and Nigeria, too, have the same educational and vocational opportunities as men. Increasing numbers are working for a living. This change in status and position of women is already reflected in the attitude of the Canadian courts to maintenance awards; such awards to wives are no longer automatic, as they used to be in the past. The idea that upon marriage the husband assumes the duty to support the wife for the duration of their joint lives seems incompatible with the acceptance of the very idea of divorce. A needy spouse should be awarded only a "rehabilitative maintenance" for a limited period. After that the social services should take over, if need be. Duty to maintain minor children should be imposed on both the parents to the extent of their ability, but the difficulty or impossibility of making suitable arrangements in this respect should not be a bar to divorce. The best interests of the children of a marriage cannot possibly be served by forcing the parents to live together; the children may well become the targets of one or both parents' frustration at not being able to dissolve the marriage because of them. Moreover, young children would seem better off with one loving parent than with two perpetually quarrelling parents. It is submitted accordingly that there should be no bars to the granting of divorce.

This wonderfully optimistic, Canadian-inspired and individual-centred approach has clearly not been adopted by the Indian courts when considering divorces and, in particular, with reference to supervising maintenance arrangements. It is amazing that an Indian writer could be so blinkered as to overlook the impossibility of any form of state-sponsored social services taking responsibility for the maintenance of stranded women and children in India. This was clearly not the way forward. Appropriate Indian social realism is reflected in an article on polygamy and women's rights of maintenance by Sagade (1989: 336), who emphasises straight away:

> Matrimony creates a number of rights and obligations on the part of the spouses against each other, maintenance being one of them. A husband is under an obligation to maintain his wife during coverture and even upon separation and divorce.

However, I do not accept Sagade's view that an Indian woman would only have a right to maintenance if she starts litigation, since married women manifestly have an inherent, pre-existing claim which they can use to good effect in private bargaining and without recourse to courts. Tradition remains eminently useful here, and our ignorance of informal processes of bargaining in India's homes cannot underpin an argument that only state law would help women. Sagade's legally centralist view is therefore too court-centred, too much focused on the protection mechanisms of the modern law as a guarantor of access to court proceedings. In reality, a combination of old and new concepts seems to have worked its way through the Indian case law on post-divorce maintenance. It is precisely because of the fact that Indian women have such pre-existing claims, which are underpinned by social and moral norms (and are thus legal postulates in Chiba's sense) that women are able to justify access to courts in the first place.

At the same time, it remains a fact that women who did go to court in India during the 1990s to claim maintenance have tended to come out victorious, if the facts of their case were right and the husband had the necessary resources. This shows us that the Indian courts have managed, during the 1990s, to distance themselves from tempting modern delusions about the independence of individuals. Instead, they have redefined the traditional norms about the supposed dependence of women on men in a productive fashion and as a matter of public policy on social welfare. In essence, the reasoning has been that if women are said to be dependent on men, then men have an inherent obligation to maintain them.

As with regard to divorce law itself, failure to develop such a broad, welfare-oriented policy would have damaged the financial interests of many women and children, allowing male egoism and chauvinism to prevail over national concerns of social welfare. It would have put private interest over public interest, another indication that modern Indian state policies have increasingly become focused on social welfare issues rather than the protection of private property claims. There can be no doubt that failure to go down this route would have been immensely dangerous in socio-economic terms and would have been especially detrimental to Indian women and children.

In *Preeti Singh v. Sandeep Singh*, AIR 1995 SC 1851, we can see how vigilantly the Supreme Court now monitors the financial arrangements between parties to a divorce by mutual consent. This is also being followed at High Court level. In *Sreelatha v. Deepthy Kumar*, AIR 1998 Ker 97, a couple had, after prolonged litigation, agreed to present a petition for divorce by mutual consent. A. R. Lakshmanan J carefully examined the facts and circumstances of the case, and the parties themselves, before he pronounced himself satisfied with the financial arrangements, in this case two lump sum payments to the wife over a total of Rs. 175,000/-. It was explicitly held that the divorce should only become effective after the payment of the second instalment.

Several important cases, discussed in the context of divorce law in ch. 2.5 above, illustrated the readiness of the Indian Supreme Court to overlook technical and procedural hurdles in order to achieve 'complete justice' in accordance with Article 142 of the Indian Constitution. *Chanderkala Trivedi v. Dr. S. P. Trivedi*, 1993 (4) SCC 232 was one such case in which the Supreme Court granted divorce to a couple who had been at war for many years through the courts and had finally reached the Supreme Court. There was no proper statutory ground for granting divorce, but in the absence of the breakdown principle, divorce was granted on condition that the husband made sufficient financial provisions for the wife.[47]

In *Uma Wanti v. Arjan Dev*, AIR 1995 P&H 312, a wife appealed against the divorce decree granted to the husband on the ground of her mental unsoundness, cruelty and desertion. Dr. (Mrs.) Saksena J refused the wife's appeal and therefore confirmed the divorce, seeing that "[t]he husband could not live in peace in the company of the appellant" (p. 315). In view of the fact that the wife had alleged dowry-related violence, the financial arrangements in this case are interesting. The wife had asked for Rs. 150,000/- as permanent alimony and, says the learned judge, "[a]s she stands divorced, she needs money for the rehabilitation" (p. 315). However, the husband claimed he could afford only about Rs. 18,000 to 20,000/-. The wife was awarded a lump sum of Rs. 35,000/-, to be paid by the husband within four months, or the divorce would automatically stand vacated (p. 315).[48]

Concern for the welfare of the wife is also evident in *Teerth Ram v. Parvati Devi*, AIR 1995 Raj 86, where G. C. Mital CJ noted with evident disapproval that the husband had been refusing to honour his marital obligations, saying at p. 87:

> ... for a period of 11 years, the husband did not pay a penny to the wife or the child. It was the husband who could have created confidence in the wife by providing means to the wife. On the contrary, we find that the wife had to go to [a] court of law ... in the year 1979 ... and then the husband did not send any penny to the wife.

The wife, having filed repeated petitions for maintenance, had not been granted relief by any of the courts during the 1980s, despite the fact that she had a son to look after. This, in itself, confirms how bad the situation could be for women during the 1980s, even if they managed to approach a court. The learned Chief Justice noted explicitly that the husband had only filed a suit for divorce once he knew that his wife had lost the maintenance cases. The husband was refused a decree of divorce and thus, in effect, reminded of his obligations to maintain his wife and son. It was held at p. 87:

> The parties have been married for 24 years and their son is 16 years old today. We are not satisfied that the husband has established a ground to have a decree for divorce. It cannot be held that [the] wife has permanently deserted the husband with no intention to come back. The wife has no intention to break the matrimonial home for

> good. On the contrary, she wants the husband to establish an independent matrimonial home where she could live with him.... Facts may differ from case to case. In this case it cannot be held that [the] wife will be considered to have deserted the husband without sufficient reasons.

We can be sure that if the husband had offered adequate financial support for the wife and son, the court might have given him a divorce. There is not a word in this judgment about the need to protect women, but the effect of this decision is very much to remind husbands that they cannot do as they please and forget about their obligations. In *Rajee v. Baburao*, AIR 1996 Mad 262, we find confirmation of the fact that Indian courts are now also tougher on men who make slanderous allegations of adultery against their wife, whether out of mischief or in order to avoid paying maintenance. In this case, exemplary costs of Rs. 10,000/- were awarded to the wife and a decree of divorce was refused.

In *Kanchan Devi v. Promod Kumar Mittal*, AIR 1996 SC 3192, the marriage had broken down a long time ago. The wife had made repeated petitions for maintenance and there was a long history of litigation. Finally, the husband had agreed to pay the wife a lump sum of Rs. 60,000/- and this was underwritten by the Supreme Court under its exceptional powers under Article 142 of the Constitution. This is another case in which everybody concerned seems to agree that it is better to settle such protracted marital disputes through adequate financial arrangements.

Cases on the position of bigamously or incompletely married wives are still being reported. An interesting recent example with complex facts is found in *Ranjit Kumar Bhattacharyya v. Sabita Bhattacharyya*, AIR 1996 Cal 301. This was, *inter alia*, a petition of a widowed Hindu woman involved in an alleged marital union with a Christian husband. However, this man was already married to a Christian lady, and since the Hindu woman was therefore not party to a legally valid marriage, the court decided that she could not claim maintenance from the 'husband' under s. 125 of the *Criminal Procedure Code*, 1973 as a 'wife'. At pp. 307–308, this judgment discusses in detail the legal position regarding a wife's maintenance under classical Hindu law and the changes introduced by modern Hindu law. However, while the Hindu woman was not a legally wedded wife, the court was not prepared to send her away without relief from a husband who had fathered her child and had maintained a long-standing relationship. This approach by the court does not amount to applying a full presumption of marriage, but it recognises the polygamous cohabitation that took place. It was held, at p. 309:

> ... we should not be unmindful of the fact that admittedly, the appellant lived with the respondent No. 1 for quite some years, as a result of which a child was born and it is obvious that no woman would not surrender to a man completely, for years together, unless,

> there is some assurance and/or act on the part of the man which may induce the woman at least to believe that she is his wife. ...
>
> ... For such immoral activities, the appellant should not be spared altogether, though the damage that has been caused by the appellant to the respondent No. 1 both physically and mentally cannot be compensated in any way. We, therefore, direct the appellant No. 1 to pay to the respondent No. 1 Rs. 30,000/- as damages for his above misdeeds within four months from the date of drawing up of the decree.

This decision, which could also, of course, be read as punishment for polygamy, constitutes another innovative use of the concept of compensation in the context of modern Indian family law. Its effect in terms of maintenance provisions, undoubtedly, is to place a cohabiting woman somewhat on par with a married woman, and thus to extend the welfare net of modern Indian family law to such women. This is further evidence of the creative treatment of modern Indian polygamy, which is not criminalised, but is brought within the ambit of tort law.

Ashok Hurra v. Rupa Bipin Zaveri, AIR 1997 SC 1266, is a case involving originally a divorce petition by mutual consent from two highly-educated people. However, the wife at some point withdrew her consent to the divorce petition. The bulk of the discussion in this case, therefore, concerns the right of a party to withdraw from a joint petition, which was challenged, but nevertheless upheld. It appears that the wife was using her refusal to consent as a tactical device to squeeze more money out of the husband. It was held by Paripoornan J, at p. 1273:

> Appropriate safeguard or provision for the respondent/wife to enable her to have a decent living should be made. The appellant is a well to do person and is a Doctor. He seems to be affluent [sic] being a member of the medical fraternity. But his conduct during litigation is not above board. The suggestion or offer of a lump sum payment of rupees four to five lakhs, towards provision for [the] wife, is totally insufficient, in modern days of high cost of living and particularly for a woman of the status of the respondent. At least, a sum of about Rs. 10,000/- p.m. will be necessary for a reasonable living. Taking into account all aspects appearing in the case, more so the conduct of the parties and the admissions, contained in the joint petition filed in Court, we hold that the respondent (wife) should be paid, a lump sum of rupees ten lakhs (Rs. 10 lakhs) (and her costs in this litigation as estimated by us) on or before 10–12–1997 ... as a condition precedent for the decree passed by this court to take effect.

Here again, then, the Indian Supreme Court seizes the chance to produce a scheme for divorcing couples, on a case-by-case basis, in which the husband is bound to maintain the former wife at an appropriate level. It appears that a lump sum payment is preferred by the Court, so that the matter may be settled once and for all, mindful of the scope for defaulting on high monthly payments which the Court could otherwise impose. It is also remarkable that in this case, too, the Supreme Court expresses displeasure about the fact of the husband's manifest polygamy, but no criminal penalties are imposed on the man. Instead, it seems that the Court focuses its attention on determining the best possible post-divorce 'deal' for the wife who finds herself pushed out of the marriage. This is part of India's new social realism, evidently, learning to live with divorce litigation and the effects of resulting polygamy if those proceedings drag on for too long.

K. Sujatha v. Government of Andhra Pradesh, AIR 1997 AP 266, is first and foremost a dowry case, involving a young couple who are lawyers and had a 'love marriage', which was later not accepted by the young man's parents, who wanted to extract dowry from the wife's side. This complicated matter could have been left by the High Court to take its normal course through the courts. However, M. N. Rao J interfered in the interests of justice and equity and said, at p. 268:

> But such a course of action, in our considered view, would amount to taking a sterile view of the nature of the jurisdiction, powers and functions of this court under Article 226 of the Constitution of India. Conventional strict scrutiny is sometimes strict in theory and fatal in law. Law and equity slide into each other compelling the Constitutional courts to render complete justice untrammelled by procedural technicalities and legal complexities by taking a holistic view eschewing compartmental scrutiny through the lens of law for the sake of compliance with legal formalism. When new situations of an unprecedented nature arise for consideration, new solutions without any roots in precedents must, in our view, need to be evolved to lend human touch to administration of justice ... Adhering to this purposive legalism, we propose to deal with the factual situation.

The facts, it turned out, were that the husband had indeed married the petitioner, but without the agreement of his father, who later showed his displeasure and had virtually ordered the son to denounce the marriage. The wife was thus forced to assert her status, but parental involvement on both sides led to unfulfilled dowry demands and a total breakdown of relations. It was evident that the court needed to act, and it was held, at pp. 270–271:

> We are satisfied that humanly it is not possible for any woman enmeshed in adversities like [the] petitioner to retain mental poise and continue the battle on several fronts. Realising all this, she got a representation made through her advocate before us that "enough is enough. I am tired of this life. From out of the hard earned money of my parents, already a good part of it was spent towards dowry, marriage and litigation expenses. If at least this is compensated in a sum of Rs. 2 lakhs, I would treat the whole thing as a bad dream and

> look forward to a new chapter in life". We were surprised that a meagre sum of Rs. 2 lakhs was asked by the petitioner only to compensate the expenses incurred by her in this entire sordid affair.

It is extremely significant that the learned judge then proceeded to award the wife just this sum, out of which Rs. 100,000/- had been given as dowry by the woman's father, plus Rs. 10,000/- as costs, without any further debate. Before directing the husband and his father to deposit Rs. 200,000/- in court within eight weeks, it was said, at p. 271:

> The so called compensation of Rs. 2 lakhs she asked, in our opinion, is far less than the amount she would have spent in the unequal battle to save her and her family's prestige and her social status both as a woman and also as a member of the legal profession. The request made by her is very just and reasonable.

Not a word is mentioned about the future of this marriage, which obviously subsists in law. Perhaps, to achieve 'complete justice', as the judge indicated, this matter could also have been taken up, although it was not asked for by the petitioner. This confirms, again, that the courts are focusing more on the financial arrangements between the spouses. Given that the wife had said so clearly that she wanted to put the whole episode behind her, a divorce decree might have been given. On the other hand, as we saw in ch. 2.5, the Supreme Court alone has reserved itself the right to act in such a manner in exceptional circumstances. In the present case, it should be simple for the spouses to bring about a divorce.

In *Satyabhama Nayak v. Narendra Kumar Nayak*, AIR 1997 Ori 47, it transpires that a Family Court had rushed through a joint petition for divorce and had granted divorce although the statutory waiting periods were not yet complete. The family court had also made a maintenance arrangement, which involved the husband in paying a lump sum of Rs. 40,000/- at a time for the wife and son.

The High Court launched into some long, interesting lectures on marriage and divorce and their function in maintaining the stability of society (pp. 49–51). Rather than granting this couple, who had agreed to divorce, a divorce by mutual consent, the High Court sent the matter back to the Family Court. It was also held, at p. 52:

> A precondition of lump sum payment of Rs. 40,000/- has been imposed. Such a condition is not sanctioned in the Act. Looked at from this angle, the order is indefensible.

Technically, therefore, this is a correct decision. It refuses to accept the reality of mass breakdown of marriages in Indian society today and seeks to operate against judicial enthusiasm for the principle of 'irretrievable breakdown'. This is evident from the way in which the High Court's criticism of the actions of the Family Court judge is phrased. We read at p. 52:

> The course adopted by the learned Judge, Family Court, is not sanctioned in law. He has proceeded on the basis that since the parties wanted divorce by consent that has to be at once granted. Procedure for divorce by mutual consent is laid down ...

This decision therefore sticks to procedural proprietry and does not underwrite the speedy dissolution of marriages, even in cases where a husband has agreed to make what is considered by the Court an adequate financial arrangement.

In a number of recent cases, the courts have dealt with the rights of women and children in cases where litigation on divorce or maintenance is pending in court and the husband dies. These cases are discussed in ch. 5. 8 below.

To conclude this section, therefore, we see that Indian courts today are increasingly prepared to grant divorce, provided the arrangements are backed by adequate provisions for the wife and any children of the parties. Some scholarly discussion of this issue has come to the conclusion that the breakdown principle may be useful in certain cases, especially where women themselves have property, but not in cases where women are being virtually pushed out of marriages. Thus, the debates about irretrievable breakdown and maintenance provisions for divorced wives coalesce here. Sivaramayya (1993: 56) rightly warns that the concerns and predilections of educated urban women cannot be applied to all Indian women, arguing that "... one must be sure that a vocal minority does not jeopardize the interests of a silent majority especially the under-privileged and rural women". Sivaramayya (1993: 60) therefore concludes that debates about divorce reforms and the breakdown principle are perennially returning to the same issue:

> Thus we are back to square one, namely, unless backed up by property rights and economic security the ground should not be introduced. Otherwise a woman seeking the ground under the pressure or false impression or by cajoling will not be protected.

A similar point was made by Vijay Sharma (1994: 150) concerning the consequences of allowing for easier divorces. Warning against copying the West, she wrote:

> Actually the mentality and the socio-economic conditions of Hindu society cannot be equated with Western society. Therefore, we should not blindly borrow any western concept and incorporate it in any Indian legislation without looking into its pros and cons. No doubt in many cases one of the spouses suffers and the relief of divorce may relieve that spouse from the hardship but while granting relief of divorce the court should be cautious and look into all aspects including socio-economic protection to the spouse particularly the Hindu woman and the future of children so that there may not be any disaster as an aftermath of divorce.

Sivaramayya (1993: 60–61) refers to several proposals made about improving the status and property rights of women on divorce. It appears that despite (or probably because of) the absence of any legislative action, the Indian courts have sought to devise feasible solutions in individual cases, which will allow divorced women to live in dignity. Our findings regarding the court cases are matched well with the conclusions on the subject of divorce produced by Vijay Sharma (1994: 363–364):

> It is submitted that the Researcher is not against the liberalization of divorce law but [sic] the question is whether or not proposed amendment will actually benefit Hindu women?
>
> In the Hindu society despite the fact that education amongst females is spreading, and in the urban areas many of them are becoming financially independent, still a large percentage of Hindu females are illiterate and economically dependent. Illiteracy and economic dependence on men is more evident in cases of females living in villages ...
>
> Though the proposed amendment gives the women the authority to contest divorce petition on the ground of financial hardship, yet for most of the married women whether literate or illiterate, money is not the only consideration. Even today, a woman is respected if she is married and she is looked down upon if she is unmarried, widow or divorcee. Despite the increasing rate of literacy and urbanization, but men and women in Hindu society have not become progressive in their outlook and they are still traditional and custom bound. Widow's remarriages, and remarriages of divorced women have not yet become a regular feature in the present Hindu society. Therefore, a common Hindu woman wants a husband and matrimonial home. Since she is aware that as long as she is wife, she is entitled to certain amount of protection in the society. Since Independence the Government has enacted so many laws for the protection of married Hindu women, but their implementation is not an easy task. For example, despite maintenance orders passed by courts in favour of women, men often refuse to pay the maintenance, and therefore, to get the maintenance amount consistently is a difficult task.
>
> ... Therefore, it is suggested that the government should first review the existing laws enacted for the protection of married women and ensure that certain fundamental changes made in law are carried out to give an equal status to women in the matrimonial home, and satisfy that they have at least adequate financial and other means to meet their day to day requirement. Irretrievable breakdown of marriage should not be introduced without such safeguards.

If we test these wise warnings against our analysis of the recent case law on maintenance in the present chapter, we see that the Indian judges, indeed, have largely followed this strategy, refusing increasingly to grant easy divorces without consideration of the financial and other arrangements for the welfare of the wife and any children.

Turning now again to the most recent developments in Indian law relating to Muslim divorced women's right to maintenance, we see precisely the same social welfare concerns and judicial strategies with regard to Muslim wives. Despite the outward appearance of difference between Muslim personal law and Hindu personal law, it should become evident that in modern Indian law there is now a uniformity of approach and policy on this subject which is largely judge-driven. That this is not entirely so will transpire from our analysis of the aftermath of the *Shah Bano* case and the resulting *Muslim Women (Protection of Rights on Divorce) Act* of 1986. This will show us that the modern Indian state (here meaning legislature and judiciary combined) has indeed developed a coherent and consistent policy that seeks to protect divorced wives and their children. However, as we saw already, the overriding social welfare concern in both Hindu and Muslim law has probably been to save the state itself from claims by destitute individuals.

The Shah Bano aftermath and the 1986 Act

The reactions to the *Shah Bano* decision, *Mohd. Ahmed Khan* AIR 1985 SC 945, have varied enormously.[49] Tahir Mahmood (1986: 84–85) vigorously opposed the social welfare-oriented interpretations of the various judgments that preceded the *Shah Bano* case on his favourite ground, namely that Muslim law had been misunderstood and misinterpreted in Indian law. Emphasising the conceptual differences between Hindu and Christian concepts of marriage on the one side and Muslim law on the other, Mahmood went too far.[50] According to his interpretation, Muslim husbands have no obligations towards a divorced wife beyond the *iddat* period. Mahmood (1986: 86–87) wrote:

> The fact is that in the Islamic matrimonial culture neither there is an inter-familial transplantation of the girl on her marriage, nor are her parents or guardians perpetually absolved, after that, of their liabilities towards her. In Islam, since marriage is always a dissoluble union, the parents' liability to maintain the unmarried daughter remains only *suspended* during her married life. On the dissolution of her marriage, whether by her husband's death or by divorce and, in the latter case, whether at her own instance or otherwise, the liability is *revived* and must continue to be discharged until she remarries.
>
> ... As a natural corollary to its concept of marriage and policy on divorce, after the dissolution of a marriage Islam does not keep the parties tagged to each other for the rest of their lives. It encourages both of them [depending on their age] to get remarried – against the remarriage of a divorcee, either male or female, there being no taboo in Islamic law or culture. The law keeps both parties to a dissolved marriage wholly free to look after their new responsibilities.

I have already highlighted that at the same time Mahmood (1986: 127) was arguing that the modern Indian judiciary had gone too far, as he put it, by "gradually turning divorce into a sort of an insurance deal offering far more lucrative benefits than available in marriage". In his view, absolving divorced wives from all kinds of traditional obligations without depriving them of the benefits of married life amounted to favourable treatment by the law. This would not only violate basic principles of Muslim law but could be dangerous in social terms. We see here, again, unspoken lurking references to fears about *zina* as a result of allowing women to become economically independent and thus no longer dependent on male supervision of their movements.

In remarkable contrast, Danial Latifi (1985: 385–400) supports not only the *Shah Bano* decision but also the methods by which it was reached, highlighting the social need to do justice. Latifi (1985: 398) concludes:

> From the above there appears ample and respectable Islamic authority for the proposition that under the Muslim law the divorcing husband, in appropriate cases, is bound to provide maintenance for his divorced wife until death or remarriage. He may also be liable to pay compensation particularly in cases of *talaq ul bidaat.*

It was indicated above that the *Shah Bano* decision led to riots and deeply divided the Muslim community.[51] Amendments suggested by traditionalists put the burden of supporting Muslim divorced women without blood relatives (who would otherwise normally support them) onto *Waqf* Boards or private *waqfs*, in other words, essentially on charitable Muslim institutions. This strategy, which also keeps such matters within Muslim control rather than state supervision, is problematic for a number of reasons: *Waqf* Boards or *waqfs* may simply be unable to help, or they may be unwilling to assist women with living relatives who should assist, but refuse to maintain the divorced female relative.

The *Muslim Women (Protection of Rights on Divorce) Act,* 1986 appeared to take such suggestions on board in s. 4(2). Otherwise, however, this Act has done precisely what its name suggests and has proved rather beneficial to divorced Muslim wives who were unable to maintain themselves appropriately after the *iddat* period. As we shall see, first of all, s. 3 of the 1986 Act holds the husband himself liable for the maintenance of the divorced wife; only then is it the turn of relatives and, ultimately, of any *Waqf* Board. Thus, the 1986 Act has not taken away the divorced Muslim woman's right to claim maintenance from the former husband, but has in fact reiterated and strengthened it. The potential recourse of a woman to her relatives and the *Waqf* Boards are no more than a fallback position in case the husband proves totally unable to maintain the former wife. Nowhere else does the state itself step in to provide maintenance for destitute Muslim divorcees.

The 1986 Act was the first codification of Muslim law in India after the *DMMA* of 1939 and remains the only Indian Muslim law statute passed after independence. It is a very short Act, with only seven sections, and only three sections with substantive rules. It was passed in a rush, but evidently not without due deliberation behind closed doors. It appears that during the public, heated debates about the Act after the *Shah Bano* case, attention was deliberately focused on sections 4 and 5 of the Act, rather than the all-important s. 3, which concerns the continuing liabilities of the former husband. In other words, it became an unsubstantiated but powerful *a priori* assumption that the purpose of the 1986 Act would be to nullify the effects of the *Shah Bano* decision. In section 3 of the Act, for those who care to read rather than peddle communal politics, it was made quite clear that the first source of support for a divorced Muslim wife remained her former husband. Section 3 of the 1986 Act provides:

> 3. Mahr or other properties of Muslim woman to be given to her at the time of divorce.–
> (1) Notwithstanding anything contained in any other law for the time being in force, a divorced woman shall be entitled to –
> (a) a reasonable and fair provision and maintenance to be made and paid to her within the iddat period by her former husband;
> (b) where she herself maintains the children born to her before or after the divorce, a reasonable and fair provision and maintenance to be made and paid by her former husband for a period of two years from the respective dates of birth of such children;
> (c) an amount equal to the sum of mahr or dower agreed to be paid to her at the time of her marriage or at any time thereafter according to Muslim law; and
> (d) all the properties given to her before or at the time of marriage or after her marriage by her relatives or friends or the husband or any relatives of the husband or his friends.
> (2) Where a reasonable and fair provision and maintenance or the amount of mahr or dower due has not been made or paid or the properties referred to in clause (d) of sub-section (1) have not been delivered to a divorced woman on her divorce, she or anyone duly authorised by her may, on her behalf, make an application to a Magistrate for an order for payment of such provision and maintenance, mahr or dower, or the delivery of properties, as the case may be.
> (3) Where an application has been made under sub-section (2) by a divorced woman, the Magistrate may, if he is satisfied that –
> (a) her husband having sufficient means, has failed or neglected to make or pay her within the iddat period a reasonable and fair provision and maintenance for her and the children; or
> (b) the amount equal to the sum of mahr or dower has not been paid or that the properties referred to in clause (d) of sub-section (1) have not been delivered to her make an order, within one month of the date of the filing of the application, directing her

former husband to pay such reasonable and fair provision and maintenance to the divorced woman as he may determine as fit and proper having regard to the needs of the divorced woman, the standard of life enjoyed by her during her marriage and the means of her former husband or, as the case may be, for the payment of such mahr or dower or the delivery of such properties referred to in clause (d) of sub-section (1) to the divorced woman:

Provided that if the Magistrate finds it impracticable to dispose of the application within the said period, he may, for reasons to be recorded by him, dispose of the application after the said period.

(4) If any person against whom an order has been made under sub-section (3) fails without sufficient cause to comply with the order, the Magistrate may issue a warrant for levying the amount of maintenance or mahr or dower due in the manner provided for levying fines under the Code of Criminal Procedure, 1973, and may sentence such person, for the whole or part of any amount remaining unpaid after the execution of the warrant, to imprisonment for a term which may extend to one year or until payment if sooner made, subject to such person being heard in defence and the said sentence being imposed according to the provisions of the said Code.

Section 4(1) of the Act focuses on the obligations of a divorced woman's relatives to provide for her if she is unable to maintain herself after the *iddat* period. However, this section only comes into operation if the former husband cannot or does not assist the woman.[52] Section 4(2) then provides a further safety net by laying down that, in the absence of any financial support from the woman's own family, the State *Wakf* Board may be directed by a Magistrate to assist such a woman. There was much outcry over the new obligations on the *Wakf* Boards in s. 4(2), in particular.[53]

Section 5 of the Act enables a husband and wife (or ex-wife, as she might be) to opt jointly to be governed by sections 125–128 of the *Code of Criminal Procedure*, 1973 instead of the 1986 Act. Since the financial limit of Rs. 500/- under the 1973 Code is more stringent for the woman than the 1986 Act, which carries no financial limit, it may in fact be to the advantage of Muslim men to opt for the application of the 1973 Code (see Mahmood 1990: 304).

A first substantive issue arose in cases where a petition for maintenance had been pending under s. 125 or s. 127 of the 1973 Code on 19th May 1986, when the 1986 Act was promulgated. Section 7 of the 1986 Act anticipated this scenario and provides:

7. Transitional provisions. –
Every application by a divorced woman under Section 125 or under Section 127 of the Code of Criminal Procedure, 1973 pending before a Magistrate on the commencement of this Act, shall, notwithstanding anything contained in that Code and subject to the provisions of

> Section 5 of this Act, be disposed of by such Magistrate in accordance with the provisions of this Act.

It was therefore correctly held in *Abdul Gafoor Kunju v. Pathumma Beevi*, 1989(1) KLT 337, that a divorced Muslim wife is no longer entitled to invoke the provisions of s. 127 of the 1973 Code after the 1986 Act came into force.[54]

Subanu v. A. M. Abdul Gafoor, AIR 1987 SC 1103, concerned the old issue of the interrelationship between the Muslim husband's right to marry up to four wives and his obligations towards a wife who objects to polygamous arrangements and seeks separate maintenance. The case also asked whether a Muslim wife whose husband has married again is worse off in terms of maintenance than a former wife whose husband merely took a mistress. The answer to that point was in the negative. The husband's defence was that Muslim law allowed him to marry again, so the first wife should not be allowed to live separately and claim maintenance from him. He had offered to take his wife back and to maintain her (p. 1109). This popular strategy, often employed to save cash expenditure, since it is cheaper to maintain a former wife in one's own home than to provide money for her to live separately, was not accepted. Natarajan J was quick to refuse the husband's offer and said, at p. 1109:

> It is, therefore, obvious that the offer was only a make-believe one and not a genuine and sincere offer. On the basis of such an insincere offer the appellant's rights cannot be negated or defeated.

After *Shah Bano*, therefore, Indian judges remained alert to the socio-economic needs of divorced Muslim wives, and retained a keen sense for the need to be socially activist as well as protective about women's rights. Many Muslim men, on the other hand, would continue to avoid their responsibilities. Not surprisingly, the intricate wording of s. 3 in the 1986 Act soon gave rise to a large number of maintenance petitions by divorced Muslim wives. In this way, some High Courts became extremely alert to the need for protecting Muslim wives through creative interpretation of the statutory text to avoid a *Shah Bano* situation.

In remarkable contrast, almost all the academic writing on the 1986 Act proceeded on misguided assumptions about the negative effects of that Act, and many writers have refused to accept (often without looking at any evidence at all) that Indian judges could be innovative, compassionate lawmakers. Much of the secondary literature is politicised commentary (not to say, blatant nonsense) by people who do not read reported judgments before they start writing. Even prominent legal writers followed the *Shah Bano* bandwagon (see Iyer 1987) and some have for a long time refused to see the beneficial effects of the 1986 Act.[55]

The misguided interpretations of activists and scholars are also reflected in the fate of numerous constitutional challenges to the 1986 Act, most of which were filed immediately in 1986.[56] These petitions have been kept pending by the Supreme Court, which has until quite recently (see further below) kept an ominous, but evidently purposeful silence on the matter.[57] It seems now that keeping such cases pending for a long time was not a matter of judicial inefficiency, but a clever strategy of refusing to play with the dangerous fire of communal politics. It appears that these petitions have been treated as lacking *bona fide* status and have simply been allowed to gather dust, while the positive, pro-women case law under s. 3 of the 1986 Act has been building up.[58]

While the creative, welfare-oriented judicial interpretations of s. 3 of the 1986 Act are still not confirmed by a Supreme Court verdict,[59] many High Court cases from all around the country now support the view that a divorcing Muslim husband remains liable for his former wife's welfare.[60] It is no longer a view concentrated in just a few High Courts, and only very few cases go the other way.[61] The Kerala High Court's detailed reasoning in *Ali v. Sufaira*, 1988(2) KLT 94, which is not the first case decided under the 1986 Act but the most articulate, has probably had most impact on the development of the case law and has been cited several times as the leading case on the matter.

Ali v. Sufaira concerns several cases on the same point of law. In the first case, the divorced woman had claimed Rs. 30,000/- as reasonable and fair provision for her life, Rs. 22,500/- as *iddat* money, Rs. 11,500/- as *mahr* and the return of properties to the value of 1.5 million rupees. This shows at once that these litigants were not impoverished, desperately poor people, but middle-class Muslim wives who could probably afford to argue over principles of jurisprudence. The Magistrate had accepted the wife's case in principle, but had granted her substantially lower sums than she had asked for, so that both the husband and the wife appealed. In the Kerala High Court, Sreedharan J clearly identified that the most important issue before him was the extent of the liability cast on a Muslim husband at the time of divorce (p. 95).

While referring back to the *Shah Bano* case, the judge considered in detail the wording of s. 3 of the 1986 Act, highlighting that in s. 3(1)(a) a Muslim woman is entitled to "a reasonable and fair provision and maintenance to be made and paid to her within the *iddat* period". The former husband was pleading that his liabilities had ended after the *iddat* period, thus implying that 'provision' and 'maintenance' were one and the same thing. Sreedharan J quite correctly saw a complex task of statutory interpretation in this case: What was the precise meaning of these particular words in s. 3(1)(a) of the 1986 Act? Considering the Preamble of the 1986 Act, as well as the Statement of Objects and Reasons, as published in the Official Gazette of 25 February 1986, the learned judge found that the unmistakable object of the 1986 Act was to protect the interests of divorced Muslim women. Thus, looking at the complex wording of s. 3(1)(a), it was held at pp. 97–98:

> In interpreting a provision in a statute it is important to remember that the Parliament does not waste its breath unnecessarily ... The

> courts are duty bound to examine and give meaning to every word of the statute in its context. ... We cannot assume a mistake in an Act of Parliament. ... The presumption is always against superfluity in a statute. ... The Parliament must be taken to have decided to provide the divorced woman with maintenance for the period of iddat and also a reasonable and fair provision for her. Both of these should be made and paid to her during the iddat.

Interestingly, it was also held, at p. 98, that s. 4 of the Act "does not absolve the former husband from making a 'reasonable and fair provision' for the lady's life". Next, having distinguished 'provision' and 'maintenance', the judge turned to the classical Muslim law on the subject, as found in Sura II, verses 236–237 and 241–242 of the Qur'an.[62] The conclusion of this inquiry is found at pp. 99–100:

> From this it is clear that the Muslim who believes in God must give a reasonable amount by way of gift or maintenance to the divorced lady. That gift or maintenance is not limited to the period of iddat. It is for her future livelihood because – God wishes to see all well. The gift is to depend on the capacity of the husband. The gift, to be paid by the husband at the time of divorce, as commanded by the Quran, is recognised in sub-clause (a) of Clause (1) of S. 3 of the Act. This liability is cast upon the husband on account of the past advantage received by him by reason of the relationship with the divorced woman or on account of the past dis-advantage suffered by her by reason of matrimonial consortium, it is in the nature of a compensatory gift or a solatium to sustain the woman for her life after the divorce. In accordance with the principles of Islamic equity the said provision or compensation or support from the former husband is [the] wife's right. This right has been given legislative recognition in the above provision. So, I find it difficult to accept the argument that the only liability of the former husband is to pay maintenance to the divorced Muslim woman during the period of iddat only.

It was therefore held, at pp. 100–101, that under s. 3(1)(a) of the 1986 Act "a divorced Muslim woman is not only entitled to maintenance for the period of iddat from the former husband but also to a reasonable and fair provision for her future". This provision would have to be made within the *iddat* period, but with a view to the wife's socio-economic welfare beyond the end of that period.

The decision in *Ali v. Sufaira* could not be much clearer. The position was subsequently developed further in a number of cases from Kerala and other Indian High Courts. Important cases on the same lines are *Aliyar v. Pathu*, 1988(2) KLT 446; *Arab Ahemadhia Abdalla v. Arab Bail Mohmuna Saiyadbhai*, AIR 1988 Guj 141 and *Ahammed v. Aysha*, 1990(1) KLT 172. *Alavi v. Safia*, 1992(1) KLT 649, defends the rights of a divorced woman who allegedly lives in adultery, a device used by many Indian men to defeat maintenance claims from an existing or former wife.[63] *Hyderkhan v. Meharunnissa*, 1992(2) KLT 330 held that the 1986 Act has retrospective operation and confirmed (at p. 333), again with reference to Qur'anic verses, that "there is no logic in holding that the Act for the first time introduced a burden on the Muslim husband to provide for reasonable and fair provision and maintenance to the divorced wife".

Thus, the basic principle today is that a divorced Muslim woman in India, finding at the end of the *iddat* period that her former husband has not made reasonable and fair provisions for her, has an instant case under s. 3 of the 1986 Act against him. The case is to be decided within a tight time-frame (see s. 3(3) of the 1986 Act as cited above), a further support mechanism for women who may not have the means to go to court and to wait a long time for a positive decision.

Concerning the quantum of maintenance awarded, the cases show that much depends on the financial standing of the spouses. But what are the criteria, the needs of the wife or the means of the husband? In *Ahammed v. Aysha* 1990(1) KLT 712, the former husband claimed that his ex-wife was better off than himself, so her claim to maintenance should fail. Jagannadha Raju J disagreed, saying at p. 174:

> If we compare and contrast the provisions of S. 3 of the Act with similar provisions in the other enactments, we find that even a millionaire wife who lives in luxury and affluence is certainly entitled to claim maintenance and other reliefs from her former husband under S. 3. There is no requirement of the wife being unable to maintain herself for granting maintenance or for payment of fair and reasonable provision as contemplated under S. 3.

Only a few reported cases oppose these pro-women interpretations of the 1986 Act.[64] The leading case on the male-centred view is *Usman Khan Bahamani v. Fathimunnisa Begum*, AIR 1990 AP 225, decided by a majority of a bench of three judges. Two major questions arose, regarding the position of pending maintenance applications under sections 125–128 of the 1973 Code when the 1986 Act came into force, and the extent of a divorced Muslim woman's right under s. 3 of the 1986 Act. The answer to the first point was provided by s. 7 of the 1986 Act itself (see above). Regarding the extent of the Muslim ex-husband's liability, the learned judges took a wide historical perspective and re-examined the precise wording of s. 3(1)(a) of the 1986 Act. They were particularly interested in the phrase "within the iddat period", concluding at p. 231 that "there is nothing in the section which can be read to mean that the husband is liable to make reasonable and fair provision and maintenance beyond the period of Iddat". The majority verdict then continued, at p. 231:

> The word "within" indicates two things that the liability of the husband to make a reasonable and fair provision and maintenance is limited to the period of Iddat only and it is already seen in the

statement of the objects and reasons that the principle of Muslim law limits the husband's liability to provide maintenance to the divorced wife for the period of Iddat only.

This lengthy judgment, a detailed analysis of Muslim law principles, textbooks and various judicial decisions, looks impressive and to some extent persuasive. However, the majority decision in this case is based on quite circuitous reasoning and refuses to make use of the idealistic spirit in the relevant Qur'anic provisions. It also clearly ignores the intended social purpose of the 1986 Act in terms of protecting the rights of divorced Muslim wives. As we saw above, both the Qur'anic provisions and modern state law as found in s. 125 of the *Criminal Procedure Code* – and now in the 1986 Act – suggest that men who divorce their wives should be considerate towards them and have moral, if not legal, obligations regarding their welfare. The analysis of traditional Muslim law in this case remains therefore open to criticism.

Latifi (1991: 29) has rightly commented that the majority verdict in *Usman Khan* refused to give due meaning to the expression 'fair and reasonable provision' and behaved as though these words had been deleted from s. 3 of the 1986 Act. In the minority view of Bhaskar Rao J in *Usman Khan*, the words 'within the iddat period' were indeed interpreted very differently. We read at p. 245:

> The words in Sec. 3(1)(a) "within the Iddat period" lay stress on the urgency in making or paying and they cannot be read as confining the liability to the limited period of iddat, save in so far as maintenance is concerned since the Muslim Law is settled on that aspect. Interpreting the distinct liability of making a reasonable and fair provision as having been confined to the period of Iddat would not only render the very Section 5 on the statute otiose but also defeats the specific purpose of casting that liability on the former husband. ...

In view of the clear distinction between 'maintenance' and 'provision' in the text of the statute, the dissenting judge concluded on p. 246:

> Accordingly, I am of the firm view that the maintenance contemplated by Sec. 3(1)(a) of the Act is limited to the Iddat period while the fair and reasonable provision to be made in terms of the same section runs for the future much beyond the iddat period.

Tahir Mahmood (1989: 228–229) provided an extended, instructive comment on this case, referring also to an earlier ruling of Bhaskar Rao J to the effect that a Muslim husband's obligation to provide maintenance and to make provision extended beyond the *iddat* period. As Mahmood confirms, the judge had modified his view in *Usman Khan* and had held (see the quote immediately above) that maintenance was restricted only to the *iddat* period, while the 'reasonable and fair provision' under the 1986 Act was different from maintenance and was clearly not restricted to the *iddat* period. Mahmood (1989: 230) then introduced his own view on the matter into the discussion:

> The author is convinced that the 'fair and reasonable provision' spoken about in the Muslim Women Act is different from maintenance of *'iddat* period – it rather represents what the Qur'an calls *mata'* [compensation for an arbitrary divorce or for a woman divorced for none of her fault]. However, since under the Qur'anic law *mata'* is payable in deserving cases *only* and not unconditionally to every female divorcee – guidelines for ordering and fixing 'fair and reasonable provision' under the Act should be provided either by legislation or by the process of judicial law-making. It will be wrong on the part of courts to take it as a mandatory provision of general application; but in a suitable case *mata'* must be awarded in addition to maintenance of *'iddat.*

This argument confirms that in traditional Muslim jurisprudence the concept of some kind of compensation for the divorced Muslim wife, in the form of *mata* or *mutat*, was not unknown.[65] Referring to the potential of abuse of such protective provisions by women, Professor Mahmood reiterated that under the Qur'anic law compensation of this kind was only payable in deserving cases, not unconditionally to every divorced woman. He suggested, therefore, that guidelines for fair and reasonable provisions should be provided either by legislation or by the process of judicial law-making.[66] The 1986 Act should not give an absolute right of continued maintenance to all divorced women irrespective of circumstances. After all, as Mahmood (1990: 304) points out, a man who wanted to provide maintenance to his divorced wife for the rest of her life was not prevented from doing so by any provision of Muslim law. However, not many Muslim men would act with such benevolence. It is a fact of life all over South Asia that Muslim men are unwilling to share their resources fairly with former wives, preferring instead various forms of desertion and non-implementation of even the most basic protective mechanisms provided under the Muslim personal law.

In view of such well-established evidence, it is certainly not a reasonable and realistic suggestion in South Asia today that the modern state should be held responsible for divorced women and their children. However, it is precisely this which appears to have been argued by Mahmood (1990: 304) in the context of s. 4(2) of the 1986 Act:

> According to the principles of Islamic law a member of the society who is unable to maintain himself or herself is the liability of the State. Where the Muslims are not the rulers and therefore the State cannot be compelled to fulfil this legal obligation, this liability passes on to the Muslim community in general.

One may find it surprising that a leading author on Muslim law, undoubtedly aware of the extra-legal nature of Muslim family laws, should suggest that the state be made liable to provide social welfare. This was not quite the case in traditional Muslim law. Mahmood's above statement should, therefore, probably be understood differently. He does not suggest that the modern state itself should pay; just like the Muslim ruler was not directly liable for the provision of maintenance to destitute individuals. In both cases, the state's duty would be to mobilise resources from within society for the purposes of social welfare.

If we interpret Mahmood's comments in this way, it is no longer clear why he should have objected so vociferously to the strategy of the modern Indian state in holding divorcing Muslim men responsible for the social and economic welfare of their ex-wives. The provisions of s. 3 in the 1986 Act introduce neither a conflict with the rules of traditional Muslim law concerning *mata*, as Mahmood himself explained, nor would they give rise to objections on public policy grounds. It seems that Mahmood was merely concerned that modern, individualistic Muslim women might exploit such provisions for their own selfish interests, as indicated by his comments in this respect, already quoted above. That kind of exploitation remains, of course, a possibility, but this should not distract from the much larger problem faced by divorced Muslim wives.

We can see, therefore, that the new scheme for the protection of divorced Muslim wives under s. 3 of the 1986 Act appears to have developed a gender-balanced and welfare-focused framework which Professor Mahmood would regard as Islamic and should recognise as socially constructive and economically sensible. Surely, not every divorced Muslim woman in India would have an automatic predatory claim under the 1986 Act against the former husband, as Mahmood's arguments seemed to suggest. Safeguards exist for the man, too. If the provisions which he makes are fair and reasonable in the particular circumstances of the couple, the divorced woman can raise no further claim.[67] As we saw, the former wife of a poor ex-husband will have to suffer poverty as well. Section 3(3)(a) of the 1986 Act provides clearly that the husband must have sufficient means to be held liable under this section. Further, it is clearly provided in s. 3(1)(a) in the 1986 Act that a divorced Muslim wife only has a claim for further support if her former husband has not made appropriate arrangements by the time the *iddat* period expires. If he has fulfilled his obligations towards the ex-wife adequately, or he has no means to be supportive, the divorced wife would have no further justifiable claim under s. 3. Instead, the next layer of the protective framework of the 1986 Act comes into effect and the provisions of s. 4 may be activated, if necessary. The matter is, basically, as simple as that.

The real problems must be located in the realm of society: To what extent will Indian Muslim women learn to use this law and gain the confidence to go to court to claim their rights? This is a matter of legal education, and the empowering of women, not a question of statutory provision. Further, looking beyond litigation as an immediate consequence of supportive provisions in a new statute, the really crucial issue is perhaps to what extent Muslim husbands will internalise, and turn into reality, the traditional and yet new obligation that the modern social welfare law has so firmly underwritten. While it appears that more women will be bold enough to claim their financial entitlements, men will continue to obfuscate. Evidently, this new tax on matrimonial freedom was never going to be a measure that men (of any religion) would warmly embrace and eagerly implement. As our above discussion has shown, there are actually no Muslim issues in this conflict of interests; it is a universal human problem.

Academic writers and commentators have used the *Shah Bano* affair and its aftermath as a paradigm for India's alleged backwardness and supposedly medieval approach to women's rights. The whole affair has also been used to discredit Islam and the allegedly backward Muslim male population of India. It was convenient to peddle the assertion that the 1986 Act had nullified the beneficial effects of *Shah Bano*, long after the case law had clearly said the exact opposite. So much for critical scholarship which forgets to take account of the truth and operates blinkers that give no credit to indigenous modernity.

It is quite interesting to recount how modernist politicking and traditional Islamic concerns joined hands in this venture. Particularly obnoxious examples of what parades as modernist scholarship of the highest calibre are found in comments by an Asian American writer, Veena Talwar Oldenburg (1994).[68] The *Shah Bano* case scenario is here viewed as proof of the continuing victimisation of women by fundamentalist forces. Oldenburg (1994: 122–123) wrote:

> A prolonged and bitter fight of Muslim women, Indian liberals of all religions, and women's organizations ended in their defeat when Rajiv Gandhi's government overturned the Supreme Court's judgement by an Act of Parliament ... The Act of Parliament shredded the secular constitution of the country ...

This volley blasts the messages that governments are bad, anything religious is backward, and Indian men cannot be trusted to make rules that help women. Among such politics of public consciousness, what is the role of legal analysis? In such demagogic fashion, scholars are re-stating, if not inventing, Indian law for their readership; a clear case of misrepresentation of facts.

A Muslim law specialist (Shabbir 1988: 287–288) discussed the fierce debates on this issue and praised 'Mr. Clean', Rajiv Gandhi, for honouring the sentiments of the Muslim community and "realising the truth" that personal laws have a right to exist under the Indian constitution. Shabbir (1988: 287) then alleged:

> The contents of the Act nullify the evil aspects of legislation and judicial pronouncements in the area of maintenance of Muslim divorcee which constitutes one of the segments of the Muslim Personal Laws in India.

Shabbir (1988: 288) further asserted that "our Legislature had the minimal intention of simply superseding the verdict of the Supreme Court of India in *Shah Bano*'s case in order to please the fundamentalists and religious orthodoxy". V. R. Krishna Iyer (1987) lamented the fact that Rajiv Gandhi let himself be pushed into introducing the 1986 Act and admitted (at p. XV) that he was puzzled:

> A riddle beyond me to decode, save on the score of politicking communalism to magnet obscurantist Muslim votes, was the sudden decision of the Prime Minister to introduce a bizarre bill to provide for the protection(!) of divorced Muslim women in truncated, distorted and illusory manner. It was neither fish, nor flesh nor good red herring. ... With blitzkrieg speed, the Islamic communal bill was introduced into the Lok Sabha and after a brief spell, moved with military relentlessness into the later stages with numerical success. Today that bill ... is on the statute book.

At p. XVI, he calls it "a primitive anti-woman bill". Evidently, such comments do not focus on the desperate need of maintenance for divorced Muslim wives. They are political rhetoric, pushing the respective author's political agenda, and merely use the *Shah Bano* issue for that purpose. Krishna Iyer (1987: 12) clearly assumed that a woman could not claim maintenance beyond the *iddat* period under s. 3 of the Act. Lateef (1990: 121–122) assumed that, despite pleas by Muslim women, the government had given in to conservative demands and had disposed of the problem by forcing divorced women to seek help from their natal families or from Muslim *wakfs*. More recent commentaries took some time to understand the full impact of the 1986 Act. Diwan and Diwan (1991: 155) introduced a separate chapter on the 1986 Act, clearly marking its importance and wrote:

> With a view to abrogate [the] Shah Bano judgment, the Government introduced in Parliament, the Muslim Women (Protection of Rights on Divorce) Bill, 1986. It is a very hastily drafted measure, the avowed purpose of which is obviously to succumb to the pressure of the fundamentalists.

Diwan and Diwan (1991: 157) concluded this analysis by saying that after the enactment of the 1986 Act, the husband's obligation to maintain his wife does not extend beyond the *iddat* period, and thus noted that the Act proposes to impose this obligation on her paternal relatives. However, the same study in its 1991 edition has a new section II (pp. 158–165), in which the authors totally revise their earlier position, evidently after having studied the first batch of reported cases under the 1986 Act from the High Courts of Gujarat and Kerala. They now speak as legal scholars and say that, undoubtedly, the Act itself is operating in favour women and reflect legal reality, concluding at p. 163:

> In our submission on reading section 3 and section 4 together it is abundantly clear that Parliament wanted to protect fully the divorced woman so that she does not become destitute or is not thrown on the streets without roof over her head and without any means for sustaining herself.

Even some of the most recent writing on the 1986 Act, however, remains confused and unduly critical, and is often not aware of the significant progress in the case law.[69] Meanwhile, the Kerala High Court has authoritatively confirmed in *Kunhammed Haji v. Amina*, 1995(1) KLT 765, that the 1988 cases of *Ali* and *Aliyar* remain good law, and that the distinction of 'provision' and 'maintenance' refers to two different entitlements of divorced Muslim wives. The Indian Supreme Court has continued to keep a low profile on this issue. Questions about the constitutionality of the 1986 Act have now probably been overtaken by events.

A recent case decided by the Supreme Court, *Tamil Nadu Wakf Board v. Syed Fatima Nachi*, 1996(2) KLT 410 [SC], concerns s. 4 of the 1986 Act.[70] In this case, a divorced Muslim wife had claimed Rs. 750/- per month as maintenance from a *Wakf* Board because none of her relatives were in a position to maintain her. Notably, this very first Supreme Court case on the matter is not reported in the *All India Reporter*.[71] It was held, at p. 413, that sub-sections (1) and (2) of s. 4 in the 1986 Act are not mutually exclusive, but that the State *Wakf* Board comes "last in line to bear the burden" of destitute women's maintenance. The social welfare dimension of the 1986 Act was underlined by Punchhi J at p. 414:

> It is futile for a divorced woman seeking succour to run after relatives, be it her children, parents, relatives or other relatives, who are not possessed of means to offer her maintenance and in fighting litigations in succession against them, dragging them to courts of law in order to obtain negative orders justificatory to the last resort of moving against the State Wakf Board. In our considered view, she would instead be entitled to plead and prove such relevant facts in one proceeding . . . It is . . . open for the State Wakf Board to controvert that the relations mentioned in the provision, or some of them, have the means to pay maintenance to her.

For obvious reasons, this decision does not make any reference to the liability of the modern welfare state. However, it is really surprising that this case also does not mention the potential role of the ex-husband and the existence of the protective provisions under s. 3 in the 1986 Act.

Taken as a whole, therefore, the legal provisions under the 1986 Act establish that an Indian Muslim ex-husband today is expected, first of all, to maintain his ex-wife during the *iddat* period.[72] In addition, he also has to make reasonable provision for the woman's life beyond the *iddat* period. The extent of this provision depends on the facts and circumstances of the couple. If such provisions have not been put into place by the end of the *iddat* period, the wife may have a claim against the recalcitrant ex-husband under s. 3 of the 1986 Act.

The long, intensive debates in Indian law have clearly shown that the Muslim husband's responsibility beyond the *iddat* period was already well-established, at least in principle, in the Qur'anic foundations. Modern Indian Muslim law has creatively used such classical foundations to facilitate access to social welfare provisions for divorced Muslim women. At least under Indian law, they can now claim a reasonable and fair provision if they feel that they are being treated unjustly. Whether one calls this 'compensation', 'provision' or some form of 'maintenance' does not really matter. Traditional Muslim law, as well as modern Indian law, at the end of the day, seem to concur in agreeing that what is fair and reasonable depends on the circumstances of the spouses. This position is now beginning to be understood by Indian writers, who have studied the subject in depth. Thus, Shiv Sahai Singh (1993: 381) concludes, quite appropriately:

> The judicial approach towards the maintenance of the spouses under various personal laws is more realistic and pragmatic to that of legislative approach in achieving the cherished goals of welfare state to secure social and especially gender justice.

Significantly, therefore, this remarkable development of modern Indian law on the issue of post-divorce maintenance, whether with reference to Hindus, Muslims, or now even Christians,[73] has been achieved without burdening the state's coffers. By re-defining social norms and re-invigorating traditional social obligations regarding the duties of men who wish to divorce, the state has cleverly done its job of protecting divorced wives of any religion. However, this was not achieved directly, by paying for the casualties of broken marriages, but indirectly, through attempts to effect changes in society which would re-establish a social welfare net that was increasingly shot through with gaping holes. Reading both divorce law and post-divorce maintenance law together, as should be done, we see that modern India's increasingly less liberal approach to granting easy divorces does link in neatly with the new, vigorously monitored requirement that men who wish to divorce should pay for this privilege by helping, to the best of their abilities, in the complex task of maintaining their former wives and, most certainly, their children.

Today, the combined effect of creative judicial interpretation of the general criminal law, as well as the various personal laws, has provided an increasingly effective social welfare network which protects the modern state as well as women and children. Mainly found in sections 125 and 127 of the *Criminal Procedure Code* 1973, together with relevant provisions of the Hindu law, as well as the skilfully drafted provisions of the *Muslim Women (Protection of Rights on Divorce) Act* of 1986, modern India's statutory law on the issue of post-divorce maintenance entitlements is certainly not a watertight, foolproof insurance system against male egoism and obstinacy. However, this statutory legal armoury has been given sharp teeth by creative judicial interpretation and a vigilant judiciary, manifestly conscious of social welfare agenda. In a developing country with an impoverished central state which has, quite evidently, different priorities for public spending outlays, this looks like a financially sustainable compromise between law and society, between central state and local community, and ultimately between men and women. The task in this field of law is no longer to create new statutes, or to develop new case law. The primary task now is to monitor vigorously that women in need, and especially destitute women and children, do not fall through this particular net of social welfare.

Notes

1 Some judges cannot resist the temptation to pronounce on big issues of the future, but this does not mean that they would lose sight of the social realities in front of them. A good example of this duality of concerns is found in *Sarla Mudgal*, AIR 1995 SC 1531 and the dicta of Justice Kuldip Singh.

2 See in particular his important *Critique of modern Hindu law* (Derrett 1970), in which he argued vigorously for stronger use of Indian principles.

3 Detailed research on this aspect would probably unearth much comment on the drawbacks of Western welfare ideology and observations about the manifest crisis of modern Western state welfare systems.

4 Certainly the credit would not go to scholars, who have been singularly focused on modernisation and individualisation agenda and have persistently refused to see, as we shall analyse in detail in chapter 4.3 below, that the judicial vision of viable post-divorce maintenance for discarded wives can be implemented in a modern society.

5 That includes myself at first; see chapter 2.3 above, where I, too, was saying that the 1986 Act was designed to nullify *Shah Bano*. See, however, chapter 4.2 below, written in 1994.

6 *India Today* regularly speaks of the concerns of 'the chattering classes' but seems unwilling to reflect on how much its writing is in fact dominated by such perspectives.

7 At the same time, the traditional system upheld patriarchal concepts and was therefore often portrayed as oppressive rather than protective.

8 In particular s. 488 of the *Criminal Procedure Code* of 1898, which had several predecessors since 1865.

9 Preeti Sharma (1990: 74–83) discusses the concept of maintenance under traditional Hindu law.

10 This is linked to the idea that, on marriage, a Hindu wife becomes a member of the husband's family and cannot then, as it were, go back to her natal family. However, there are many different local traditions about this issue, and the above-stated norm seems to apply mainly to North Indian Hindus.

11 As we saw, this was clearly confirmed by the Supreme Court in the recent case of *M. Govindaraju v. K. Munisami Gounder*, AIR 1997 SC 10.

12 See for example the concept of 'women's property' (*stridhanam*) as a separate category apart from individual male property and the Mitakshara joint family property system, in which women were not entitled to a place as co-parceners or co-sharers in the family funds but remained entitled to maintenance from the common stock.

13 I have already mentioned that such statements, often quoted from the *Manusmriti* and other old cultural texts, have been understood as laying down the perpetual dependence of all Hindu women on men. That is clearly only part of the message which such ancient texts of uncertain origin contain.

14 The leading case on Hindu widows' inheritance rights under s. 14 of the *Hindu Succession Act*, 1956 is *V. Tulasamma v. V. Sesha Reddi*, AIR 1977 SC 1944, establishing the principle of the 'pre-existing right'. For details see ch. 5.8 below.

15 This was confirmed in *M. Abdul Karim v. P. K. Nabeesa*, AIR 1988 Ker 288, a case involving Shafi'i law, holding that a Muslim wife is entitled to past maintenance even in the absence of an agreement to that effect.

16 See *Kadeeja v. Aboobacker*, 1995(1) KLT 563, which reiterates the general principle, at p. 563, that "a husband is bound to maintain his wife and children even if he is necessitous".

17 For details on Muslim inheritance law see now Pearl and Menski (1998: 439–487).

18 *Mohd. Shamsuddin v. Noor Johan Begum* AIR 1955 Hyd 144; *Chandbi Badesha Mujawar v. Badesha Balwad Mujawar* [1960] 62 BomLR 866.

19 It was held in *K. Raza Khan v. Mumtaz Khatoon*, [1976] 1 AnWR 1, that the rights of Muslim wives under such provisions are independent and irrespective of their rights under the Muslim personal law.

20 For details see a good discussion in Mahmood (1986: 82–83).

21 This has been noted by many authors. Parashar (1992: 164) confirms that it had been brought to the notice of the government that in some cases, when Muslim women asked for maintenance, men had avoided the application of s. 488 of the 1898 Code by divorcing their wives extra-judicially.

22 For details see Pearl and Menski (1998: 306) with reference to further cases.

23 There are other aspects to this case, interestingly questions about the ownership of joint wedding presents under s. 27 HMA, which the judge also decided against the woman, although this was manifestly an early dowry case.

24 In *Bankim Chandra Roy v. Anjali Roy*, AIR 1972 Pat 80, it had also been held that no monthly allowance can be granted under s. 24 HMA for the support of the children.

25 The learned judge then proceeded to follow two other cases, which clearly considered the social environment of the litigants and the particular needs of the women and children involved in the case. See *D. Thimmappa v. R. Nagaveni*, AIR 1976 Kant 215 and *Baboolal v. Prem Lata*, AIR 1974 Raj 93.

26 For further details and commentary see e.g. Diwan and Diwan (1991: 137).

27 See e.g. *Savitri v. Govind Singh Rawat*, AIR 1986 SC 984, where the Supreme Court held that under s. 125 of the new *Criminal Procedure Code*, interim maintenance could be granted to an indigent wife.

28 Parashar (1992: 9) uses the example of the debates about sections 125–127 to illustrate the pervasive influence of religion on modern Indian law-making. She asserts that, following persistent objections of the Muslim *Ulema*, "the government suddenly did a *volte-face* and capitulated to their demands".

29 Many authors have commented on this. See *ibid.*: 9–10.

30 A useful discussion on this is found in Bharatiya (1996: 92–96).

31 *Rukhsana Parvin v. Shaikh Mohomed Hussein Mohomed Akbar* (1977)79 BomLR 123.

32 E.g. *Hajuben Suleman v. Ibrahim Gandabhai* 18 [1977] GujLR 133; *Khurshid Khan Amin Khan v. Husnabanu* 1976 (78) BomLR 240.

33 *Hajuben Suleman v. Ibrahim Gandabhai* 18 [1977] GujLR 133.

34 *Bai Tahira v. Ali Hussain*, AIR 1979 SC 362, *Fuzlunbi v. K. Khader Vali*, AIR 1980 SC 1730 and finally *Mohd. Ahmed Khan v. Shah Bano Begum*, AIR 1985 SC 945, the famous *Shah Bano* case, which gave rise to the MWPRDA of 1986, discussed further below.

35 That Bill, which sought to nullify the effects of *Bai Tahira*, was never passed and the MP who unsuccessfully brought the Bill wrote a book instead, see Banatwalla (1992). For details see Kusum (1980: 412–413) and Jain (1988: 291–292).

36 See to the same effect *Thilothama v. Kunjappan*, 1983 KLT 90, a case on the position of customary dues under a specific local Hindu enactment. This case confirms that the new maintenance law was not simply directed against Muslims, but was promoted to protect all destitute or needy Indian women.

37 For details see p. 951 of the judgment. The reaction of official bodies like the All India Muslim Personal Law Board was to suggest that this was a rule only for pious Muslims. For details see for example Diwan and Diwan (1991: 138–139); Mahmood (1990: 305–306).

38 The legal principle itself had already been applied in *Bai Tahira*, AIR 1979 SC 362, so that, to some extent, *Shah Bano* did not constitute a new law.

39 Many writers opposed the judgment, see e.g. Mahmood (1986: 88–94), who noted, at p. 82, that "for the past about ten years a *Shari'at* vs. Cr. P. C. war is being fought in the judicial corridors of this country". Latifi (1985: 385–400) defended the decision and argued, at p. 399, that "[t]o deny the Indian courts the jurisdiction to look, in appropriate cases, at the Holy Quran, would be to deny the Indian Muslims the right to be governed by Islamic law".

40 To date, neither Pakistan nor Bangladesh, despite the well-meaning efforts in *Hefzur Rahman v. Shamsun Nahar Begum*, 1995(15) BLD 34, seem willing to accept that message.

41 I have already referred to the important case of *Soundarammal*, AIR 1980 Mad 294 in this context. Anand (1992: 185) called for the reconstruction of maintenance law as a law of compensation and advocated the introduction of one-off lump-sum payments as well as "matrimonial insurance policies". For detailed discussions see Diwan (1990b); Preeti Sharma (1990); Vijay Sharma (1994) as well as several articles in Sarkar and Sivaramayya (eds.) (1994).

42 An important case in this regard, as we saw, was *Sumitra Devi*, AIR 1985 SC 765.

43 Another case of this type is reported at 1979 CriLR (Guj) 489.

44 On the other hand, where a polygamously married Hindu wife makes a claim for maintenance under s. 125 of the secular 1973 Code, as in *Yamunabai v. Anantrao*, AIR 1988 SC 644, the courts cannot apply the wide definition of 'Hindu wife'. In *Yamunabai*, consequently, it was held that the expression 'wife' means 'legally wedded wife' and excludes a polygamously married Hindu wife. Sagade (1989: 342–344) discusses this issue and argues elaborately for the extension of the protective principle under s. 25 HMA to cases under s. 125 of the 1973 Code.

45 *K. Vimla v. K. Veeraswamy*, (1991) SCJ 282.

46 It is evident from many cases that husbands were not happy. A particularly bad case of contempt of court is found in *Jai Singh v. Khimi Bhiklu*, AIR 1978 HP 45, discussed further below, where the husband was deliberately and persistently ignoring the orders of the Court.

47 As we also saw, in *Romesh Chander v. Savitri*, AIR 1995 SC 851, the husband was required by the Supreme Court to transfer the only house in his name to the wife and to deliver possession to her before his divorce decree would become effective.

48 This appears to reflect recognition of the fact that the wife's family probably did provide some dowry, which the husband would otherwise claim for himself, although this is blatantly against the law, as found in s. 6 of the *Dowry Prohibition Act*, 1961.

49 Gani (1988: 12) highlights correctly that the Supreme Court judgments in *Bai Tahira* in 1979 and *Fuzlunbi* in 1980 did not stir any public controversy

amongst the Muslims. For an extended discussion, Latifi (1985) and Mahmood (1986: 88–94) are especially useful. See also Pearl (1987: 74), Gani (1988), Mahmood (1990); Lateef (1990: 192–201).

50 Mahmood (1986: 85), while comparing Hindu and Muslim law, overstates the Hindu law principle that on marriage "every girl would be *finally and perpetually* transferred to her husband's family". Such a principle exists in Hindu law, but is neither binding nor universal. This is reflected in the social observation that it does not appear to be followed in general practice among most Hindus today.

51 On opinion surveys at the time see Rao (1985: 575–577). Alka Singh (1992: 142–143 and 160–161) confirms that many Muslims were in favour of the *Shah Bano* decision. See also Shiv Sahai Singh (1993: 339–365) with much evidence to the effect that the Muslim community in different regions of the country was in favour of post-divorce maintenance.

52 Latifi (1986: 620) envisaged difficulties for female claimants, saying that "this ill-considered and hastily concocted legislation is likely to disturb the peace of Muslim families. Oddly enough, the Act does not empower the magistrate to enforce his order under section 4(1) in case of default by anyone ordered to pay maintenance".

53 Gani (1988: 40) reports that immediately on the introduction of the Bill, the Chairman of the Madhya Pradesh *Wakf* Board welcomed it, only to add that he would appeal to the Centre to allocate money to the Board for those purposes because of its poor financial condition. The spokesmen of the Uttar Pradesh and Bihar *Wakf* Boards have also complained of their incapacity to support women. For details on this issue see also Lateef (1990: 195).

54 For very early cases under the 1986 Act and excerpts from several early unreported cases, see Jain (1988). Further case references are found in Mahmood (1989: 230–232). Where a husband files a case, s. 7 of the 1986 Act does not apply, see *Anwaruddin Ahmad v. State*, 1989 CriLJ (NOC) 20 (Cal). *Shamsudeen v. Sabhiya* 1988(2) KLT 392, held that an earlier final order for maintenance under the 1973 Code was not disturbed by the promulgation of the 1986 Act. See also *Idris Ali v. Ramesha Khatun*, AIR 1989 Gau 24. In *Mytheen v. Saphiya*, 1993(2) KLT 322, it was held that if a wife has signed away her right to maintenance, she cannot reclaim it later. Cases on the maintenance of children and parents are still governed by sections 125–128 of the 1973 Code.

55 The list would be too long to cite. Danial Latifi used strong language to criticise the key provisions of the 1986 Act, which "could mean almost anything" (Latifi 1986: 617). Iyer (1987: 13) complained about "long clauses and crude drafting", asserting at p. 12 that alimony cannot be claimed under s. 3 of the 1986 Act for the period beyond the brief *iddat*. Diwan and Diwan (1991: 155–165) provide a curious, interesting mixture of old and new views, but at least this is explained by the authors in a note at p. 155.

56 Negative reactions abound. See e.g. Carroll (1986) and Iyer (1987).

57 For details see Jain (1988: 289–290) and Mahmood (1990: 305 and 310). Like many others, Pearl (1987: 74) speculated on whether the 1986 Act would be struck down as unconstitutional.

58 It can be safely assumed that legal challenges to the authority of the Indian state to legislate on matters of Muslim law would be treated as lacking standing as well as *bona fides*. *Bishnu Charan Mohanty v. Union of India*, AIR 1993 Or 176, upheld the constitutional validity of s. 5 of the 1986 Act. It was held that it does not discriminate on the basis of religion and as such does not violate Article 15 of the Constitution. Meanwhile, *Syed Fazal Pookoya Thangal v. Union of India*, 1993(1) KLT 860, has confirmed that s. 4(2) of the 1986 Act is not unconstitutional.

59 Latifi (1986: 617–618) speculated that s. 3 of the Act could mean almost anything and argued at p. 618 that "[u]ntil the Supreme Court pronounces on this nobody will know what this section really means".

60 See Mahmood (1990) and ch. 4.2 above with further case references. Even the more patriarchal North Indian High Courts have now fallen in line. *Amjum Hassan Siddiqui v. Salma B*, AIR 1992 All 322, discusses the jurisdiction of Family Courts in such proceedings, but does not question the positive interpretation of the 1986 Act. for divorced Muslim wives.

61 The only major decision holding that a husband is not liable to maintain his ex-wife beyond the *iddat* period appears to be the High Court case of *Usman Khan Bahamani v. Fathimunnisa Begum* AIR 1990 AP 225. *Raja Mohammed v. Moimoon*, 1992(2) KLT SN 1, was decided by the Madras High Court and appears to rely on the wording employed in *Usman Khan* without saying so.

62 Bhat J in *Aliyar v. Pathu*, 1988(2) KLT 446, at pp. 457–458, also made reference to these sources and came in essence to the same conclusion.

63 This case, also reported as *M. Alavi v. T. V. Safia*, AIR 1993 Ker 2, will have raised a few eyebrows because it protects a divorced woman who had allegedly been living in adultery.

64 Apart from the case discussed below, I only found one case decided by the Madras High Court, but reported in the KLT: *Raja Mohammed v. Moimoon*, 1992(2) KLT SN 1. This strange case appears to rely on the wording employed in *Usman Khan*.

65 For details on this important subject, with further references, see Pearl and Menski (1998: 219–220).

66 See in particular Mahmood (1989: 230) and Mahmood (1990: 300).

67 In this regard, then, we are back to the leading principle of *Bai Tahira*, AIR 1979 SC 362. However, what is adequate in terms of provision may remain contested.

68 This is in an article on the *Roop Kanwar* case of *sati* in 1987 (see Hawley 1994).

69 Parihar (1994: 227) still complains that the language of the 1986 Act is "clumsy and ambiguous" and asserts at p. 234 that "the Act of 1986 is in fact against the protection of Muslim women's rights".

70 See earlier *The Secretary, Tamil Nadu Wakf Board v. Syed Fatima Nochi*, AIR 1995 Mad 88.

71 It appears that in a number of High Court cases, various *Wakf* Boards had earlier claimed that it would be against their constitution to have to provide maintenance for destitute ex-wives. In *Syed Fazal Pookoya Thangal v. Union of India*, AIR 1993 Ker 308, it was argued without success that s. 4(2) of the 1986 Act is unconstitutional (see Latifi, 1993: 170). Parihar (1994: 229) claimed that the 1986 Act "is a sin against the constitution of Wakfs", since they are religious and charitable trusts created to perform specified holy acts, rather than serving social welfare purposes. I do not see why these two matters should be treated as strictly separate.

72 This is, of course, entirely in line with traditional Islamic scholarship, but it is manifestly not a guaranteed entitlement in South Asian Muslim societies on account of widespread desertion and abandonment of wives. Judicial criticism of this was voiced in the Bangladeshi case of *Hefzur Rahman v. Shamsun Nahar Begum*, (1995) 15 BLD 34.

73 On the new activism in Christian law see *Myra Joseph Braz Dias v. Joseph Braz Dias*, AIR 1992 Bom 142, which challenges the statutory limit for the wife's maintenance (one-fifth of the husband's income) as unconstitutional, and emphasises the need for legislative action.

Chapter Five

Joint family and property law

Will individualism work?

5.1 Modernity and the family in Indian law

Joint family law used to be widely seen as the key element of Indian family law and in many ways it still remains in that position today. However, the emergence of new areas of law within the modern systems of family law regulation, as well as the recent prominence given to contentious issues like the maintenance entitlements of divorced wives, divorce law itself, or dowry-related problems, have created a powerful impression that joint family law is less important than it used to be. In reality, questions about the relative entitlement of certain individuals to support from joint family funds, or the extent of the interest of one individual in another person's individual property clearly remain within the umbrella of the old law. We have already seen, in ch. 4 above, that this goes for maintenance entitlements of divorced wives and children. Much could also have been said about the hotly debated issues surrounding dowry, which have not been included in the present study (see in detail Menski 1998b).

The less evident prominence of joint family law issues in the general Indian law reports today has other, more formal and administrative reasons as well. The modern judicial system has developed in such a way that only certain types of cases will now work their way through the normal court hierarchy of District and Sessions Courts, Additional District and Sessions Courts, the various layers of possible appeals before a High Court and finally the Supreme Court. Many areas of the law are being processed today in specialised tribunals, with their own law reports and separate literature. The law may only converge at the very top of the judicial hierarchy, when appeals from a tribunal lie to a High Court or the Supreme Court. This even goes, to some extent, for joint family law itself, which has gradually been turning into a specialist field of tax law, with its own, long-established law reporting mechanisms. We should be aware that in this context adherence to joint family property principles has been widely treated as a form of creative accounting for purposes of tax evasion.

We are not concerned in this chapter with the technicalities of Hindu joint family law,[1] or with fine points of Muslim inheritance and succession law.[2] On both subject areas, detailed textbooks and practice handbooks exist,[3] and those topics bristle with technical detail and mind-boggling complexities that most readers would find tedious and unnecessarily complicated. For our present purposes, at any rate, such intricacies go too far, given that the focus of the present book lies in explaining and analysing the progression of modern Indian law through the 1980s and 1990s to a socially conscious, welfare-oriented system of family law regulation.

Although this may not be evident at first sight, the present chapter is closely linked to previous discussions in this book. When we consider the position of an Indian individual, male or female, old or young, of whatever religious background, a complexity of legal rules come into play, determining the network of expectations and entitlements, both social and legal, that this individual may have. Our focus in the present discussion relates closely to the ever-present, inherent conflict between the individual and the group, more specifically between individual assertions of property rights and claims on that individual by a group, whether it be a family, a clan, a caste, or the entire religious community to which an individual belongs.

One could say quite a lot here about uniformity and diversity, about discrimination and preferential treatment (simply another, specific form of discrimination) in modern Indian law. We shall reserve those issues for chapter 6 below. In the present context, it seems most relevant to consider how modern Indian law has made sense of the never-ending conflicts between individuals of different social and legal standing within the context of social groups. In that respect, we are mainly concerned with the joint family, whether it be a small nuclear unit or a huge extended family of the type which one still finds in social reality.[4] Joint families, of course, continue to exist in the realm of the invisible as well, and state law has not been able to abolish that aspect of the joint family system, while fiddling with legal rules about succession within the sphere of the official law.

For, we must not ignore, in the present context, that the first underlying principle of joint family law is the existence of visible *and* invisible links between individuals sharing a common ancestor several generations back.[5] These invisible links are created through birth into a particular bloodline, most often a patriliny. While modernity and modern laws tend to deny the legal relevance of such links, although they cannot do so entirely, lest there be chaos,[6] society may treat the images of interlinkedness at several levels in quite a different way.

Modern assumptions about the inherent superiority of the paradigms of modernity are, in essence, diametrically opposed to ancient Hindu and Muslim religious traditions, their underlying concepts and their present manifestations. Modernity, in that sense, too, opposes anything 'religious' in its wider sense. By declaring 'religion' virtually irrelevant for daily legal life, restricting it to the level of personal psychology rather than recognising its public impact, modernity and legal centralist axioms cooperate to bolster their own claims to supremacy. The ideologies of modernity, in that sense, have been a most convenient tool for legal centralism.

Religious traditions, however, have also experienced development and modernity, although that is constantly denied by modernists and traditionalists alike who operate with their own hidden agenda. Thus, the static nature of 'tradition' is constantly asserted, as though that was an unshakeable truth rather than a convenient myth. We need not be detained by such confusions: All over the world, and not just in India, a re-appraisal of the role of religion and of 'tradition' within the context of post-modernity is currently under way. Our analysis of modern Indian marriage laws in ch. 1 has confirmed, in many ways, that 'tradition' or 'custom' may be a useful legal concept today, but what exactly 'custom' is, and how inherently flexible it may turn out to be, have remained most difficult issues, and not only for lawyers. Tradition, at the end of the day, is not controllable by modernity from the outside. It develops its own forms of supra-modernity, as it might now be called (Yilmaz 1999), by flexible adjustment to new circumstances. We should not behave as though we had remained unaware all along that religion and tradition are not really dysfunctional and irrelevant today.

As a specialist in South Asian culture and law, I frequently encounter, as a kind of professional hazard, arguments to the effect that 'tradition' has an inherently negative impact and that cultural traditions are bad for women, so what is one doing by researching 'tradition'?[7] Modernity and a commitment to progress, on the other hand, demand secularisation and the atomisation of society, so that individuals may be empowered to act as independent entities, free from invisible and visible constraints on personal autonomy.[8] Respect for joint family systems and related arrangements is therefore immediately seen as evidence of conservative, backward thinking and male chauvinism. In terms of political correctness, as we seem to call this today, arguing for the family system has become 'wrong thinking', while the 'correct' truth seems to lie in arguments for individualism and freedom from those invisible ties of 'tradition'. But how adequate is this? How can we portray ties of any kind merely as a negative element? Do not such links also protect? As always, more than one perspective on such issues may be taken. A holistic approach to such questions cannot just shut out certain ideologically questionable elements and declare them irrelevant.

In the traditional Hindu conceptual framework of reference, individual property rights for males were, of course, well-known. They were matched, however, by the ancient concept of *stridhanam*, individual property rights for women, an important issue which remains incompletely researched, and over which many conflicting claims are still made.[9] All of this is then overlaid by the principles of Hindu joint family law of various kinds; the *Mitakshara* system is the most dominant, but it is clearly not the only one in operation.[10]

In post-colonial India, the importance and key position of this concept of overlapping and competing networks has been challenged in many ways. It appears that the aim has been to create an atomistic system of absolute individual property rights by dismantling and legally abolishing various joint family concepts such as the *Mitakshara* birthright and the pious obligation.[11] On the road to modernity, which is supposed to lead towards individualism and freedom to contract, the binding ties of joint Hindu family arrangements were supposed to be cut; traditional obligations were to be negated in order to free individuals from all kinds of bondages. The invisible blood links of the joint family systems have been portrayed as representing trip wires for enterprising individuals, unwanted shackles which need to be shaken off as fast and as completely as possible. Joint family ideology is perceived as involving burdensome, lurking loyalties to others which women, in particular (as much of the literature asserts) would find difficult to ignore.

Thus, the Indian family has virtually been treated as an obstacle to development.[12] And yet, as will have become more than evident from our discussions in the previous chapters, modern India's developments in family law during the 1980s and 1990s could not have done away with this cornerstone of society. The state, in effect, desperately needs the family, and its inherent potential for support networks, to provide the kind of social welfare structures that modern Indian law has been developing, and which the state itself cannot finance, as we clearly saw. Realising that many of the huge constitutional and legislative promises of the modern Indian state are programmatic rather than reflective of social reality, the judges, more than anyone else,[13] have recognised that the ancient models of family support remain extremely relevant today.

At the same time, the academic literature on Indian family law has moved further and further towards celebrating individualism, focusing in particular on granting women autonomy and increased rights over their own, separate property. This has been a tempting, and increasingly high-profile agenda (see Agarwal 1994), and most authors, evidently middle-class and predominantly female, seem to have assumed that the world would be in order if only women had a say over their own property. While this is perfectly appropriate for women who have property and who have the will and desire to assert their own individual rights, academics and social reformers have tended to overlook the concerns of 'little people', of those women who own little or no property in their own right, and who are thus dependent on the willingness of others to share resources.[14] The concerns of such individuals began to interest me during the 1980s and were a motivation to write about the unforeseen impact of state laws on the lives of such people (see chapters 5.2, 5.4 and 5.6 below).

In many areas of legal discussion, notably divorce,[15] one can study most interesting clashes between the individualistic predilections of academic authors and legal reformers on the one hand, and social realities 'on the ground', which do not match those exciting academic and legal dreams.

Contentious issues arise with reference to virtually all fields of law in modern South Asia. In particular, one could write much about the implications of concepts of property law in relation to the persistent presence of bonded labour in all South Asian jurisdictions. Or we might reflect for a moment on why married women are murdered in India, every day of the year, on account of so-called dowry problems (see now in detail Menski 1998b). The gruesome evidence appears to show that women themselves are treated as property, and can thus be disposed of as and when others please. Such modern forms of virtual slavery and total disregard for what seems to be called 'human rights' are not peculiar to Hindus, however, and they occur not only in South Asia.[16] Still, much of the literature tends to overlook this, immediately blaming Hindu and Muslim cultural traditions for socio-economic problems that are clearly of a universal nature and concern not only gender relations. Do we care to know about the statistics on murdered wives in the USA?[17]

Challenges to the beautified axioms of modernity have come up in various ways. Unless supposedly free-floating, modern, independent individuals have the financial resources to purchase themselves space, both real and mental, to protect their individuality from the interference of others, or simply to live and enjoy it, how will they be able to maintain such imagined freedoms? In the process of protecting their own élitist concerns, such privileged individuals (for that is what they turn out to be, when compared to the majority) subordinate other individuals, less fortunate than those resourceful few, by purchasing the services of others for specific tasks. Remarkably, feminist literature has also begun to acknowledge that there is a problem. It is not recognised that traditional status relationships are being replaced by multiple forms of contract, so that at the end of the day, the borderlines between tradition and modernity, status and contract, individualism and groupism, even servant and master, remain not perfectly neat and easily definable.

In other words, modernity reproduces its own hierarchical status relationships. It does not get round the supposed problems of inequality, it might even make things worse (Stern 1993). The escalating statistics on dowry murders, for example, cannot easily be explained. The simplest shortcut, evidently dishonest but academically convenient, has been to blame religious and cultural traditions,[18] rather than modern consumption-driven greed for more resources. Turning marriage arrangements into a speculative enterprise akin to lottery deals, today's potentially murderous husbands have become mixed up over modernity and tradition. If they have not been trained to respect basic human principles, more and more women will go up in flames because modernity, not tradition, has failed to protect their very existence. We are slowly beginning to understand today that the modern dowry drama plays out the tensions between tradition and modernity, between ruthless individualism and greed, on the one hand, and reliance on basic ethical norms of traditionality and interlinkedness on the other. Are we not already aware of the fact that women who sense the danger of being burnt alive still do not want to escape? It is too simple to blame the victim for being traditional, however. The analytical spotlight should be on the murderers, who seem to act decidedly modern, rolling the acquisition of dowry riches and a trouble-free instant divorce into one convenient strategy of advancing individual desires at any cost. Dowry murder, then, becomes an eminently modern form of divorce: Burn the woman, save on post-divorce maintenance, and even grow rich in the process by keeping the unfortunate woman's dowry, if you can! These are aberrations of crude individualism, masquerading as models for a modern, consumerist society. Evidently, they find few restraints in the ethical norms of modernity, where the survival of the fittest has, once again, become the dominant rule.

While all this politicking about modernity and tradition, as well as uniformity and plurality (see ch. 6.1) has been in ferment, modernity itself has been challenged and questioned in many ways. In India – but the point is, of course, that this happens not only in India – it became evident to the rulers themselves, decades ago, that the axioms of modern autonomous individuality are unworkable in the socio-legal practicalities of the modern world. Nehru's dreams of modernity notwithstanding, the growing social and legal realism of the 1970s became a matter of political survival. If India's leadership had not listened to the emerging cracks in the volcano of poverty and legal deprivation, Indian democracy would simply not be what it is today, still functioning against all odds, as specialist writers are busy to assert, but cannot explain.[19] In other words, and plainly obvious to leaders such as Mrs. Gandhi during the 1970s, the poor were becoming poorer and more numerous, while the fashionable élite was playing roulette with the resources of the nation.

It is easy to say that things in India are not any better now. The point for our present analysis, so much must be emphasised, is that there was a gradual realisation, at the highest level, that something had to be done to arrest the slow process of manifest maldevelopment. Something, indeed, *was* done, through the much-maligned and incompletely analysed Emergency of 1975, whose undoubtedly cathartic effects I discussed in the introduction to this book.

To reiterate that argument here, Mrs. Gandhi patently acted like a classical Hindu ruler in the face of a modern national emergency. She knew that the modern state would not be able to pay for social welfare structures, that she could not tackle the massive poverty by throwing money at the problem. The entire system of governance would need to be re-adjusted to reflect awareness of the critical balance between dominant private interests and concerns and the faltering concepts of public accountability and duties to the nation. Acting as she did, outwardly as a cruel dictator, Mrs. Gandhi moved the Indian colossus along to post-modernity, utilising invisible axioms of South Asian culture to redirect and re-focus the development of the nation and its people.

This requires some explanations here. For Hindus, the basic axiom of universal interlinkedness with all other creations (the classical *rta/dharma* complex which so many modern scholars abhor, or are simply not aware of) means, in a philosophical sense, that an individual can never be an absolutely autonomous individual in the invisible sphere of life. One can only strive towards achieving visible independence and autonomy, no more. For Muslims, too, submission to the Divine will and awareness of a final judgment create invisible bonds which individuals may not emphasise, but they know that these ties continue to exist. Similarly for adherents of other religious and cultural traditions, there are networks of invisible bondages that nobody can shake off. Attempts to do so merely confirm the strength and tenacious hold of such links, not their non-persistence.

The result is not necessarily a fatalistic submission to religion and tradition, but a particular sense of awareness of one's own roles, and the place of others. This leads to a cultural complex which makes distinctions between the private and the public spheres mere constructs with which one can play in the most exciting ways. In other words, awareness of being tied to the created world can also be turned into an asset, a safety net, within which many freedoms exist. Any individual's actions, most evidently illustrated by the concept of *karma* as automatic consequence of any action (and, for that matter, inaction), play a role in this system.[20] This basic awareness of the role of 'action' does not allow South Asian individuals to hide behind axioms of immovable rigidity in anything they know, while they cannot fully shake off the latent sense of being tied into a duty-focused framework of reference either. Not all of this is duty-focused, however. The very same cultural complex contains a more or less constant realisation that others have duties towards oneself, which one may well wish to call upon in some form, thus claiming what other cultures emphasise as 'rights'.

Too much has, in my view, been made of the binding nature of these duty-centred ties and the resulting obligations and limitations when it comes to women, lower caste people and anyone who is dependent (or is declared to be dependent) on others in some way. Too little attention has been paid to the flexible operation of such awareness of being interlinked and the resultant duties of those who are supposed to be more powerful and more resourceful, in charge of others rather than being controlled. In other words, women, the poor, anyone, may have an inherent right to call upon others to activate such invisible ties and linkages. The more privileged, therefore, have obligations and duties rather than just rights, and such rights and duties do not need to be reciprocal, since they may be symbiotically linked. Such ties can be potentially limitless and they are often treated as morally and socially binding. Naturally, this is not a simple matter to discuss in the context of a book on family law, but it is precisely this cultural phenomenon of interlinkedness that is becoming increasingly relevant in understanding modern Indian family laws. Studying interlinkedness in itself is a tough task; nothing ever works in a linear fashion the moment we start to look at life as a web of networks. Law itself is clearly a dynamic field of social activity, rather than merely a linear continuum This is another reason why it is has been so difficult to make sense of recent developments in modern Indian family law which might look traditional, but have turned out to be signs of supra-modernity.

Too much of the legal literature, in its modernising fervour and ambitiousness, has been impressed by individualism and has thus sought to empower the individual at the expense of the group. What happened to Indian law during this process is evident from the analysis of the first two decades of modern Indian legal history, in constitutional as well as family law. Protecting the strong individual by inheriting the colonial legal model, while holding out the carrot of independence and autonomy to everyone through constitutional guarantees of equal treatment and non-discrimination, post-colonial Indian law tilted more and more in favour of those who could hire lawyers and could use the legal procedures to claim respect for their arguments. The result was, as I explained in the introduction, a social and legal system in which the imbalances between rich and poor, big and small, men and women, grew larger rather than becoming less pronounced. Promises of social and legal equality were increasingly shown to be a hollow myth of modernity, a political lie. As the crisis of Indian law grew, something had to happen to avoid a violent explosion that would disrupt the entire set-up of modern, post-colonial India.

I analysed in the introduction to this book why and how Mrs. Gandhi played the role of the violent dictator. She reminded Indians of the uncomfortable fact that developmental aims were not achieved, that maldevelopments had taken centre-stage, that individualised privileges of the élite made a mockery of textbook wisdoms about the supposedly important and equally legitimate concerns of the underprivileged masses. During the 1960s and 1970s, Indian state law had become increasingly an instrument of blatant oppression. The in-built biases of the official law towards the strong and resourceful constantly distorted delicate balances in favour of the individualistic, egoistic designs of the upper classes.[21] Exploitation of superiority became legally underwritten, despite a democratic, equality-centred ideological framework, which is clearly more idealistic than real.

This is where Mrs. Gandhi came in, dictating secularism and socialism into the Preamble of the Indian Constitution, and thereby effecting a re-balancing of private and public interest in the most fundamental way possible. One of the well-guarded secrets of the miraculous functioning of Indian democracy during the 1980s and 1990s has been that the new regime of legal concepts induced by the Emergency, whether by design or by default, has re-focused attention on the concerns of hundreds of millions of disadvantaged people. This helps to explain why modern Indian family law has become more restrictive on divorce, but more lenient towards bigamy and child marriages, and definitely tougher on men who do not fulfil their financial obligations towards others in the family.

It appears that, in this roundabout way, modern Indian law has not just rediscovered the usefulness of the family. What has been realised, evidently somewhere at the highest level, is the essential need to make family structures work as a social welfare mechanism for modern India. Official recognition that a strategy of ruthless, tie-less individualisation cannot be conducive to public welfare in a system which still protects individual property rights – and therefore still disproportionately supports the stronger, the 'big fish' – has induced a prolonged and ongoing process of re-balancing basic rules of Indian family law. This, in essence, is what we have been able to observe and analyse in the concluding sections of all the major chapters above.

It would be too much to expect that the new social welfare-oriented jurisprudential rationale and legal policy should appear in real life as a straightforward beacon of light that guides everyone and unites the nation. Far from it. As we saw in the previous chapters, the academic discourses about legal development and modernisation in India have continued to be dominated by axiomatic modernisation ideologies and vociferous disagreements among scholars and policy-makers. Judges, too, have adhered, well into the 1980s, to the contested axioms of modernity without thinking in depth about the social effects of their decisions. Thus, the two trends have been working side by side, and therefore, in effect, probably against each other. Did they cancel each other out, to some extent? What has been our evidence?

This issue first struck me when I began to research the effects of the *Kerala Joint Hindu Family System (Abolition) Act*, 1975 in Kerala during the mid-1980s. By then, public interest litigation strategies had begun to make their mark. I was taking part in legal aid camps in Kerala with a group of students, and we found it contradictory that one law should promote individualism and should assert private rights and entitlements, while another law in the same legal system demanded a public interest perspective and recognition of the needs of others. Surely, in social reality 'on the ground', these conceptual clashes would come out in litigation, or in stalemate scenarios.

Examining the intentions, policies and effects of the 1975 Act in Kerala, I soon found confirmation (if any was needed) that the concepts of 'official law' and 'unofficial law', as explained at the time by Chiba (1986) and others, existed in real life (see chapters 5.2 and 5.4 below). Today we are even more sure that there is indeed a mind-set in Kerala which operates on the basis that the Act has fundamentally changed property relations in the joint family. This is confirmed by the use of legislation, and it clearly comes out of the case law that has built up in the meantime (see ch. 5.8 below). Co-existing with this, however, and remarkably at the unofficial legal level, we discover (and must take note of) the operation of a different mind-set. Here it remains a fact that members of a family will continue to live as though they were joint owners of the little property that they may call their own. As a matter of traditional obligation, the family will pool such meagre resources and will help any individual member in need, as and when possible. As a result, girls from poor families will be given a decent marriage at the expense of the family.[22] Such girls, as individual owners of their separate shares in the family property, would in most cases never have been able to afford a feast at that level of sophistication. In other words, even if we only look at the simple example of marriage, family solidarity has remained an asset, an active survival mechanism. However, all of this undercuts and contradicts the letter of the modern official law. The unofficial law of extended or nuclear family solidarity, with its clearly articulated welfare orientation (I would say here that actions speak louder than pious words) stands in open contradiction to the modern official law. The modern law is a largely urban phenomenon (although that contrast oversimplifies the matter) and is very clearly a law for the upper classes, especially those families who have enough property to be concerned about individual shares. Otherwise, the modern law and its implications in life are manifestly irrelevant, if not positively harmful, for those who barely own the ground on which they sleep.

The collection of articles reprinted in this chapter focuses, from various angles, on my long-standing concern in recognising the potential benefits of family support for individuals. I have included an article by Dr. Lucy Carroll, which seemed to me too individualistic and took too little account of the concerns and needs of real people in Kerala. As my response to that article shows (ch. 5.6 below), when legal scholars write about another society from an armchair perspective, there is no guarantee that such writing makes any sense to the people about whom it purports to be concerned.

In this field of law, then, we need to test at a greater depth what people in India itself actually want for themselves. This will never be an easy task. In fact, we can predict quite contradictory expectations which will not marry up to realistic proposals for legal reform. The current strategy of the modern Indian state, pursued at state level rather than by the central government, has been directed at increasing the claims of women over ancestral property, by promulgating new laws that virtually equate daughters to sons in terms of their legal position vis-à-vis the joint family. This seems quite appropriate, given that other areas of the law, notably again maintenance law, have held daughters accountable for the welfare and maintenance of their aged parents, putting them on a par with their brothers.[23]

I remain as concerned today as more than a decade ago, however, that the modernising statutory reforms carry the risk of promoting individualism to a level where the inter-familial solidarity is broken down by modern assertions of individualised ownership. In the light of new legal developments in various segments of Indian family law, this would not appear to be a healthy development. While I am certainly not saying that individualism as such is a bad thing, promoting ruthless egoism and lack of concern for those nearest to oneself cannot serve as a healthy base for economically sustainable social welfare policies in a country of approximately a billion people. It seems very appropriate, therefore, that the modern legislative interventions and their individualising trends have been tempered by judicial directions that remind individuals of their obligations within a family framework. In fact, looking back at the MWPRDA of 1986 and the sustained activism of the Indian High Courts in securing maintenance rights for divorced wives, one might even venture to conclude that the Indian legislature and the judiciary are actually pulling the same cart, and in the same direction.

At the same time, as we shall see in ch. 5. 8 below, when certain individuals seek to exploit the new social welfare orientation of the supra-modern law, and want to use the newly invigorated family protection networks for their own selfish ends, the courts may step in to curb and control such new forms of legal abuse. This reflects an explicit recognition in today's Indian law of a new symbiosis between family and individual. This is not the widely wished-for modern scenario of individual autonomy, however. Rather, we find a reconstructed form of ancient models of social organisation in which individuals, as interlinked components of complex societies, are supported by the organs of the state, prominently the courts, in defining their rights through the duties of others. In this scenario, the Indian state needs the family: It cannot afford to discard its resources and potential as a support mechanism for individuals in urgent need of assistance.

5.2 Legislative overkill and the *Kerala Joint Hindu Family System (Abolition) Act*, 1975*

[From: 1986 *KLT*. Journal section, pp. 17–20]

In medical science, it is considered of fundamental importance that the patient should be protected against potential evil side-effects of a medicine or other medical treatment. The same standard of care does not seem to prevail in the legal field; this seems so particularly when the perceived patient is sought to be freed from disabilities and unwanted ties, usually of tradition in some form or another, which a zealous legislative body wants to remove or destroy. The problem could be studied almost anywhere in the world. My colleague Professor A. Allott in *The limits of law* (London, 1980) gives a lot of evidence of such cases. In India, a prime example of such unreflected administration of a popular legislative drug, the bitter-sweet pill of social engineering through law, appears to be the *Kerala Joint Hindu Family System (Abolition) Act*, 1975 (Act 30 of 1976), which came into force on 1–12–1976. My concern here is with the side-effects of such legislation on the common man who is subject to such forms of legislative overkill, and who may one day find that his customary obligation system has been shattered, that his traditional rights and duties have been dissolved or radically changed by some legal process that remained unknown to him.

*The author gratefully acknowledges financial support of the British Academy.

Since modern law proceeds on the assumption that ignorance of the law is no defence, the law-making agencies would seem to be under a definite obligation to exercise every possible care to avoid oversights.

Since the 1975 Act applies only to Kerala, it is hardly known outside the state. A number of practising lawyers have commented upon some aspects of the Act's operation in this Journal, but I have doubts whether the full implications of this piece of social engineering have been grasped by those who have been, or will be, concerned with it. The only somewhat detailed study of the Act and its operation is provided by Shri P. Parameswaran Moothath, who has published the full text of the Act with a (now rather outdated) introduction and useful short notes (Cochin, 1984).

The intention of Kerala Act 30 of 1976 seems quite clear. It is "An Act to abolish the joint family system among Hindus in the State of Kerala". Primarily, so it appears, the legislature wanted to abolish large Hindu joint families in which, at least potentially, one powerful individual, the *karta* or *karnavan*, determined the life of junior members of the family by virtue of his power of control over the family assets. Concern to curb abuses in this situation is apparent from the debates of the Kerala Assembly in 1973, when the Act was introduced as a Bill. However, when this became law in 1976, all joint Hindu families were abolished, also those which, in sociological terms, would be counted as nuclear families. This is because the criterion for a joint Hindu family is not primarily the number of persons involved, but community of property. So the typical nuclear family of father, mother and their children was also vitally affected and, as we shall see, in more than one way.

By repealing twelve earlier Acts on Hindu law applicable in Kerala the 1975 Act also sought to abolish the confusing multitude of Hindu personal laws in the state. The creation of a uniform law for all Hindus had been recommended by the First and Second Report of the Law Commission of Kerala. However, the way in which this was done may serve as a warning to those who intend on pushing through uniform legal provisions for the whole of India; a piece of legislation fixed on creating uniformity on paper may add to the confusion as to what the law actually is, and it may be counter-productive and even dangerous, unless possible side-effects are fully taken into account.

The 1975 Act did not achieve total uniformity, however. S. 4(1) and 4(2) of the Act continue to distinguish between Mitakshara law and other forms of Hindu law. S. 4(2) gives total equality in terms of property rights to Hindu females, because here the deemed partition takes place on a *per capita* basis. Under s. 4(1), on the other hand, the Mitakshara Hindu daughter, as in the rest of India, gets no share in the family property unless she becomes an heiress under the provisions of the *Hindu Succession Act*, 1956. For example, under s. 8 of that Act, if her father died intestate, as would normally be the case.

Now, the Mitakshara daughter's right to marriage expenses appears to be saved by the proviso to s. 4(1) of the Act, but since the coparcenary property has been legislated away and separate co-owners have been created on 1–12–1976, it must have become extremely difficult for a young woman in this situation to obtain the support of all brothers, unless everybody contributes their due share willingly. I note that the same proviso gives the sister or daughter the right to recover such dues, if necessary in a suit, but in the meantime, considering delays of justice and other hazards, how will she get married? Fortunately, the quite realistic approach of Hindus in Kerala continues to be that marriage of one's daughter or sister is a family matter, as a result of which every family member contributes towards it, even though great hardship may have to be undergone. But the 1975 Act would seem to encourage the egoistic individual in such situations and to allow a mischievous brother loopholes for substantial delays in making his contribution. As a result, again, women will suffer, as so often when legal reforms turn sour against them.

It appears that the provisions of the 1975 Act have not yet been fully tested in the Courts of Kerala, because otherwise a glaring oversight which I shall drawn attention to further below would have become known. So far, only two questions have come up before the High Court of the State: Firstly, what is the position of those 12 earlier Acts on Hindu law that were repealed by the 1975 Act? Though there is by no means agreement of all concerned, the prevailing opinion seems to be that the 1975 Act has repealed all the 12 earlier Acts *in toto (Kesavan v. Krishnamma*, 1985 KLT 17). In the absence of any provisions for marriage and divorce in the 1975 Act, the *Hindu Marriage Act*, 1955 is deemed to apply to such matrimonial matters as may arise in Kerala. The further question whether s. 29(2) of the *Hindu Marriage Act*, 1955 saves some aspects of the various Hindu personal laws in Kerala does not concern us here; it would, however, warrant detailed discussion.

Regarding the second point of law so far decided by the High Court of Kerala, we find a very interesting and again not uncontroversial situation. The question is whether a suit, filed before 1–12–1976, can still be disposed of under the old Acts that now stand repealed. This point has clearly been answered in the affirmative (*Gopalakrishnan Nair v. Sarasamma*, 1981 KLT 810; *Krishnan Namboodiri v. Unnikrishnan*, 1982 KLT 640; *Balasubramoniam v. Nalini*, 1983 KLT 998). Indeed, recently this principle was expanded, in *Kesavan v. Krishnamma*, 1985 KLT 17, to extend to cases where the cause of action arose prior to 1–12–1976. This seems a dangerous proposition; it is undesirable that Advocates in Kerala should be able to argue that a particular cause of action arose when the couple, now locked in litigation, got united in wedlock, i.e. to contend that all trouble in their client's life started at the time of marriage. No doubt such argumentation will not be accepted.

As indicated, nine years after the coming into force of Act 30 of 1976 there are still no cases on the full implications of the Act on matters of joint family property. It would be interesting to know whether such cases have come up before the lower courts of Kerala and whether they have formed for example, a matter of discussion in Panchayats. Many members of the legal profession in Kerala will be well-placed to provide details on this matter and should feel encouraged to participate in the present discussion. I find it rather astonishing, to say the least, that this glaring legislative oversight that I am about to point out has not yet been noticed; at least we have no evidence that such realisation has been made public, and the most pernicious side-effect of Act 30 of 1976 is yet to make itself felt. There is a sword of Damocles hanging over the head of so many Hindu families in Kerala. What will the High Court do when this drama begins to unfold itself? Will Act 30 of 1976 be held unconstitutional? Let us first see what actually happened.

S. 4 of the 1975 Act provides for an automatic transformation of Hindu joint family property from coparcenary property held jointly to property held by the various members of the family as tenants-in-common, each such member (I have already pointed out that s. 4(1) and 4(2) define who is entitled to a share) having acquired, as from 1–12–1976, the status of absolute owner of his or her respective share. Now let us take the easiest possible case, because I have no interest in confusing anyone with intricacies of Hindu joint family law, however exciting an intellectual exercise that may be. Let us take a Hindu joint family consisting of father, mother and their two sons. In this easy case even the distinction between s. 4(1) and s. 4(2) of the Act does not apply and as from 1–12–1976 there were four co-owners, each holding an equal share of 1/4 of the former joint family property as absolute owners. Now let a further son be born after 1–12–1976; that poor fellow is not entitled to any share of the property at all, during the lifetime of his father, because s. 3 of the 1975 Act has also taken away the Hindu son's birth-right! Since so far Hindus in Kerala seem unaware of this dangerous situation, the side-effects of this bitter-sweet pill will not be felt at this stage.

Now let the father die intestate in 1986. What are the respective shares of the surviving members of the family? Since we have to apply s. 8 of the *Hindu Succession Act*, 1956 the answer must be that the widow and the two oldest sons still hold their 1/4 share each, plus a fourth share of the deceased's share 5/16, while the youngest son gets only 1/16. The conclusion is thus inevitable that Act 30 of 1976 has the effect of creating a most inequitable form of distribution of the former joint family property even as between male siblings, the criterion being merely the date of birth of the respective individual.

What will the High Court of Kerala do if such a case comes up? I have shown the present case to a number of practicing lawyers and to many Kerala Hindus actually affected by this Act. The reaction, apart from astonishment and initial disbelief, has been very varied. The hard view, taken only by a few practice-oriented lawyers, was to accept the legislative consequences as inevitable, because "this is the law". Most practitioners felt that an equitable solution would have to be found, and that this was a bad law requiring judicial intervention or legislative amendment. The fact that no such case seems to have reached the courts may well be interpreted as proof that the common Keralite has not lost his common sense and refuses to accept that such a law could seriously claim to govern his life and that of his family. For the people I spoke to, it was definite that their families would make arrangements to give an equal share to the younger son, and various methods were suggested.

The fact remains, however, that an egoistic individual, armed with Act 30 of 1976, the official law of Kerala, could try and take advantage of the present situation. That itself is undesirable.

The warning example of Kerala leads me to conclude here with some general comments on the problem of legislative overkill in India. As we have seen, the major reason for introducing the 1975 Act seems to have been that there were some abuses of the joint family system among Hindus by unscrupulous individuals who took advantage of their positions of power. We may safely state that in the majority of Hindu families there were no such problems. But then, would a doctor prescribe a particular drug to all his patients just because a few of them happened to suffer from a particular form of disease? Moreover, would he enforce the taking of his drug or treatment on everybody? Let us note that the modern law keeps doing precisely that.

The argument that the position of the doctor and the legislator are fundamentally different does not seem acceptable. Both are supposed to serve the public and to work for the common good. The unfortunate patient in the present case, the joint Hindu family, may not die; it may have enough resistance power to recover from this onslaught on family solidarity. In fact there is much evidence that this Act has had absolutely no effect on the local level. Either way, this is not a healthy situation. We may just as well have less of these modern laws if they are ineffective anyway because they remain unnoticed and somewhat fictitious. Such laws as exist should more precisely take into account people's needs.

Now, what are people's needs in this respect? In India, since no comprehensive system of social welfare exists, it is unrealistic to expect that unemployment benefit will ever be introduced. Similarly, provisions for old age pensions and the like exist only for those who could afford to contribute to them in the first place, not for the common man who continues to look for, and to rely on, the support of his family in times of crisis or in old age. If the side-effect of some modern laws is to destroy family solidarity and the individual's sense of responsibility towards the other members of the family, these laws are not suitable for Indian conditions and detrimental to the needs of the overwhelming majority of Indians. The strengthening of individualism, if this leads to the promotion of egoism can hardly lead to greater social welfare under present Indian conditions. To expect that such conditions will change seems hardly realistic in view of India's rapidly growing population.

Readers will be aware that many of the social problems in the West are due to excessive individualisation; the survival of the destitute or indigent individual being guaranteed by the State, there is purely in economic terms, no immediate need for family solidarity. In India such an approach is unrealistic. Enactments like the one discussed here actually endanger the position of women and the poor. Since Indian villagers remain perfectly capable to manage their family affairs sensibly (and by that I mean sensibly in view of their circumstances, not by the standards of some fashionable urbanites) modern Indian laws must not legislate away this family solidarity and must try to preserve the strength of flexible family arrangements, which seem to be the only means of ensuring survival for the many rural and urban poor. I strongly feel that the time has come for India to shed the remainders of colonial attitudes and complexes and to develop a critical self-consciousness and a sense of pride in her indigenous ethic models and behavioural patterns, which are, after all, irrespective of religion, caste and the like, closely linked with ecological and socio-economic realities. Law, in India as anywhere else, cannot stand apart and seek to enforce its own body of rules, and one would hope that those concerned with the future development of laws in India will be good physicians ready to listen to all the bodies and souls that they claim to be responsible for.

5.3 Legislative overkill

O. V. Abdulkhader

[From: 1986 *KLT*, Journal section, p. 33]

Dr. W. F. Menski at page 17 of 1986 KLT Journal has described the effect of Kerala Act 30/1976 as a case of legislative overkill. According to [the] Concise Oxford Dictionary the word "overkill" means amount by which (capacity for) destruction (lit. or fig.) exceeds what is necessary for victory over or annihilation of [an] enemy. If it is suggested that the Act in question has by extra force removed at one stroke an ancient system, it will be misleading. The Act in fact recognises a long-existing state of affairs in the shape of break-up of joint families, which had really started decades earlier and their supplantation by individual families. The concept of joint family owes its origin to a static social system with a stationary population. From the bullock-cart age of its origin to the present day space age, much has happened in Kerala society as elsewhere. There is no possibility of retracing the steps. With the proliferation of population with perhaps just a family house in ruins as the only joint family asset, the share due to a member was not worth speaking of and the general run of joint family property was of little value, except to the manager!

The accent should be not so much on the legal abolition of the joint family system in Kerala, but on the factual disappearance of it which preceded it. Even when joint family system was flourishing, personal properties existed side by side. And individual families were minding their own affairs, and where such existed augmenting their income with that from the meagre share in joint family assets, at irregular intervals. One cannot, however, overlook some recent disturbing trends in society. With the passage of time religious and moral attitudes to life are giving place to irreligious and a-moral forces. Consider the increasing prevalence of suicides among all communities. The waning of influence of religious and moral inhibitions, if not arrested by inculcation from birth of proper outlook on life and universe, will lead to other vices, which are the bane of western society.

If advocates from Kerala have been indifferent to the impact of Act 30/76, the reason has to be sought in a historical setting. For one thing even before effecting formal partition, at least within living memory, the rule had been to set separate individual residences. And most of joint properties had got partitioned by the seventies. For another, the operation of the *Land Reforms Act* sounded a death-knell to the joint family system by vesting tenanted lands in the cultivating tenants in absolute right and by causing surrender of excess lands in direct possession. Joint family assets were mostly in agricultural and forest lands. Joint families owning private forests came to grief with the enactment of the *Private Forests Vesting and Assignment Act* 1971. Act 30/76 came, one may submit, at the close of this period of reforms and was only a piece of consequential legislation in Kerala.

Yet it has worked hardship in an unforeseen way. Dr. Menski has given an inkling of this problem. This writer submits that Act 30/76 has had the effect of obliterating Marumakkathayam and Aliyasanthana system of inheritance and enthroning the remaining provisions of the *Hindu Succession Act*, as suggested by this writer in 1983 KLT Journal 43. Though the ostensible idea behind the Act was only abolition of joint family system, its collateral effect has been damaging to certain classes of Marumakkathayi and Aliyasanthana heirs in some situations. But few in Kerala will regret the legal passing of [the] joint family system.

5.4 Legislative overkill – A rejoinder

[From: 1986 *KLT*, Journal section, pp. 63–65]

At p. 33 of 1986 KLT Journal our learned friend Shri O. V. Abdulkhader has commented on my discussion of Act 30 of 1976, which is found at 1986 KLT Journal, p. 17. I agree that by speaking of "overkill" I have used a rather drastic expression, but have I overstated what I wanted to say? The reality of what has happened here is drastic!

The learned commentator suggests that the joint family system of Kerala was virtually dead before it was abolished by the legislature. In other words, the "legislative overdose" merely finished off a little mouse that was already old and very weak and was on the point of dying anyway. As a piece of "consequential legislation" Act 30 of 1976 looks logical in the view of the commentator, almost as an inevitable consequence of progressive legal development. But let us reflect further on what has happened.

First of all, I did not suggest that Act 30 of 1976 has "by extra force removed at one stroke an ancient system" and I am sorry if I have been misunderstood. On the contrary, I maintain that the said Act may purport to have abolished the joint family system among the Hindus of Kerala, but de facto this system continues to exist, and we cannot just close our eyes and point to the legal document itself.

This assertion would seem to be in total opposition to Shri Abdulkhader's position. But the difficulty is rather easily resolved: we seem to be speaking different languages, and use different concepts to describe one and the same reality. The evidence that my commentator presents about the disappearance of the joint family system in Kerala is, of course, a lawyer's view of the world, expressed in legal language. When I spoke to lawyers in Kerala, indeed the very same picture emerged. But as soon as I ventured out of the legal chambers, I received a consistently very different picture: there can be no doubt that the joint Hindu family continues to exist in Kerala, in a variety of forms. What has happened and here I totally concur with my learned friend from Tellicherry, is that the large joint Hindu families have been breaking up and are now virtually non-existent. Shri Abdulkhader very rightly points out the various other legislative measures that have contributed to this development and have speeded up the process of dissolution of large joint Hindu families.

But what is a joint family? Let us speak one language here and not disagree over fundamentals. Professor Derrett spends much time discussing what would be a minimum number of persons to constitute a joint Hindu family. Surely it does not have to be a large clan!

If we take an average family, of father, mother and their children, all Hindus, this is, legally speaking, a joint Hindu family. But sociologists call this a nuclear family and it appears that many legislators did not see the difference. I do not think it could be argued that such joint families (no doubt they continue to exist in Kerala today) are not affected by Act 30 of 1976. So here is a crucial factor that has been overlooked in our discussion so far, and I am grateful to my commentator for pointing this out. So when he concludes that "few in Kerala will regret the legal passing of joint family system", I think we have to understand that few (or few lawyers?) in Kerala will regret the legal passing of the large joint Hindu families.

Directly from this point, of course, follows my argumentation of 'overkill'. Legislative eagerness to limit the influence of the large joint families has also swept away, by what I would call a legal fiction, the small joint family. If I may venture a prediction here, such families will continue to exist, no matter what the modern law has to say on this point. The same system continues among 'Asians' in Britain, despite non-recognition by the common law, as a very recent study by one of my students has conclusively shown. But the system does not survive without change, it adapts to new circumstances, among which there may be reformed legal provisions. How these processes of adaptation work would be interesting to look at in the context of the Kerala joint family systems. I concur with Shri Abdulkhader in emphasising that far-reaching consequences may result from Act 30 of 1976 for members of Marumakkathayam and Aliyasanthana joint families. Again, the argument has been advanced there that the process of change pre-dated legal reform, but the case is far too complex to be discussed here.

Let us now turn to the second important aspect of the overkill syndrome in the case of Act 30 of 1976. What this Act sought to abolish were certain traditional ties existing between members of joint Hindu families, really their interdependence in terms of property rights. By creating, no doubt not for the first time, an individualistic pattern of property ownership, the modern legislation also impaired, but luckily not yet destroyed, other aspects of joint family life, above all family solidarity. One gets a distinct feeling, though, that the 'enemy', as perceived in the form of tradition, was not merely the joint Hindu family system but the family itself. China, it may be remembered, tried this in her recent past, smashing the power of the clans and making the individual the basic unit of society. But more recent legislation, e.g. the *Marriage Law of the People's Republic* of China, 1980, esp. Articles 15, 22 and 23, again emphasises the importance of family ties and of duties within the family, particularly when it comes to looking after weak and infirm members of the family. The welfare state in modern India and China, so much is clearly visible, exists to a large extent on paper rather than in social reality. In India, the Directive Principles of State Policy are no doubt very impressive and potentially powerful instruments of legal reform, but the very highly idealistic principles do not improve the daily existence of so many millions of people, especially those who are poorest. In this wider context I wanted to emphasise that Act 30 of 1976, must be seen as another piece of programmatic legislation that has been designed, apparently, to rid the country of traditions that are supposed to be outdated and negative for the purposes of the active individual. What I have indeed only indicated so far is the fact that Act 30 of 1976, once officially applied and enforced in its present form, will cause tremendous hardship to weak family members, while it strengthens those egoistic individuals who have the wits and the means to use the legal machinery and provisions for their own ends. As stated before, we do not know sufficiently well what is actually happening out in the country, but commonsense would tell us, and Shri Abdulkhader indicates this too, viz. that very poor people, who may have hardly anything to share, better stand by each other rather than insisting on individual shares. If all a family owns is a hut in ruins, if there are no shares worth speaking of, and perhaps not even a regular income, legal reforms that strengthen the individual will work havoc among the poor. Rather than sharing the little that may be available, the stronger members will assert their position to be detriment of the already downtrodden.

My commentator points to some recent disturbing trends in society. Is he not trying to say the same as I did, both of us in a roundabout way? We both seem to plead for a society in which moral attitudes to life are dominant, in which the individual should be able to find a suitable balance between his or her own needs and those of society, or indeed, of the universe. Such high, idealistic aims are not promoted by legislation that gives ready weapons to greedy individuals. Under the excuse of being 'modern' and 'progressive', such elements are being given further opportunities to destroy the subtle networks of mutual support that a family is able to give in all societies. Shri Abdulkhader speaks of Western societies and their vices in this context. But nobody forces modern India to accept and introduce socially and morally undesirable legislative models imported from abroad. The time may indeed have come now for a critical review of the modern Indian legislators' approach to their function. If, as Professor Derrett at one stage claimed, the bow-tie society of Delhi and other capitals makes laws merely because these suit a particular group of people, who often happen to be the makers of such rules, then it may be time to remind us that India is a country of more than 750 million people, of enormous diversity and gigantic daily needs, and that less legislative interference and more visible action may at times be appropriate. Against many, and mainly Western, predictions India's democratic model is seen to be functioning, but it functions in an Indian way, along novel lines. Significantly, this involves giving much regard to local needs and particular circumstances in individual cases, not dogmatising, centralised rule making on ideological lines. The Kerala villager who happily ignores such legislation as Act 30 of 1976 knows much better than any legislator what is appropriate in his circumstances, no matter how full of idealism and learning the law-maker may be. Act 30 of 1976 is symptomatic of the aspiration of modern legal systems all over the world to regulate all aspects of man's existence. However, while traditional obligation systems are destroyed in this way, the modern system often does not provide for the casualties of such new rules. As I pointed out, who will help Kerala brides to finance their marriages if their brothers refuse their traditional roles? I am not pleading for a return to medieval times, but, to use Shri Abdulkhader's imagery, the slow pace of the bullock cart may be a safer way to ensure survival and harmony than miracle devices of the modern world. Space ships, we have seen, explode in seconds, nuclear power may bring silent disaster even accidentally, excessive mechanisation brings more unemployment, and well-sounding legal reforms may bring human misery rather than better justice. Let Act 30 of 1976 be scrapped, it appears superfluous and contributive to an improper outlook on life.

5.5 Kerala Joint Hindu Family System (Abolition) Act, 1976: Women and society the beneficiaries

Lucy Carroll

[From: 1993(1) *KLT*, Journal section, pp. 45–48]

'Let Act 30 of 1976 be scrapped; it appears superfluous and contributive to an improper outlook on life.' Thus proclaimed Dr. W. F. Menski in an article (1986 KLT J 63 at 65) which has belatedly come to my attention. (See also 1986 KLT 17).

It is more than a little surprising that anyone could possibly talk about the Kerala Act without mentioning the position of the Mitakshara daughter, who even after the *Hindu Succession Act*, 1956, is in a grossly inferior position vis-à-vis a son in regard to rights in or to family property. There are only two ways of dealing with the problem: giving daughters birthrights comparable to those of sons, or abolishing male birthrights. Kerala boldly opted for the latter alternative; this step should be applauded.

Dr. Menski draws attention to what he considers a 'glaring oversight' and 'the most pernicious side-effect of Act 30 of 1976.' (1986 KLT, pp. 18, 19) Postulating a family consisting of father, mother, and two sons on the day the Act came into force, he compares the shares taken by these two sons with that taken by a third subsequently-born son. On the father's death, each of the three sons will take (under the *Hindu Succession Act*) one-fourth of the father's share (assuming his widow is present). By virtue of the partition occasioned by the coming into force of the 1976 Act, the father's share is one-fourth; thus each son takes 1/16. However, the two elder sons who were alive at the time the Act came into force and participated in the partition already have shares of one-fourth each. Thus, while the son born subsequent to the partition takes only 1/16, the two elder sons end up with a total of 5/16 each. This result is neither surprising nor unprecedented; nor is it grounds for scrapping the Act.

Firstly, let it be remembered that the Mitakshara daughter, is under the *Hindu Succession Act*, 1956 in exactly the same position of the son born after the 1976 Act on whom Menski expends such sympathy. While her brothers take from birth a share equal to that of their father, the daughter has no birthright and can only claim, after 1956, a share (with her brothers and mother, if alive) of her father's share.

Secondly, the situation to which Menski draws attention can only happen once; it will only occur in the present generation. The existing sons retain the share they acquired through the birthright; subsequently-born sons, whether of the transitional generation or later generations, do not take shares by right of birth. Only in the transitional generation is it possible that sons in existence on the coming into force of the Act and subsequently-born sons might co-exist together. If the subsequently-born son of the transitional generation takes a share less than he would if he had been lucky enough to be born a generation later, so also does the existing daughter.

Mitakshara daughters benefit not at all in the transitional generation. It might have been more satisfactory if all Mitakshara property could have been distributed per capita to all members of the family, but this was avoided, obviously because such a course would have involved divesting sons who had already acquired rights by birth, a step which would certainly have raised protests and would probably have involved constitutional issues.

Once the partition consequent upon the coming into force of the 1976 Act has taken place, all property passes by succession and sons and daughters will inherit equally on an intestacy. Again Menski's comment that as regards Mitakshara Hindus, 'the ... daughter, as in the rest of India gets no share in the family property unless she becomes an heiress under the provisions of the *Hindu Succession Act*, 1956 (1986 KLT p.18), is unenlightening. The implied criticism or comparison (with Mitakshara sons? with non-Mitakshara daughters?) only applies in the transitional generation. After that, all property will pass by succession. A son, no less than a daughter, will get no share in the family property unless he becomes an heir under the provisions of the *Hindu Succession Act*, 1956.

Thirdly, the situation to which Menski calls attention is far from unique or unusual. It is analogous to what occurs when there is a partition among father and sons during the lifetime of the father and other sons are conceived and born subsequent to the partition. The subsequently-born sons will take considerably less than the sons born before the partition. The result in this case, no less than in the case which so disturbs Menski, might be termed 'a most inequitable form of distribution of the former joint family property ... between male siblings, the criterion being merely the date of birth of the respective individual' with respect to the partition. (1986 KLT p. 19). The possibility that an 'inequitable' share of the former joint family property might go to sons conceived subsequent to a voluntary partition could only be prevented by barring all Mitakshara partitions during the lifetime of the father. I wonder that Menski has not (at least as far as I am aware) suggested such a 'reform'.

From the perspective of the Mitakshara daughter, the distribution of joint family property has *always* been 'inequitable'. The Kerala Act of 1976 remedied this basic defect; that some individuals might suffer a similar *transient* 'inequality' in the transitional generation is the cost of the kind of fundamental reform to which Kerala has courageously committed itself.

Having said all this, it might be worth considering an amendment to the 1976 Kerala Act detailing a special rule of succession to the property of a Mitakshara male who was a co-parcener with sons at the time the 1976 Act came into force and who died leaving *either daughters or after-born sons*. This special rule should give preference to the children (*daughters and after-born sons*) who did not participate in the partition occasioned by the 1976 Act as heirs to the share the father took on that partition and to his self-acquired property, provided that the preferential entitlement would not exceed an amount equivalent to the share that the existing sons had taken on the partition. It should be remembered that according to Mitakshara law prior to the HSA, the son born after a partition was heir to the father's self-acquired property in preference to the separated sons.

I doubt very much that the 1976 Kerala statute was enacted simply or even mainly because 'there were some abuses of the joint family system among Hindus by unscrupulous individuals who took advantages of their positions of power.' (1986 KLT p. 20.) Surely a major thrust behind the legislation was that there was simply no other effective way of guaranteeing the right of the Mitakshara daughter to an equitable share of patrimony.

The ouster of daughters was something that happened routinely, in every Mitakshara family; it was not a matter affecting only a 'few' such families; the *Hindu Succession Act* had done little to redress the situation. By 1976 the virtual exclusion of the Mitakshara daughter could simply no longer be justified. This is a question that Mitakshara Hindus in other parts of India are going to have to deal with sooner rather than later. As befitting a progressive state with a highly literate populace, Kerala has shown the way.

Dr. Menski professes concern for the daughter whose 'egoistic' brother may not be willing to contribute toward her marriage expenses. (1986 KLT pp. 18, 65) To a large extent this is again a problem confined to the transitional generation, involving the daughter who did not get a share when the property was partitioned among the coparceners upon the coming into force of the 1976 Act; S. 4(1) of the Act expressly attempts to protect her.

As for future generations, as long as her father is alive, the girl's brothers have no claim on his property; if her father is dead, she will have inherited a share equivalent to that taken by her brother. Hopefully, she will be more practical and more far-sighted than to waste money on frivolous and extravagant celebrations designed more to glorify her kinsmen than to contribute to the welfare of the bride, the matrimonial couple, or their children.

Whether because her father has access to a smaller purse and/or because the girl herself has more to say about precisely how the money is spent and/or because her brothers are less willing to dip into their own pockets, the Kerala Act may be expected to mitigate wasteful and extravagant expenditure on marriages and dowries. I have previously argued (e.g. in a paper presented at the University of Texas, Austin, 2 April 1986) that the problem of dowry cannot and will not be resolved until the question of equalising the daughter's rights in the patrimony is directly addressed. In the absence of such fundamental reform, the attempt to render illegal dowry transactions is to negate even further the daughter's rights in her family of birth. While it would be a gross over-simplification to suggest that exclusion from inheritance is the single cause of the dowry system as it presently exists in India, the problem of dowry must be seen in the context of other property rights of the daughter, and criticism and condemnation of the dowry system must be coupled with advocacy of reform of the daughter's rights as an heir to the property of her natal family. Again, Kerala's dramatic step in abolishing male birthrights in Mitakshara joint family property can only be applauded.

To the extent that the Kerala statute recognises daughters as equal, and equally important and valuable, members of the family as sons; and to the extent that it discourages extravagant and wasteful expenditure and mitigates the dowry evil, it certainly cannot be said to be either 'superfluous' or 'contributive to an improper outlook on life.' (1986 KLT p. 65.) Precisely the opposite!

The matter that concerns me about the 1976 Act is that henceforth, there being no birthrights, all of the father's property will pass on his death under the *Hindu Succession Act*. This means that daughters and sons inherit equally – if the father dies intestate. But there is no restriction on the power of a Hindu to will away his property as he pleases. By disposing of his entire property by will in favour of his son, a father could effectively disinherit his daughter.

Here Muslim law offers a solution – and in evolving a Uniform Civil Code, the potential contributions on offer from this impressive corpus of legal thought and jurisprudence should not be under-estimated. (An example already incorporated into law is the 'option of puberty' clause added to the *Hindu Marriage Act* in 1976. See Lucy Carroll, 'Muslim family law in South Asia: The right to avoid an arranged marriage contracted during minority,' *Journal of the Indian Law Institute*, 23 (1981): 149–180). In Muslim law an individual may not dispose of more than one-third of his estate by means of a will without the concurrence of his heirs. Sunnis take the matter a step further and ban all bequests in favour of an heir (even within the one-third limit) without the concurrence of the other heirs.

The Kerala legislators would do well to consider amending the *Hindu Succession Act* so as to impose limits on the testate power of Hindus in order to ensure that the rights given to the daughter by one hand are not taken away by another.

5.6 Egoism versus family solidarity: Women's property rights in Kerala

[From: 1993(2) *KLT*, Journal section, pp. 45–48]

At 1993(1) *KLT*, J 45–48, Dr. Lucy Carroll argues that I have disregarded the legitimate claims and concerns of the Mitakshara Hindu daughter while criticising some of the effects of the *Kerala Joint Hindu Family System (Abolition) Act*, 1975. Surely, one could have said more about the daughter, but what I wrote a few years ago was based on extensive fieldwork in Kerala in 1985/86, focused on the lack of fit between the officially declared urban-based law and 'people's law' in the villages. There was, as far as I could see, no evidence of concern on the part of the urban lawmakers about the rights of the Mitakshara daughter. At any rate, in Kerala there are other kinds of Hindu daughters who have traditionally had better rights.

Clearly, some of the problems that my fieldwork identified are of a transitional nature and are not unique; pointing them out was designed to show that a modern Act that seeks to strengthen individualism, and thus egoism, causes some new difficulties that the lawmakers may not have anticipated. That the new law would not work in favour of weaker members of society, including women and children, was probably clear from the start: the 1975 Act seems to have been passed to protect propertied interests, not for the benefit of the poor. Talking to villagers in 1986, I learnt that, in their view, individualising law reforms cannot trigger off that precious human quality, concern for others; it may actually damage it beyond retrieval. The traditional status-based system, on the other hand, emphasising duties rather than rights, appeared to guarantee women a better deal, since the men were under moral pressure to fulfill their obligations.

I would have been glad to find evidence that the legislators who created the 1975 Act actually had a significant improvement of the position of Kerala's women in mind. But there was no such evidence. Maybe among the numerous readers of the KLT there are some persons who can enlighten us on this. As far as I know, Dr. Carroll is wrong to simply assert that a major thrust behind the 1975 Act must have been a will to improve the lot of the Mitakshara daughter. If that had been so, the law could have offered Mitakshara daughters a better deal and Kerala could have opted, as Andhra Pradesh has done, by the *Hindu Succession* (*Andhra Pradesh Amendment*) Act of 1985, for making daughters totally equal to sons as coparceners. Abolishing the birthright, in Kerala, did not indicate an explicit need or desire to assist women, the reform focused on male interests as far as Mitakshara Hindus in the state were concerned. Significantly, the Act itself is silent on this issue, nor have the cases under this Act made explicit policy comments in this regard.

This shows that it does not help our understanding of South Asian family laws if European or North American lawyers expound on such matters from an armchair perspective. Socio-legal realities in South Asia continue to have their own flavour and, this was a major result of the Kerala case study, may develop quite differently from the officially stated law.

The concern that I professed for the daughters was voiced by my informants during village fieldwork in 1986. The issue is certainly not a transitional problem, it is at the core of South Asian family arrangements about property matters. Imagine a basically landless family – all too common now – that owns a few cents with a house on it and perhaps some coconut trees. The parents have several children, boys and girls, and want to arrange the marriage of a daughter. Which form of state law will help this family to have a 'decent wedding'? For poor people, too, this now seems to be a wedding on which you spend in the region of Rs. 10,000/-. My fieldwork shows that the arrangements made by families in such circumstances disregard individual property rights; family solidarity is the need of the hour. Thus, uncles, sons and brothers are called upon, the latter ultimately to the extent of being unable to marry till well into their thirties. The obligation to assist a sister in getting married clearly overrides the egoistic concerns of the male.

It is too simplistic for a Western legal scholar, however feminist and outspoken, to denigrate the South Asian marriage systems as 'frivolous and extravagant celebrations designed more to glorify her kinsmen than to contribute to the welfare of the bride.', as Dr. Carroll stated (p. 47). Western egocentric hybris may see Indian weddings as wasteful, but how can one object to people's desire to 'marry in style' in principle? For the majority of people, this is still a once-in-a-lifetime occasion that needs to be celebrated and auspiciously completed. There is certainly some scope for economising in many cases, but what is extravagant and frivolous about giving a simple little party to relatives and neighbours, which is all a poor family can afford? People the world over, unless they merely cohabit, indulge in such 'frivolous' feasting. Poor Keralites, too, in their own small way, take their marriages very seriously as important family affairs. Lest we restrict marriage to the sterile procedure of signing a contract, which no legal system in the world has achieved to the total exclusion of all other forms of marriage, who are we Western scholars to deny South Asians their claim to have this probably most important rite of passage marked in a socially meaningful way?

Using so many words here, I am not excusing excesses of the dowry problem for a moment. However, we should never forget that dowry, apparently, becomes only a matter of concern when there is breakdown of relations between the participating families. Nobody takes rich people to court, simply for giving and taking a huge dowry. Celebrating one's marriage and the dowry problem are not exactly the same issue and it is fundamentally wrong to assume that all Indian marriages involve a dowry of some kind or another. In this context, I see the Keralite 'donation' that the bride's side is expected to make as a contribution to the expenses of the wedding, admittedly a form of dowry, but not the one that causes the legal problems that North Indians, in particular, are so familiar with.

Dr. Carroll very rightly emphasises the fundamental connection between dowry and women's property. While they are intimately linked, there is no simple legal solution to either problem. Blaming Indians for wasting money on marriage is certainly not a constructive approach. What has the modern law to offer here?

My evidence from Kerala in 1986, confirmed in 1992, was quite clear on this. A legal improvement of the daughter's property rights would only be of help if there is substantial property to distribute. At any rate, at the time of marriage it is not the daughter who pays for her marriage, but her natal family. Thus, the people's law saves daughters, as my informants so clearly indicated, from being deprived of a decent wedding. Brothers, uncles, everyone will rally round to bear and share the burden. If a daughter or sister has all this done for her, how then can she sit back and insist on a separate share of property as well? My apprehension, expressed in 1986, that giving women their own property rights may leave them on their own when it comes to bearing the marriage expenses, has been confirmed by more recent fieldwork.

Here, as elsewhere, Western women's concerns are out of fit with the realities of South Asian societies. The Hindu daughter cannot have it both ways, and I doubt whether many women in Kerala would take Dr. Carroll's path of claiming separate property rights and foregoing the enjoyments of an 'extravagant' marriage and the solidarity of their family. Elsewhere, Asians in Britain included, women are known to renounce their shares in favour of male relatives, in exchange for goodwill and solidarity in times of need. Of course, this gives them a position of moral strength, but the Mitakshara system embodies that same moral principle. If this is unpalatable to modern feminists, so be it.

I have not come across any evidence to suggest that the Kerala Act of 1975 has, as speculated by Dr. Carroll, mitigated wasteful and extravagant expenditure on marriage and dowries. Again, it would be most welcome if readers of the KLT could enlighten us on this point. The question would be whether some families now make conscious decisions to spend less on marriage because individual property rights have reduced willingness to share and to contribute. Perhaps some bright students could apply their minds to this.

Dr. Carroll also, and rightly, alerts us to the scope for male deviousness in willing away property to disinherit Hindu females. One fails to see, though, how recourse to Islamic law can offer a realistic remedy that will work in practice. Muslim women, too, complain of being disinherited, despite the clear stipulations of Qur'anic shares. The political gesture of copying another rule of Muslim law into Hindu law, or into the illusory uniform civil code provisions, would be quite pleasant. But where is the meaningful remedy for women faced with male chauvinism and greed? As indicated, legislation *per se* is of limited value.

Here, a secular judicial approach in Kerala shows some promise. What we need is astute judges and judicial alertness to the plight of women, not more legislation, however refined. In *Lakshmi v. Valliyammal*, 1992(2) KLT 873, we find a case under s. 39 of the *Transfer of Property Act*, 1882 (clearly a secular Act) which illustrates the scope for judicial creativity, which is now so prominent in Indian cases concerning maintenance for women and children.

This is actually a Hindu *Shah Bano* situation. An unpleasant old man had alienated his property to defeat his wife's claim to maintenance. He had simply given it to a younger mistress. The older woman, whose claim as wife is disputed in revolting fashion, had grown old bearing nine children and found herself deprived of financial support. Mr. Justice Balasubramanyan of the Kerala High Court astutely ruled that the husband's gift to his lover was vitiated by the clear intention to defeat the old lady's claim for maintenance. Thus, the wife had a charge upon the properties of the husband. Lawyers will note the good use made here of the leading case of *V. Tulasamma*, AIR 1977 SC 1944, which can be applied to all Hindu females and would, thus, assist a Mitakshara daughter in peril. I venture to suggest that this case could even assist a Hindu daughter where her egoistic brothers have decided that they cannot contribute to her marriage expenses.

In conclusion, if we want to fix our gaze on formal equality between the sexes, we may have to bear with encouraged egoism. Recent developments in various areas of Indian law concerning the property rights of women show that an unambiguous recognition of legal inequality works, in fact, to the advantage of women. Alert judges rather than pompous legislators or Western scholars can be the most efficient protectors of the legitimate financial interests of Indian women. As so often, the judiciary in Kerala has been playing a leading role in this process, emphasising moral obligations over the cold and sterile concept of legal rights.

5.7 Matrilineal succession law in Kerala: An aborted challenge to women's property rights

[From: 1993(2) *KLT*, Journal section, pp. 50–56]

The issue in its wider context

In the important recent test case of *Chellamma Kamalamma*, 1993(1) KLT 174 FB, a Full Bench of the Kerala High Court led by Jagannadha Rao, CJ was called upon to consider whether two earlier decisions by the same court, reported in *Madhavi Amma*, 1988(2) KLT 964 and *Bhaskaran*, 1990(2) KLT 749 were correct. In the earlier cases, the respective judges had held, without much explanation, that s. 17 of the *Hindu Succession Act*, 1956 (HSA) has not been rendered inoperative after the coming into force of the *Kerala (Hindu Joint Family System Abolition) Act* of 1975 (the 1975 Act), which had, no doubt, abolished the joint Hindu family law in the state of Kerala.

The test case concerns succession to the property of a female Hindu from a matrilineal community. Typically, where the deceased woman died childless, the succession struggle is between her mother, on the one hand, claiming inheritance based on matrilineal principles, and the deceased's husband on the other, whose claim arises from patrilineal principles. The simple facts in *Chellamma Kamalamma*, 1993(1) KLT 174 FB gave no rise to any dispute. But which law applied to those facts after the death of a Marumakkathayi female from Kerala?

Since the HSA made special provisions for succession in matrilineal communities, s. 17 of that Act has the effect of preferring the mother's right to that of the husband. Not surprisingly in our male-dominated world, the representatives of the patrilineal principle have again gone to great lengths to defeat the female principle. But they have lost the battle, at least so far, and for some good reasons. My argument here is that the majority verdict of the Kerala High Court in *Chellamma Kamalamma*, 1993(1) KLT 174B looks shaky on purely legal technical grounds, but that it is correct and highly appropriate as far as the social consequences of the decision are concerned.

Regrettably, the lawyers and judges involved in *Chellamma Kamalamma's* case got so carried away and partly side-tracked in their fine-tuned legal argumentation that they overlooked the wider social and political implications of the decision they were called upon to produce. At least the case report does not disclose any such concerns, which may well have arisen in the elaborate opinions provided by three senior members of the Kerala Bar (see p. 181 of the case report).

If the purpose of certain sections of the HSA, prominently sections 7 and 17, was to save various aspects of matrilineal family law in India, prevalent in South India, with the famed Marumakkathayam system the most prominent among them, any decision that renders those sections ineffective would simply kill off the matrilineal legal systems of India, at least in Kerala. If that is the price we are prepared to pay for legal uniformity, so be it; as always, I have grave reservations about such an overzealous reformist approach. Firstly, it damages the property rights of women and their dependants and strengthens the already superior rights of men. Thus, to declare s. 17 HSA ineffective changes the balance in favour of men and the male principle, which cannot be constitutionally sound, nor socially acceptable in many families of South India. Further, weakening (if not abolishing) the matrilineal principles of succession will impose, on the matrilineal families of Kerala at any rate, the North Indian system of succession, which is not really alien, but has radically different effects, as the cases show all to clearly.

The hidden political dimension

What we need to understand, then, is that the current struggle over the effectiveness of s. 17 HSA is also an eminently political matter, in terms of gender politics as well as the Indian struggles over legal uniformity. Courts are probably wise not to indicate this in so many words. In the present case, though, it seems that legal technicalities have taken up all mental energy. This is not healthy. From the study of the High Court cases before us, it seems that the various advocates have narrowly concerned themselves with their clients' interest. The judges, too, have addressed their minds to many legal niceties and appear to have shut out any consideration of the wider dimensions. *Chellamma Kamalamma*, 1993(1) KLT 174 FB, certainly represents a serious attempt to solve the current conundrum and is a typical test case, but it could have said a bit more about the socio-legal dimensions of the issue. Without this, as I shall show below, our basic understanding of the law itself may suffer.

Thus, to hold now that s. 17 HSA is rendered ineffective – we shall see that s. 7 HSA has already been ineffective since 1976 – would mean to impose North Indian succession law on those South Indians that used to live by a radically different tradition. This ex-post re-writing of the HSA goes too far, in my view, since it wipes away the legal safeguards for South Indian patterns of inheritance and succession in the HSA, which was designed as an all-India law, explicitly taking account of legal diversity. Within it, South Indian laws and traditions are just as valid and valuable as North Indian ones. Even though the trend worldwide goes against matrilineal systems (see various examples in African countries, whether Tanzania or Ghana), there is no logical reason for this. It simply reflects the continuing onslaught of male chauvinism and brash North Indian-style principles that see women as the property of men.

Surely, if the *Hindu Marriage Act*, 1955 can explicitly save South Indian marriage customs in sections 5(iv) and 5(v), as well as by implication in sections 7 and 29(2), then the HSA must retain similar mechanisms to allow continuity for the various South Indian matrilineal systems of succession.

The fatal flaw in the understanding of Marumakkathayam law

I have warned repeatedly, at 1986 KLT J 17–20, 1986 KLT J 63–65 and now at 1993(2) KLT J 45 that the *Kerala* (*Hindu Joint Family System Abolition*) *Act* of 1975 took too little account of the social dimension and the implications of the legal reforms brought about by that Act. Is this another example of a miraculous wonderdrug with disastrous side-effects (see 1990(2) KLT J 3–10)? If it is now argued that the 1975 Act has rendered whole important sections of the HSA otiose, some thinking has to be started over the social consequences of such wide-ranging legal changes that were, surely, not anticipated by the eager law-makers in the 1970s.

In my writing so far, I have been complaining about the lack of fit between the officially passed law and the rules that Kerala villagers continue to apply to themselves. In this situation, it may pay off to go to court and to challenge the continued application of traditional law. Clearly, such acts of egoism are not restricted to male litigants, though it must be said that behind female claimants there are mostly male lawyers. Thus, the stubbornness of female claimants, such as in *Madhavi Amma*, 1988(2) KLT 964, seems to be a major factor leading us now to very interesting and controversial questions concerning the position of the official law itself.

The current controversy has focused entirely on the official law and has led to interesting but quite confused legal arguments. At first sight, it is indeed the correct position, as now authoritatively restated by the learned Chief Justice in *Chellamma Kamalamma*, 1993(1) KLT 174 FB, at pp. 192 and 193, that all joint Hindu family law of Kerala stands abolished with effect from 1–12–1976. But there is a fatal flaw in this reasoning. What precisely is the Marumakkathayam law? As correctly noted throughout the judgment, the 1975 Act affected the various Hindu joint family laws and turned all jointly owned property into individually owned shares. But has this change in the law also affected those parts of the Marumakkathayam law which are concerned with succession to individual property? With respect, the statement of the learned Chief Justice that no part of the Marumakkathayam law can be said to be in existence after 1–12–1976 (p. 193) cannot be correct. The Marumakkathayam law in Kerala is still alive, and long may it live! But it is now restricted to rules concerning succession to individual property. S. 17 HSA applies precisely to such property only, not to joint family property.

Clarifying the law

When I started my research for this article, I focused (as almost always) on the social dimensions of the legal problem, developing the working hypothesis that in succession struggles a good law should ensure gender equity. I appreciate that busy mainstream lawyers may not be interested in resolving the conflicts between official law and real local practice, but now the nature of the official law itself has come under scrutiny in the courts of Kerala and no lawyer can afford to ignore the issue: Has the 1975 Kerala Act really rendered s. 17 of the *Hindu Succession Act,* 1956 otiose and ineffective, thus depriving matrilineal families of their old-established rules on all kinds of succession?

What we witness here is confusion among the law makers and the legal profession about what actually is the law that was official passed. This problem, although by no means unique, seems particularly acute in the Indian family law set up, where legislation (and case law, for that matter) may be produced at central and state level, but it is potentially an issue in every legal system. While the doctrine of precedent is supposed to take care of conflicting positions taken by courts at different levels, in the realm of legislature there is much scope for confusion. More often than not, the legislators have not considered the implications and side-effects of a new enactment, so that we find bad drafting and inconsistencies in the law, requiring judicial intervention.

But the current Kerala problem is not quite of this kind, it would seem. When the 1975 Act was created, one was clearly concerned to abolish the incidents of the joint Hindu family in the state and to provide for separate ownership of property rather than joint family sharing. Out went the birthright and aspects of the pious obligation, in came the strengthened notion of individual property rights. Following on from this, the next step must be a succession regime that concerns itself with allocating shares in a deceased individual's property to the right claimants.

Precisely here lies the problem for Kerala. As correctly stated in the test case, the 1975 Act does not really cover succession, it only concerns the abolition of the joint family holdings. Any legal disputes over succession are still referred to under the regime of the relevant central Act, which is the *Hindu Succession Act*, 1956. The central issue for Kerala (and, in some respects, adjacent states) concerns rights of inheritance to females from the matrilineal systems of Hindu law, mainly those governed by the Marumakkathayam law. After Marumakkathyam law has virtually been abolished by the 1975 Act in Kerala, and s. 7 HSA has been rendered ineffective to that extent, has s. 17 of the HSA also lost its relevance for Keralites?

In a nutshell, the argument for the male principle has been this: S. 17 HSA makes special provisions respecting persons governed by Marumakkathayam and Aliyasanthana laws, but such persons do no longer exist in Kerala; thus s. 17 is now ineffective. This argument, as Mr. Justice Radhakrishna Menon has said in *Madhavi Amma,* 1988(2) KLT 964, at 966), is "really attractive". The learned judge, then, came to the conclusion that s. 7 of the 1975 Act "has no manner of impact on the order of succession prescribed under S. 17 of the Succession Act" (p. 967), but he did not tell us why this should be so.

In this case, the mother of a deceased man was trying to appropriate the whole of his inheritance for herself, though her son was married and had left a widow who, however, followed him to the heavenly abode a week later. The couple being childless, the heirs of the deceased male under s. 8 HSA were his mother and his widow, both taking an equal half share. This was not a share in real estate, rather a certain amount of insurance money, which would not have been worked out by the time the widow herself died. The mother-in-law, seeing a chance for quick enrichment, one must suspect, sought to claim the entire insurance amount for herself, while a female relative of the deceased widow – her identity is not further specified in the case report – claimed the widow's half share exclusively for herself as an heir under s. 17 of the HSA, 1956.

In support of the mother-in-law's claim, her lawyers resorted to the new situation created by the 1975 Act in Kerala. I am not sure whether it is the first case in which this point has been argued; whoever invented it deserves much credit for originality. The deaths having occurred in 1982, the petitioner's lawyers simply said that there were no Marumakkathayis in Kerala after the abolition of the system by the 1975 Act. Thus s. 17 of the HSA could not apply, instead the succession was governed by s. 15 HSA and his client was entitled to the full insurance amount. For, in accordance with the provisions of s. 15 HSA, in the absence of offspring, the property of a female Hindu dying intestate would devolve upon the heirs of the husband, here the greedy mother-in-law to the exclusion of all other claimants.

On the other hand, if one applied s. 17 HSA, then a rather different sequence of statutory heirs comes into play: the heirs of the husband have been relegated to the last slot in the section, while preference is given to the heirs of the mother. This is how the female relative of the deceased widow in *Madhavi Amma*, 1988(2) KLT 964, came in as a claimant. She ultimately won her case for a half share in the insurance amount because the learned single Judge found that s. 17 of the HSA had not been affected by s. 7 of the 1975 Kerala Act. In other words, s. 17 of the HSA continues to protect matrilineal based inheritance rights where these are relevant.

The test case of *Chellamma Kamalamma*, 1993(1) KLT 174 FB, questioned the correctness of this verdict as well as the decision made by a bench of two judges in *Bhaskaran*, 1990(2) KLT 749.

In this case, Ramakrishna J spent more time on the interpretation of certain non-statutory insurance regulations and the definition of 'family' than on the question that concerns us here. But he made an unequivocal decision, without referring to *Madhavi Amma*, 1988(2) KLT 964, to the effect that s.7 of the 1975 Act in Kerala "does not in any manner interfere with the mode of succession reflected in S.17 of the Hindu Succession Act" (p. 754). The court, therefore, rejected an appeal by a husband whose wife had died childless in 1978, against the lower courts decision to make the deceased's mother the sole heir under s. 17 of the HSA. Of course, the application of s. 15 HSA, as claimed by the husband, would have made him the sole heir. Though there is not as much as an inkling of social comment in this case, it needs to be emphasised how radically different the two alternatives before the court were. In my view, to find in favour of the female principle is the socially correct and preferable approach. A Marumakkathayi marrying a woman from this community should know that he neither owns his wife, nor her property.

Thus, both cases discussed above uphold and protect the preferential inheritance rights for women or heirs claiming through women in Kerala. I can find no fault with this either in terms of gender equality, nor legislative policy. It would surely be a retrograde step if Kerala's laws were to deprive matrilineal people of their old-established rights that provide a viable counterbalance to male domination.

This does not mean that the abolition of the joint family systems in Kerala as from 1–12–1976 was, per se, a bad thing, though I have my reservations. Traditions, where it causes social problems, may legitimately be curtailed or even superseded. Thus, to turn all property into absolutely owned shares was the most important effect of the 1975 Act; readers will have to make up their own minds whether this was good or bad.

Now, to what extent should this important change in the law have any effects on the various regimes of succession that prevail in Kerala? Without doubt, what the 1975 Act has abolished are the joint family aspects of Marumakkathayam law. Thus, there is no more joint family property to distribute, and s. 7 of the HSA, 1956 has indeed been rendered ineffective since 1–12–1976 for Kerala Hindus; there simply are no longer any shares in this kind of joint Hindu family property to distribute. This issue may be regarded as clearly settled.

What about s. 17 of the HSA, though? Like sections 8, 10 and 15 of the HSA, s. 17 applies to separate property only. The class of persons who owns such property was increased by millions of Kerala Hindus on 1–12–1976, precisely the new owners of separate shares that the 1975 Act gave to everyone who had an interest in joint family property that would otherwise have passed under s. 7 HSA. Surely it goes too far to argue now that the basis for the application of s. 17 HSA has been legislated away by the 1975 Act because it abolished the Marumakkathayam law in its entirety?

The socio-legal argument here, as far as Kerala is concerned, must be that the law-makers, in this case the judges, should uphold the rights of the matrilineal people of Kerala to inherit through females rather than males on account of the principle of non-discrimination. The legal argument, I would suggest is that the Marumakkathayam law (like the Mitakshara law, of course) is composed not only of a system of joint family property law, but contains also rules on the ownership of, and succession to, individual property. The rules of the Marumakkathayam law of Kerala regarding succession to individual property have clearly not been affected by the 1975 Act. Thus, the argument that s. 17 HSA does no longer apply to the Marumakkathayis of Kerala must be faulty, since the Marumakkathayam law of Kerala, though only as far as its rules concerning individual property and succession are concerned, is still fully alive. That these rules are heavily influenced by family, local and caste custom will be known throughout the state. That most people will, therefore, find amicable settlements within their community and without recourse to the state courts, is also clear. Lawyers acting for greedy individuals who think they can exploit the current legal insecurity should beware: To argue that s. 17 of the HSA has been rendered entirely ineffective is not going to lead them anywhere. The attempted total abolition of the Marumakkathayam system has simply not happened. An important part of that law is still alive, and long may it live!

If the above argument is correct, the five categories of potential claimants listed by Jagannadha Rao, CJ in *Chellama Kamalamma*, 1993(1) KLT 174 FB, at p. 193 need to be looked at afresh. Categories (i) and (iii) are clearly governed by s. 17 HSA, but what is the position of heirs to persons governed by Marumakkathayam law, whether living on 18–6–1956 (when the HSA came into force) or born on or after that date, who died on or after 1–12–1976, when the 1975 Kerala Act came into force? The learned Chief Justice has correctly argued that it is not difficult to identify this class of persons (see p. 194). He then goes on to state that "such persons once identified need not, in our view, continue to be governed by the Marumakkathyam law on their death" (p. 194). My view would be, as stated above, that such persons continue to be governed by Marumakkathayam law as far as it refers to individual property. Thus, once the class of persons has been identified, succession to their property can be regulated as laid down in s. 17 HSA, as before the passing of the 1975 Act. This means, by implication, that also succession to Marumakkathayis born on or after 1–12–1976 continues to be governed by s. 17 HSA. Obviously, in their case it can only be separate property that falls for succession.

To hold, as the learned Chief Justice does in effect (see p. 200), that his fifth category of persons has already irrevocably lost its claim to inheritance under s. 17, might seek to avoid the harshness of the sudden death of the Marumakkathayam system on 1–12–1976 and the envisaged ineffectiveness of s. 17 HSA. Instead, it would mean slow death for the Marumakkathayam system and s. 17 HSA, as the class of persons born after 1–12–1976 naturally increases, while the older class can no longer be replenished and will gradually die off. Thus, the application of s. 17 HSA would only cease when the last Marumakkathayi Keralite born before 1–12–1976 has died. The argument of the learned Chief Justice, then, gives a limited lease of life, as it were, to the continued application of s. 17 HSA and the Marumakkathyam system in Kerala. I have already shown that this argument cannot be maintained due to the lack of distinction between the joint family property and individual property dimensions of Marumakkathayam law.

The Marumakkathayam law lives on

Thus, I find neither the majority view in *Chellamma Kamalamma*, 1993(1) KLT 174 FB, nor at all the dissenting view given by Krishnamoorthy J doing justice to the problem posed before the court. Considering the wider context of this difficult problem, the law must come to a conclusion that helps the women of Kerala and upholds the matrilineal traditions of this great state. It is not a matter of recent sociological enlightenment that women tend to be deprived of legal rights by official legal systems that work on Upendra Baxi's principle of 'the long purses' deciding the law. The learned judges in *Madhavi Amma*, 1988(2) KLT 964 and *Bhaskaran*, 1990(2) KLT 749, have done a splendid job to defend women's rights, though that was not what their judgments tell us. It is entirely proper that a superior court should examine the correctness of such verdicts, but wider issues of socio-legal policy making must inform such decisions. Law, do we need to be remained, is more than a technical craft. To some extent, one can read *Chellamma Kamalamma*, 1993(1) KLT 174 FB as an example of the waste of precious judicial time by lawyer-induced obfuscations. At the end of the day, the solution seems so simple, but we must admit that we have learnt from aberrant arguments. To follow them could have ruined the social fabric of Kerala society.

In a constitutional democracy supposedly based on equal rights, there is every justification for having two or more principles of succession side by side. In Kerala, the 1975 Act abolished all joint family interests, not just the matrilineal ones, leaving the field entirely to individual property rights. The matrilineal principle of succession to individual property, even though it may hurt men, is alive and well in Kerala, though it seems for the moment buried under the rubble of *Chellamma Kamalamma's* case. The Marumakkathayam law, I was glad to find, is not entirely dead.

5.8 Joint family law in India today

The traditional scenario

Under the older law on the joint family, the concerns of men appeared to be predominant, but one could just as well argue that the concerns of the family group were always put above the interests of any individual.[24] In the old Mitakshara law, men alone were participants in the joint family coparcenary. This gave them rights, but also important duties towards others in the family. The coparcenary was the group of males, linked through common blood particles, who partook in the joint family property in equal shares. Women and children, on the other hand, had claims to maintenance and support on this joint family. Male children, thus, were at once coparceners,[25] as well as being entitled to the fullest possible support of the family. This demonstrates and confirms the manifest importance of legal rules on guardianship (see Derrett 1970: 172–192).

The respective shares of the males as coparceners, with the birth of new members and the death of others, represented a constantly fluctuating interest through the birth right and the principle of 'survivorship'. The extent of shares might never be worked out 'by metes and bounds' if the family remained joint and no partition occurred. The birth right, however, turned into a pious obligation if the family had debts. A Hindu male could not more or less politely decline a negative inheritance, he had to bear and share the burden.[26]

The extent of individual interests might have to be ascertained if there was a formal partition. Here some interesting questions come into play. For example, is it beneficial for a man to produce lots of sons, so that his branch of the family will be given more property than others? Or should partition take place per branch, rather than per head? As always, and prominently under Anglo-Indian law, lawyers were kept in bread by arguing both positions.[27]

The latent conflicts between individual property rights and an individual's interest in the joint family manifested themselves in much litigation. It would never be simple to ascertain, for example, whether a particular item of property was purely part of the joint family property, and thus subject to many restrictions in terms of an individual's rights of disposal. A set of presumptions was applied by the courts, operating in favour of jointness and seeking to achieve equitable arrangements.[28] Where a man asserted individual property rights, he had to prove that this was indeed his self-acquired property and not, in fact, joint family property over which this individual might have some right of usufruct or authority, but not an absolute right of disposal.

Tensions between the assertion of individuality and private interests, and the concerns and expectations of the group and the joint family as a corporate body, are not a new phenomenon. The British intervened at some point, through the promulgation of the *Hindu Gains of Learning Act* of 1930, to strengthen individual enterprise and to free at least some individuals from the traditional obligations and expectations of joint family life. This Act, claiming in the Preamble "to remove doubt as to the rights of a member of a Hindu undivided family in property acquired by him by means of his learning" seems to be a typical law taking account of élite interests. It was not much used in litigation, however, and its impact appears to have been relatively minimal.

The traditional Anglo-Hindu law that developed on the subject of the joint Hindu family, as well as its post-Independence manifestations, are an enormously complex subject in its own right.[29] For our present discussion, we need to focus on the relationship between individual members of a family and the interests of the family as a whole. The latter needed to be preserved and strengthened against individualistic, predatory claims at all times, otherwise strong individuals in a joint family would walk off with the assets of the family and leave others in despair and destitution. No doubt, this often happened in a male-dominated, patriarchal set-up, where the constraints of individual conscience were not strong enough to withstand egoistic inclinations.

Much of the litigation focusing on joint family law is therefore concerned, in one way or another, to restrain individualism and to protect various aspects of the joint family rather than an individual member. A key player in such litigation was often the *karta* or manager of the joint family, normally the oldest male, or another suitable person. While the traditional law was based on the assumption that only men could be managers of joint family property, real life dictated that, in many situations, women would have to, and could, act as managers. They would then receive *de facto* recognition, however reluctant it might be given. While this aspect, too, was therefore never uncontroversial, the more important concern of the law was to curb as well as to facilitate the powers of the manager. He alone could represent the family to the outside world as a legal personality, while the other coparceners were, in that sense, perpetual legal minors, like the women and children of the family. The manager's powers needed to be put under control, so that an unscrupulous or simply imprudent manager could not do what he wanted at the expense of everyone else in this family. Professor Derrett's favourite examples were a man who bought himself an elephant, or a Mercedes in later days, and let the family bear the costs of such luxury. Would every member of the family be bound in law to contribute to the never-ending expenses for a voracious pachiderm or the costs of maintaining a petrol-thirsty status symbol? The answer tended to be in the affirmative, not on account of animal rights or a soft corner for those who claim status through appropriate symbols, but because the law was mainly concerned to ensure that managers of joint families could make business and investment decisions without having to convene a major shareholders' meeting on every little issue. Thus, if the transaction concerned was not illegal, or could in any way be said to be for the benefit of the family, it would be supported judicially.

What, however, if the manager himself, or his friends, indulged in costly habits involving, say, alcohol, women and gambling? Anglo-Hindu law developed marvellously complex and interesting rules to restrain men in wasting away the family's assets.[30] Other issues were less straightforward because they did not involve actions which might lead to open social criticism. Thus, could a manager keep a mistress, in effect another wife, at the expense of the joint family? Such situations frequently arose, and the law responded by attempting to lay down some criteria for what was permissible, and what was not. The concept of *avyavaharika* debts, or 'tainted' debts, attempted to make distinctions between merely keeping a mistress in a marriage-like relationship and visiting a number of attractive ladies who then expected to be paid. Here again, we see that the Anglo-Hindu law and its post-colonial acolytes sought to find a balance between unrestrained individualism and a sense of responsibility for the concerns of the joint family as a whole. Interestingly, Derrett (1970: 102) noticed that more recent developments had strengthened the social welfare approach at the expense of the individual coparcener:

> More recent decisions, basing themselves on a feeling that the pious obligation must be confined within narrow limits, tend to take the

> view that if it is right to compensate the injured person, as it obviously must be, the sons' interests cannot escape: it cannot be "pious" to refuse to support the father in meeting his conscientious liabilities.

Professor Derrett (1970: 103), farsighted as ever, predicted that a realistic approach would eventually prevail:

> The courts will (I feel free to predict) eventually hold sons liable for all amounts of damages awarded against the father, no matter how deliberate and malicious the injury he committed may have been.

In addition to potential disputes between coparceners, who might disagree about any transaction conducted on behalf of the family by any of them, the joint family had of course very important responsibilities for its non-coparcenary members. These were, first of all, women and children. This group of claimants on the funds of the joint family could be composed of all kinds of people: severely disabled male members who were not treated as coparceners, properly married wives, re-married wives, concubines, and all kinds of children in innumerable categories.[31]

The main difficulty for such claimants against joint family funds and assets would probably have been that the nature of their entitlements was only in a very general way supported by the state legal system. We have seen in ch. 4.3 above that s. 488 of the *Criminal Procedure Code*, 1898 entitled wives and children to claim maintenance from a male who refused to maintain them.[32] While such provisions certainly did not remain unused, how useful could litigation be if the men simply refused to fulfil their traditional obligations and chose to ignore them?

Such problems added to the general impression that women and children were not getting a fair deal in the traditional joint family system, and that they should be provided with more entitlements in their own right, rather than remaining at the mercy of the male custodians of a family's assets. In other words, modern legal development would seek to reduce, if not abolish altogether, the phenomenon of legal dependency of adults, male or female, on others. One way forward would be to smash the joint family and to atomise legal entitlements to property by attaching them to individuals rather than the family as an institution.

Post-colonial developments

In the vigorous debates about the reforms of Hindu law and its proposed uniform codification during the 1950s,[33] no agreement could be reached on the reforming process of the complex joint Hindu family laws and of property and succession laws generally. The *Hindu Succession Act* of 1956 is only one of four major Acts promulgated in 1955–56. India did not produce a uniform Code for all Hindus at that time, nor has the appetite for the unification of laws led to further amendments in that direction.[34] The overall picture is that the Hindu joint family was by no means obliterated, and it was certainly not abolished by law. On the other hand, several important reforms were made. Some of these have had significant impact with regard to the issues debated in this book.

It must suffice here to highlight a few major problems that have arisen. The legislative promise to treat women as equals to men was only half-heartedly implemented with respect to the rights of inheritance of Hindu daughters. While before the 1956 Act Hindu daughters never had a claim to their own absolute entitlement in the deceased father's share of the joint family property, various sections of the HSA, 1956 have changed that.[35] A daughter can now inherit from her father in equal proportions with her brother(s) at the non-testamentary stage of succession.[36] However, while this seems well-established in the case law, it remains a fact that a daughter is not in fact treated equally by this method of distribution of assets, since the effects of the old law are still making themselves felt. At the first stage of distribution of assets, the daughter still goes empty-handed, in fact she is simply not in the picture, since she is not entitled to a share in the coparcenary cake.[37] It is only at the second stage of distribution of assets, when her share in the property of her deceased father is to be determined, that a daughter will receive equal treatment. As we shall see further below, this perpetual disadvantaging of daughters may work both ways, since it also continues to give daughters a claim on family solidarity which extends, especially for poor people, much beyond the limits of the actual property owned by members of the family.

Another much-contested issue in the context of the new succession law has been the nature of the entitlements of Hindu widows. Following an enormous line of cases and much dispute over even the most basic principles, it is now securely confirmed that Hindu widows have so-called 'pre-existing' claims on the joint family or the family assets, basically as a result of their status as the wife of a coparcener. Not surprisingly, as the atrociously bad recent case of *Surjit Kaur v. Garja Singh*, AIR 1994 SC 135 SC showed, the male relatives of a deceased man may try every trick in the book to claim that such a woman is not in fact a widow, but was merely a concubine, or even less than that. As we saw in ch. 1.5 above, it took Indian law some time to work out that in order to protect widowed women from such challenges to their entitlement, the traditional concepts of sacramental marriage would be useful, and that presumptions of the validity of marriage would be most appropriate in such circumstances.

The legal position of Hindu widows had already been significantly improved during the British time by the *Hindu Women's Right to Property Act*, 1937. This Act assisted women in asserting their claims vis-à-vis the husband's joint family, and allowed them through a legal fiction to slip into the shoes of the deceased husband at the time of his death. This new law was introduced with the proviso that any property such acquired would not belong to the widow absolutely. Instead, it would constitute a 'limited estate' or 'life estate', which would remain joint family property, and would revert on the woman's death or remarriage to the common stock. Legal problems arose, predictably, over the extent of the widow's right to deal with this property in any way she pleased. If she could not sell it, could she mortgage it or otherwise use her possessions prudently? How much could she give away *inter vivos*, and on what grounds? The widow's powers of alienation became a bone of contention in many cases, and the law maintained an uneasy balance between joint family claims and individual freedom.

Section 14 of the *Hindu Succession Act*, 1956 then abolished the 'limited estate', replacing it with an absolute right of the widow to hold and alienate any property in her possession. We see here another example of clashes between concepts of absolute, individual right to property and some form of joint family supervision over an individual's right to enjoy what they hold and appear to own. S. 14 of the HSA 1956 provided as follows:

> 14. *Property of a female Hindu to be her absolute property.* –
> (1) Any property possessed by a female Hindu, whether acquired before or after the commencement of this Act, shall be held by her as full owner thereof and not as a limited owner.
>
> Explanation. –
> In this sub-section, "property" includes both movable and immovable property acquired by a female Hindu by inheritance or devise, or at a partition or in lieu of maintenance or arrears of maintenance, or by gift from any person, whether a relative or not, before, at or after her marriage, or by her own skill or exertion, or by purchase or by prescription, or in any other manner whatsoever, and also any such property held by her as stridhana immediately before the commencement of this Act.
> (2) Nothing contained in sub-section (1) shall apply to any property acquired by way of gift or under a will or any other instrument or under a decree or order of a civil Court or under an award where the terms of the gift, will, or other instrument or the decree, order or award prescribe a restricted estate in such property.

The important question now was whether a Hindu widow who had been given, or had in any other form acquired, any property that was traditionally treated as a limited estate, would now be able to claim full and absolute ownership. The somewhat self-contradictory provisions of sections 14(1) and 14(2) became one of the most fiercely contested Indian legal provisions ever, and consequently an enormous case law developed under this section. Significantly, again, until the early 1970s, the Indian courts appeared to be holding out in favour of the joint family, male-focused perspective.[38] They did this mainly by refusing to acknowledge that Hindu wives had inherent rights in the assets of the husband's joint family and by relying on technical interpretations of certain words in the statute. In *T. V. Velmurugayya Pillai v. K. V. Lakshmana Perumal*, 1974 II MLJ 295, it was held by the Madras High Court that the widow in question had merely obtained a 'restricted estate' in 1930, and that this therefore did not enlarge into full ownership in 1956. In *Naraini Devi*, 1976(1) SCC 574, the Supreme Court somewhat ingeniously held that this widow had only acquired a life interest in the rent from the property, not in the property itself and thus had only a 'restricted estate' under s. 14(2).[39]

Perhaps it is not a co-incidence that by 1977, i.e. at the time when the Emergency had begun to make significant impact, the Supreme Court made a huge effort to implement and clarify the law on this subject. Until that time many widows had found themselves unprotected against male greed, in the majority of cases, before the various High Courts and even the Supreme Court (see n. 15 above). The leading case on the extent of Hindu widows' rights under s. 14 of the *Hindu Succession Act* of 1956, *V. Tulasamma v. Vaddeboyina Sesha Reddi*, AIR 1977 SC 1944, can be read as evidence of Emergency-induced judicial activism in the field of family law. This landmark case, decided by a bench of three judges including P. N. Bhagwati J, firmly established the principle of the 'pre-existing right' of Hindu widows. It thus implemented the old maintenance-focused law in a socially constructive fashion by giving Hindu widows their own, absolute right to property and freeing them from male interference.

In this case, the husband had died in 1931, leaving a step-brother and his widow. The widow was eventually given property to enjoy as a limited estate and had continued to hold these properties also after 1956. She then alienated some of this property in 1960 and 1961 and the husband's brother protested. By the time this case went to the Supreme Court, an enormous case law had built up, but the issue itself had remained unresolved and had become a gold mine for lawyers. With definite touches of social criticism, but speaking very much as a Supreme Court judge who is professionally concerned to clarify the law, Bhagwati J vigorously criticised the ambivalent, bad drafting of s. 14 HSA and highlighted such waste of resources as a consequence of this lack of clarity in the statute. He blamed inadequate legal drafting, although it should have been very clear that the social purpose of the 1956 Act had been to improve the legal position of women. He might just as well have given a social welfare lecture to Indian men. The time for that, however, was not yet ripe. Instead, Bhagwati J said, at pp. 1945–1946:

> It is indeed unfortunate that that though it became evident as far back as 1967 that sub-sections (1) and (2) of Section 14 were presenting serious difficulties of construction in cases where property was received by a Hindu female in lieu of maintenance and the instrument granting such property prescribed a restricted estate for her in the property and divergence of judicial opinion was creating a situation which might well be described as chaotic, robbing the law of that modicum of certainty which it must always possess in order to guide the affairs of men, the legislature, for all these years did not care to

> step in to remove the constructional dilemma facing the courts and adopted an attitude of indifference and inaction, untroubled and unmoved by the large number of cases on this point encumbering the files of different courts in the country, when by the simple expedient of an amendment, it could have silenced judicial conflict and put an end to needless litigation. This is a classic instance of a statutory provision which, by reason of its inapt draftmanship, has created endless confusion for litigants and proved a paradise for lawyers. It illustrates forcibly the need of an authority or body to be set up by the Government or the Legislature which would constantly keep in touch with the adjudicatory authorities in the country as also with the legal profession and immediately respond by making recommendations for suitable amendments whenever it is found that a particular statutory provision is, by reason of inapt language or unhappy draftmanship, creating difficulty of construction or is otherwise inadequate or defective or is not well conceived and is consequently counter-productive of the result it was intended to achieve. If there is a close inter-action between the adjudicatory wing of the State and a dynamic and ever-alert authority or body which responds swiftly to the drawbacks and deficiencies in the law in action, much of the time and money, which is at present expended in fruitless litigation, would be saved and law would achieve a certain amount of clarity, certainty and simplicity which alone can make it easily intelligible to the people.

Reading this learned and detailed judgment, it become quite evident that this was not the first Supreme Court case on the matter to accept Hindu women's rights in this way. It was evident that men all over India were fighting the pro-women reforms through litigation. It was necessary that the highest court in the land should pronounce authoritatively on this matter. Bhagwati J explained in detail, at pp. 1947–1948, that section 14(1) clearly took a wide ambit and was designed to fulfil a beneficial social purpose, while section 14(2) was more in the nature of an exception and should not be strictly construed, otherwise the social purpose of the entire Act would be defeated. At p. 1948, the nature of the Hindu widow's pre-existing right is further discussed in some detail.

The main judgment, given by Fazal Ali J, contains an immensely learned dissertation on the subject of the Hindu wife's rights in the matrimonial home and in relation to the husband's family after the husband's death. This judge also demonstrated in detail how the old Hindu law (from which he copiously cited) and Anglo-Hindu law on the subject had protected Hindu widows by placing obligations even on the purchaser of joint family property, if a widow's sustenance depended on income from such property. There were, thus, several protective mechanisms already in the old law, which explicitly strengthened the bargaining power and the rightful claims of the Hindu widow. There could be no doubt that the 1956 Act had gone beyond such protective mechanisms, and that its underlying purpose was to act as a protective form of social welfare legislation. Significantly, however, these precise words are not used and the emphasis was instead placed on gender equality. It was held by Fazal Ali J at p. 1966:

> ... the Act of 1956 has made revolutionary and far-reaching changes in the Hindu Society and every attempt should be made to carry out the spirit of the Act which has undoubtedly supplied a long felt need and tried to do away with the invidious distinction between a Hindu male and female in matters of intestate succession.

Following a detailed review of the case law, Fazal Ali J explicitly overruled the bad decisions in *Naraini Devi*, (1976) 1 SCC 574 and held, at p. 1977:

> Indeed, if the contrary view is accepted, it will, in my opinion, set at naught the legislative process of a part of Hindu Law of the intestate succession and curb the social urges and aspirations of the Hindu women, particularly in the International Year of Women, by reviving a highly detestable legacy which was sought to be buried by the Parliament after independence so that the new legislation may march with the times.

There is much talk about modernity and gender equality here and no direct reference to the needs of destitute women, especially widows. The decision itself, however, could not be any clearer. In this case, the Supreme Court authoritatively emphasised and explained in detail the nature of the pre-existing rights of a Hindu female marrying into a Hindu joint family, and the consequent entitlements of Hindu widows to their own absolute share of property after the husband's death. In other words, this decision firmly held the Hindu family liable for the future maintenance of Hindu widows. It thus matches admirably well with the general maintenance law that the Indian courts were developing at that time.

Perhaps it was too optimistic to hope that this important Supreme Court case would settle the issue.[40] There continued to be a long line of cases in which male relatives questioned the consequences of s. 14 HSA and the entitlements of Hindu widows by arguing that, in the particular facts and circumstances of their case, the property that the widow holds is not 'possessed' by her.[41] However, almost all these cases have upheld the pro-women interpretation of s. 14 HSA.[42]

Some of these cases are remarkable for the audacity of the claimants. In *Partap Singh v. Union of India*, AIR 1985 SC 1695, a Sikh appellant went all the way to the Supreme Court, fighting windmills, to try and defeat a widow's entitlement to absolute property rights. Realising that the law under s. 14 HSA was against him, he tried a constitutional petition, alleging that this pro-women law blatantly discriminated against men and was therefore violative of Articles 14 and 15(1) of the Constitution. His lawyer also cited the long passage from the judgment of Bhagwati J in *Vaddeboyina Tulasamma*, AIR 1977 SC 1944 (as cited above) to argue that the law was clearly unsatisfactory, because it was vague and uncertain. One need not say much about this case; it was thrown out with some terse comments from Venkataramiah J at pp. 1697–1698:

> There is now hardly any justification for the males belonging to the Hindu community to raise any objection to the beneficient provisions contained in section 14(1) of the Act on the ground of hostile discrimination. The above provision is further protected by the express provision contained in clause (3) of Article 15, since it is a special provision enacted for the benefit of Hindu women. We do not find any merit in the Writ Petition.

This was, of course, a Sikh petitioner. The case therefore represents some evidence of Sikh opposition to being governed by modern Hindu law. This is so not merely for ideological or religious reasons. As the above case demonstrates with utmost clarity, the modernised Hindu law of succession interfered with the customary property law arrangements of this important agricultural community, and thus led to much disquiet.

Jagannathan Pillai v. Kunjithapadam Pillai, AIR 1987 SC 1493 was another landmark case on the subject and firmly underwrites *V. Tulasamma*, AIR 1977 SC 1944 without even mentioning that case. The purpose of this judgment appears to be to explicitly overrule the High Courts of Orissa and Andhra Pradesh in some old cases that were deemed unsatisfactory. Further positive decisions from the Supreme Court are found in *Gulwant Kaur v. Mohinder Singh*, AIR 1987 SC 2251 and *Gopal Singh v. Dile Ram*, AIR 1987 SC 2394.

We should not assume, however, that all Indian widows with a potential claim to absolute property rights would now be able to assert their position. The dangers for women in asserting their claims against men are well-illustrated in a murder case from the 1970s, *Dinkar Bandhu Deshmukh v. State*, AIR 1970 Bom 438. A Hindu widow had asserted her property rights against the deceased husband's brothers and had been murdered, together with one of her helpers, during the harvest operations in a contested field. A death sentence had been passed and the murderers appealed. Despite the involvement of Ram Jethmalani as counsel, this case, centred on criminal evidence, dismisses the appeal against sentencing and the judge concludes, at p. 448:

> In my opinion, however, there is no extenuating circumstance whatsoever as far as accused No. 2 is concerned. The conduct of both the accused person appears to have been to create a false sense of confidence and security in Housabai, a helpless woman who had come to work on her own field, and thereafter to trap her unawares in the manner in which they have done. I, therefore, hold that the maximum penalty of the law has rightly been inflicted upon accused No. 2.

This tough and uncompromising treatment of the murderers of, as the judge himself put it, a "helpless woman who had come to work on her own field" was probably not an exception. While I have not seen other reported cases on this subject, Dhagamwar's research suggests that many women will find it difficult to assert their claim in a court of law and/or against other members of the family (see especially Dhagamwar 1992).

Joint family law during the 1990s

During the 1990s, there are notably fewer reported cases on s. 14 HSA, which may simply be a reflection of the fact that the law has now been fully clarified. In addition, it would appear that the earlier prominence of joint family litigation between competing males is no longer as pronounced as before. However, we must of course not assume that all decided cases are reported, and a perusal of specialist law journals such as the *Income Tax Reports* confirms that litigation in that field remains vigorous. However, litigation is also becoming increasingly expensive, and the old techniques of family arrangements and the more or less informal settlements of competing claims continue to be useful alternatives.

Some of the reported cases from the 1990s create the impression that women are now appearing as litigants in property-related cases where the conflict of interests lies mainly between different women, rather than between the male-dominated clan and a female claimant. In *Kanchan Dakuani v. Tarini Dakuani*, AIR 1992 Ori 159, we see a fight between two sisters over their mother's property. Their widowed mother had executed a deed in favour of one of her daughters many years ago, prior to the HSA 1956. However, this daughter never cared properly for her mother, as she had undoubtedly hoped. The mother then executed a further deed in favour of her second daughter in 1975.

The High Court correctly applied the law under s. 14 HSA and held that, since the first transfer of property was made prior to the HSA, from 1956 onwards this right to property vested in the daughter and matured into full, absolute ownership of the property. Hence, the mother had no legal right to make a second transfer deed of the same property in 1975. This is a legally correct decision, but it is socially extremely undesirable, showing that a socially irresponsible individual can get away with claiming the benefits of the modern law without fulfilling corresponding obligations.

This case may be unusual in that it involved two sisters. However, it is not a unique case at all. I have spoken to many aged Indians, male and female, who are hesitant to make transfer deeds of property in favour of their offspring, fearing that once the absolute property right has been granted, the beneficiaries will only see their own benefit and will not reciprocate by caring for the donors of such property. This phenomenon appears to disturb many Indians; it is of utmost social relevance as many Indians now tend to live longer.

Within the context of new research on ageing in India, and in view of demographic changes (Zachariah and Rajan 1997), there is now a need for legal research that links issues of joint family obligations to the increasing incidence of assertions of individual rights in property. The modern legal system, having promoted this kind of individualism to some extent, will now need to monitor that individualism does not turn into selfish egoism and ends in selfish exploitation of others. Failure to do so on the part of the state might well mean irresponsible complicity in the development of gaping holes in India's patchy social welfare net for the older sections of the population.

The Indian courts appear to have developed some sensitivity to such issues since the late 1980s.[43] In two cases concerning the rights of a married daughter to reside in the family dwelling, a right explicitly protected by s. 23 HSA of 1956, the question is whether a married woman can leave her husband and may then simply claim a legal right to live in her natal home. In *Kalamma v. Veeramma*, AIR 1992 Kant 362, it was held that a married daughter who had merely deserted her husband was not entitled to claim such a right of residence. In other words, the duty to maintain her and to look after her welfare was still with the husband. However, in *Sripatinath Neogi v. Ira Rani Sur,* AIR 1992 Cal 60, it was held that a daughter who was separated from her husband and had resided with her parents in the dwelling house before their death could not be turned out by her brothers. Here we see that the courts will need to be alert in order to achieve equitable solutions in cases of conflicts of interests.

Another recent set of cases concerns protection mechanisms for wives and children after the husband or father has died. Legal insecurities may arise when there was litigation pending between the spouses at the time of the man's death and the precise status of the wife may need to be ascertained. *Yallawwa v. Shantavva*, AIR 1997 SC 35, holds that when a decree of divorce has been obtained against the wife and the husband then dies, the wife does not lose her right of appeal on account of the husband's death. This kind of decision definitely protects the social and financial position of the woman who, in this case, was an illiterate lady whose circumstances the court carefully took into account.[44]

Finally, our discussion has demonstrated that daughters were not given fully equal treatment under the provisions of the HSA 1956. In this context, it may be useful to return to the discussions about dowry and marriage expenses. It is a traditional obligation of the joint family and/or the father of a girl to provide her marriage expenses and to send her off to the new family in style, at whatever level. The links with the dowry problem will be evident: Some recent research suggests that some families will make strategic use of dowry incentives, virtually to purchase for their daughter the best possible groom.[45] It is doubtful whether such strategies always work to the benefit of a daughter, however, since offering 'dowry sweeteners' upfront for greedy in-laws may actually generate appetite for more transfers of property and thus endanger the daughter's very existence.

Dowry-related problems of domestic violence apart, which may have many other underlying reasons, the fact that daughters normally leave their natal home on marriage and join the husband's family as a more or less full member involves complex property transactions between two families, not just the passage of one individual from one family to another. This is an immensely complicated scenario, in which new research is urgently needed, for Hindus as much as for Muslims and other communities. The simple, tempting argument that granting daughters individual property rights will avoid the so-called dowry problems or close the book on questions of succession, because dowry amounts to pre-mortem inheritance, can certainly not be maintained.

In precisely this context, a number of interesting questions about the balance between private ownership and family property arose. A complex case about marriage gifts, *Meenakshamma v. M. C. Nanjundappa*, AIR 1993 Kant 12, was contested not under the HSA, but under traditional Hindu law. The main issue here was whether a daughter who, at the time of her marriage, had been given a large number of presents could still claim a share in the inheritance from her father. In essence, thus, the question was whether daughters would be able to take twice. Significantly, in *Meenakshamma*, the court vigorously defended the rights of daughters to inheritance under the HSA in addition to receiving gifts from the family. At the same time, the court was concerned to work out an equitable balance of interests between the various claimants, giving something to everyone.

This kind of case will probably become more prominent now, since the assumptions and practices in various parts of India concerning dowry transactions in marriages constitute an interference with the processes of determining how succession should develop. The claims of daughters against the joint family in general and their father and mother in particular, arise today as much from traditional notions of family solidarity and obligations as from modern social welfare concerns and considerations of status. Nobody would send their daughter to a new home virtually naked. Girls from even the poorest families expect their family to provide for them at this critical point of their life. As I pointed out in various articles years ago (see ch. 5.2, 5.4 and 5.6 above), Indian brides from modest backgrounds, and certainly really poor girls, tend to get a more than fair deal out of the current interplay of traditional joint family obligations, at the cost of the family (often their brothers) and without any recourse to the law of the state at all. Recent fieldwork experience in Kerala has powerfully reinforced that message: Even among the poorest, there is simply no marriage without what we have got used to calling 'dowry', a phenomenon that needs to be looked at afresh in the light of social evidence from outside the middle classes.

Whether encouraging litigiousness to promote individual claims is a useful strategy for the modern Indian system of property and succession law remains a matter of grave doubt to me. Sensible people ought to be able to talk to each other and find an equitable solution outside the fora of the official courts. What the courts have done, and evidently have done well, is to help women implement their enlarged claims to separate, absolute ownership of segments of family property if others in the family are unwilling to share the group's resources and intended to push certain individuals out of the family. It must be doubted whether the official courts would ever be able to assist truly impoverished women in turning the moral and social obligations of mutual support from their natal families into legal rights. Here, again, modern Indian society and law need to rely on traditions of interlinkedness and sharing as a basic parameter of social welfare.

Rather than claiming absolute equality and making this a focal point for discussion of issues of property and succession, I continue to think that equitable balancing of claims and interests in a sustainable form should be the priority. In the particular cultural, social and economic circumstances within which modern Indian law applies, hundreds of millions of potential claimants to tiny shares of individual property could never be fully satisfied. They could not be more or less safely cushioned against emergencies, unless they could count on informal networks of support from within the family. If we found earlier that modern Indian family law needs the family to maintain a sustainable system of social welfare, we must reiterate here that most Indians today probably realise that they, as legally autonomous individuals, may need the family, too.

Notes

1 For Hindu joint family law, see Sontheimer (1977) and virtually all the large practice handbooks, such as *Mayne's Hindu law* in its various editions (Kuppuswami, 1986) and *Mulla's Hindu law* (Desai, 1990).

2 On Muslim law of inheritance and succession, the leading study remains Coulson (1971), but see also Powers (1986) and Khan (1999).

3 See also Diwan and Diwan (1995) for Hindu law; Pearl and Menski (1998, ch. 11).

4 But see the argument in ch. 5.3 below that such families have long disappeared.

5 On these principles, see Sontheimer (1977); Derrett (1977); Diwan and Diwan (1995: 250ff.).

6 Otherwise, for example, how could any legal system operate a scheme of inheritance based on interpersonal relations?

7 I have recently called this 'academic gagging' (Menski, 1998a) in the context of the *sati* debate, opposing American scholars who have been trying to argue that research on this phenomenon signifies a betrayal of Indian women.

8 Modernity, however, can hardly be restraint-free, it merely replaces one set of ties with another. On modern living styles in India, allegedly without joint family ideology, see Jain (1999) in typical *India Today* style.

9 See in detail Narang (1990) and Pathak and Sharma (1992). Recent litigation in London showed that the *stridhanam* literature contains many points of potential and actual conflict with joint family law principles. The same, of course, applies to the concept of individual male property.

10 On South Indian forms, in particular the *Marumakkathayam* law of Kerala, see Variar (1969) and ch. 6.7 below on their continuing relevance.

11 For details on such concepts see Derrett (1963b; 1970) and Sontheimer (1977).

12 On concepts of the family, a leading study remains Kapadia (1955), subsequently re-published in many editions.

13 Certainly the credit wouldn't go to scholars, who have been singularly focused on modernisation and individualisation agenda and have even refused to see, as we shall analyse in detail in chapter 4.3 below, that the judicial vision of viable post-divorce maintenance for discarded wives can be implemented in a modern society.

14 Gulati (1981) brings several examples of poor South Indian women who realised that they are better off without men, and acted accordingly.

15 On the dangers of projecting individualism as the magic cure, see Dhagamwar (1987), an excellent study on the economic dependency of most married women and their resulting inability to opt for divorce.

16 The pain of having to confront systematic – some people prefer to call it systemic – recent killings of non-white people in countries like Britain, Germany and the USA should be a reminder that 'our' house is not in order, either.

17 Significantly, new literature on domestic violence in the USA is keenly focusing on evidence of marital violence against South Asian immigrant women, thus 'othering' them and distracting from the realities of marital violence among 'white' Americans. On this issue see now Abraham (1998).

18 A popular explanatory model has been that ever since India elected a nationalist Hindu government, dowry-related violence has increased. Such assumptions are hard to prove, either way, but they are powerful in the public mind.

19 I encountered incredulity and considerable scepticism about my views on Indian democracy. See the entry on 'Hinduism' in Lipset, Seymour Martin (ed.) [1995]: *The Encyclopedia of Democracy*. Washington DC and London: Congressional Quarterly Inc. and Routledge, Vol. II, pp. 561–565.

20 See in this respect the emphasis on the role of the individual's conscience (*atmanastusti*) in classical Hindu law as a source of legal norms (Menski 1997: 17–19).

21 This is well-reflected in Bardhan (1984), for example, and in the powerful writing of Professor Upendra Baxi (1982; 1985).

22 Note that Dr. Lucy Carroll in chapter 5.5 below dismisses this as wasteful expenditure and thus refuses to acknowledge the social value of celebrating rites of passage.

23 See especially *Vijaya Manohar Arhat v. Kashirao Rajaram Sawai*, AIR 1987 SC 1100, in which it was held that a married daughter is liable to maintain her parent, and that both male and female children share such obligations.

24 Derrett (1970: 60) writes that the family "is sometimes called an ancient "welfare-state" mechanism. It is also a test; it is a laboratory in which members are continually subjected to education for living and to an examination of character". This evidently refers to the continuous need for self-restraint. For detailed analysis of joint Hindu family principles see Derrett (1970: 52–121).

25 From birth or, according to some traditions, from the time of conception.

26 There are important links between these kinds of concepts and the continuing problems over bonded labour in modern South Asian laws today.

27 On partitions and the many sub-issues arising therefrom see in detail Derrett (1963b: 317–345) and Derrett (1970: 145–171).

28 See in detail Derrett (1963b: 335–336).

29 Apart from Sontheimer (1977), see also Derrett (1963b: 244–345) and Diwan and Diwan (1995).

30 A cynic could say that the law developed because the growing class of lawyers became rather interested in creaming off surplus family assets, which would otherwise be 'wasted' on potentially unsavoury activities.

31 For example, he classical literature enumerates many different types of sons, and leaves no doubt that not every son is automatically entitled to full membership of the joint family, even though there may be a claim on the family in terms of maintenance.

32 It should be noted, at least, that the first version of this law was already introduced in 1865. This reflects awareness about the issue of maintenance in the context of the family at a very early stage of British intervention in the legal framework.

33 For details see especially Derrett (1957).

34 If anything, the fact that individual states in India can promulgate their own laws in this area has led to further pluralisation of legal provisions. On the other hand, the trend is towards granting larger legal rights to daughters as coparceners, although only a few states, significantly those of the South, have taken that step so far.

35 For details see especially Derrett (1970: 213–219).

36 The leading cases are: *Rangubai v. Laxman Lalji Patil*, AIR 1966 Bom 169; *Gurupad Khandappa Magdum v. Hirabai Khandappa Magdum*, AIR 1978 SC 1239; *Raj Rani v. The Chief Settlement Commissioner, Delhi*, AIR 1984 SC 1234.

37 This would now, of course, be different in those states where the daughter has been added to the group of coparceners, i.e. Andhra Pradesh, Tamil Nadu and Maharashtra. The situation in Kerala, where the Hindu joint family law was officially abolished by the 1975 Act (see ch. 5.2 above), is quite different and would have to be the subject of a specialist study.

38 For some instructive cases see *Thayammal v. Salammal*, AIR 1972 Mad 83; see also *T. V. Velmurugayya*, 1974 II MLJ 295 and then *Naraini Devi v. Ramo Devi*, (1976) 1 SCC 574, which defined away the woman's right through a breathtakingly blinkered approach, speaking of a 'restricted estate'. *V. Tulasamma,* AIR 1977 SC 1944, is the leading case in this field and contains an extremely detailed review of the earlier cases.

39 The Supreme Court apologised for this decision in *V. Tulasamma*, AIR 1977 SC 1944, at p. 1977.

40 *Bai Vajia v. Thakobhai Chelabhai*, AIR 1979 SC 993 duly followed *Tulasamma*'s case of 1977.

41 For such cases, following *Tulasamma*, see for example *Chockalingam Pillai v. Alamelu Ammal*, AIR 1982 Mad 29; *Padma Vati Ahuja v. Desaundhi Ram*, AIR 1986 P&H 155.

42 See, however, cases that went the other way: In *Suraj Mal v. Babu Lal*, AIR 1985 Del 95, a widow had accepted a right to maintenance prior to the 1937 Act and it was held that s. 14 was not attracted, since this widow did not 'possess' any property that could have matured into her own absolute property.

43 On the entitlements to maintenance for parents see the leading case of *Vijaya*, AIR 1987 SC 1100.

44 See also *Ghambir Chand Kotwal v. Santosh Kumari*, AIR 1997 J & K 116 and *Suresh Bala v. Rajbir Singh*, AIR 1997 P&H 74.

45 See especially an article by Bisakha Sen, an economist, in Menski (1998b: 75–95).

Chapter Six

The Uniform Civil Code debate

Changing agenda

6.1 The uncritical acceptance of uniformity as an ideological problem

There is something seriously wrong with the debates about the issue of legal uniformity, which is the subject of the present chapter. We saw in ch. 5. 1 above that the allegedly unlimited potential for universal application of the axioms of modernity has purposely and systematically overlooked cultural specificities, ethnic diversities, religious pluralism, in a sense all kinds of pluralism. There is supposed to be only one good truth, a belief in a bright future in which law (rather than religion) is in control of everything. In this new system, therefore, by implication, lawyers and politicians have untrammelled power over individuals and their lives. This is legal centralism in action, a form of legalised dictatorship which looks wonderful in its idealised modern dressing. However, in a huge country like India with its multiple hybridities, the axioms of legal centralism and of uniformity simply do not work in daily practice, where the diversities and pluralities of 'little people' and of basic human existence re-assert themselves most powerfully all the time. Not surprisingly, this is even recognised by some of the most recent literature on the subject. Thus, it has been reported that Professor S. P. Sathe, who had taken it upon himself to draft a uniform civil code during the 1980s, ended up expressing his reservations about the feasibility of total legal uniformity. Kiran Deshta (1995: 58) writes, partly quoting Professor Sathe:

> He stated that in the process of compiling all the provisions of the existing personal laws governing different religious communities, he has run into difficulty in extracting the religious from the non-religious components of these laws. Professor Sathe opined that the task appears [sic] to be more difficult than I originally thought and all I can anticipate at the moment is that some plurality may have to be provided for even in a uniform civil code.

Deshta (1995: 59) concludes her own discussion on this subject with the critical comment that "[o]ne is left with the impression that many of the writers were only putting off the day when serious thinking on this subject would have to be done". Such comments do not advance our knowledge, and are hardly constructive.

The underlying problems in this area have their roots not only in biased jurisprudential politics, but also in strangely inadequate reconstructions of South Asian history which reverberate until now and keep confusing even the brightest of minds. The so-called Orientalist, traditional understanding of India, the purported Aryanisation of South Asia, its Muslim domination for a long time and the significant Muslim influence in modern times are only some of the major factors that make any reading of South Asian history and development a most complex task. Starting from contested and vague beginnings, Hindu culture has all along refused to become a monotheistic, mono-focused, monocultural, centralised system of human organisation.[1] From the start, it appears, there were so many different views and perceptions about key issues of religion, culture and life that the ancient South Asians did not find it possible to aim for unifying agreement. In other ancient cultures – so we are led to believe – similar complex diversities appear to have given rise to axiomatic and centralising, uniformising positions that were somehow asserted by a dominant elite, whether political or religious. Christianity developed a belief system that had to be shared, or one was not part of the system. So did Islam later. A long time before that, however, the people we now refer to as Hindus had agreed to disagree, and had explicitly allowed for pluralism in every sphere of life.

This open recognition of the reality of pluralism can be observed in every sphere of Hindu life and can be studied on the basis of very ancient material, recorded in difficult languages and not designed to teach us today about the people's perceptions at that time. Within the conceptual framework of an understanding of cosmic Order which encompasses everyone and everything,[2] inter-relational systems were perceived to be crucial. Nobody was perceived as an isolated, autonomous individual. Everybody, including gods and other higher beings, had roles to play in relation to the universe, society, clan, family, and those closest in one's personal life. The husband-wife symbiosis became a focal point of attention and concern. Relations between people in different occupations and walks of life were clearly seen as the key element of a socio-economic pattern of organisation in which division of labour occurred, and was needed to maintain order and increase efficiency. The resulting representations, whether we take the sacrament of marriage (*samskara*) as an ideally indissoluble tie between a male and a female, or the so-called caste system as an image of all body parts functioning together in a complex symbiotic relationship, have all been misread and misrepresented subsequently. Outsiders and insiders alike have come to view them as complex mechanisms of 'tradition' whose main purpose was to suppress some and elevate others. In other words, ancient Hindu culture has been presented as only emphasising difference and diversity, rather than being engaged in constantly balancing this with symbiotic understandings of commonality, equality and uniformity. There is no space here to go into the history of such biased misrepresentations.

It should at least be noted, however, that more researchers today are questioning the commonly accepted reading of ancient Indian traditions as uniform patterns of rules that are distinctly and typically non-modern and are focused on maintaining diversities rather than striving for uniformity. There is some awareness that if *everybody* is treated as different, then there can actually be equality in difference.[3] This means going away from the idea that one group or the other in a particular society is 'dominant' or is the standard-setting majority to which everything else has to be oriented. In one important sense, of course, the post-colonial Indian model of secularism tried to achieve exactly that sort of scenario, where the voices of all would be heard in equal measure.[4]

However, modern India's secularism continues to be seriously misunderstood as a cheap copy of Western, anti-religious policies, rather than explicit recognition of the elementary fact of human interlinkedness with many different higher entities. Through our dominant, some say Orientalist, reading of ancient Indian culture, where we constantly emphasise Brahmin perspectives and claims, and thus disregard other voices, we have deprived ourselves of the chance to understand the indigenous concepts of relative equality which continue to underpin South Asian societies. By emphasising cosmic interlinkedness of everything and everyone, ancient Hindu culture provided an external reference point and thus gave the clear message that everybody and everything, in their own way, had a role to play in relation to a higher entity. We can take the image of the primeval man's body parts as segments of the *varna* system, as found in Rigveda 10.90, to test the theory of equitable symbiosis: The feet (the lowest castes) are just as necessary as the head (the Brahmin castes) for the full functioning of the whole complex system called 'man'. One simply cannot do without the other. This kind of message is easily lost today in the communal battles of majorities and minorities, in the escalating gender warfare of academia, and between the loud assertions (which tolerate little dissent) that uniform Western legal systems can, somehow, guarantee all citizens equal rights through the 'rule of law'.

Even if we take only the central elements of the 'old order', *rita* as an understanding of macrocosmic ordering and *dharma* as its more individualised, microcosmic system of obligations, or duties upon everyone to do the 'right thing', we cannot but recognise that pluralism forms the epistemological basis of traditional Indian cultures. Modernist researchers may not like such basic facts and concepts, but they cannot really define them away on that account. Scholars cannot really rewrite the documents of ancient history and their concepts, but many people have tried to do just that, even today.[5] Thus, academic endeavours to represent ancient Indian concepts not as they probably were, but as *we* see them, have led to multiple confusions. Modern talk of 'envisioning' rather than objectively 'knowing' assists this process of blurring the dimly lit boundaries between objective knowledge and 'construction'. It provides in this respect a new unlimited licence for academics to speculate.

In fact, matters are much worse. Approaching the third millennium, we remain unable to make sense of the time before the first millennium, which somehow legitimises ideologically motivated 'constructions' of every type, the idealising 'golden age' pattern as well as the 'dark ages' school of thought. Scholarly politics are at their worst, it seems, when some modernists now declare certain sections of the past irrelevant (see footnote 5 above). It is not that academics are stupid, they are simply selective and often mischievous.

To focus on the key issue arising with reference to our present topic, researchers realise the systemic importance of pluralism in ancient India, but often do not like it and hence downplay or outrightly deny it. The result is a reading of ancient Indian history and culture that emphasises monolithic concepts such as the suppression of women and low-caste people and marginalises all traces of evidence of symbiotic interactions between males and females, high and low castes, and so on. There is some scholarship which accepts that the ancient Indian sources have not just sub-texts of various kinds, but multiple layers of comment and perspectives on one and the same issue, reflecting a plurality of views which cannot be anything other than confusing, but which constituted social reality. Precisely this, we must emphasise, is Hindu culture, having agreed long ago to disagree over the very basic 'bricks' of culture and allowing a plurality of perceptions, aware of the somehow unquestioned reality of cosmic interlinkedness. Because of that particular super-axiom of cosmic Order, nothing else in Hindu culture can ever be axiomatic, recognising systemically that there are always going to be different perspectives on one and the same issue. Most Western reading of Hindu tradition, however,[6] has remained mono-focused. It has declared the suppression of women, the caste system, polytheism, and many other 'questionable' practices as unacceptable. Academic study of South Asia has turned largely into ideologically-motivated criticism, devoid of sympathy for the object of study, often full of contempt for it. The point of study, then, becomes the confirmation of one's own superiority. Notably, this is also a technique used by some Muslim writers, for whom systemic pluralism is also an ideological problem.

To define the ancient system and its inherent pluralisms away, or to ignore them as though they did not exist, amounts to intellectual dishonesty. One takes academic shortcuts – we have to do this all the time as a management strategy – but when it comes to intercultural studies and comparative perspectives, there is more to this technique than a desire for efficiency and brevity. Scholarship on South Asia has tended to create a seriously distorted image of ancient India (and now of modern India, Pakistan, and Bangladesh) that suits us and our arguments, rather than trying to reflect conceptual and social reality as closely as possible. Ultimately, this prominent – not to say dominant – academic methodology has had enormous implications for how we read and understand modern Indian law today.

Having spent years on studying Vedic concepts and their implications, someone like myself can still not claim to know precisely what the Vedic Indians did or thought. Of course, we will never know. However, the existing texts, in their variant readings,[7] tell us in enormous detail what some people thought a long time back. We do not know why they thought like this, and what precisely they were trying to express, but we have the evidence of words. Piecing together subjective representations of such distant past elements of culture, we have built up a mosaic of detail that remains marked by pluralism and diversity, not only by time and space.

In view of such evidence,[8] the civilisational network of the roots of Hinduism and ancient South Asian 'tradition' could never be reduced to a single stem or theory, a uniform system of drawing sustenance for the magnificent giant tree called 'India' today. The increasingly complex and ideologically bitchy, often personalised, current debates about labels like 'India', 'Hindu', 'Brahmanism', 'Bengali', and so on, instructive and exciting as they may be, divert us from the basic fact that, at the end of the day, all of this desperate effort to define and distinguish takes place within a wider framework of reference in which all of these categories remain conceptually interlinked. Does one create autonomy by denying linkages, whether visible or invisible? Some recent writing in the context of communal politics and Indian ethnicity rightly suggested that India contains 'the other' within itself all the time (Nandy et al. 1995) and that there is no point in denying this.

While this is not the right place to provide a comprehensive critique of legal centralism,[9] some of the essays reprinted in this chapter come back to such fundamental concerns. We know that modernity treats the maintenance of plural legal systems as evidence of backwardness (see now again Deshta 1995: 2). Countries that operate a personal law system, in effect many countries in the South, are therefore perceived to suffer a deficit of modernisation and are under pressure to follow the dominant legal model of uniform legal regulation. India is only one of the many countries in which this has become a huge political issue.[10] Here, Article 44 of the Constitution, 1950 anticipated the eventual introduction of a uniform civil code, but 50 years later this programmatic aim has still not been achieved, and has in fact remained "no more than a distant mirage" (Allott 1980: 216).

Countries like Turkey, on the other hand, following the West and abolishing the personal law system, have been held up as good models. The realisation that such uniformising efforts created new legal problems and were not necessarily conducive to justice has been suppressed for a long time but is now being researched in more detail.[11] Legal uniformity *per se* does not guarantee human rights and equal justice, especially not where socio-economic inequalities – over which law has only limited authority, despite the axioms of legal centralism – continue to exist.

It ought to be universally recognised that all human societies retain elements of socio-economic inequality despite legal and political assertions to the effect that equality before the law is a marker of legal modernity. As we know only too well, most academic legal writing is not seriously interested in socio-legal analysis and in real comparison.[12] In their academic writing, it appears, few scholars will openly admit that the West and modern legal systems have exactly the same problems of implementing equal justice and human rights guarantees as those supposedly backward legal systems that take into account differential statuses.

Having declared ancient India hostile to recognition of equality, whether based on gender or caste, any element of 'tradition' in modern Indian law has been treated with contempt and has been answered by loud calls for legal reforms. We have seen, in the previous chapters, how unrealistic some of those calls have been, but how tenaciously modernist scholars and activists have stuck to them, even in the face of legal evidence to the contrary. For example, despite most vigorous demands for introducing the breakdown principle into Hindu divorce law, we saw that neither modern Indian legislation nor the courts have gone as far as accepting the principle as a guiding yardstick for today's legal practice. Individualism may be a modern value, but it was not found suitable as a conceptual basis for developments in modern Indian laws.

In this particular context, it is important to highlight again that the concept of 'irretrievable breakdown' itself was never unknown to Indian law, anyway. Thus, it is more than a bit dishonest of modernity to occupy the position that the breakdown principle belongs to *its* realm, when this is manifestly not so.[13] In fact, by the 1980s, it was also becoming clear to many female activists that following modernity would not, by itself, alleviate the sufferings of Indian women. We saw in ch. 4 above that recent developments in Indian post-divorce maintenance laws confirm the readiness of the state to ignore the axioms of formal legal uniformity, while both legislature and judiciary will nevertheless seek to achieve parity of legal provisions. Thus, as Vasudha Dhagamwar (1989) clearly identified, modern Indian law had various options to work towards greater equality, and it would never be an easy strategy to simply impose a uniform civil code overnight. In fact, examining the chequered history of legal uniformisation in India so far, Dhagamwar (1989: 76) courageously stuck to her agenda of arguing for a uniform civil code, but warned:

> A Uniform Civil Code that is compulsory from the beginning would by-pass all these problems and create many of its own. Voluntary or compulsory, it seems that if and when the Uniform Civil Code is introduced, there is a strong possibility of a period of deep social unrest taking place. Unless the government is prepared to ride out this period, if it then gives in to those who don't want the Uniform Civil Code, more damage will be done by introducing than by withholding the Uniform Civil Code.

Such eminently sensible and realistic comments are rare. It is highly significant that even well-known authors, and this includes high-profile Indian judges such as V. R. Krishna Iyer (1987), in their selective blindness to Indian cultural concepts and sometimes unqualified admiration of Western-style modernity, have peddled the myth of legal uniformity as a tool for the desperate desire to modernise Indian laws. In that context the superior social policy aim has often been an improvement of the socio-legal position of women. However, looking back at that literature, how much of it is merely ideological shadow boxing in ivory towers or a reflection of drawing room discussions among élite participants? How much of this is actually concerned about the realities of common people's lives and about justice for them?

Here again, selective blindness to ancient Indian socio-legal traditions must be identified as a key factor in scholarly politics. Without understanding the plural legal nature of ancient Indian laws prior to colonial intervention,[14] modern commentators simply do not have command over the necessary tools to reconstruct – and understand – a modernity that makes productive use of the past. Even if they wanted to, they lack the relevant basic skills.[15] The result of such philosophising speculation is often deeply unsatisfactory: Making constructive use of the past involves complex processes of thinking, which most scholars have either been unwilling or unable to follow. The favoured rationale appears to be that the past has nothing to teach us; the faster we overcome its remnants, the better. If the past is assumed to contain relevant elements, these are often 'imagined' along the lines of our predilections, so that the mythical authors of ancient *shastras* turn into law givers! A lot of nonsense has been written – and continues to be written – about Indian legal developments old and new.

For example, in an important study about women and family law reform in modern India, Parashar (1992: 46) seems to claim that the British introduced the personal law system into India and implies that post-colonial legal reform, therefore, must incorporate abolition of that system. Readers should note that the author also claims a more or less exclusive 'religious' status for personal laws, which later (pp. 47–48 and 63–76) enables her to attack the religious nature of personal laws. Parashar (1992: 46) wrote:

> Before the introduction of British law in India no distinction was made between territorial and personal laws. Hindu law and later Islamic law applied to an individual who followed a particular religion and not because the person was situated in a particular territory. With some exceptions Hindu and Islamic religious laws were intended only for the followers of these religions. Furthermore, the religious laws covered all areas of conduct and no distinction was made between personal and public or between religious and secular laws. The division between personal and other spheres of law was first introduced in India by

> English administrators who, early on, decided to leave the personal laws of the natives undisturbed, ostensibly because they formed a part of the religion of the natives. Meanwhile over a period of time all other aspects of law, which were equally religious under the Hindu and Islamic systems, were modified by the British administrators. The introduction of this distinction, and the subsequent different treatment of personal laws from all other aspects of law, form part of the foundation for present day claims that religious personal laws cannot be modified by the State.

This chain of argumentation contains several much-repeated misunderstandings of Indian legal 'tradition'. First of all, one does not need to be a legal specialist to recognise that, under Muslim rule in India, Hindu, Christian, Parsi and other personal laws continued to be applied, as well as the Muslim personal law.[16] This occurred on a personal as well as territorial basis, since there has never been one unified Hindu law or Muslim law in the subcontinent. Even earlier, too, under Hindu domination, apart from Hindu law, Christian, Parsi and Muslim laws were also treated as personal laws, and different Hindu laws, again based on territory as much as religion, were in operation. If anything, Hindu culture can claim to have invented the personal law system.[17] The critical issue in this debate is not, however, who invented the personal law system first. Rather, why are scholars arguing that the modern state law needs to dominate people's lives right down to the household level by providing uniform legal regulation? Looking at the matter from this angle, we may realise that calls for uniform legal regulation are in effect underwriting legal centralist aspirations which can easily slide into dictatorial abuses.

In her subsequent debate, Parashar (1992: 47–48) tries to demonstrate that personal laws are not really 'religious' and that, hence, the state has an inherent right to override them in order to achieve justice. This blind belief in the inherent justice of uniform, Western-type egalitarian laws mars most of the older writing, but also some of the most recent studies on the subject of legal uniformity.[18]

It has been a convenient diversion for this debate that Muslims in India have often tried to argue that the general law of the country should not apply to them and that their *shariat* law should be left undisturbed by the state. Such arguments were also put forward by Hindus in India during the post-Independence debates on the reforms and codification of Hindu law (for details see Derrett 1957). A quick glance across the border shows that in essence the same arguments were advanced by Muslims in Pakistan. The Muslim-dominated state there, significantly, ignored those objections and introduced the *Muslim Family Laws Ordinance* of 1961.[19] Pakistan thus reformed its majority Muslim law, while India did the same for its majority Hindu law in 1955–1956. This is a typical South Asian pattern of state activity, focusing on the respective majority law but ignoring, for all kinds of reasons, the minority personal laws. This comparison demonstrates that the debates have not really been about religion, or about a particular religious law, but about the extent of state control over the respective majority population, in other words about nation building and identity formation more than effective legal regulation or a concern for substantive justice.

We know today that after the *Shah Bano* case, when Muslims went on the rampage demanding the non-application of the *Criminal Procedure Code*, 1973 to themselves and pushing for a separate law, the modern Indian state was self-assured enough to play its own leading role in this strategic game. Thus, the demonstrators were in effect punished by the swift implementation of a separate personal law rule for Muslims, as found in the MWPRDA of 1986, which did not (as we know today) give Muslim men the freedom from financial responsibility for their ex-wives that they wanted. While superficial, politicised analysis saw the 1986 Act as a disaster for the Indian nation and a step back in terms of legal uniformity policies, the actual application of the 1986 Act, as we saw in ch. 4.3, has taught Indian Muslims important lessons. The modern Indian state has been willing to relax its programmatic policy of uniformisation of law in formal terms, but not with regard to substantive provisions. Thus, a Muslim ex-husband of a divorced wife is today worse off than his non-Muslim co-citizens. This is not what anyone expected, and certainly not what the literature told us until very recently. The Muslim community leaders realised this fast, and they have thereafter stopped protesting about preservation of their separate laws – knowing that the state would seize upon this to institute further legal reforms.[20]

In this scenario of legislative stalemate and hidden communal agenda, the courts have played an important role in keeping the debate about legal uniformity in India alive. Every now and then, a case would be reported in which some judges voiced their disquiet about continuing legal inequalities in modern Indian law. I shall show in ch. 6.8 below that this ebb and flow of arguments has kept the Indian uniform civil code debate on the agenda, but it has not led anywhere.

In fact, following the coming into power of the so-called nationalist Bharatiya Janata Party (BJP) government, and hence a Hindu-dominated political force at the federal centre, rather than the secular Congress or a mixed bag of regional parties, the agenda of legal uniformity itself dramatically changed, almost overnight. The movement towards legal uniformity in India has now more or less entirely collapsed, since the lobbyists of uniformity suddenly realised, to their horror, that in a Hindu-dominated India their argument for legal uniformity would amount to underwriting a reconstructed version of Hindu ideology, rather than the envisaged transfer to a supposedly culture-neutral, Western-style model. Intense soul-searching seems to be going on at present (see also Mahmood 1995: 135–139).

Meanwhile, however, the courts have constantly had to deal with practical questions brought before them, and a pattern is emerging that moves India in the direction of legal uniformity, but not through abolition of the personal law system. The key example of the MWPRDA of 1986 showed the modern Indian state, first of all, that constructing a viable social welfare net through reliance on societal resources was possible. This policy aim has been perceived, by judges and governments alike, as more important than playing with the politics of legal uniformity. Secondly, the 1986 Act confirmed for the central government of this huge country that a policy of uniformisation of laws did not necessarily have to go through the arduous route of a uniform civil code. Legal uniformity, in substantive if not formal terms, could also be achieved through the harmonisation of parallel provisions in the concurrent personal laws. This policy has been pursued for Muslims in 1986 by making s. 3 of the MWPRDA similar to s. 125 of the CrPC, and for Christians during the 1990s by the recent judicial re-writing of section 10 in the extremely outdated *Indian Divorce Act*, 1869.[21]

Together with this, we find renewed emphasis in modern India's justice orientation on an age-old, systemic and therefore indigenous strategy which considers problems on a case-by-case basis. Since the late 1980s, modern Indian law has visibly moved further away from attempts to lay down uniformly binding legal rules for all citizens. Probably the most impressive example of this policy within the realm of family law is the strategy of the Supreme Court to grant divorce on the basis of irretrievable breakdown to some couples 'in special circumstances' (see ch. 2.5 above), while refusing to open the floodgates of divorce for all Indian couples.

To increase the woes of modernist legal scholars, public opinion in India is not as vigorously in favour of legal uniformity as some academic writing suggests. Shiv Sahai Singh (1993: 323) reports:

> Leading members of the majority communities agree that it may be premature to aim at a Uniform Civil Code which will be applicable to all citizens in a country like India, but they think that the time has come to codify personal law of each community by highlighting its best points.

The most elaborate case for legal unification to date has been put by Dhagamwar (1989), whose study was based on wide consultation with many individuals from different communities. However, the recorded voices tend to be 'enlightened' figures and few people seem to have been convinced by the arguments in that study.[22] Looking back over the 1980s and 1990s, I have consistently argued against legal uniformity in India, as will be evident from the series of reprinted articles in this chapter. My starting point was, originally, that in view of its own legal history and millennia of experience, and with almost a billion people to take account of, India would find it conceptually and practically impossible to govern everyone by the same rule system. It seems to me that during the late 1980s, the Indian state itself finally recognised this and has now changed its policy, thereby leaving a huge question mark over the precise interpretation of Article 44 in the Indian Constitution of 1950, which reads:

> 44. *Uniform civil code for the citizens.* –
> The State shall endeavour to secure for the citizens a uniform civil code throughout the territory of India.

The classic interpretation of this Article implied a mandate for introducing a straightforward uniform civil code for all Indians, thus abolishing the personal law system and streamlining Indian law in this respect.[23] However, this model solution, clearly designed to copy the West, is no longer as attractive as it once seemed, in fact it is now seen by many as positively obnoxious. As more and more scholars and lawyers realise that the modern Indian legal system remains – and will need to remain – a culture-specific political construct serving a gigantic population in the process of nation-building rather than direct legal regulation of every little human action, the ambition for legislation has waned altogether. During the 1990s, mental energy has increasingly been redirected towards judicial concerns for justice and equity and the legislature has blatantly refused to act and to promulgate what Allott (1980) would have called 'phantom laws'. This has become a definite pattern during the past few years.[24]

Instead of seeking to fit the enormous square peg of litigation into an equally large round hole of uniform family law legislation, supra-modern Indian law today appears to have changed direction. More and more, the sharp edges of the case-law are being smoothed by judicial activism and by a judiciary that sees its major task as balancing competing claims in scenarios of irreconcilable competition for social welfare-oriented resources. A re-invigorated awareness of the importance of justice, equity and good conscience, which in India never meant the exclusive application of English legal principles anyway, can be observed as well.[25] This works in many ways for the benefit of women, and certainly for children, although such comments should not be read to mean that everything is well in the state of India. No legal system in the world has achieved perfect justice, nor will this ever happen, since human deviancy always invents new scenarios of conflict and the law follows disputes rather than preventing their genesis in the first place.

The most important point with which to conclude our present legal analysis is therefore this: Indian law has now finally abandoned the Western legal axioms of uniformity and rejects the norm that states must have uniform laws to be called modern states. Indian modernity has retained decidedly Indian characteristics. Not surprisingly, especially if one knows something about ancient Indian legal history, it turns out that the Western axiom is probably false, anyway. The complex, federal Indian legal system shows that uniformity of legal provisions is manifestly not a pre-condition for modernity and for justice. These are not new messages at all if we take a cross-cultural, diachronic approach. All we know today better, and quite firmly so, is that the remarkable post-colonial Indian optimism about the scope for following Western legal structures and concepts was quite misguided. These are historical lessons which countries like Russia and Yugoslavia have ignored at their peril.

While Mother India still claims all of her many different children as her own, she continues to recognise that they will live to a large extent on their own terms and by their own rules. In terms of Chiba's (1986) analysis of legal pluralism, the official Indian law has been building recognition mechanisms for a multitude of unofficial laws and for legal postulates into the basic structure of modern Indian law, thereby refuting the ideological superiority of legal uniformity as an axiomatic component of modernity in modern democracies of the South.

6.2 Towards a scientific jurisprudence

[From: 1988(2) *KLT*, Journal section, pp. 14–17]

In his article 'The crisis in jurisprudence', at AIR 1987 Journal section 39–42, Shri Markanday Katju has rightly pointed out that jurisprudence has very often been treated as an ideological tool to serve vested interests. On the other hand, he argues, even basic problems have not been solved, and the impression is created that "Western jurisprudence has come to a grinding halt" (p. 39).

The purpose of my response is certainly not to defend Western jurisprudence, which could indeed be said to be in a deep muddle, but to point out a different way forward than Shri Katju suggests.

It may be taken as a fact that jurisprudence has indeed often become little but intellectual jugglery. In my view this has as much to do with many scholars' delight in the obscure and unusual, which afford opportunity to display brilliance and to confuse others, as with the common desire among mankind to predict a golden future on the basis of scanty evidence. But why talk about Western jurisprudence? Jurisprudence the world over has not been raised to the level of a science, and this is the real problem. In my submission, non-Western legal systems have a lot to contribute to a science of jurisprudence; for reasons I shall explain below this is not a widely-shared opinion.

As a matter of fact, many Asian and African legal systems are much older than Western legal systems, and they may have approached 'law' in a rather different way than Austinian jurisprudence did in the 19th century. Islamic jurisprudence, above all, has built up an impressive body of literature, based on its own perception of the world, and of principles of interpretation. Classical Hindu jurisprudence, almost forgotten now, similarly produced much evidence of serious intellectual labour. Ancient Chinese jurisprudence is becoming better known now. Historically speaking, much law had been in existence before the Western jurisprudents, even the Roman ones, began to think about the subject. The trouble with jurisprudence as a science is that even such very basic historical facts have been systematically suppressed. Jurisprudence has been largely eurocentric, and this continues to be so.

We know now that early writers like Sir Henry Maine did not understand the nature of non-European legal systems; Austin was building his theories on an inherent assumption of Western superiority. How can such theories, culturally blinkered as they are, be a suitable foundation for a universal science of jurisprudence? Truly scientific jurisprudence, it is submitted, must be comparative jurisprudence.

Small, but significant beginnings have been made recently in this field, and those lines are worth pursuing. A. N. Allott: *The limits of law*. London 1980, which is partly a critical response to the Hart concept of law, indicates that traditional law is a culture-bound local phenomenon, not neatly separable from aspects of order in society like religion and morality. Modern law, however, is to a certain extent identifiable as a separate factor of social control. Allott also wrote, unusual for an English law professor, that law of course claims to govern its subjects in so many ways, but that in reality these subjects of law never lose the capacity to develop their own forms of law. This may well be in reaction to some form of official law or imposed law. It is likely that he wrote this because he spent many years of his life in Africa, observing the legal effects of colonial rule there, thus coming to very different conclusions than Austin or Hart could possible have reached.

But Allott's study went further. He observed that in England itself, law was not the all- powerful controller of human behaviour. The subjects of English law, too, did not order their lives only in accordance with positive law. In other words, law had limits, not just in so-called underdeveloped countries, where the resources for a 'proper' court system may be lacking and where disputes traditionally did not necessarily reach the officially provided arenas of dispute settlement. Such realisations are easier to achieve when one is aware of the place of local dispute settlement procedures in traditional and modern China, for example, or in India or Africa.

In a separate chapter of his book (pp. 259–286), Allott took the example of cohabitation, that recently very common 'social phenomenon' in English law, which has now been officially recognised by the legal system as a 'legal phenomenon', to illustrate his concept of the limits of official law in England itself. He also indicated that in Britain now, the presence of millions of non-English residents would have important implications on the legal system in the near future. The official law would have to take notice of new sets of facts, and English law would soon find itself modified as a result of multicultural realities. Not even a decade later, much of what he wrote has been realised as true, but the official attitude continues to be extremely reluctant to admit this.

Recently, I have been able to show that Hindus, Muslims and Sikhs in Britain have, over the past two decades or so, been developing their own methods of complying with the requirements of English law (See 1988(1) *KLT* Journal, p. 56). As a result, we now find new forms of Hindu, Muslim and even Sikh laws in Britain, officially ignored, but acting as powerful and authoritative mechanisms of ordering the lives of Asian residents in Britain. A new compromise has been found here between traditional laws and the requirements of a modern uniform national law.

Also very recently, an important comparative legal study of Asian laws appeared under the editorship of an experienced Japanese scholar of law: Masaji Chiba (ed.): *Asian indigenous law in interaction with received law.* London and New York 1986. Here it is argued, not dissimilar to Allott's approach, that official law and unofficial law, plus legal postulates, contribute to the working out of the actual legal systems in modern Asian countries. This is an elaboration on Ehrlich's concept of 'living law', and it strongly refutes the officially perceived view that state law is the law that one has to study to understand a legal system. The various contributors, including U. Baxi for India, provide excellent material for a comparative study of jurisprudence.

Studies of this kind, it is submitted, are urgently needed to make jurisprudence a legal subject of more than superficial relevance. The crisis of jurisprudence in India, so elaborately described by U. Baxi, Shri Katju and others, is largely due to a superficial reliance on the biased ideas of famous Western schools of jurisprudence. So let us begin to think about how to gather material for an Indian jurisprudence that can be fed into this international science.

At once, a major difficulty in India is lack of knowledge about the traditional legal systems. How many legal scholars now know Sanskrit, Arabic or Persian and would thus be able to have a fresh look at the historical development of indigenous legal systems of India, assessing them for the purpose of jurisprudential inquiry? How many of us would be ready to shed deep-rooted pre-conceived notions of the superiority of Western law models, to attempt an unbiased account of ancient Hindu legal systems, of the origins and development of Muslim laws in the subcontinent, of the history of Christian laws in India? I have put plurals everywhere, since the very diverse picture of a multitude of different legal systems operating side by side at any one time is still far too often overlooked. There is, and has never been, one Hindu law, one Muslim law, nor one Christian law of India, there are many.

Precisely here our major current difficulties in jurisprudence as a science become obvious. Legal science as a whole is geared, for reasons of its own that we need not go into here, towards uniformity, clarity, ambiguity-avoidance, to name but a few. All these values are Western conceptual fragments that have been uncritically adopted by Indian legal science as values, to the extent that the Constitution of India has a Directive Principle of State Policy placing (it would appear) the State under a duty to work towards a uniform civil code. I am not saying that this is a bad thing in itself, there are certainly good and valid reasons for having such a constitutional directive. But the concept of legal uniformity in India has become, inevitably, a political, ideological tool, and powerful vested interests will tell the jurisprudent that one should not wake sleeping lions by reminding present-day Indians of the traditional diversity of the Indian legal systems. In order words, to look at a past of communally different laws will quickly be seen as an attempt to strengthen communalism. But have we considered sufficiently well in India that enforced uniformity may provoke communalism? There are several recent and current reminders of this uncomfortable truth.

If even those countries that produced the unifying legal ideologies are now beginning to accept, however reluctantly, that there are basic human facts of legal diversity that cannot be ignored by any legal system concerned with justice, India has little reason to continue to pursue a policy of legal unification. The problem is, significantly, not an Indian one, it is a universal issue. But again, how many scholars in India have looked to Tanzania or Kenya, to take but two prominent examples of modern countries that have been left with the same misguided colonial heritage as India?

Shri Katju gave the excellent advice to treat jurisprudence as a science. But to take this seriously will inevitably meet powerful objections. It will be an uncomfortable science, since it will demask certain ideologies as what they really are. Jurisprudence, as Shri Katju rightly stresses, has been a useful ancillary tool of government; it is thus a political force. But if we become afraid to state the truth, because it displeases the great and powerful, we may just as well have no science of jurisprudence. So let us face the fact that our research may yield facts about law that lawyers do not like to know. As it happens, Shri Katju indicates what these would be, since his own theory of "progressive positive law" operates with purported axioms that need to be seen in their ideological context, too.

I would not be concerned to discuss at length whether jurisprudence can be a science or not. It depends, clearly, on what scholars make of it. Shri Katju rightly points out that we must free it from prejudices, subjectivism and vested interests (p. 41). Perhaps, this is ultimately never possible, so we must try to use our scientific methods with this fundamental problem in mind and not become overconfident about our own theories.

Shri Katju adopts too uncritically, in my humble submission, theories like the dependence of law on the economic system, raising the axioms of "our scientific age" and of 'progress' to the extent of man's "mastery over nature" all of which require "more and more positive law" (p. 42). With respect, I see no difference between this Indian model of "progressive positive law" and what has been called by Shri Katju himself "clumsy, superficial approaches which never seriously tackled the subject" (p. 41), among them the various schools of jurisprudence in the 20th century. At best, this new approach could yield some ideas about the modern study of Indian laws in context. But this new theory gives no indication of respect for unofficial laws and legal postulates, in Chiba's terminology, i.e. for people's ideas about law. It will consequently be incapable of throwing light on the crucial questions of interrelation of official and unofficial laws in modern India, ultimately of the nature of the modern legal system itself. This admittedly very sophisticated theory of progressive positive law closes its eyes to social realities in so many ways. It does not see, for example, that customary laws continue to be powerful regulators of social and economic relations in India, not just in backward, rural areas. In summary, it adopts too uncritically the positivist theories of law coupled with a 'social engineering through law' approach.

This, I submit with great respect to Shri Katju's legal expertise and learning, is not the way forward. At the same time, I am not in a position to suggest an easy remedy. I think there is none. But in view of what I indicated above about comparative legal studies as the basic foundation for a study of jurisprudence, I feel that Indian legal scholarship will do well to look to the past and to present evidence from a number of countries rather than fixing its gaze to an uncertain future. We cannot anticipate properly what we are heading for unless we have an adequate understanding of past processes and learn to evaluate, in such light, the present abundance of confusion. In India, whether we like it or not, the roots for historical and current processes of legal development lie in the more or less holy books and in the minds of the various communities, not in some holy books of Western scholarship on law or political science. Indian law will never become a Western system of law; to strive for it is a big fallacy based on the inadequate understanding of purported universal 'axioms'.

Jurisprudence, if it wishes to lift itself out to this current crisis everywhere in the world, better acknowledges, with all consequences, that it requires a fundamentally open- minded and open-ended approach to the issues under debate. We can all speculate about the future and strive for some ideal goals; but in the meantime, there are real people living real lives which are very often adversely affected by laws unsuitable to their subjects, or which have nothing to do with the official laws that claim so much authority. Such situations will not change by appeals to the scientific age or the axiom of progress. Jurisprudence, then, even in a future-oriented country like India, must not ignore past and present in favour of predicting a better future which promises unrealistic goals.

6.3 Uniformity of laws in India and England

[From: Vol. 7 No. 11 [June 1988] *Journal of Law and Society* (Peshawar), pp. 11–26]

This article invites readers [sic] to familiarise themselves with a new area of English law that is likely to achieve more importance in the future and in a number of countries, and that is particularly relevant to Indian lawyers, legal scholars and legislators. A proper name for this subject has not yet been found, but recently the first detailed study on the topic appeared, written by a Senior Lecturer in Law at Southampton University in the UK (Sebastian M. Poulter: *English law and ethnic minority customs*. London: Butterworths 1986). This very important and excellent study has the effect, *inter alia*, that the legal profession in England can no longer pretend that the issues raised in the book do not exist. A most impressive collection of material, including reference to many unreported cases, indicates that this study represents only the tip of an iceberg; much more research of this kind is needed, and is likely to be conducted before we enter the 21st century.

Dr. Poulter's attempts "to provide a systematic description of those provisions of English law which tend to impinge upon ethnic minority customs" (p. vi) redress a balance. As is rightly argued, the relationship between English law and the cultures of the ethnic minorities has so far tended to be overlooked. Such ethnic minorities are very prominently Indians, Pakistanis and Bangladeshis, who are all classed as 'Asians' in England. Now, rather than developing along secular lines, and merging into one uniform group of 'Asians' or even into the 'host community', most ethnic minorities in Britain have been forming distinctive groups along regional and religious lines, so that even the English are now becoming more aware of the distinctions between Panjabi Muslim and Panjabi Hindus, the Sikhs, Gujarati Muslims and Hindus, Maharashtrians, Tamils, Bangladeshis, and a number of other groups, whose claims for separate provision in terms of language and culture, as well as religion, are increasingly being recognised. Detailed fieldwork in a number of cities in England has shown that the more 'Asians' there are in one place, the greater will be their claim for recognition of separate cultural identities. Thus, larger cities in Britain now have a variety of mosques, gurudwaras and Hindu temples catering for different regional groups and/or sects, rather than for all Muslims, all Sikhs or all Hindus, as was very often the case decades ago when there were fewer 'Asians'. So England currently witnesses a constantly increasing assertion of diverse cultural identities. This has tremendous implications in the sphere of law.

Exact figures on ethnic minorities do not exist, since the UK Census has so far been unable to count people according to ethnic criteria and has preferred to class the children of 'Asians' and other immigrants born in the UK as British. As a result, quoted figures vary tremendously and this insecurity is easily exploited to support conflicting claims. It is thought that several million members of ethnic minority groups live in Britain now. Out of a total population of about 54 million this is a significant share, and the many more than ten lakhs 'Asians' figure prominently and are highly visible. Since ethnic minorities tend to concentrate in the central parts of England, and there again in certain urban centres, both in inner-city and suburban areas, one very often finds a situation now, locally, that the actual ethnic minority are the white English natives. Some areas of English cities are now totally dominated by 'Asians' and in some cases Afro-Caribbeans. This has implications on all levels, including local and now also national politics. In such cases of residential segregation, for which there are a number of precedents in India (the *mohallah* concept, the *bazar* as a concentration of particular trades), cultural diversities and with them legal particularities assert themselves quite powerfully. After an initial period of dispersion and confusion, during which first individuals and later families concentrated on economic betterment, 'Asian' communities in Britain (the same process is under way in the USA now) have been getting together to establish community centres as visible expressions of the age-old links of communal and clan support and control. The number of such centres, as ofHindu temples, gurudwaras and mosques, is rising fast. These places of worship often have a multiplicity of functions, they provide cohesion for the community, strengthen group identity, emphasise the borders to other groups, and provide a forum for innumerable 'leaders' to seek influence in a number of ways. Both religious and cultural diversities are in this way perpetuated and even strengthened in Britain.

But while in India such local and communal concentrations and particularities are an accepted fact of life and of history, 'Asians' in Britain have had to fight for recognition of their cultural particularities. Poulter's study is concerned with some of these situations. Unfortunately, however the viewpoint that the author has chosen overlooks the perspective of the ethnic minorities themselves.

The scheme of the book is impressive and systematically arranged: Every chapter begins with a discussion of what the author calls 'ethnic customs' in their respective traditional context. Then follow very detailed 'policy considerations' which ask whether the application and rationale of such customs makes sense in an English setting. The third limb of argument is a detailed analysis of the relevant provisions of English law, and the treatment finishes with the assessment of the scope for legal reform, which often takes the form of a concluding discussion and summary of the 'policy considerations'.

By proceeding in this way, the discussion takes a particular turn, mainly because of the underlying assumption that the ethnic 'customs' need to be put in line with the requirement of English law, which seems to provide the superior standard within the conceptual framework of the book. Detailed insight is, thus, provided into the current difficulties over the acceptance of ethnic minority 'customs' in English law. In certain respects, little appears to have changed since the British colonial administrators first came into contact with the traditional laws of their Asian and African subjects. But now such former subjects have become citizens and demand, or at least expect, to be treated differently than centuries ago.

More critically, as a consequence of Poulter's approach, it is overlooked that the ethnic minorities themselves, ever since they arrived in England, have been adjusting to the new legal environment. Poulter's method thus ignores a crucial dimension: It fails to notice a third layer of law that has, at least in the perception of the ethnic minorities themselves, a most important role to play. There is more to consider than English law and ethnic minority 'customs'. The latter, a broad collective term, as the author explains (p. 3), refers to "the widest possible range of social practices found among the ethnic minorities which are, in one way or another, affected by the provisions of English law". What Poulter examines here are the laws of the ethnic minorities at their point of contact with the English legal system; the official laws, not really the customary laws, also as they have subsequently developed in the respective foreign jurisdiction. For example, the Hindu law of marriage and divorce in India is considered a relevant factor here. But how much weight can be given to the provisions of the *Marriage Laws (Amendment) Act*, 1976, which came at a time when most 'Asians' had long settled in Britain? And how relevant are such provisions for East African 'Asians', for example, who may for generations have had minimal contact with India?

Obviously, writing on the subject in the mid-eighties, we cannot pretend that nothing has happened to ethnic 'customs' in England since about 1960, when many 'Asian' immigrants started coming. I would imagine that the demands of English law virtually hit the immigrants the moment they set foot anywhere on the British Isles. Significantly, this 'hitting' happens today in India itself, as many unsuccessful applicants for British visas discover. The process of learning, in either case, is painful and takes some time. Since certain common rules must, of necessity, be followed, but there are so many rules, sooner or later some conflict will arise. To avoid such conflicts, 'Asians' and other minorities have often initially sought to ensure compliance with this body of strange rules, but there are limits to this. Most immigrants did not come to Britain expecting to 'do as the Romans do', as Poulter rightly recognises (p. v.). The desire to maintain one's own distinct culture and traditions, coupled with ignorance of many requirements of English law, put most immigrants on a course of confrontation. In the absence of official recognition of these problems, a solution had to be found by the people themselves, and as a result, many ethnic 'customs' changed and were modified in Britain. It is this dimension that Poulter's approach overlooks, and some of the discussions in the book are therefore rather academic, with little relevance to the actual situation. Thus Poulter is led by the Muslim demand for the recognition of *talaq* in English law into arguing that "[t]here seems a reasonable argument for at least recognising the validity of extra-judicial consensual divorces which take place in England, provided they are so recognised by the countries where the parties are domiciled or of which they are national" (p. 125). In fact, English law has been doing this for some time now, through a 'special procedure', which leads to a so-called 'quickie divorce', i.e. merely an administrative act of legal recognition of a couple's agreement to divorce. How this agreement has been reached seems not to interest the state, so long as at the point of registration the impression is created and maintained that this is a divorce by mutual consent. This seems to be the English equivalent of divorce by mutual consent under s. 13-B of the *Hindu Marriage Act*, 1955 (as amended in 1976) and s. 28 of the *Special Marriage Act*, 1954.

Now, in England as in India, the official act of registering an agreed divorce is only the very last act of a presumably, at least potentially, complex drama that was fought out between the spouses, in the families concerned, or even before some council of caste or clan elders. So far, we know very little about customary divorce procedures among ethnic minorities in Britain, but contrary to frequent claims 'Asians' in Britain are getting divorced, and many have learnt to present an acceptable case to the agents of the English legal system. The rather uncomplicated 'special procedure' that is now available has, with a bit of adjustment and goodwill, allowed ethnic minorities in Britain to maintain their customary procedures of divorce almost unmodified. Much of the controversy over the *talaq* divorces in Britain appears, therefore, purely political wrangling. What needs to be investigated now is whether the existing customary procedures of divorce settlements among 'Asians' in Britain give women a fair deal.

While we know far too little about divorce among 'Asians' in Britain, the process of multi-layered adjustment to a new legal environment is much better known in the area of solemnisation of marriages. As I have shown recently ('Legal pluralism in the Hindu marriage', in R. Burghart (ed.): *Hinduism in Great Britain*. London: Tavistock 1987, pp. 180–200), 'Asians' in Britain had to 'learn the law' in this area very rapidly at a stage in the early seventies, when marriages were beginning to become more common in communities here. To their utter dismay, some families found that their daughters, who had been married in a customary Hindu, Sikh or Muslim marriage ritual in England, were not in fact validly married in the eyes of English law. The young 'husband' could (and a few did) walk away after the first night, or a few nights, and the women and their relations had no legal remedies and hid in shame. Such news travelled very rapidly. More recently, the same learning process has been taking place in some parts of India. In Gujarat in particular, a 'dreamboy' from England could marry an innocent girl in a customary ceremony, often with great pomp, only to disappear after a few nights, leaving the 'wife' and her family in shambles. Even if such a marriage remains valid under Indian law, what do you do if the 'husband' escaped to England?

In England, the need to register marriages under the provisions of English law was thus brought home to all 'Asians' with some force, and now there is total compliance with this legal requirement. But, can we argue that 'Asians' are now following the English law of marriage? My fieldwork shows that the registration ceremony of English law has been built into the customary 'Asian' patterns of marriage solemnisation in such a way that it constitutes something like an engagement in the eyes of the 'Asian' spouses and their families. The state makes a contract with the couple that they are henceforth recognised as husband and wife. But execution of the rights and duties between the spouses remains in abeyance till they have undergone the religious, customary wedding ritual. Till then, the 'wife' will stay with her parents, the 'husband' has no conjugal rights. The day of the 'Asian' wedding is later remembered as the wedding day, the now famous videos are shot then, while the registered marriage tends to be a rather dry and almost unimportant procedure that can be dealt with in a lunchbreak. The desire to display wealth and status has effected some changes here, so that an 'Asian' wedding in England may now be a series of posh celebrations and receptions, but in either case one is not much concerned with the couple's relationship vis-à-vis the state, but very concerned with the community.

The state itself is content with this minimal role. If you have followed the prescribed registration procedures, you are taken to be husband and wife, and cannot simply opt out of the marriage again, as was tried in some nullity cases under English law that make amusing reading. On the surface, thus, there is legal uniformity in English law. Below the surface, the customary diversities prevalent in the various ethnic minorities are allowed to prosper, and there is much evidence that new forms of customary procedures of marriage have been developing among 'Asians' in Britain. From the viewpoint of the English legal system as well as the 'Asians' themselves, however, an acceptable balance has been found in this area of the law between respecting ethnic minority customs and demanding adherence to uniform legal standards.

If the state is content to require compliance with certain minimum standards of administrative procedures only, ethnic minority cultures would seem to have tremendously wide free space to act out their customary patterns of life. In a country like Britain, it would appear that this has always been seen as a value in itself. But now, as so very diverse and different cultural patterns claim recognition, one is tempted to draw lines. This is extremely dangerous, as it discriminates between different communities. Thus there are many indications in England that Afro-Caribbean and also African customary laws find it much harder to gain respect and recognition than 'Asian' cultural patterns. One reason is apparently that West Indians and Africans are presumed and almost expected to be Christian, i.e. complying with what are seen as Christian standards, which are, however, European Christian standards. 'Asians' on the other hand, are mostly members of Oriental religious traditions that often demand a different way of life, which seems to be accepted more easily. There has of course been tremendous pressure from Muslims in particular, for a greater recognition of ethnic religious and cultural patterns of life in England. Again, where official reaction has been negative, often the communities themselves have got together to organise remedies, which in turn exert their own pressures.

The total picture one gains is, thus, that in Britain today ethnic minority customs, however defined, are claiming recognition in a legal system that has traditionally considered itself uniform. The great reluctance of this purported uniform legal system to accept and adapt to the new diversities has become untenable in some areas of the law, as Poulter's book well illustrates. If English law today maintains this fiction of uniformity somewhat successfully, it appears to have managed to do this by retreating, in some cases, to a position of demanding little more than compliance with some fairly simple administrative procedures that have legal consequences. As we have seen, the underlying legal diversities have been relegated to the status of unrecognised customs, but they have not been outlawed.

What, now, can Indian law today take from the issues raised by Poulter's book with regard to uniformity and diversity in modern English law?

The current English situation appears almost as a variation of a familiar Indian theme: cultural and legal diversities have to compete for official recognition at the state level, while at the same time the lives of ethnically and culturally very diverse peoples continue to be determined by such diversities irrespective of their legal status. The state's desire for the maintenance or achievement of uniform legal standards is diametrically opposed to the religious and cultural diversities of the people. In neither case, though, has the official unifying state machinery been able to score a victory: English law today is under pressure to accommodate more diversities to remain a just and equitable legal system, while Indian law is unable to discard and disregard the traditional diversities. Is uniformity of laws an unachievable aim?

We find the modern Indian legal system on a thorny road to self-inflicted uniformity that nobody really wants to advance on. The constitutional provision of Article 44 sits there, causing multiple anxieties. The project of a Uniform Civil Code, though much debated, must still be seen as a "distant mirage" (A. Allott: *The limits of law*. London: Butterworths 1980, p. 216). Half-hearted tinkering with an optional Uniform Civil Code seems pointless and counterproductive, since it contributes to communal tensions. Actually, the country already has a rudimentary uniform civil code, the *Special Marriage Act*, 1954; this has to be applied in some cases, but is otherwise far too little known, not free from flaws, and is apparently little used. Indian legislators are rightly apprehensive about possible backlashes of new legislation, and the Supreme Court appears to have become afraid of its own courage. The *Shah Bano* case and its consequences have shown the deep divisions of opinion in the country and have raised the question of feasibility of legal uniformity in a particular way. The 1986 Act securing 'rights' to divorced Muslim women was certainly a step away from legal uniformity.

Many legal scholars have expressed doubts about the benefits of total unification of laws in India, but these are not taken seriously enough. The real people of India, not their representatives, seem to show in so many was that for them unification of laws, if it involves rash abolition of their traditional patterns of life, remains undesirable. The abolition of Hindu law in Kerala shows this very clearly (see 1986 Kerala Law Times, Journal section, pp. 177–200 and pp. 63–65). The common Indian will overlook and ignore such reforms with the result that the gap between official law and actual 'living law' becomes wider all the time.

The issue of ethnic minorities and their claim for separate treatment is not new to India at all. Nowadays, however, there are new conflict situations: would a colony of settlers from Tamil Nadu, resident in Bombay for a long time, be able to claim exemption from some local laws? The official answer may not satisfy a comparative lawyer who is aware of the strength of customary laws. Indian legal studies should address themselves to such questions, in the national interest.

Historically, India is of course in a very different position from England. Already the ancient Hindu law expressly respected legal diversity through the consequent application of the concept of *dharma*, with its most important actual source being individual conscience (*atmanastusti*). We know that traditional Hindu law perceived uniformity of laws as leading to injustice. Similarly, the Islamic law that developed during the long Mughal reign in the subcontinent, encompassed in the term *sharia*, which implies a unity of religious experience and belief, did not demand uniformity of legal rules. Moreover, for a minority religious and legal system it must have been expedient to respect the demands of the other legal systems. So, when the British came to start their Raj, they found tremendous diversity and they realised (e.g. the 1772 Declaration by Warren Hastings) that at least in certain areas of the law they would never be able to enforce total uniformity. To my knowledge, it has not yet been analysed in detail how it happened that 'the people of India' gave themselves a constitutional provision promoting uniformity of all laws. So in India now, as in Britain, though for different reasons, the state seeks legal uniformity, while the people expect recognition of diversities. How can this be reconciled without causing injustice?

Wholesale and forcible unification of the Indian legal system will, it is submitted, never be a realistic option. The introduction of an optional uniform civil code seems pointless: it will increase the diversity of legal rules, and it is thus doubtful whether it can promote uniformity at all. If there is so much resistance to a uniform civil code as such, surely a viable alternative would be to reform the existing personal laws and the concurrent general law on roughly similar lines. To date, only the laws of the Hindu majority have been subjected to this process, so that there is now little difference between the *Hindu Marriage Act* of 1955, as amended, and the *Special Marriage Act* of 1954, which was similarly amended. Of course, Hindus and others governed by this personal law system (the Sikhs in particular) are not entirely happy with their secularised and rather Westernised modern legal system, and legal scholars including Professor Derrett have criticised the gradual destruction of the socio-cultural fabric of the country through law. India, it is widely felt, will never succumb to total secularisation and unification. Events in England today give much credence to that view.

It is not entirely clear why only the Hindu law has been so heavily reformed since independence. Of course, attempts to modify the Muslim law of India would cause resentment, to say the least. But even the minor personal laws were not touched and allowed to become so outdated that the Supreme Court felt constrained to point this out (*Jorden Diengdeh*, AIR 1985 SC 935, at 940–941). Other well-known recent cases have contributed to a rising awareness of the need for reform of the Christian law of India, which is still much influenced by church law (see *Kurian v. Alphonsa* at 1986 KLT 731). The Parsis, or rather some of their astute community leaders, have just managed to persuade Parliament to reform their personal law to preempt the merging of their jealously maintained separate identity. Nobody seems to know what the Jews of India think about this matter.

It appears that the original plan of the makers of India's Constitution was that members of the minority groups would gradually submit voluntarily to a secularised uniform legal system. This calculation has definitely proved wrong. Both the secularised Hindu law and the secularised general law have been suspected of being Hindu, by Tahir Mahmood and others, explaining thus that there is great reluctance by members of other communities to follow these so-called secularised laws. But Hindu bias or not, the people of India (including the Hindus) are apparently not ready to be governed by a uniform secularised system of family laws of any description. The issue is, therefore, not one of communal rivalries and tensions, as it is made to look all the time. In truth, the opposing poles are clearly the official state law and people's law. The state, with its centralising, bureaucratic tendencies and its obvious and necessary concern over maintaining national unity seeks to develop uniform standards in all areas of life, including law. On the other hand it appears still, does it not, that all communities in India are united in their desire to maintain regional and local, religious and cultural diversities, and a plurality of laws.

It would almost appear as a matter of commonsense that India's hugeness (like the whole of Europe!) must preclude total uniformity. The United States, too, do not have an entirely uniform legal system. Why is India so obsessed with the concept of uniformity? Is it more than a distant mirage, a vision of some politicians who may be worried that their huge area of influence may break up? It is, at last, becoming increasingly apparent that the discussions have been sidetracked by communal issues all the time.

The central problem, as indicated above, is that the state, despite democratic processes of election etc, is unrepresentative of its people. In fact, the people have to be protected from the state at times, since the concept of public interest (and of law) is a different one depending on whether you walk in the corridors of power or work in someone else's field.

The official concept of law is that of statute and case law. Since independence, within the framework of the Constitution, a body of official laws has grown up that claims to serve the interest of all Indian citizens alike. This body of laws, so far, appears to provide recognition of legal diversities, to some extent. But these laws are not known to the overwhelmingly rural population of India. This is not, however, because these people are ignorant as is always hastily argued. In reality, their lives are determined by other laws, which are well known, much of them customary, much dependent on the situation at the particular place and time. Those laws are ignored and often unrecognised by the state. But they exist, and they continue to develop, as any system of living law does. Whether they are developing in the right way is an entirely different matter, which is not for discussion here.

So the official Indian legal system, including the personal law system, does not constitute the totality of the actual Indian law. The 'living law' of India today is a combination of the official legal system and the innumerable 'unofficial' local laws that determine most people's lives.

The parallels with the situation of 'Asians' in Britain today are remarkable. In either case, the existing plurality of laws should not be seen as a negative phenomenon, as a relapse into the 'primitive' stage of customary laws. Certainly in England, we cannot talk about lack of 'development'. England, at any rate, has managed to maintain a fiction of legal uniformity, while in India, since time immemorial, local, ethnic and religious diversities have become entrenched, even in the official legal system, and continue to determine much of the living law.

The fairly recent demand for recognition of ethnic diversities in English law shows that the colonial masters' experience of Indian, other Oriental and African laws has not provided many useful lessons. As Poulter's study demonstrates, English law today remains fixed to its fiction of common law and continues to overlook the disparity between official law and customary laws. The English legal system, therefore, finds itself troubled, as its Indian counterpart, by politically motivated and communalised claims resisting legal uniformity. At the same time, ethnic British-based customary laws are entrenching themselves in the living law of British 'Asians', and the official law can do little about it, because it refuses to realise and recognise what has been happening.

At least in this regard, Indian law with its express recognition of personal laws appears more realistic. But, as outlined above, the disparity between official law and actual law is also a feature of the personal law system of India. So the question arises whether any amount of legal reform in the official legal system, including the personal laws, could have any direct implications on the ground. We see that not even the general law is effective in enforcing uniform standards: Drastic amendments to the *Dowry Prohibition Act* have not abolished the problem of dowry deaths, let alone dowry itself, child marriages continue to exist, and murders take place all over the country, as though no *Indian Penal Code* existed. But this should not be called lawlessness. Rather, here are open conflicts of laws and moral standards, and these conflicts have not been resolved by any new legislation. So even if against all odds India were to give herself a Uniform Civil Code, there is little chance that this would be followed on a large scale. In other words, in seeking to implement a Uniform Civil Code, India is now following a perceived Western model of development that is showing itself to be unworkable, even in the West.

Is there a way out of the dilemma? Recent developments in the English legal system seem to show that even without full official admission of the recognition of diversities, a state of legal uniformity can be maintained that satisfies both the official doctrine and the people governed by such laws. This can happen in two ways. Firstly, there is the partial relaxation of otherwise uniform legal rules. Thus it was found expedient in England, after much pressure, to pass the *Motor-Cycle Crash Helmets (Religious Exemption) Act,* 1976 exempting Sikhs from the legal requirement to wear crash helmets. Regarding marriage laws, Quakers and Jews have long had special provisions under English law. Secondly, the state may renounce its claim to regulate all activities of its citizens and be content to expect compliance with minimum standards and, more importantly here, some uniform administrative procedures that have legal implications. As we saw, the truly secular approach to marriage solemnisation in English law, the demand to follow merely a short, dry process of official registration which created a legal status in the eyes of the state, leaves sufficient freedom to the spouses and their families to follow such customary procedures of marriage solemnisation as they wish, or to follow none. Similarly, the 'special procedure' for divorce under English law is but an administrative act to recognition of a couple's agreement to divorce, which is thus given legal validity. How this agreement was reached remains a matter for the spouses and their families; it may be regulated ad hoc, by customary procedures, or according to religious rules.

It may strike readers that both these forms of renunciation of the state's claim for absolute uniformity are already found in Indian law. Since, unlike Britain, India starts from a position of explicit recognition of legal diversity, to provide exemptions for religious minorities (e.g. the Sikhs' permission to carry a *kirpan*) or local peculiarities (e.g. the relaxation on prohibited degrees in marriage in sections 5(iv) and (v) of the *Hindu Marriage Act*, 1955) is fairly common practice anyway. One might fear, though, that too many exemptions may be provided to those who shout loudest, thus making a total mockery of the system itself, as happened in the case of the 1986 Act purporting to 'protect' Muslim divorced women.

But what about the state's renunciation to regulate customary procedures, and to implement instead nationally uniform standards of administration? If all new marriages in India were to be registered compulsorily under a uniform procedure from the year 2000 or so, even illiterate village people would, after due publicity, quickly learn about this, since the value of women and their virginity or purity is understood everywhere, and few people would like to see their daughter or sister abandoned after a sham marriage. Admittedly, the problem of regulating cohabitation would remain, as it does in English law. But all sections in any matrimonial legislation dealing with solemnisation of marriage could be repealed in favour of compulsory provision for registration of marriage, leading to much greater security over the status of many Indian marriages.

Similarly, when it comes to divorce, Indian law should insist on a uniform process of registration, no matter how the divorce was brought about, provided the divorce is by mutual consent. Thus, as in England now, a Muslim husband could still give a *talaq* to his wife; as a devout Muslim she would have to agree to a registered divorce. The sensitive issue of duress should not be disregarded, of course, and the question of maintenance must figure somewhere, but in principle this approach seems preferable to the present one, where the state, despite a multitude of legal regulations, does not seem to be able to create certainty over the status of many marriages in the context of divorce proceedings. Provisions must also be made in cases where one spouse has good reason to resist a divorce, and for the opposite situation, i.e. where one of the spouses just walks out of a marriage, making a mockery even of customary processes of divorce settlement. Or should we assume that this is a custom in some communities? Here, as in the case of marriage solemnisation, doubts are not out of place whether the state will ever achieve complete legal regulation.

If India wishes to embark on the road to legal uniformity in the personal laws, other matters could be dealt with similarly. Thus a consequential step would be to allow polygamous marriages to all Indians, but on condition that these are registered and are approved on a variety of acceptable grounds, among which infertility might figure side by side with the Qur'anic sanctioning of polygamy under certain conditions.

To proceed in this way, identifying the special needs of people rather than discussing communal anxieties over cultural and legal imperialism all the time, would create an official legal system (which could be called Uniform Civil Code) which would maintain the fiction of legal uniformity, but would still allow a considerable extent of legal diversity. Only in this way can the distrust and tension between the official state law and people's customary law be overcome.

Once it has been fully realised that religious freedom is no longer endangered by such laws, people's laws may even develop in such a way as to accept the minimum legal requirements of the state as perfectly sufficient. So far, in England, few 'Asians' have abandoned the customary forms of marriage solemnisation altogether, and it seems unlikely that many will ever do it. Since the English 'white wedding', too, experiences some form of revival, the Indian legislature should not rely on the quite uncertain prediction that with increased modernity and 'development', local custom and religion will become less important. Evidence from all over the world suggests just the opposite. Therefore the legal system of India should be better directed towards a course of compromise with religious and cultural diversities, which are there to stay, no matter what the state law chooses to say.

Some of the above proposals may seem too radical at the present moment, because the wounds of hurt communal feelings are still so very fresh. There may indeed be another path which India, rather than England, can go. Before I turn to that, finally, I must however comment on a new Indian book that reached me while I was writing this essay. The title to Tahir Mahmood's *Personal laws in crisis* (New Delhi: Metropolitan 1986) sounds doubtful about the position of personal laws, but this exciting and sensible study makes, in fact, a powerful plea for the maintenance of diversity in modern Indian law, and for the retention of the personal law system, at least for the time being. The author suggests, *inter alia* that the central term 'uniform' has been misinterpreted (p. 31) to mean something 'common' and 'westernised', and shows very clearly that to call India a 'common-law country' is a straight-forward misrepresentation of facts, no matter how much sentimental value may be attached to such an expression. Mahmood demonstrates convincingly that the Indian legal diversities are not based on religious differences alone, but also on regional variations, and he exposes the false search for uniformity in Indian laws. The book advocates that there should first be uniformity within the various personal laws. In the author's words, (p. 47), "Removal of inter-territorial, sectarian and custom-based diversities within each of the personal laws" is essential to achieve the constitutional ideal of uniformity in civil laws. A cautious approach is advocated, though, since inside the privacy of homes the requirements of constitutional law can only have a limited application (pp. 48–49).

With respect, these suggestions vastly overestimate the state's power to 'remove' local diversities. More importantly, the real issue of uniformity of all civil laws in India is sidetracked. Uniformity within any one personal law does not guarantee total legal uniformity. The author, very cleverly, does not tell us directly what standards should be applied in reforming and unifying the various personal laws. He speaks of "our own concept of secularism" (p. 48) and argues, in his final appeal, for greater recognition of customary procedures of dispute settlement (pp. 135–136). While all this makes good sense, it does not explain away the underlying customary ideal of absolute diversity, so that the crucial question is consistently avoided: How do we, at the end of the day, achieve greater uniformity between the various personal laws? It appears that this book, a series of public lectures, does not discuss this issue at all. One gets the impression, though, that the author's message is really to abandon the futile search for legal uniformity along Western lines. That would seem to put an end to the discussion about the implementation of Article 44 of the Indian Constitution.

But perhaps not all is lost. Let us consider, finally, whether there is a viable compromise solution. It may be submitted, as indicated earlier, that a gradual reform of all personal laws along similar lines may be a suitable option. As shown above, the Hindu law of India was already subjected to this reform process, and there are now demands for the other personal laws to follow suit. Significantly, both Tahir Mahmood and I have independently argued that dangerous overdoses have been administered to the Hindu personal law, that excessive Westernisation and individualism has been infused into this personal law, which now contrasts so very much with the living Hindu law of India. It would be essential, therefore, that the central standards one wishes to follow as guidelines for such reforms should be subjected to detailed scrutiny. Mahmood's book, and his earlier works, are useful here since they show, for example, that the Muslim law of India is not so averse to reform and development as has often been made out. A constructive process of gradual, piecemeal reform of the individual personal laws would indeed seem possible, provided it is ensured that common standards are being maintained in the process. It is surprising how many common rules there are already, and how few areas of fundamental difference there really are.

The state, however, must not dictate such reforms from above, as has hitherto happened. Detailed consideration must be given to the Indian people's perceptions of their laws, i.e. to be precise, their customs. The results will inevitably be that the need to respect and maintain legal diversity in Indian law will be fully recognised. But if the official legal system really wishes to maintain the fiction of uniformity, let the necessary steps be taken, cautiously. While the laws of England and other countries (what about Tanzania, which is in a similar position?) may provide some models, India will have to develop her own combination of legal rules to suit her circumstances, i.e. those of her people. It is pointless to try to ape any other legal system. The creative force of ethnic minority customs in modern English law should impress the Indian legislature and should make us reconsider many 'established' positions in Indian laws. In India, such creative forces are infinitely stronger, and they have a legitimate claim for recognition that even the Constitution does not deny. So let the people's voice be better heard in the process of law reform, and the Indian law of the future will be much more just and equitable than it is now. Surely, justice should come before uniformity in the ranking of values.

6.4 Uniform Civil Code in India: A false model for development?

[From: 1990(2) *KLT*, Journal section, pp. 3–10]

An important new study on the vexed question of the Uniform Civil Code (Vasudha Dhagamwar: *Towards the uniform civil code*, Bombay: Tripathi 1989) prompts me to comment on the feasibility of such a wide-ranging and ambitious project for India as a whole.

Regular readers of KLT will be aware that I have been arguing, on the basis of experience in Kerala, that much of centralised law-making, particularly if it is designed to affect the way local 'little' people regulate their daily lives, will not per se lead to the desired results. Thus, I argued (at KLT 1986 J 17–20 and 63–65), that the official abolition of joint Hindu family law in Kerala through the promulgation of the *Kerala Joint Hindu Family System (Abolition) Act*, 1975 was not in fact effective as far as most Kerala villagers were concerned. I have no reason today to abandon this argument, despite the dictum of Mr. Justice U. L. Bhat in *Saraswathy Warassiar v. Parukutty Warassiar*, KLT 1988(1) 638, at 640, para 7, to the effect that s. 4 of the 1975 Act has created certain legal facts. One notes the carefully chosen words of the learned Judge at p. 641 that "it would be open to the plaintiffs to sue for partition claiming share on per capita basis". This seems to indicate that the legal facts undoubtedly created by the statute have to be reinforced by litigation in cases where there is no assent to these new legal facts. In other words, a local citizen, when faced with opposition from other family members to his or her individualistic claims, may have to drag them to court to assert a right that the statute has already granted to this individual. It could, of course, be argued that it is in the nature of many legal rights that they have to be re-inforced and operationalised by court action. However, this approach to legal rights can hardly be an asset for a legal system of a country with many millions of people who are dependent for survival on the goodwill of their close kin. Quite apart from problems of access to courts, financial barriers etc., I do not consider it a realistic option for most people to fight their families to assert their individual rights, though this will undoubtedly happen in some cases. In social reality, as I observed in numerous cases in Kerala and elsewhere, there is a definite preference for informal family arrangements and consensual sorting out of individual claims and ambitions without the aid of courts. Some lawyers have told me that a man in Kerala may now go as far as spending a fortune in legal fees on ascertaining his right over a single coconut tree. Such experiences illustrate one of my major points here: Modern state law, like the 1975 Kerala Act, is often imperfectly implemented and exists more on the statute book than in reality. It may be proudly held up as the 'official law' of the state, but the 'living law' can be remarkably different. Of course, lawyers never tend to suffer from such discrepancies. It is only confused individuals who cannot make sense of competing obligation systems who get caught in the nets of legal conflicts and often have to pay dearly for their trust in the 'progressive' law.

Whether one likes it or not, these are, in a nutshell, the major effects of what I called 'legislative overkill' in Kerala. It seems to me that the implementation of a Uniform Civil Code for the whole of India could be a far worse form of legislative overkill than the 1975 Kerala Act.

In my KLT essays of 1986, medical images had a prominent place; we discovered subsequently that Professor Tahir Mahmood [*Personal laws in crisis*. New Delhi: Metropolitan 1986] was writing in similar terms. There can be no doubt that all of independent India's major leaders have been seeing themselves as doctors in charge of an ailing patient. Thus, more or less brilliantly conceived prescriptions for a better future have been dominating much of the agenda of Indian legal development. One of the favourite strategies has been to prescribe a number of medicines, often with the specific aim to rejuvenate and develop the patient's ancient body into something more in line with the second half of the 20th century. Not unexpectedly, the doctors did not agree among themselves, but once the *ayurvedins* and *hakims* had been sidelined by the believers in the new religion of progress and development, the patient was given little option but to swallow large amounts of legal drugs.

One wonderdrug, in particular, was recommended for boosting the country's immune system against communal fevers and for strengthening the general health of the body, e.g. national unity. Remarkable reticence about the true nature of this rather colourless and neutralising drug has been maintained up to now. It was offered to the nation under the label of 'Uniform Civil Code' and is found in Art. 44 of the Indian Constitution of 1950 which provides that "The State shall endeavour to secure for the citizens a uniform civil code throughout the territory of India".

What did this well-sounding Directive Principle of State Policy mean? It appears that a major intended effect of this promised wonderdrug was to turn a newly created nation, still suffering from the recent wounds of communal frenzy, into a peaceful haven for all communities. Thus, the intention must have been to tackle what was perceived as the cancer-like spread of the traditional systems of differential statuses and inequalities, and to curtail and ultimately eliminate the various systems of communal personal law based primarily on religious distinctions.

The vision was that in the new secular body politic all members would be equal before the law, if not in reality, and that differences of race, religion, caste, class and gender would rather sooner than later, be wiped away to create a standard breed of 'the new Indian' as an individual with a dominant loyalty to the central state.

These rosy perceptions of the future have now lost much of their attractiveness for the country's legal doctors. During the 1980s, there has been much talk of a 'crisis' of the Indian legal system (Upendra Baxi: *The crisis of the Indian legal system*. New Delhi: Vikas 1982) and of personal laws (Tahir Mahmood, as above). We now realise that what was prescribed to India in the 1950s is not untypical of legal prescription in the name of 'development' generally. The only difficulty is that nobody in the 1940s and 1950s knew quite how the new medicines would work, what their actual implications would be and what, more importantly, would be their side-effects.

Some 40 years later, some doctors of India's political and legal system are still advertising the miraculous wonderdrug as a panacea for all the ills of modern Indian legal development. Article 44 has gathered dust, but is still found in the shopwindow of the Indian Constitution. Yet the optimism about the effectiveness of the superdrug has largely evaporated. The experts now carry a professional mien of distance and give their advice in guarded tones, even though there is no American-style insurance policy that a frustrated, ill-treated patient could seek to invoke. Self-doubt plagues the profession. One is now almost ready to contemplate alternative medicines; the *ayurvedic* type is beginning to be back in fashion, *panchayats* are debated again, and it does not even seem to matter what political persuasion the new doctors adhere to, their messages signal a loss of confidence in the ability of officious and formal state law to regulate the daily lives of the common citizen.

The patient, in the meantime, has developed vigorously, beating all odds. There may be all kind of cancer raging in the vast belly, and some ailments have definitely got worse. Like many bad (or sensible?) patients this one has obstinately refused to take all the medicines. But the doctors have definitely connived in this by failing to ensure that the drugs, once prescribed, were consistently applied and their effects monitored. After 40 years of somewhat haphazard treatment, the patient is still alive and well, with no vital bits missing, despite the threat of peripheral parts to fall off. But the immune system remains impaired, the communal temperature has gone up, and there are many danger signs.

Not that the end is near, though. As the world's largest functioning democracy settles down under a new leadership, the patient's ailments are likely to be re-assessed and the treatment will be continued. One may wonder how: There are not many options of therapy for the Indian disease of diversity. In fact, an appropriate diagnostic analysis should question the definition of 'disease' in this case. The problem itself will never ever go away. Perhaps our doctors' diagnosis so far has been wrong? What if we consider that diversity, in itself, may be an asset for legal regulation rather than a problem?

Our doctors, of course, in their customary self-engrossment with their powers, have so far largely overlooked the innate forces of immunity against injections of modern uniformising wonderdrugs. One knows and accepts that some limbs may be numbed for a while, shocked into submission by the new chemistry, and may look and behave almost as desired by the wonderdoctors. But what happens after a couple of years when the initial effects may have been modified? What if after a while 'the system' re-asserts itself and the effects of the treatment are slowly taken away, not necessarily completely, but in such a way that the originally projected cure will not be achieved.

Vasudha Dhagamwar's new book contains much evidence of the resilience of the Indian body of traditions and the consequent rejection of recently implanted legal tissue. This timely and splendid study focuses to some extent on the fundamental uniformising legal and political pressures in modern India. These present a basically irreconcilable clash between the aims of the ambitious 'social engineering through law' school of thought and persisting social realities of a perceived 'traditional' type. This, as the study indicates, more between the lines than openly admitting it, has led to the slowly growing realisation that modern India can and will never become a mere copy of the so-called advanced and developed modern Western democracies. Indeed, the reluctance to admit this is felt throughout the book; a sense of urgency is expressed several times, a feeling of panic almost: if we don't act now, and soon, all progress will be lost!

But it would be quite wrong to imagine that a boat could be missed or has been missed already. This is a modern case of Waiting for Godot. Fundamental misconceptions have confused the issues that this book seeks to address, creating immense tensions. Any debate on the Uniform Civil Code, therefore, seems as much emotional as it is political and legal. The author admits deep frustration over lack of agreement and progress, leading to phrases like "barren controversy" (p. 71) and the view that the last four decades have been "a sad waste of time" (*id.*).

As one of India's leading socio-legal scholars, Dhagamwar is far too experienced to rush into an apparently easy option. She displays some due cautiousness and declares open-mindedness, but this is perhaps little more than half-hearted rhetoric. As the title subtly indicates, this study is rather too concerned, apart from raising the issue, to propel developments in the direction of greater legal uniformity and progress. It is apparently one of the book's major premises that legal uniformity will more or less automatically follow from swallowing the legal wonderdrug of the Uniform Civil Code. But the argumentation fails to convince, the author simply tries too hard to push her own perception of the issue. Yet the book is very useful indeed and admirable as a bold attempt to give the complex issue of legal uniformity in modern India a higher place on the agenda.

As the author is, at the same time, so very aware of the major difficulties of enforcing legal uniformity in a country like India, the main discussion in the book ends with a remarkably open-ended conclusion which is probably designed to challenge us into debate. Here is a prominent 'mainstream' lawyer (with due reservations about the term, as expressed p. 63) who seems to indicate her own ambivalence about the feasibility of truly uniform civil code:

> Voluntary or compulsory, it seems that if and when the Uniform Civil Code is introduced, there is a strong possibility of a period of deep social unrest taking place. Unless the government is prepared to ride out this period, if it then gives in to those who don't want the Uniform Civil Code, more damage will be done by introducing than by withholding the Uniform Civil Code (p. 76).

This statement seems to say that there are basically two options: Implement a Uniform Civil Code, irrespective of all the likely negative side-effects, or abandon it altogether. The suggestion that India should have a Uniform Civil Code, even if prolonged bloodshed follows seems rather disturbing. How desperate have we become? Should we hope for a 'benign' emergency dictatorship à la Mrs. Gandhi that is bold enough to impose uniformity from above, arguing that, in the long run, the bitter medicine will prove beneficial? The author's anguish is coming through many passages of this book; it poses serious questions, but offers no ready answers.

Clearly, thus, modern India's élite legal thinkers, realising that they are so very remote from the masses, are currently in a healthy crisis of self-assessment: one still feels the urge to recommend and prescribe the old wonderdrug to the nation, but there is much evidence that it has not worked so far, and does not work elsewhere.

Apparently also in this context, we are beginning to witness a growing realisation that the élites of India have a duty not to devise remedies that suit mainly their own aims. The public interest element, so noticeably strengthened in the 1980s, is also beginning to assert itself in this debate. For, if a few enlightened individuals manage to separate law and religion, as is proudly asserted (p. 51), the average Indian cannot and may never want to do this, and would thus be alienated from the state by forced reforms along 'secular' non-communal lines. A consideration of public interest cannot overlook this important fact.

Dhagamwar's book, apart from discussing the issue of legal uniformity, contains an interesting range of material about different areas of the law, notably on adoption law. The perhaps necessarily rushed and sketchy treatment of many specific legal topics shows, however, that there is clearly no point in doggedly pursuing legal uniformity in India with reference to any one legal topic. In each case, as is only too apparent, the attempts to devise total uniformity are soon running aground, often because of vocal

Muslim opposition. But it would be unfair, and the author resists this temptation well, to blame the Muslims of India for the ills of the system. At the same time, the valid point is made that the discussion has become dominated by Muslim issues and concerns and that the government has listened and reacted too much to conservative Muslims.

Still, much of this book, too, is firmly in the grip of this predicament. It is not a coincidence, as I have indicated elsewhere (see 1988(1) KLT, J 56–66), that we find the same situation in Britain today.

It seems a bit too simple to accept the argument of some of Dhagamwar's informants that communalism is so strong in India because different communities do not have the same status in law (p. 50 and 83). Rather, apart from competition for scare resources and politicking community leaders, whose role is rightly castigated by the author in various contexts, the state itself has significantly contributed to the communal tensions, but not, as Dhagamwar consistently argues in many contexts, by respecting diversity and backpeddling on uniformity, but, in the first instance, by its own uncoordinated and unreflected programme of secularisation and uniformisation, now perceived as threatening by almost all communities, even the Hindu majority. For, did we not know for decades that the Hindu never really agreed to the secularising reforms of their personal laws, and that such reforms as were made often show half-heartedness, either on the part of the legislators or the judges who applied the law or both (J. D. M. Derrett: *The death of a marriage law.* New Delhi: Vikas 1978)? Dhagamwar's study shows that, far from developing consistently towards greater legal uniformity, modern Indian law has oscillated between extremes. So one abolished, as J. D. M. Derrett put it in his *Critique of modern Hindu law* (Bombay 1970: 310), major elements of tradition laws "in a euphoric moment", while one reintroduced traditional elements in other contexts. More recently, the great euphoria (of course only in some quarters!) following the *Shah Bano* case of 1985 was rapidly smothered by the much misunderstood *Muslim Women (Protection of Rights on Divorce)* Act 1986 that appears to treat Muslim divorced wives differently from others. In Kerala, of course, the cases of *Ali*, 1988(2) KLT 94] and *Aliyar*, 1988(2) KLT 446 have now opened up the debate again, and we can be sure that the last word has not been spoken on this controversy.

The consequent muddles into which modern Indian family laws have been thrown, appearing hopelessly inefficient and confused to the uninitiated outsider, are not to be interpreted as welcome evidence of the persistently alleged Indian inability to be efficient, but are rather splendid proof of the conceptual blindness with which some self-styled experts applied the new wonderdrug of legal uniformity in India. What we see, in virtually every legal context, and not just in Kerala, is the apparent incompatibility of much of the new law with the thinking of common Indians, who as Dhagamwar notes, are far too busy with their own little worlds to philosophise about legal uniformity. This, she comes close to arguing, gives a mandate to those that have a long-term vision of modern

Indian law. I find this extremely dangerous, precisely the kind of doctor's approach that claims to know best what is good for the patient without listening to his or her perception of the presumed illness first. My diagnosis is rather that the communal fevers of modern India have been, over decades, aggravated by the discomfort caused due to the impending threat of abolition of one's traditions and the consequent inner rejection of what is perceived as foreign or alien tissue.

There is clearly no easy cure, no patently obvious remedy. But an urgent reassessment of the whole topic is asked for and is thankfully stimulated by Dhagamwar's splendid efforts. It does not help, though, to put wholesome blame on tradition; one needs to be more open-minded.

The author also notes the disappointing contribution of academics to the debate so far (p. 47). She attempts to stimulate and generate discussion by interviewing a rather small and limited panel of community leaders (or those presenting themselves as such) and eminent legal experts. The study, thus, also offers a wide variety of opinions from the simplistic and demagogic to the legal philosophy of a leading light like Upendra Baxi. This evidence, often duplicating the author's earlier discussion, which is to an extent based on the responses of her informants, fills a major part of the book in seven substantial appendices. The material thus collected is perhaps not representative of anything other than the respective individuals, but it illustrates the lamentable state of the debate: there is a lot of politicking and infighting among the 'experts' shining through, quibbling over little details and outrageous episodes rather than giving attention to the important conceptual issues involved here. This is clearly a case of the blind leading the blind, and all the rhetoric about 'experts' and 'masses' is quite meaningless. In her final concluding discussion (pp. 158–162), Dhagamwar brings evidence of amazing examples of local legal uniformity that make all communalist politicians look like desperate agitators and show the proponents of a Uniform Civil Code in no better light.

What is clearly needed now is a major re-assessment of some very fundamental issues in the debate on legal uniformity in India: To what extent does modern India need legal uniformity at all? Is it in fact counterproductive for the political unity of such a diverse and vast nation to press for uniformity in each and every respect (p. 44)? Further, is the personal law system really as suppressive and divisive as Dhagamwar's study seems to make out? It seems far too simplistic to argue that a personal law system, perpetuating differential statuses, creates only barriers and injustice (p. 62): The differentiation of statuses also makes for, and strengthens, links between individuals, and these remain of crucial relevance to most individuals anywhere in the world. This is certainly the case in India and, interestingly, in modern China too, where the modern law has again begun to remind individuals more openly of their social responsibilities. In India, this attitude has been phrased in terms of the fundamental duties of Article 51A of the Constitution, or in important court cases like *Vijaya Manohar Arbat*, AIR 1987 SC 1100, where it was held that a Hindu daughter, also after marriage, has a duty to maintain her aged parents. I fail to see how one can argue in favour of the preservation of traditional links of support for tribals, as Dhagamwar does, but not for the (more 'civilised'?) average Indian!

Further, is there, as Baxi indicates (p. 36), scope in not only contemplating but fully accepting, legal pluralism rather than uniformity? Should India not be proud of her immense diversity and take this as an asset rather then something that needs to be legislated away? This question must be asked with renewed vigour today, especially since the American model of the 'melting pot' is now just a haunting sceleton in the legal wonderdoctor's cabinet. In the context of modern Indian law, how useful are the various legal concepts found in the world? Have we got our perceptions of state law and the various kinds and levels of non-state law right? Is it correct to assume, for example, as Dhagamwar does (p. 54), that Indian criminal law operates and is applied in a uniform way? If we have so much evidence that the various steps towards unification have been so painful and unsure, and that the technique of gradually codifying all personal laws separately will not work since it does not necessarily lead to absolute uniformity, why do we remain fixed to the idea of a Uniform Civil Code?

Dhagamwar's book provides a suitably disturbing response, guided by the author's "rare courage of conviction" which is candidly emphasised in Upendra Baxi's preface. While I find the laudable aims of Dhagamwar's important study fully accomplished, fundamental reservations about the book's evaluation of modern Indian legal development remain at the back of one's mind.

Since the book was written, apparently in 1986, many dramatic events have taken place that make updating of its factual material inevitable. We seem to have moved a little bit closer to legal uniformity. While the issue of legal uniformity is still as unresolved as it was when Dhagamwar wrote, the Parsis of India have decided on a reformed law for themselves. We now find this in the *Parsi Marriage and Divorce (Amendment) Act,* 1988, which often reads like a carbon copy of the much-amended *Hindu Marriage Act* of 1955, thus pursuing the strategy of harmonising individual personal laws along similar lines. The Christians of India have not been able to react with equal speed, and predictions about legal development in this field remain unsure, as far as I am aware. Quite crucially, as we saw, the *Shah Bano* controversy over the rights of divorced Muslim wives to maintenance is still far from over. The 'illness' of lack of legal uniformity in India has still not been cured by any of the modern prescriptions, and I venture to predict that there is no cure for legal diversity other than to accept it as part of human existence. Dhagamwar, too, seems unconvinced about the feasibility of a strategy of codifying the various personal laws first (p. 70) and urges for a very basic policy decision for or against the Uniform Civil Code.

In my submission, it would be unrealistic to refuse to accept that the operation of human societies generally is based on and results in distinctions and diversity. These have always been there, and are going to remain a dominant fact of life. What a good law probably needs to do is to ensure a balance of rights and duties as between individuals and groups of people. Diversity *per se*, no matter how hard the law strives to create equality and uniformity, will never be abolished by statute or case law. Whether one can begin to work towards greater legal uniformity without antagonising large sections of the population is, in my view, a most difficult issue. If one looks at the Indian policies of protective discrimination, one finds the same conceptual problem: To hope for absolute equality and total legal uniformity is, as I said, like waiting for Godot.

The desire to create a national legal system has always been seen as a legitimate aim for a modern nation state, but this does not, by itself, mean total legal uniformity, which remains an ideal model of legal regulation, not a realistically workable concept. Experts on modern India's legal ills must no longer allow themselves to be misguided and blinded by the apparently so persuasive Western models of legal uniformity. Firstly, these have often allowed much more diversity than some modern Indian legal prescriptions have been prepared to concede. Secondly, many Western-type and socialist uniform, secular laws have run into severe difficulties due to the strengthening of grass-roots public interest elements, which feed on local diversity and reject unnecessary centralisation. Such movements thus often appear populist or 'ethnic', challenging the inherent inequalities created and perpetuated by uniform national laws in many countries. Such laws have regularly *purported to* be uniform and secular, but they have also favoured certain dominant power structures. Whether we think of the Indian ruling classes in P. Bardhan's model in *The political economy of development in India*, Oxford: Basil Blackwell 1984, or of the successive toppling of East German élites in the recent past, of the current controversy in England about blasphemy laws that protect only certain religious faiths, or of Russia's difficulties in persuading national minorities that the centralised system serves them well, centrally imposed legal uniformity may, at best, remain an ideal goal. For a country like India, it looks more like a false, inappropriate model altogether.

This conclusion, however, does not automatically and totally deny the value of a certain extent of legal uniformity. But no useful purpose is, in modern India, served by ignoring the patient's healthy grass-roots awareness of the whole body as a complex and immensely diverse system that cannot be drugged into submission by a powerful dosis of legal wonderdrugs like the Uniform Civil Code.

6.5 Review of: Vasudha Dhagamwar [1989]: *Towards the Uniform Civil Code*. Bombay: N. M. Tripathi

[From: Vol. 53 No. 3 [1990] *BSOAS*, pp. 543–546]

Soon after Independence in 1947, India's new guardians prescribed a number of medicines for the country which aimed to foster its growth into a modern, secular democracy. One such miracle-cure in particular was intended to conquer communal tensions and promote a healthy body politic, i.e. national unity. Labelled the 'Uniform Civil Code' it was enshrined in Article 44 of the Indian Constitution of 1950 which provides that "[t]he State shall endeavour to secure for the citizens a uniform civil code throughout the territory of India".

Clearly it was hoped that the newly created nation, still suffering the effects of recent communal strife, could thereby be transformed into a peaceful home for all communities in India. This was to be the antidote to what was seen at the time as the spreading canker of traditional systems of differential statuses and inequalities. It was intended to curtail and ultimately eliminate the system of personal laws based on religious distinctions. In the new, secular, body politic it was envisaged that all members would be equal before the law, if not in reality, and that differences of race, religion, caste, class and gender would gradually be wiped out to create a standard breed of 'the new Indian' as an individual with a dominant loyalty to the central state.

The flaw in this rosy prescription for the future, which is not untypical of legal prescription generally, was that nobody in the 1940s and 50s knew quite how it would work in practice, what its true implications were and what, if any, would be the side-effects.

This, then, is the context of the book under review, which contains much evidence of the resilience of the Indian body of traditions and the effectiveness of its rejection of such a foreign implant as a constitutional directive for legal uniformity. Dhagamwar's splendid study focuses on the fundamental contradictions between forms of societal resistance and legal and political pressures towards uniformity in modern India, in other words, the basically irreconcilable clash between the aims of the 'social engineering through law' school of thought and the social realities perceived as 'traditional'. This, as the study under review indicates, though more between the lines than explicitly, has led to a gradual realisation that modern India can never and will never become a mere copy of the so-called advanced modern Western democracies. The reluctance to admit this openly makes itself felt throughout the book, and an odd sense of urgency, of panic almost, comes to the surface more than once: We must act now or all the progress made will be lost!

In this reviewer's opinion, it would be quite wrong to suppose that India could be about to miss some crucial boat. Fundamental misconceptions have clouded the issues this book seek to address, reflecting the immense tensions that mark a debate in which what is at stake is as much emotional as it is political and legal. The result has been a deep frustration with the lack of agreement and progress, giving rise here to phrases like "barren controversy" (p. 71) and the view that the last four decades have been "a sad waste of time" (*id.*). The author, one of India's leading socio-legal scholars, proceeds with some caution and her claim to an open mind is largely rhetorical. For, as the title indicates, the book aims not just to raise the issue, but to propel developments in the direction of greater legal uniformity and progress. It seems to be a major premise of the study that progress will follow more or less automatically from acceptance of the legal cure-all. The argument fails to convince, but the work is nevertheless very valuable; indeed, it is an admirable and bold attempt to give the complex issue of legal uniformity in modern India a higher place on the agenda.

Dhagamwar is far too experienced to be unaware of the major difficulties of enforcing legal uniformity in a country like India. The main discussion, thus, ends with a remarkable open-ended conclusion, challenging debate. Here is a prominent 'mainstream' lawyer (with due reservations on this term as expressed on p. 63) who indicates that implementing a truly uniform civil code may indeed never be possible:

> Voluntary or compulsory, it seems that if and when the Uniform Civil Code is introduced, there is a strong possibility of a period of deep social unrest taking place. Unless the government is prepared to ride out this period, if it then gives in to those who don't want the Uniform Civil Code, more damage will be done by introducing than by withholding the Uniform Civil Code. (p. 76)

How is one to interpret this? Let us have a Uniform Civil Code even if bloodshed follows? Let us hope for a dictatorship that is bold enough to impose it, just as Mrs. Gandhi prescribed a lot of bitter pills which were ultimately beneficial? None of this is intended by the author, I think, but the sense of anguish in the face of a dilemma comes through many passages in the book. The élite of India's legal thinkers clearly realises its remoteness from the mass of people and is currently undergoing a crisis of self-assessment; on the one hand, there is still the urge to press on with the idea of the uniform code, but on the other, the evidence is that it has not worked so far, and does not work elsewhere.

We are thus beginning to witness a growing awareness in India that the élite has a duty not to devise remedies that suit mainly its own aims. The public interest element, so noticeably strengthened in the 1980s, is also beginning to assert itself in this debate. For, if a few enlightened individuals do manage to separate law and religion, as is proudly asserted here (p. 51), the average Indian cannot, and may never want to do so, and would be alienated from the state by further reforms along 'secular', non-communal lines.

The present book contains an interesting mixture of discussion of principles and examples of particular legal issues, with much material on adoption law. The perhaps unavoidably condensed and sketchy discussion of specific legal topics shows that there is clearly no point in doggedly pursuing legal uniformity with reference to any one legal topic. In each case, the attempts to devise total uniformity have soon run aground, often because of vocal Muslim opposition. But it would be unfair, and the author resists this temptation well, to blame the Muslims of India for the ills of the system. At the same time, the valid point is made that the discussion has become dominated by Muslim issues and concerns and that the government has listened and reacted, disproportionately, to pressure from conservative Muslims. Still, much of this book, too, is firmly in the grip of the same predicament, and it is not a coincidence that we find a parallel situation in Britain today.

It seems too simple to accept the argument that communalism is so strong in India because different communities do not have the same status in law (pp. 50 and 83). Rather, apart from competition for scarce resources, and the politicking of community leaders, rightly castigated by Dhagamwar in various contexts, the state itself has significantly contributed to communal tensions, but not, as Dhagamwar consistently argues in many contexts, by respecting diversity and back-pedalling on uniformity. In the first instance, it is the uncoordinated and ill-thought-out programme of secularisation and promotion of uniformity which is perceived as threatening by almost all communities, even the Hindu majority. For, it has been known for decades that the Hindus never really agreed to the secularising reforms of their personal laws, and that such reform as were made often reflect half-heartedness, on the part of legislators as well as judges. Dhagamwar's study shows that, far from developing consistently towards greater legal uniformity, modern Indian law has oscillated between extremes. So, as J. D. M. Derrett put it in his *Critique of modern Hindu law* (Bombay, 1970: 310), major elements of traditional laws were abolished "in a euphoric moment", while traditional elements were re-introduced in other contexts. The consequent confusion into which modern Indian family laws have been thrown, giving an impression of hopeless muddle to the uninitiated outsider, is not to be interpreted as evidence of the oft-alleged Indian inefficiency, but as splendid proof of the conceptual blindness with which certain self-styled experts have studied the issue of legal uniformity. Apparent in virtually every legal context is the incompatibility of much of the new law with the thinking of ordinary Indians who, as Dhagamwar notes, are far too busy with their own lives to philosophise on legal uniformity, which, she comes close to arguing, gives a mandate to those who have a long-term perspective on modern Indian law. In the meantime, however, I would argue that communal tensions have been worsened over the decades precisely by the threatened abolition of traditions.

There is no obvious remedy. But an urgent reassessment of the whole topic is both called for and stimulated by the author's efforts here. It is, however, unhelpful to place wholesale blame on 'tradition' from the start.

The author notes the disappointing contribution of academics to the debate so far (p. 47). She attempts to generate discussion by interviewing a fairly restricted panel of community leaders (or those presenting themselves as such) and eminent legal experts. The study does thus offer a wide variety of opinion, ranging from the simplistic and demagogic to the reflective legal philosophy of a leading light like Upendra Baxi. This evidence, which in many cases retraces the ground of the author's earlier discussion, fills a major part of the book in seven substantial appendices (pp. 80ff.). The material perhaps represents no more than the individuals concerned, but it illustrates the lamentable state of the debate: What emerges is much politicking and in-fighting among the 'experts', quibbles over detail and extreme cases, rather than any attention paid to the great conceptual issues involved. In her concluding discussion (pp. 158–62), Dhagamwar introduces examples of local legal uniformity that make all communalist politicians look like desperate agitators and show proponents of a Uniform Civil Code in no better light.

Clearly, a major discussion of very fundamental issues is needed: Would modern India benefit from legal uniformity at all, or is it in fact counter-productive for the political unity of such a diverse and vast nation to press for uniformity in each and every respect (p. 44)? Is the personal law system really as wrong and divisive as Dhagamwar seems to make out? As already indicated, it is far too simplistic to argue that a personal law system, perpetuating differential statuses, creates only barriers and injustice (p. 62); the differentiation of statuses also makes for, and strengthens, links between individuals, and these remain of crucial relevance to most people anywhere in the world. This is certainly the case in India (as in modern China), where the modern law has again begun to remind individuals more expressly of their social responsibilities, whether in terms of the fundamental duties of Article 51A of the Constitution, or in important court cases like *Vijaya*, AIR 1987 SC 1100. I fail to see how one can argue in favour of preservation of such links for tribals, as Dhagamwar does, but not for the (more 'civilised'?) average Indian.

Further, is there, as Baxi indicates (p. 36), scope for not only contemplating, but fully accepting, legal pluralism rather than uniformity? Should not India be proud of her immense diversity in every possible way and take this as an asset rather than something than needs to be legislated away? In the context of modern Indian law, how useful are the diverse legal concepts found across the world? Is our perception of state law and the various kinds and levels of non-state law right? Is it correct to assume, as the author does (p. 54), that Indian criminal law operates and is applied in a uniform way? If we have so much evidence that the various steps towards unification have been so painful and unsure, and that the technique of gradually codifying all personal laws separately will not work, since it does not necessarily lead to absolute uniformity, why do we remain wedded to the idea of a Uniform Civil Code?

Dhagamwar's book provides a suitably disturbing response to those problems, informed by the author's 'rare courage of conviction', as emphasised in the preface. This reviewer finds the aims of study fully accomplished and, despite fundamental reservations about the evaluation of modern Indian legal developments as presented by Dhagamwar, hopes that we can now venture to take the next steps in this minefield of socio-legal research.

Since the book was written (apparently in 1986), many dramatic events have taken place that make the need for updating of its factual material inevitable. While the issue of legal uniformity is still as unresolved as it was then, the Parsis of India have decided on a reformed law for themselves (now found in the *Parsi Marriage and Divorce (Amendment) Act*, 1988), while the Christians have not been able to react with equal speed. Crucially, the *Shah Bano* controversy over the rights of divorced Muslim wives to maintenance is still far from over. There are now two 1988 cases from the High Court of Kerala on the interpretation of the controversial *Muslim Women (Protection of Rights on Divorce) Act*, 1986, which seem to confirm the view that the 'experts' on modern India's legal ills have, once again, been confounded by the resilient immunity of 'the system'.

6.6 Muslim polygamy and the Special Marriage Act

S. A. Karim

[From: 1992(1) *KLT*, Journal section, p. 6]

In *Anwar Ahamed v. State of Uttar Pradesh and another*, reported in Criminal Law Journal, page 717, Mr. Justice S. I. Jafri of the Allahabad High Court held that a second marriage solemnised under the *Special Marriage Act*, 1954 amounts to bigamy and is punishable under s. 494 of the *Indian Penal Code*, and that the *Special Marriage Act* supersedes the Muslim personal law (*shariath*). With due respect, I submit this interpretation and finding seems erroneous and needs re-consideration.

Anwar Ahamed had married Hasin Begum according to *shariath*. While the first marriage subsisted, he married another lady, Nusrath Sulthana alias Shirin, under the *Special Marriage Act*. The husband and both wives are Muslims.

Now, it is obvious that the *Hindu Marriage Act*, 1955 provides for monogamy among Hindus under s. 5(i) read with s. 11. Similarly, s. 4 of the *Special Marriage Act* 1954 leaves no doubt that marriages under this Act are monogamous. Also, under s. 60(2) of the *Indian Christian Marriage Act* of 1872, monogamy is prescribed. Since the Parsi law also enforces monogamy, all codified personal laws of India are unanimous on the position regarding monogamy.

The position is entirely different in Muslim personal law. A Muslim man, under *shariath* as well as the current law of India, is permitted to have four wives at the same time, but not more, with the condition that he should be just between them. It is well-known that this rule reflects the conditions prevailing in Arabia when the Arabs fought several wars and a large number of men died in them, so that many women became widows and there were more women than men. To avoid the resultant contingency of immorality and destitution, *shariath* dictated that able-bodied men may have more than one wife, but limited their number to four. Before this theory came into existence men had kept any number of spouses. Might was the right prevailing then. This is the brief history of the four wife theory. Though indirect legislative restrictions have been imposed in India, marriage and divorce of Muslims are still governed under *shariath*.

The objects and reasons stated in the *Special Marriage Act* touch several aspects of the *Hindu Marriage Act*. It never refers to the marriage laws of either Muslims, Christians, Parsis or Jews. This indicates the *Special Marriage Act* is intended only for Hindus. When Parliament enacted this Act, *shariath* was in force. If the legislature had desired to bring Muslims under the *Special Marriage Act*, it would have stated so. In the absence of such a reference, s. 43 of the *Special Marriage Act* cannot be interpreted to include Muslims.

Shariath permits the existence of more than one wife at a time. It does not mean all the marriages shall be under the Muslim personal law. A man who comes under *shariath* cannot be found guilty under another Act for another marriage, as long as he has not violated the terms of *shariath*. In the instant case, both marriages are legal and within the ambit of *shariath*. Thus, s. 43 of the *Special Marriage Act* has no relevance and the conviction for bigamy under s. 494 *Indian Penal Code* is illegal and void.

6.7 Much water has flowed down the Ganges: Muslim polygamy, the Special Marriage Act and judicial collusion

[From: 1993(2) *KLT*, Journal section, pp. 19–22]

At 1992(1) KLT J 6 (see also 1991 CriLJ, J 127–128), our learned friend S. A. Karim of Thiruvananthapuram argued that the decision of the Allahabad High Court in *Anwar Ahmed,* 1991 CriLJ 717 needs reconsideration because the *Special Marriage Act*, 1954 does not apply to Muslims. This is an attractive argument which is, however, as the learned High Court judge aptly put it, “a fallacious contention”. Apart from the Muslim element in this debate, this particular case demonstrates the continued leniency of Indian judges towards bigamists.

Basically, there was no dispute about the facts of the case, though the case report itself is somewhat confusing about various dates. As far as I can see, Anwar Ahmed had married a Muslim woman some time ago and had then contracted a second marriage with another Muslim woman in 1981. This marriage was registered under the *Special Marriage Act*, 1954 and was, it appears, only subsequently solemnised in a *nikah* some four months later. To achieve registration under the 1954 Act, the husband had concealed the fact of his first marriage, which was clearly an offense punishable under s. 494 of the *Indian Penal Code*, 1860.

The husband’s revision petition before the Allahabad High Court was only admitted on the question of sentence. Anwar Ahmed has been sentenced to undergo rigorous imprisonment for three years. His defence was that as a Muslim he could have up to four wives and, further, that the provisions of the *Special Marriage Act* cannot take precedence over his personal law. This latter argument, pursued with some vigour by Mr. Karim also, would certainly bail out the husband. Mr. Karim has argued that the 1954 Act does not apply to Muslims because it does not specifically mention them. However, a close study of the objects and reasons of the 1954 Act, of which Mr. Karim seems to be aware, reveals its purpose as "to provide a special form of marriage which can be taken advantage of by any person in India and by Indian nationals in foreign countries irrespective of their faith which either party to the marriage may profess".

I fail to see how one can interpret this to mean (see 1991 CriLJ 127, at 128) that the 1954 Act is "mainly intended to legalise the marriage of Indian nationals in foreign countries irrespective of the faith of the spouses" and can then proceed to argue that the *Special Marriage Act* does not apply to Muslims. Surely, they are included under "any person in India" and "Indian nationals in foreign countries"? Further, as was also noticed by Mr. Karim, the Act specifically indicates that its provisions apply irrespective of faith, which is fully appropriate for a secular statute. The argument that his Act does not apply to Muslims, therefore, is not tenable and was rightly thrown out by the learned judge. The *Special Marriage Act*, 1954 is with few exceptions, an optional law, and can be used by any Indian who is attracted by its provisions.

Mr. Karim's argument in support of the polygamous husband, namely that "both marriages are legal and within the ambit of *shariath*" (1992(1) KLT J 6) would appear to be correct, as long as we assume that the husband did not move beyond the realm of *shariat*. But that is not what he did: By attempting to register his second marriage under the *Special Marriage Act*, he brought himself within the umbrella of the secular law of India and committed a crime in the process. We are not told what his reasons were for doing so, but it does not appear to be the case that the husband was ignorant of the law, nor would I compare him to an unfortunate insect fatally attracted by the glistening spider's web of India's optional Uniform Civil Code. Anwar Ahmed clearly knew what he did, wanting to sanctify his desire by fraud, for which he was duly punished.

Muslim reluctance to acknowledge the superiority of any form of state law in modern India is now an issue which is similarly politicised in several European countries with substantial Muslim minorities. It is not helpful if Muslim lawyers, in India or anywhere else, are seeking to construct obfuscating arguments to 'protect' Muslim law from some kind of secular onslaught. More often than not, as in this case, the real purpose is to assist and protect a devious man. The object of the appeal was, one assumes, to have the husband's sentence reduced; that object was indeed achieved. So why harp on about the Muslim element in this case? It may be fashionable, but only helps to stir up communalist arguments, the last thing any sensible Keralite should wish to see.

In my view, the more important legal issue raised by this case is the judicial handling of polygamy. Here we see no evidence at all of India's famed judicial activism, rather the opposite: Continued male collusion between judges, lawyers and polygamists to defeat the claims of female victims of polygamy. The case report does not tell us why the first wife pressed the prosecution after so many years, but possibly this was so because of some trouble over maintenance. Not a single comment in the case report shows any concern about the superseded woman, who could well turn out to be a Shah Bano-type lady.

The learned judge, in reducing the husband's sentence from three years to the time already served in prison, refers to the fact that the offence occurred many years ago. As he puts it, "much water has flowed down the Ganges" since then (p. 719) and, astonishingly, "I see no reason to impose retributive punishment just to satisfy certain provisions of law" (*id.*). In other words, the learned judge, while upholding the superior status of the *Special Marriage Act* vis-à-vis the Muslim personal law if a Muslim chooses to opt for the former, shares the well-known attitude of Indian judges that polygamy is really only a small cavalier's delict and that the law, if anything, should protect the polygamist from unduly harsh victimisation. Nothing seems to have changed since Professor Derrett, ages ago, noted this attitude to polygamy in 'A round-up of bigamous marriages' at 1967 (69) *Bombay Law Reporter*, J 84–93.

The present case, thus, throws some interesting light on the current sentencing policies of Indian judges for bigamists. It confirms that, even in 1991, India's polygamists can count on judicial sympathy. This case is, therefore, in illustrious company. After all, India's leading case on the punishment for polygamy (*Gopal*, AIR 1979 SC 713) contained a lecture to the nation about the seriousness of the offence, followed by a reduction of the bigamist's sentence to the time already served. *Gopal* is not referred to in the judgment, but it is probably not wrong to assume some continuing empathy here among many male members of the Indian higher judiciary.

Readers will be aware that I have argued against the total and strict abolition of polygamy in India (see 1990(1) KLT J 50–69 and 1991(2) KLT J 20–24), but the argumentation used to free Anwar Ahmed reeks of male collusion and does not bode well for women in India. One wonders how this particular approach can be matched with the stiffer attitude to polygamy found in *Baby*, AIR 1981 Bom 283, and especially in the much-underrated case of *Sumitra Devi*, AIR 1985 SC 765, in which the Supreme Court overruled itself and, at a stroke, got rid of the very unsatisfactory earlier leading cases of *Bhaurao Shankar*, AIR 1965 SC 1564 and *Kanwal* Ram, AIR 1966 SC 614.

In remarkable contrast to the law on maintenance for divorced wives, the Indian higher judiciary's position on polygamy lacks any element of judicial activism in favour of the concerns of women. This, and not communalist politics, is the focal point of *Anwar Ahmed's* case that Indian lawyers should pay attention to.

In this context, the Pakistani case of *Faheemuddin,* PLD 1991 SC 1074, a very interesting public interest petition concerning the right of the second wife to prosecute her husband for polygamy under the *Muslim Family Laws Ordinance* of 1961, might serve to show that South Asian women of any faith, anywhere, still have to wait for much more water to flow down the Ganges before they may have effective remedies against the trickery of polygamous husbands. True, the lady in *Faheemuddin* was given standing to prosecute him, but what is she going to gain other than some revenge, or a divorce? At least, however, Muhammad Afzal Zullah, CJ (as he then was), took the arguments of the female complainant seriously and made no attempt to collude with the polygamist and his legal advisers. Mr. Karim and others would do well to study such judgments; they might realise that Indian Muslims are well-protected by the secular Indian legal framework and that polygamy at the whim and fancy of any husband cannot be a right worth defending, whether in a secular or an Islamic context.

6.8 Legal uniformity in India: A political football

We saw in ch. 6.1 that India's post-colonial dream of achieving better justice through uniform legal provisions in the form of 'one law for all Indians' never turned into a reality. As we began to see, there are many reasons for this. From the start, the uniformising framework of the Constitution of India, 1950 and the continued presence of the personal law system clashed conceptually and in actual daily practice. Apart from creating space for the personal law system as part of the official law, the Indian Constitution itself recognised in many ways that the people of India were not equal citizens in social reality and that mere declarations about formal equality would be counter-productive. Several articles of the Constitution, therefore, took explicit account of this.[26]

Challenges to the continued presence of the personal law system were entirely expected. They have been systematically rebuked.[27] Much of the litigation in this field concerned Indian Muslims, some of whom have persistently claimed that the modern Indian state law should not be interfering in their religious personal law and in the norm systems underlying their traditional *shariah* law. In *Shahulameedu v. Subaida Beevi*, 1970 KLT 4, V. R. Krishna Iyer J heard an appeal by a Muslim husband who had been refusing to pay maintenance to his wife, on the ground that she had been disobedient by leaving him, and hence he was not liable for her maintenance. We have already discussed this case in the context of polygamy and maintenance, since the main ground for the wife's refusal to live with the husband was her objection to his polygamous arrangements. The case was heard under s. 488 of the old *Criminal Procedure Code* of 1898, a uniform legal provision applying to all Indian husbands. An amendment to that section in Indian law, introducing s. 488(3) by the *Code of Criminal Procedure (Amendment) Act* of 1949, appeared to suggest that a man might not be liable to pay maintenance to the wife if he offered to maintain her in his own home. However, the proviso to this new section also stated that if a husband had married another wife and the existing wife objected, then this would constitute a just ground for her refusal to live with the husband.

The factual situation in *Shahulameedu* exactly matched this scenario and the husband was arguing that the new law created injustice for Muslim men, who had the right to marry up to four women at the same time. In 1949, of course, even a Hindu husband could have brought a similar argument to claim his 'entitlement' to polygamy. Krishna Iyer J remained firm, saying at p. 6:

> But the amendment incorporated by Act 9 of 1949 expresses the moral consensus of the community that a woman should not be driven to live with her husband who has transferred his affections to another woman either by marrying her or by keeping her as a mistress. The argument is that while this wholesome rule may apply to the rest of Indian humanity, Muslims should be excused out of this civilized law, because the fundamental assumption in the provision is that it is obnoxious to marry a second wife while the first is alive and this assumption does not hold good in the case of the Muslims of India who under their personal law enjoy the privilege of four wives simultaneously.

This argument was powerfully rebuked by the learned judge, *inter alia* with reference to several earlier cases from the 1950s, cited in this report,[28] which had all held that Muslims might well claim the right to marry several wives, but when it came to maintaining them, they were subject to the general laws of India. The popular argument, to the effect that it was a fundamental right for Muslims to marry up to four wives as a matter of freedom of religion under Article 25 of the Indian Constitution, had also been rebuked earlier on the ground that the right to marry up to four wives was not a matter of religion.[29]

The upshot of all these cases has been that when there is a conflict between a rule of the Muslim personal law and a rule of the general Indian law, the latter would prevail and would override the rule of the personal law.[30] Krishna Iyer J, however, was not content to just apply the law. In typical activist fashion, he made further comments on legal policy, in this case related to legal uniformity, holding at pp. 9–10:

> The Indian Constitution directs that the State should endeavour to have a uniform civil code applicable to the entire Indian humanity and, indeed, when motivated by a high public policy, S. 488 of the Criminal Procedure Code has made such a law, it would be improper for an Indian Court to exclude any section of the community born and bread up on Indian earth from the benefits of that law, importing religious privilege of a somewhat obscurantist order. I have no doubt that it behoves the Courts in India to enforce Section 488(3) of the Code of Criminal Procedure in favour of Indian women, Hindu, Muslim or other. I will be failing in my duty if I accede to the argument of the petitioner that Muslim women should be denied the advantage of para. 2 of the proviso to Section 488(3).

It was thus concluded, at p. 11, that "there is hardly any doubt that neither the reliance on Art. 25 of the Constitution nor the refuge under the sanctions of the Koran can save a Muslim husband from meeting his statutory obligations ...".

The tensions between legal uniformity and diversity have also been debated with reference to provisions on divorce (see especially Shiv Sahai Singh 1993). Joseph Minattur (1980: 170–171) was particularly concerned with the disadvantaged legal position of Christian spouses, who could not escape from an irretrievably broken marriage and wrote:

> If irretrievable breakdown of marriage is made the only ground for judicial declaration of divorce applicable to all communities and religious groups in India there will be equality of treatment not only between men and women but also between various religious groups. Perhaps one has to wait for the adoption of a uniform civil code for such unification of laws.

We see here again how different legal agenda were intersecting, and how, in a sense, India has been waiting for the miraculous wonderdrug, as I called it during the late 1980s, of the uniform civil code. However, no action in this respect was taken by the legislature. It is significant that judges took up the cause of legal uniformity and commented on the perceived need for a uniform civil code in a number of important cases during the latter half of the 1980s, in particular.

In *Jorden Diengdeh v. S. S. Chopra*, AIR 1985 SC 935, decided about three weeks after the famous *Shah Bano* case, which we shall discuss further below, the Supreme Court heard an appeal against refusal to grant a divorce to a couple, married in 1975 under the *Indian Christian Marriage Act* of 1872, who could now not obtain a legally valid divorce, despite the fact that their marriage had broken down irretrievably (for details see also Mahmood 1995). The wife was a Christian from Eastern India, while the husband was a Sikh. The wife's petition for nullity of marriage had been refused and the High Court had granted a decree for judicial separation on the ground of cruelty, based on the husband's alleged impotence. The wife insisted that she wanted nothing less than nullity, or a divorce on the ground of irretrievable breakdown; she obviously wanted to get rid of this marriage. However, the court's hands were tied, since the provisions of the *Indian Divorce Act*, 1869 contained no grounds which could have assisted the wife. The judgment in this case, given by Chinappa Reddy J, starts immediately with the key issue of legal uniformity. We read at pp. 935–936:

> It was just the other day that a Constitution Bench of this court had to emphasise the urgency of infusing life into Art. 44 of the Constitution which provides that "The State shall endeavour to secure for the citizens a uniform civil code throughout the territory of India." The present case is yet another which focusses attention on the immediate and compulsive need for a uniform civil code. The totally

> unsatisfactory state of affairs consequent on the lack of a uniform civil code is exposed by the facts of the present case. ...

The learned judge then quoted *verbatim* from the *Shah Bano* case to the effect that in the absence of legislative action the courts would have to take the initiative. The judgment itself is a comparative analysis of the various provisions on divorce under the respective personal laws of India. The conclusion of this judgment cannot resolve the predicament of the two spouses, who remain tied together in matrimony, but are at least allowed to live separately. It was held, concluding the judgment at pp. 940–941:

> It is thus seen that the law relating to judicial separation, divorce and nullity of marriage is far, far from uniform. Surely the time has now come for a complete reform of the law of marriage and [to] make a uniform law applicable to all people irrespective of religion or caste. It appears to be necessary to introduce irretrievable breakdown of marriage and mutual consent as grounds of divorce in all cases. The case before us is an illustration of a case where the parties are bound together [sic] by a marital tie which is better untied. There is no point or purpose to be served by the continuance of a marriage which has so completely and signally broken down. We suggest that the time has come for the intervention of the legislature in these matters to provide for a uniform code of marriage and divorce and to provide by law for a way out of the unhappy situations in which couples like the present have found themselves. We direct that a copy of this order may be forwarded to the Ministry of Law and Justice for such action as they may deem fit to take.

Nothing was done in this field, however, as we shall see further below. At the same time as *Jorden Diengdeh*, the Supreme Court's decision in the *Shah Bano* case grabbed the national and even international headlines. In *Mohd. Ahmed Khan v. Shah Bano Begum*, AIR 1985 SC 945, discussed in detail in ch. 4.3 above, the Indian Supreme Court reiterated and elaborated on the conclusion, reached earlier in cases like *Bai Tahira*, AIR 1979 SC 362, that there was really no conflict between the provisions of the Qur'an and the revised Indian *Criminal Procedure Code*, 1973 in terms of the Muslim husband's obligations to provide maintenance for a divorced wife beyond the *iddat* period. It was therefore firmly held that the husband in this case had such an obligation (p. 950).

During the course of the judgment, the Supreme Court had to deal again with the argument that Muslim personal law should be exempt from certain aspects of the general Indian law. That contention, too, was firmly laid to rest in this judgment. The Court then, finally, commented on the issue of the uniform civil code and in the process, it appears, upset a lot of people. It was said, at pp. 954–955:

> It is also a matter of regret that Article 44 of our Constitution has remained a dead letter. It provides that. . . . There is no evidence of any official activity for framing a common civil code for the country. A belief seems to have gained ground that it is for the Muslim community to take a lead in the matter of reforms of their personal law. A common Civil Code will help the cause of national integration by removing disparate loyalties to laws which have conflicting ideologies. No community is likely to bell the cat by making gratuitous concessions on this issue. It is the State which is charged with the duty of securing a uniform civil code for the citizens of the country and, unquestionably, it has the legislative competence to do so. A counsel in the case whispered, somewhat audibly, that legislative competence is one thing, the political courage to use that competence is quite another. We understand the difficulties involved in bringing persons of different faiths and persuasions on a common platform. But, a beginning has to be made if the Constitution is to have any meaning. Inevitably, the role of the reformer has to be assumed by the courts because, it is beyond the endurance of sensitive minds to allow injustice to be suffered when it is so palpable. But piecemeal attempts of courts to bridge the gaps between personal laws cannot take the place of a common Civil Code. Justice to all is a far more satisfactory way of dispensing justice than justice from case to case.

The Court further referred, at pp. 954–955, to the arguments in favour of a uniform civil code by Tahir Mahmood (1977), other statements from the same author, and also made a brief reference to the Report of the Commission on Marriage and Family Laws in Pakistan. This Commission had expressed itself hopeful to the effect that Muslim law was capable of modern evolution. Such comments underpinned the firm view of the Supreme Court that rules of traditional Muslim law could not be used as a device to treat divorced Muslim wives differently from other Indian wives in the same position.

The *Shah Bano* case, as we saw in ch. 4.3 above, was quickly followed by the promulgation of the MWPRDA, 1986. This Act was, on the one hand, perceived as an unwarranted interference in Muslim personal law, on the other hand it was almost universally understood as an Act that took Indian Muslims out of the ambit of the 1973 *Criminal Procedure Code,* and thus damaged the interests of Muslim wives. We can see now that both these perspectives were misguided. As to the first point of criticism, Lateef (1990: 195) has emphasised:

> To the purists on the All India Muslim Personal Law Board to whom any government interference was anathema, it must be pointed out that with the passage of this bill the Government of India has indeed legislated on Muslim law; it has interfered in the Shariat, because there is no provision in the latter for maintaining divorced Muslim

> women through waqfs or charitable organisations. If in fact the government were to provide funds to waqf boards for maintenance such interference becomes direct and institutionalized.

However, this did not happen. The government of India would clearly have no interest, let alone the means, to supply Muslim *waqfs*, which anyway command enormous resources of their own, with additional social welfare funds. Recent case law, however, centres partly on the role of Waqf Boards, which evidently still see a need to protect their position against potential claimants under s. 4(1)(2) of the MWPRDA, 1986.[31]

The second point of criticism, that the 1986 Act was contrary to India's policy aims of legal uniformisation, and that it damaged the interests of divorced Muslim wives, has elicited vociferous comment by many authors (see ch. 4.3 above). V. R. Krishna Iyer (1987) became one of the most vocal critics of the 1986 Act. This learned writer was initially under the impression that the 1986 Act had damaged the material interests of Muslim women. Iyer (1987: XVI) called this "a primitive anti-woman bill". Already prior to the promulgation of the Act, Iyer (1987: XVI–XVII) had vigorously attacked the Bill:

> The bill is an injustice to our Republic's secular principle; it is an injustice to women's basic rights and, therefore, violative of human rights; it is an injustice to the egalitarian policy in our Constitution in Arts. 14 and 21 and 25; it is a vindictive injustice to Muslim women selling the soul of the State's humanism to obscurantist fundamentalists; it is an injustice to the holy Quran which insists on payment of maintenance of divorced women in distress; it is an injustice to the 21st century because it throws us back to the 6th century to buy Islamic votes through the noisy illusion of electoral support of fundamentalists whose hold on the liberal Muslim intelligentsia and the suffering masses of women is marginal; it is an ultra vires injustice to the law of Wakfs because Wakfs are not trusts to look after privatised wrongs inflicted by irresponsible talaqs; it is an injustice to family integrity because it is fraught with potential for litigation between close relatives. It is an injustice to pragmatic working of the law because, functionally speaking the provisions lead the destitute to several cases in search of a pittance; it is an injustice to national stability, because the secular credibility of the Government will be a casualty.

Such vigorous criticism highlights the fact that the 1986 Act, being a legislative provision under Muslim personal law rather than under the general law, violates the Directive Principle of legal uniformity as found in Article 44 of the Indian Constitution of 1950. However, that is more a point of communal politics. It is more important for the present discussion, and for the development of Muslim law on this point, to understand that s. 3 of the *Muslim Women (Protection of Rights on Divorce) Act,* 1986 offers a more or less instant remedy today to any divorced Muslim wife in India who, at the end of the *iddat* period, finds that her ex-husband has not made reasonable provisions for her future maintenance. Iyer (1987) and many others were therefore totally misguided in their reading of the provisions of the 1986 Act.

As we saw in ch. 4.3, therefore, the personal law politics were a mere diversion. Both in Hindu and Muslim law on the subject of post-divorce maintenance arrangements, thus our conclusion in ch. 4.3 above, divorcing husbands are now, in principle if not in practice, held liable for their ex-wife's future maintenance until her death or remarriage. This shows us that the politicking over questions of legal uniformity in this area of the law missed the point of legal substance with regard to modern India's social welfare arrangements.

After the late 1980s, the focus in criticism of lack of legal uniformity shifted for a while to Christian law. As indicated in *Jorden Diengdeh*, AIR 1985 SC 935, which we discussed above, several new cases, mainly from Kerala, highlighted the unsatisfactory legal position under s. 10 of the *Indian Divorce Act* of 1869. This section basically provided only very restricted grounds for divorce to persons married under the *Indian Christian Marriage Act* of 1872, and was especially harsh on women. The need for equal legal treatment for Christian wives was, therefore, vigorously canvassed. In *Mary Soniz Zachariah*, 1990(1) KLT 130, it was held that s. 10 of the *Indian Divorce Act* is unconstitutional, but Parliament did not react. Finally, in *Mary Sonia Zachariah*, 1995(1) KLT 644, s. 10 of the 1869 Act was judicially redrafted to achieve the desired result of putting Christian women on a par with other Indian claimants for divorce in the same situation. Here again, we see that Indian legal development has recently progressed along the route of harmonisation of the various personal laws, rather than full-scale legal intervention through a uniform civil code.

While *Mary Sonia Zachariah* tackled only the divorce ground of cruelty under s. 10 of the 1869 Act, *Ammini E. J. v. Union of India*, AIR 1995 Ker 252, is a further case under s. 10 of the *Indian Divorce Act*. This case tackles the equally long-standing gender discrimination in Indian Christian law regarding adultery as a ground for divorce. While it was sufficient for a Christian husband to prove adultery *simpliciter*, a Christian wife would have to prove aggravated adultery. This discriminatory provision was struck down by a Special Bench of the Kerala High Court in this landmark case as violative of Articles 14, 15 and 21 in the Indian Constitution. The process of legal uniformisation was thus driven still further. Remarkably, no legislative intervention of any kind has followed this series of acts of judicial activism and law-making.

At roughly the same time, the much-debated and controversial case of *Sarla Mudgal v. Union of India*, AIR 1995 SC 1531, again raised the issue of the uniform civil code, asserting that the persistence of different personal laws led to embarrassing and unacceptable situations which legal uniformity would be able to avoid. In essence, this case concerned legal problems caused for women and children when a Hindu husband decides to convert to Islam to be able to make polygamous arrangements.

In this judgment, Kuldip Singh J immediately highlighted the pressing need for implementation of a uniform civil code, starting his judgment at p. 1532 with the following words:

> "The State shall endeavour to secure for the citizens a uniform civil code through-out the territory of India" is an unequivocal mandate under Article 44 of the Constitution of India which seeks to introduce a uniform personal law – a decisive step towards national consolidation.

Noting that India's first Prime Minister had said in 1954 that India was not yet ripe for the introduction of such a code, the learned judge criticised the subsequent legislative inaction (*id.*):

> It appears that even 41 years thereafter, the Rulers of the day are not in a mood to retrieve Article 44 from the cold storage where it is lying since 1949. The Governments – which have come and gone – have so far failed to make any effort towards "unified personal law for all Indians". The reasons are too obvious to be stated. The utmost that has been done is to codify the Hindu law . . . When more than 80% of the citizens have already been brought under the codified personal law there is no justification whatsoever to keep in abeyance, any more, the introduction of "uniform civil code" for all citizens in the territory of India.

Looking at the facts of the cases before him, the learned judge then argued that devious husbands could abuse India's legal pluralism within the personal law sphere. It was said at p. 1533:

> Till the time we achieve the goal – uniform civil code for all the citizens of India – there is an open inducement to a Hindu husband, who wants to enter into a second marriage while the first marriage is subsisting, to become a Muslim. Since monogamy is the law for Hindus and the Muslim law permits as many as four wives in India, errand Hindu husband embraces Islam to circumvent the provisions of the Hindu law and to escape from penal consequences.

Having held that "the second marriage of a Hindu husband after his conversion to Islam is a void marriage in terms of Section 494, I.P.C." (p. 1537), Kuldip Singh J returned to the issue of legal uniformity and further held, at p. 1538:

> Article 44 is based on the concept that there is no necessary connection between religion and personal law in a civilised society. Article 25 guarantees religious freedom whereas Article 44 seeks to divest religion from social relations and personal law. Marriage, succession and like matters of a secular character cannot be brought

> within the guarantee enshrined under Articles 25, 26 and 27. The personal law of the Hindus, such as relating to marriage, succession and the like have all a sacramental origin, in the same manner as in the case of the Muslims or the Christians. The Hindus along with Sikhs, Buddhists and Jains have forsaken their sentiments in the cause of national unity and integration, some other communities would not, though the Constitution enjoins the establishment of a "common civil Code" for the whole of India.

These comments gave rise to vigorous criticism, given the insinuation that Muslims were somehow blocking progress in this respect.[32] Kuldip Singh J went further and demanded legislative action, holding at p. 1539:

> The successive Governments till date have been wholly remiss in their duty of implementing the constitutional mandate under Article 44 of the Constitution of India.
>
> We, therefore, request the Government of India through the Prime Minister of the country to have a fresh look at Article 44 of the Constitution of India and "endeavour to secure for the citizens a uniform civil code throughout the territory of India"
>
> We further direct the Government of India through Secretary, Ministry of Law and Justice to file an affidavit of a responsible officer in this Court in August, 1996 indicating therein the steps taken and efforts made, by the Government of India, towards securing a "uniform civil code" for the citizens of India.

R. M. Sahai J concurred with this judgment but added some observations of his own with respect to the question of a uniform civil code. In essence, the learned judge emphasised the pervasive importance of religion in modern India and noted explicitly, at pp. 1539–1540, that "[r]eligion is more than mere matter of faith". At the same time, however, he called for a rational approach to law and held, at p. 1540:

> But these are matters of faith. Reason and logic have little role to play. The sentiments and emotions have to be cooled and tempered by sincere effort. But today there is no Raja Ram Mohan Rai who single handed brought about that atmosphere which paved the way for Sati abolition. Nor is a statement of Pt. Nehru who could pilot through, successfully, the Hindu Succession Act and Hindu Marriage Act revolutionising the customary Hindu Law. The desirability of uniform Code can hardly be doubted. But it can concretize only when social climate is properly built up by elite of the society, statesmen among leaders who instead of gaining personal mileage rise above and awaken the masses to accept the change.

Pointing further to legal reforms of polygamy in many Muslim countries, and thus indicating the potential for legal reform also for Muslims, Sahai J concluded, at p. 1540:

> Therefore, a unified code is imperative both for protection of the oppressed and promotion of national unity and solidarity. But the first step should be to rationalise the personal law of the minorities to develop religious and cultural amity. The Government would be well advised to entrust the responsibility to the Law Commission which may in consultation with Minorities Commission examine the matter and bring about the comprehensive legislation in keeping with modern day concept of human rights for women.
>
> The Government may also consider feasibility of appointing a Committee to enact Conversion of Religion Act, immediately, to check the abuse of religion by any person. The law may provide that every citizen who changes his religion cannot marry another wife unless he divorces his first wife. The provision should be made applicable to every person whether he is a Hindu or a Muslim or a Christian or a Sikh or a Jain or a Budh. Provision may be made for maintenance and succession etc. also to avoid clash of interest after death.
>
> This would go a long way to solve the problem and pave the way for a uniform civil code.

The scathing criticism of this judgment produced by Tahir Mahmood (1995) is an indication that the two learned judges in this case mixed up a number of agenda and, in the process, upset alert commentators like Professor Mahmood, who saw in this judgment lurking anti-Muslim sentiments and little more than "some invidious remarks apparently made without much thought" (Mahmood 1995: 36). The reaction of the Government to this judgment has been entirely negative, too. It was widely reported in the Indian press during 1997 that the Indian government had refused to contemplate the introduction of a uniform civil code. As indicated, the agenda of this debate have changed significantly since the nationalist Bharatiya Janata Party came to power in Delhi and in some Indian states, and the so-called modernist voices are no longer calling for a uniform civil code for fear that it will simply turn out to be a Hinduised code.

At the same time, as our discussion of various legal subjects in this book confirmed, there has been much legal development in the direction of uniformisation of legal provisions in modern Indian law. This, however, has taken place within the context of explicit recognition of the many Indian diversities. Significantly, in his epilogue of discussions on legal uniformity, Mahmood (1995: 161–182) tells us that he views India as a complex mosaic. He compares the country as a whole to a traditional Hindu joint family, in which all members of the family (which are in this image the various communities of India) have an inherent inalienable birthright and corresponding pious obligations. It is not surprising to read whom Mahmood entrusts with the task of managing this complex interlinked system. He writes, at p. 162:

> The role of the *karta* -the 'pious obligation' of not allowing any member-community to arrogate to itself any particular right exclusively or of usurping the rights of others – is to be played, in the *sanyukt parivar*[33] of Indian communities, by none else but the judiciary.

Mahmood (1995: 169) then produces a defence of the place of religion in modern India, but goes much further when he writes:

> The fact is that religion can never be rooted out from private and public life of India. Indeed it need not be. The Constitution does not say it should be. Respect for religion and religious values – is in fact one of the basic philosophies of the Constitution. What the Constitution insists on is not eradication of religion itself from the society but eradication of abuse and exploitation of religion by anybody – by men against women, by politicians against masses, by bigots against the enlightened, by one community against another, by the majority against the minorities.

I found myself in agreement with much of what Mahmood wrote in this epilogue. In his view, too, a uniform civil code for India is simply impracticable (see p. 171), which does not mean that there should be no legal reforms in the direction of legal uniformisation, but they should not be made for the sake of political agenda and for the purpose of uniformising alone. Mahmood (1995: 171–172) also seems to concur with Sahai J in *Sarla Mudgal*, as cited above, that in India today, nobody is in a position to promote agreement on legal reforms of the kind that are needed.

Mahmood further concurs with my arguments to the effect that the existing academic writing on the subject has remained confused, is often misleading, and is simply, in many cases, thoroughly inadequate. Thus, Abrol (1990: 65–66) pointedly claims that the existence of personal laws has held India back from advancing to nationhood, and peddles the simplistic myth that a uniform civil code would reduce communal tensions (p. 72). Even the most recent writing in leading Indian law journals on this issue has remained woefully flat and confused,[34] and I was not at all impressed with a recent, supposedly leading study on the subject of the uniform civil code (Deshta 1995), which makes many relevant points, but creates an overall picture of total confusion. This prevailing muddle of conceptual and political issues promotes an atmosphere in which the issue of a uniform civil code for India can be easily exploited and misused as a political football.

Notes

1 In that respect it is remarkably similar to African cultures, about which much more could – and should – be written from this particular angle.

2 On the *rita/dharma* complex of Order/order see Menski (1997) and Miller (1985).

3 Significantly, such realisations may arise today in so-called immigration countries, like Australia, during the process of re-focusing their identity in ethnic and cultural terms and debating 'citizenship'. For an exciting example of such thinking, which is manifestly not new in view of the age-old Hindu experience, see Castles [1994], who speaks of an equality of respect and discusses in detail what he calls 'equity' as a basis for multicultural citizenship.

4 On Muslim sensibilities in this respect, see Mahmood (1995: 41).

5 On a critique of attempts to declare tradition irrelevant and dangerous, because scholars no longer know how to read it, and are afraid to learn more about politically incorrect matters, see Menski (1998a) in the context of recent *sati* debates.

6 And of course a lot of enthusiastic South Asian scholarship, to the extent that many South Asians have become ashamed of being part of that 'questionable' culture and would love to be accepted as part of the superior 'other'.

7 In my experience, there are often good reasons for such variant readings. While Western scholars have sometimes insinuated that the old seers did not know their Sanskrit or fantasised, the deficiencies all too often lie with us.

8 There is growing realisation today that a lot of the older writing on South Asian cultures is not in English and has therefore remained inaccessible to the dominant Anglophone circles of scholarship. That, too, remains problematic. It is another element of plurality that academics should be concerned about.

9 On this see Griffiths (1986) and indirectly Chiba (1986).

10 In several African countries, especially in East Africa, extensive debates about unification of laws have yielded much published material. For an overview see Allott (1980), who confirms that the Ethiopian unification model was a disaster and that other countries wisely refrained from imposing total unification.

11 See in detail Hooker (1975) but now in critical perspective Yilmaz (1999), providing detailed evidence of the persistence of legal plurality in terms of concepts and arrangements among Turkish, Pakistani and British Muslims.

12 For some strong words of criticism about the unsatisfactory level of comparative analysis, which are entirely justified, see Legrand (1996). Tamanaha (1993) poked fun at legal pluralism but seems to miss the key points of the debate. More positive comments have been made in India, where this branch of law should certainly be more developed. See Bakshi (1984).

13 Muslim scholars, too, have contested the claim of Western modernists to ownership of the breakdown principle, which is manifest in the institutions of *talaq*, *khul* and *mubaraat*, hence in all aspects of traditional Muslim divorce law.

14 Here we reap the fruits of incomplete education, when history and culture start arbitrarily somewhere, and the earlier periods are somehow just 'dark'. This is not a hidden argument for compulsory Sanskrit or 'Vedic' education, but a plea for recognition that our knowledge has huge gaps, of which scholars should be more aware and which they should perhaps flag up instead of pretending omniscience.

15 There were some attempts in the 1980s and early 1990s by Indian legal scholars to start a debate about the relevance of the past. This did not get anywhere because modern lawyers are not well-equipped to conduct that kind of debate. See Dhavan (1992) and Chhatrapati Singh (1990). Compare Jois (1990; 1997), taking a different approach, which has been challenged as too idealising, but certainly contains more depth.

16 Other separate legal entities were the Sikh, Buddhist and Jaina law, as well as Jewish law, and a number of unspecified personal laws for 'others' like Armenians and some Chinese residents. For more details on this discussion, see also Mahmood (1995).

17 However, that claim will be contested by evidence that Africans, the Chinese, and probably all other early people, knew and operated the concept of personal laws.

18 See in particular Khodie (1975); more recently Deshta (1995); Deolekar (1995).

19 Pearl and Menski (1998) show in detail how the actual operation of the 1961 Ordinance has undermined the purported reform agenda of the modern state and has led to a reconstruction of modern Pakistani law which is a most intricate compromise between the Muslim personal law as found in the unreformed *shariat*, which continues to exist, and the Muslim personal law of the 1961 Ordinance.

20 This appears to account for the extremely low profile of the Indian Muslim leadership on questions of the 'triple *talaq*', which many people see as violative of Muslim women's basic rights, although it should be taken as a recognised fact that modern Western divorce law also fails to protect unwanted spouses against unilateral repudiation of the marital tie.

21 The recent reform of Christian divorce law through judicial pronouncements rather than legislative activity is a most interesting example of modern South Asian law-making. The key cases in this respect were briefly discussed in chapter 2 above.

22 Mahmood (1995) is extremely critical of this study. For my own views see chapters 6.4 and 6.5 below.

23 Mahmood (1995: 121–134) examines in some detail what the project of the uniform civil code implies and finds that it does not contain a clear mandate to unify all laws, merely advice to 'endeavour to secure' legal uniformity.

24 We shall see in ch. 6.8 below that the central government's response to Mr. Justice Kuldip Singh's call for legislation in *Sarla Mudgal*, AIR 1995 SC 1531, has been a blatant refusal. During July 1998, it was further reported in the Indian press that the government had decided not to enact the draft Marriage Bill proposed jointly by the National Commission for Women and the Department of Women and Child Development. One of the reasons given was that this would impinge on the personal laws, but proposed measures like compulsory registration of marriages would patently not work, anyway.

25 On justice, equity and good conscience in British India see excellently Derrett (1962).

26 This is not the place to go into much detail. Examples that could be discussed would be related, in particular, to Article 13 of the Constitution and the meaning of 'law', to Articles 14–16, allowing the state to make special provisions for women, children and other disadvantaged sections of the Indian population, and to Article 372.

27 Again, we have no space for details here. See impressively Jain (1990: 580–651). Probably the most important early case was *State of Bombay v. Narasu Appa Mali*, AIR 1952 Bom 84.

28 They are *Maiki v. Hemraj*, AIR 1954 All 30; *Rajeshwariamma v. K. M. Viswanath*, AIR 1954 Mys 31, *Bhanwarlal v. Vitabai*, AIR 1957 MP 221 and *Syed Ahmad v. Naghath Parveen Taj Begum*, AIR 1958 Mys 128.

29 See *Badruddin v. Aisha Begum*, 1957 AllLJ 300.

30 In *Mohamed Haneefa v. Mariam Bi*, AIR 1969 Mad 414, it was held that the proviso to s. 488(3) of the 1898 Code applied to all parties irrespective of their personal law. The Supreme Court of India confirmed that position in *Nanak Chand v. Chandra Kishore Agarwale*, 1969(1) SCWR 1176 with reference to a Hindu law case under the HAMA, 1956.

31 See for example *The Secretary, Tamil Nadu Waqf Board v. Syed Fatima Nachi*, AIR 1996 SC 2423.

32 For more detail, albeit often marred by excessive polemics, see Mahmood (1995).

33 Basically, within the context of the Indian joint family of communities.

34 See Reddy (1996), who appreciates *Sarla Mudgal*, but otherwise says nothing new or useful. In fact, this author also appears to be misguided on the effects of the MWPRDA of 1986.

Concluding analysis

In the six major chapters of this book, we have seen exciting evidence to the effect that the Indian judiciary has, in particular during the late 1980s and 1990s, exhibited a more holistic and confident approach to its own central role in India's legal development. We saw that this process was shaped significantly by the judicial experience of total powerlessness during Mrs. Gandhi's Emergency. This probably gave some judges a bad taste of their own medicine and made them more open to thinking about reforming and modernising Indian law in ways which would not simply and somewhat blindly follow Western model jurisprudence and 'rule of law' concepts. Some strongly-worded decisions were reported, reminding Indian judges of their duties to their own people in the new post-colonial phase of modern India. An important statement in this regard was made, in a landlord-tenant dispute that went right up to the Supreme Court,[1] by V. R. Krishna Iyer J in *Rattan Lal v. Vardesh Chander*, (1976) 2 SCC 103, at pp. 114–115:

> We have to part company with the precedents of the British-Indian period tying our non-statutory areas of law to vintage English law, christening it "justice, equity and good conscience". After all, conscience is the finer texture of norms woven from the ethos and life-style of a community and since British and Indian ways of life vary so much the validity of an Anglophilic bias in Bharat's justice, equity and good conscience is questionable today. The great values that bind law to life spell out the text of justice, equity and good conscience and Cardozo has crystallized the concept thus: "Life caste the mould of conduct which will some day become fixed as law". Free India has to find its conscience in our rugged realities – and no more in alien legal thought. In a larger sense, the *insignia* of creativity in law, as in life, is freedom from subtle alien bondage, not a silent spring nor a hothouse flower.

The realisation that life drives law, not the other way round, contradicts not only the dominant Western model approach to legal positivism and legal centralism, it is also typically Indian. It is evident from the writings of

Professor Derrett and of V. R. Krishna Iyer, both amazingly prolific authors, that the former argued much more for the re-invigoration of ancient principles (as well as, at least in his earlier writings, for following Western models), while the latter emphasised the need for a re-orientation of modern Indian justice as a matter of harmonising law and life. To an extent, we see here the differences between the foreign, Orientalist scholar's approach and the Indian judge's somewhat more pragmatic view. However, it would be doing injustice to both writers to pigeon-hole them into one or the other category. They both took a holistic perspective and merely emphasised certain aspects of that holism more than others. In particular, as a sitting judge who had sworn allegiance to the secular Indian Constitution, V. R. Krishna Iyer could not possibly have discussed the development of modern Indian law in terms of a resurgence of Hindu principles.[2] Professor Derrett, however, as a world-renowned scholar of Hindu law, had in a sense a *dharmic* as well as professional obligation to discuss his subject from that angle. Here, we are trying to combine this disparate approaches for a fresh analysis.

Indian family law today shows what modern development specialists would call a 'sustainable' form of family law regulation by the state. While Northern, and Northern-influenced Southern scholarship still largely maintains the images of colonial importation of secular laws to achieve modernity and propel development, to support women's and children's rights and a host of other desirable aims, modern Indian family laws have in the past two decades found their own path. Many Indian judges, as Krishna Iyer's above quote demonstrated, have long ago begun to question those colonial shackles of the mind which told Indians that their own traditions and values were not usable for a bright future.

The developments which this book analyses are neatly falling in line with evidence from other Asian economies that the modern Asian (or more generally, Southern) state would seek to curtail its financial commitments to many sections of activity, including the realm of family law. This is only partly because there are better, traditional agencies to take care of such issues. The modern state, especially in huge countries such as India, China or Indonesia, simply does not have the resources to fund social welfare provisions in the family law area for the casualties of broken family life.

This perspective is bound to be misinterpreted as some form of new rightism with a South Asian tinge. But we must beware of quick judgments of this type – right and left have lost their meaning, and maybe never had any comparable meaning, in the political arenas of the South. Of course, in South Asia, as elsewhere, family law tells us much about politics. Politicised obfuscations about family law have been the order of the day in India, as well as in Pakistan. Since Professor Derrett stopped writing about Indian family law in the 1980s, nobody has bothered to analyse Indian family laws in much depth by focusing merely on the law.[3] Most of the recent research on Indian law has been driven by politicised agenda of one kind or the other, often by ideological concerns about women's rights. More recently, human rights has rapidly become a new fashion topic in India, too, and Indian developments in family law are beginning to be viewed through that prism which involves, again, foreign perspectives and outside concerns.

In this context, it appears that critical legal analysis has been mixed up with criticism for the sake of asserting cultural superiority. I have often come across objections to my legal analysis in classes in London, with students claiming that those assessments are too positive and assertive, not gloomy enough about the dark realities of South Asia and not sceptical enough about human rights violations, religious discrimination and lack of effective minority protection, everything really.

The result of such prolonged politicking over the representations of Indian laws and their development has been that we have remained in the dark about many recent developments which have not reached national headlines and NGO agendas. In some cases, most evidently the post-*Shah Bano* scenario and the interpretation of the MWPRDA of 1986, the 'expert' literature has remained seriously deficient for a long time. The enormous size of almost any aspect of Indian law is of course a factor that militates against easy analysis, but these are not valid excuses. With a massive Supreme Court, 17 High Courts and a jurisdiction the size of Europe, with sheer limitless diversity, one may ask where to start, but the case reports on specific legal topics have been giving surprisingly clear messages. It is not impossible to analyse the complexities of Indian law, but it is certainly not an easy task.

The extremely impressive labours of Paras Diwan, a man whose work I admire yet must constantly be critical of, have created an impression that everything about Indian family law can be said between the covers of a book on the law. Yet the unwary are trapped at once: Authoritative positions are taken on each and every point of the law, but how authoritative are they in the Indian legal setting, where the facts and circumstances of a case continue to be a major element in decision making? More particularly, how relevant (and thus, ultimately, how correct) can a particular North Indian position be if Southern Indians follow different rules? Professor Diwan wrote very much as a North Indian law professor, and this fact needs to be explicitly recognised if one wants to understand the impact of his research and writing.

Much of the evidence about the North-South divide within India is constantly hushed up in the name of national unity and integrity of the nation, as though regional diversity was some kind of disease of the national immune system. It is a fact that many Southern Indians appear to be viewing many issues in a different way from Northerners. Notably they perceive their women differently, and they behave differently towards them as a result. For example, I would argue that it makes a crucial difference to the marital life of a couple whether the marriage is consummated in the home of the bride (as in many cases in South India) or in a space under the authority and jurisdiction of the husband's family. A different balance and mix of patrilineality and matrilineality has been maintained throughout

South Indian cultures. This shows up in the analysis of modern Indian family laws in many ways, for example in significantly lower figures of dowry deaths in the South. It is thus more than a little imprecise to speak of anything Indian as though it were possible to encapsulate it in a few general statements.

Through the supra-modern reconstruction processes which we observed in the major chapters of this book, the Indian state of the 1990s has reverted to a familiar role, acting mainly as arbiter of competing claims in society rather than a top-down rule-maker for all citizens. The legal institutions of the post-modern state, certainly the superior courts, but even to an extent Parliament, have developed a keener sense of accountability for the social welfare of the citizens, in other words, they are viewing themselves more as responsible servants of a supervening order than as rulers of a body politic. These are subtle shifts in emphasis that do not exclude the possibility of massive abuses of power and multiple instances of refusal to be held accountable. Perhaps this picture would have become clearer if we had also managed to include in this book studies on the recent developments of Indian public law. Alas, that must wait and will be the subject of a further study.

Studying Indian legal developments mainly from the perspective of family laws, we have been able to ascertain significant changes in the basic reasoning that underpins important paradigm shifts in the law. Unable to provide the resources for even basic survival, the post-Emergency state, to some extent guided by an increasingly activist Supreme Court in this endeavour, has now become far less of an instrument of convenience for the 'men with long purses' that Upendra Baxi spoke of. Rather, the Indian superior courts constitute today a powerful support mechanism for the socially and economically disadvantaged – not by paying all social welfare bills, but by redistributing the burdens of moral and social expectations under legal supervision. A case in point is that of divorced Muslim wives, but as we saw in ch. 4.3 above, the new-found activism extends to all divorced wives because the Indian state is desperate to save its resources. Cynics could say that, somehow, the Indian state has money for nuclear experiments and increases in the defence budget, but not for its deprived women, but where is it written that the state's *dharma* is to pay the social welfare bills? Drawing from the experience of ancient Indian forms of legal organisation, such as the 'soft' or 'segmentary' state (see Ingalls 1954), but also in view of traditional Muslim concepts of the role of the state, modern Indian law has declined to follow more ambitious Western models that seemed to promise citizens a comprehensive welfare net. In retrospect, given that the ambitious Western social welfare models now face cash-starvation and resource depletion, this was probably quite a wise move.

In the complex bargaining processes over the distribution of resources within society, the Indian courts, in particular, now appear to have a clear sense of direction: Those who need to claim their rights but whose voice is not heard will be treated as *bona fide* claimants and will probably be given support, while those individuals who refuse to work out an equitable balance and egoistically insist on enforcement of their perspective, will be taken to task and may even be punished by new techniques like punitive damages. This approach, tough on some and soft on others, is reflective of a general tradition-focused awareness that contextual justice is better than uniform legal regulation, that cases need to be looked at in their own right, and that unwarranted litigation should be discouraged.

The latter element, in particular, amounts to another argument for saving precious state resources. Particularly with reference to marriage and divorce, we have clearly seen that the state's unwillingness to earmark resources for bureaucratised social regulation mechanisms is matched with renunciation of even basic control functions, which Western legal systems jealously guard. Thus, Indian law makes no attempt – to the surprise of many Western lawyers – to insist on full records of births and deaths, let alone of marriages and divorces. What we have called DIY marriages and divorces here, in which there is social registration of family events but no bureaucratic back-up service of compulsory official documentation, has become a standard pattern in Indian law, not a deviation from the official norm. While this does create its own legal problems if particular legal statuses are seriously challenged, this method of legal regulation – especially in a country of close to a billion people – is evidently much cheaper than fully bureaucratised registration systems which will turn out to be practically irrelevant for most citizens and which might still not be fool-proof for all cases anyway.

Western axioms of legal regulation, therefore, have increasingly been seen to be irrelevant and unsuitable for post-modern Indian legal regulation. Certain political agenda, such as uniformity of law, have consequently had to be downgraded, while specific social welfare aims have been given higher priority. In other words, Indian law today does not really concern itself specifically with the issue whether its development veers towards legal uniformity or not. What counts more heavily is the socio-economic result, the protective potential of the new legal regime in terms of safeguarding the survival of disadvantaged individuals by the redistribution of *social* burdens. Naturally, this has been most evident in the field of maintenance laws, but we have seen how the same kind of thinking has also influenced the modified legal approaches to divorce and to polygamy. Shiv Sahai Singh (1993: 381) attempted to put this observation as follows:

> The judicial approach towards the maintenance of the spouses under various personal laws is more realistic and pragmatic to that of legislative approach in achieving the cherished goals of [the] welfare state to secure social and especially gender-justice.

Justice, then, is less defined today by ideological criteria than by tangible financially measurable outcomes. This helps to explain why post-modern Indian family law has continued to condone polygamy and now forces many warring couples to stay together in matrimony. Within the parameters of modernist debates, 'tradition' and 'modernity' have long ago acquired values of their own, and have been put into the straightjacket of a simplistic binary opposition. However, all of this breaks down in the context of our present analysis of post-modern Indian family laws. The recent developments in Indian law are showing us that such simplistic antagonisms are merely fictitious, ideological positions, not solid building bricks for a better socio-legal reality that would help the many millions of Indians whose lives depend on familial solidarity.

Much of the current literature on Indian family laws is dominated by an oddly slanted approach to the continued presence of Muslim personal laws in the context of the Indian legal system. The new developments of Indian family law show, again through the example of maintenance law, but also with regard to polygamy, that a judicially supervised Muslim personal law can very well remain an integral part of India's national legal system. There is neither justification nor need to legislate such personal laws away, given that law and religion are so closely linked, and that India's unity in diversity actually thrives on the plurality of personal law regulation. So, as Singh (1993:10–11) emphasises, the state has the power to legislate – and even to legislate away – the personal law system, but whether this would be an appropriate legal policy remains doubtful. While Singh (1993: 11) is right to emphasise that "[i]n India the Muslim law acquired binding force not because of its divine origin but from the Constitution of India", such a statement merely asserts legal centralism and puts the state's laws above God's law. In the very next sentence, Singh (1993: 11) therefore legitimises the legal authority of the state to interfere in the Muslim personal law:

> The state, therefore, can validly enact measures of social welfare and reform with respect to the matters governed by the Muslim law.

However, there is no need to insist on legislative interference in this form, since effective legal intervention can also be brought about by judicial involvement. In either case, writers like Singh appear to me to have paid far too much attention to the supposed recalcitrance of Indian Muslims and have spent far too little mental energy on trying to research and understand the actual details of recent Indian legal developments. It seems that the judicial approaches to India's constantly contested plural legal realities can only be appreciated through reading the relevant judgments in their original.

In the same vein, the uniform civil code debates, as we found, have been more about the politics of governance and nation building, and in that connection about Muslim marginalisation, than about deep analysis of meaningful recent legal developments. At the end of the day, legal uniformity has been demasked as a convenient device to prop up legal centralist axioms rather than a viable programme for India's legal future.

The conclusions we have reached in the various chapters of this book match surprisingly well with the research results of one of Britain's leading analysts of British colonial influence on India. Washbrook (1991: 203) wrote in this respect:

> In effect, the supreme flexibility of Indian social logic defeated the wider purposes of the colonial-modern ideology of language, not by outright resistance but by epistemological subversion. Indeed, that would seem to have been the fate not only of the ideology of language but of virtually all the ideas and artefacts of the 'modern' era. Indian society has accommodated, and then subverted to its own predilections, the entire gamut of Western invention – from Marxism to democracy to the internal combustion engine. By so doing, it has plotted its own idiosyncratic course in the context of an increasingly uniform world, and has repeatedly exposed the piety and the contradiction of that perspective on modern history which would speak of the latter simply as 'the triumph of the West'.

Notably, this kind of post-modern development is not restricted to the Indian subcontinent. As Asians overseas have turned into an influential transnational community, they have also re-asserted their Indianness, in specific ways, in places like Britain,[4] Canada and the USA. In the long run, then, as the emerging comparisons with the legal experience of South Asian migrants and others in countries of the North confirm (see also ch. 6.3 above), more pressure for pluralistic accommodation will be directed towards the purportedly uniform legal systems of the Western world. While those legal systems are struggling to maintain the fiction (see to this effect already Griffiths 1986) that justice can only be achieved by combining equality axioms and uniformity of legal provisions, in other words, by following so-called Western-style 'rule of law' models, Asian and African jurisdictions demonstrate the viability of alternative models of legal regulation. Our analysis of keys issues in the recent genesis of Indian family laws shows convincingly that South Asian indigenous models of legal development, rather than Western blueprints, have been a useful tool in constructing a uniquely modern system of legal regulation.

Notes

1 The hapless tenant in this case was relying on 'justice, equity and good conscience' in the form of the modern technical argument that he should be protected against eviction from the property because there had been no written notice to quit. Krishna Iyer J held that in the realities of Indian life, written notice was not a requirement recognisable under 'justice, equity and good conscience'.

2 See very interestingly Jois (1990) and the much more openly Hindu approach in Jois (1997).

3 Saying this, I am aware of the work of Paras Diwan, but regrettably his voluminous work lacks analysis and is more in the nature of comprehensive compilation.

4 See especially Ballard (1994: 1–35) on the emergence of what he calls *desh pardesh*, a home abroad, and the reconstruction processes which that involved among such South Asians.

Table of cases

India

Bangladesh

Pakistan

List of statutes

India

China

England

Pakistan and Bangladesh

USSR

Bibliography

[Note: This bibliography contains all references from the introductory and concluding sections in every chapter of this book. The original references from the reprinted articles have been left as in the original text, but have also been included here. However, the bibliographical details of chapter 3.2 are found only in the footnotes to that reprinted article].

Abandan-Unat, Nermin (ed.) [1986]: *Women in the developing world: The evidence from Turkey*. Denver: University of Denver.

Abraham, Margaret [1998]: 'Speaking the unspeakable: Marital violence against South Asian immigrant women in the United States'. In: Vol. 5 No. 2 [July-Dec. 1998] *Indian Journal of Gender Studies*, pp. 215–241.

Abrol, Anam [1990]: 'Attitude of 'Hindus' and 'other religious' communities towards uniform civil code'. In: 1990(2) *KLT*, Journal section, pp. 65–72.

Agarwal, Bina [1994]: *A field of her own. Gender and land rights in South Asia*. Cambridge: CUP

Agarwal, Bina [1995]: 'Gender and legal rights in agricultural land in India', In: Vol. 30 No. 12 [25 March 1995] *Economic and Political Weekly*, pp. 39–55.

Agrawala, Rajkumari and A. Ramanamma [1994]: 'Women and the family law'. In: Sarkar, Lotika and B. Sivaramayya (eds.): *Women and law. Contemporary problems*. New Delhi: Vikas, pp. 248–269.

Ahmad, Furqan [1994]: *Triple talaq. An analytical study with emphasis on socio-legal aspects*. New Delhi: Regency.

Ahmad, Shahbano [1992]: 'Methodological problems in the study of Muslim women'. In: Anjum, Mohini (ed.): *Muslim women in India*. New Delhi: Radiant, pp. 24–33.

Ahuja, Sangeeta [1997]: *People, law and justice. Casebook on public interest litigation*. Vols. I and II. London and Hyderabad: Sangam Books and Orient Longman.

Altekar, A. S. [1978]: *The position of women in Hindu civilization*. 2nd ed. Delhi et al.: Motilal Banarsidass.

Anand, R. D. [1992]: 'Let the maintenance jurisprudence have a heart'. In: Vol. 39 No. 1 *Panjab University Law Review*, pp. 173–185.

Anjum, Mohini (ed.) [1992]: *Muslim women in India*. New Delhi: Radiant.

Arora, K. K. [1986]: 'Polygamy – A negation of Quran'. In: Saraf, D. N. (ed.): *Social policy, law and protection of weaker sections of society*. Lucknow: Eastern Book Co, pp. 368–375.

Asif, Zaheda [1991]: *A treatise on the law of maintenance*. Bangalore: Lawyers' Law Book.

Bakshi, P. M. [1984]: 'East and West: The legal systems and their convergence'. In: Vol. 26 No. 3 [July-Sept.] *JILI*, pp. 222–254.
Banatwalla, G. M. [1992]: *Religion and politics in India*. Bombay: Banatwalla.
Bardhan, Pranab [1984]: *The political economy of development in India*. Oxford: Basil Blackwell.
Baxi, Upendra [1982]: *The crisis of the Indian legal system*. New Delhi: Vikas.
Baxi, Upendra [1985]: *Courage, craft and contention. The Indian Supreme Court in the eighties*. Bombay: N. M. Tripathi.
Baxi, Upendra [1986]: *Towards a sociology of Indian law*. New Delhi: Satvahan.
Bharatiya, V. P. [1996]: *Syed Khalid Rashid's Muslim law*. 3rd rev. ed. Lucknow: Eastern Book Co.
Bhatia, K. L. (ed.) [1990]: *Judicial activism and social change*. New Delhi: Deep & Deep.
Bhatnagar, J. P. [1992]: *Muslim women and their rights*. 2nd ed. Allahabad: Ashoka Law House.
Bhattacharjee, A. M. [1985]: *Muslim law and the Constitution*. Calcutta: Eastern Law House.
Bhattacharjee, A. M. [1994a]: *Muslim law and the Constitution*. 2nd ed. Calcutta and New Delhi: Eastern Law House.
Bhattacharjee, A. M. [1994b]: *Hindu law and the Constitution*. Calcutta and New Delhi: Eastern Law House.
Bhattacharjee, A. M. [1996]: *Matrimonial laws and the Constitution*. Calcutta and New Delhi: Eastern Law House.
Bhatty, Zarina [1991]: 'Islamic fundamentalism and Muslim women in India'. In: Swarup, Hem Lata and Sarojini Bisaria (eds.): *Women, politics and religion*. Etawah: A.C. Brothers, pp. 145–151.
Boparai, Harinder [1981]: 'The expansion of matrimonial cruelty'. In: Vol. 23 No. 1 [Jan. – March] *JILI*, pp. 34–89.
Boparai, Harinder [1984]: 'Reappraisal of bars to divorce. A comparative study'. In: Vol. 26 No. 3 [July-Sept. 1984] *JILI*, pp. 255–287.
Carroll, Lucy [1981]: 'Muslim family law in South Asia: The right to avoid an arranged marriage contracted during minority'. In: Vol. 23 No. 2 *JILI*, pp. 149–180.
Carroll, Lucy [1985]: 'The mahr and Muslim divorcee's right to maintenance'. In: Vol. 27 No. 3 [July-Sept.] *JILI*, pp. 487–495.
Carroll, Lucy [1986]: 'The Muslim Women (Protection of Rights on Divorce) Act 1986: A retrogressive precedent of dubious constitutionality'. In: Vol. 28 No. 3 [July – Sept.] *JILI*, pp. 364–376.
Castles, Stephen [1994]: 'Democracy and multicultural citizenship. Australian debates and their relevance for Western Europe'. In: Bauböck, Rainer (ed.): *From aliens to citizens. Redefining the status of immigrants in Europe*. Aldershot et al.: Avebury, pp. 3–27.
Chiba, Masaji (ed.) [1986]: *Asian indigenous law in interaction with received law*. London and New York: KPI.
Choudhary, J. N. [1988]: *Divorce in Indian society*. Jaipur: Printwell.
Committee on the Status of Women in India [1974]: *Towards equality. Report of the Committee....* New Delhi: Government of India.
Cosar, Fatma Mansur [1978]: 'Women in Turkish society'. In: Beck, Lois and Nikki Keddie (eds.): *Women in the Muslim world*. Cambridge, MA and London: Harvard University Press, pp. 124–140.
Coulson, Noel J. [1971]: *Succession in the Muslim family*. Cambridge: Cambridge University Press.
Deolekar, Madhu [1995]: *India needs a common civil code*. Mumbai: Vivek Vyaspeeth.

Derrett, J. Duncan M. [1957]: *Hindu law past and present*. Calcutta: A. Mukherjee & Co.
Derrett, J. Duncan M. [1962]: 'Justice, equity and good conscience in India'. In: (1962) 64 *BomLR*, Journal section, pp. 129–138 and 145–152.
Derrett, J. Duncan M. [1963a]: 'Divorce by caste custom'. In: (1963) 65 *BomLR*, Journal section, pp. 161–169.
Derrett, J. Duncan M. [1963b]: *An introduction to modern Hindu law*. London and Bombay: Oxford University Press.
Derrett, J. Duncan M. [1967]: 'A round-up of polygamous marriages'. In: (1967) 69 *BomLR*, Journal section, pp. 84–93.
Derrett, J. Duncan M. [1968]: *Religion, law and the state in India*. London: Faber and Faber.
Derrett, J. Duncan M. [1970]: *A critique of modern Hindu law*. Bombay: N. M. Tripathi.
Derrett, J. Duncan M. [1973]: 'Hindu matrimonial freedom, child marriages, and Muslim divorce reform. Some notes'. In: (1973) 75 *BomLR*, Journal section, pp. 29–34.
Derrett, J. Duncan M. [1975]: 'Matrimonial freedom: A step 'forward' in Bombay'. In: (1975) 77 *BomLR*, Journal section, pp. 8–10.
Derrett, J. Duncan M. [1977]: 'The development of the concept of property in India c. A.D. 800–1800'. In: Derrett, J. D. M. (ed.): *Essays in classical and modern Hindu law*, Vol. II, Leiden: E. J. Brill, pp. 8–130.
Derrett, J. Duncan M. [1978]: *The death of a marriage law. Epitaph for the rishis*. New Delhi et al.: Vikas.
Derrett, J. Duncan M. [1981]: 'When is an 'own wrong' not a wrong?'. In: (1981) I *Madras Law Journal*, Journal section, pp. 13–16.
Desai, Sunderlal T. (ed.) [1990]: *Mulla's principles of Hindu law*. 16th ed. Bombay: N. M. Tripathi.
Deshpande, V. S. [1993]: 'Monogamy in India'. In: Kusum (ed.): *Women – March towards dignity. Social and legal perspectives*. New Delhi: Regency, pp. 22–33.
Deshta, Kiran [1995]: *Uniform civil code: In retrospect and prospect*. New Delhi: Deep & Deep.
Devasia, Leelamma and V. V. Devasia (ed.) [1990]: *Women in India. Equality, social justice and development*. New Delhi: Indian Social Institute.
Dhagamwar, Vasudha [1987]: *Women and divorce*. Bombay and New Delhi: Somaiya.
Dhagamwar, Vasudha [1989]: *Towards the uniform civil code*. Bombay: Tripathi.
Dhagamwar, Vasudha [1992]: *Law, power and justice. The protection of personal rights in the Indian Penal Code*. 2nd ed. New Delhi et al.: Sage.
Dhavan, Rajeev [1992]: 'Dharmasastra and modern Indian society: A preliminary exploration'. In: Vol. 34 No. 4 [Oct.-Dec. 1994] *JILI*, pp. 515–540.
Diwan, Paras [1977]: *Muslim law in modern India*. Allahabad: Allahabad Law Agency.
Diwan, Paras [1980]: 'Technological niyoga and nirodh and social engineering through law'. In: Vol. 22 No. 4 *JILI*, pp. 445–465.
Diwan, Paras [1984]: 'Hindu law'. In: *ASIL 1984*. New Delhi: ILI, pp. 258–294.
Diwan, Paras [1985]: 'Hindu law'. In: *ASIL 1985*. New Delhi: ILI, pp. 99–135.
Diwan, Paras [1986]: 'Hindu law'. In: *ASIL 1986*. New Delhi: ILI, pp. 128–154.
Diwan, Paras [1987]: 'Hindu law'. In: *ASIL 1987*. New Delhi: ILI, pp. 291–311.
Diwan, Paras [1988]: 'Hindu law'. In: *ASIL 1988*. New Delhi: ILI, pp. 301–322.
Diwan, Paras [1989]: 'Hindu law'. In: *ASIL 1989*. New Delhi: ILI, pp. 213–225.
Diwan, Paras [1990a]: 'Hindu law'. In: *ASIL 1990*. New Delhi: ILI, pp. 125–136.
Diwan, Paras [1990b]: *Law of maintenance in India*. New Delhi: Deep & Deep.
Diwan, Paras [1991]: 'Hindu law'. In: *ASIL 1991*. New Delhi: ILI, pp. 83–104.
Diwan, Paras [1992]: 'Hindu law'. In: *ASIL 1992*. New Delhi: ILI, pp. 157–175.

Diwan, Paras [1993a]: 'Hindu law'. In: *ASIL 1993*. New Delhi: ILI, pp. 155–167.

Diwan, Paras [1993b]: *Private international law*. New Delhi: Deep & Deep.

Diwan, Paras [1994]: 'Hindu law'. In: *ASIL 1994*. New Delhi: ILI, pp. 295–304.

Diwan, Paras and Peeyushi Diwan [1991]: *Muslim law in modern India*. 5th ed. Allahabad: Allahabad Law Agency

Diwan, Paras and Peeyushi Diwan [1995]: *Modern Hindu law*. 10th ed. Allahabad: Allahabad Law Agency.

Dube, Leela [1992]: 'Women in a matrilineal Muslim community'. In: Anjum, Mohini (ed.): *Muslim women in India*. New Delhi: Radiant, pp. 99–111.

Engineer, A. A. [1992]: *The rights of women in Islam*. New Delhi: Sterling.

Ganai, Nisar Ahmed [1990]: 'Judicial contribution to Muslim matrimonial law in a changing society in India: Some policy perspectives'. In: Bhatia, K. L. (ed.): *Judicial activism and social change*. New Delhi: Deep & Deep, pp. 406–427.

Gani, H. A. [1988]: *Reform of Muslim personal law*. New Delhi: Deep & Deep.

Ghouse, Mohammad [1973]: *Security, society and law in India*. New Delhi: Vikas.

Griffiths, John [1986]: 'What is legal pluralism?'. In: Vol. 24 *Journal of Legal Pluralism and Unofficial Law*, pp. 1–55.

Gulati, Leela [1981]: *Profiles of female poverty*. Delhi: Hindustan Publishing.

Gupta, R. L. [1979]: *The medico-legal aspects of sexual offences*. 2nd ed. Lucknow: Eastern Book Co.

Haq, M. Fazlul [1988]: 'Amend the law and make divorce easy for Hindus'. In: 1988(1) *KLT*, Journal section, pp. 45–47.

Hamilton, Charles [1891] *The Hedaya, or guide: A commentary on the Mussulman laws*. Vols. I-IV. London: T. Bensley.

Harman, William P. [1989]: *The sacred marriage of a Hindu goddess*. Delhi: Motilal Banarsidass.

Hawley, John Stratton (ed.) [1994]: *Sati, the blessing and the curse. The burning of wives in India*. New York and Oxford: Oxford University Press.

Hershman, Paul [1981]: *Punjabi kinship and marriage*. Delhi: Hindustan Publishing.

Hussain, S. Jaffer [1983]: *Marriage breakdown and divorce law reform in contemporary society. A comparative study of USA, UK and India*. New Delhi: Concept.

Ingalls, D. H. H. [1954]: 'Authority and law in ancient India'. In: Vol. 17 *Journal of the American Oriental Society*, pp. 34–45.

Iqbal, Safia [1989]: *Women and Islamic law*. Lahore: Islamic Publications.

Iyer, V. R. Krishna [1987]: *The Muslim Women (Protection of Rights on Divorce) Act*. Lucknow: Eastern Book Co.

Jain, Kiran B. [1988]: 'Writs against, rulings under and suggested amendments to the Muslim Women (Protection of Rights on Divorce) Act, 1986: An overview'. In: Vol. 8 No. 4 *Islamic and Comparative Law Quarterly*, pp. 289–313.

Jain, Madhu [1999]: 'Friends as family'. In: [22 March 1999] *India Today International*, pp. 30–34.

Jain, M. L. [1961]: 'Validity of Hindu marriage solemnised without performing any customary ritual or ceremony'. In: *AIR* 1961, Journal section, pp. 84–86.

Jain, M. P. [1990]: *Outlines of Indian legal history*. 5th ed. Bombay: N. M. Tripathi.

Jain, S. C. [1983]: *The law relating to marriage and divorce*. 3rd ed. Delhi: Surjeet.

Jois, Rama [1990]: *Seeds of modern public law in ancient Indian jurisprudence*. Lucknow: Eastern Book Co.

Jois, Rama [1997]: *Dharma. The global ethic*. 2nd ed. Mumbai: Bharatiya Vidya Bhavan.

Jolly, Julius [1975]: *Hindu law and custom*. Reprint. Varanasi and Delhi: Bhartiya Publishing House.

Kant, Anjani [1996]: 'Right of maintenance to Indian women'. In: Vol. 38 No. 3 [July-Sept. 1996] *JILI*, pp. 392–404.

Kapadia, K. M. [1955]: *Marriage and family in India*. 1st ed. Calcutta et al.: Oxford University Press. [printed in several subsequent editions].

Khan, Hamid [1999]: *Islamic law of inheritance*. 2nd ed. Karachi and London: Pakistan Law House and Platinium.

Khan, M. Mustafa Ali [1989]: 'Islamic polygamy – A blessing in disguise'. In: 1989(1) *KLT*, Journal section, pp. 47–58.

Khanam, Firdous [c. 1960]: *Attitudes of men and women towards polygyny*. Lahore: Alnaseem.

Khodie, Narmada (ed.) [1975]: *Readings in uniform civil code*. Bombay: Thacker.

Khodie, Narmada [1994]: 'Maintenance provisions'. In: Sarkar, Lotika and B. Sivaramayya (eds.): *Women and law. Contemporary problems*. New Delhi: Vikas, pp. 210–218.

Küng, Hans and Karl-Josef Kuschel (eds.) [1993]: *A global ethic. The declaration of the Parliament of the World's Religions*. London: SCM Press.

Kuppuswami, Aladi (ed.) [1986]: *Mayne's treatise on Hindu law and usage*. 12th ed. New Delhi: Bharat Law House.

Kusum [1980]: 'Maintenance of a divorced Muslim wife: A critique of the proposed law'. In: Vol. 22 No. 3 [July-Sept.] *JILI*, pp. 408–413.

Kusum [1987]: 'Divorce by mutual consent'. In: Vol. 29 No. 1 [Jan.-March 1987] *JILI*, pp. 110–114.

Kusum (ed.) [1993]: *Women – March towards dignity. Socio-legal perspectives*. New Delhi: Regency.

Larivière, Richard W. [1991]: 'Matrimonial remedies for women in classical Hindu law: Alternatives to divorce'. In: Leslie, Julia (ed.): *Rules and remedies in classical Hindu law*. Leiden et al.: Brill, pp. 37–45.

Lateef, Shahida [1990]: *Muslim women in India. Political and private realities: 1890s –1980s*. New Delhi: Zed Books.

Latifi, Danial [1985]: 'Muslim law'. In: *ASIL 1985*. New Delhi: ILI, pp. 385–404.

Latifi, Danial [1986]: 'Muslim law'. In: *ASIL 1986*. New Delhi: ILI, pp. 615–636.

Legrand, Pierre [1996]: 'How to compare now'. In: Vol. 16 No. 2 [July 1996] *Legal Studies*, pp. 232–242.

Madan, T. N. [1987]: 'Secularism in its place'. In: Vol. 46 *Journal of Asian Studies*, pp. 747–759.

Madan, T. N. (ed.) [1991]: *Religion in India*. Delhi et al.: OUP.

Mahmood, Tahir [1976]: *An Indian civil code and Islamic law*. Bombay: Tripathi.

Mahmood, Tahir [1977]: *Muslim personal law. Role of the state in the subcontinent*. New Delhi et al.: Vikas.

Mahmood, Tahir [1978]: *Civil marriage law. Perspectives and prospects*. New Delhi: ILI.

Mahmood, Tahir [1986]: *Personal laws in crisis*. New Delhi: Metropolitan.

Mahmood, Tahir [1989]: 'Muslim law'. In: *ASIL 1989*. New Delhi: ILI, pp. 227–239.

Mahmood, Tahir [1990]: 'Islamic family law. Latest developments in India'. In: Mallat, Chibli and Jane Connors (eds.): *Islamic family law*. London: Graham & Trotman, pp. 295–320.

Mahmood, Tahir [1991]: 'Freedom of conscience and conversion to a minority religion – legal parameters and social realities'. In: Mahmood, Tahir (ed.): *Minorities and state at the Indian law. An anthology*. New Delhi: Institute of Objective Studies. pp. 56–81.

Mahmood, Tahir [1995]: *Uniform civil code. Fictions and facts*. New Delhi: India and Islam Research Council.

Malhotra, Anil and Ranjit Malhotra [1998]: 'Validity of marriages in the context of unmarried cohabitation under Hindu law'. In: [May 1998] *International Family Law*, pp. 46–48.

Malik, H. K. S. [1981]: *Testamentary disposition of property under the Hindu Succession Act 1956*. Delhi: Commercial Law Publications.

Manohar, V. R. and W. W. Chitaley (eds.) [1989]: *The AIR Manual. Civil and Criminal Law.* 5th ed. Nagpur. [Vols. 1–].

Mathur, K. S. [1962]: 'Validity of Hindu marriages solemnised without any customary ritual or ceremony'. In: *AIR* 1962, Journal section, pp. 27–28.

Mehta, Rama [1975]: *Divorced Hindu woman.* Delhi et al.: Vikas.

Menski, Werner F. [1984]: *Role and ritual in the Hindu marriage.* London: SOAS. [Unpublished PhD thesis].

Menski, Werner F. [1985]: 'Solemnisation of Hindu marriages: the law and reality'. In: 1985 *KLT*, Journal section, pp. 1–10. [= ch. 1.3]

Menski, Werner F. [1987]: 'Legal pluralism in the Hindu marriage'. In: Burghart, Richard (ed.): *Hinduism in Great Britain. The perpetuation of religion in an alien cultural milieu.* London: Tavistock 1987, pp. 180–200.

Menski, Werner [1988]: 'English family law and ethnic laws in Britain'. In: 1988(1) *KLT*, Journal section, pp. 56–66.

Menski, Werner [1989]: 'Hindu talaq: On a progressive divorce law for India'. In: 1989(1) *KLT*, Journal section, pp. 23–30. [= ch. 2.4]

Menski, Werner [1990]: 'The reform of Islamic family law and a uniform civil code for India'. In: Mallat, Chibli and Jane Connors (eds.): *Islamic family law.* London: Graham&Trotman, pp. 253–293.

Menski, Werner F. [1997]: *Indian legal systems past and present.* London: SOAS.

Menski, Werner F. [1998a]: 'Sati: A review article'. In: Vol. 61 Part 1 *BSOAS*, pp. 74–81.

Menski, Werner F. (ed.) [1998b]: *South Asians and the dowry problem.* Stoke-on-Trent: Trentham Books.

Midha, Seema [1990]: 'Women, law and social justice'. In: Devasia, Leelamma and V. V. Devasia (ed.): *Women in India. Equality, social justice and development.* New Delhi: Indian Social Institute, pp. 69–78.

Miller, Jeanine [1985]: *The vision of cosmic order in the Vedas.* London et al.: Routledge & Kegan Paul.

Minattur, Joseph [1980]: 'Women and the law: Constitutional rights and continuing inequalities'. In: De Souza, Alfred (ed.): *Women in contemporary India and South Asia.* 2nd rev. ed. New Delhi: Manohar, pp. 165–178.

Mishra, Srikanta [1994]: *Ancient Hindu marriage law and practice.* New Delhi: Deep & Deep.

Moothath, Parameswaran [1984]: *The Kerala Joint Hindu Family System (Abolition) Act 1975. With short notes.* Cochin: Law Books Centre.

Morgan, Peggy and Marcus Braybrooke (eds.) [1998]: *Testing the global ethic. Voices from religious traditions on moral values.* Oxford and Ada, MI: International Interfaith Centre, World Congress of Faiths and CoNexus Press.

Mukhopadhyay, Maitrayee [1985]: *Silver shackles. Women and development in India.* Reprint, Oxford: Oxfam.

Nandy, Ashis et al. [1995]: *Creating a nationality. The Ramjanmabhumi movement and fear of the self.* Delhi et al.: Oxford University Press.

Narang, Bhim Sain [1990]: *Concept of stridhana in ancient India.* Delhi: Parimal.

Narang, Sudesh (ed.) [1988]: *Dharmashastra in contemporary times.* Delhi: Nag.

Nijjar, Manjit Singh [1994]: *Nullity of marriage under Hindu law.* New Delhi: Deep & Deep.

O'Flaherty, Wendy Doniger and J. Duncan M. Derrett (eds.) [1978]: *The concept of duty in South Asia.* London and New Delhi: SOAS and Vikas.

Oldenburg, Veena Talwar [1994]: 'The Roop Kanwar case: Feminist responses'. In: Hawley, John Stratton (ed.): *Sati, the blessing and the curse. The burning of wives in India.* New York and Oxford: Oxford University Press, pp. 101–130.

Parihar, Lalita [1990]: 'Supreme Court: A doughty champion of the Muslim divorcees' right to maintenance'. In: Bhatia, K. L. (ed.): *Judicial activism and social change.* New Delhi: Deep & Deep, pp. 365–383.

Parihar, Lalita [1994]: 'Right to maintenance of Muslim divorcees'. In: Sarkar, Lotika and B. Sivaramayya (eds.): *Women and law. Contemporary problems.* New Delhi: Vikas, pp. 219–236.

Parashar, Archana [1992]: *Women and family law reform in India. Uniform Civil Code and gender equality.* New Delhi et al: Sage.

Parashar, Archana [1994]: 'Conflicting situations in marriage'. In: Sarkar, Lotika and B. Sivaramayya (eds.): *Women and law. Contemporary problems.* New Delhi: Vikas, pp. 195–209.

Pathak, J. K. and B. K. Sharma [1992]: *Law of stridhana.* Allahabad: The Law Book Company.

Pearl, David [1987]: *A textbook on Muslim personal law.* 2nd ed. London et al.: Croom Helm.

Pearl, David and Werner Menski [1998]: *Muslim family law.* 3rd ed. London: Sweet & Maxwell.

Poulter, Sebastian S. [1986]: *English law and ethnic minority customs.* London: Butterworths.

Powers, David S. [1986]: *Studies in Qur'an and hadith. The formation of the Islamic law of inheritance.* Berkeley et al.: University of California Press.

Purohit, Nishi [1989]: *Divorce under modern Hindu law.* Pune: C. T. J. Publications.

Qureshi, Mohammed A. [1978]: *Marriage and matrimonial remedies. A uniform civil code for India.* Delhi: Concept.

Rao, P. Koteswar [1985]: 'Shah Bano's case and uniform civil code – A survey of public opinion among Muslim community at Tirupati'. In: Vol. 27 No. 4 [Oct.-Dec.] *JILI*, pp. 572–577.

Ray, S. K. [1985]: *Hindu Succession Act, 1956.* Calcutta: Kamal Law House.

Reddy, D. Sura [1996]: 'Article 44: A dead letter?'. In: Vol. 38 No. 3 [July-Sept. 1996] JILI, pp. 405–409.

Sachdeva, Sanjiv [1993]: *The primary purpose rule in British immigration law.* Stoke-on-Trent: Trentham Books.

Sagade, Jaya [1989]: 'Polygamy and women's right of maintenance: Survey of judicial decisions'. In: Vol. 31 No. 3 [July-Sept. 1989] *JILI*, pp. 336–345.

Sampath, B. N. [1983]: 'Hindu law'. In: *ASIL 1983*, pp. 283–317.

Sarkar, Golapchandra [1986]: *Hindu law of inheritance as in Viramitrodaya of Mitramisra.* Repr. Delhi: Gian Publishing House.

Shabbir, Mohammad [1988]: *Muslim personal law and judiciary.* Allahabad: Law Book Co.

Shabbir, Mohammad [1991]: *Parsi law in India.* 5th ed. Allahabad: Law Book Company.

Shams, Shamsuddin (ed.) [1991]: *Women, law and social change.* New Delhi: Ashish.

Sharma, B. K. [1989]: *Divorce law in India. Inter-spousal conflicts in relation to maintenance, property and custody of children.* New Delhi: Deep & Deep.

Sharma, B. K. and Vijay Nagpal [1992]: 'Let them bury the marriage breakdown theory: Its Indian perspective'. In: Vol. 39 No. 1 *Panjab University Law Review*, pp. 83–97.

Sharma, Mani Ram [1993]: *Marriage in ancient India.* Delhi: Agam Kala Prakashan.

Sharma, Preeti [1990]: *Hindu women's right to maintenance.* New Delhi: Deep & Deep.

Sharma, Vijay [1994]: *Protection to women in matrimonial home.* New Delhi: Deep & Deep.

Shastri, Madhu [1990]: *Status of Hindu women.* Jaipur: RBSA Publishers.

Siddiqi, Zakia A. (ed.) [1993]: *Muslim women. Problems and prospects.* New Delhi: M.D. Publications.

Singh, Alka [1992]: *Women in Muslim personal law.* Jaipur: Rawat.

Singh, Chhatrapati [1990]: 'Dharmasastras and contemporary jurisprudence'. In: Vol. 32 No. 2 [April-June 1990] *JILI*, pp. 171–188.

Singh, Indu Prakash [1989]: *Women, law and social change in India*. London: Sangam.

Singh, Indu Prakash [1990]: *Indian women. The captured beings*. New Delhi: Intellectual.

Singh, Indu Prakash [1992]: 'Indian Muslim women: Prisoners of the capitalist patriarchate'. In: Anjum, Mohini (ed.): *Muslim women in India*. New Delhi: Radiant, pp. 34–66.

Singh, Ranbir [1991]: 'Women and compulsory registration of Hindu marriages: Need for uniform legislation'. In: Shams, Shamsuddin (ed.): *Women, law and social change*. New Delhi: Ashish, pp. 39–54.

Singh, Shiv Sahai [1993]: *Unification of divorce laws in India*. New Delhi: Deep & Deep.

Singh, Shyam [1990]: 'Bigamy – An impediment to matrimonial relief under Hindu law'. In: Bhatia, K. L. (ed.): *Judicial activism and social change*. New Delhi: Deep & Deep, pp. 428–435.

Singh, Subhash Chandra [1996]: 'Polygamy, Islam and change'. In: *AIR* 1996, Journal section, pp. 178–184.

Sinha, S. N. and N. K. Basu [1992]: *The history of marriage and prostitution. (Vedas to Vatsyayana)*. New Delhi: Khama.

Sivaramayya, B. [1993]: 'Irretrievable breakdown of marriage as a ground for divorce: Gateway to liberation or oppression?'. In: Kusum (ed.): *Women. March towards dignity. Socio-legal perspectives*. New Delhi: Regency, pp. 56–62.

Sontheimer, Günther-Dietz [1977]: *The joint Hindu family. Its evolution as a legal institution*. New Delhi: Munshiram Manoharlal.

Sontheimer, Günther-Dietz and Parameswara Kota Aithal (eds.) [1982]: *Indology and law. Studies in honour of Professor J. Duncan M. Derrett*. Wiesbaden: Steiner.

Sorabjee, Soli [1991]: 'Women, constitution and courts'. In: Shams, Shamsuddin (ed.): *Women, law and social change*. New Delhi: Ashish, pp. 259–266.

van der Sprenkel, Sybille [1977]: *Legal institutions in Manchu China*. Reprint. London: Athlone.

Stern, Robert W. [1993]: *Changing India: Bourgeois revolution on the subcontinent*. Cambridge et al.: Cambridge University Press.

Swarup, Hem Lata (ed.) [1991]: *Women, politics and religion*. Etawah: A.C. Brothers.

Tamanaha, Brian Z. [1993]: 'The folly of the 'social scientific' concept of legal pluralism'. In: Vol. 20 No. 2 [Summer 1993] *Journal of Law and Society*, pp. 192-217.

Thapalyal, Abha [1986]: 'Proving bigamy: Unfair burden?'. In: 1986 (4) *SCC*, Journal section, pp. 11–18.

Towards equality. Report of the Committee on the Status of women in India. New Delhi: Government of India.

Variar, K. Sreedhara [1969]: *Marumakkathayam and allied systems of law in the Kerala state*. Cochin: Author.

Verma, B. R. [1988]: *Muslim marriage, maintenance and dissolution*. 2nd ed. Allahabad: Law Book Co.

Vyas, Mohan K. [1993]: *National integration and the law*. New Delhi: Deep & Deep.

Washbrook, David [1991]: "To each a language of his own': Language, culture and society in colonial India'. In: Corfield, Penelope J. (ed.): *Language, history and class*. Oxford: Basil Blackwell, pp. 179–203.

Weber, Jörg [1997]: *Customary divorce and Hindu law in India*. London: SOAS [Unpublished MA Dissertation].

Yilmaz, Ihsan [1999]: *Dynamic legal pluralism and the reconstruction of unofficial Muslim laws in English, Turkish and Pakistani laws*. London: SOAS. [Unpublished PhD thesis].

Zachariah, K. C. and S. Irudaya Rajan (eds.) [1997]: *Kerala's demographic transition. Determinants and consequences*. New Delhi et al.: Sage.

Index